S0-BQY-041

WORD TRACES

W O R D

T R A C E S

Readings of Paul Celan

Edited by Aris Fioretos

The Johns Hopkins

University Press

Baltimore and London

© 1994 The Johns Hopkins University Press
All rights reserved
Printed in the United States of America on acid-free paper

The Johns Hopkins University Press
2715 North Charles Street
Baltimore, Maryland 21218-4319
The Johns Hopkins Press Ltd., London

Frontispiece photograph: Paul Celan, © 1963, by Lütfi Özkök

Library of Congress Cataloging-in-Publication Data

Word traces : readings of Paul Celan / edited by Aris Fioretos.
    p.   cm.
    Includes bibliographical references and index.
    ISBN 0-8018-4525-4 (hc : alk. paper).—ISBN 0-8018-4767-2
(pbk. : alk. paper)   1. Celan, Paul—Criticism and
interpretation.   I. Fioretos, Aris.
PT2605.E4Z96   1994
831'.914—dc20   92-44195

A catalog record for this book is available from the British Library.

DEIN VOM WACHEN stößiger Traum.
Mit der zwölfmal schrauben-
förmig in sein
Horn gekerbten
Wortspur.

Der letzte Stoß, den er führt.

Die in der senk-
rechten, schmalen
Tagschlucht nach oben
stakende Fähre:

sie setzt
Wundgelesenes über.

Contents

Ein Kritiker ist ein Leser, der wiederkäut
   —Friedrich Schlegel

Preface

In late March 1970, less than a month before he died, Paul Celan met with friends and acquaintances, among them Martin Heidegger, at Gerhart Baumann's home in Freiburg. According to Baumann's account, Celan was presented with a recently published essay which juxtaposed his poetry with that of Mallarmé. After having read it, he turned to his host "in an agitated state of mind." "What offended him," Baumann observes, "what had called forth his vehement rejection, was the comparing juxtaposition. Celan opposed any attempt at comparison and insisted on the incomparable."[1]

The role of Celan's poetry in postwar literature has received ample attention. Surely one of the most rapidly growing secondary literatures, Celan scholarship recognized early the centrality of his work for an understanding of the position of poetry in a period of particularly distressed self-examination. It would even be fair to argue that, together with the writings of Kafka, those of Celan have provided the major point of reference with regard to which the discipline of *Germanistik* has tended to define itself methodologically since the war. Few oeuvres in modern German can have received as subtly detailed or as philologically thorough attention as that of Celan—for that matter, few in any other language, either. During his short lifetime (Celan would have turned fifty in the year of his death) dissertations had already been produced; a great deal of scholarly work had been promulgated in the form of papers, essays, and seminars; and critical differences of opinion were articulated in that particularly implacable manner characteristic of academic discourse. By now, Celan scholarship has a *Jahrbuch*, colloquia are arranged frequently, and a five-volume edition of Celan's more or less finalized work is currently being replaced by a text-critical edition of his complete writings. Hardly surprisingly, the differences of opinion, too, have graduated into minor *Streite der Fakultäten*.

Yet even today, when the awareness of Celan's crucial position in contemporary poetry and poetics may appear in greater evidence than ever before, there are few attempts made to register the way in which his writing insists on its incomparability. Studies of Celan in the context of the literature of the Holocaust are certainly numerous, as are studies orienting themselves in his work by means of biographical coordinates; the attempt to understand Celan as the last or latest representative of a tradition in German letters running from Hölderlin through Rilke has been made over and over, albeit with varying success, as has the endeavor to interpret his poetics with reference to the ideas of thinkers as diverse as Adorno and Freud, Buber and Habermas, Benjamin and Heidegger. A structurally defining component of these endeavors is, of course, comparison, and one would be hard pressed to argue that an understanding of Celan can be dissociated rigorously from that principle.

Nonetheless, it may be claimed that if Celan's poetry is not analyzed with regard to the particular way in which it articulates the relation between literature and its other—or, put differently, between language and reference—attempts to read his poetry would run the risk of neutralizing it by introducing categories such as "the Hölderlinian tradition," "hermeticism," or "poetry after Auschwitz." These categories are as necessary as they are legitimate; furthermore, and with justification, they point to contexts in which Celan's oeuvre must, at least initially, be situated. These contexts, which become available only by means of comparison, would then open spaces in which the singularity of Celan's poetry could resonate as that which would have no counterpart.

One may ask, however, to what extent contexts can be read and still remain contexts, and also in what measure such categories do not domesticate what is essentially other. Indisputably, Celan's highly charged poems refer to conditions, situations, and events of tormenting importance, as necessary as they are difficult to address. When he invokes the caesura, for example, Celan (who was surely aware of the term's theoretical implications in Hölderlin and Benjamin) may also be using a term from metrics as a designation for that which has been named the Shoah. "Ich trink Wein" ("I Drink Wine"), a poem partly about Hölderlin collected in the posthumous 1976 volume *Zeitgehöft*, speaks of one instance of such a caesura, more precisely of the "king's caesura."[2] When drastically initialized, Celan's two-noun "Königszäsur" becomes *KZ*, the abbreviation for "concentration camp"—itself a concentrated name for that which remains incomparable.

But if a significant portion of Celan's poetry concerns the necessity of finding words for grave historical circumstances, a crucial part of what is at stake in it pertains to the difficulty of doing so. His texts, that is, are not only made up *of* references to important historical events, but are also *about* the possibility of such reference. As such, they reflect on how language relates to the necessity of referring to something other than itself, and thus on the indispensability of an aspect of it about which it cannot provide knowledge.

Insofar as they reflect upon the medium in which they are articulated, Celan's texts also present a language which appears at odds with
itself. In greater measure than most other poetry, then, Celan's demands
to be read with particular attention not only to its intention toward language, to reiterate the celebrated formula of Benjamin, but also to its
thematization of such intention. Moreover, it requires a reading able to
take into account those components of the poem that may not be verbal,
but which nonetheless participate in its manner of making a difference.
"The truth," Celan once remarked in a letter to his editor Gottfried
Bermann Fischer, "is in the detail." [3] The contraction of a word may
prove to offer unexpected possibilities of meaning here, an anagram
may contain an oblique commentary to what is thematized in a poem,
and a quotation can turn out to be the nucleus in a drama of charged
historical significance. In the case of Celan, old categories of understanding demand to be reconsidered, abandoned, or resharpened, and
the "punctuation mark"—a "Satzzeichen" which in the 1967 *Atemwende*
poem "Solve" characteristically stands for

> den unzähligen zu
> nennenden un-
> aussprechlichen
> Namen aus-
> einandergeflohenen, ge-
> borgenen
> Schrift
>   (*GW* 2:82)

> (the sequestered writ that
> has dis-
> persed
> into the
> countless, un-
> utterable,
> to be uttered
> names)
>   (*P* 257)

—may also be that particular sign attesting to why the distinction between the poetic text considered as the representation of spoken language (troped on "conversation," for example) and its definition as a
written construction (troped on a "message in a bottle," say) is so vital
in his poetry.

While they often engage in comparisons as necessary as they may be insufficient, the essays collected in this volume emphasize various facets of that which eludes comparison in Celan. Some underscore the way in which his poetry engages in and relates to contemporary philosophy, especially as articulated by Heidegger (Pöggeler, Schmidt, and Lacoue-Labarthe); some stress the poetics of singularity as well as of alterity which emerges from Celan's prize addresses in Bremen and Darmstadt but also from his actual poetic production (Derrida, Fynsk, Golb, and Hamacher); while others pursue the problematization of interpretability and history in his works (Olsson, Frey, and Fioretos) or discuss Celan's radicalization of the work of the translator (Frey, Pepper, and Olschner).

Several of the essays ask how interpretation can be conceived of as an activity already taken into account by Celan's writing; some address the effects arising from this complication; and others ask what the implications of Celan's poetics are for a theorization of the relationship between literature, history, and philosophy. In various ways, however, the essays all address the central question of how Celan may be read today and what is involved in such a reading—not least for an understanding of the position of contemporary criticism. This pursuit involves the far from trivial suggestion that poems remain "en route," as Celan puts it in his Bremen prize address: "they are headed toward. / Toward what? Toward something open, inhabitable, an approachable you, perhaps, an approachable reality" (*GW* 3:186/*CP* 35).

The articulation of such a critical "toward" is at stake in Celan's poetry as well as in the reading of it. In large part, therefore, the following essays are critical in a double sense: they demonstrate an awareness of the problematic intersection of language and reference (the apostrophic "you" being the figure par excellence of reference) operative not only in Celan's poems themselves, but also articulating the relationship between his poetry and the analysis of it; moreover, they are critical because they may serve as a ground for subsequent readings.

Containing translations of already published texts as well as original contributions, the volume's ambition is to bring independent but interrelated studies of Celan's poetry into a constellation. The particular desire of this ambition is to provide an occasion to examine and pursue the literary, philosophical, and historical implications of an instance of poetic activity which so far has received relatively scant attention in the Anglo-American academy. Despite continuous scholarship on the Continent, Celan's poetry remains less often discussed in the English-speaking world, where his influence has been primarily on poets and writers. For a long time, and for many reasons, it could not have been otherwise. Celan's texts are of a density and linguistic inventiveness that

can only be converted in acts of translation as faithful as they are betraying: faithful in that particular meaning must be conveyed in the act
of linguistic transfer; betraying in that this act, by virtue of being a
transfer from one signifying system to another, necessarily will fail to
convey the internal tensions between the various idioms constituting
the original.[4]

The difficulties of translation, however, do not amount to the sole
cause of the lack of a widespread critical reception of Celan in the
Anglo-American world, one that moves beyond the scholarly article or
conference paper.[5] Paradoxically, though perhaps not altogether surprisingly, it was not until Celan had been received critically in France
that his poetry began to make its way more solidly across the Atlantic.
This detour is probably due to the orientation of contemporary theory
toward French philosophy and *its* relationship to the German tradition.[6]
Thus some of the volume's contributions, notably those by Derrida and
Lacoue-Labarthe, provide examples of the reception of Celan in
France, his country of adoption. (Other examples of this reception, such
as those of Blanchot and Lévinas, can be found in English translation
elsewhere, whereas yet others, such as those of Martine Broda and Jean
Greisch, still await translation.) Other contributions contained in the
volume, by Pöggeler and Frey, for instance, offer instances of two
particularly dominant aspects of the ongoing scholarship in German,
Celan's native as much as adopted tongue; while the essays of Hamacher
and Olschner are written at the intersection of Continental and Anglo-
American academic pursuits.

But there were, of course, early and incisive attempts to introduce Celan into the English-speaking world of letters—notably by
Jerry Glenn and James K. Lyon.[7] Since then, many essays have indeed
been produced on his poetry, among which those by John Felstiner,
Rainer Nägele, Elizabeth Petuchowski, Howard Stern, and Shira Wolosky stand out as of particular interest.[8] Notwithstanding this important work, however, a thorough critical reception of Celan in
the Anglo-American world still remains a matter for the future. By
juxtaposing some of the more attentive readings of Celan by foreign
scholars with new essays by their English-speaking colleagues, it
is the desire of the present volume to provide indices toward such a
future.

In a sense, translation is the art of loss—as for Celan, also an accomplished translator, all poetry must exist in relation to loss. In his
Bremen address, speaking of the place from which he has come
(a "place" as much a *topos* in literature as a place localizable in any geography), Celan says of this relation:

Only this one thing remained reachable, close and un-lost amid all losses: language.

Yes, it, language, remained un-lost, in spite of everything. But it had to go through its own lack of answers, through terrifying silence, through the thousand darknesses of murderous speech. It went through and gave no words for what was happening; but went through it. Went through and could surface again, "enriched" by it all. (*GW* 3:185–86/*CP* 34 [trans. modified])

This sarcastically twisted "enrichment," with its deadly deepening of verbal meaning, stands in close proximity to memory in Celan. In the "Meridian," he explicitly approaches the way in which linguistic density is linked to memory, especially to what is termed—by way of Benjamin—"eingedenk bleiben," when speaking of "a kind of concentration mindful of all our dates [*eine aller unserer Daten eingedenk bleibende Konzentration*]" (*GW* 3:198/*CP* 50). This highly charged "concentration" relates to the notion of reading (*Lesen*) at work in Celan's poetry, often understood etymologically (as "plucking" or "gathering") and at once close to and decisively different from, for example, that found in Heidegger.

The difference articulating such comparison—a comparison hardly arbitrary in the sense that, besides Benjamin, Heidegger and Celan must be considered the most insistent *advocati lectionis* in twentieth-century German thought about language—may be illuminated by a passage from a letter Heidegger wrote to Emil Staiger on December 28, 1950. "But to read," he adds in a postscript to the letter, "what else is that than to gather [*sammeln*]: to collect oneself in focusing on the unspoken in what is spoken [*sich versammeln in der Sammlung auf das Ungesprochene im Gesprochenen*]?"[9] In the case of Celan's poetry—for which dispersal, as "Solve" indicates, is a central category, and for which any "gathering" must remain a profoundly problematic, if necessary, activity—reading demands not so much a "focusing on the unspoken in what is spoken" as a double-edged concentration on that which remains strictly unspeakable. This unspeakability, expressionless as the caesura in Hölderlin, "unutterable" as the "countless . . . names" in "Solve," could be argued to be the marker of what, finally, lacks comparison in Celan.

The impossibility of naming the incomparable—the Bremen address can only describe it as that which happened ("das, was geschah")—is an impossibility the effects of which require reading. For even if incomparability may elude conceptualization—and what is a concept if it does not erase, in the name of generality, the singularity of that which cannot be compared?—it still remains possible to address it critically. Thus, while resisting appropriation in a positivistic vocabulary, incomparability may nonetheless be described and theorized in terms of the effects it produces in a given act of reception. The engagement in such acts of reading describes the collected effort of the essays included in this volume.

"No work of art claims that it is incomparable," Peter Szondi remarks in his treatise on "philological cognition," since "this would be claimed, in any event, only by the artist or the critic." Yet, he argues, "it demands that it simply not be compared." [10] This demand is also the imperative to read Celan. [11] Philology, "the art of reading slowly," as Roman Jakobson is said to have termed it, [12] may be a particularly instructive practice of tracing patiently the effects of this demand. Celan's interest in dictionaries of various kinds, records of etymology and entomology, the vocabularies of geology, mineralogy, and meteorology, and facts of flora and fauna, is well attested, and some of the more compelling studies that have been made of his poetry are guided by minute attention to philological detail—attention, of course, being a state of cognition of particular significance in Celan: the "Meridian" quotes Benjamin's Kafka essay quoting Malebranche ("Attention is the natural prayer of the soul"), but also argues for the "attention which the poem pays to all that it encounters" (*GW* 3:190/*CP* 50); and in a letter to Hans Bender in May 1960, Celan defines poems as "gifts to the attentive" (*GW* 3:178/*CP* 26). Yet, as Jakobson's phrase suggests, philology does not only intimate the attentive gathering, often compendious and painstaking, of empirical data, but also the patient tracking of the traces, marks, and remains of these data (the German word for "attention," *Aufmerksamkeit*, contains the morpheme *–merk–*, derivative of *merken*, "to mark"). As Celan's "Give the Word" puts it with characteristic simplicity, what it recognizes as occurring may be the coming of a man: "Es kommt ein Mensch" (*GW* 2:93/*P* 265).

One particular trace of these words may be tracked back to one of Hölderlin's late hymns, entitled "Der Einzige" and explicitly concerned with a "man." In the third version of "The Only One," it is said that "a trace of a word nonetheless remains, however, which a man perceives. The place, though, was the desert":

Es bleibt aber eine Spur
Doch eines Wortes; die ein Mann erhascht. Der Ort war aber

Die Wüste. [13]

This "trace of a word," of which Celan's words, in their turn, may be a trace, is itself a trace of another word: it refers to Matt. 4:4, where Christ (the "only one" of the poem's title) is tried after having spent forty days fasting in the desert. He is asked to convert stones into bread;

given the limitations of the language of man, however, a language in which words may do a great deal but can hardly transform themselves into the bread of which the Bible speaks, Christ answers by referring to some words in Deut. 8:3—which in their turn are traces of those in Exod. 16:15, where God made bread fall from heaven. In Hölderlin, then, to "remain" (*bleiben*) within those "limits drawn by language" mentioned in the "Meridian" (*GW* 3:197/*CP* 49) is necessarily to refer to other traces of words. Given the inability of an arbitrary system of signifiers to become their signifieds, language will never provide man with food for thought in the way bread can, but will always remain only traces of traces of traces . . .

As has been pointed out, the particular "trace of a word" in "The Only One" is not only available as a chain of signifying regression into an ever-deeper textual anteriority, but also materially as its own turning-into-trace: the *Wort* of which the poem speaks disperses in the movement of the text's articulation and becomes itself a trace at the very site of dispersal: in that "*W*üste" which is its "*Ort*."[14] In effect, the "place" at which the vestiges of the word are "perceived" proves to be the desert in question: the poem's "word" turns into a "trace," and its text amounts to the very *topos* of this dispersal.

In the passage suggesting that the poem remains aware of the "limits drawn by language," the "Meridian" also speaks of an attention to "the possibilities it opens" (*GW* 3:197/*CP* 49). Poetry, then, is defined equally by the limitations of language (rather than those of bread), as by the possibilities of something yet to come—the promise of "an "approachable reality," thus providing that charting of an actuality which is, in fact, an "addressable reality" according to the Bremen acceptance speech (*ansprechbare Wirklichkeit*). "Such realities are, I think, at stake in a poem" (*GW* 3:186/*CP* 35). Indeed, the "word" of Hölderlin *is* itself only in the passage between that to which it no longer amounts (word) and that which it becomes (trace). In order to survive as the trace of itself, this *Wort* must waste itself semantically and become that *W*üste which is the *Ort* for such a devastating event. The traces of this movement—*W* . . . *ort*—become the remnants in a "desert" in which the language of man will never provide any sustenance other than a meaning that runs the risk of always being further dispersed, an erring without semantic stability.

Celan's late poem "Mit den Sackgassen" ("To Speak With"), contained in the 1971 *Schneepart*, mentions such an "expatriate / meaning" ("expatriierten / Bedeutung") and suggests:

> dieses
> Brot kauen, mit
> Schreibzähnen.
>   (*GW* 2:358)

(to chew
this bread, with
writing teeth.)
  (*LP* 119)

In a text characterized by linguistic terseness, the "bread" in question is that white, unwritten material which, in the form of a blank space, precedes the final stanza of the poem and which can never be assimilated into understanding. To chew it with "writing teeth" may be to take part in this bread in an act of receptive activity, yet without ever being able to digest it comprehensively. It is a bread that no act of reading while writing, however sharp its teeth, can capture or swallow except by transcribing it into something else. As in the case of that "inedible writing" mentioned in a late fragment of Hölderlin's "Patmos,"[15] Celan's poetry demands to be read with the greatest care and attention—"precision" and "philological exactness" being two highly valorized categories in Celan[16]—in a process also aware of those constitutive elements of otherness which may not be assimilable or turned into meaning.

The most accurate mode of reception of this poetry is that of commemoration or *eingedenk bleiben*, in which reading quite literally is what remains. Such *bleiben* may well require a "connoisseurship of the 'word'" similar to the one heralded by Nietzsche, for whom philology had "nothing but delicate, continuous work to do and achieves nothing if it does not achieve it *lento*."[17] Elsewhere, in conjunction with this particular "art of reading," Nietzsche explicitly demands "something that has been unlearned most thoroughly nowadays . . . : *rumination*."[18] But if the fourfold art of explication required by classical hermeneutics is troped here on the four bellies of a cow, and if the experience of "modernity" remains one of the important categories in any understanding of Celan (*pace* Nietzsche), it is probably the patient *Wiederkäuen* uniting these forms of "rumination" which describes most adequately the proper activity of reading his poems.

What remains incomparable, today, in Celan's poetry, are its traces of words—its remnants of expatriated meaning—which cannot be assimilated successfully in the "digestion" of any interpretation. Here, the poem may be both "word spew" ("Wortaufschüttung" [*GW* 2:29]) and an "unmouthed lip" ("Entmündigte Lippe" [*GW* 2:36]). Faced with this sort of music, in which a "singable remnant" ("Singbarer Rest" [*GW* 2:36]) will always be left over, reading will have to amount to a concentration mindful of those particular dates which also mark the poem's singular contusions. Yet by trying "to make the wound legible," as Celan's friend and colleague Nelly Sachs suggested in a late poem,[19] reading also amounts to a precarious activity in which memory is converted into meaning, traces are transformed into words—an activity, that is, whose problematic character partly consists in the fact that "signs [may also be] interpreted / to shame" ("Zeichen zuschanden- / gedeutet"), as "Warum aus dem Ungeschöpften" in *Schneepart* puts it (*GW* 2:364). Thus, as is indicated by the poem providing the title of this volume, "Dein vom Wachen," the fate of reading may be to understand at the expense of inflicting pain—albeit hermeneutically, by way of transcription; to read to the quick as well as to carry across "the wound-read":

> sie setzt
> Wundgelesenes über.[20]

Exploring the tension between *über-setzen* with separable prefix, "to take across," and *übersetzen* with unseparable prefix, "to translate," Celan's poem speaks of carrying through and across that which has been read to the quick. The wound mentioned—one inflicted by reading—is the wound of language. During the twenty-five years Celan wrote in German, this wound both healed and deepened. Yet to say that it is readable may prove problematic, as Jacques Derrida points out in his contribution to this volume: "for it is also unreadable, and this is why it wears out reading to the very marrow." "But," he adds, the wound "belongs to the experience of reading . . . even . . . to that of translation, for the *setzt . . . über*, which could not be translated by 'translates' under any circumstances, also passes over this grammatical impossibility to beckon toward the translation of this reading-wound, passing over the border to the other side, the side of the other."

The particular cognition brought about by the otherness of Celan's poetry is tantamount to an experience of that which is incomparably present in its reading. To address it critically is to disregard that for which one wants this otherness to pass in the name of letting that pass which is bound to occur in it. "Philological cognition," then, may also imply an attention to the necessary incomparability of the other, or an ethics of reading. As the "Meridian" says about the apostrophized "you," "come about by dint of being named and addressed": it "brings its otherness into the present. . . . [In] this immediacy and proximity it gives voice to what is most its, the other's, own: its time" (*GW* 3:198–99/*CP* 50 [trans. modified]).

"The hopes I have left are small," Celan writes in the letter to Bender already mentioned, "I try to hold on to what remains for me [*das mir Verbliebene*]" (*GW* 3:178/*CP* 26 [trans. modified]). The remnants making up Celan's poetry, the traces constituting his words, "remain" to be addressed. In the engagement of this critical address, in the promise of this "toward," his poetry may be given time and voice—its incomparable time, its incomparable voice.

The essays collected in this volume were all finalized in the earlier xix
part of 1990. Only the Bibliography and references in a few notes have
since been slightly updated.

A. F.

Baltimore, Maryland
September 1992

NOTES

Epigraph: "A critic is a reader who ruminates." "Athenaeum-Fragmente,"
in *Kritische Friedrich-Schlegel-Ausgabe*, ed. Ernst Behler et al. (Paderborn: Schönigh, 1958–80), 2:149.

1. *Erinnerungen an Paul Celan* (Frankfort: Suhrkamp, 1986), 84. The essay
referred to was Gerhard Neumann, "Die 'absolute' Metapher. Ein Abgrenzungsversuch am Beispiel Stéphane Mallarmés und Paul Celans," *Poetica* (Amsterdam) 3, nos. 1–2 (1970), 188–225.

2. *GW* 3:108/*LP* 189. For readings, see Bernhard Böschenstein, "Hölderlin
und Celan," *Hölderlin-Jahrbuch* 23 (1982–83), 147–55; and Klaus Manger, "Die
Königszäsur. Zu Hölderlins Gegenwart in Celans Gedicht," *Hölderlin-Jahrbuch*
23 (1982–83), 156–65.

3. *Paul Celan. Materialien*, ed. Werner Hamacher and Winfried Menninghaus (Frankfort: Suhrkamp, 1988), 24. The letter is dated January 8, 1964.

4. The first larger pieces of translation into English appeared within a year
or so after Celan's death. Yet despite this initial introduction, which showed an
impressive sensitivity to verbal idiosyncracies, it was not until the mid-eighties
that Celan was translated more extensively into English. For references, see the
Select Bibliography.

5. At present, there are two published secondary studies of his poetry in
English (Jerry Glenn's slim volume, which appeared twenty years ago, and Amy
D. Colin's recently published study of the early Celan) as well as a collection of
essays in which several of the contributions are in English (the proceedings of
a conference at the University of Washington, Seattle, edited by Colin). See
Glenn, *Paul Celan* (New York: Twayne, 1973), Colin, *Paul Celan: Holograms of
Darkness* (Bloomington: Indiana University Press, 1991), and Colin, ed., *Argu-
mentum e silentio* (Berlin: de Gruyter, 1987). Monographs by John Felstiner (on
Celan and translation) and Joel Golb (on Celan and tradition) are currently
under way, however, as is a collection of essays edited by Haskell M. Block.

6. The special issue on "Translating Tradition: Paul Celan in France," published a few years ago by *Acts* (8/9 [1988]), may serve as an indicative example.

7. See, e.g., Jerry Glenn, "Celan's Transformation of Benn's *Südwort*: An
Interpretation of the Poem 'Sprachgitter,'" *German Life and Letters* 21, no. 1
(1967), 11–17; James K. Lyon, "Paul Celan's Language of Stone: The Geology
of the Poetic Landscape," *Colloquia Germanica* 8, nos. 3–4 (1974), 298–317; and
the special Celan issue of *Studies in Twentieth Century Literature* 8, no. 1 (1983),
edited by Lyon. For further references, see the Select Bibliography.

8. See, e.g., John Felstiner, "Paul Celan in Translation: 'Du sei wie du,'" *Studies in Twentieth Century Literature* 8, no. 1 (1983), 91–100, "Kafka and the Golem: Translating Paul Celan," *Prooftexts* 6, no. 2 (1986), 172–83, "Mother Tongue, Holy Tongue: On Translating and Not Translating Paul Celan," *Comparative Literature* 38, no. 2 (1986), 113–36, and "'Ziv, That Light': Translation and Tradition in Paul Celan," *New Literary History* 18, no. 3 (1987), 611–63; Rainer Nägele, "Paul Celan: Configurations of Freud," in *Reading after Freud: Essays on Goethe, Hölderlin, Habermas, Nietzsche, Brecht, Celan, and Freud* (New York: Columbia University Press, 1987), 135–68; Elizabeth Petuchowski, "A New Approach to Paul Celan's 'Argumentum e silentio,'" *Deutsche Vierteljahrsschrift für Literaturwissenschaft und Geistesgeschichte* 52, no. 1 (1978), 111–36, and "Bilingual and Multilingual *Wortspiele* in the Poetry of Paul Celan," *Deutsche Vierteljahrsschrift für Literaturwissenschaft und Geistesgeschichte* 52, no. 4 (1978), 635–51; Howard Stern, "Verbal Mimesis: The Case of 'Die Winzer,'" *Studies in Twentieth-Century Literature* 8, no. 1 (1983), 23–39; and Shira Wolosky, "Paul Celan's Linguistic Mysticism," *Studies in Twentieth Century Literature* 10, no. 2 (1986), 191–211, and "Mystical Language and Mystical Silence in Paul Celan's 'Dein Hinübersein,'" in Colin, ed., *Argumentum e silentio*, 364–74. For further references, see the Select Bibliography.

9. "Ein Briefwechsel mit Martin Heidegger," in Emil Staiger, *Die Kunst der Interpretation der Kunst. Studien zur deutschen Literaturgeschichte* (Zürich: Atlantis, 1955), 48. Martin Heidegger, "An Exchange of Letters between Staiger and Heidegger," trans. Beryl Lang and Christine Ebel, *PMLA* 105, no. 3 (1990), 426 (trans. modified). A study of the precarious relationship between Benjaminian and Heideggerian elements in Celan's writing would have to take into account, among other things, the opening lines of the Bremen address with its thematization of the etymology bringing together "thinking" and "thanking" (*denken* and *danken*) by way of "the semantic fields of memory and devotion" (*GW* 3:185/*CP* 33). While the reference to Heidegger seems clear here—in particular to the Heidegger of *Was heißt Denken?*—its bearing on Benjamin's treatment of *Eingedenken* cannot be overlooked. Elsewhere, in a forthcoming study entitled "Concentration," I discuss this issue at greater length.

10. "Über philologische Erkenntnis," in *Schriften*, ed. Wolfgang Fietkau (Frankfort: Suhrkamp, 1978), 1:276. "On Textual Understanding," in Peter Szondi, *On Textual Understanding and Other Essays*, trans. Harvey Mendelsohn (Minneapolis: University of Minnesota Press, 1986), 14.

11. For a personal assessment of Celan and the imperative, see Esther Beatrice Cameron, "Paul Celan, Dichter des Imperativs. Ein Brief," *Bulletin des Leo Baeck Instituts* 59 (1981), 55–91.

12. Cf. Calvert Watkins, "What Is Philology?" *Comparative Literature Studies* 27, no. 1 (1990), 25.

13. *Sämtliche Werke*, ed. Friedrich Beißner (Stuttgart: Kolhammer, 1951), 2(1):163.

14. Cf. Hans-Jost Frey, "Textrevision bei Hölderlin," in *Der unendliche Text* (Frankfort: Suhrkamp, 1990), 104–5, to whom this discussion is indebted. Any analysis of the relationship between *Ort* and *Wort* in Celan, of the significance of this *topos* as well as of its place in his writings, will have to take into account a poem such as "Deine Augen im Arm," collected in *Fadensonnen*,

in which it is stated: "Mach den Ort aus, machs Wort aus" (*GW* 2:123). Investigating the nature of negative prefixes in German, the poem goes on to say: "Vermessen, entmessen, verortet, entwortet, // entwo"—words which recall, among other poems, "Eingewohnt–Entwohnt" (*GW* 2:156). Compare also the crucial lines of "Engführung"—

Der Ort, wo sie lagen, er hat
einen Namen, er hat
keinen. Sie lagen nicht dort. Etwas
lag zwischen ihnen . . .
  (*GW* 1:198)

The place where they lay, it has
a name—it has
none. They did not lie there. Something
lay between them . . .
  (*P* 137)

—with its deictic play on *er* ("he") lying "between" "D*er* Ort," that is, "dort."

15. *Sämtliche Werke*, 2(1):185. For a study in light of this *topos* in Hölderlin, see Rainer Nägele, *Text, Geschichte und Subjektivität in Hölderlins Dichtung. "Uneßbarer Schrift gleich"* (Stuttgart: Metzler, 1985).

16. The most precise formulation of the importance of "precision" (*Präzision*) may be found in Celan's response to the Flinker questionnaire in 1958. See *GW* 3:167/*CP* 15–16. As for "exactness" (*Genauigkeit*), Celan, in a letter to the Mandelstam translator Gleb Struve on January 29, 1959, refers to his "constant effort at philological exactness." See *Paul Celan. Materialien*, ed. Werner Hamacher and Winfried Menninghaus (Frankfort: Suhrkamp, 1988), 12.

17. "Vorrede," *Morgenröte*, in Friedrich Nietzsche, *Werke*, ed. Karl Schlechta (Frankfurt am Main: Ullstein, 1981), 2:16. "Preface," in Friedrich Nietzsche, *Daybreak: Thoughts on the Prejudices of Morality*, trans. R. J. Hollingdale (Cambridge: Cambridge University Press, 1982), 3.

18. "Vorrede," *Zur Genealogie der Moral*, in *Werke*, 3:216. "Preface," in Friedrich Nietzsche, *On the Genealogy of Morals*, trans. Walter Kaufmann (New York: Vintage, 1967), 23.

19. "Immer wieder neue Sintflut," in Nelly Sachs, *Suche nach Lebenden* (Frankfort Main: Suhrkamp, 1971), 37. "New Flood Again and Again," in Nelly Sachs, *O the Chimneys*, trans. Michael Hamburger (New York: Farrar, Straus, & Giroux, 1967), 265 (trans. modified).

20. *GW* 2:24. In the Lynch-Jankowsky translation, the poem reads:

YOUR WAKING'S BUCK DREAM.
With the word trace, screw-
shaped, carved
twelve times
into its horn.

The last stab that it makes.

The ferry, poling
up through the
vertical, narrow
day-cleft:

it carries across
the wound-read.
(*65 Poems* 56 [trans. modified])

Acknowledgments

The editor wishes to thank Alan Udoff, Baltimore Hebrew University, for the original suggestion that instigated the project; Eric Halpern, of the Johns Hopkins University Press, for his commitment to it; and Sarah Roff, the Johns Hopkins University, for her editorial assistance in the course of preparing this volume. A grant from the Yale University Mellon–West European Studies Project made copyediting easier, and a fellowship from The Getty Center for the History of Art and the Humanities, Santa Monica, California, facilitated final corrections.

Several of the essays have previously appeared elsewhere, in part or in whole: Chapter 1 appeared as Jacques Derrida, *Schibboleth pour Paul Celan* (Paris: Galilée, 1986), and in an earlier, shorter English version as "Shibboleth," in *Midrash and Literature*, ed. Geoffrey H. Hartman and Sanford Budick (New Haven: Yale University Press, 1986), 307–47, copyright © Editions Galilée for the French, and copyright © Yale University Press for the English; a shorter version of Chapter 2, Otto Pöggeler, "Sein und Nichts. Mystische Elemente bei Heidegger und Celan," appeared in *Zu dir hin*, ed. Wolfgang Böhme (Frankfort: Insel, 1987), 270–301; Chapter 4, here entitled "Catastrophe," appeared as a section of Philippe Lacoue-Labarthe, *La poésie comme expérience* (Paris: Bourgois, 1986), 61–103, copyright © Christian Bourgois Editeur; Chapter 7, Werner Hamacher, "Die Sekunde der Inversion. Bewegungen einer Figur durch Celans Gedichte," appeared in *Paul Celan. Materialien*, ed. Werner Hamacher and Winfried Menninghaus (Frankfort: Suhrkamp, 1988), 81–126, and in an earlier English version as "The Second of Inversion: Movements of a Figure through Celan's Poetry," trans. William D. Jewett, in *Yale French Studies* 69 (1985), 276–311, copyright © Suhrkamp Verlag for the German; Chapter 8, here entitled "Spectral Analysis: A Commentary on 'Solve' and 'Coagula,'" appeared as a section of Anders Olsson, *Den okända texten* (Stockholm: Bonniers, 1987), 125–37, copyright © Albert Bonniers Förlag AB; Chapter 9, Hans-Jost Frey, "Zwischentextlichkeit von Celans Gedicht: 'Zwölf Jahre' und 'Auf Reisen,'" appeared in *Der unendliche Text* (Frankfort: Suhrkamp, 1990), 52–75, copyright © Suhrkamp Verlag; portions of Chapter 10, Aris Fioretos, "Ingenting," appeared as Afterword to

Jacques Derrida, *Schibboleth för Paul Celan*, trans. Aris Fioretos and Hans Ruin (Stockholm: Symposion, 1990), 129–52, and partly in an earlier English version as "Nothing: Reading Paul Celan's 'Engführung,'" in *Comparative Literature Studies* 27, no. 2 (1990), 158–68, copyright © Symposion Bokförlag och Tryckeri AB for the Swedish, and copyright © Pennsylvania State University for the English; and Chapter 11, Hans-Jost Frey, "Die Beziehung zwischen Übersetzung und Original als Text," appeared in *Der unendliche Text* (Frankfort: Suhrkamp, 1990), 38–50, copyright © Suhrkamp Verlag. Permission to reprint is gratefully acknowledged.

Throughout, the German original of Celan's poems is from *Gesammelte Werke*, ed. Beda Allemann and Stefan Reichert, in collaboration with Rolf Bücher (Frankfort: Suhrkamp, 1983), 5 vols., and reprinted by permission of Deutsche Verlagsanstalt (vol. 1); S. Fischer Verlag (vol. 1); and Suhrkamp Verlag (remaining vols.). Translations by Jerry Glenn are taken from Paul Celan, "The Meridian," in *Chicago Review* 29, no. 3 (1978), 29–40, copyright © University of Chicago Press; translations by Michael Hamburger from *Poems by Paul Celan* (New York: Persea Books, 1989), copyright © Persea Books; translations by Brian Lynch and Peter Jankowsky from Paul Celan, *65 Poems* (Dublin: Raven Arts Press, 1985), copyright © Raven Arts Press; translations by Joachim Neugroschel from Paul Celan, *Speech-Grille and Selected Poems* (New York: Dutton, 1971); translations by Rosmarie Waldrop from Paul Celan, *Collected Prose* (Manchester: Carcanet, 1986), copyright © Carcanet Press; and translations by Katherine Washburn and Margret Guillemin from Paul Celan, *Last Poems* (San Francisco: North Point Press, 1986), © North Point Press. Permission to reprint is in all cases gratefully acknowledged.

Abbreviations

Throughout, references to Celan's work are to *Gesam-melte Werke*, ed. Beda Allemann and Stefan Reichert, in collaboration with Rolf Bücher (Frankfort: Suhrkamp, 1983), 5 vols., using the abbreviation *GW*, followed by arabic numerals designating volume and page; and to *Das Frühwerk*, ed. Barbara Wiedemann (Frankfort: Suhrkamp, 1989), abbreviated as *F*. English translations are from *The Poems of Paul Celan*, trans. Michael Hamburger (New York: Persea Books, 1989), abbreviated as *P*, or in the cases where Hamburger does not offer English renditions, either from Paul Celan, *Last Poems*, trans. Katherine Washburn and Margret Guillemin (San Francisco: North Point Press, 1986), abbreviated as *LP*; from Paul Celan, *Speech-Grille and Selected Poems*, trans. Joachim Neugroschel (New York: Dutton, 1971), abbreviated as *SG*; or from Paul Celan, *65 Poems*, trans. Brian Lynch and Peter Jankowsky (Dublin: Raven Arts Press, 1985). At times, the translations have been modified (and duly noted). Celan's prose texts are quoted from Paul Celan, *Collected Prose*, trans. Rosmarie Waldrop (Manchester: Carcanet, 1986), using the abbreviation *CP*.

"GIVE THE WORD"

Shibboleth

For Paul Celan

Jacques Derrida
Translated by Joshua Wilner

I

One time alone: circumcision takes place but once.

Such, at least, is the appearance we receive, and the tradition of the appearance, we do not say of the semblance.

We will have to circle around this appearance. Not so much in order to circumscribe or circumvent some *truth* of circumcision—that must be given up for essential reasons. But rather to let ourselves be approached by the resistance that "once" may offer thought. And it is a question of offering, and of that which such resistance *gives* one to think. As for resistance, this will be our theme as well, calling up the last war, all wars, clandestine activity, demarcation lines, discrimination, passports and passwords.

Before we ask ourselves what, if anything, is meant by the word "once," and the word "time" in "one time alone"; before interpreting, as philosophers or philosophers of language, as hermeneuts or poeticians, the meaning or truth of what one speaks of in English as "once," we should no doubt keep a long and thoughtful while to those linguistic borders where, as you know, only those who know how to pronounce *shibboleth* are granted passage and, indeed, life. "Once," "one time"—nothing, one would think, could be easier to translate: "une fois," "einmal," "una volta." We will find ourselves returning more than once to the vicissitudes of latinity, to the Spanish "vez," to the whole syntax of *vicem, vice, vices, vicibus, vicissim, in vicem, vice versa,* and even *vicarius,* to its turns, returns, replacements, and supplantings, voltes and revolutions. For the moment, a single remark: the semantic registers of all these idioms do not *immediately* translate one another; they appear heterogeneous. One speaks of "time" in the English "one time," but not in

3

"once," or "einmal," or any of the French, Italian, or Spanish locutions. The Latin idioms resort rather to the figure of the turn or volte, the turnabout. And yet, despite this border, the crossing of ordinary translation takes place every day without the least uncertainty, each time that the semantics of the everyday imposes its conventions. Each time that it effaces the idiom.

If a circumcision takes place one time only, this time is thus, *at once, at the same time*, the first and last time. This is the appearance—archaeology and eschatology—that we will have to circle around, as around the ring that it traces, carves out, or sets off. This ring or annulation is at once the seal of an alliance or wedding band,[1] the circling back on itself of an anniversary date, and the year's recurrence.

I will speak then about circumcision and the one-and-only time, in other words, of what *comes* to mark itself as the one-and-only time: what one sometimes calls a *date*.

My main concern will not be to speak about the date so much as to listen to Celan speak about it. Better still, to watch as he gives himself over to the inscription of invisible, perhaps unreadable, dates: anniversaries, rings, constellations, and repetitions of singular, unique, *unrepeatable* events: "unwiederholbar," this is his word.

How can one date what does not repeat if dating also calls for some form of recurrence, if it recalls in the readability of a repetition? But how date anything other than that which does not repeat?

Having just named the unrepeatable (*unwiederholbar*) and marked the borders of translation, I am led to cite here the poem Celan entitled, in French, "A la pointe acérée,"[2] not because it has any direct connection with the surgery of circumcision, but because it seeks its way in the night along paths of questions "Nach / dem Unwiederholbaren," after the unrepeatable. I will limit myself at first to these small pebbles of white chalk on a board, a sort of nonwriting in which the concretion of language hardens:

Ungeschriebenes, zu
Sprache verhärtet . . .

(Unwritten things, hardened
into language . . .)[3]

Without writing, un-writing, the unwritten switches over to a question of reading on a board or tablet which you perhaps are. You are a board or a door: much later, we will see how a word can address itself, indeed confide itself to a door, count on a door open to the other.

Tür du davor einst, Tafel

(Door you in front of it once, tablet)

(And with this "einst" it is again a question of one time, one time alone)

mit dem getöteten
Kreidestern drauf:
ihn
hat nun ein—lesendes?—Aug.
    (*GW* 1:251)

(with the killed
chalk star on it: that
a—reading?—eye has now.
    (*P* 195 [trans. modified])

We could have followed in this poem the ever discrete, discontinuous, *caesuraed*, elliptical circuitry of the hour ("Waldstunde"), or of the
trace, and of the track of a wheel that turns on itself ("Radspur"). But
here what I am *after* is the question which seeks its way *after* ("nach")
the unrepeatable, through beechmast ("Buchecker"). Which may also
be read as book corners or the sharp, gaping edges of a text:

Wege dorthin
Waldstunde an
der blubbernden Radspur entlang.
Auf-
gelesene
kleine, klaffende
Buchecker: schwärzliches
Offen, von
Fingergedanken befragt
nach—
wonach?

Nach
dem Unwiederholbaren, nach
ihm, nach
allem.

Blubbernde Wege dorthin.

Etwas, das gehn kann, grußlos
wie Herzgewordenes,
kommt.
    (*GW* 1:251–52)

(Ways to that place.
Forest hour alongside
the spluttering wheeltrack.
Col-
lected
small, gaping
beechnuts: blackish
openness, asked of
by fingerthoughts
after—
after what?

After
the unrepeatable, after
it, after
everything.

Spluttering tracks to that place.

Something that can go, ungreeting
as all that's become heart,
is coming.)
        (*P* 195 [trans. modified])

Ways ("Wege"): something comes, which can go ("Etwas, das gehn kann, . . . kommt"). What is going, coming, going to come, going and coming? and becoming heart? What coming, what singular event is in question? What impossible repetition ("Nach / dem Unwiederholbaren, nach / ihm)?

How to "become heart"? Let us not, for the moment, invoke Pascal or Heidegger—who in any case suspects the first of having yielded too much to science and forgotten the original thinking of the heart. Hearing me speak of the date and of circumcision, there are those who might rush on to the "circumcised heart" of the Scriptures. That would be moving too fast and along a path of too little resistance. Celan's trenchant ellipsis requires more patience, it demands more discretion. Caesura is the law. But it gathers in the discretion of the discontinuous, in the cutting in of the relation to the other or in the interruption of address, as address itself.

It makes no sense, as you may well suppose, to dissociate in Celan's writings those *on the subject* of the date, which name the theme of the date, from the poetic traces of dating; to rely on the division between a theoretical, philosophical, hermeneutic, or even technopoetic discourse concerning the phenomenon of the date, on the one hand, and its poetic implementation,[4] on the other, is to no longer read him.

The example of the "Meridian" warns us against such a misconstruction. It is, as they say, a "discourse": one pronounced on a given occasion and at a given date—that is, an address. Its date is that of the conferral of a prize ("Rede anläßlich der Verleihung des Georg-Büchner-Preises, am 22. Oktober 1960" [*GW* 3:187]). On October 22, 1960, this address deals, in its way, with art or more precisely with the memory of art, perhaps with art as a thing of the past, Hegel would have said: it deals with "art as we already know it" but also as "a problem, and, as we can see, one that is variable, tough, long lived, let us say, eternal" (*GW* 3:188/*CP* 38). The thing of the past: "Meine Damen und Herren! Die Kunst, das ist, Sie erinnern sich . . . ," "Art, you will remember . . ." (*GW* 3:187/*CP* 37). The ironic attack of this first sentence seems to speak of a history gone by, but it does so in order to call on the memory of those who have read Büchner. Celan announces that he is going to evoke several appearances of art, in particular in *Woyzeck* and *Leonce und Lena*: you remember. A thing from our past that comes back in memory, but also a problem for the future, an eternal problem, and above all a way toward poetry. Not poetry, but a way in view of poetry, one way only, one among others and not the shortest. "This would mean art is the distance poetry must cover, no less and no more. I know that there are other, shorter, routes. But poetry, too, can be ahead. *La poésie, elle aussi, brûle nos étapes*" (*GW* 3:194/*CP* 44–45).

At this crossing of ways between art and poetry, in this place to which poetry makes its way at times without even the patience of a path, lies the enigma of the date.

It seems to resist every philosophical question and mode of questioning, every objectification, every theoretico-hermeneutic thematization.

Celan shows this poetically: by a *mise-en-oeuvre* of the date. In this address itself. He begins by citing several dates: 1909, the date of a work devoted to Jakob Michael Lenz by a university lecturer in Moscow, M. N. Rosanov; then the night of May 23–24, 1792, a date itself cited, already mentioned in this work, the date of Lenz's death in Moscow. Then Celan *mentions* the date which appears this time on the first page of Büchner's *Lenz*, "the Lenz who 'on the 20th of January was walking through the mountains'" (*GW* 3:194/*CP* 46).

Who was walking through the mountains, *on this date?*

He, Lenz, Celan insists, he and not the artist preoccupied by the questions of art. He, as an "I," "er als ein Ich." This "I" who is not the artist obsessed by questions of art, those posed to him by art—Celan does not rule out that it may be the poet; but in any case it is not the artist.

The singular turn of this syntagm, "he as an I," will support the whole logic of individuation, of that "sign of individuation" which each poem constitutes. The poem is "one person's language become shape" ("gestaltgewordene Sprache eines Einzelnen" [*GW* 3:197–98/*CP* 49]). Singularity but also solitude: the only one, the poem is alone ("einsam"). And from within the most intimate essence of its solitude, it is en route ("unterwegs"), "aspiring to a present," following the French translation of André du Bouchet[5] ("und seinem innersten Wesen nach Gegenwart und Präsenz" [*GW* 3:198/*CP* 49 (trans. modified)]). Insofar as alone, the only one, the poem would keep itself then, perhaps, within the "secrecy of encounter."

The only one: singularity, solitude, the secrecy of encounter. What assigns the only one to its date? For example: there was a 20th of January. A date of this kind will have permitted its being written, alone, unique, exempt from repetition. Yet this absolute property can be transcribed, exported, deported, expropriated, reappropriated, repeated in its utter singularity. Indeed, this has to be if the date is to expose itself, to risk losing itself in readability. This absolute property can enunciate, as its sign of individuation, something like the essence of the poem, the only one. Celan prefers to say, of "every poem," better still, of "each poem." "Vielleicht darf man sagen, daß jedem Gedicht sein '20. Jänner' eingeschrieben bleibt?": "Perhaps we can say that each poem remains marked by its own 20th of January?" (*GW* 3:196/*CP* 47 [trans. modified]). Here is a generality: to the keeping of each poem, thus of every poem, the inscription of a date, of this date, for example a "20th of January," is entrusted. But despite the generality of this law, the example remains irreplaceable. And what must remain, committed to the keeping, in other words to the truth of each poem, is the irreplaceable itself: the example offers its example only on condition that it holds for no other. But it offers its example in that very fact, and the only example possible, the one which it alone offers: the only one.

Today, on this day, at this date. And this marking of today tells us perhaps something of the essence of the poem today, for us now. Not the essence of poetic modernity or postmodernity, not the essence of an epoch or a period in some history of poetry, but what happens "today" "anew" to poetry, to poems, what happens to them at this date.

What happens to them at this date is precisely the date, a certain experience of the date. One no doubt very ancient, dateless, but absolutely new at this date. And new because, for the first time, it here shows itself or is sought after, "most plainly" ("am deutlichsten"). Clarity, distinction, sharpness, readability, this is what today would be *new*. What thus becomes readable is not, it must be understood, the date *itself*, but only the poetic experience of the date, that which a date, *this one*, ordains in our relation to it, a certain poetic seeking. "Perhaps the newness of poems written today is that they try most plainly to be mindful of this kind of date?" ("Vielleicht ist das Neue an den Gedichten, die heute geschrieben werden, gerade dies: daß hier am deutlichsten versucht wird, solcher Daten eingedenk zu bleiben?") (*GW* 3:196/*CP* 47).

This question concerning the date, this hypothesis ("Perhaps . . ."), is dated by Celan; it relates *today* to every poem *today*, to what is new in each poetic work of our time, each of which, at this date, would share the singularity of dating (transitively), of remaining mindful of dates ("Daten eingedenk zu bleiben"). The poetic today would perhaps be dated by an inscription of the date or at least a certain coming to light, newly, of a poetic necessity which, for its part, does not date from to-day. Granted.

But—the sentences which we have just heard are followed by three "Buts": three times "But."

The first, the least energetic and the least oppositional, raises again the same questions concerning the traces of the other *as I*: how can some *other* irreplaceable and singular date, the date of the other, the date for the other, be deciphered, transcribed, or appropriated? How can I appropriate it for myself? Or rather, how can I transcribe myself into it? And how can the memory of such a date still dispose of a future? What dates to come do we prepare in such a transcription? Here, then, is the first "But." The ellipsis of the sentence is more economical than I can convey and its gripping sobriety can only register, which is to say, date itself, from within its idiom, a certain way of inhabiting and dealing with the idiom (signed: Celan from a certain place in the German language, which was his property alone). "But do we not all transcribe ourselves out of such dates? And to what dates to come do we ascribe ourselves?" ("Aber schreiben wir uns nicht alle von solchen Daten her? Und welchen Daten schreiben wir uns zu?") (*GW* 3:196/*CP* 47 [variant trans.]).

Here the second "But" is sounded, but only after a blank space, the mark of a very long silence, the time of a meditation through which the preceding question makes its way. It leaves the trace of an affirmation, over against which arises, at least to complicate it, a second affirmation. And its force of opposition reaches the point of exclamation: "But the poem speaks! It is mindful of its dates, but it speaks. True, it speaks only on its own, its very own behalf" ("Aber das Gedicht spricht ja! Es bleibt seiner Daten eingedenk, aber—es spricht. Gewiß, es spricht immer nur in seiner eigenen, allereigensten Sache") (*GW* 3:196/*CP* 48 [trans. modified]).

What does this "but" mean? No doubt that *despite* the date, in spite of its memory rooted in the singularity of an event, the poem speaks; to all and in general, to the other first of all. The "but" seems to carry the poem's utterance beyond its date: if the poem recalls a date, calls itself back to its date, to the date *on which* it is written or *of which* it writes, as of which it writes, nonetheless it speaks! to all, to the other, to whoever does not share the experience or the knowledge of the singularity thus dated: *as of* or *from* a given place, a given day, a given month, a given year. In the preceding phrase, the ambiguous force of *von* collects in itself in advance all of our paradoxes ("Aber schreiben wir uns nicht alle von solchen Daten her?"): we write *of* the date, *about* certain dates, but also *as of* certain dates, *at* [à] certain dates. But the English "at," like the French "à," may be turned by the ambiguous force of its own idiom toward a future of unknown destination, something which was not literally said by any given sentence of Celan's, but which doubtless corresponds to the general logic of this discourse, as made explicit in the sentence that follows, "Und welchen Daten schreiben wir uns zu?" To what dates do we ascribe ourselves, what dates do we appropriate, now, but also, in more ambiguous fashion, turned toward what dates to come do we write ourselves, do we transcribe ourselves? As if writing *at* a certain date meant not only writing on a given day, at a given hour, but also writing to [*à*] the date, addressing oneself to it, committing oneself to the date as to the other, the date past as well as the promised date.

What is this "to" of "to come"[6]—as date?

Yet the poem speaks. Despite the date, even if it also speaks thanks to it, of it, as of it, to it, and speaks always of itself, "on its own, very own behalf" (*CP* 48), "in seiner eigenen, allereigensten Sache" (*GW* 3:196), in its own name, without ever compromising with the absolute singularity, the inalienable propriety of that which convokes it. And yet, the inalienable must speak of the other, and to the other, it must speak. The date provokes the poem, but the latter speaks! And it speaks of what provokes it, *to* the date which provokes it, thus convoked from the future of the *same* date, in other words from its recurrence at *another* date.

How are we to understand the exclamation? Why this exclamation point after the "but" of what would seem in no way to be a rhetorical objection? One might find it surprising. I think that it confers the accent, it accentuates and marks the tone, of admiration, of astonishment in the face of poetic exclamation itself. The poet exclaims—faced with the miracle that makes clamor, poetic acclamation, possible: the poem speaks! and it speaks to the date of which it speaks! Instead of walling it up and reducing it to the silence of singularity, a date gives it its chance, the chance to speak to the other!

If the poem is *due* its date, due to its date, owes itself to its date as its own inmost concern (*Sache*) or signature, if it owes itself to its secret, it speaks of this date only insofar as it acquits itself, so to speak, of a given date—and of that date which is also a gift—releasing itself from the date without denying it, and above all without disavowing it. It absolves itself of it so that its utterance may resonate and proclaim beyond a singularity which might otherwise remain undecipherable, mute, and immured in its date—in the unrepeatable. One must, while preserving its memory, speak of the date that already speaks of itself: the date, by its mere occurrence, by the inscription of a sign as a memorandum, will have broken the silence of pure singularity. But to speak of it, one must also efface it, make it readable, audible, intelligible *beyond the pure singularity* of which it speaks. Now the beyond of absolute singularity, the chance of the poem's exclamation, is not the simple effacement of the date in a generality, but its *effacement faced with* another date, the one *to which* it speaks, the date of an other strangely wed or joined in the secrecy of an encounter, a chance secret, with the same date. I will offer— by way of clarification—some examples in a moment.

What takes place in this experience of the date, experience itself? and of a date which must be effaced in order to be preserved, in order to preserve the commemoration of the event, that advent of the unique in thrall to the poem which must exceed it and which alone, by itself, may transport it, deliver it to understanding beyond the unreadability of its cipher? What takes place is perhaps what Celan calls a little further on "Geheimnis der Begegnung," "the secrecy of encounter" (*GW* 3:198/*CP* 49 [trans. modified]).

Encounter—in the word "encounter" two values come together without which there would be no date:[7] "encounter" as it suggests the random occurrence, the chance meeting, the coincidence or conjuncture that comes to seal one or more than one event *once*, at a given hour, on a given day, in a given month, in a given region; and "encounter" as it suggests an encounter with the other, the ineluctable singularity out of which and destined for which the poem speaks. In its otherness and its solitude (which is also that of the poem, "alone," "solitary"), it may inhabit the conjunction of one and the same date. This is what happens.

What happens, if something happens, is this; and this encounter, in an idiom, of all the meanings of encounter.

But—a third time, a third "but" opens a new paragraph. It begins with a "But I think," it closes with a "today and here," and it is the signature of an "Aber ich denke" . . . "heute und hier":

> But I think—and this will hardly surprise you—that the poem has always hoped, for this very reason, to speak also on behalf of the *strange*—no, I can no longer use this word here—*on behalf of the Other*—who knows, perhaps of an *altogether other.*
>
> This "who knows" which I have reached is all I can add here, today, to the old hopes. (*GW* 3:196/*CP* 48)

The "altogether other" thus opens the thought of the poem to some thing or some concern (*Sache*: "in eines Anderen Sache zu sprechen ... in eines ganz Anderen Sache") the otherness of which must not contradict but rather enter into alliance with, in expropriating, the "inmost concern" just in question, that due to which the poem speaks at its date, as of its date, and always "in seiner eigenen, allereigensten Sache." Several singular events may conjoin, enter into alliance, *concentrate* in the same date, which thus becomes both the same and other, altogether other as the same, capable of speaking to the other of the other, to the one who cannot decipher one or another absolutely closed date, a tomb closed over the event that it marks. This gathered multiplicity Celan calls by a strong and charged name: *concentration*. A little further on he speaks of the poem's "attentiveness" ("Aufmerksamkeit") to all that it encounters. This attentiveness would be rather a kind of concentration which remains mindful of "all our dates" ("eine aller unserer Daten eingedenk bleibende Konzentration") (*GW* 3:198/*CP* 50). The word can become a terrible word for memory. But one can understand it *at once* in that register in which one speaks of the gathering of the soul, of the heart, and of "spiritual concentration," as, for example, in the experience of prayer (and Celan cites Benjamin citing Malebranche in his essay on Kafka: "attention is the natural prayer of the soul" [*GW* 3:198/*CP* 50]), and in that other sense in which concentration gathers around the same anamnetic center a multiplicity of dates, "all our dates" coming to conjoin or constellate in a single occurrence or a single place: in truth in a single poem, in *the only one*, in that poem which is each time, we have seen, alone, the only one, solitary and singular.

This is perhaps what goes on in the exemplary act of the "Meridian." This discourse, this address, this speech act (*Rede*) is not—not only—a treatise or a metadiscourse *on the subject of* the date, but rather the habitation, by a poem, of its own date, its poetic *mise-en-oeuvre* as well, making of a date which is the poet's own a date for the other, the date of the other, or, inversely, for the gift comes around like an anniversary, a step by which the poet ascribes or commits himself to the date of the other. In the unique ring of its constellation, one and the "same" date commemorates heterogeneous events, each suddenly neighboring the other, even as one knows that they remain, and must continue to remain, infinitely foreign. It is just this which is called the encounter, the encounter of the other, "the secrecy of encounter"—and precisely here the Meridian is discovered. There was a 20th of January, that of Lenz who "on the 20th of January was walking through the mountains." And then at the *same* date, on *another* 20th of January, Celan encounters, he encounters the other and he encounters himself at the intersection of this date with itself, with itself as other, as the date of the other. And yet this takes place but once, and always anew, each time but once, the each-time-but-one-time-alone alone constituting a generic law. One would have to resituate here the question of the transcendental schematism, of the imagination and of time, as a question of the date—*of the once*. And one would have to reread what Celan had said earlier about images:

13

> Then what are images?
> What has been, what can be perceived, again and again, and only here, only now. Hence the poem is the place where all tropes and metaphors want to be led *ad absurdum*. (*GW* 3:199/*CP* 51)

This radical *ad absurdum*, the impossibility of that which, each time once alone, has meaning only on condition of having no meaning, no ideal or general meaning, or which has meaning only so as to invoke, in order to betray it, the concept, law, or genre, is the pure poem. Now the pure poem does not exist, or rather, it is that "which does not exist" ("das es nicht gibt!"). To the question: of what do I speak when I speak not of poems but of the poem, Celan answers: "I speak of the poem which does not exist! / The absolute poem—no, it certainly does not, cannot exist!" (*GW* 3:199/*CP* 51 [trans. modified]).

But if the absolute poem does not take place, if there is none ("es gibt nicht"), there is the image, the each time once alone, the poetic of the date and the secrecy of encounter: the other-I, a 20th of January which was also mine after having been that of Lenz. Here:

> Several years ago, I wrote a little quatrain:
>
> "Voices from the path through nettles:
> *Come to us on your hands.*
> Alone with your lamp.
> Only your hand to read."
>
> And a year ago, I commemorated a missed encounter in the Engadine valley by putting a little story on paper where I had a man "like Lenz" walk through the mountains.
> Both the one time and the other, I had transcribed myself from a "20th of January," from my "20th of January."
> I . . . encountered myself. (*GW* 3:201/*CP* 52–53 [trans. modified])

I encountered myself—myself like the other, one 20th of January *like* another, and *like* Lenz, as Lenz *himself*, "wie Lenz": the quotation marks around the expression set off, in the text, what is strange in the figure.

This "like" is also the signal of another appearance summoned within the same comparison. This man whom I described, wrote, signed, was *just like* Lenz, almost like Lenz himself, *as* Lenz. The *wie* almost has the force of an *als*. But *at the same time*, it is myself since in this figure of the other, as the other, it is myself whom I encountered at this date. The "like" is the co-signature of the date, the very figure or image, each time, of the other, "the one time and the other," one time *like* the other time ("das eine wie das andere Mal"). Such would be the anniversary turn of the date. In the "Meridian," it is also the finding, the encountering of the place of encounter, the discovery of the meridian itself:

> I am also, since I am again at my point of departure, searching for my own place of origin.
> I am looking for all of this with my imprecise, because nervous, finger on a map—a child's map, I must admit.
> None of these places can be found. They do not exist. But I know where they ought to exist, especially now and . . . I find something else!
> . . . I find something which consoles me a bit for having walked this impossible road in your presence, this road of the impossible.
> I find the connective which, like the poem, leads to encounters.
> I find something—like language—immaterial, yet earthly, terrestrial, something in the shape of a circle which, via both poles, rejoins itself and on the way serenely crosses even the tropes: I find . . . a *meridian*. (*GW* 3:202/*CP* 54–55 [trans. modified])

Almost the last word of the text, near the signature. What Celan finds or discovers *all at once*, invents if one may say so, more and less than a fiction, is not only a meridian, the Meridian, but the word and the image, the trope "meridian" which offers the example of the law, in its inexhaustible polytropy, and which binds ("das Verbindende," both that which binds and that which connects or acts as intermediary), which provokes in broad daylight, *at noon*, at midday, the encounter of the other in a single place, at a single point, that of the poem, of this poem: "in the here and now of the poem—and the poem has only this one, unique, momentary present—even in this immediacy and nearness, that which is addressed gives voice to what is most its own: its time, the time of the other" (*GW* 3:198–99/*CP* 50 [trans. modified]).

II

A date would be the gnomon of these meridians.

Does one ever speak of a date? But does one ever speak without speaking of a date? Of it and as of it?

Whether one will or not, whether or not one knows it, acknowledges it or dissembles it, an utterance is always dated. What I am going to hazard concerning the date in general, concerning that which a generality may say or gainsay where the date is concerned, concerning the gnomon of Paul Celan,[8] will all be dated in its turn.

Under certain conditions at least, what dating amounts to is signing. To inscribe a date, to enter it, is not simply to sign as of a given year, month, day, or hour (all words which haunt the whole of Celan's text), but also to sign from a given place. Certain poems are "dated" Zürich, Tübingen, Todtnauberg, Paris, Jerusalem, Lyon, Tel Aviv, Vienna, Assisi, Cologne, Geneva, Brest, etc. At the beginning or at the end of a letter, the date consigns a "now" of the calendar or of the clock ("alle Uhren und Kalender": second page of the "Meridian" [GW 3:188/ CP 38]), as well as the "here," in their proper names, of the country, region, or house. It marks in this way, at the point of the gnomon, the provenance of what is *given*, or, in any case, sent; of what is, whether or not it arrives, destined. *Addressing its date*, what an address or discourse declares about the concept or meaning of the date is not, by this fact, dated, in the sense in which one says of something that it dates in order to imply that it has aged, or aged badly; in speaking of a discourse as dated, our intention is not to disqualify or invalidate it, but rather to signify that it is, at the least, marked by its date, signed by it or remarked in a singular manner. What is thus remarked is its point of *departure*, that to which it no doubt belongs but from which it departs in order to address itself to the other: a certain imparting.[9]

It is concerning this singular remarking that I am going to hazard in my turn some remarks—in memory of some missives dated from Paul Celan.

What is a date? Do we have the right to pose such a question, and in this form? The form of the question "what is" has a provenance. It has its place of origin and its language. It dates. That it is dated does not discredit it, but if we had the time, we could draw certain philosophical inferences from this fact, inferences indeed *about* the philosophical regime that this question governs.

Has anyone ever been concerned with the question "what is a date?" The "you" who is told "Nirgends / fragt es nach dir," nowhere is there any asking about you, nowhere any concern with you, is a date, of that we may be certain *a priori*. This you, which must be an I, like the *er als ein Ich* of a moment ago, always figures an irreplaceable singularity. Only another singularity, just as irreplaceable, can take its place without substituting for it. One addresses this you as one addresses a date, the here and now of a commemorable provenance.

As it reaches me, at least, the question "what is a date?" presupposes two things.

First of all, the question "what is . . ." has a history or provenance; it is signed, engaged, or commanded by a place, a time, a language or a network of languages, in other words by a date in relation to whose essence this question's power is hence limited, its claim finite, and its very pertinence contestable. This fact is not unrelated to what our symposium calls "the philosophical implications" of Celan's work. Perhaps philosophy, as such, and insofar as it makes use of the question "what is

... ?," has nothing essential to say about what bears Celan's date or about what Celan says or makes of the date—and which might in its turn say something to us, perhaps, about philosophy.

On the other hand, and this is a second presupposition, in the inscription of a date, in the explicit and coded phenomenon of dating, *what is dated must not be dated.* The date: yes and no, Celan would say, as he does more than once.

> Sprich—
> Doch scheide das Nein nicht vom Ja.
> Gib deinem Spruch auch den Sinn:
> gib ihm den Schatten.
>
> Gib ihm Schatten genug,
> gib ihm so viel,
> als du um dich verteilt weißt zwischen
> Mittnacht und Mittag und Mittnacht.
>
> (Speak—
> But keep yes and no unsplit.
> And give your say this meaning:
> give it the shade.
>
> Give it shade enough
> give it as much
> as you know has been dealt out between
> midnight and midday and midnight.)[10]

Again the meridian. It is necessary that the mark which one calls a date must be *marked off,* in a singular manner, detached from the very thing that it dates; and that in this de-marcation, this deportation, it become readable, that it become readable, precisely, as a date in wresting or exempting itself from itself, from its immediate adherence, from the here and now; in freeing itself from what it nonetheless remains, a date. It is necessary that the unrepeatable (*das Unwiederholbare*) be repeated in it, effacing in itself the irreducible singularity which it denotes. It is necessary that in a certain manner it divide itself in repeating, and in the same stroke encipher or encrypt itself. Like *physis*, a date loves to encrypt itself. It must efface itself in order to become readable, to render itself unreadable in its very readability. For if it does not annul in itself the unique marking which connects it to an event without witness, without other witness, it remains intact but absolutely indecipherable. It is no longer even what it has to be, what it will have had to be, its essence and its destination, it no longer keeps its promise, that of a date.

How, then, can that which is dated, while at the same time marking a date, not date? This question, whether one finds this hopeful or troubling, cannot be formulated in this way in all languages. It remains barely translatable. I insist on this because what a date, always bound up with some proper name, gives us to think, commemorate, or bless, as well as to cross in a possible-impossible translation, is, each time, an idiom. And if the idiomatic form of my question may appear untranslatable, this is because it plays on the double functioning of the verb "to date." In French or in English. Transitively: I date a poem. Intransitively: a poem dates if it ages, if it has a history, and is of a certain age.

To ask "What is a date?" is not to wonder about the meaning of the word "date." Nor is it to inquire into established or putative etymology, though this may not be without interest for us. It might, in fact, lead us to think about gifts and literality, and, in particular, the giving of the letter: *data littera*, the first words of a formula for indicating the date. This would set us on the trace of the first word, of the initial or the opening of a letter, of the first letter of a letter—but also of something given[11] or sent. The sense of the date as something given or sent will carry us beyond the question given in the form "what is?" A date is not something which is there, since it withdraws in order to appear, but if *there is no* absolute poem ("Das absolute Gedicht—nein, das gibt es gewiß nicht, das kann es nicht geben!"), says Celan, perhaps there are (*es gibt*) dates—even if they do not exist.

I will associate for the moment, in a preliminary and disorderly way, the values of the given and the proper name (for a date functions like a proper name) with three other essential values:

1. That of the missive within the strict limits of the epistolary code.

2. The re-marking of place and time, at the point of the here and now.

3. The signature: if the date is an initial, it may come at the letter's end and in all cases, whether at the beginning or the end, have the force of a signed commitment, of an obligation, a promise or an oath (*sacramentum*). In its essence, a signature is always dated and has value only on this account. It dates and it has a date. And prior to being mentioned, the inscription of a date (here, now, this day, etc.) always entails a kind of signature: whoever inscribes the year, the day, the place, in short, the present of a "here and now," attests thereby to his or her own presence at the act of inscription.

Celan dated all his poems. I am not thinking here, in the first place, of a kind of dating which one might—mistakenly, but conveniently— call "external," that is, the mention of the date on which a poem was written. In its conventional form such mention lies in some ways outside the poem. One is certainly not entitled to push to the limit the distinction between such an external notation of the date and a more essential

18

incorporation of the date within a poem wherein it forms a part, a poem itself. In a certain way, as we will see, Celan's poetry tends to displace, indeed, to efface such a limit. But supposing we maintain for clarity of exposition the provisional hypothesis, we will concern ourselves first of all with a dating which is registered *in* the body of the poem, *in* one of its parts, and under a form which accords with the traditional code (for example, "the 13th of February"), and then with a nonconventional, noncalendrical form of dating, one which would merge entirely, without residue, with the general organization of the poetic text.

In "Eden," that memorable reading of a poem from *Schneepart*, "Du liegst im großen Gelausche" (*GW* 2:334), Szondi recalls that an indication of date accompanied its first publication: "Berlin 22./23. 12. 1967."[12] We know how Szondi turned to account these dates and his chance to have been the intimate witness of, and at times actor in, or party to, the experiences commemorated, displaced, and ciphered by the poem. We also know with what rigor and modesty he posed the problems of this *situation*, both with regard to the poem's genesis and with regard to the competence of its decipherers. With him, we must take into account the following fact: as the intimate and lucid witness of all the chance happenings and all the necessities that intersected in Celan's passing through Berlin *at this date*, Szondi was the only one able to bequeath us the irreplaceable passwords of access to the poem, a priceless *shibboleth*, a luminous, clamorous swarm of notes, so many signs of gratitude for a deciphering and translation of the enigma. And yet, left to itself without witness, without the alerted complicity of a decipherer, without even the "external" knowledge of its date, a certain internal necessity of the poem would nonetheless *speak* to us, in the sense in which Celan says of the poem, "But it speaks!" beyond what appears to confine it within the dated singularity of an individual experience.

Szondi was the first to acknowledge this. He set this enigma before himself with an admirable lucidity and prudence. How is one to give an account of this: concerning the circumstances in which the poem was written, or better, concerning those which it names, codes, disguises, or dates in its own body, concerning the secrets of which it partakes, witnessing is *at once* indispensable, *essential* to the reading of the poem, to the partaking which it becomes in its turn, and finally *supplementary*, *nonessential*, merely the guarantee of an excess of intelligibility which the poem can also forgo. *At once* essential and inessential. This *at once* derives, this is my hypothesis, from the structure of the date.

(I will not here give myself over to my own commemorations, I will not give over my dates. Permit me nevertheless to recall here that in my encounter with Paul Celan and in the friendship which subsequently bound us, such a short time before his death, Peter Szondi was always the mediator and witness, the common friend who presented us to one another in Paris, although we were already working there at the same institution. And this took place a few months after a visit which I made to the university in Berlin, at Szondi's invitation, in July 1968, just a short time after the month of December 1967 of which I spoke a moment ago.)

What does Szondi recall for us, from the outset of his reading? That Celan suppressed the poem's date for the first collection. It does not figure in the *Ausgewählte Gedichte* edited by Reichert in 1970.[13] This conforms, according to Szondi, with Celan's customary practice: "The poems are dated in the manuscript, but not in the published versions."[14]

But the retraction of what we are calling the "external" date does not do away with the internal dating. And while the latter harbors in its turn, as I will try to show, a force of self-effacement, what is involved in that case is another structure, that of the inscription of the date itself.

We will be concerned then with the date as a cut or incision which the poem bears in its body like a memory, like, at times, several memories in one, the mark of a provenance, of a place and of a time. To speak of an incision or cut is to say that the poem is entered into, that it begins in the wounding of its date.

If we had the time, we should patiently analyze the modalities of dating. There are many. In this typology, the most conventional form of dating, dating in the so-called literal or strict sense, involves marking a missive with coded signs. It entails reference to charts, and the utilization of systems of notation and spatio-temporal plottings said to be "objective": the calendar (year, month, day), the clock (the hours, whether or not they are named—and how often will Celan have named them, here or there, but only to restore them to the night of their ciphered silence: "sie werden die Stunde nicht nennen," "they will not name the hour" [*GW* 1:125/*P* 91]), toponomy, and first of all the names of cities. These coded marks all share a common resource, but also a dramatic and fatally equivocal power. Assigning or consigning absolute singularity, they must mark themselves off simultaneously, *at one and the same time*, and from themselves, by the possibility of commemoration. In effect, they mark only insofar as their readability enunciates the possibility of a recurrence. Not the absolute recurrence of that which precisely cannot return: a birth or circumcision takes place but once, nothing could be more self-evident. But rather the spectral return of that which, unique in its occurrence, will never return. A date is a specter. But the spectral return of this impossible recurrence is marked *in* the date; it seals or specifies itself in the sort of anniversary ring secured by the code. For example by the calendar. The anniversary ring inscribes the possibility of repetition, but also the circuit of return to the city whose name a date bears. The first inscription of a date signifies this possibility: that which cannot come back will come back as such, not only in memory, like all remembrance, but also at the same date, at an in any case analogous date, for example each February 13 . . . And each time, at the same date, what one commemorates will be the date *of* that which could never come back. This latter will have signed and sealed the unique, the unrepeatable; but to do so, it will have had to offer itself for reading in a form sufficiently coded, readable, and decipherable for the indecipherable to *appear* in the analogy of the anniversary ring (February 13, 1962 is *analogous* to February 13, 1936), even if it appears *as* indecipherable.

One is tempted to associate here all of Celan's rings with this alliance between the date and itself *as* other. There are many and they are all unique. I will cite only one; it imposes itself here, since it seals in the same beeswax—and the fingers themselves are of wax—the alliance, the letter, the ciphered name, the hive of the hours, and the writing of what is not written:

MIT BRIEF UND UHR

Wachs,
Ungeschriebnes zu siegeln,
das deinen Namen
erriet,
das deinen Namen
verschlüsselt.

Kommst du nun, schwimmendes Licht?

Finger, wächsern auch sie,
durch fremde,
schmerzende Ringe gezogen.
Fortgeschmolzen die Kuppen.

Kommst du, schwimmendes Licht?

Zeitleer die Waben der Uhr,
bräutlich das Immentausend,
reisebereit.

Komm, schwimmendes Licht.
    (*GW* 1:154)

(WITH LETTER AND CLOCK

Wax
to seal the unwritten

that guessed
your name,
that enciphers
your name.

Swimming light, will you come now?

Fingers, waxen too,
drawn
through strange, painful rings.
The tips melted away.

Swimming light, will you come?

Empty of time the honeycomb cells of the clock,
bridal the thousand of bees,
ready to leave.

Swimming light, come.)
    (*P* 107)

Clock and ring are quite close again in "Chymisch" (*GW* 1:227–28/
P 178–81). A ring awakens on our finger, and the fingers are the ring
itself, in "Es war Erde in ihnen" (*GW* 1:211/*P* 153). But above all, since
a date is never without a letter to be deciphered, I think of the ring of
the carrier-pigeon at the end of "La Contrescarpe." The carrier-pigeon
transports, transfers, or translates a coded message, but this is not a metaphor. It departs at its date, that of its sending, and it must return from
the other place to the same one, that from which it came, completing a
round trip. Now the question of the cipher is posed by Celan not only
with regard to the message but also with regard to the ring itself, sign
of belonging and alliance, and condition of return. The cipher of the
seal, the imprint of the ring, *counts*, perhaps more than the content of
the message. As with *shibboleth*, the meaning of the word matters less
than, let us say, its signifying form once it becomes a password, a mark
of belonging, the manifestation of an alliance:

Scherte die Brieftaube aus, war ihr Ring
zu entziffern? (All das
Gewölk um sie her—es war lesbar.) Litt es
der Schwarm? Und verstand,
und flog wie sie fortblieb?
    (*GW* 1:282)

(Did the carrier-pigeon sheer off, was its ring
decipherable? [All that
cloud around it—it was readable.] Did the
flock endure it? And understand,
and fly as the other went on?)

A date gets carried away, transported; it takes off, takes itself off—
and thus effaces itself in its very readability. Effacement is not something that befalls it like an accident; it affects neither its meaning nor
its readability; it merges, on the contrary, with reading's very access to
that which a date may still signify. But if readability effaces the date, the
very thing which it offers for reading, this strange process will have begun with the very inscription of the date. The date must conceal within
itself some stigma of singularity if it is to last longer—and this lasting
is the poem—than that which it commemorates. This is its only chance
of assuring its spectral return. Effacement or concealment, this annulment in the annulation of return belongs to the movement of dating.
And so what must be commemorated, *at once* gathered together and repeated, is, *at the same time*, the date's annihilation, a kind of nothing,
or ash.

Ash awaits us.

III

Let us keep for the moment to those dates that we recognize
through the language-grid of the calendar, the day, the month, and
sometimes the year.

First case: a date relates to an event which, at least *in appearance and
outwardly*, is distinct from the actual writing of the poem and the moment of its signing. The metonymy of the date (a date is always also a
metonymy) designates part of an event or a sequence of events by way
of recalling the whole. The mention "13th of February" forms a part of
what happened on that day, only a part, but it stands for the whole in a
given context. What happened on that day, in the first case which we
are going to consider, is not, in appearance and outwardly, the advent
of the poem.

The example then is that of the first line of "In eins" ("In One"). It
begins with "Dreizehnter Feber," "Thirteenth of February."

What is gathered and commemorated in the single time of this *in
eins*, in one poetic stroke? And is it a matter, moreover, of one commemoration? The "in one," "all at once," several times at once, seems to
constellate in the uniqueness of a date. But this date, in being unique
and *the only one*, all alone, the lone of its kind—is it one?

And what if there were more than one thirteenth of February? Not only because the thirteenth of February recurs, becoming each year its own *revenant*, but first of all because a multiplicity of events, dispersed (for example, on a political map of Europe, among other places), at different periods, in foreign idioms, may have conjoined at the heart of the same anniversary.

IN EINS

> Dreizehnter Feber. Im Herzmund
> erwachtes Schibboleth. Mit dir,
> Peuple
> de Paris. *No pasarán.*
>   (*GW* 1:270)

(IN ONE

> Thirteenth of February. In the heart's mouth
> An awakened shibboleth. With you,
> Peuple
> de Paris. *No pasarán.*)
>   (*P* 206)

Like the rest of the poem, and well in excess of what I could say concerning them, these first lines are *evidently* ciphered.

Ciphered, in full evidence: in several senses and in several languages.

Ciphered, first of all, in that they include a cipher, the cipher of the number thirteen. This is one of those numbers where chance and necessity cross and in crossing are both at once consigned. Within its strictures a ligament binds together, in a manner at once both significant and insignificant, fatality and its opposite: chance and coming-due, coincidence in the event, what *falls*—well or ill—together.

> DIE ZAHLEN, im Bund
> mit der Bilder Verhängnis
> und Gegen-
> verhängnis.
>   (*GW* 2:17)

(THE NUMBERS, bonded
> with the images' doom
> and their counter-
> doom.)
>   (*65 Poems* 49)

Und Zahlen waren
mitverwoben in das
Unzählbare. Eins und Tausend . . .
(*GW* 1:280)

(And numbers were
interwoven into the
numberless. One and a thousand . . .)

Even before the number thirteen, the "one" of the title "In eins"
announces the con-signing and co-signing of a multiple singularity.
From the title and the opening onwards, cipher, and then date, are incorporated in the poem. They give access to the poem which they are,
but a ciphered access.

These first lines are ciphered in another sense: more than others,
they are untranslatable. I am not thinking here of all the poetic challenges with which this great poet-translator confronts poet-translators.
No, I will limit myself here to the aporia (to the barred passage, *no
pasarán*: this is what "aporia" means). What seems to bar the passage of
translation is the multiplicity of languages in a single poem, all at once.
Four languages, like a series of proper names or signatures, like the face
of a seal.

Like the title and the date, the first line is in German. But with the
second line, a second language, an apparently Hebrew word, arises in
the "heart's mouth": *shibboleth*.

Dreizehnter Feber. Im Herzmund
erwachtes Schibboleth. Mit dir, . . .

(Thirteenth of February. In the heart's mouth
an awakened shibboleth. With you, . . .)

This second language could well be a first language, the language
of the morning, the language of origin speaking of the heart, from the
heart and from the East. Language in Hebrew is lip, and does not Celan
elsewhere (we will come to it) call words circumcised, as one speaks of
the "circumcised heart"? Let this be for the moment. *Shibboleth*, this
word I have called Hebrew, is found, as you know, in a whole family
of languages: Phoenician, Judeo-Aramaic, Syriac. It is traversed by a
multiplicity of meanings: river, stream, ear of grain, olive-twig. But beyond these meanings, it has acquired the value of a password. It was
used during or after war, at the crossing of a border under watch. The
word mattered less for its meaning than for the way in which it was
pronounced. The relation to the meaning or to the thing was suspended, neutralized, bracketed: the opposite, one could say, of a phe-
nomenological "epokhe" which preserves, first of all, the meaning. The

Ephraimites had been defeated by the army of Jephthah; in order to
keep the soldiers from escaping across the river (*shibboleth* also means   25
river, of course, but that is not necessarily the reason it was chosen),
each person was required to say *shibboleth*. Now the Ephraimites were
known for their inability to pronounce correctly the *shi* of *shibboleth*,
which became for them, in consequence, an "unpronounceable name";
they said *sibboleth*, and, at that invisible border between *shi* and *si*, betrayed themselves to the sentinel at the risk of death. They betrayed
their difference in rendering themselves indifferent to the diacritical
difference between *shi* and *si*; they marked themselves as unable to remark a mark thus coded.

This happened at the border of the Jordan. We are at another border, another barred passage in the fourth language of the strophe: *no
pasarán*. February 1936: the electoral victory of the *Frente Popular*, the
eve of civil war. *No pasarán*: la Pasionaria, the no to Franco, to the Pha-
lange supported by Mussolini's troops and Hitler's Condor legion.
Rallying cry and sign, clamor and banderoles during the siege of
Madrid, three years later, *no pasarán* was a *shibboleth* for the Republican
people, for their allies, for the International Brigades. What passed this
cry, what passed despite it, was the Second World War, the war of extermination. A repetition of the first, certainly, but also of that dress rehearsal [*répétition générale*], its own future anterior, which was the Spanish Civil War. This is the dated structure of the dress rehearsal:
everything happens as if the Second World War had already begun in
February of 1936, in a slaughter at once civil and international, violating
or reclosing the borders, leaving ever so many wounds in the body of a
single country—grievous figure of a metonymy. Spanish is allotted to
the central strophe, which transcribes, in short, a kind of Spanish *shibboleth*, a password, not a word in passing, but a silent word transmitted
like a symbolon or handclasp, a rallying sign, a sign of membership and
political watchword.

er sprach
uns das Wort in die Hand, das wir brauchten, es war
Hirten-Spanisch, . . .

im Eislicht des Kreuzers "Aurora" . . .

(into our hands
he spoke the word that we needed, it was
shepherd-Spanish, . . .

in icelight of the cruiser "Aurora" . . .)[15]

Amidst the German, the Hebrew, and the Spanish, in French, the
People of Paris:

Mit dir,
Peuple
de Paris. *No pasarán.*

(With you,
Peuple
de Paris. *No pasarán.*)

It is not written in italics, no more than is *shibboleth*. The italics are
reserved for *No pasarán* and the last line, *Friede den Hütten!*, "Peace
to the cottages!," the terrible irony of which must surely aim at
someone.

The multiplicity of languages may concelebrate, *all at once*, at the
same date, the poetic and political anniversary of singular events, spread
like stars over the map of Europe, and henceforth conjoined by a secret
affinity: the fall of Vienna and the fall of Madrid, for as we will see,
Vienna and Madrid are associated in the same line by another poem,
entitled "Schibboleth"; and still other memories of February, the beginnings of the October Revolution with the incidents tied not only to the
cruiser Aurora and to Petrograd, both of which are named in the poem,
but in fact to the Peter and Paul Fortress. It is the last stanza of "In
eins" which recalls other "unforgettable" singularities, the Tuscan for
example, which I will not here undertake to decipher.

"Aurora":
die Bruderhand, winkend mit der
von den wortgroßen Augen
genommenen Binde—Petropolis, der
Unvergessenen Wanderstadt lag
auch dir toskanisch zu Herzen.

Friede den Hütten!

("Aurora":
the brotherly hand, waving with
the blindfold removed from
his word-wide eyes—Petropolis, the
roving city of those unforgotten,
was Tuscanly close to your heart also.

Peace to the cottages!)

But already within the habitation of a single language, for example
French, a discontinuous swarm of events may be commemorated all at

once, *at the same date*, which consequently takes on the strange, coincident, *unheimlich* dimensions of a cryptic predestination.

The date itself resembles a *shibboleth*. It gives ciphered access to this collocation, to this secret configuration of places for memory.

The series thus constellated becomes all the more ample and numerous as the date remains relatively indeterminate. If Celan does not specify the day (13) and says only "February," ("Februar," this time and not *Feber*), as in the poem entitled "Schibboleth," the memory swells even further with demonstrations of the same kind, of the same political significance, which were able to bring the people of Paris, that is, the people of the left, together in the surge of a single impulse to proclaim, like the Republicans of Madrid, *No pasarán*. One sole example: it is on the twelfth of February, 1934, after the failure of the attempt to form a Common Front of the Right, with Doriot, after the riot of February 6, that a huge march takes place which spontaneously regroups the masses and the leadership of the parties of the left. This was the origin of the Popular Front.

But if, in "In eins," Celan specifies the thirteenth of February, (*Dreizehnter Feber*), one may think of February 13, 1962. I consign this hypothesis to those who may know something about or can testify to the so-called "external" date of the poem; I am unaware of it, but should my hypothesis be factually false, it would still designate the power of those dates to come to which, Celan says, we write and ascribe ourselves. A date always remains a kind of *hypothesis*, the support for a, by definition, unlimited number of projections of memory. The slightest indetermination (the day and the month without the year, for example) increases the chances, and the chances of a future anterior. The date is a future anterior; it gives the time one assigns to anniversaries to come. Thus on the thirteenth of February 1962, Celan was in Paris. *Die Niemandsrose*, the collection in which "In eins" appears, is not published until 1963. On the other hand, in moving from one poem to the other, from "Schibboleth," published eight years before, to "In eins," Celan specifies "Thirteenth of February" where the earlier poem said only "February." Thus something must have happened. February 13, 1962 is the day of the funeral for the Métro Charonne massacre victims, an anti-OAS demonstration at the end of the Algerian war. Several hundred thousand Parisians, the people of Paris, are marching. Two days after, the meetings begin which lead to the Evian accords. These people of Paris are still the people of the Commune, the people with whom one must band together: "Mit dir, / Peuple / de Paris." In the same event, at the same date, national and civil war, the end of one and the beginning—*as* the beginning of the other.

Like the date, *shibboleth* is marked several times, several times in one, "in eins," *at once*. A marked multiplicity but also a marking one.

On the one hand, indeed, within the poem, it names, as is evident, the password or rallying cry, a right of access or sign of membership in all the political situations along the historical borders which are brought together in the poem's *configuration*. This *visa*, it will be said, is the *shibboleth*; it determines a theme, a meaning or a content.

But on the other hand, as cryptic or numerical cipher, *shibboleth* also spells the anniversary date's singular power of gathering together. This anniversary grants access to the date's memory, its future, but also to the poem—itself. *Shibboleth* is the *shibboleth* for the right to the poem which calls itself a *shibboleth*, its own *shibboleth* at the very moment that it commemorates others. *Shibboleth* is its title, whether or not it appears in that place, as in one of the two poems.

This does not mean—two things.

On the one hand, this does not mean that the events commemorated in this fantastic constellation are nonpoetic events, suddenly transfigured by an incantation. No, I believe that for Celan the signifying conjunction of all these dramas and historical actors will have *constituted* the dated signature, the dating of the poem.

Nor does this mean, on the other hand, that possession of the *shibboleth* effaces the cipher, holds the key to the crypt, and guarantees transparency of meaning. The crypt remains, the *shibboleth* remains secret, the passage uncertain, and the poem only unveils this secret to confirm that there is something secret there, withdrawn, forever beyond the reach of hermeneutic exhaustion. A nonhermetic secret, it remains, and the date with it, heterogeneous to all interpretative totalization, eradicating the hermeneutic principle. There is no one meaning, from the moment that there is date and *shibboleth*, no longer a sole originary meaning.

A *shibboleth*, the word *shibboleth*, if it is one, names, in the broadest extension of its generality or its usage, every insignificant arbitrary mark, for example the phonemic difference between *shi* and *si*, as that difference becomes discriminative, decisive, and divisive. The difference has no meaning in and of itself, but it becomes what one must know how to recognize and above all to mark if one is to get on, to get over the border of a place or the threshold of a poem, to see oneself granted asylum or the legitimate habitation of a language. So as no longer to be beyond the law. And to inhabit a language, one must already have a *shibboleth* at one's disposal: not simply understand the meaning of the word, not simply *know* this meaning or know how a word *should* be pronounced (the difference of *h* between *shi* and *si*: this the Ephraimites knew), but *be able* to say it as one ought, as one ought to be able to say it. It does not suffice to know the difference; one must be capable of it, must be able to do it, or know how to do it—and doing here means *marking*. It is this differential mark which it is not enough to know like a theorem which is the secret. A secret without secrecy. The right of alliance involves no hidden secret, no meaning concealed in a crypt.

In the word, the difference between *shi* and *si* has no meaning. But it is the ciphered mark which one must *be able to partake of* with the other, and this differential power must be inscribed in oneself, that is, in one's own body, just as much as in the body of one's own language, and the one to the same extent as the other. This inscription of difference in the body (for example by the phonatory ability to pronounce this or that) is nonetheless not natural, is in no way an innate organic faculty. Its very origin presupposes participation in a cultural and linguistic community, in a milieu of apprenticeship, in short an alliance.

Shibboleth does not cipher something. It is not only a cipher, and the cipher of the poem; it is now, emerging from that nonmeaning where it keeps itself in reserve, the cipher *of* the cipher, the ciphered manifestation of the cipher as such. And when a cipher manifests itself as what it is, that is to say, in encrypting itself, this is not in order to say to us: I am a cipher. It may still conceal from us, without the slightest hidden intention, the secret which it shelters in its readability. It moves, touches, fascinates, or seduces us all the more. The ellipsis and caesura of discretion inhabit it; there is nothing it can do about it. This pass is a passion before becoming a calculated risk, prior to any strategy, any poetics of ciphering intended, as with Joyce, to keep the professors busy for generations. Even supposing that this exhausts Joyce's first and true desire, something I do not believe, nothing seems to me more foreign to Celan.

Multiplicity and migration of languages, certainly, and within language itself. Babel: named in "Hinausgekrönt," after the "Ghetto-Rose" and that phallic figure knotted in the heart of the poem ("phallisch gebündelt"), this is also its last word, both its address and its envoy.

> Und es steigt eine Erde herauf, die unsre,
> diese.
> Und wir schicken
> keinen der Unsern hinunter
> zu dir,
> Babel.
> > (*GW* 1:272)

> (And an earth rises up, ours,
> this one.
> And we'll send
> none of our people down

to you,
Babel.)
     (P 211)

Address and envoy of the poem, yes, but what seems to be said to Babel, addressed to it, is that nothing will be addressed to it. One will send it nothing, nothing from us, none of ours.

Multiplicity and migration of languages, certainly, and within language. Your country, it says, migrates all over, like language. The country itself migrates and transports its borders. It displaces itself like those names and those stones which one gives as a pledge, from hand to hand, and the hand is given, too, and what gets detached, sundered, torn away, can gather itself together anew in the symbol, the pledge, the promise, the alliance, the imparted word, the migration of the imparted word.

> —was abriß, wächst wieder zusammen—
> da hast du sie, da nimm sie dir, da hast du alle beide,
> den Namen, den Namen, die Hand, die Hand,
> da nimm sie dir zum Unterpfand,
> er nimmt auch das, und du hast
> wieder, was dein ist, was sein war,
>
> Windmühlen
>
> stoßen dir Luft in die Lunge.
>   *(GW* 1:284)

> (—what was severed joins up again—
> there you have it, so take it, there you have them both,
> the name, the name, the hand, the hand,
> so take them, keep them as a pledge,
> he takes it too, and you have
> again what is yours, what was his,
>
> windmills
>
> push air into your lungs.)
>   *(P* 217)

Chance and risk of the windmill—language which holds as much of wind and of illusion as it draws from breath and spirit, from the breathing bestowed. We will not recall all the coded trails of this immense poem ("Es ist alles anders"), from Russia—"the name of Osip"— to Moravia, to the Prague cemetery ("the pebble from / the Moravian hollow / which your thought carried to Prague, / on to the graves, to

the grave, into life") and "near Normandy-Niemen," of the emigration
of the country itself, and of its name. Like language:

> wie heißt es, dein Land
> hinterm Berg, hinterm Jahr?
> Ich weiß, wie es heißt.
> [...]
> es wandert überall, wie die Sprache,
> wirf sie weg, wirf sie weg,
> dann hast du sie wieder, wie ihn,
> den Kieselstein aus
> der Mährischen Senke,
> den dein Gedanke nach Prag trug.
> > (*GW* 1:285)

> (what is it called, your country
> behind the mountain, behind the year?
> I know what it's called.
> [...]
> it wanders off everywhere, like language,
> throw it away, throw it away,
> then you'll have it again, like that other thing.
> the pebble from
> the Moravian hollow
> which your thought carried to Prague.)
> > (*P* 219)

Multiplicity and migration of languages, certainly, and within language itself, Babel within *a single* language. *Shibboleth* marks the multiplicity within language, insignificant difference as the condition of
meaning. But by the same token, the insignificance of language, of the
properly linguistic body: it can only take on meaning in relation to a
place. By place, I mean just as much the relation to a border, country,
house, or threshold, as any site, any *situation* in general from within
which, practically, pragmatically, alliances are formed, contracts, codes,
and conventions established which give meaning to the insignificant,
institute passwords, bend language to what exceeds it, make of it a moment of gesture and of step, secondarize or "reject" it in order to find
it again.

Multiplicity within language, or rather heterogeneity. One should
specify that untranslatability is not only connected with the difficult
passage (*no pasarán*), the aporia, or impasse which would isolate one poetic language from another. Babel is also this *impossible possible step*,[16] beyond hope of transaction, tied to the multiplicity of languages within
the uniqueness of the poetic inscription: several times in one, several

languages in a single poetic act. The uniqueness of the poem, itself yet another date and *shibboleth*, forges and seals, in a single idiom, *in eins*, the poetic events, a multiplicity of languages and of equally singular dates. "In eins": within the unity and within the uniqueness of this poem, the four languages are certainly not untranslatable, neither among themselves nor into other languages. But what will always remain untranslatable into any *other* language whatsoever is the marked difference of languages in the poem. We spoke of the *doing* which does not reduce to *knowing*, and of that *being able to do the difference* which is what *marking* comes to. This is what goes on and what comes about here. Everything seems, in principle, by right, translatable, except for the mark of the difference among the languages within the same poetic event. Let us consider for example the excellent French translation of "In eins." The German is translated into French, as is normal. *Schibboleth* and *no pasarán* are left untranslated, which respects the foreignness of these words in the principal medium, the German idiom of what one calls the original version. But in preserving, and how could one not, the French of this version in the translation, "Avec toi, / Peuple / de Paris," the translation must efface the very thing which it preserves, the foreign effect of the French (unitalicized) in the poem, and that which places it in configuration with all those ciphers, passwords, and *shibboleths* that date and sign the poem, "In eins," in the at once dissociated, rent, and adjoined, rejoined, regathered unity of its singularities. There is no remedy to which translation could have recourse here, none at least in the body of the poem. No one is to blame; moreover, there is nothing to bring before the bar of translation. The *shibboleth*, here again, does not resist translation by reason of some inaccessibility of its meaning to transference, by reason of some semantic secret, but by virtue of that in it which forms the cut of a nonsignifying difference in the body of the written or oral mark, written in speech as a mark within a mark, an incision marking the very mark itself. On both sides of the historical, political, and linguistic border (a border is never natural), the meaning, the different meanings of the word *shibboleth* are known: river, ear of grain, olive twig. One even knows how it should be pronounced. But a single trial determines that some cannot while others can pronounce it with the heart's mouth. The first will not pass, the others will pass the line—of the place, of the country, of the community, of what takes place in a language, in languages as poems. Every poem has its own language; it is one time alone its own language, even and especially if several languages *are able* to cross there. From this *point of view*, which may become a watch tower, the vigilance of a sentinel, one sees well: the value of the *shibboleth* may always, and tragically, be inverted. Tragically because the inversion sometimes overtakes the initiative of subjects, the good will of men, their mastery of language and politics. Watchword or password in the struggle against oppression, exclusion, fascism, and racism, it may also corrupt its differential value, which is the condition of alliance and of the poem, making of it a discriminatory limit, the grillwork of policing, of normalization, and of methodical subjugation.

I V

Inserted in the second line of "In eins," the word "schibboleth" forms the title of a longer and earlier poem, published in 1955 in the collection *Vom Schwelle zu Schwelle*. *Shibboleth* could also serve, by metonymy, as the title of the collection. It speaks in effect of the threshold, of the crossing of the threshold ("Schwelle"), of that which permits one to pass or to cross, to transfer from one threshold to another: to translate. Here in the earlier poem, one meets with more or less the same configuration of events, sealed by the same February anniversary, the linking of the capitals, Vienna and Madrid, substituted perhaps for the linking, in "In eins," of Paris, Madrid, and Petropolis. *No pasarán* already figures in close conjunction with *shibboleth*. Again we are dealing, no doubt, with the memory of February 1936–39, though this time neither the day (13), nor the year appear. Which leads one to think, given the seeming absence of references to France and the French language, that, in fact, another date is in question this time, in the otherness of which other Februaries, and then a certain thirteenth of February, come together, overdetermining the "Sprachgitter" of the signature. The play of resemblances and differences, the *shibboleth between* the two poems, could occasion an interminable analysis.

Apart from its presence as title, the word *shibboleth* almost directly precedes "February" and *no pasarán*, in a strophe which one might call openhearted, opened here again through the heart, through the single word "heart" (in "In eins," it will also be *Im Herzmund*, in the heart's mouth, in the first line):

Herz:
gib dich auch hier zu erkennen,
hier, in der Mitte des Marktes.
Ruf's, das Schibboleth, hinaus
in die Fremde der Heimat:
Februar. No pasaran.

(Heart:
make yourself known even here,
here, in the midst of the market.
Call it out, the shibboleth,

into the alien homeland:
February. No pasaran.)
(*SG* 73)

Strangeness, estrangement in one's own home, not being at home, being called away from one's homeland or away from home in one's homeland, the "shall not" pass [*ce pas du "ne pas"*], which secures and threatens every border crossing in and out of oneself, this moment of the *shibboleth* is re-marked in the date in the month of and in the word *February.* The difference is hardly translatable: *Februar* in "Schibboleth," *Feber* (*Dreizehnter Feber*) in "In eins," a *shibboleth in February* perhaps leading back, through a play of archaism and Austrian, to some no doubt falsely attributed etymology of *februarius* as the moment of fever, access, crisis, inflammation.[17]

The two poems beckon to one another, kindred, complicitous, allies, but as different as they can possibly be. They bear and do not bear the same date. A *shibboleth* secures the passage from one to the other in the difference, within sameness, of the same date, between *Februar* and *Feber.* They speak, in the same language, two different languages. They partake of it.

We make use here of the word *partaking*, as elsewhere *imparting*, to render the ambiguities of the French *partage*, a word which names difference, the line of demarcation, the parting of the waters, scission, caesura as well as participation, that which is divided because it is shared or held in common, imparted and partaken of.[18]

Fascinated by a resemblance at once semantic and formal and which nonetheless has no linguistico-historical explanation, I will hazard a comparison between the imparted or partaken as *shibboleth* and as *symbolon*: In both cases of S-B-L, a pledge is transmitted to another, "er sprach / uns das Wort in die Hand" ("he spoke / the word in our hand"), a word or a piece of a word, the complementary part of an object divided in two to seal an alliance, a tessera. This is the moment of engagement, of signing, of the pact or contract, of the promise, of the ring.[19]

The signature of the date plays a role here. Beyond the singular event which it marks and of which it would be the detachable proper name, capable of outliving and thus of calling, of recalling, the vanished as vanished, its very ash, it gathers together, like a title (*titulus* includes a sense of gathering), a more or less apparent and secret conjunction of singularities which partake of, and in the future will continue to partake of, the *same* date.

There is no limit assignable to such a conjunction. It is determined by the future to which a fracture promises it. No testimony, no knowledge, not even Celan's, could by definition exhaust its deciphering. First of all, because there is no absolute witness for an external decoding. Celan may always have imparted one more *shibboleth*: under cover of a word, a cipher, or a letter. Second, he would not have claimed himself to have totalized the possible and compossible meanings of a constellation. Finally and above all, the poem is destined to remain *alone*; it is destined for this from its first breath, alone with the vanishing of the witnesses and the witnesses of witnesses. And of the poet.

The date is a witness, but one may very well bless it without knowing all of that for which and of those for whom it bears witness. It is always possible that there may no longer be any witness for this witness. We are going to approach this affinity slowly between a date, a name—and ash. The last words of "Aschenglorie":

Niemand
zeugt für den
Zeugen.
(*GW* 2:72)

(No one
bears witness for the
witness.)
(*SG* 241)

Folded or refolded in the simplicity of the singular, a certain repetition thus assures the minimal and "internal" readability of the poem, even in the absence of a witness, of a signatory or of anyone who might have some knowledge concerning the historical reference of the poetic legacy. This in any case is what is signified, if one can still speak in this way, by the word or title *shibboleth*. Not this or that meaning derived from its language of origin: river, ear of grain, olive-twig, or indeed the other meanings which it takes on in the two poems. It signifies: there is *shibboleth*, there is something of a crypt; it remains incalculable, it does not conceal a single determinate secret, a semantic content waiting for the one who holds a key behind the door. If there is indeed a door, we will come to this, it does not present itself in this way. If this crypt is symbolic, this does not in the last analysis derive from some tropic or rhetoric. To be sure, the symbolic dimension never disappears, and at times it takes on thematic values. But what the poem marks, what enters and incises languages in the form of a date, is that there is a partaking of the *shibboleth*, a partaking at once open and closed. The date (signature, moment, place, gathering of singular marks) always functions as a *shibboleth*. It shows that there is something not shown, that there is ciphered singularity: irreducible to any concept, to any knowledge, even to a history or tradition, be it of a religious kind. A ciphered singularity which gathers a multiplicity *in eins*, and through whose grid a poem remains readable: "Aber das Gedicht spricht ja!" The poem speaks, even should none of its references be intelligible, none other than the Other, the one to whom it addresses itself and to whom it speaks in saying that it speaks to him. Even if it does not reach and leave its mark on, at least it calls to, the Other. Address takes place.

In a language, in the poetic writing of a language, there is nothing but *shibboleth*. Like the date, like a name, it permits anniversaries, alliances, returns, commemorations—even if there should be no trace, what one commonly calls a trace, the subsistent presence of a remainder, even if there should be scarcely an ash of what we thus still date, celebrate, commemorate, or bless.

We will keep, for the moment, to conventional dating, as it is coded in a calendar or public toponymy. "Tübingen, Jänner" (*Jänner*, in the old style or the Austrian, also heralds *Feber*) is at once the title of a poem, a date, and a signature. Like a *shibboleth*, it takes into its consignment enigma and memory, citing the enigma:

> Ihre—"ein
> Rätsel ist Rein-
> entsprungenes"—, ihre
> Erinnerung an
> schwimmende Hölderlintürme, möwen-
> umschwirrt.
>
> (Their—"an enigma
> is the purely
> originated"—, their
> memory of
> Hölderlin towers afloat, circled
> by whirring gulls.)[20]

In parentheses, "La Contrescarpe" writes, "(*Quatorze / juillets . . .*)" (*GW* 1:283). Like the title of the poem, the date is in French in the original and thus untranslatable. Untranslatable first and foremost into French. It does not suffice to transcribe it in italics.

Moreover the date, incorporated in the poem, is overdetermined in several ways. For one, it commemorates quite evidently that which, for two centuries now, every July 14 may commemorate. At times, in many places in western culture, July 14 becomes the emblem of the commemorative ceremony in general. It then figures a political and revolutionary anniversary in general, whether past or to come: the anniversary, in other words the return, and by revolution, of the revolutionary.

What is more, "(*Quatorze / juillets . . .*)" is written here with an *s*. In its disorthography, this inaudible mark of the plural insists on the plurality of rings. The anniversaries do not signal only, necessarily, the return of the same original July 14. Other more or less secret events, other rings, anniversaries, and alliances, other partakings partake perhaps of the same date. A parenthesis, as its name indicates, *sets alongside*: *aside*. The same parenthesis *sets aside*, in reserve, other "quatorze juillet": "(*Quatorze / juillets. Et plus de neuf autres.*)" One may read either nine other fourteenths of July or 14 + 9 = 23 Julys, or 23 months of July, 23 anniversaries, etc. When I say that I do not know what other anniversaries the poem thus turns itself toward, the last thing this means is "I don't want to know," "This doesn't interest me," or that I am forgoing all interpretation, all use of the resources of hermeneutics, philosophy, historical knowledge, or biographical testimony. "I don't know" signals a situation. In what I have elsewhere called its *remnance*, the poem speaks beyond knowledge. It writes, and what it writes is, first of all, this very fact, that it is addressed and destined beyond knowledge, inscribing dates and signatures which one may encounter and bless, without knowing everything of what they date or sign. Blessing beyond knowledge, commemorating through forgetting or the unimparted secret, partaking yet in the unimpartable. The "Quatorze / juillets" form the cut of an unrepeatable (*unwiederholbar*) singularity. But they repeat the unique in the ring. A tropic sets anniversaries turning around the same. Moreover, the whole of the poem multiplies the signs of other events associated with July 14. One is thus led to think that "Quatorze / juillets" is not a listed date, the date of public and political history, but perhaps, who knows, the date which signs in secret, the private seal which at least marks with its initials or flourishes the advent of this particular poem, the sublime tearing open which I prefer to leave intact. Such a signature would make up part of the constellation. Let us merely recall, without further commentary, that "Gespräch im Gebirg" ("Conversation in the Mountains"), also says "and July is not July" ("der Juli ist kein Juli") (*GW* 3:170/*CP* 19). This in the course of a meditation on the Jew, son of a Jew, whose name is "unpronounceable" (*GW* 3:169/*CP* 17) and who has nothing of his own, nothing that is not borrowed, so that, like a date, what is proper to the Jew is to have no property or essence. Jewish is not Jewish. We will come back to this, as to this other fact: for the Ephraimites, in another way, *shibboleth* was also an unpronounceable name. One knows what this cost them.

We have spoken often of "constellations": several heterogeneous singularities are consigned in the starry configuration of a single dated mark. Let us recall here the "constellations of November" ("Novembersternen").[21] They are associated with an ear, not of grain as in *shibboleth*, but of corn:

BEIM HAGELKORN, im
brandigen Mais-
kolben, daheim,
den späten, den harten
Novembersternen gehorsam:

in den Herzfaden die
Gespräche der Würmer geknüpft—:

eine Sehne, von der
deine Pfeilschrift schwirrt,
Schütze.
      (GW 2:22)

(WITH THE HAILSTONE, in
the rust-blighted ear
of maize, at home,
obedient to the late, the hard
November stars:

woven into your heart-thread, the
conversations of worms—:

a bowstring, from which
your arrow-script whirrs,
archer.)
      (65 Poems 54 [trans. modified])

The months come back as well, and especially March, and especially September. Among other places, in "Huhediblu" (GW 1:275–77).
The return of the month is registered here, without mention of the
year, in this way signing the marking off of the date, its partaking and
its deportation. The ring's condition and the fate of all archival re-
cording. A date marks itself and becomes readable only in freeing itself
from the singularity which it nonetheless recalls. It is readable in its
ideality; its body becomes an ideal object: always the same, traversing
the different experiences which point to or constitute it, objective, guaranteed by codes. This ideality carries forgetting into memory, but it is
the memory of forgetting itself, the truth of forgetting. The reference
to a singular event is annulled in the ring's annulation, when a month
recalls and annually annuls a year. This is the moment when the year
turns on itself. Poles and tropes, one recalls the "Meridian." A date:
always a turning-about, a volte-face, una volta, a revolt, or a revolution.
It replaces itself in its vicissitudes. Commemorating what may always
be forgotten in the absence of a witness, the date is exposed in its very
essence or destination. It is offered up to annihilation, but in truth it
offers itself up. The threat does not come from without, it is not connected to the possibility of some accident suddenly destroying the archive's material support. The date is threatened in its coming due, in its
conservation and its readability, by them, insofar as it remains, and permits itself to be read. Risking the annulment of what it saves from for-

getting, it may always become no one's and nothing's date, the essence without essence of ash in which one no longer even knows what one day, one time alone, under some proper name, was consumed. The name partakes of this destiny of ash along with the date. This does not happen *empirically*, like a fact which might come about once under certain conditions and which one could avoid at other times, for example by multiplying precautions—or simply by chance. It is incident to the date's erratic essence to become readable and commemorative only in effacing that which it will have designated, in becoming each time no one's date.

No one's—the possessive may be understood in two contradictory senses, which nonetheless form an alliance in the same tragedy. *Either . . . Or.*

Either the date remains encrypted, supposing, for example, that behind the allusion in "Huhediblu" to September ("unterm / Datum des Nimmermenschtags im September"), and beyond a certain number of identifiable things or persons, Celan has named and ciphered an event which he alone, or alone with but a few others, is able to commemorate. And those who commemorate are mortals, one must start with that. Then the date of this "Nevermansday in September" is destined, at least to this extent, to no longer signify at all *one day* for the survivors, that is to say, essentially, for the reader, interpreter, or guardian of the poem. Finite survival, this is their lot. In this case, a date becomes, from the moment that it crosses the threshold of this survival or spectral return, from the moment, therefore, that it crosses the threshold of the poem, no one's date, nevermansday. The name *September* crops up in a poem, a poem which "speaks!"; it lends itself to reading to the extent that it is caught up in, catches itself up in a network of marks which signify and are, by convention, intelligible; it has its share in the "beauty" of the poem. But to the same extent, and here is the affect of bereavement which makes for this "beauty," it pays for its readability with the terrible tribute of lost singularity. Mourning reading itself. What is encrypted, dated in the date, is effaced; the date is marked in marking itself off, and all the losses, all the beings whom we lament in this mourning, all the griefs are gathered in the poem of a date whose effacement does not await effacement.

Or, in line with an apparently inverse hypothesis, nothing is encrypted in the date. It makes itself available to all. And then the result is the same. The other's singularity is incinerated. The September rose, the no one's rose. "Die Nichts-, die / Niemandsrose" of "Psalm" belongs, to so speak, to the same generation as "die September- / rosen" of "Huhediblu"; "unterm / Datum des Nimmermenschtags im September" belongs to the same generation too as the untranslatable envoy, when the quasi-citation, metonymizing the flower of rhetoric, displacing the order of attribution, concludes the poem in *French,* without italics: "Oh quand refleuriront, oh roses, vos septembres?" ("Oh when will they reflower, oh roses, your Septembers?") (*GW* 1:277). The future belongs to the date, the plural month, the round of future Septembers. One awaits less the return of the flowers, their blossoming to come, than the re-flowering of returns. One does not place flowers on the stone of a date, one does not await a season, spring or autumn, one does not await the roses of this time, but the time of the roses, the dated time. What counts, what is born, flowers, opens, is not the flower, it is the date. It counts, and *September*, moreover, includes a cipher, or rather a number, in its name.

Either/Or. This does not constitute a choice; the date's double demarcation does not make two. The two phenomena do not contradict each other, they are not juxtaposed, not even in the poem. The sameness of all dating is gathered and constituted here. The possibility of reading and of recurrence, the ring, the anniversary and its keeping, the *truth* of the poem, its very reason, its essential *raison d'être*, its chance and its sense, this is also its madness.

A date is mad, that is the truth.

And we are mad for dates.

For those ashes which dates are. Celan knew, one may praise or bless ashes. No religion is needed. Perhaps because a religion begins there, before religion, in the blessing of dates, of names, and of ashes.

A date is mad: it is never what it is, what it says it is, always more or less than what it is. What it is, is either what it is or what it is not. It does not reside in being, in some sense of being; it is on this condition that its mad incantation becomes music. It *remains* without being, by force of music, remains for song, "Singbarer Rest," this is the opening or the title of a poem which *begins* by speaking of the remainder (*GW* 2:36/*SG* 231). It begins with the remainder—which is not and which is not the being—allowing a wordless ("lautlos") song to be heard therein, a perhaps inaudible or inarticulate song, yet a song whose turn and whose line, whose outline or contour ("Umriß") no doubt derives from the cutting, sharpened, concise, but also rounded, circumvenient form of a sickle, of yet another writing, of a sickle-script ("Sichelschrift"). This writing-sickle does not round what it slices, since it does not avoid it, not altogether, but rather cuts in coming around, all the way around. Another turning, another trope: rounding and coming around are not the same thing for this sickle which perhaps inscribes letters in cutting, all around. Shall one say that it circumcises words in silence, when speech is muted (*lautlos*) so that song may come: *singbarer Rest*? This will resonate later: "beschneide das Wort," "circumcise the word" (*GW* 1:242).

"Singbarer Rest" or "cello-einsatz / von hinter dem Schmerz" ("cello entry / from behind pain"), that other poem which sets into musical play something indecipherable or unsignifying ("Undeutbares"). It closes on these words which say so little, and more than all, henceforth unforgettable and made to pass unperceived from memory, in the scanning of their untranslatable simplicity:

> alles ist weniger, als
> es ist,
> alles ist mehr.
>> (*GW* 2:76)

> (everything is less, than
> it is,
> everything is more.)
>> (*P* 253 [trans. modified])

What is most untranslatable here has to do at once with the scansion, or the caesura, and the absence of negation, whether grammatical or not. The ambiguous *als*, emphasized by its position at the end of the line, after the pause of the comma, disengages the *als es ist* (as it is, insofar as it is, as such, such as it is) from the apparent syntax of comparison with which it nonetheless plays.

If I say that the sense of a date opens into madness, a kind of "Wahnsinn," this is not to move you: only to enunciate what *there is to read* in a date, in the injunction or chance of every reading.

Wahnsinn: the madness of the date, the madness of "when," the delirious sense of "wann." The madness of the homophony (*Wahn/wann*) is not a play on words by Celan, any more than was the resemblance just before between *shibboleth* and *symbolon*, between Hebrew and Greek, and, here, Germanic. Madness slumbers in this aleatory encounter, this chance among heterogeneities which breaks into making sense and dating. Prior to the *Wahn/wann* of "Huhediblu," Scripture, the epistle, the epistolary, indeed epistolary espittle, cross missives with the name of the prophet, the trace and the posthumous, the postscript and the date:

> Und—ja—
> die Bälge der Feme-Poeten
> lurchen und vespern und wispern und vipern,
> episteln.
> Geunktes, aus
> Hand- und Fingergekröse, darüber
> schriftfern eines
> Propheten Name spurt, als
> An- und Bei- und Afterschrift, unterm
> Datum des Nimmermenschtags im September—:
>> (*GW* 1:275)

42

(And—yes—
the windbags of the poet-proscribers
toady and vesper and whisper and viper,
epistle.
Croaked things, out of
hand- and finger-tripe, on which
far from writing the
name of a prophet leaves its traces, as
at- and by- and behindscript, under the
date of Nevermansday in September—:)

The question "When?," *Wann?*, which, bearing first of all upon the
roses (when do the roses of September flower?), comes to bear finally
on the date itself ("Oh quand refleuriront, oh roses, vos septembres?"),
becomes, in the interval, mad itself:

Wann,
wann blühen, wann,
wann blühen die, hühendiblüh,
huhediblu, ja sie, die September-
rosen?

Hüh—on tue . . . Ja wann?

Wann, wannwann,
Wahnwann, ja Wahn,—
Bruder . . .
 (*GW* 1:275)

(When
when bloom, when,
when bloom the, hoomendibloom,
hoohedibloo, yes them, the September-
roses?

Hoo—on tue . . . when then?

When, whenwhen,
manywhens, yes mania—
brother . . .)

The date's annulment in the anonymity of nothing as in that of the
ring, this given of the date leaves its trace in the poem. This trace is the
poem. What it comes to is not simply the trace of something, of a non-
trace which happened, which took place in that it was lived through in

one sense of the word and asks to be commemorated. It is also this, certainly, but it is first of all the trace *as* date, that which is bound to mark itself off if it is to mark, to bereave itself if it is to remain. It must expose its secret, risk losing it if it is to keep it. It must blur the border, crossing and recrossing it, between readability and unreadability. The unreadable is readable as unreadable, unreadable insofar as readable; this is the madness or fire which consumes a date from within. Here is what renders it ash, here is what renders ash from the first moment. And during the finite time of incineration, the password is transmitted, there is communication, the *shibboleth* circulates from hand to hand, from mouth to ear, from heart to heart—among a few, a finite number, always. For it can vanish with them, be left as an indecipherable sign, and yet a universal one (by right, in principle): a token, a symbol, a tessera, a trope, a table, or a code.

Despite appearances, there is no contradiction here which could be organized dialectically. To illustrate the paradoxes of this universalization of the "this, here, now" or of the "when," one might have cited the beginning of the *Phänomenologie des Geistes.*[22] But ellipsis, discontinuity, caesura, or discretion do not allow themselves here to be reduced or sublated (*aufgehoben*). No dialectic of sense-certainty can reassure us in the matter of an archive's safekeeping.

This is the gift of the poem, and of the date, their condition made up of distress and hope, the chance and the turn, the shift of tones, the "Wechsel der Töne."[23] This annulment of the return without return is not brought upon experience by the only poem, the poem which there is not ("Ich spreche ja von dem Gedicht, das es nicht gibt!"), any more than there is the date which nonetheless is there (*es gibt*)—to give. Annulment is at work everywhere that a date inscribes its *here* and *now* within iterability, *when* it consigns itself to losing its senses, in self-forgetfulness, succeeding thus only in effacing itself. Trace, or ash. These names stand for others. A date's destiny is analogous to that of every name, every proper name. Is there another desire than that of dating? of leaving a date? of fixing a date? of praising or blessing a commemoration without whose enunciation no event would take place?

Yet desire gets carried away. It gets carried away in praising or blessing the given letter, a date which, in order to be what it is, must give itself to be read in ash, in the nonbeing of its being, that remainder without remainder one calls ash. Of a date *itself*, nothing remains, nothing of what it dates, nothing of what is dated by it. No one remains—*a priori*. This "nothing" or "no one" does not befall the date after the fact, like a loss—of something or someone; nor is it an abstract negativity which one could plan for here, and there avoid.

We use "nothing" and "no one" in the grammatical sense in which they are neither positive nor negative. Despite the artifice or arbitrariness of this situation, the grammatical suspension is not unrelated to that in which Celan's *Nichts* and *Niemand* may resonate. Especially when he writes, in "Psalm":

> Gelobt seist du, Niemand.
>   (*GW* 1:225)

> (Praised be your name, no one.)
>   (*P* 175)

Or the following, in "Einmal" ("Once"), in which a certain "ichten" remains so difficult to translate; it repeats, in some sort, the annihilated without negation in what also sounds like the production or constitution of an "I" ("ich"), one and infinite, once and endlessly, the step between nothing ("Nichts") and light ("Licht"):

> Eins und Unendlich,
> vernichtet,
> ichten.

> Licht war. Rettung.

> (One and Infinite,
> annihilated,
> ied.

> Light was. Salvation.)[24]

If the date becomes readable, its *shibboleth* says to you: "I" (almost nothing, once alone, once alone endlessly recommenced but ended in that very act, in the de-termination in advance of its repetition), I am, I am only a cipher commemorating just that which will have been consigned to oblivion, destined to become name, for a finite time, the time of a rose, name of nothing, "voices of no one," *name of no one*: ash.

The poem's desire or gift, the date is borne, in a movement of blessing, toward ash.

I am not presupposing in this way some essence of blessing, realized here in a strange example. I am not saying: you know, we know, what a blessing is, well then, here is one that addresses itself to the ash. No, the essence of benediction enunciates itself perhaps from within poetic prayer, the song of remains without being, the experience of ashes in the incineration of the date, from within the experience of the date *as* incineration. The latter will no longer designate, in this place, the *operation* at times decided on or rejected by someone asking himself whether or not to proceed with the cremation, the destruction by fire, with no remains other than ashes, of this living being or of this archive. The incineration of which I speak takes place prior to any operation, it burns from within. The date is consumed by incineration in that expiring which is its production, genesis, or inscription: its essence and its chance.

Like the September roses, the no one's rose calls for the blessing of that which remains of that which does not remain, what does not remain in this remainder (*singbarer Rest*), the dust or ash. It sings, *yes, amen,* to this nothing which remains (a nothing does not remain), and even to the desert in which there would be no one left to bless the ashes. "Psalm," again:

Niemand knetet uns wieder aus Erde und Lehm,
niemand bespricht unsern Staub.
Niemand.

Gelobt seist du, Niemand.
Dir zulieb wollen
wir blühn.
Dir
entgegen.

Ein Nichts
waren wir, sind wir, werden
wir bleiben, blühend:
Die Nichts-, die
Niemandsrose.
  (*GW* 1:225)

(No one moulds us again out of earth and clay,
no one conjures our dust.
No one.

Praised be your name, no one.
For your sake
we shall flower.
Towards
you.

A nothing
we were, are, shall

remain, flowering:
the nothing-, the
no one's rose.)
    (P 175)

To address no one is not exactly not to address oneself to any one. To speak to no one, *in the risk*, each time, singularly, that there is no one to bless, no one for blessing—is this not the only chance for blessing? for an act of faith? What would a blessing be that was sure of itself? A judgment, a certitude, a dogma.

I have suggested the following: that date, ash, and name were or will be the same, this same never holding in the present. And this same remains to be blessed. To be sung. It remains nowhere, the same, but in blessing's call, it calls for the blessing which calls it. But the response is never assured, it is *given*, but by that very fact incalculable, nowhere a given, given in advance. "Chymisch":

Große, graue,
wie alles Verlorene nahe
Schwestergestalt:

Alle die Namen, alle die mit-
verbrannten
Namen. Soviel
zu segnende Asche. Soviel
gewonnenes Land
über
den leichten, so leichten
Seelen-
ringen.
    (GW 1:227)

(Great, gray,
sisterly shape
near like all that is lost:

All the names, all those
names
burnt with the rest. So much
ash to be blessed. So much
land won
above
the weightless, so weightless

rings
of souls.)
        (*P* 179)

There is ash, perhaps, but an ash is not. This remainder *seems* to remain of what was, and was presently; it seems to nourish itself or quench its thirst at the spring of being-present, but it emerges from being, it uses up in advance the being from which it seems to draw. The remnance of the remainder—ash, almost nothing—is not the being-that-remains, if, at least, one understands by that a being-that-subsists. What is drawn, sucked up, drunk ("geschöpft") with the scoop ("Kelle"; the spring or fountain, "Quelle," is not far), with the ash-scoop, with the ash-ladle ("mit der Aschenkelle") comes out of the tub of being ("aus dem Seinstrog"). It comes from it perhaps, but it comes out of it, and it comes out clean, soapy ("seifig"). This is why, in this scene of laundering and of ash (the fountain is not far), it is better to speak of a tub of being than of a manger or trough (*Trog*):

MIT DER ASCHENKELLE GESCHÖPFT
aus dem Seinstrog,
seifig . . .
        (*GW* 2:236)

(DRAWN WITH THE ASH-LADLE
from the tub of being,
soapy . . .)
        (*LP* 7 [trans. modified])

All the rings, all the ashes—there are ever so many and each time unique—pass through the giving of a blessed date. Each tear. Innumerable gifts, ciphered beyond counting by ever so many poems, we will not cite them.

V

Until now, we have always been speaking of dates that are coded, not only ciphered, but coded by the conventional grid of a calendar. The poem can mention these dates while incorporating them in its phrase: itself a daybook. The date thus marked does not necessarily correspond with that of the writing, with the event of the poem. It represents its theme rather than its signature.

While there is a certain necessity to this distinction, it appears nonetheless to be limited in pertinence. Where is this limit to be situated?

It has the form of the ring. By reason of the revolution of which we are speaking, the commemorating date and the commemorated date tend to rejoin and conjoin in a secret anniversary. The poem is this anniversary which it sings or blesses, the giving of this ring, the seal of an alliance and of a promise. It *belongs to* the same date as the one it blesses, gives and gives back again the date to which it *at once both* belongs and is destined. At this point, in this place which is always already passed, always yet to come, the border is effaced between the poem's external occasion, its "empirical" date, and its internal genealogy. A *shibboleth* also crosses this border: for a poetic date, for a blessed date, the difference between the empirical and the essential, between the contingency of the outer and the necessity of the inner, no longer has any place. This no-place, this utopia, is the taking place or occurrence of the poem as blessing, that (perhaps) absolute poem that Celan said does not exist ("das es nicht gibt!").

With this distinction between the empirical and the essential, a limit is blurred, that of the philosophical as such, philosophical distinction itself. Philosophy finds itself, *rediscovers* itself, in the vicinity of the poetic, indeed of literature. It finds itself there, for the indecision of this limit is perhaps what most provokes it to thought. It finds itself there, it does not necessarily lose itself there as those believe, in their tranquil credulity, who believe that they know where this limit is situated and timorously keep within it, ingenuously, although without innocence, stripped of what one must call the *philosophical experience*: a certain questioning crossing of limits, unsureness as to the border of the philosophical field—and above all the *experience of language*, an experience always as poetic, or literary, as it is philosophical.

Whence the privilege of what we are calling the code: the institution of the calendar which permits one to call off, to class (*calare*), the years, the months, the days; or of the clock which spaces and sounds the revolution of the hours. Like the calendar, the clock names the return of the other, of the wholly other in the same. But by *Uhr* and *Stunde*, named in so many poems, we must understand something else and something more than themes or objects. The hour writes, the hour speaks; it calls or assigns the poem, provokes it, convokes, apostrophizes, and addresses it, it and the poet whom the hour claims; it summons it at its hour. "Nacht" speaks of a "Zuspruch der Stunde": an exhortation, perhaps a consolation, but first of all a word addressed (*GW* 1:170/*P* 123). And to this *Zuspruch* responds elsewhere a "Gespräch" of the hour, a dialogue, a conversation with the turning hour, the sharing of a word with it:

Diese Stunde, deine Stunde,
ihr Gespräch mit meinem Munde.

Mit dem Mund, mit seinem Schweigen,
mit den Worten, die sich weigern.
   (*GW* 1:216)

(This hour, your hour,
Its dialogue with my mouth.

With the mouth, with its silence,
with words refusing their compliance.)

Just as much as a sundial or any other chart, the mark of the hour assigns the subject its place, occasions it; its address seizes hold of the signatory or the poet even before he has himself marked or given the hour. Mallarmé spoke of the initiative returning to words: it also returns to the hour. The poet is provoked, in other words constituted by it. He is revealed to himself, as such, from within it. Discontinuous return and round of the hours, the here of the clock hand spaces the now. This discretion, this "caesura of the hours" (*Stundenzäsur*), cadence, chance, and sufferance, scans the poem from its origin. But this poetic of rhythm or of spacing concerns not only the form of the language, it also says something about the origin of meaning, and of the meaning of language. "Und mit dem Buch aus Tarussa" inscribes in its heart the "caesura of the hours." The poem speaks of rhythm, rhyme, respiration ("mit / geatmeten Steppen- / halmen geschrieben ins Herz / der Stundenzäsur," "with / breathed steppe- / grass written in the heart / of the caesura of the hours"), but also of language, the rhythm of language, the "language-scale, word-scale, home- / scale of exile" ("Sprachwaage, Wortwaage, Heimat- / waage Exile") (*GW* 2:288/*SG* 209 [trans. modified]). The Bremen address sees an affinity between this question of the meaning of language, of its sense and its place for an exile (German for a poet of the German language who was not German), and "the question as to which sense is clockwise" ("Uhrzeigersinn"):

> Only one thing remained reachable, close and secure amid all losses: language . . .
>   In this language I tried, during those years and the years after, to write poems: in order to speak, to orient myself, to find out where I was, where I was going . . .
>   It meant movement, you see, something happening [*Ereignis*], being *en route* [*Unterwegssein*], an attempt to find a direction. Whenever I ask about the sense of it, I remind myself that this implies *the question as to which sense is clockwise.*
>   For the poem does not stand outside time. True, it claims the infinite

and tries to reach across time—but across, not above. (*GW* 3:185–86/*CP* 34 [emphasis added])

The annulment, again, of the annulation of the ring. The turning on itself of the hour. Consumption, becoming-ash, burning up or incineration of a date: on the hour, in the hour itself, at each hour. This is the threat of the absolute crypt: nonrecurrence, unreadability, amnesia with nothing left, but nonrecurrence *as* recurrence, *in* recurrence itself. Such a risk is no more inessential, no more an accident of the hour or the day, than the possibility itself of recurrence, which carries with it both a chance and a threat, at once, each time.

Forgive me if I do not name, here, the holocaust, that is to say literally, as I chose to call it elsewhere, the all-consuming, except to say this: there is certainly today the date of that holocaust we know, the hell of our memory; but there is a holocaust for every date, and somewhere in the world at every hour. Every hour counts its holocaust. Every hour is unique, whether it comes back, and this is the wheel that turns on itself, or whether, the last, it comes no more, no more than the sister, its own, the same, its other revenant:

> Geh, deine Stunde
> hat keine Schwestern, du bist—
> bist zuhause. Ein Rad, langsam,
> rollt aus sich selber, die Speichen
> klettern,
> [. . .]
> Jahre.
> Jahre, Jahre, ein Finger
> tastet hinab und hinan
> [. . .]
> Kam, kam.
> Kam ein Wort, kam,
> kam durch die Nacht,
> wollt leuchten, wollt leuchten.
>   (*GW* 1:197–99)

> (Go, your hour
> has no sisters, you are—
> are at home. A wheel, slow,
> rolls on its own, the spokes
> climb,
> [. . .]
> Years.
> Years, years, a finger
> feels down and up,

[. . .]
Came, came.
Came a word, came,
came through the night,
wanted to shine, wanted to shine.
  (*P* 137–41; *SG* 155–59 [trans. modified])

And further on, in the same poem, which I thus have to divide up and on which these divisions inflict a measureless violence, since they wound not only the body of the song but first of all the rhythm of its own caesuras, cutting into the cuts, the wounds and the scars, and the very sutures spoken of by precisely *this* poem, the focus of so many readings, further on then, ashes, ashes repeated, ashes of ashes, night in night, night and night—but the two words (*Asche, Nacht*) call to one another, with their terrifying echo, only in this language:

Asche.
Asche, Asche.
Nacht.
Nacht-und-Nacht.
  (*GW* 1:199)

(Ash.
Ash, ash.
Night.
Night-and-night.)
  (*P* 141)

There is the commemorated date and the date of the commemoration, the commemorating. But how is one to distinguish, today, when an anniversary's hour has come? How is one to differentiate between the date of which the poem speaks and that of the poem, when I write this, here, now, to recall that other here, now, which was another but virtually at the same date?

Virtually: not so much because this hour, today, at this date, this *dated* here and now is not rigorously the same as, merely analogous to, the other, but because the originary date, as coded mark of the other here-now, was *already* a sort of *fiction*, telling of singularity only in the fable of conventions and generalities, of what are in any case iterable marks.

Ashes in truth. If the date which is mentioned, commemorated, blessed, sung tends to merge with its recurrence in the mentioning, commemorating, blessing, and singing of it, how then is one to distinguish, in a poetic signature, between the *constative* value of a certain truth (here is when it took place) and that other order of truth which would be associated with poetic *performativity* (I sign this, here now, at this date)? Is a date true? What is the truth of this fiction, the untrue truth of this truth? Here, this, now, is a *shibboleth*. This is—*shibboleth*.

VI

Let us now move beyond that in language which classifies the marks of dating according to the conventional fictions of the calendar or the clock.

Radicalizing and generalizing, we may say, without artifice, that poetic writing offers itself up to dating in its entirety. The Bremen address recalls this: a poem is en route from a place toward "something open" ("an approachable you"), and it makes its way "across" time, it is never "timeless." It is all cipher of singularity, offering its place and recalling it, offering and recalling its time at the risk of losing them in the holocaustic generality of recurrence and the readability of the concept, in the anniversary repetition of the unrepeatable. Wherever a signature has entered into an idiom, leaving in language the trace of an incision which is *at once* unique and iterable, cryptic and readable, there is date. Not *the* absolute date, there is none, no more than there is an "absolute poem"; but date, the madness of "when," the *wann/Wahnsinn*, the unthinkable *Einmal*, the terrifying ambiguity of the *shibboleth*, sign of belonging and threat of discrimination, indiscernible differentiation between alliance and war.

A date discerns and concerns a place, it is a *situation*. It may give rise to calculations. But in the final analysis, it ceases to be calculable. The crypt ceases to be the result of a concealment, the work of a hermetic poet, one skilled in the ways of concealment or anxious to seduce with ciphers. A date fascinates, but it is not *made* to fascinate. The crypt occurs (it is the poet's passion, not his action) wherever a singular incision marks language. As one might engrave a date in a tree, burning the bark with figures of fire. But the voice of the poem carries beyond the singular cut. I mean by this that the cut becomes readable for certain of those who have no part in the event or the constellation of events consigned to it, for those excluded from partaking, yet who may thus partake and impart.

Seen from the side of this generality or repeatable universality of meaning, insofar as its sense is repeatable in this way, a poem acquires the status of a philosopheme. It may offer itself as the object of a hermeneutic labor which, for the purposes of its "internal" reading, does not require access to the singular secret once partaken of by a finite number of witnesses or participants. The poem itself is already such a hermeneutic event, its writing is a matter of *hermeneuein*, it proceeds from it. Looking at it from the side of the universal meaning which corresponds to the date, to that in it which might come again, in a publicly commemorated recurrence, one may always speak, as does one of the titles of the symposium, of "philosophical implications." But looking at it from the other side, from the side of an irreducibly singular dating and an untranslatable incision, if some such thing existed in all purity, there would be no "philosophical implication." The possibility of a philosophical reading would encounter here, in fact, as would any hermeneutics, its limit.

This limit would also be the symmetrical limit of a formal poetics, one concerned or confident about being able to keep meaning set apart, in an isolated state. Such a limit does not signify the failure of philosophical hermeneutics or formal analysis, and even less does it indicate the necessity of their renunciation. It turns us back first of all toward the effaced but common provenance, toward the *possibility*, of both philosophical hermeneutics and of formal poetics. Both presuppose the date, the mark incised in language, of a proper name or an idiomatic event. What they thus suppose, they forget, it will be said. To be sure, but the forgetting belongs to the structure of what they forget: one can only recall it to oneself in forgetting it. The date *succeeds only in effacing itself*; its mark effaces it *a priori*.

This is what I suggested in a somewhat elliptical way when I began by saying: the question "what is?" dates. Philosophy, hermeneutics, and poetics can only come into being within idioms, within languages, the body of events and dates a metalinguistic overview of which one could not say is impossible—but rather that it is guaranteed, from within, so to speak, by the structure of marking off which pertains to the date's iterability, that is to say to its essential annulment. The effacement of the date or of the name inside the ring: here is the origin of philosophy, of hermeneutics, of poetics, their sendoff.

Annulling it in its repetition, what is sent presupposes and disavows the date—in other words the *shibboleth*. And we ought to distinguish— but how?—between *shibboleth* and "the" or "a" *shibboleth*. How to interpret this phrase or indication: "this = *shibboleth*"? This deictic, here, now? Go and know.

————

Formally, at least, the affirmation of Judaism has the same structure as that of the date. By affirmation, I also mean the claim, the engagement which does not limit itself to the acknowledgment of a fact but which invokes a responsibility. "We are all Jews" means, in this case, "We take it on, we take it upon ourselves," "We undertake to be it" and not only "It turns out that in fact we are it"—and means this even if the engagement cannot be reduced to the decisional act of an abstract will, but is rooted within the accepted memory of an unchosen destination. The "same structure as that of the date," we said. Is this only a formal analogy? When someone says, "we Jews," does he intend the reappropriation of some essence, the acknowledgment of a belonging, a sense of partaking?

Yes and no, once again. Celan recalls that there is no Jewish property. This is at least a common theme as well as the title of a general question: "do you hear me, you do, it's me, me, me and whom you hear, whom you think you hear, me and the other . . . because the Jew, you know, what does he have that is really his own, that is not borrowed, taken and not returned?" ("hörst du mich, ich bins, ich, ich und der, den du hörst, zu hören vermeinst, ich und der andre . . . denn der Jud, du weißts, was hat er schon, das ihm auch wirklich gehört, das nicht geborgt wär, ausgeliehen und nicht zurückgegeben?") (*GW* 3:169/*CP* 17). The Jew is also the other, myself and the other; I am Jewish in saying: the Jew is the other who has no essence, who has nothing of his own or whose own essence is not to have one. Thus, *at one and the same time*, both the alleged universality of Jewish witnessing ("All poets are Jews," says Marina Tsvetayeva, cited in epigraph to "Und mit dem Buch aus Tarussa" [*GW* 1:287/*SG* 207]) and the incommunicable secret of the Judaic idiom, the singularity of "his name, his unpronounceable name," *sein Name, der unaussprechliche*.

The "name," the Jew's "unpronounceable," his proper name, is it a name? It says more than one can say:

—it says *shibboleth*, the word which is unpronounceable in the sense that it *cannot* be pronounced by one who does not partake of the covenant or alliance. The Ephraimite *knows* how one *ought* to but *cannot* pronounce it. This is the fact that serves the law;

—it says the name of God, which *must* not be pronounced by whoever partakes of the covenant or alliance. The Jew *can* pronounce it but *must not*; he cannot pronounce it. The law commands the fact;

—it says the name of the Jew, which the non-Jew has trouble pronouncing, which he does not know how or does not want to pronounce correctly, and which he scorns or destroys for that very reason; he expels it as foreign and uncouth,[25] he replaces it with a derisive name which is easier to pronounce or classify, as has happened at times on both sides of the Atlantic.

Its unpronounceability keeps and destroys the name; it keeps it, like the name of God, or dooms it to annihilation among the ashes.

Apparently different or contradictory, these two possibilities can always cross the border and exchange with one another.

The Jew, the name Jew, also exchanges with the *shibboleth*, is exchanged for it. Prior even to any use of the pledge, or to becoming its victim, prior to any division between communal division and discriminatory division, whether safe or lost, master or proscript, Jew and *shibboleth* partake of each other. Witness to the universal, but by virtue of absolute singularity, dated, marked, incised, caesuraed—by virtue of and in the name of the other.

(And I will also add that, in its fearful political ambiguity, *shibboleth* could today name the State of Israel, the present state of the State of Israel. This deserves more than a parenthesis, it will be said. Yes. But what I say in parentheses is this: that it is a question here of nothing but this, everywhere and beyond the borders of this parenthesis.)

Witness to the universal by virtue of absolute singularity, by virtue of and in the name of the other, the stranger, you toward whom I must take a step which, without bringing me nearer to you, without exchanging myself with you, without being assured passage, lets the word pass and assigns us, if not to the one, at least to the same. We were already assigned to it, dwelling beneath the same contrary wind. Let the word pass across the barbed frontier, across, this time, the grid of language or thanks to it. The passage of the other, toward the other—respect *of* the same, of a same that respects the otherness of the other. Why did Celan choose the word "Passat," the name of a wind, to say, in "Sprachgitter" (in parentheses) "We are strangers"?

(Wär ich wie du. Wärst du wie ich.
Standen wir nicht
unter *einem* Passat?
Wir sind Fremde.)
    (*GW* 1:167)

([Were I like you. Were you like me.
Did we not stand
under *one* tradewind?
We are strangers.])
    (*SG* 109)

Strangers. Both strangers, the two of us. Strangers each to the other? Strangers the two of us to yet others, third parties? Both—the two of them, one *like* the other, *unter* einem *Passat*.

The impossible impulse to designate the "Judaic," Jewishness—yours and not only mine, always something inappropriable of the other's—may be read, for example, in the poem dated, this is its title, "Zürich, zum Storchen." It is dedicated—every date is dedicated—to Nelly Sachs. The semantics of I and you figure here just as paradoxically (you, you are [a] me). This paradox exceeds any measure of being. Again the disproportion of too much or too little. You, the word *you*, may be addressed to the other as well as to myself, to oneself as other. Each time it overruns the *economy* of the discourse, its self-proximity:

Vom Zuviel war die Rede, vom
Zuwenig. Von Du

und Aber-Du, von
der Trübung durch Helles, von
Jüdischem, von
deinem Gott
[. . .]
Von deinem Gott war die Rede, ich sprach
gegen ihn.
(*GW* 1:214)

(Of too much was our talk, of
too little. Of the You
and You-Again, of
how clarity troubles, of
Jewishness, of
your God.
[. . .]
Of your God was our talk, I spoke
against him.)
(*P* 157)

(Second parenthesis: I have abstained on several occasions from interpellating Heidegger or evoking his interpellation. Its necessity can escape no one. It is for the same reason that I will say nothing in this place of what there is to be said of other thinkers, Buber, Lévinas, Blanchot, and still others.)

The "you," the "yours," may be addressed to the other as Jew but also to the self as other, as another Jew or as other than Jew. Is this a true alternative? "Die Schleuse," "The Lock Gate," addresses you, and your mourning, "all this mourning / of yours" ("aller dieser deiner / Trauer"): to tell you that what has been lost, and beyond a trace, is the word, a word which opens, like a *shibboleth*, on what is most intimate. Now this lost word, the word that is to be mourned, is not only the word "that had remained with me": "sister." It is also, and even more grievously, if this can be said, the word that opens the possibility of mourning what has been lost beyond a trace (the exterminated family, the incineration of the family name in the figure of the sister—for the word is "sister"—at the final hour which no longer has a sister—"your hour / has no sisters.") It is the very word which grants access to Jewish mourning: "*Kaddish.*" This word addressed me, sought me, like the hour's interpellation; it came before me, it sought me out ("mich suchte"), it took the initiative. But then I lost it, like the word that had remained with me: "sister." I lost the word that had remained with me, I lost the one that sought me out to mourn the one that had remained with me:

An einen Mund,
dem es ein Tausendwort war,
verlor—
verlor ich ein Wort,
das mir verblieben war:
Schwester.

An
die Vielgötterei
verlor ich ein Wort, das mich suchte:
Kaddisch.
     (GW 1:222)

(To a mouth
for which it was one of a thousand
I lost—
I lost a word
that had remained with me:
sister.

To
the worship of many gods
I lost a word that was looking for me:
Kaddish.)
       (P 169)

Lost the word "sister" that had remained with me, lost the word
"kaddish" that sought me to live the loss, lost too "my Jew's spot" ("wo /
mein Judenfleck . . . ?") (*GW* 1:229), lost my "Jew's curl," which was
also a "human curl" ("Judenlocke, wirst nicht grau . . . Menschenlocke,
wirst nicht grau.") (*GW* 1:244/*P* 189).

The loss cannot be worse than when it extends to the death of the
name, to the extinction of the proper name which a date, bereaved commemoration, remains. It crosses that boundary where mourning itself is
denied us, the interiorization of the other in memory (*Erinnerung*), the
preserving of the other in a sepulcher or epitaph. For in securing a sepulcher, the date would still make room for mourning, for what one calls
its work. Whereas Celan also names the incinerated beyond of the date,
words lost without sepulcher, "wie unbestattete Worte." But once dead,
and without sepulcher, these words of mourning which are themselves
incinerated may yet return. They come back then as phantoms. One
hears them roaming about the stelae,

wie unbestattete Worte,
streunend

im Bannkreis erreichter
Ziele und Stelen und Wiegen.
(*GW* 1:287)

(like unsepulchered words,
roaming
in the orbit of attained
goals and stelae and cradles.)
(*SG* 207)

Spectral errancy of words. This spectral return does not befall words by accident, following a death which would come to some or spare others. The spectral return is partaken of by *all* words, from their first emergence. They will always have been phantoms, and this law governs the relationship in them between body and soul. One cannot say that we know this *because* we have experience of death and of mourning. That experience comes to us from our relation to this spectral return of the mark, then of language, then of the word, then of the name. What one calls poetry or literature, art itself (let us not distinguish them for the moment), in other words a certain experience of language, of the mark or of the trait *as such*, is nothing perhaps but an intense familiarity with the ineluctable originarity of the specter. One can naturally translate it into the ineluctable loss of the origin. Mourning, the experience of mourning, the *crossing* of its limit too, so that it would be hard to see here a law governing a theme or a genre. It is experience, and as such, for poetry, for literature, for art itself.

V I I

There is an event, a rite of passage, which seems to mark the legitimate entry of the Jew into his community and which takes place, as we said at the outset, but once alone, on an absolutely specific date: the circumcision. This at least is how it appears.

Circumcision: may one say that it is precisely of this ciphered wound, this wound to be deciphered, that Celan speaks at the end of "Dein vom Wachen" (*GW* 2:24/*65 Poems* 56)? "Sie setzt / Wundgelesenes über" ("it carries across / the wound-read"), these lines speak in any case of a passing beyond, over that which is *read* to the quick, to the point of bleeding, to the point of wounding, reaching that place where the cipher is painfully inscribed in the body itself. This body may be that of the "reader-gatherer," as Jean Launay's French translation rightly suggests,[26] but also the one on which a cipher offers itself to be read because it has remained there like the mark of a wound. Thus the wound, or its scar, becomes significant, it is joined by some thread to reading. To say that it is readable would be literally abusive, for it is also unreadable, and this is why it wears out reading to the very marrow. But it belongs to the experience of reading. I would even say to that of translation, for the *setzt . . . über*, which could not be translated by "translates" under any circumstances, also passes over this grammatical impossibility to beckon toward the translation of this reading-wound, passing over the border to the other side, the side of the other.

In the literality of its word (*Beschneidung*), circumcision appears rarely in Celan's text, at least as far as I know. The example to which I will return in a moment concerns the circumcision of a word. But does one ever circumcise without circumcising a word? a name? And how can one ever circumcise a name without doing something to the body? First of all to the body of the name which finds itself recalled by the wound to its condition as word, then as carnal mark, written, spaced, and inscribed in a network of other marks, at once both endowed with and deprived of singularity.

If the word *circumcision* appears rarely in its literality, other than in connection with the circumcision of the word, by contrast the *tropic* of circumcision disposes cuts, caesuras, ciphered alliances, and wounded rings throughout the text. The wound, the very experience of reading, is also universal. It is tied to both the differential marks and the destination of language: the inaccessibility of the other returns there in the same, dates and sets turning the ring. To say "all poets are Jews" is to state something which marks *and* annuls the mark of a circumcision. It is tropic. All those who deal with or inhabit language as poets are Jews— but in a tropic sense. And the one who says this, consequently, speaking as a poet and by trope, never presents himself literally as a Jew. He asks: what is literality in this case?

What the trope (again an intersection with the "Meridian") comes to, then, is locating the Jew not only *as* a poet but also in every man circumcised by language or led to circumcise a language. I am not prepared to deal here with the question of the semantic charge of circumcision; I will not enumerate all the usages which the rich lexicon of circumcision may authorize in the language of the Scriptures, well beyond the consecrated operation which consists in excising the prepuce. The "spiritualization," as one often says, the "interiorization" which consists in extending the meaning of the word beyond the sense of the cut into the flesh does not date from Saint Paul; it is not limited to the circumcision of the soul or the heart.

Keeping ourselves to a minimal semantic network, "circumcision" seems to involve *at least* three significations:

1. The cut which incises the male sexual member, entering and passing around it to form a circumvenient ring;
2. A name given to the moment of covenant or alliance and of legitimate entry into the community: a *shibboleth* which cuts and divides,

then distinguishes, for example, by virtue of the language and the name which is given to each of them, one circumcision from another, the Jewish from the Egyptian operation from which it is said to derive, or, indeed, the Muslim operation which resembles it, or many others.

3. The experience of blessing and of purification.

Now a certain tropic may displace the literality of membership in the Jewish community, if one could still speak of belonging to a community to which, we are reminded by "Gespräch im Gebirg," nothing properly belongs, among all these meanings. In that case, those who have the experience, a certain concise experience of circumcision, circumcised and circumcisers, are, in all the senses of this word, Jews. Anyone or no one may be a Jew. Jew, no one's name, the only one. No one's circumcision.

If all the poets are Jews, they are all, the poets, circumcised or circumcisers. This gives rise, in Celan's text, to a tropic of circumcision which turns from the *Wundgelesenes* toward all ciphered wounds, all cut words, notably in "Engführung," where the thread can be followed which passes through "points of suture" ("Nahtstellen"), closed up tears or scars, words to be cut off which were not cut off, membranes stitched back together, etc. (*GW* 1:199/P 139).

We said a moment ago "no one's circumcision." The evocation of the exterminated race designates the race and root of no one: black erection in the sky, verge and testicle, race and root of no one. Uprooting of the race, but equally so of the sex ("Geschlecht") in "Radix, Matrix":

Wer,
wer wars, jene
Geschlecht, jenes gemordete, jenes
schwarz in den Himmel stehende:
Rute und Hode—?

(Wurzel.
Wurzel Abrahams. Wurzel Jesse. Niemandes
Wurzel—o
unser.)
    (*GW* 1:239)

(Who,
who was it, that
lineage, the murdered, that looms
black in the sky:
rod and bulb—?

[Root.
Abraham's root. Jesse's root. No one's
root—o
ours.])
      (*P* 187)

Circumcise: the word appears once in the imperative mode: *beschneide*.

But the grammar of the verb, the modality of the imperative, does not necessarily signify an imperious order. Injunction, appeal, desire, supplication, prayer, these also may be conveyed through the same grammar.

This word, this word of command—injunction or appeal, desire, supplication, or prayer—bears this time *upon the word*. The verb has the word as its object, it speaks about an operation to be performed on the verbum, on the word. The word says: circumcise the word. Its complement is the word, or rather the Word: "beschneide das Wort."

Let us read this poem: "Einem, der vor der Tür stand" (*GW* 1:242–43).

It concerns the circumcision of the Word. The interpellation apostrophizes a rabbi, a circumciser no doubt. Not any rabbi, but Rabbi Löw:

Rabbi, knirschte ich, Rabbi
Löw:

Diesem
beschneide das Wort.

(Rabbi, I grated, Rabbi
Löw:

For this one
circumcise the word.)

This word to be circumcised, this word *of someone's* to be circumcised, this word to be circumcised for someone, this word which must thus be given, and given *once* circumcised, we may understand this word as an opened word.

Like a wound, you will say. Yes and no. Opened, first of all, like a door: opened to the stranger, to the other, to the neighbor, to the guest, to whomever. To whomever no doubt in the figure of the absolute future (the one who will come, more precisely who *would come*, for the coming of this future, *the one* to come, must be neither assured nor calculable), thus in the figure of the monstrous creature. The absolute future can only announce itself in the form of monstrosity, beyond all anticipated forms and norms, beyond all genres or kinds. And I am passing over here what the apparition of Rabbi Löw may recall for us of the Golem, the inventor of the monster: the narrative is given over in the poem to a transmutation, a transfigurative translation, meticulous in its letter and detail—yet another stone in the Prague cemetery—but totally emancipated. The translation is beholden to the narrative, but absolved from and having no relationship with this same literality.

A word opened to whomever in the figure as well, perhaps, of some prophet Elijah, of his phantom or double. He is mistakable, through this monstration of monstrosity, but one must know how to recognize him. Elijah is the one to whom hospitality is due, promised, prescribed. He may come, one must know this, at any moment. He may cause the event of his coming to happen at each instant. I will situate in this place that which speaks of or summons the coming of the event ("kommen," "geschehen") in so many of Celan's poems.

The prophet Elijah is not named by Celan, and perhaps he was not thinking of him. I take the risk of recalling as well that Elijah is not only the guest, the one to whom, as *relationship* itself, the door of the word must be opened. Elijah is not simply a messianic and eschatological prophet. By God's command, according to the tradition, he must be present at all circumcisions, each time, every time. He watches over them. The one who holds the circumcised infant must be seated on what is called Elijah's chair (Kise Eliyahu). How could he be absent from this poem which says "Diesem / beschneide das Wort"?

Here in this very place, in the poem, the monster, or Elijah, the guest or the other, stands before the door, at the poem's first step, on the threshold of the text. "Einem, der vor der Tür stand" is its title. He stands before the door as before the law. We may think of Kafka's "Vor dem Gesetz," "Before the Law," but also of everything which, in Judaism, associates the door and the law.

And the one who says "I," the poet, if you like, one of those poets "all" of whom "are Jews," no doubt opens the door to him, but the door turns into the word. What he opens to him is not the door, but the word:

EINEM, DER VOR DER TÜR STAND, eines
Abends:
ihm
tat ich mein Wort auf—: . . .

(TO ONE, WHO STOOD BEFORE THE DOOR, one
evening:
to him
I opened my word—: . . .)

Let us call this—by way of allegory—an *allegory*, the bearing of a word for the other, to the other or from the other. The allegory follows the revolution or *vicissitude* of the hours, from evening to morning, the times *in their turns* (*in vicem, vice versa*). The vicissitude begins one evening, *eines Abends*, in the Occident of the poem. The poet, the one who says I, opens the word and addresses himself to the Rabbi, to the *Mohel*, to the one whom he appoints as circumciser since he says to him, "circumcise." What does he ask of him? To close the door of the evening and to open the door of the morning (*die Morgentür*). If the door speaks the word, he now, once the word is circumcised, asks it for the word of morning, the Oriental word, the poem of the origin.

> Wirf auch die Abendtür zu, Rabbi.
> . . . .
> Reiß die Morgentür auf, Ra- —

> (Slam shut the evening door too, Rabbi.
> . . . .
> Fling the morning door open, Ra- —)

A violent opening and closing. *Aufreißen* is to open brusquely, rapidly and wide, to break or sometimes to *rend* in one stroke, like a veil. *Zuwerfen* marks as well some brutality; the door is slammed, as though in someone's direction, signifying its closing to someone. As for *Ra-*, the name interrupted at the final caesura, the first syllable of an appellation that is not completed and finally remains in the mouth, the Rabbi cut in two, this is perhaps the Egyptian God as well, the sun or light, at the opening of the "morning door."

I will not attempt to read or decipher this poem. A poem about the poem, it also names the becoming-poetic of the word, its becoming-Jewish, in short, if "all poets are Jews." It describes the becoming-circumcised of the word of origin, its circumcision. It is a narrative of circumcision.

I use this word, *circumcision*, to designate an operation, the surgical act of cutting, but also and equally the state, the quality, the condition of being circumcised. In this second sense, one may speak of the circumcision of a word or utterance, as one also speaks of the concision of a discourse. Circumcision will designate being circumcised or circumscribed. Blake's *Jerusalem*, that great poem of circumcision, regularly associates these three turns or turns of speech, these three revolutions: *circumcision, circumscription*, and *circumference*, for example, that of the four senses which are also four faces turned toward the four cardinal points, from the west ("the Tongue") to the east ("the Nostrils"), from the north ("the Ear") to the south ("the Eye": "Eyed as the Peacock"): "Circumscribing & Circumcising the excrementitious / Husk & Cov-

ering into Vacuum evaporating revealing the lineaments of Man . . . re-
joicing in Unity / In the Four Senses in the Outline the Circumference & Form, for ever / In the Forgiveness of Sins which is Self
Annihilation. it is the Covenant of Jehovah."[27]

I have cited this "covenant" of Blake's to emphasize that, in all of
what we are calling its tropic dimensions, circumcision remains a matter
of the body. It offers itself for writing and for reading on the body. Or
rather: the sense of the senses, the body, offers itself for thinking, signifying, interpreting thus, as it is revealed through *this* response to the
question "What is the body proper, said to be proper?": a place of circumcision.

Before Saint Paul, the Bible writes of the circumcision or uncir-
cumcision of the lips, which is to say, in this tongue, of the tongue
(Exod. 6:12, 30), of the ears (Jer. 6:10), and of the heart (Lev. 26:41).

The opposition of the clean and the unclean, the proper and the
improper, the pure and the impure, coincides often with that of the circumcised and the uncircumcised, extending without limit the semantic
field of circumcision and thus defining it only at the limits of definition,
of limitation, of circumscription itself, which is to say, conferring on it
a singular indefiniteness.

The circumcision of a word must thus be understood as an event of
the body. There is an essential analogy between this event, on the one
hand, and the diacritical difference between *shibboleth* and *sibboleth*, on
the other. It is in the body, by reason of a certain impotence *coming over*
their vocal organs, but an impotence of the body *proper,* of the already
cultivated body, limited by a barrier neither organic nor natural, that
the Ephraimites experienced their inability to pronounce what they
nonetheless knew ought to be pronounced *shibboleth*—and not *sibboleth.*

An "unpronounceable name" for some, *shibboleth* is a circumcised
word. For this one, Rabbi, circumcise the word, *beschneide das Wort.*
Give him the word of partaking, impart it to him, also, to this one also.

———

One must pretend to close a lecture, and to have encompassed one's
topic. I will limit myself in concluding to some remarks or questions.

The word which is to be circumcised: here it is, first of all, opened,
like a door, offered, given, or at least promised to the other.

The other remains indeterminate—unnamed in the poem. He has
no identifiable face, he simply has a face since he must see the door, and
receive the word, even if this face remains invisible. It never shows itself
in the poem. It is *no one,* anyone, the neighbor *or* the stranger, for with
the other it comes to the same.

The one who is not yet named, the one who perhaps awaits his
name, awaits its bestowal by a circumcision, is the one-and-only, the

unique, *this one*. He draws the whole poem toward him, destines it for himself, the destinatory, inspires it toward his own pole in absolute dis-symmetry.

The other, *this one*, is always, as it were, placed *at the head, alone*, very much alone on a line—a poetic line. It is to him, *to this one* (*Diesem*) that one must open, give, circumcise, *for him* that the living Nothing must be inscribed in the heart ("diesem / schreib das lebendige / Nichts ins Gemüt"): to him, for him, this one: *ihm*, then *Diesem, diesem, diesem, Diesem*, four times the same demonstrative pronoun, the same word framing a strophe, four times alone on a line, twice, to begin and to end, in the grammar of the capital.

ihm
tat ich mein Wort auf
[...]
Diesem
beschneide das Wort,
diesem
schreib das lebendige
Nichts ins Gemüt,
diesem
spreize die zwei
Krüppelfinger zum heil-
bringenden Spruch.
Diesem.

(to him
I opened my word
[...]
for this one,
circumcise the word,
for this one
write the living
Nothing in the heart,
for this one
spread the two
cripple-fingers in the
hallowing sentence.
This one.)

The offering of this word for circumcision is indeed the giving of a word, of one's word, since it is said that "I open my word," *mein Wort*. Given word, promise, engagement, signature, date, saving word also in the form of a poem or a decision (*Spruch*: sentence or aphorism, strophe or poem, sentence or verdict, decision of justice: circumcision would be *just* this, this decision of the word, its sentence, inscribed right in the body, just in the heart, *precisely*).

This word of opening permits one to pass through the doorway. It is yet another *shibboleth*, the very *shibboleth* at the origin of all the others, and yet one among others, *in a given language*.

The *shibboleth* is given or promised by *me* (*mein Wort*) to the singular other, "this one," that he may partake of it and enter, or leave, that he may pass through the doorway, across the line, the border, the threshold.

Yet this word, which is given or promised, in any case, opened, offered to the other, also asks. It asks intercession, or rather it intercedes with the Rabbi—still an other—that he might bestow, him, the third, the value of circumcision on this word—the *shibboleth* of the community before the law, the sign of the covenant. The Rabbi is a wise man invested with this right; he has the knowledge, and the power to circumcise the word. He is the guardian and the guarantor; it is through him that the transmission of the *shibboleth* passes just as the doorway is crossed. And this doorway is nothing other than circumcision as *shibboleth*, the place of decision for the right of access to the legitimate community, the covenant or alliance, the given name of a singular individual, but the *dated* name, singular but inscribed right on the body, on a given day in a genealogical classification, one could say in a calendar. The name counts *at once both once and several times*. There is a turning and a vicissitude of names.

The intercessor seems to hold all the powers and all the rights, whether one thinks of the poem's intercession, of mine, or of the Rabbi's. This—a *shibboleth*—intercedes. But here the knowledge and power are annulled of themselves. The knowledge and the power of Rabbi Löw are annulled, his knowing—being able—to circumcise, which amount in truth to the same thing, which are but one—are immediately annihilated in the *object-less*. They know how and are able to infinitely, but must also infinitely annihilate themselves. For the writing of circumcision which *I* ask of him, for which I intercede with the intercessor, is a *writing of Nothing*. It performs its operation on Nothing, an incisive surgery which, to the point of bleeding, to the point of wounding ("Wundgeschriebene," one might say this time), embeds the inscription of Nothing in the flesh, in the living word, in the flesh of the pronounceable and circumcised word: "Diesem / beschneide das Wort, / diesem schreib das lebendige / Nichts ins Gemüt." Write, slice, inscribe, cut, separate, "schreiben," "schneiden," "scheiden." But Nothing. One gives the word, one's word, in inscribing this Nothing in the heart; thus one should not cut in, but on the contrary allow the word passage. In "Engführung," it is said of a stone, that of the threshold perhaps, or of the path, or of the first circumcisers, that "it / was hospitable, it / did not cut in": "er / war gastlich, er / fiel nicht ins Wort" (*GW* 1:201/*P* 143). As often, the break in the line comes after the pronoun.

How can one write nothing?

(Let us place here, not to close it, put on the contrary so as to leave it open, like a wound, the necessity of an immense parenthesis: for the question of Nothing and the meaning of being in Celan, of a truth of being which *passes* through the *experience* of Nothing, for the question, here, of circumcision left unanswered and dated "Todtnauberg" [*GW* 2:255–56/*P* 293], when it was, in effect, put to another kind of wise man, one summer's day in 1967.)[28]

No one's circumcision, the word's circumcision by the incision of Nothing in the circumcised heart of the other, of this one, you.

Circumcise the word for him, circumcise his word, what is meant by this demand? More than one can *mean-to-say*, more and less than this or that meaning, more or less than this determination. Circumcision is also a *determination*: it defines and it decides. But to ask for circumcision is not to ask for something determinate, a meaning or an object.

The circumcised word is *first of all* written, at once both incised and excised in a body, which may be the body of a language and which in any case always binds the body to language: the word which is entered into, wounded in order to be what it is, the word cut into, written because cut into, caesuraed in its origin, with the poem.

The circumcised word is, *next of all*, readable, starting from *nothing*, but readable, *to be read* to the point of wounding and to the point of bleeding (*Wundgelesene*).

By the same stroke, as it were, the circumcised word grants access to the community, to the covenant or alliance, to the partaking of a language, in a language. And in the Jewish language as poetic language, if all poetic language is, like all the poets according to the epigraph, Jewish in essence; but this essence promises itself only through disidentification, that expropriation in the nothing of that non-essence of which we have spoken. The Germanic language, like any other, but here with what privilege, must be circumcised by a rabbi, and the rabbi becomes then a poet, reveals the poet in him. How can the German language receive circumcision at this poem's date, that is to say, following the holocaust, the solution, the final cremation, the ash of all? How is one to bless these ashes in German?

Finally, *fourth* and in consequence, at once both readable and secret, mark of belonging and of exclusion, the wound of partaking, the circumcised word reminds us also of what I will call the *double edge* of a *shibboleth*. The mark of a covenant or alliance, it also *intervenes*, it interdicts, it signifies the sentence of exclusion, of discrimination, indeed of extermination. One may, thanks to the *shibboleth*, recognize and be recognized by one's own, for better and for worse, in the cleaving of partaking: on the one hand, for the sake of the partaking and the ring of the covenant, but also, on the other hand, for the purpose of denying the other, of denying him passage or life. A cleaving always refuses the other, the meaning of the one—a given cleaving—proscribes the other. Because of the *shibboleth* and exactly to the extent that one may make use of it, one may see it turned against oneself: then it is the circumcised who are proscribed or held at the border, excluded from the community, put to death, or reduced to ashes: at the mere sight, in the mere name, at the first reading of a wound.

How is one to guard oneself against this double edge? With what? With nothing. Perhaps Nothing, the annulment of all literal circumcision, the effacement of this *determinate* mark, perhaps the inscription as circumcision of Nothing or nothing in circumcision. Perhaps Rabbi Löw understood himself to be asked or ordered to do this, *precisely* this, nothing, the inscription of "the living Nothing in the heart." Perhaps, but precisely: this would not reduce the demand to nothing.

There must be circumcision, circumcision of the word, writing, and it must take place once, precisely, each time one time, the one time only.

This time awaits its coming, as its vicissitude. It awaits a date, and this date can only be poetic, an incision in the body of language. It remains to come, always. How are we to transcribe ourselves into a date?, Celan asks.

When we speak here of a date to come for circumcision, we are not yet speaking, not necessarily, of history. We are not speaking of the date *in* the history of an individual (we know for example that this date was variable before it was fixed, for Jews, at the eighth day after birth) or *in* the history of Judaism (we know that other peoples practiced it already and still do; a shibboleth passes the blade of a slight difference between several circumcisions. We also know that circumcision only becomes law at a certain date; the first codes of Israel did not make a ritual injunction of it).

No, the circumcision of the word is not dated in history. In this sense, it has no age, but calls forth the date. It opens the word to the other, and the door, it opens history and the poem and philosophy and hermeneutics and religion. Of all that calls itself—of the name and the blessing of the name, of yes and of no, it sets turning the ring, to affirm or to annul.

I have kept you too long and ask your pardon.

Permit me to let fall, by way of envoy or *shibboleth*, that is to say, in the economy of an ellipsis which circulates only in the partaking and imparting of a given language, here my own, by way of signature here, today, this: circumcision—dates.

Seattle, October 14, 1984

NOTES

In its first version (published in English), this text was given as a lecture at the "International Paul Celan Symposium" at the University of Washington, Seattle, in October 1984. Despite certain revisions and some new developments, the plan of exposition, the rhythm, and the tone of the lecture have been preserved as far as possible.

1. *Translator's Note*. "Alliance" denotes a broader range of meanings in French than in English, including marriage and the biblical covenant.

2. The title of the poem alludes to Baudelaire's "*Confiteor* de l'artiste": "et il n'est pas de pointe plus acérée que celle de l'Infini" ("and there is no point more piercing than that of the Infinite") (*Oeuvres complètes*, ed. Claude Pichois [Paris: Gallimard, 1975], 1:278), as confirmed by Werner Hamacher's very beautiful text, "The Second of Inversion: Movements of a Figure through Celan's Poetry": "Celan reported in conversation that he borrowed this text's title from a note by Baudelaire, cited in Hofmannsthal's journal under the date June 29, 1917." Trans. William D. Jewett, in *Yale French Studies* 69 (1985), 308. Werner Hamacher, "Die Sekunde der Inversion. Bewegungen einer Figur durch Celans Gedichte," in *Paul Celan. Materialien*, ed. Werner Hamacher and Winfried Menninghaus (Frankfort: Suhrkamp, 1988), 117.

3. *GW* 1:251/*P* 193. I wish first of all to express an immense debt and to render hommage to those who have taken on the responsibility and the risk of translating Celan's texts, every letter of which, as we know, and every blank space, every breath and caesura, defies translation, yet calls for and provokes it at the same time. The enigma of the *shibboleth*, as will be confirmed, merges completely with that of translation, in its essential dimension. I am therefore not going to deal with it in a note, before having even started. Whoever has read Celan will have passed through the experience of translation, of its limits, its aporias, its exigencies, I mean those of the original poem which also *demands* to be translated. In general, I have abstained from translating, above all from retranslating. I did not want to seem to want, however little, to amend a first attempt. In the approach to texts such as these, lessons and polemics have no place. It may happen, to be sure, that I more readily go along with one or another participant in the debate which is currently under way in France on this subject. One thinks, first of all, of the essays by Henri Meschonnic ("On appelle cela traduire Celan," in *Pour la poétique* [Paris: Gallimard, 1973], 2:367–405); by Jean Launay ("Une lecture de Paul Celan," *Po&sie* 9 [1979], 3–8); and by Philippe Lacoue-Labarthe ("Deux poèmes de Paul Celan," in *La poésie comme expérience* ([Paris: Bourgois, 1986], 11–58), especially where formidable qualities of tone, the Mallarmean for example, are at issue.

T.N. Whenever possible, I have used available English translations of Celan's poetry and prose, although sometimes I have had to modify these in the interest of a more exact articulation between Derrida's text and the passages he cites.

4. *T.N. mise en oeuvre*; "setting-to-work," but also, in the idiom of the text, "setting-(in)to-(the)-work." In subsequent occurrences, I have simply retained the French phrase.

5. "Le Méridien," in *Strette* (Paris: Mercure de France, 1971), 191.

6. *T.N. l'à venir*; cf. *l'avenir*.

7. *T.N.* The distinction that Derrida develops in the following paragraph is clearer in French, since the French word for "encounter," *rencontre*, is also employed in the phrase *de rencontre*, meaning "chance," "passing," "casual," etc. Thus, for example, "le secret d'une *rencontre*" is "the secrecy of an *encounter*"; "un secret *de rencontre*" is "a chance secret."

8. *T.N. au gnomon de Paul Celan*; cf. *au nom de Paul Celan*, "in the name of Paul Celan."

9. *T.N. Partage* in French signifies at once division, participation through sharing in what is divided, and the share apportioned. It will be translated in most cases by either "imparting" or "partaking," in one case by "cleaving."

10. *GW* 1:135/*P* 99. We will return below to the question of that which links the word, and the word as decree, aphorism, sentence, verdict, judgment (*Spruch*), to decision and circumcision, on the one hand, and to the date and the hour, on the other. Here, the imparting or distribution (*Verteilung*), and the gift of shade, that which gives meaning to the *Spruch*, to the word as judgment (*Urteil*), spreads or distributes the origin of meaning, that is, the shade, *between the hours*, between complete shade and the absence of shade, midnight and midday and midnight. The shade is imparted, spread out, or apportioned (*verteilt*) among the hours. And this imparting of shade *gives meaning*.

11. The date and the gift. The debt as well. Beyond etymology, this is the shade which would give meaning, here, to all our questions. This lecture had already been delivered, and the second version written, when I had the chance to read the manuscript of Jean Greisch's then unpublished text, "Zeitgehöft et Anwesen (La dia-chronie du poème)," in *Contre-jour*, ed. Martine Broda (Paris: Cerf, 1986), 167–83. I would like to thank him here. I refer the reader to these rich analyses concerning Celan. Here, I will have to be content with calling attention to two precious references both of which I owe to Jean Greisch. First of all, he recalls the text of Heidegger which "transforms the 'Datum' into a donation": "Moreover, poetic time differs in accordance with the essence [*Wesenart*] of poetry and the poets. For each essential poem figures [*dichtet*] equally, and in a new way, the essence of making poetry. This holds even more for the poetry of Hölderlin in a particular and unique sense. For the 'now' of his poetry there is no date conforming to the calendar. Moreover, there is no need here of any date. For this 'now' which is called and which itself calls is itself in a more originary sense a date—which is to say: a given, a gift, given, that is, by the calling" ("Überdies ist die dichterische Zeit auch jeweils wieder verschieden je nach der Wesenart der Dichtung und der Dichter. Denn jede wesentliche Dichtung dichtet ja auch das Wesen des Dichtens selbst 'neu'. Von Hölderlins Dichtung gilt dies noch in einem besonderen und einzigen Sinn. Für das 'Jetzt' seiner Dichtung gibt es kein kalendermäßiges Datum. Auch bedarf es hier überhaupt keines Datum. Denn dieses gerufene und selbst rufende 'Jetzt' ist selbst, in einem ursprunglicheren Sinne ein Datum, will sagen—ein Gegebenes, eine Gabe; gegeben nämlich durch die Berufung"). Martin Heidegger, *Hölderlins Hymne "Der Ister"*, Gesamtausgabe (Frankfort: Klostermann, 1984), 43:8. Jean Greisch also recalls and analyzes the passage that Heidegger devotes to "data-bility" (*Datierbarkeit*) in *Die Grundprobleme der Phänomenologie*, ed Friedrich-Wilhelm von Herrmann (Frankfort: Klostermann, 1975), vol. 24. I cite a few excerpts. They touch on a problem, that of the relationship between the calen-

drical and the noncalendrical date, which we will address directly a little further on: "By the term 'datability' we denote this relational structure of the now as now-when, of the at-the-time as at-the-time-when, and of the then as then-when. Every now dates itself as 'now, when such and such is occurring, happening, or in existence' . . . The date itself does not need to be calendrical in the narrower sense. The calendar date is only one particular mode of everyday dating. The indefiniteness of the date does not imply a shortcoming in datability as essential structure of the now, at-the-time, and then . . . The time that is commonly conceived as a sequence of nows must be taken as this dating relation. This relation should not be overlooked and suppressed. Nevertheless, the common conception of time as a sequence of nows is just as little aware of the moment of pre-calendrical datability as that of significance . . . Why could time-structures as elemental as those of significance and datability remain hidden from the traditional time concept? Why did it overlook them and why did it have to overlook them? We shall learn how to understand this from the structure of temporality itself" (370–72). Martin Heidegger, *The Basic Problems of Phenomenology*, trans. Albert Hofstadter (Bloomington: Indiana University Press, 1975), 262–63. The third volume of Paul Ricoeur's great book *Temps et récit: le temps raconté* (Paris: Seuil, 1985) includes in particular a rich analysis of calendrical time and the institution of the calendar. This "institution constitutes the invention of a third-time," between "lived time" and "cosmic time." The "transcendental" analysis proposed, above and beyond the genetic and sociological approaches, is developed specifically by means of a critique of the Heideggerian concept of "common time" and the elaboration of a philosophy of the trace which is both close to and different from that of Levinas.

12. *Schriften*, ed. Wolfgang Fietkau (Frankfort: Suhrkamp, 1978), 2:390.

13. *T.N. Ausgewählte Gedichte*, ed. Klaus Reichert (Frankfort: Suhrkamp, 1970).

14. "Eden," 391.

15. Martine Broda devotes "a long parenthesis" to this "shepherd-Spanish" in "Bouteilles, cailloux, shibboleths: un nom dans la main," in *Dans la main de personne* (Paris: Cerf, 1986), 95–105.

16. *T.N. ce* pas impossible; both "this impossible step" and "this not impossible."

17. *Feber*: Austrian dialect for *Februar. Jänner*, occurring in other poems, goes back (like *Jenner*) to the beginnings of Middle-High German and remains in use up through the nineteenth century, and even today in Austria, and here and there in Switzerland and Alsace.

18. Cf. Jean-Luc Nancy, *Le Partage des voix* (Paris: Galilée, 1982). *T.N.* Among its other meanings, *partage des voix* is the French idiom for a split, that is to say tied, vote.

19. It would have been appropriate to do it everywhere, but I chose to recall Freud's *shibboleths* here, at the moment of this allusion to the ring, for example the one symbolizing the alliance of the founders of psychoanalysis. Freud often used this word, *shibboleth*, to designate that which "distinguishes the followers of psychoanalysis from those who are opposed to it" ("Drei Abhandlungen zur Sexualtheorie," in *Gesammelte Werke* [London: Imago, 1940–68], 5:128; "Three Essays on the Theory of Sexuality," in Sigmund Freud, *The Stan-*

dard Edition of the Complete Psychological Works, ed. and trans. James Strachey [London: Hogarth, 1953–66], 7:226), or "Dreams, the shibboleth of psychoanalysis" ("Zur Geschichte der psychoanalytischen Bewegung," in *Gesammelte Werke*, 13:239; "On the History of the Psycho-Analytic Movement," in *Standard Edition*, 14:57). Cf. also "Das Ich und das Es," in *Gesammelte Werke*, 13:239 ("The Ego and the Id," in *Standard Edition*, 19:13) and "Neue Folge der Vorlesungen: Zur Einführung in die Psychoanalyse," in *Gesammelte Werke*, 15:6 ("New Introductory Lectures on Psychoanalysis," in *Standard Edition*, 22:7). The motif of the *shibboleth* was discussed in the course of a seminar arranged around Wladimir Granoff, Marie Moscovici, Robert Pujol, and Jean-Michel Rey in conjunction with a symposium at Cerisy-la-Salle. Cf. *Les fins de l'homme* (Paris: Galilée, 1981), 185–86.

20. *GW* 1:226/*P* 177. Concerning *Jänner*, Lacoue-Labarthe suggests an "allusion to the disconcerting manner in which Hölderlin dated his so-called 'poems of madness,'" *La Poésie comme expérience*, 27–28. In this regard, one may also recall the title and first line of the poem "Eingejännert" (*GW* 2:351).

21. *T.N.* The translation of the poem cited in the French text renders *Novembersternen* as *Constellation de Novembre*, a rendering motivated by the allusion to Saggitarius in the poem's last line (*Schütze*).

22. *T.N.* Cf. "Die sinnliche Gewissheit; oder das Dieses und das Meinen," in George Wilhelm Friedrich Hegel, *Phänomenologie das Geistes*, ed. Johannes Hoffmeister (Hamburg: Meiner, 1952), 79–89. "Sense-Certainty: Or the 'This' and the 'Meaning,'" in G. W. F. Hegel, *Phenomenology of the Spirit*, trans. A. V. Miller (Oxford: Oxford University Press, 1977), 58–67.

23. *T.N.* Cf. Friedrich Hölderlin, *Sämtliche Werke*, ed. Friedrich Beißner (Stuttgart: Kolhammer, 1951), 4:266–72. "On the Difference of Poetic Modes," in Friedrich Hölderlin, *Essays and Letters on Theory*, ed. and trans. Thomas Pfau (Albany: State University of New York Press, 1988), 83–88.

24. *GW* 2:107/*P* 271. With regard to *ichten*, Henri Meschonnic writes: "It seems that one should take this for the preterit of an infinitive *ichten* found in Grimm: 'to become I,' 'to create an I'—a genesis. In addition, *ichten* is between—*nicht* and *Licht*. Between the two, it partakes of both through its signifier—of nothingness and of light." *Pour la poétique*, 374.

25. *T.N. comme "un nom à coucher dehors"*; i.e., a long, unpronounceable name.

26. *T.N.* "Le Méridien. Discours prononcé à l'occasion de la remise du prix Georg Büchner," *Po&sie* 9 (1979), 68–82.

27. IV. pl. 98, ll. 18–23. *T.N.* William Blake, *The Complete Poetry and Prose*, ed. David V. Erdman (Berkeley and Los Angeles: University of California Press, 1982), 257.

28. On the secret of this encounter, on that which came to pass there or not, Philippe Lacoue-Labarthe poses, it seems to me, the essential questions, the just one. Cf. *La Poésie comme expérience*.

THOUGHT AND POETRY

Mystical Elements in Heidegger's
Thought and Celan's Poetry

Otto Pöggeler
Translated by Henry Pickford

With his paths of thought Martin Heidegger has exerted an influence upon our age as no other philosopher has done, and indeed his influence extends far beyond the realm of academic philosophy. Of course, in this regard Heidegger's philosophy has been interpreted in the most varied of ways. For some, Heidegger's works are footnotes to Aristotle: if Aristotle is the classical philosopher who gives thinking a homeland across the centuries, then Heidegger is the one who leads Aristotelian metaphysics as well as his practical philosophy forward to the questions of our tempestuous age. Others, however, pay closer attention to how Heidegger attempts a new approach by means of Husserl's phenomenology, and in so doing how he tries to demonstrate that wanting-to-have-a-conscience is more than a "theory," that art and technology stand in a conflictual relationship, and so on. Lukács attacked Heidegger as being an extreme exponent of an irrational tradition; surprisingly, this interpretation could also be positively valorized: today's world is such that just this irrationalism is capable of breaking out of a closed circuit of senselessness. Is not Heidegger, who was once held to be an existential philosopher, the philosopher who, with his critique of logos and subjectivity, rather enriches the understanding of structures by pointing to the ungraspable in the movement of such structures? Heidegger can join Nietzsche, who in *Zur Genealogie der Moral* attempts to deal with history through a hermeneutics of suspicion. The inversion of this rather liberal interpretation into its conservative counterpart is then not difficult, and thus Heidegger is also held to be a mystic. This latter characterization, as when offered by representatives of a supposedly academic philosophy, often has the tone of dismissal, but not always. Significantly, it is an American book that treats *The Mystical Element in Heidegger's Thought* in a balanced manner. And at least since Heidegger's discourse on Nothing in the 1929 Freiburg inaugural lecture *Was ist Metaphysik?*, attempts have been made in Japan to come to grips with Heidegger's thinking from the perspective of a perceived elective affinity, namely, with Zen Buddhism.[1]

Heidegger himself liked to refer theological visitors to Meister Eckhart. When Bernhard Welte spoke with Heidegger about the funeral oration shortly before Heidegger's death, the talk turned again to Eckhart, about whom Welte was giving lectures; Heidegger turned the conversation toward the question of detachment (*Abgeschiedenheit*). Welte then wrote his book *Meister Eckhart. Gedanken zu seinen Gedanken* in remembrance of friends such as Heinrich Ochsner and Heidegger.[2] In this book, Eckhart is seen in overall harmony with Zen Buddhism, but also with Thomas Aquinas, the metaphysical tradition, and Heidegger in their crucial experiences; in addition, the problem of evil, which has accosted us in a new severity, is approached from these experiences. Should we not, however, in place of such a harmony first establish the diversity of the fundamental experiences? Heidegger's thinking has also exerted its influence in other areas; thus Paul Celan writes in his poem "Todtnauberg" that he wrote a line in the book Heidegger kept in his hut on the mountain, "von / einer Hoffnung, heute, / auf eines Denkenden / kommendes / Wort / im Herzen" (*GW* 2:255) ("about / a hope, today, / of a thinking man's / coming / word / in the heart" [*P* 293]). In 1947 Heidegger had published a small text, sometimes called a "hut-booklet," in which simple, everyday experiences around Todtnauberg were worked into poems and adages. There it is written that thinking succeeds when it has the matter before the eyes and the hearing of the heart attuned to the word. Does this text belong in the center of Heidegger's late thinking or is it rather a mere private jotting, with no relevance to his philosophy? Perhaps the word in the heart, of which both Heidegger and Celan speak, is the mystical word? The present essay will pursue this question, and with it the question of how mysticism confronts us today, or how mystical elements exist in thought and literature.

In accordance with his background, the young Heidegger began his studies in Freiburg with four semesters of Catholic theology. Thus in the winter semester of 1910–11, he attended the two-hour lecture course "History of Medieval Mysticism" by Josef Sauer. When he wrote his *Habilitationsschrift* in philosophy in 1915 on a tractate (falsely) ascribed to Duns Scotus, he promised other investigations into how Eckhart's mysticism might obtain its philosophical interpretation and value. Heidegger prefaced his *Habilitationsvortrag* with a sentence of Eckhart: "Time is that which changes and varies, Eternity simply stays." This sentence is from a sermon on a verse out of the proverbs of Solomon

(Prov. 31:27–31). Solomon's proverb speaks of the wife and housewife, who has illuminated the paths around her house and not idly eaten her bread. Since the text on the nineteenth of November served as an epistle for the feast of Saint Elizabeth of Hungary, Eckhart also had occasion to speak of true poverty and giving alms to the poor. But in Eckhart's allegorical interpretation the house means the soul, the paths being powers of the soul. With its uppermost powers the soul touches the changeless eternity of God; therefore the soul is formed after God, while God is formed only after himself: "His image is that he knows himself completely, and is nothing but light." At the lowermost powers, however, the soul encounters time and thus is subject to the principle of change. Yet man can direct toward the good everything that seeks entrance into his soul, for example, to guard himself from the evil that he sees. With the uppermost powers the soul comes to know God and wants that which God wants; the soul takes hold of God with its desirous and vexatious power, and here the soul can fall prey to the sin of pride. Eckhart says: "The soul cannot bear anything being above it. I believe it cannot even bear that God is above it; if he is not in it, and it is not just as well off as he himself, then it can never come to rest." That the soul comes to rest, in that it is in God and God is in it, is the main concern of Eckhart, but he develops the orientation of the traditional Neoplatonic understanding of knowing and thinking further to the emphasis on striving; therefore he can return to wisdom literature.[3]

At the root of Eckhart's distinction between eternity and time lies the result of two thousand years of philosophical elaboration. According to Plato's *Timaeus*, time is the image of eternity. When in the Ostrogothic empire of Italy the attempt to bring together the Roman patricians and the Germanic conquerors collapsed, the imprisoned statesman and philosopher Boethius, intellectually reconciled the philosophical orientation of Reason toward the eternal with the Christian doctrine of salvation, and placed the concept of providence above the concept of fate, as bound up with time. That which is dispersed and isolated in time is in eternity or *aeternitas* at once present in an ordered structure. The young Heidegger adopted this metaphysical tradition; indeed, he wished to construct it anew from the standpoint of modern philosophy. With the Tübingen Catholic theological school, Heidegger wished to recoup Hegel's overall view of history and system, and with his teacher Rickert to reconnect the transient structure of values to the conception of an eternal value system. Yet after his military service, Heidegger wrote on January 9, 1919, to his patron, the theologian Engelbert Krebs—the author of significant works on medieval philosophy and mysticism—that he had set aside every particular academic problem during the last two years and had struggled toward a fundamental clarification of his philosophical position. This clarification had so developed that Heidegger could no longer enter into extraphilosophical

connections (such as those encompassed by the philosophical instruc-
tion for theologians). Heidegger wrote: "Epistemological judgments,
encroaching upon the theory of historical understanding [*Erkennen*],
have made the system of Catholicism problematic and unacceptable for
me—not however Christianity and metaphysics (this nevertheless in a
new sense) . . . It is hard to live as a philosopher—the inner truthfulness
with oneself and with regard to that for which one is supposed to be a
teacher requires sacrifices, renunciations, and struggles, which remain
forever foreign to the scientific craftsman."

In the meantime the phenomenologist Edmund Husserl had come
to Freiburg and Heidegger had joined him. In March 1919, Husserl
marveled in a letter to the Marburg theologian Rudolf Otto that among
his students Protestants became Catholics and Catholics (such as Heidegger) turned Protestant, although in arch-Catholic Freiburg he did
not want to seem a corrupter of youth, but to have an influence on
Catholics, Protestants, and Jews. Through Heidegger and his friend
Ochsner, Husserl had become acquainted with Otto's book *Das Heilige*.
The book launches the beginning of a phenomenology of religion, yet
reminds Husserl of the image of the angels who cover their eyes with
their wings: the metaphysician and the theologian bear away the phenomenologist, who was the first to offer an unbiased analysis of religious phenomena.[4] Heidegger would undertake the elaboration of such
a phenomenology of religion. In other letters, Husserl reports that for
his project Heidegger was working with texts such as the Galatians letter. What the young Heidegger himself understood by phenomenology,
in his struggle with his teacher Husserl, he presented in the winter of
1919–20, in a lecture course on "Fundamental Problems of Phenomenology." Although his course on "The Philosophical Principles of Medieval Mysticism" announced for that same semester was not held due
to time constraints, the significance of mysticism for Heidegger is evident in the more general lecture. In it he shows that the concentration
upon the individual world which has today become self-evident, had to
be discovered first in the earliest Christian community and then had to
prevail against being buried by the classical sciences in violent intellectual eruptions—in Augustine, medieval mysticism, Luther, and Kier-
kegaard. In the winter of 1920–21, Heidegger gave the lecture course
"Introduction to the Phenomenology of Religion." There he also aimed
at displacing the concept that Otto used to approach the phenomenon
of the holy: the distinction between rational and irrational. In religion
it is a matter not of the irrational, but of the actual life experience as a
historical one. If life is concentrated in the life of the self, then this self
is historical; it is always already placed in a context, must persevere in
its concern for itself against self-deterioration, and thus must seize the
moment or *kairos* from the uncertainty of the future. The apostle Paul
referred to *kairos* as the hour of salvation, when in First Thessalonians

he spoke of the return of Christ which suddenly and unpredictably descends upon humanity. In the next semester, in a lecture course on Augustine and Neoplatonism, Heidegger attempted to show that Augustine also begins with this real historical life experience, but that he adulterates it by adopting the "aesthetic" Neoplatonic philosophy and ancient classical ontology. Augustine claims that our heart is restless until it abides in God; behind this idea of coming to rest in God can one not detect the concept of eternity as stationary *aeternitas*? But who tells us that God in this way is eternity and peace, and not abruptly (ever and abruptly) the hour of salvation? Because exegesis at that time newly discovered the strange eschatology of Jesus, theology was prevented from clearing away the philosophical macroformations and rethinking the concept of eternity. Is there not evident in Eckhart an ambiguity similar to that which Heidegger finds in Augustine? In any case, Heidegger does not pursue the traditional attempt to break through the diversity and variability of time to reach the unity of the remaining Now of eternity, and thus to rob time and history of its import.

It is only momentarily surprising that in 1920 Heidegger sent *The Imitation of Christ* to Karl Löwith as a gift, in that this book traces the mystical tradition back to the simple and practical questions of everyday life. Heidegger's concern for such is reflected in the inscription on the lintel above the door of the house that he built after his return from Marburg to Freiburg. It is a verse out of the Proverbs of Solomon (4:23), in Luther's translation: "Behüte dein Herz mit allem Fleiß; denn daraus geht das Leben" ("Keep your heart with all vigilance; for from it flows the springs of life"). Before he brought together in his later works *Denken, Danken,* and *Andenken* (thinking, thanking, and remembrance), Heidegger had gone through this tradition of wisdom literature as well. He entered into a new relationship to speculation and mysticism exactly in the moment when he parted from his teachers and friends Husserl and Bultmann to go his own way. After the Freiburg inaugural lecture *Was ist Metaphysik?* in 1929, Heidegger spoke of Nothing and Abyss in a manner immediately reminiscent of the mystical tradition. In 1935 the book *Meister Eckhart* by Käte Bröcker-Oltmanns appeared, seeking to understand Eckhart from the vantage point of Heidegger's philosophy. What Heidegger himself said about Eckhart in these years appears ambiguous. In the lectures on Hölderlin in 1934–35, he speaks of the beginning of German philosophy with Eckhart, and then relates this beginning to the inceptive thinking of Heraclitus, which in its confrontation with Oriental fatalism redefined fate and had been taken up again by Hegel and Hölderlin.[5] A year later, the lecture *Die Frage nach dem Ding* denies that we must search for the beginning of modern philosophy in Eckhart; rather it lies in Descartes. More decisive than Heidegger is Walter Schulz in his well-known book *Der Gott der neuzeitlichen Metaphysik.* He discerns two main trajectories that lead to modern philosophy: one defines God as pure power of will and leads "from Ockham through Descartes to Luther"; the other conceives of God "as intelligence and therefore as subject in the modern sense" and leads from Eckhart to Cusanus and further to Bruno as well as others. How a line from Descartes, who was born in 1596, can lead to Luther, who died in 1546, is indeed difficult to follow, regardless of how questionable the entire sketch remains. Heidegger's apparent ambiguity is more sincere: despite Eckhart's discussion of being and intelligence, one should not simply lay claim to him for modern philosophy, which is decisively determined by the Cartesian approach of trying to assure methodological certainty.

In the 1930s, Heidegger meditates upon the sentence of Hölderlin: "Es ereignet sich aber das Wahre" ("But that which is true occurs"). Truth, the unconcealment of being, had come to pass for Hölderlin and his contemporaries in an overpowering and exemplary manner in Greece; then the gods had fled, however, as Hölderlin said in his poem "Germanien": the temples, statues, and customs had decayed, and only legend remained like smoke from graves for those in doubt. Can this destiny (*Geschick*) be turned around, and can thinking aid in preparing this turn by intentionally and explicitly attempting to think how truth occurs? Even in 1942 Heidegger expressed the hope for Germany, in his lecture course "Hölderlin's Hymns," "that a 'guest-house' and home [*Stift*] would be established and built for the gods, which the temples of the Greeks cannot fulfill anymore."[6] But then the battle of Stalingrad was fought, the final solution of the Jewish question and Auschwitz began, and the atomic bomb ended the Second World War. There remained a Germany upon which the names of the death camps lay as guilt and shame, and Heidegger must have told himself that he too was to bear this guilt and shame.

In the following years Heidegger referred not only to Hölderlin's great hymns but also to the smaller poems from the time after Hölderlin's collapse, in which a simple verse plays with the view of a landscape or with the course of the seasons. The connection to Eckhart grows more pronounced; his sermons were also written in a time of political decline and religious discord, though admittedly in the time of a new migration into the cities rather than congregations. It is not so much Eckhart the master of reading who interests Heidegger, as Eckhart the master of living, who through mysticism wishes to lead his audience to a new life. In the small narrative "Der Feldweg," Heidegger speaks of his native Meßkirch and with it of a simplicity which preserves the riddle of that which is great and abiding. "In the insignificance of the ever same it conceals its blessing," Heidegger writes, and continues: "The extent of all the grown things which linger around the field path bestows world. In the unexpressed of its language, as the venerable master of reading and living Eckhart says, is God first God." Heidegger here alludes to the sermon *Misit dominus manum suam*. There Eckhart says that the creatures wish to speak God in all of their works, and yet God remains unspoken. Eckhart's "mystical" approach lies in his concern for a proof of God that would confirm the existence of an eternal god of creation based on the createdness of things or their order. Man should rather also be rid of this God of creation, as the sermon *Beati pauperes spiritu* says: man, who like God is "knowing" (*Erkennen*), belongs through his eternal determination to the divine self-knowing; man must break through into the incomprehensible and unsayable, the desert of the godhead, but can accomplish this only in detachment (*Abgeschiedenheit*), not by moving from things (to a beyond). In his lecture "Das Ding," however, Heidegger criticizes Eckhart's reductionist concept of the thing. Is the unspoken in speaking of things the same for Eckhart and for Heidegger? In the postwar years Heidegger not only constantly quoted Eckhart, but he also translated Lao Tzu with the help of a Chinese acquaintance. Does the relationship to Lao Tzu strengthen Heidegger's relationship to Eckhart, or does it indicate another form of "mysticism"? If we wish to answer this question, we must examine the materials in order to determine how Heidegger's thought incorporates mystical elements.

In a conversation from 1944–45, Heidegger specifically discussed a fundamental concern of mysticism, "releasement" (*Gelassenheit*). While on a walk along a field path, a researcher, a scholar, and a teacher inquire about the essence of thinking, which is indeed the distinguishing characteristic of man. The teacher, in whom we should see the least distorted self-portrait of Heidegger, puts forward the seemingly paradoxical thesis that we must look away from thinking in order to catch sight of the essence of it. Usually we accept thinking to be a representing (*Vorstellen*); as a placing-in-front and a placing-toward-oneself, representing is a desire and therefore an endowment of man. For instance, it transmits (but also "blocks") the jug-ness as the view (*eidos*), in which we first can make out the jug as jug. The various views belong in the field of vision of a horizon. We transcend the jug to the jug-ness and then further, beyond this view of the jug-ness, to the horizon. Thus this representing is governed by transcendence, a going-beyond. With this discourse of view, horizon, and transcendence, Heidegger summarizes the development of his confrontation with his teacher Husserl in 1928. He makes the so-called "turn" when he continues and claims that this horizon in truth is the other of itself: it is the horizon only of our representing, because in itself it is the region, from and in which first of all that which is, is encountered. This region is a "range" (*Weite*), the distance and unavailability of which the "while" (*Weile*), and thus nearness, first furnishes. When thinking sets itself free in this while and range, when it properly or from the outset has overcome all placing-in-front and placing-toward-oneself and remains engaged in the letting-be of the encounter, then thinking is released. We come to the essence of thinking, namely to *Gelassenheit*, therefore, only when we look away from thinking as simple representation and are mindful that this thinking is used for the while and range which allows the encounter to happen.

As the researcher, scholar, and teacher carry on their conversation, the three draw attention to the fact that things in modernity have become objects for physics. Therefore, the range allowing encounter has a history; since physics comes from this history, the methodological analysis of the procedure of physics remains "historical." Indeed, when the ancient world, for example, starts from the proposition "force equals mass times speed," one cannot simply set this proposition beside its modern counterpart "force equals mass times acceleration" and call the first one false. Rather, one must reflect historically upon the fundamental approach. The Greeks started from simple phenomena of motion: the faster one runs, the more force one uses. The Greeks evidently were reluctant to break down the phenomena into components, and thus they had a destiny for the art which represents totalities and which has remained unsurpassed. Modern physics breaks down and analyzes phenomena of motion, for instance separating the force of friction from the applied force. If one removes the oppositional forces such as the force of friction, one can indeed say in regard to the idealized relations that force is not proportional to speed, but to acceleration. In this way, it is eventually possible to hold rockets on course in near weightless space. Yet one can no longer create Greek works of art. It may be the task of physicists and technicians to maintain such rockets in their course, but man as a thinking being will have to ask further which space he wants to give in his life to science, on one hand, and to art, on the other. This thinking must enter into that history in which being finds itself in a varied Being, and art and technology enter into shifting constellations. Heidegger says thinking must "urgently," with the "thinking heart," be admitted into the "unpreconceivable" ("das Unvordenkliche"), which is not to be mastered by thought, but which man nonetheless must forethink. Ten years after this discussion Heidegger read a paper in his native Meßkirch on *Gelassenheit* and published both texts under the title *Gelassenheit*. The Meßkirch paper deals with our relationship to the technological world and to the atomic age. Heidegger starts from the position that the philosophical tradition from Plato to Hegel and Nietzsche has always resolutely conceived of thinking as representation and thus as will. The sciences are only followers of this so-called metaphysic; from the very beginning they are of the technological essence, that is, oriented toward opportunistic grasping and production. Today's technology does not even know objects anymore, but only an interchangeable and exploitable standing reserve. The person, too, is transformed into such a standing reserve. Consequently, he or she can end up just as well in an affluent society as in a perfected death camp or in an atomic war. The intimacies of life—procreation, birth, and death—become technological problems as much as the balance of terror between the great empires or the economic circulation between the so-called developed and underdeveloped countries. The *Gelassenheit* accepts this world, the atomic age, as a task; yet it is *Gelassenheit* only when it does not let itself be charmed by technology, indicates the limits and boundaries of technology, and remains open for the mystery.

But why are there such things as the statues of the Greeks, the experiments of Galileo, the technological adventures and threats of our age? Classical philosophy and science start from the position that nothing is without a ground: according to Leibniz, the ground can be provided for truths of reason as well as for truths of fact. Thus that which is enters an openness, for which man, in providing a ground, gives an account to himself. The ground for this openness itself is missing, however; the question why there is altogether something and not nothing receives no answer. Eckhart's sermon *Mulier, venit hora* tells of the man who in the time of his hour finds his eternal destiny in God, thus becoming the son of God and in the completion of the union with God also the father of this son. But how is it that man finds his destiny in God or the godhead? In various ways, Eckhart poses this question, ultimately in the dialogue "Why do you live?—Verily, I do not know! But I enjoy living!"[7] Life in the godhead is an abyss and without a reason. Heidegger's lecture *Der Satz vom Grund* summons Eckhart as a witness, that "the most extreme rigor and profundity of thinking" belongs "to genuine and great mysticism." He quotes the thought expressed in popular form, contained in the verses of Angelus Silesius: "The rose is without a why; it blooms, because it blooms." The "because" appears to provide a ground, but it says that the rose blooms without reason. It does not bloom so that man may see it, but rather because according to its definition it comes out of the abyssal eternal godhead. Heidegger understands the *Weil* ("because") also as a *Dieweilen* ("meantime"): the rose blooms in its time and place, in that comprehensive history in which that which is, is. One may offer various grounds for why the rose blooms: the good soil, the passing season, the human need for beautiful gardens, and the labor of the gardener. If the evolution of life had not taken a particular turn at one time, perhaps we would be living today in the gloomy and colorless world of scrub grass and not in this charming interplay of flowers and insects, which in its turn is cared for by man in his raising of roses. For the mystical breakthrough, however, it is a matter of experiencing through the rose, and through itself as well, the eternal determination from a final "without why." In this sense, Heidegger appropriates the mystical discourse of ground and abyss, *Grund* and *Ab-*

grund. But the importance lies in the fact that he alters this discourse in a particular way: the while and range, which imparts things to us, is not only without reason and abyssal, it is ungrounded: in preserving a certain openness, it withdraws and displaces another one. For example, in the age of analytical scientific experiment and technology, it withdraws from us an art such as the Greeks had.

If one goes along with this train of thought, it is no longer possible, as the young Heidegger still thought, to relate time to eternity in the way Eckhart had. Thus in Heidegger's discussion of *Gelassenheit*, one reads that although there is "much good" to be learned from "older masters of thinking" such as Eckhart, Eckhart still conceives of *Gelassenheit* in relation to the will, that is, as a "relinquishing of one's own sinful will in favor of the divine will."[8] If one reads the *Reden der Unterscheidung*, which the Erfurt prior reads to his brothers when seeking advice, one sees that Eckhart indeed approaches *Gelassenheit* from the direction mentioned above. If one reads the famous sermon *Beati pauperes spiritu*, however, one sees how Eckhart moves beyond these thoughts. The people who superficially occupy themselves with penances are ultimately "donkeys," this sermon says in complete severity. He who is poor in spirit should not only desire to fulfill the will of God, but must also not-desire, as if he were not born. Equally well, he must be rid of the God whom we seek as the creator of nature. In this way he is able to accept himself according to the determination that he has in the union with the godhead. Eckhart takes up the thought which seeks to provide a ground for everything and finally finds it in the godhead.

This path is criticized by Heidegger, who wishes to take a different direction from the outset. The metaphysical tradition, as he remarks in the lecture *Was heißt Denken?*, leads to two different summits: its final term is in the one case God, who as will eternally wills itself and so is collected in itself, and in the other case the world, which, eternally recurring, circles within itself. In both cases, however, it is the spirit of vengeance, which cannot bear the transitory and so turns against time and the "it was" ("es war"). In both cases man unjustly brings the abyssal-ungrounded while and range, out of which any thing encounters him, to rest in a final term. In comparison, as *Gelassenheit* thinking "thanks" this range, which bids us to think and thus to allow the encounter. We speak of thanking at the completion of something and the settlement of a transaction or a matter; Heidegger also considers *Abgeschiedenheit* from the perspective of this thanking, that is, from the perspective of a final completion of the range mentioned above.[9] Such a thanking can produce itself by all means in that which Heidegger, in his critique of Eckhart's reductionist thing-concept, called "thing": in a ritualistic performance, in a work of art, or in custom. Moreover, Heidegger too places the range under the measure of eternity. Eternity then signifies neither the aggregate in a highest term nor the eternal recurrence, but rather the fulfillment in the instant, which in its uniqueness and singularity possesses the freedom of withdrawal. Taking up the language of religious experience, Hölderlin says that everything heavenly is "schnellvergänglich," "swiftly-transitory." Referring to this speech in his Hölderlin lecture of 1934–35, Heidegger speaks of the "transitoriness," that is, the "stride past" ("Vorbeigang") of the eternal. In this lecture Heidegger also believes that he can bring into contiguity Eckhart and Heraclitus on the one hand, with Hölderlin on the other. When with Heraclitus he conceives of the range as play without a reason, and with Parmenides thinks of the identity of Being and thinking as "behest" ("Geheiß"), thus as a coming into language, Heidegger can truly stride past the actual pre-Socratic thought and draw Eckhart's experiences thoroughly into it.

The play of the range is "appropriation" or "event" (Ereignis), because that which is finds its Being and its own in it. In his later work, Heidegger also names this appropriation "expropriation" (Enteignis), because the range is expropriated into the thing, the thing expropriated into the range. Since thing and range are "stilled" in each other, Heidegger speaks of the play of stillness. One can adduce many parallels from Eckhart to this manner of speaking. Of Gelassenheit, the sermon Beati pauperes spiritu says that not only does it know nothing and want nothing, but also has nothing: just as the answer (Ant-wort) is completely absorbed in the offered word (Zuspruch) from which it lives, so too the appropriation of the place of Gelassenheit in the Entwerden of the mystical stillness is completely absorbed in that to which it—Gelassenheit—belongs. Gelassenheit has no "place," and it is precisely this "abruptness of the bridgeless turning-in" which Heidegger calls Enteignis.[10] Yet he conceives of the reciprocal self-transference of range and thing in such a way that it is incompatible with the initial theological position of Eckhart. Nonetheless, there is an agreement between Heidegger and Lao Tzu. Lao Tzu's seventh chapter says that only he who does not live his own life completes his ownmost essence. According to the sixteenth chapter, our downfall must be a descent into that stillness. This is Tao, that way which alone remains the unchangeable amidst constant change. The root of the Chinese sign for "change," I, is supposed to mean "new moon"; in contrast it is inconceivable that Greek thinkers (Heraclitus himself) would orient themselves by the changing moon, and not by the law of the ever-recurring motion of the stars. Yet Heidegger, too, says in Unterwegs zur Sprache: "Perhaps in the word 'way,' Tao, is concealed the mystery of all mysteries of the contemplative saying." Earth and heaven appear to Tao: the open sky of light and the self-closing earth beget all that is.

When Heidegger adopts this discourse, then, it indicates a departure from Eckhart: can we assume that when we transcend things in general and the god of creation, that we arrive at pure openness, the flowing light of the godhead? Who tells us that this "nothing" is pure, divine plenitude? Is it not that light reaches us only out of the darkness? That this reciprocal play of darkness and light is the range of earth and sky, which furnishes things? The Nothing and the void in things make them usable for this interplay and thus for the Tao, as Lao Tzu says in the eleventh chapter and Heidegger explicates the example of the jug in his lecture on the thing. When we ask from the perspective of today's state of knowledge what a jug actually is, we should remember that perhaps three billion years of evolution have passed on this planet, and that the human species has used stones during the last two-and-a-half million years. Just recently, less than ten thousand years ago, man invented the art of pottery and so experienced the jug. In the jug man could cook potatoes and thus transform something inedible into something edible. Yet the marvelously adaptable jug could also be used for sacrificial libations and thus could transform the place where one lived into a site for the holy and the divine. Through their very emptiness, things such as the jug bring into contact earth and sky, divinities and mortals.

Heidegger calls this interplay and interreflection in the "thing" a "mirror play" (*Spiegelspiel*). Eckhart, too, knew this self-reflection: the Father is reflected in the Son (according to the doctrine of the Trinity); through the uncreated, the spark of light which he has in himself, man participates in the light of the godhead. But for Heidegger man is the mortal, who is already on the path that shows light only together with darkness, the divine only in an abrupt passing by. Indeed, Heidegger's thoughts on the divine bear a weight not found in Lao Tzu, indicating that he remains close to Hölderlin and therefore also close to the attempt to recuperate what was once myth in a cultic conception of art. Nonetheless, the setting out *of* Hölderlin, as well as the setting out *with* him, failed; thus the later Heidegger turns toward Hölderlin's fragmentary poems and the resonance they find with the poems of Trakl. While for Eckhart detachment (*Abgeschiedenheit*) was a central term, a *Grundwort*, Heidegger now defines *Abgeschiedenheit* as the place of the poet Trakl. According to Trakl, the departed (*die Abgeschiedenen*) are those called into the downfall, yet who find a new beginning in their downfall—namely, the transformation. During his visits in Provence, Heidegger identified his concerns with Cézanne's art. Cézanne's paintings show us the things nearest at hand—familiar people, a cliff, the Sainte Victoire. The paintings point to these things in such a way that in the mystery of the encounter the range out of which the things emerge and into which they recede is also present.

Through the experience of the simplest things (the times of the day and the seasons), the hut-booklet *Aus der Erfahrung des Denkens* attempts to return a troubled thinking to the way. Way and weighing scales (that which remains the same in change and that which gives a weight), but also footbridge and legend (that which the individual can build and that which comprehends every individual thinking and speaking), should come together in a gait which bears the loss of the divine and the open question. One could well say that in this way a sick person can find a new orientation, but when a philosopher after the Second World War speaks of the experiences of thinking, he cannot omit Auschwitz and Hiroshima. Heidegger spoke of "Gewissen-haben-wollen" in *Sein und Zeit*; he bore the responsibility in 1933 Germany. Can he write in his 1944–45 discussion of *Gelassenheit*, that in the area in which *Gelassenheit* is involved ("eingelassen"), there is "nothing to answer for," because this "region of the word" answers for itself? That there, "everything is in the best order only then, when no one has been there"?[11] Is such a use of mysticism anything other than an evasion of actual experience, an excuse to thwart the guilt, a blindness to the reality of destruction and evil?

According to Heidegger's *Brief über den Humanismus*, in this demarcated region together with salvation and the sacred there appears also the wrathful, the destructive and evil, for this region is a way to which belongs the passage and consequently destruction. If this is so, however, why does Heidegger juxtapose the mortals with the divinities and not with the demons? The only way out appears to be the overcoming of evil in a new beginning; the condemnation of evil seems only to make things worse. In both Eckhart (in his East-Asiatic meditation) and Heidegger, the opposition of good and evil becomes secondary. Eckhart adopts the philosophical doctrine of Being and the fulfillment of Being in being good, but he then says that whoever calls God a being or calls God good commits such an injustice as if he called the sun black: "God is neither good nor better nor the very best." The gnat, the soul, and the highest angel are equally in God, and our valuations—which erect world orders—only wrong the life of the godhead. We can be only an "epithet" (*Beiwort*) to its word (which according to Heidegger, is to answer to the word that answers for itself). Is it possible, then, for evil to be turned to good or be overcome in the godhead? It is said of martyrs that they had their being in God; for our part we should not lament a mortal life: "One should be dead to the ground, so that neither body nor pain touches us."

Nietzsche extended this line of reasoning further: whoever bears the word "rightly" in the mouth, all too often wants only to be "righted" in the revenge of the subjected, who invoke the fiction of a good God or a righteousness contra life. According to Nietzsche (and Heidegger), however, the moral God is refuted by the tragic God. Ariadne must not only lament Theseus, who abandoned her; she ought to be blessed in her very grief and experience the divine. But would one want to offer this advice to the dead of Auschwitz and Hiroshima?

When Paul Celan speaks of the "coming word in the heart" in "Todtnauberg," the question is raised how a Holocaust survivor can understand such a "mystical" discourse. Yet already in Celan's juvenilia, one finds the "black sister"—that sister and bride called "black, but yet dear" in one of the fundamental books of mysticism, the Song of Songs.[12] For Celan this sister is black because she has been burned in the death camps. Thus he molds or constructs for himself, but also for the sisterly helping and loving, the form of the burned and therefore also "regal" ("Königliche"). Through its very title, the 1963 collection *Die Niemandsrose* recalls the mystical rose; in the poem "With All My Thoughts" ("Mit allen Gedanken" [*GW* 1:221]) the poet exits the world:

MIT ALLEN GEDANKEN ging ich
hinaus aus der Welt: da warst du,
du meine Leise, du meine Offne, und—
du empfingst uns.

Wer
sagt, daß uns alles erstarb,
da uns das Aug brach?
Alles erwachte, alles hob an.

Groß kam eine Sonne geschwommen, hell
standen ihr Seele und Seele entgegen, klar,
gebieterisch schwiegen sie ihr
ihre Bahn vor.

Leicht
tat sich dein Schoß auf, still
stieg ein Hauch in den Äther,
und was sich wölkte, wars nicht,
wars nicht Gestalt und von uns her,
wars nicht
so gut wie ein Name?

(WITH ALL MY THOUGHTS I
went out of the world: and there you were,
you my quiet, my open one, and—
you received us.

Who
says that everything died for us

when our eyes broke?
Everything awakened, everything began.

Great, a sun came drifting, bright
a soul and a soul confronted it, clear,
masterfully their silence mapped out
an orbit for the sun.

Easily
your lap opened, tranquilly
a breath rose up to the aether
and that which made clouds, was it not,
was it not a shape come from us,
was it not
as good as a name?)
    (*P* 167)

There, outside, where everything dies and grows, he is received by the gentle one, the open one (*die Leise, die Offene*), who in another passage is also called the true one (*die Wahre*). Both, "soul and soul" (*Seele und Seele*), are able to fore-silence the course of a sun drifting near. In the tradition, the sun, the eye of heaven, stands for God, who as an unmoved clarity resting in itself provides the world with order and meaning. Yet after "the sun, and not only it" ("die Sonne, und nicht nur sie") has perished (as Celan says in "Gespräch im Gebirg" [*GW* 3:169]), the encounter of which our poem speaks is able to put at least "one" sun on its course. The gentle and open one, beyond the world, receives not only the poet, but rather herself *and* the poet. Thus she bears a vaulted breath, which is as good as a name but has its form (*Gestalt*) from this encounter. A cloud once showed Israel the way through the desert; the name was the name of God. The breath to which Celan owes his poems must therefore stand for this cloud and this name. Yet who is the one whom the poet meets? In a cycle with a mystical thematic, the 1968 collection *Fadensonnen* contains the poem "Aus Engelsmaterie." There one reads: "He, the enlivening-righteous, slept you to me, sister" ("Er, der Belebend-Gerechte, schlief dich mir zu, Schwester" [*GW* 3:196]). The Kabbalah distinguishes between the *En-sof*, the hidden ground or unground of the divinity, and the *Sefiroth*, the manifestations and *logoi* in which God appears and speaks to us. The first *Sefirah* and highest crown is Nothing, the seventh is the Enlivening-Righteous One (*Zaddik*). In the Tree of Life of the *Sefiroth*, the Righteous One unites with the Lost One, the tenth *Sefirah*: the *Shekhinah*. He is the Righteous in that he maintains the forces of life within their boundaries and watches over them. Following the uninhibited use of sexual images in Jewish mysticism, Celan thus has the Righteous One "sleep" the *Shekhi-*

nah "to" the poet. For Celan, the *Shekhinah* is God's dwelling among people, the community of God, but also exile, the burned sister who cannot be revived by the survivors but who precisely through this Not and Nothing gestures to the primordial ground. This can only be called divine if righteousness is one of its manifestations, that is, if righteousness befalls those murdered. In this sense, Celan's poems are a remembrance of the dead.

The last three poems of the 1970 collection *Lichtzwang* (*GW* 2:326–28) directly include mystical expressions. The antepenultimate poem speaks with Eckhart's sermon *Beati pauperes spiritu* of becoming free of God, and with the sermon *Surge. Illuminare Jerusalem* of the deheightening (that is, of God), which is an "innering" (*Innigung*). The penultimate poem finds a new relationship to Jerusalem from the latter sermon. From liturgy, Eckhart undertakes the "Arise, shine, Jerusalem," with which Third Isaiah continues Second Isaiah's hopes of Zion, when the exultants might have turned back: God will create a new heaven and a new earth; Jerusalem will console her own like a mother. In the posthumous 1976 collection *Zeitgehöft*, a poem from the cycle of Celan's journey to Jerusalem speaks of this consolation. If one overlooks the introductory poem, which was composed earlier, this poem appears exactly in the middle of the cycle. Moreover, at its center (after eight lines and before eight lines) is the imploring verse: "Say that Jerusalem *is*" ("Sag, daß Jerusalem *ist*") (*GW* 3:105/*P* 345). But how is Jerusalem? It should be the messianic city of peace, and yet it is the city of strife. The Messiah should come through the Gate of Mercy (since according to the Christian interpretation the Messiah in Jesus has already entered through the gate; they call this gate the Golden Gate, whereby the gold stands for the radiance of eternity). The Moslems have walled up the gate, however, and as an additional obstacle they have buried their dead before the gate, since the Messiah is not supposed to walk over dead. Inside and outside form such a dichotomy that it remains uncrossable; only the sleep of mystical unification through love leads toward the Gate of Mercy. Thus the poet loses his You to itself—that is, the mystical Jerusalem to the actual one. He, too, finds consolation in Jerusalem, since Jerusalem is his "snow-solace" (*Schneetrost*).

At the beginning of 1943, Celan had written about his mother and "the snow-pain of the Ukraine" in "Es fällt nun, Mutter" ("It Falls Now, Mother" [*F* 68]). In the fall of 1942 Celan's father was murdered in the camps of the Ukraine; his skeleton was, as the poem "Schwarze Flocken" says, "snowy," atomized (*GW* 3:25). Apparently Celan's mother soon followed him into death. For Celan, snow is the frozen water of life, the dead, which may yet rise again if righteousness befalls them. Because those murdered in the Holocaust are granted righteousness, so too Celan can find solace in Jerusalem. Then the snowflakes are no longer black or pushed back into gray, but rather white—that is, the accepted fatal event that belongs as much to the burned and the lost ones as to the poet. The reality—the Holocaust as well as the actual unrest in Jerusalem—is recorded without modification. Yet this reality is placed under a standard that was constructed from the mystical and religious tradition and is now incorporated in the poetry: if there is a "God" and from him solace and peace, he must be just and therefore bring righteousness to the victims. Only from this righteousness is that sisterly close power to be encountered, which stands for the lost and the burned, but also for that which helps.

The poem "Die Pole" is not only in the middle of the entire Jerusalem cycle (*GW* 3:105); in terms of length no other poem matches it. Yet all the poems of the cycle invoke the reality of Jerusalem from various perspectives, including the small poem immediately preceding the cycle:

DIE POSAUNENSTELLE
tief im glühenden
Leertext,
in Fackelhöhe,
im Zeitloch:

hör dich ein
mit dem Mund.
    (*GW* 3:104)

(THE TRUMPET PART
deep in the glowing
lacuna
at lamp height
in the time hole:

listen your way in
with your mouth.)
    (*P* 343)

Like so many other late poems of Celan, this one is divided into two halves by a colon. The first stanza summons up a definite situation; from this, after the colon, the second stanza draws a conclusion in the form of an imperative. Yet can one hear at all with the mouth? It is a matter of hearing oneself "into" the empty text with the trumpet passage, thus into a text which does not make any statement in particular, but changes into a trumpet blast. Nonetheless, that which is thus announced cannot be actuated without assistance. It is with the mouth which blows the trumpet or enunciates poems that one must hear oneself into something which exceeds human understanding and speech.

Of what trumpet passage does the poem speak? Since Luther the word "shofar" has been translated as "trumpet." The trumpet sounded when the Lord in Sinai convoked his people into a covenant, and Moses received the ten commandments. The people camped below, and the mountain above spewed lightning (or torches), but with its sound the trumpet showed that the revelation in which God proclaimed himself Lord exceeded all linguistic formulation. Thus the text remains ultimately an empty text (*Leertext*), even when commandments are formulated.[13] The "shofar" or the trumpet is the instrument which announces the holy days and the Hebrew Jubilee, thus ultimately the messianic era. History *in toto*, which in Jerusalem itself was and continues to be shaped by rise and fall, renewal and abiding hope, is taken up into the *Posaunenstelle*. Yet can one assume, with poems which confront us with the reality of Jerusalem, that a book is alluded to (even when it is the Book of Books) when the poem speaks of a "passage" (*Stelle*)? Could not a certain place in Jerusalem be intended? Two years before Celan came to Jerusalem, Jewish troops conquered the Old City, which had long been divided, in the Six Day War. Hence the Western Wall, the sacred remains of the temple, became accessible again to the Jews. On this occasion the senior rabbi of the army, General Shlomo Goren, sounded the ram's horn: the trumpet, the shofar. (Later excavation revealed a stone which indicated that on this spot the shofar was blown already in ancient times.)

Could Celan not have meant this *Posaunenstelle* and the temple remains in an entirely "realistic" manner? The first and second temples of the Jews had been destroyed along with the Hadrianic temple and the Christian churches, and so one may truly say that the remains of the wall lie deep in a glowing empty text. For Celan, the script which must be read is never the script of a book, but rather the world itself. The great conclusion of *Sprachgitter*, "Engführung," searches out the terrain of an extermination camp as a script to be read and a trace to be followed (*GW* 1:197–204). The poem "Unlesbarkeit," contained in the 1971 volume *Schneepart*, indicates the "unreadability of this / world" ("Unlesbarkeit dieser / Welt"), in which the "split-hour" ("Spaltstunde") receives justice, and a You emerges from its "deepest" ("Tiefstes") and from it itself "for ever" ("für immer") (*GW* 2:338). The poem "Aus Engelsmaterie," discussed above, sees Jewish mysticism and Eastern Jewry with its terrible fate "dispersed from the East, to be retrieved in the West" ("von Osten gestreut, einzubringen im Westen"), but as burning script! The view of the Western Wall of the temple shows that this burning script in Jerusalem is a *glühender Leertext*, a "glowing empty text"—the reality accosts us, but from the destroying and consuming fire, from the "emptiness," which may not remain simply something negative. The trumpet position, at the remains of the temple wall, is deeply embedded within this empty text and nonetheless "into the torch's height" (*in Fackelhöhe*): in that height, in which the torch raised up gives light and shows a way. This place lies also "in the time-hole" (*im Zeitloch*). Philosophers such as Sartre have made Hegel responsible for talk of a "hole in being." Hegel referred to Leibniz's thought that the structure of the world would break apart completely if one atom in the world were to be destroyed. Yet this destruction, leaving behind a hole, seems to be established in the negativity and freedom of man, so that a compact being is sublated. In Celan, this hole is radicalized and bound up with time: time and history continually interrupt their way and—beginning anew—point to an other history; the "dead point" (*toter Punkt*) of the interruption, which summons up the Other, is indicated by the "split-hours" (*Spaltstunden*) and the "leap-years," which as Jubilees (*Halljahre*) are to bring deliverance from the chains of history. In this sense, perhaps, there is no place better where one may see history than at the Western Wall of the temple in Jerusalem, at the center of the world. In the Jerusalem poems Celan always stringently distinguishes the apostrophized You from the I. Yet at the conclusion of our poem, when he says *hör dich ein*, Celan seems to be issuing an imperative to himself. Or should the You here also be understood as Jerusalem, the earthly and the heavenly? Is it the same as the monstrous empty text, as the temple remains show it? In that case, the poem would be nothing other than the echo of that reality which nonetheless first must be gained.

Repeatedly Celan's cycle of poems conjures up the reality of Jerusalem. The very first poem following the introductory poem speaks of an overwhelming experience: that Jerusalem now surrounds the poet and his You. The poem also names particulars: the "ship of the Danes" ("Dänenschiff"), a memorial in a square in Jerusalem that commemorates the Danes, who in the time of persecution saved Jews with ships sent across the straits (*GW* 3:96). The poet and his You also thank this ship for making possible the rescue and transport to another country and another time. Absalom's grave (the monument in Kidron Valley) and Gethsemane are named as well. Finally, the poet and his You are in Abu Tor, a quarter lying to the south of the Old City:

DAS LEUCHTEN, ja jenes, das
Abu Tor
auf uns zureiten sah, als wir
ineinander verwaisten, vor Leben,
nicht nur von den Handwurzeln her—:

eine Goldboje, aus
Tempeltiefen,

maß die Gefahr aus, die uns
still unterlag.
(*GW* 3:100)

(THE SHINING, the very one, which
Abu Tor
saw riding toward us, when we
were orphaned into each other, before life,
not only from the carpi—:

a golden buoy, out of
the depths of the temple,
measured out the danger, which
calmly succumbed to us.)

This poem, too, is divided into two stanzas by a colon (and additionally with a dash). In order to describe the situation, the first stanza uses an independent substantive, which is then explained by apposition and relative clauses: *das Leuchten*. The second stanza explains what this "shining" effects and what happens to it. The poet is in Abu Tor, an Arab village. If one gazes down from the slope there, one sees the Hinnom Valley. When King Manasse introduced the cult of Moloch from Moab, he bought (or seized) from one Ben-Hinnom a plot of land in this ravinelike valley for a cult in which children would be sacrificed as burnt offerings. Thus one could later form the name for the diabolical fire in which the condemned were burned from the name of the former landowner. On the other side of the ravine rises the mountain which today is called Mount Zion; there one is shown David's grave, but also the towering church Dormitio Sanctae Mariae. According to one tradition, Jesus's mother slept at the site of this church. Behind Mount Zion stands the southwest corner of the City Wall; turning to the right, one sees above the distant City Wall (and today also above the TV antennas of the nearby Arab houses and shelters) the shining of the golden cupola of the Dome of the Rock.

Once again, the poet must explicitly confirm that it is "that" (*jenes*) shining of the cupola of the mosque which Abu Tor saw ride toward him and his You. According to the poem "Bei Wein und Verlorenheit" ("Over Wine and Lostness") in *Die Niemandsrose* (*GW* 1:213), he even rides God into that distance which alone can be God's nearness. Are the thoughts of the Prophet Jeremiah not also incorporated in that the voice of a wrathful God roars even in the very snorting of the steed of the conquering enemy army which falls upon Jerusalem? In this way, the shining of the mosque's cupola rides toward the poet and his companion. The two in the Arab village do not forget the alienation and enmity (after so many other enmities) that has broken out between

Arabs and Jews, and which can always break out anew. In the Jerusalem cycle, the poem "Der Königsweg" ("The Way of the King") (*GW* 3:306) speaks of the Gate of Forgiveness and the Lion Gate in the Eastern Wall (also called St. Stephen's Gate) when it has the mark of the lion (which stands for Judas) "redeathed" ("umtodet") by the counter-mark, the star of the Islamic half-moon swimming upside down and "umsumpft." The poem then closes by speaking of the wound, which the poet and his You are to fathom.

With the many eyes of its children and all the craftsmen, who diligently hammer even on the Sabbath, Abu Tor sees the shining riding from the cupola of the Dome of the Rock toward the two people, who "become orphaned into one another" (*ineinander verwaisen*). A child is orphaned when it loses its parents (as the poet was orphaned, when in 1942 his mother and father were murdered in camps on the Bug River). But *verwaisen* also means to be cut off from one's origins or descent, to lose their sheltering closeness. Thus the two in the Arab village are cut off from their Jewish origins when they gaze at the mosque's cupola. Finally, *verwaisen* also means that the Creation has lost its meaning, yet can regain that meaning after a break and by a new attempt (the poem "Verwaist" in *Fadensonnen* speaks of this [*GW* 2:212]). In "Das Leuchten," the poet and his You are orphaned into one another. The companion is at once comfortingly close and as alone and forsaken as the poet himself. In this she exhibits the characteristics of the *Shekhinah*, who with her brightness binds men with the concealed divine origin, while at the same time being the banished one who wanders through the misery of exile. Both are orphaned into one another "vor Leben, und nicht nur von den Handwurzeln her." The carpus is the location of the finger's activity, which could be the finger which writes or the finger which is raised in giving an oath. Thus in Celan, hand and finger may always stand for writing and poetry. Yet what takes place in our poem is not literature and is not effected through reading and the literary tradition: it is life itself, which here completely unites the poet in his solitude and isolation with the companion, who invokes the mystical tradition of Jewish exile.

The second stanza calls the shining from the mosque's cupola a "golden buoy" (*Goldboje*). Buoys indicate the way out into the ocean; those which row out upon the sea that tomorrow will evaporate in the poem "Inselhin," contained in the 1955 collection *Von Schwelle zu Schwelle*, are "ensounded by sinking buoys" ("umläutet von sinkenden Bojen") (*GW* 1:141). If the water is the water of life, then the sea stands for universal life which is one with death—at once the origin, out of which all life comes, and the terminus, to which all rivers return. The poem "Anabasis," in *Die Niemandsrose* (*GW* 1:256–57) speaks of the return to the sea and to the homeland: "buoys of sorrow" ("Kummerbojen") mark the way, yet the muffled ringing of their "dum, dun, un" dissolves into the *unde suspirat cor* of Mozart's "Exsultate, jubilate." In this soprano motet the language of the heart is awakened in the encounter with love: *Tu virginum corona, tu nobis pacem dona, tu consolare affectus, unde suspirat cor. Alleluja.* Buoys measure out the danger of the shallows, but they also indicate the way to the open. The buoy of "Das Leuchten" links the indication of danger with gold, which stands for the brightness of eternity. The buoy of the gilded mosque cupola ascends the nearby hill "out of the depths of the temple" (*aus Tempeltiefen*). In the Bible, Abraham encounters the king and priest Melchisedek in Jerusalem; the latter greets the patriarch with "bread and wine." David then conquers the city through the cunning of his commander and makes the city into the capital of his empire; his son Solomon then built the first temple there. There follows, however, the varied history of the destruction and reconstruction of new temples—by the Babylonians and Jews, by Hadrian, by the Byzantines, by the Muslims. According to tradition, the last of these temples—the Dome of the Rock—still stands above the rock Moriah, where Abraham was to sacrifice his son, and where Mohammed ascended to heaven. The golden cupola of the Dome of the Rock rises up just as actually "out of the depths of the temple."

The second stanza not only calls the cupola of the Dome of the Rock a golden buoy, but also says that this buoy measures out the danger—that danger which nonetheless "calmly succumbed" (*still unterlag*) to them both in Abu Tor (so that, on the contrary, they did *not* succumb to the danger). If the sacred binds the peoples with gold, intimating the infinite, it also divides the peoples; such confrontations belong to the most terrible, turning into religious wars and ideological confrontations. The confrontation of religions is always bound up with the struggle of peoples, as in Jerusalem, the intersection of the routes from Asia Minor to Egypt and from Asia Minor and Egypt into the Near East. The danger measured out by the temple and delimited by "golden buoys" can become a danger which emanates from the temple, strengthened through its one-sided binding and rabid energy. This danger succumbs to the poet, however, who encounters his You, and in this You finds a life-force that does not fear banishment and death. It is the thought of peace which has united with the "mystical" conception of Jerusalem: the buildings of man wrest order from chaos, thus reflecting the cosmogony. Yet Zion, the Near Eastern city atop the high mountain, is with its temple a likeness of the canopy of the firmament which descends upon the earth and brings to humanity the completely Other: peace as the standard of their coexistence.

When visiting the temple in Jerusalem's Old City, if one leaves one's shoes before the entrance of the Dome of the Rock and steps inside, one finds oneself in not only the edifice considered the greatest artwork of Jerusalem, but an overpowering quiet, which induces an imageless contemplation and pushes all other thoughts away. Thus it is not surprising that Islam, this complete submission to the will of the one God, could produce a lyric in modern Persian writing that is at the same time mystical. One may well ask, as Rückert did of Hafiz, whether such literature speaks of the sensory or the supersensory, or ultimately of a "unsupersensory" mystery. In his own way, Goethe was able to adopt Hafiz in his *West-östlicher Divan*. Celan's view, however, originates from a completely different tradition, and thus from another world than the one familiar to us from Goethe, from Abu Tor across to the Dome of the Rock: it is the view of one who has escaped the Holocaust, one for whom, after so many expulsions and exterminations, exile remains as close and oppressive as it does for the Jewish mystic of Safed, for instance. Thus the companion You can take on the lineaments of the *Shekhinah* figure, for Celan's lyric poetry from the very beginning has sought to overcome hate and enmity by turning to that which is closest and to love; that is, he has sought that peace which Jerusalem had promised its peoples. The shining, then, streaming from the golden cupola of the Dome of the Rock, can ultimately be taken into the old *Auf werde Licht, Jerusalem.*

Yet how should one approach the succeeding poem, "Du gleißende" ("You Glistening"), in which the apostrophized You becomes a "glistening / tumor / of a blinding in the universe" ("gleißende / Tochtergeschwulst / einer Blendung im All") (*GW* 3:101)? Does this poem not recall a space flight or a science fiction story of the War of the Worlds rather than mysticism? What does the poem actually say? In the universe there was the explosion from a superabundance of light; a metastasis of this blinding was seized by "supra-celestial reconnaissance troops" ("überhimmlischen Suchtrupps") and shifted into the "gazing god-bereft star-piled blueness" ("sehendes gottentratenes Sternhaufen-Blau"). This glistening secondary growth then "reeks musk" ("wildenzt") before the hungry pores as a "fellow sun, between two bright shots abyss" ("Mitsonne, zwischen zwei Hellschüssen Abgrund"). Does this discourse remain intelligible? Do these "supra-celestial reconnaissance troops" go beyond all the galaxies and the Milky Way? Perhaps the discourse is actually functioning, here, with a linguistic analogy: the supraterrestrial (*das Überirdische*) is the heavenly (*das Himmlische*) as the supracelestial (*das Überhimmlische*) is the terrestrial (*das Irdische*). Completely in the realm of the terrestrial, the searching troops (supposedly "supracelestial") have here taken up the tumor of a blinding, just as Celan's poems took up the blinding light of Jewish mysticism. This tumor is subsequently displaced into the blueness (the celestial-transcendental) of that heap of stars which orient life, and which therefore are gazing, yet bereft of God in the sense of Eckhart's elimination of God for the sake of the godhead and the union. This simple metastasis of a blinding can be an "accompanying sun" (*Mitsonne*), namely to *wildenzen* (which means "to smell strongly of wild game") before our pores. By the *Hellschüsse*, blinding and light are related to the abyss, which according to Eckhart's mysticism is the "without because" (*Ohne Warum*) of the godhead and according to Jewish mysticism is the *En-sof*. In his poems Celan brings together brightness and echo, so the *Hellschüsse* from the abyss could also refer to the call which in the Jewish Jubilee bestows freedom upon those enslaved.

Should we really ascribe a "mystical" interpretation to the passage about the blinding? Such ascribing would be more feasible if other poems also suggest this interpretation. The phrase "ummuttert von Blendung" occurs in the poem "Eingewohnt-entwohnt" in *Fadensonnen* (*GW* 2:156). The beginning of the poem is evidently a play on words, concatenating two words into one: "Eingewohnt-entwohnt, / einentwohnt." What is this? Is it more than the empty disarticulation of language, at best as in so-called "concrete poetry"? Yet the *Einwohnung*, "inhabiting," is most likely the inhabiting of God among human beings. *Entwohnung* signifies the loss of all dwelling and of all cities: exile— perhaps also the renunciation of dwelling and homeland thus, as the answer offers itself up as an unbecoming of the comfort of the word. Celan takes *Einwohen* and *Entwohen* together and has both sides of the *Shekhinah*. Hence the third stanza can speak of the "obedient darkness" ("gehorsame Finsternis"): the darkness with its horror is full and fully there; yet it is obedient, because it is received from the reference to a final entity. If we reflect upon the medieval pogroms, upon the expulsion of the Jews from Spain, upon the last Holocaust, then we must accede to Celan, when he says, from within the mystical tradition, that the darkness lies "three / blood-hours behind / the glance-source" ("drei / Blutstunden hinterm / Blickquell"). There is no eye at this spot that could or might be allowed to see, rather only "coldlight-ocelli, / mothered round from blinding" ("Kaltlicht-Ozellen, / ummuttert von Blendung"). Ocelli, or "simple eyes," "eyespots," are quasi-eyes of primitive organisms. These animals have a sensitivity to light; at least they can react to light and thereby orient themselves. That which blinds in the blinding mothering round is Nothing. The next stanzas speak of Nothing which is "dreizehnlötig" ("thirteen-soldered") and bears within itself the absolute disaster. This Nothing draws itself over the You as "Glückshaut" during the departure. Is it the departure of the poet or the departure of the *Shekhinah*, which will once again unite with the "higher" *Shekhinah* or even with the "Enlivening-righteous one" (*Belebend-Gerechten*)? This either-or does not exist: the poet lives from and with the *Shekhinah*, only from her is he a poet.

The mystical doctrine teaches one to close one's eyes and be silent, in order to gain another orientation for living through an ungrounded experience where other methods of orientation fail. In this regard Thomas Aquinas spoke of a *cognitio dei experimentalis*. If there are mystical elements in Celan's lyric poetry, they serve as an orientation beyond the usual vision. Thus Celan alludes to the rudimentary ocelli, which nonetheless are "mothered round" from blinding. This blinding is not the self-blinding of Oedipus the seeker of knowledge, who could not yet bear actual self-knowledge. The blinding occurs out of a Nothing which contains a negative in excess, yet ultimately remains not purely negative because it raises the new sense of light and orientation like a mother (and like Jerusalem, the glowing empty-text, which consoles its people like a mother). When Celan speaks of *Kaltlicht-Ozellen* he evidently is thinking about that "luminescence" which in "Wetterfühlige Hand," contained in *Lichtzwang* (*GW* 2:309), is named by this *terminus technicus*: dead and decaying organisms in marshlands and bogs radiate bioluminescence. This "cold" light indicates that even the dead remain and will send yet one more message. The living cannot bring the dead back to life, but they can preserve a memory of them. They must allow the murdered to be vouchsafed "righteousness" (*Gerechtigkeit*), that is, by reversing the judgment that claims those lives were unworthy of life. On this way, the comforting closeness (*helfende Nähe*) can also remain, as well as the love it affords, a closeness to which the distance of the Other belongs, who places us under an obligation.

The Jewish mystical tradition holds that a divine primordial ground is only accessible across the "Nothing," attainable across the always threatened closeness and righteousness. Thus the *Urgrund* is not simply the heavenly as the supraterrestrial, but rather the supraheavenly as the completely terrestrial (the mystery of the suprasensory, as Rückert said). This *Urgrund* is concretely actual, in our social existence, as the messianic call for peace, which places beneath its standard just such a city with so much actual strife and furnishes Jerusalem with a promise. Celan could have drawn upon this mystical tradition for interpretive markers within his creative work, which remains fully independent and integral to our age. For this very reason the fulfillment of his poetic path lay in the final encounter with Jerusalem.

We speak comfortably of East-West mysticism. In so doing the Asiatic, or at least the East-Asiatic, appears as a complete whole, with which Eckhart as a representative of the West again forms a unity. Yet besides the Eckhartian mysticism, there are others in the West, for instance Jewish mysticism; and Taoism, for that matter, is not the same as Zen Buddhism. Japanese philosophers influenced by Zen Buddhism felt their affinity with Heidegger's 1929 discourse on Nothing. Heidegger acknowledged the power of reflection in Zen Buddhism, yet he himself issues no koans to confuse self-consciousness in favor of immediate experience. Kôichi Tsujimura, an attentive student of Heidegger and the Zen Buddhist tradition, also found in Heidegger's treatment of history and epochality elements that depart from Zen Buddhism, at least in its traditional form.[14] Indeed, it was thought possible to confirm Heidegger's affinity with Zen Buddhism based on interviews with him, yet the question remains whether a philosopher in general and Heidegger in particular can be interviewed while "under way." Particularly regarding mysticism, interviews are irrelevant. Heidegger's characterization of the Japanese experience in his conversation with a Japanese is not based on Zen Buddhism; ancient Chinese was more important for Heidegger's encounter with East Asia. Of course China was as flooded with Buddhism as the ancient Mediterranean culture was with oriental religiosity: the reverse influence of Taoism on Mahayana Buddhism thus contributed to the formation of Zen Buddhism. But did Heidegger not always seek the "modern"?

We cannot assume that Eastern and Western mysticism compose a whole, and further that the East and West finally agree. We often call "mystical" the intrinsic mystery in a cult or the hidden interpretation of a hermetic text. Do the mystics of all peoples and ages experience the same thing, which they then interpret differently according to their various individual traditions, or does mysticism derive from fundamental experiences and religious traditions that are finally irreconcilable? For instance, does righteousness refer to the divine *Ungrund*, or is the godhead beyond good and evil? According to some Western positions, the East-Asian approach, and especially Buddhism, should even be termed "atheistic." Here, indeed, we must recall that our discourse on God also makes use of a word that adheres to certain historical experiences: the etymological dictionary states that the German word *Gott* means perhaps first of all "der Angerufene," "the called on" or "the addressed," or "das gegossene Bild," "the poured" or "cast image." In any case, our experience of God seems to be shaped by the belief that, for man, the closed earth reveals itself to heaven in the monument; that God stepped out of the monument and the pillars as a figure capable of being addressed. Yet in the history of this experience, that nameless and abyssal range (*Weite*) in which things rest might have gotten somewhat lost, having endured more strongly in the East Asian experience.

It is ill-advised to construe too quickly a unity or a synthesis among mystical traditions. Perhaps we are not even capable of grasping simply the unity of a single thinker's approach, say that of Eckhart. Eckhart interprets the parables of the Bible not only as parables, that is, parabolically and allegorically, but also as stories to be understood historically. Does the *Lebemeister* not transfer that which should remain historical revelation into an ever possible transhistorical event of the birth of God in the soul? Does he not thereby return theology to (an admittedly theological) philosophy? The *Lesemeister* Eckhart, however, gave up the idea of completing his philosophical work in order to assume an important position in the management of his order and to lead his brothers (but also nuns and laymen) as *Lebemeister*. In this activity he always began with the Bible. In view of his background, Heidegger was close to this "mysticism." Of course one cannot overlook the question of whether this proximity to mysticism does not also contain a certain danger: can the striving for an immediate and ultimate experience, just when it is vouchsafed, rather not induce a vertigo and a loss of orientation in real life? Does Heidegger neglect the search for an orientation constructed from the bottom up, in provisional but relatively sure knowledge? When he refers to the "path" or "way" (*Weg*) of Lao Tzu, then not only the question of whether he comprehends the historical Lao Tzu or the historical *Tao Te Ching* arises, but also how exactly this "way" is a way and how it reaches places where we could stay. When Heidegger seeks the closeness of poetry as thinker, he also approaches the mythological; since the latter abides in legend, it also stands in opposition to the silence of mysticism. One should by no means hastily restrict Heidegger to a particular religious tradition because of his manifest affinity to the religious. In his Trakl interpretation, he draws our attention to the fact that in his last productive poem, "Grodek," Trakl calls upon neither God nor Christ, but upon the "swaying shadow of the sister" ("schwankenden Schatten der Schwester"). In the poem "Klage," eternity is called the "icy surge" ("eisige Woge"). "Is this a Christian thought?" asks Heidegger, and answers: "It is not even Christian despair." Heidegger's affinity to the mythological precludes a warning which the first patriarch of Zen, the Bodi Darma, gave to the emperor of China: "Too light-hearted. Nothing holy!"[15] When Heidegger names only the "divinities" in his approach to the dimension of the propitious and catastrophic, he may have overlooked that this approach also can be concentrated in the seductive and destructive "Powers and Forces," of which a poem from Celan's *Fadensonnen* (and a graphic print by his wife) relates the following:

MÄCHTE, GEWALTEN.

Dahinter, im Bambus:
bellende Lepra, symphonisch.

Vincents verschenktes
Ohr
ist am Ziel.
    (*GW* 2:209)

(POWERS, DOMINIONS.

Behind them, in the bamboo:
barking leprosy, symphonic.

Vincent's posted
ear
has reached its destination.)
    (*P* 281)

When Aion darkens, he no longer shows those bright divine forms who gave man the image from which he could understand himself in the great age of the Greeks. The way of the world rolls forth powers and forces that incite self-destruction, embodied in the leading ideas of men, in myths and rituals, but also in distorted institutions and tendencies. The Letter of Jude, which is found at the end of the New Testament, says of these powers that they had not retained the dominion which was originally entrusted to them; by having lost their "dwelling," their power became simply their own self-authority and thus the temptation to ruin. Against this temptation the Christian Gospel states that devotion to ungrounded love which liberates from all self-willed authority. Thus in Romans 8:38, the Apostle Paul declares that neither death, nor life, nor powers, nor forces can sever him from God's love, which appeared in Christ. In Celan's poem, however, the powers and forces stand for that which threatens our own age, and so leprosy is named immediately following them, which symphonically barks after them in the bamboo. This disease, known from innumerable statistics and appeals for aid to combat it, stands as symptom for the tensions today defining and separating North and South, the industrial nations and the so-called underdeveloped lands, and thus constituting a fundamental injustice of our time. Also named, however, is that absurd gesture, which was supposed to be the gesture of love for Vincent van Gogh at the very end of his short life: such love, or rather what was actually sought in that love, is established as a standard for that modern art which van Gogh still represents. Like Heidegger, Celan is convinced that art should show the path to salvation to people ensnared in an age of catastrophe. But Celan does not succumb to the nostalgia that seeks the fourfold image of Earth and Sky, Mortal and Divine. Celan's realism does not overlook the ever-accompanying dangers of seduction.

Thus perhaps the way in which Celan adopts elements of the mystical tradition offers a correction of Heidegger's approach. It is true, one should not criticize Heidegger's path rashly, for instance by disqualifying it as "aesthetic" rather than "ethical." Above all, one should not condemn him as did the fools from the archbishopric in Cologne and the papal court in Avignon in their judgment on Eckhart, when tailoring his theses to match their insipid understanding. If Heidegger rejects the usual discourse on responsibility, he does so by attempting to trace it back to a reflection of the manner in which the person can be a complete "answer" (*Antwort*). Thus he inquires into the borders of what we ourselves—running the danger of moralistic presumption—can do and can assure on the one hand, and on the other, what perhaps can develop on a long and lonely path and be freely received only in the fortunate hour. The eighteenth chapter of the *Tao Te Ching* says that where the way has been lost, there is humanity and righteousness and then mendacity, discord, and benighted life. Do Lao Tzu and Heidegger offer themselves as sad examples of people who have irresponsibly allowed events to take their course and shirked their own responsibility? This danger may well exist, yet one must also ask the question in reverse: have we not in the meantime often enough experienced that the cry for humanity and righteousness can also corrupt all good beginnings? For example, what would be more important than the endeavor to end the brutality with which our society treats the handicapped and to give them genuine prospects? Yet such an endeavor, too, could have its function altered. It could well be that not only people 150 centimeters tall should be subsidized, but rather everyone under 160 centimeters. Requirements of this sort, however, have the tendency ultimately to declare everyone under 175 centimeters to be too small and everyone over 175 centimeters too big, and thus to submit everyone to a rampant caretaker-bureaucracy and rob them of any real possibility for improvement.

Undoubtedly, Heidegger's thought has its lapses in clarity and its obliquities from a systematic perspective, its errors from a historical perspective and its biases in application. Yet again and again, he makes a strong impression on individuals in America and Japan, France and Germany, because he conveys neither vacant acumen nor petrified erudition, but rather, if not words of life, then words that point toward life. If I were to tell when I learned most from Heidegger, I would invoke not long conversations about Aristotle and Hegel, Bultmann, Heisenberg, Klee, and Celan, but a game of boccie played between the house and the garage. Of course Heidegger won, but at that time I realized the secret of his effect: he was always fully there in whatever he was doing; thus small games found their own meaning. When he polemicized against academic life or political machinations, he did so because he missed this: that, as in the making of a jug, an endeavor coming out of a long descent is able to return into itself, so that it rests and abides in itself. When Confucius visited the wise elder Lao Tzu, he asked him, according to the beautiful legend of Chuang Tzu, what he understood by love and righteousness, and whether with his banner waving he did not perplex even more the life which had strayed from its way and its righteousness. Lao Tzu answered that the swan is white without anyone artificially cleaning it, and the raven is black without being blackened. The striving for organized righteousness is hopeless. One does not moisten the fish stranded on the shore, not even their mouths; rather one helps them back into the water. When Confucius went home, he was very distraught and for three months could not speak. After long reflection he visited the old man again, and now the two men understood each other without arguing about the principles of great words—perhaps over the simple procedure of drinking a cup of tea. Confucius had learned that the birds hatch their young, the fish spawn, and the insects undergo metamorphoses; only he who changes can go with change. In any case, we should not disturb the way in which Lao Tzu confirmed the thoughts of his great adversary: he had now attained that which is attainable.

If it is ill-advised to pass swift judgment about the different paths of Confucius or Lao Tzu, or Heidegger's way as well, by the same token we should insist on the experiences that belong to our life, and from which Celan appropriated the tradition of Jewish mysticism. The experiences of our decades once again articulate what emerged in southern France in the time of the Cathari, and then in Spain in the thirteenth century with the *Zohar*.[16] After the terrible expulsion of the Jews from Spain, people in Safed in Palestine asked what meaning the renewed exile and the experience of evil could have. Isaac Luria taught that God withdraws back into himself and therefore leaves room for forlornness and evil itself. Is this mysticism, which derives more from personal experience than historical revelation, not somewhat un-Jewish? Does it not contradict the fundamental character of the Jewish tradition when the *Shekhinah* is not simply the face that God shows to his people in each historical situation, but rather becomes a mythological figure? As does every maternal divinity, this figure has a double face: she is the bestower of life and the sisterly helper as well as the horror of death and desolation. If the feminine obtains something fascinating and daemonic in this way, it is once again something very Jewish: for example, it ensues from the position of the woman that there are no "female mystics," not even nuns as a chosen audience of a mystic. Celan, who as an only child was very close to his mother, can situate his entire literary creation around the experience of sisterly strength. Yet by no means does he limit himself to the Jewish mystical tradition: for example, he also borrows the apocalyptic Eber from Yeats's "new mythology" and with it the tradition of a lost or dispersed people such as the Celts or the Etruscans; and Mallarmé stands for him like an Irish hermit atop a lonely cliff in the sea. Celan's poems have many dimensions and therefore also an openness which should not simply be interpreted away.

Then again, Celan's poems lose a crucial dimension when their mystical elements are not taken into account. Hans-Georg Gadamer has not only written about Celan's poetry, but also interpreted in detail a particular cycle of poems, "Atemkristall."[17] He remains the sole interpreter to undertake such an arduous task, yet one may ask whether his attempt to reduce Celan's images, like Goethe's symbols, to universally comprehensible experiences does not misread an allegory which is historically and artificially composed of unintelligibility as a daring new understanding. (Gadamer, like Walter Benjamin, has demanded a new attentiveness to allegory.) Does the poem "Schläfenzange" (*GW* 2:21) really refer to the graying temple lying down like pincers around the head? Does the poem nonetheless posit the joy of a birthday against the experience of old age? These temple-pincers are more likely forceps used in childbirth, which retain the silver of their sheen even for the head into which they bit. A You and the remains of its sleep must be brought to the birth. To put it crudely, the poem is about the birthing with forceps of the *Shekhinah*, about the attempt to draw forth for our age the residue of a former mystical experience by means of highly poetic artifice.

The first exigency in reading this cycle of poems is that one is always thinking of a You when the texts speak of a You, and of the poet only when he says "I." Then the figure of the You is self-composed. This You appears in the elementary imagery of the faults and displacements of the earth as well as of snow and ice. When a text speaks of "slickensides," "fold-axes," and "cutting-points" ("Harnischstriemen," "Faltenachsen," "Durchstichpunkte"), one should not imagine a knight in armor. *Harnischstriemen* occur when rock plates slide over one another along a fault line; a geological fold with a fold axis and coordinates is produced when horizontal pressure buckles a rock plate, etc. In this geological fault, however, she—the *Shekhinah*—appears. When the great concluding poem of the cycle speaks of the radiant wind of its language, then to begin with, one must take this phrase entirely literally: as the deadly radiated wind of the atomic explosion. Do not the "human-shaped snow" ("menschen-gestaltiger Schnee") and the "penitent-snow" ("Büsserschnee") mean "the humans with their idle talk that covers everything"? Under *Büßerschnee* the lexicon provides the following information: "peaked towers, up to several meters high, of névé and glacier-ice, which always appear in groups (similar to mushrooms); formed by evaporation and melting due to sunlight."[18] From this image Celan can return to the snow imagery. Deposited snow masses, however, form honeycombed ice formations within glaciers. If the breath of the *Shekhinah* settles there in the innermost crystal, only then is the glacier a "glacier" in Celan's meaning of the term. According to "Warum dieses jähe Zuhause," contained in *Schneepart*, the poet can lower himself "glacially" ("gletschrig") in the "snowed one" ("Geschneete"), with whom he "was nowhere other" than with God (*GW* 2:363). The glacier's miracle lies in the fact that below, in the glacier milk, the frozen ice once again becomes living water: "The ice will rise again" ("Das Eis wird auferstehen"), says the poem "Eis, Eden" in *Die Niemandsrose* (*GW* 1:224). If one notices that the poem "Schläfenzange" is placed exactly in the middle of the "Atemkristall" cycle, one also sees that the last poem takes up the snow imagery of the first poem in superb expansiveness. Indeed, composed as a cycle, the poems may be read in concentric circles, reading the first and the last poems, then the second and the penultimate, and so on, onward toward the middle of the cycle.[19]

Gadamer draws attention to the penultimate poem's being completely bracketed; he interprets it as a much too personal confession and, like a "discrete dedication," spoken as an aside. The motifs of the Pietà are set into play:

> (ICH KENNE DICH, du bist die tief Gebeugte,
> ich, der Durchbohrte, bin dir untertan.
> Wo flammt ein Wort, das für uns beide zeugte?
> Du—ganz, ganz wirklich. Ich—ganz Wahn.)
>   (GW 2:30)

> ([I KNOW YOU, you are the deeply bowed,
> I, the run through, am subjected to you.
> Where blazes a word, which testified for us both?
> You—wholly, wholly real. I—wholly madness.])

One may think of personal history or the Pietà, but also of chivalric legends (for instance, as in Nerval's sonnet "El Desdichado," translated by Celan). Yet one should not omit the dimension articulated by the Jewish mystical tradition. Above all, one must emphasize that the You to whom Celan speaks is indeed "completely, completely real," whether one sees her more as the burned and lost sister or as the helping and loving one. When the poet seeks a life force in this You, which deeply determines his "I," when he incorporates mystical elements in doing so, is his literary production not "complete madness"? Whether it is or not is also a question for us. When, in Eckhart's time, the autos-da-fé were blazing in the towns along the Rhine, and the archbishops had the beghards (women who entered into conventlike communities without religious vows) drowned in the Rhine for the sake of peace and order, this appearance of mysticism signaled a crisis in the transmission of the religious tradition. For those who are convinced of the vital necessity of such a tradition, this crisis has intensified today. In the scientific civilization, science is capable of knowing many separate things, but extensive scientific research knows no answer to the existential questions (whether our world has a unique history; whether life arises diversely in the universe or rarely or perhaps just this one time on this one planet; whether material itself induces the development of life and life in turn the development of consciousness, etc.). Thus one attempts to answer such questions with the existential and experimental "knowledge" of mysticism. This way is not without its dangers. In any case, in their relationships to mysticism Heidegger and Celan show us that mysticism is no universal cure for human unrest. The ways of mysticism reveal themselves to us only when we receive them from our own experiences, and therefore are already from the outset positioned in a decision among different mystical traditions.

NOTES

1. See John D. Caputo, *The Mystical Element in Heidegger's Thought* (Columbus: Ohio State University Press, 1978). On the Japanese interest in Heidegger, see note 13.

2. Bernhard Welte, *Meister Eckhart. Gedanken zu seinen Gedanken* (Freiburg: Herder, 1979). See also Welte's report in *Erinnerung an Martin Heidegger*, ed. Günther Neske (Pfullingen: Neske, 1977), 249–56.

3. Eckhart's sermon is printed in a modern German translation as sermon no. 30 in Meister Eckhart, *Deutsche Predigten und Traktate*, ed. and trans. Josef Quint (Munich: Diogenes, 1979 [1963]), 295–98. On Heidegger's background, see Bernhard Casper, "Martin Heidegger und die Theologische Fakultät Freiburg 1909–23," in *Kirche am Oberrhein. Beiträge zur Geschichte der Bistümer Konstanz und Freiburg*, ed. Remigius Bäumer, Karl Suso Franz, and Hugo Ott (Freiburg: Herder, 1980), 534–41.

4. Husserl's letter is reprinted in *Das Maß des Verborgenen*, ed. Curd Ochwadt and Erwin Tecklenborg (Hannover: Charis, 1981), 157–60. Ochsner also relates that Heidegger already had given a paper in a private circle on August 1, 1917 on Schleiermacher's *Reden über die Religion* (p. 92). That Heidegger relied most strongly on the second discourse is indicative of his parting of ways from the metaphysical theology of Aristotle and Hegel. This was an important step taken away from the system of Catholicism and from dogmatic Protestantism toward an open Christianity, as Heidegger said in these years. On this, see also the reports concerning Heidegger's lecture course "Einleitung in die Phänomenologie der Religion." Otto Pöggeler, *Der Denkweg Martin Heideggers*, 2d rev. ed. (Pfullingen: Neske, 1983), 36–38. Otto Pöggeler, *Martin Heidegger's Path of Thinking*, trans. Daniel Magurshak and Sigmund Barber (Atlantic Highlands, N.J.: Humanities Press, 1989 [1987]), 24–26. Cf. further: Thomas Sheehan, "Heidegger's 'Introduction to the Phenomenology of Religion,' 1920–21," in *A Companion to Martin Heidegger's "Being and Time,"* ed. J. J. Kockelmans (Washington, D.C.: University Press of America, 1986), 40–62.

5. Cf. Martin Heidegger, *Hölderlins Hymnen "Germanien" und "Der Rhein"* (Frankfort: Klostermann, 1980), 134. See also Martin Heidegger, *Die Frage nach dem Ding* (Tübingen: Niemeyer, 1962), 76, and Walter Schulz, *Der Gott der neuzeitlichen Metaphysik* (Pfullingen: Neske, 1957), 14.

6. Martin Heidegger, *Hölderlins Hymne "Der Ister"* (Frankfort: Klostermann, 1984), 155. The narrative mentioned next, "Der Feldweg" (originally published in 1949), was reprinted as the "hut booklet" *Aus der Erfahrung des Denkens* (originally published in 1947). See Martin Heidegger, *Aus der Erfahrung des Denkens* (Frankfort: Klostermann, 1983), 75–86 and 87–90. The lecture on "Das Ding" appears in Martin Heidegger, *Vorträge und Aufsätze* (Pfullingen: Neske, 1954), 163–79. On Eckhart's sermon *Beati pauperes spiritu*, see No. 32 in Quint, 303–13.

7. Cf. No. 49 in Quint, 384. On the following, see Martin Heidegger, *Der Satz vom Grund* (Pfullingen: Neske, 1957), 70–75.

8. Martin Heidegger, *Gelassenheit* (Pfullingen: Neske, 1959), 36. On the following, see Quint, 53–100 and 303–9.

9. See Martin Heidegger, *Was heißt Denken?* (Tübingen: Niemeyer, 1954), 54, 159. On the following, see *Hölderlins Hymnen "Germanien" und "Der Rhein,"* 112 and 134.

10. See Martin Heidegger, *Identität und Differenz* (Pfullingen: Neske, 1957), 24; *Zur Sache des Denkens* (Tübingen: Niemeyer, 1969), 23; *Unterwegs zur Sprache* (Pfullingen: Neske, 1959), 28–33. On the following, see *Unterwegs zur Sprache*, 198. On Heidegger's attempt at a translation of Lao Tzu, see *Erinnerung an Martin Heidegger*, 119–29.

11. *Gelassenheit*, 49. On the following, see "Brief über den Humanismus," in Martin Heidegger, *Wegmarken* (Frankfort: Klostermann, 1967), 189, and Eckhart's sermons Nos. 10 and 9 in Quint, 197, 199, and 193.

12. See *F,* 38, 57, and 108. On the following, see the poem "Es fällt nun, Mutter," which names "die Schneewehn der Ukraine" (68).

13. Stéphane Moses has interpreted this poem with as much insight as detailed attentiveness. See "Patterns of Negativity in Paul Celan's 'The Trumpet Place,'" in *Languages of the Unsayable: The Play of Negativity in Literature and Literary Theory*, ed. Sanford Budick and Wolfgang Iser (New York: Columbia University Press, 1989), 209–24. Gershom Scholem has shown that the mystical tradition continually reduces the content of the Revelation. See, for example, *Zur Kabbala und ihrer Symbolik* (Frankfort: Suhrkamp, 1977), 11–48. Pioneering work on Celan's relationship to mysticism was done by Joachim Schulze. See *Celan und die Mystiker* (Bonn: Bouvier, 1976).

14. See Kôichi Tsujimura, "Martin Heideggers Denken und die Japanische Philosophie," in *Martin Heidegger zum 80. Geburtstag von seiner Heimatstadt Meßkirch 26. September 1969* (Meßkirch: Klostermann, 1969), 9–19. On the following, see "Aus einem Gespräch von der Sprache. Zwischen einem Japaner und einem Fragenden," in *Unterwegs zur Sprache*, 83–155. Phenomenologists who articulate the religious dimension in the confrontation with Heidegger can fall into a fundamental opposition: the opposition between Emmanuel Lévinas and Keiji Nishitani may well indicate the opposition between the Jewish and Zen Buddhist experiences of the world. On this, see Otto Pöggeler, *Heidegger und die hermeneutische Philosophie* (Freiburg: Alber, 1983), 353–64. The epigraph from one of Celan's poems, which Lévinas places in his second magnum opus, correctly brings out Celan's concern and indicates the "fateful affinity" between Levinas's thought and Celan's poetry. See Emmanuel Lévinas, *Autrement qu'être ou au-delà de l'essence* (The Hague: Nijhoff, 1974), 125.

15. On Trakl, see "Die Sprache im Gedicht," in *Unterwegs zur Sprache*, 76. On "the holy," see esp. Martin Heidegger, *Erläuterungen zu Hölderlins Dichtung* (Frankfurt: Klostermann, 1971). On Celan's "Mächte, Gewalten," see Heinrich Schlier, *Mächte und Gewalten im Neuen Testament* (Freiburg: Herder, 1958). When Schlier, a student of Bultmann and Heidegger, wrote the foreword to the new edition of Margarete Susman's *Das Buch Hiob und das Schicksal des jüdischen Volkes* (Freiburg: Herder, 1968), Celan said that he could not adopt the following sentence from the book for himself: "Israel should free itself of everything that it itself considers the righteousness of God, of the people's self-righteousness; it should also free itself of the intention of wanting first to under-

stand God's righteousness and only then to acknowledge it" (15). Does Celan's self-defense not have its justification, since God would be undifferentiable from a demon if he did not prove to be the righteous one? Surely it may be specifically "Jewish" to want to maintain God's "intelligibility," be it at the cost of the doctrine of God's omnipotence. In this way Hans Jonas borrowed the cabbalistic idea of the *zimzum* in his lecture "Der Gottesbegriff nach Auschwitz": the self-limitation of God's power consequently leaves it to humans and if need be to the "thirty-six righteous ones" to take care lest it come to pass—or come to pass too often—"that God must regret the letting-become of the world." Yet Jonas departs from Celan when he wishes to keep absurdity and even concealment away from the notion of God. See Fritz Stern and Hans Jonas, *Reflexionen finsterer Zeit* (Tübingen: Mohr, 1984), 85 and 80.

16. *Translator's Note.* Major work of the Jewish Kabbalah believed to have been written in the second half of the thirteenth century by Moses Ben Shem Tov de Leon.

17. *T. N. Wer bin Ich und wer bist Du? Kommentar zu Celans "Atemkristall"* (Frankfort: Suhrkamp, 1973).

18. *T. N. Das neue Fischer Lexikon in Farbe* (Frankfort: Fischer, 1981), 870.

19. In the second edition of his *Wer bin ich und wer bist Du?* (Frankfort: Suhrkamp, 1986), Gadamer willingly accepts corrections pertaining to the meaning of words such as *Harnischstriemen* and *Büßerschnee*. He remains skeptical, however, about the attempt to underscore the significance of Jewish mysticism for Celan. Indeed, he shifts a confrontation about it into the arena of erudition (153). But one does not become learned simply by reading a couple of articles by Scholem and occasionally referring to the Old Testament. If Celan used a long-ostracized tradition—i.e., Jewish mysticism—after the most frightful ostracism of the Jews as a better interpretant for his relation to the reality of our age, it has nothing to do with erudition. Celan originally wanted to end the first poem of the cycle with the following: "ich komme mit sieben / Blättern vom Sieben- / stamm" ("I come with seven / leaves from the seven- / stem"). Gadamer says to this: "I do not know what the *Siebenstamm* is." He inquires about a possible connection "with the seven-armed religious candelabra" and finds that a "very esoteric expression" was replaced in the final edition of the poem by the accessible and suitable image of the luxuriantly sprouting mulberry tree (43). Having one cycle in mind, Celan in fact did not want to say it all in the very first poem. Only the cycle as a whole elaborates on the meaning of the *Siebenstamm* (the Menorah): the survival of Israel, which at Sinai was given the *Siebenstamm* in spite of all the threats and destruction. Because the *Siebenstamm* means this, the new Israel could choose it as its national emblem. Here, erudition did not suppose—even if it did arise in opposition to the reigning intellectual-historical opinion, as Toynbee conceived of it—that extinct peoples could not once again become active historical subjects. On this question in greater detail, see my discussion of Gadamer's interpretation. Otto Pöggeler, *Spur des Worts. Zur Lyrik Paul Celans* (Freiburg: Alber, 1986), 165–245.

Denn das Schöne ist nichts
als des Schrecklichen Anfang, den wir noch grade ertragen,
und wir bewundern es so, weil es gelassen verschmäht,
uns zu zerstören. . . .
    —Rainer Maria Rilke

2

Black Milk and Blue

Celan and Heidegger on Pain and Language

Dennis J. Schmidt

"Two mouthfuls of silence"[1] mark the place of the poem for Celan, "two kinds of strangeness next to each other" ("zweierlei Fremde—dicht beieinander") (*GW* 3:195). To think the poetic place means remembering that the silence marking that place has its own contours; it also means knowing that such silence is not to be confused with mere quiet, but needs to be heard as the unvocalized voice of the poem. A voice straining itself as well as those who can hear it. A voice estranged from language, rendering the effort to listen to language in the poem rare, demanding, and painful at once. More than any other feature of the poem this demand that silence be heard is the peculiar difficulty of reading the poem. Even in the moment of its greatest fluency, the moment in which the mediating power of the word reaches out in full communicative force, language in Celan's poetry lives in the middle of mouthfuls of silence that no word can either swallow or speak.

If such poetry is to be read, if its language is to be thought, then silence must be heard along the rhythmic axis of its own idiom. Reading such poetry one is reminded that the idiom of the poetic word emphasizes itself most of all in contact with that which it cannot convert into its own, and which nonetheless cannot subvert the word away from itself. In the contact with the radically other idiom of silence, the poetic word is brought to its own brink, where it announces its own apartness

110

and inconvertibility. In that contact, that moment in which language touches us by being touched itself, the singularity of every idiom begins to emerge, and one suddenly realizes with a kind of shock that in delimiting the edges of language the poem becomes a disclosure of the peculiar singularity of those who speak. The experience that one undergoes in moving with language in the poem—a movement that is particularly radicalized and reflected upon in Celan—is an original experience, a disclosure, not merely a reminder or memento, of our finite singularity. Hölderlin already gave testimony to the originality of poetic experience when he wrote that "dichterisch wohnet der Mensch."[2] Once one understands how it is that the poetic word is simply itself, how it is to be thought as "language actualized, set free under the sign of radical individuation . . . as aware of the limits drawn by language as of the possibilities it opens" (*GW* 3:197), one also understands how it is that the poem "speaks from the aspect of our creaturely, our bodily, existence" (*GW* 3:197). It is only from this strained and compressed point, at which the singularities of language and body meet, that one begins to read the poem as language that speaks by listening to itself, thereby telling us who we are—and are not.

In what follows, my purpose will be to discuss some of the specific strains and compressions of the poetic experience as voiced by Celan. I propose to do so by taking Celan at his word, that is, by taking cues from his own efforts to articulate the nature and stakes of poetic language in the "Meridian" speech. Doing that, especially against the backdrop of Martin Heidegger's efforts to think through language in the poem as drawing attention to such original poetic experience, highlights what I take to be the guiding matrix of concerns at work in Celan's poetic thinking—a matrix uniting language, mortality, body, and catastrophic history. I believe that Heidegger—whose presence in Celan is far more prevalent than the word "backdrop" conveys—is especially instructive here because he argues more clearly than most that once language comes forward *as* language and confesses its nature as an "event" the lines binding poetry and history become visible.

In making such an argument, Heidegger calls attention to what is required if we are to read Celan's poetry, since, as Celan himself suggests, it is not until those lines become visible that one can read his work as the poetry dictated by history today. Celan persistently remarked that the experience of such a compression of language and silence is the only poetic experience that history permits after language has passed through "its own lack of answers, through a terrifying muteness, through a thousand darknesses of talk that brought death" (*GW* 3:186). Language has delivered itself over to this encounter with silence, which moves language to the site of its own idiomatization. One finds in Celan's work a play of idioms that, by returning language to its own possibilities today, persists in opening the passage between language and history and in reminding us that "the poem is not timeless" (*GW* 3:186). The history that language itself has articulated and found the words to make possible, and the "terrifying muteness" language has now to hear in itself after such history, have left poetry possible today only as an impulse of idioms—the idiom of our singularity (body and death) and the singularity of every idiom (word)—as the idiom of idioms. This idiomatic play initially becomes evident in the work of silence in the poem, for it is in this strangeness of word and silence that the place of the poem, the preeminent site of the idiom, first comes forward and into its own.

Such is the possibility of poetic experience today. Yet to think through this experience as Celan performs it one is compelled to ask if "silence" is the word most suited to name this unnameable other with which language makes contact in his poetry. Ultimately, Celan leads us to the question whether there is a word for silence just as Heidegger urges us to ask if there has yet arrived a word for the word. From the outset, both have rendered problematic just how "we" (a word that finally must be set apart since it is the question asked by every word) might receive such a word. Waiting for such words, both are drawn to speak, in the end, of the essential relation between pain and language.

———

How does one read silence?

Preliminarily, one notes that the word in the poem stands out against a certain haunting silence articulating the contours of the poem; yet the real enigma of language in the poem is that in it the word not only stands out *against* the silent space around it but also bears the traces of silence *within* itself. Even in its apartness and singularity, the word is not solid and without fissures. Even as apart, perhaps then more than ever, the word stands as an appeal and the possibility of relation. In that appeal, that availability for what stands apart from its own apartness, language in the poem preserves the essential capacity of all language to throw itself into darkness and fall mute. The poetic experience of language cannot be thought apart from this cryptic capacity and the resonance of the silence within the word as that which loves to hide. More precisely, the poetic experience of the word is the discovery that the pure word—the "absolute poem" (*GW* 3:199)—is not, and that every word only stands as a countercall, a call which is equally for its own other. One begins to read silence in this countercall of the word, in the self-encrypting withdrawal which the word itself is. It is with this in mind that Celan writes: "The poem has always hoped, for this very reason, to speak on behalf of the *strange*—no, I can no longer use this word here—*on behalf of the other*, who knows, perhaps of an *altogether other*" (*GW* 3:196).

This "altogether other" to which language in the poem, language intensified by being reflected upon itself, turns is not an other to language, an other "outside" language. What could be "other" to language for a poet speaking? It is rather the kinship of language in the poem with that which places all language at risk, a kinship which Maurice Blanchot referred to as "the silence of silence which by no means has any relation to language for it does not come from language but has already departed from it."[3] The difficulty in reading the poem comes in maintaining one's availability for silence and in understanding that the departure it marks does not lead away from the poem, but rather belongs to language itself in the poem. According to Heidegger, such departure in language marks the "place" of all poetry.[4] It is this movement of language beyond itself on the way to more of itself, not any representational potential of language linking word and abstract idea, that sets poetic language apart. Likewise, it is by virtue of this extension of language, of this life of language on the self-renewing edge of its own departure, that one must also say that language in the poem refuses to be domesticated even in returning to itself. Originary poetic experience draws near this point of departure in language. In the "Meridian," Celan obliquely echoes this curious homecoming of language in the poem when he says: "I am again at the point of my departure, searching for my own place of origin" (*GW* 3:202).

In such departure, every poem becomes the simple advance of what is otherwise unspeakable. The measure of the poem, what Hölderlin referred to as "Maaß,"[5] is the distance that language in the poem goes along the route of that advance. Needless to say, such departure and measure, the real truth of the poetic idiom, cannot be found by any ready-made calipers or calculus, especially those found in the linguistic economies of representation. Rather, in such departure as the advance of what is otherwise unspeakable, language in the poem unfolds as the advance and presence of nothing, thereby demonstrating the truth of Plato's claim that poetry speaks to the side of the soul that is *alogon* and that poets do not respect the boundaries of the *logos*. The seemingly anarchic potential of language in the poem, the measureless measure of language itself, is to be thought from this point of departure. But the point to be taken now is that language in the poem enlists silence for the word. Such enlistment marks the distance that language in the poem must move from a speech that finds the center of gravity of its language in its representational potential. It also renders every poem a reminder of its own impossibility.

When we speak specifically of Celan's poetry, however, we must remember that for him this poetic impossibility is redoubled, and that the remarkable compression of his language is to be thought from this very point. Between two mouthfuls of silence Celan wrote in German, the language of his deferred death and a language he freshened against himself.[6] There is then a double unspeakability out of which Celan writes: his language is forced to nourish itself not only against the threat of its own other, but equally on words that have turned to "black milk," "ash," and the taste of cyanide on the tongue, "bitter almonds" (*GW* 1:41, 78), by having been made serviceable for death. Silence is not alone in rendering the poem difficult, for the language in which Celan wrote, a language he called upon to move beyond itself to a point "north of the future" ("nördlich der Zukunft" [*GW* 2:14]), was nonetheless never far removed from the lacerations of pain and death held in its memory: "freely the hammers swung in the bell-frame of your silence, / the listened for reached you, / what is dead put its arm around you also" ("schwangen die Hämmer frei im Glockenstuhl deines Schweigens, / stieß das Erlauschte zu dir, / legte das Tote den Arm auch um dich") (*GW* 1:78). It is a language that speaks as an open wound even when its language is the language of mediation, that is, even when it is the bearer of love and grace. In this regard, Celan's work gives new meaning to Bataille's remark that "love smells like death."[7]

One learns of love when one knows its ineluctable relation to human fragility and mortality, and for Celan declarations of love and the memory of death arrive together. The "pendulum of love" swings at night, "between always and never" ("Nachts, wenn das Pendal der Liebe schwingt / zwischen Immer und Nie") (*GW* 1:57). Such a double arrival of love and death is not a mere quirk; rather it belongs to the truth of poetic experience: language is among the few goods that grow and expand the more they are shared. It always acts as a promise of communication, contact, and community; yet, it is equally true that by carrying us to the point of our finite singularity, poetic experience—the experience of language as language—renders mortality possible as the mortality that is ours and that keeps us apart. This is why it makes such sense to say, as does Peter Szondi, that Celan wrote on "the terrain of death and mourning."[8] One might add that he wrote equally out of the prospect of love and longing. In the end, I believe that we approach the full force of this writing once we recognize that self-sacrifice is an essential element of Celan's work, and once we understand that sacrifice is an act both of the most extreme solitude and solidarity.[9] The deepest meaning of sacrifice in the poem comes only after the self has abdicated its claims and done so without the price of a promise or exchange: "art creates distance from the I" (*GW* 3:193). But to speak of the specific self-sacrifice in Celan's poetic texts means recognizing that his language, which like all poetic language nourished itself on its own departure, finds no respite from risk—for it is the voice of treason and catastrophe—and that his tongue is the reminder of terror. First and foremost the place of sacrifice in the poem is a matter of recognizing the way in which silence belongs to Celan's poetry as the very life and renewal of its language. Ultimately, the deeper threat for Celan, one who knows that "language is the tongue,"[10] the real risk of language in his poetry is not simply of losing his voice or never finding it at all, but of having his tongue cut off. Silence is the risk of all language in every poem, but one should not forget that, for Celan, overcoming this risk, the very achievement of speech, bore the memory, the promise, of his own real silence: German remained always the language of his confrontation with death, the language of real annihilation. What Celan says of Danton applies with equal aptness to Celan himself: "We can only understand him through his death" (*GW* 3:188)—a reminder that the dominion of the word always includes the possibility of death. "Art lives on" (*GW* 3:200), but for Celan only as the enduring confrontation with death.[11]

Being between two mouthfuls of silence, and bearing the risk of death in its language, the poem lives between suffocations and is marked by a certain gasping for breath: "When I knead the / lump of air, our nourishment, / it is soured by the letter effulgence from / the dementedly open / pore" ("Wenn ich den Klumpen Luft / knete, unsere Nahrung, / säuert ihn der / Buschstabenschimmer aus / der wahnwitzig-offenen / Pore") (*GW* 2:49). But "poetry: that can mean a turn of breath" (*GW* 3:195). It is precisely the struggle to breathe, the return of breath as the small effort of the body both to absorb its world and to extend itself, which circumscribes the region and life of the poem as language which calls for voice. One knows what it means to say that language in the poem calls for voice once one knows that poetry cannot be read without being heard as spoken by a voice—even one not spoken out loud. One knows then that language in the poem is elaborating its relation to the body.[12] Bearing in mind this relation of language and breath, of poems as works of breath, we can say that although it is impossibly compressed (in the case of Celan doubly so), the poem should nonetheless be read as an advance and extension: the advance of the unspeakable and the slight extension of the body.[13] The bond holding together this advance and extension, mutually of silence and of the body, is all important, and the topic toward which I intend my remarks to lead. For the present, however, the point to be made is simply that the poem gathers these countervalent motions of compression and extension together and so stands as a "pause," as the place of "hope and thought" (*GW* 3:197). The poem lives at the site of this infinite and ambiguous compression and extension of the idioms of word and silence, the facticity of breath and body, alike. "Poetry speaks out of an ambiguous ambiguity," as Heidegger puts it.[14]

Celan repeatedly renews this point about the relation of the poem to silence in the "Meridian," when he asks about the meaning of the poem, about writing the poem—and that also means about reading the poem, since he understood that all reading is a rewriting and that every text becomes a palimpsest in being read.[15] There, Celan writes that "the poem shows . . . a strong tendency toward becoming silent," and that it "asserts itself on its own margin" (*GW* 3:197). Living on this margin binding word and silence, language in Celan's work always threatens to close itself off, to become airtight, and thus to seal off its secrets. Calling Celan's poetry "hermetic"—a tag that Celan himself refused[16]—is a way of speaking to the difficulty of language at those margins.[17] But since language, no matter how far flung toward the margins of itself, retains its name by virtue of the prospect of communication, one should not forget that this "hermeticism" is equally a way of naming a refusal or failure of the reader to hear such lapidary language. Yet according to Celan, such margins are not an option in the poem; rather, they are the margins of every poem as language which folds back upon itself. Celan gave these margins, this fold and poetic place, a name: "the meridian." This meridian, this place of the poem, Celan characterizes as a conflicted unity by saying, in a remarkably Heraclitean phrase, that it "rejoins itself by way of both poles."[18] A phrase which also echoes Heidegger's description of the poem as "the point of a spear . . . gathering together the supreme and extreme."[19] Here language bends back upon itself and lives in great tension with itself.

However else we might characterize it, language in the poem is language at the moment of its greatest concentration and density, and whatever else it might be "about," the poem needs to be read as the discourse of language with itself. To make such an assertion, however, is equally to say that all language is poetic in its truth, since, as Novalis put it, "the peculiar property of language [is] that it is solely concerned with itself."[20] It is this fold of language, the moment in which language calls attention to itself as language, which draws a line through language and holds the words of the poem together as a poem. Yet in reading Celan we are continually reminded that the countervalent idiom of silence belongs to the unity of the poem—a unity held together by a the curious necessity at work in the poem that leaves us with the knowledge that none of its words could be otherwise (a necessity dictated so singularly by the idiomatic dimension of language that the poem can only fulfill itself in its own untranslatability). At the summit of its poetic moment, the coherence of the poem is not univocal: "Do not sheer Yes from No" ("Doch scheide das Nein nicht vom Ja") (*GW* 1:135). Thus language in the poem refuses the goal of fluency which so deeply imprints itself upon our everyday relation to language, a relation to language in which language loses courage for itself and instead trails continually after its own uninterrupted reification. Here again, language in the poem is language set apart for the line of the poem, the meridian, and needs to be thought of as its own idiomatic caesura. Language which does not articulate itself—and language is always poorest at such self-articulation—plasters over this divided line defining the poem.

Celan's own syntactic chiasmus, his möbius-strip inversions, tropes, and sharp punctuation breaks, are some of the markers of the divisions along the meridian.

However, according to Celan, the poem should not only be read as a dialogue of language and the counter-rhythms of silence; it is not only this tension of countervalent idioms. For Celan, in these countervalent idioms, "the otherness gives voice to what is most its own: its time" (*GW* 3:199). Thus in order to read the poem we also need to understand that the meridian it articulates intersects another line as well, one which is temporal, and we must understand how it is that "this question also involves the question as to which sense is clockwise" (*GW* 3:186). Consequently, "we can read it in different ways, we can give it a variety of accents: the acute of the present, the grave of history . . . the circumflex . . . of eternity. I give it—*I have no other choice*—I give it an acute accent." (*GW* 3:190 [emphasis added]). Celan has "no other choice"—here he faces a necessity of his language, its own dictation—precisely because he writes in German. It is language itself, not the choice of the poet, which dictates the dates. No language is immunized against the memory of that which it has spoken or of the anticipations it has permitted. Whenever language comes to speak as language, a certain relation to history and culture works itself to the surface in the structures of memory and anticipation belonging to all language. Even if it is always more than the vessel of history and culture, language can never speak without marking its relation to both, as well as to the marginalization in silence which is peculiar to them.

Celan's own struggle with German, his effort to break down and reconfigure all received sedimentations of the language, must be understood as the search for words that have no replication in memory, a memory cut loose from the economy of retribution and revenge, yet one which retains the dignity of the name of memory. For Celan, then, the task is to stretch German beyond itself, to the point from which it can give voice to that which otherwise risks annihilation.[21] Such a project means that Celan's work stands as a forceful argument against Hegel's claim that history takes place in the "temple of *mnemosyne*,"[22] and that in history "the wounds of spirit heal and leave no scars behind."[23] Celan's poetic impulse is driven by the awareness that history is just as much the site of annihilation as of memory, and that the task of memory is to fight the risk that history will finally fall into the dark, silent site of *lethe*. "The poem . . . becomes a conversation—often it is desperate conversation" (*GW* 3:198) between language and silence, memory and forgetfulness.

While the poem "is mindful of and indebted to its dates" (*GW* 3:196), it is not governed by the calendar which it commemorates.[24] The poem is not handed its dates ready-made; rather, it is the original writing and founding of a calendar—as Jacques Derrida puts it, "poetic writing is dating through and through."[25] In this regard, the poet must be read as having a basic role in the political life of those who share a language, as well as in the decisions of history. The full significance of this act of poetic dating—as both shattering and founding at once[26]— is a topic which moves beyond my present concerns to the larger topic of the relation between language, history, and catastrophe. To allude to the direction in which such a topic takes us, however, I would merely indicate that this (re-)writing of calendars is what Benjamin discusses in the fifteenth thesis in "Über den Begriff der Geschichte," where he calls such dating a revolutionary act which "blasts the continuum of history."[27] The deepest call of language in the poem is the call that argues against its own tendency to marginalize and forget silence—the call to give voice to that which is still without voice. This call, heard on the plane of history and the cultural life sustained by a language, is the call to rewrite history, to find the dates marking the edges of silence, and to give voice to history's victims, to those dispossessed of a language. The historical—and that means of course political as well—significance of the poetic imperative, the imperative of all originary poetic experience, is precisely such enlargement and reconfiguration of the reach of language. Answering that call, the poetic imperative becomes a challenge to the polis. Again, one finds that it is Plato who ironized that poetic potential in the gesture of putting the poets in their proper place by exiling them from the polis. Celan knows this and says that "the poem searches for this place" (*GW* 3:199). But for the question at hand, the question of reading Celan by following his remarks on how we are to listen to language in the poem, such a relation of the poem to dates means finally that poetry rewrites itself as "an eternalization of nothing but mortality, and in vain" (*GW* 3:200); that is, as the perpetual call for its own rewriting and historicization. In the end, every poem is marked by the date it bears as well as by the relation between language and silence. As such it is doubly compressed and strained: both by language itself and by time.

Such remarks only hint at the beginning of several difficulties for the reader of Celan's poetry. My intent in what follows here is to draw out some of the specific difficulties that face the reader of Celan, in order to prepare the way for beginning to think through some of the questions they raise about language in his poetry. Most especially, my attention will be drawn to the real presence and pressure of silence in his writing, and to the dilemma of reading what is certainly more than "wordlessness" in his work. As an opening onto the avenue whereby the riddles of Celan's work may be addressed, I would propose a continued reading of the "Meridian" speech read specifically as a reply to Heidegger's reflections on the relation binding language and time.

The curious lack of comment on Celan's work by Heidegger notwithstanding, I believe that there are profound kinships between Heidegger and Celan as readers of language in the poem, and that these kinships—when set next to their equally profound differences (especially with regard to Celan's claim that language is obliged to answer its time)—draw both into a productive dialogue. Furthermore, to understand Celan it seems important to realize that "Heidegger" is a strange and difficult sort of raw material for him, and that Celan was deeply concerned with finding a way through Heidegger to what he spoke of as "a hope, today, / of a coming word, / thinking, / in the heart" ("einer Hoffnung, heute, / auf eines Denkenden / kommendes / Wort / im Herzen") (*GW* 2:255)

More precisely, Celan had a need to find a way to answer to Heidegger's own political engagement with the Nazis. It was a need quite independent of Heidegger's person; rather, it was rooted in what Celan perceived as Heidegger's own relation to the German language—"I see in Heidegger one who has won back the 'limpidity' of language for language"[28]—as well as to Heidegger's understanding of language in the poem. The source of Celan's need in this regard might simply be that he believed that his perceived kinship with Heidegger was on a point which was essentially a direct and unambiguous criticism of the very kind of political engagement about which Heidegger remained stubbornly silent after the war.[29] For Celan, poetry is a deeply political matter and cannot be understood as otherwise—"words are viewed as a means of changing the world, and the protest against its violence and injustice results in a critique of language,"[30] which in turn results in a critique of the world. The meridian is an axis of sharp, double-edged critique.

Read against the backdrop of Celan's persistent preoccupation with both learning from and finding a reply to Heidegger, his own concerns are simultaneously thrown into sharper relief and emerge as giving voice to a powerful rejoinder to Heidegger. This reply may be best understood as a radicalization of Heidegger's reflections on the relation of language and history. In the "Meridian" specifically, I believe that we must hear how it is that Celan is concerned with redefining Heidegger's own effort to give a precise name to the line about which Heidegger himself writes in the essay "Über 'die Linie,'" where he is answering Ernst Jünger's text diagnosing "our" time(s) as marking the date of nihilism.[31] In the choice of title, as well as in its several clear echoes of Heidegger, Celan's text itself stands in a line which clearly passes through the polar opposites of Jünger and Celan. Not just in his prose, however, but also in his poems, Celan's writing is animated by a sense of language which is given a powerful articulation in Heidegger's work. Yet to begin to speak to the ways in which Heidegger sheds light on Celan, one must begin with the extraordinary sensibility which underpins every remark on language in both their works; namely, that "language is grounded in silence. Silence is the most concealed holder of measure."[32]

"Apprends à penser avec douleur"
—Maurice Blanchot

Again, the question begins with silence.

"He speaks truly, who speaks shadows" ("Wahr spricht, wer Schatten spricht") (*GW* 1:135): the difficulty comes in writing and reading silence according to its own idiom, voice, and dialect. It is difficult because "too much of my speaking: / besieges the small / crystal in your share of silence" ("das Zuviel meiner Rede: / angelagert dem kleinen / Kristall in der Tracht deines Schweigens") (*GW* 1:157). The warning here is obvious: talk about silence tends to efface its presence relentlessly; contact with its own concept only hides the fact of its hiding. Silence in Celan's work is not a strategy, but one of the felt pressures of language itself in the poem. It is rather a "fact" which belongs to the life of the language Celan writes. The self-articulation of language in the poem—the effort to bring that "fact" of language forward—is not a matter of another discourse "about" language, it is not gained by further speech, but is always there, already granted. The difficulty comes in listening to it at the point which is always already there. So a certain reversal is requisite if we are to read the poem; reading requires the reenacting of that which always already made writing possible. We are called upon to listen back to the point from which the word becomes necessary and speaks itself in its own apartness, to the point at which the word arrives as a gift.

Even according to Celan's own presentation of the poem in the "Meridian" speech, silence must be heard as exerting its own specific pressure in the poem, and the poem cannot be read apart from this pressure. Even if the specificity of its pressure is difficult to characterize, that pressure is clear and palpable in Celan's own poetry, and is a distinguishing mark of his work. This is what Adorno acknowledged when he claimed that "Celan's poems articulate unspeakable horror by being silent, thus turning their truth content into a negative quality. They emulate a language below the helpless prattle of human beings—even below the level of organic life as such. It is the language of dead matter, of stones and stars. . . . Celan writes poetry without an aura."[33] Disabused of aura, Celan's poetry resists the tendency of language to permit its own reification. In such poetry one finds a language that is almost untranslatable—"Schweigewütiges sternt" (*GW* 3:76) ("a body that rages for silence / stars")—and that speaks from out of a history still in abeyance. A language and time in which even stones and stars speak, so that for the first time they, too, know silence, since only that which has the possibility of speech can be silent. Here "the Medusa's head" (*GW* 3:192) turns the human to stone and finds that it speaks a new language. In large measure, then, Adorno's comment is well-taken: it is a gesture in the direction of the task of hearing the place of silence in Celan's language. Yet Adorno does not go far enough, for in the end, what we need to remember is that silence confesses its presence wordlessly and according to the measure of its own uncanny ubiquity.

This confession of silence is best witnessed in the indissoluble bond of language and the body, in the bond to which Celan refers when he says that the poet speaks "from the angle of his existence, the angle of reflection of his bodily life" (*GW* 3:197). His characterization of the poem as a "turn of breath" has already pointed toward the relation of language and body in the poem, and there should be no surprise in the more extended recognition of this relation. To the extent that we acknowledge that the voice is a kind of body and understand that language in the poem calls for voice,[34] we have begun to approach the real carnality of language in the poem. It is this carnality which bears along the mutually excessive relation of sound and sense in the poem, rendering it a particular "this" which resists being taken up onto the mediating passage and plane of universality defining translation, and which equally resists being taken up as a matter of communication or "meaningful content." This is what Heidegger means as well when he writes that "language sounds and rings and vibrates, it hovers and trembles, [and this] belongs to it in the same measure as does the fact that what is said has a meaning."[35] In the poem, sound and sense each pin the other to itself so radically that neither can be thought apart from the other. The self-insistence of the poem upon its own language arises from this very point. Every poem is to be read as a "way . . . on which language becomes vocal; they are paths upon which language becomes voice . . . paths of physical life, perhaps outlines of an existence, a self-projection upon itself into the search for itself . . . A sort of homecoming" (*GW* 3:201). The poetic experience of language gives us to ourselves in an originary manner.

Yet if the sounding voice is the achievement of language in the body, if this is the bearer of the poetic word and its idiom, then the countervalent idiom, the idiom in which the body robs language of voice—the "mouthfuls of silence"—is best spoken of in terms of the moment in which the body robs us of words, that is, in the moment at which pain interrupts language. The preliminary sense of such an interruption is rather evident: pain not only actively resists expression in words, but when in profound pain we are unable to speak, we lose the capacity to speak at all. In pain, human space is contracted and compressed to the point from which language is no longer possible. In pain, the ipseity of the body and the idiom of the silence meet. Ultimately, this contraction of the human space which happens in pain, the moment at which the body silences language, must be understood as a mime of death. The arrival of pain is a reminder of the basic fact of our facticity and finitude, of the real and present presence of death for us, and of our aloneness before this fact. When Heidegger says that "all that lives is painful"[36] he means that all that lives is en route to its death and must be understood as such. In pain, the body, which is normally unmindful and mute about itself, becomes a reminder of the death it makes possible, and this reminder speaks as the pressure of silence upon language. Pain belongs to the poem just as fully as do voice and breath, and in the silence of pain, as Elaine Scarry puts it, "the edges of the self become coterminous with the edges of the body it will die with."[37] Here, then, the otherwise hidden "essential relation between death and language flashes up."[38] The gift of the word come forward as itself stings. To think that gift, to "undergo an experience of language in the poem,"[39] is to be ready to suffer a certain pain of speech—a pain that, as Nietzsche remarked of the pain of childbirth, "is to be pronounced holy."[40]

In Heidegger's case one worries that his treatment of the relation of pain and language risks mortifying the body by turning it into the mere bearer of a word or even of the idea. This worry even seems to be confirmed when one reads that "every view that tries to represent pain from the perspective of physical sensation remains cut off from the essence of pain."[41] Further, there appears to be a move to encode pain— a move which would need to be addressed in the full effort to think through Heidegger's understanding of the meaning of pain—which allows him to say that "pain, the great soul's basic trait, remains pure harmony with the holiness of blue."[42] One is drawn up abruptly by the sense of the subsequent remark that "the 'infinite torment' is consummate, perfected pain, pain that comes to the fullness of its nature."[43] In order to hear the full force of Heidegger's claims, however, one must understand that he is calling into question our sense of the body as a visible object by virtue of an attempt to rethink the relation of language and the body. In the end, "the sounding of the voice is no longer explained as something merely physiological-physical," and "the mouth is not merely a kind of organ of the body understood as an organism."[44]

A rethinking of the meanings of both pain and body is called for here, one that begins with the recognition that there is something inadequate in Yeats's description of the body, as "this flesh I purchased with my pains."[45] It is true, as Kant citing Epicurus maintained, that pain is "ultimately always of the body,"[46] but it is not true that its meaning is only a matter of the body—especially if we regard the body with any Cartesian sensibilities at all. Pain is always also—maybe this most of all—a matter of the impossibility of the sharing of our own death. Once again, the apartness of the word in the poem refers us to our own final apartness. In the end, then, the presence of silence in the poem, and the countervalent pressure exerted upon language by the body in pain, means that language in the poem is not only a matter of that which we can share, but rather, as bearing the traces of silence, that it is equally the reminder of the final failure to speak about our own apartness. Thus Celan writes that the "poem is alone . . . The one who writes it stays with it" (*GW* 3:198).

The pressure of silence in the poem, the "pain of syllables" ("Die Silbe Schmerz" [*GW* 1:280]), the realization that "pain itself has the word,"[47] is an intimation of the relation of language to death. Poetry, as the discourse of language with itself, always bears traces of this relation; it is always a discourse with death. By virtue of the relation pertaining between language and time and the original dating such a relation enables, this discourse discloses death as a historical event, not simply as an "existential" event. The poem becomes a testimony to the isolation it denies; it becomes the communication of apartness. This is why Heidegger could claim that all poetry is written from the single mood of "mourning": "The spirit which answers to pain, the spirit attuned by and to pain, is mourning."[48] Yet from this perspective Celan's poetry is distinctive in that it is not only written from the point of mourning, but also to it:

> Über aller dieser deiner
> Trauer: kein
> zweiter Himmel.
> > (*GW* 1:222)

> (Over all of this your
> mourning: no
> second heaven.)

Mourning, then, marks the place between the silences:

> schnell
> verblühn die Geräusche
> diesseits und jenseits der Trauer.
> > (*GW* 2:78)

> (quickly
> fade the sounds
> this side and that side of mourning.)

I believe that Celan was drawn to Heidegger because he found in Heidegger a kindred sensibility on precisely this score: the poetic experience of language today commits us to mourning. There is an equally deep affinity between Celan and Heidegger in the awareness that such an experience with language is ultimately a "homage to the majesty of the absurd which bespeaks the presence of human beings" (*GW* 3:190). An abyss opens in the word, a curious abyss that arrives with a reversal: "One who walks on one's head [on one's hands], has the sky as an abyss beneath" (*GW* 3:195). An abyss that Celan implores us to have the courage to witness—"*Come on hands to us*" (*GW* 3:201)—since that abyss is the site at which we gather and meet. In the abyss of the word is the "secret of the encounter" (*GW* 3:198). In those rare moments in which the gift of the word arrives, this abyssal site, the site of our apartness, opens, in the same arrival, the prospect of a sort of communion and the memory of our mortality.

Celan writes as one who has outlived his death for the moment. His work speaks from this deferral, and its language, the pressure of silence, the voice of pain, bears the traces of that deferred death which in being deferred is a double death. Reading with this in mind one knows as well that in such poetry one is the recipient of an extraordinary act of generosity, the generosity of the witness Celan bears. I say that, but do not intend such a remark to eventually return Celan's work to categories which would have us read him as a German-Jewish poet writing "about" the Holocaust—unless, of course, one is willing to say that "there is in the world a Holocaust for every date, and every hour."[49] One need not deny the truth of Celan's life, one certainly should never neglect historical singularity of death in such a lifetime, but one constricts its full force and scope if one regards him only as a poet of the Holocaust. First and foremost Celan's work is always a confrontation with death as a historical event, and as such cannot be fully understood in terms of its own history. It is rather a struggle to speak across the apartness which marks both language in the poem and the meaning of one's death as it is held out in originary poetic experience. Poetry that lives up to its name links what is always apart: "I see no difference in principle between a handshake and a poem" (*GW* 3:177). In the end, Celan's work must also be read as a declaration of hope and love, as bearing witness to our belonging together in our apartness: "Having gone this impossible way, this way of impossibility in your presence, I find something that consoles me a little bit. I find the connective and how the poem leads to encounter" (*GW* 3:202).

To complete the movement just begun, we must say that if language in the poem echoes a truth borne by the body in pain, it must equally be thought of as resonating with the truth of the body in love. The poem oscillates between those poles bent back upon one another, living between silence and song as the achievement of both. In a similar gesture Heidegger write that "[the] more joyful the joy, the purer the mourning slumbering within it. The deeper the mourning, the deeper the call of joy resting within it."[50] Paul Valéry echoes this insight when

he writes quite to the point at hand: "Is it not true that each person
will leave behind a formless mass of perceived fragments, pains broken
against the world, years lived in a minute, unfinished and chilly con-
structions, immense labors embraced in a single glance and dead? But
all these ruins have a certain rose."[51]

125

Of course, to find the connective in our apartness is to name the
secret of the poem as an impasse. It is to say, with Hölderlin, that "language, most dangerous of possessions, is given man . . . so that he might
bear witness to what he is."[52] It is also to say, with Celan, that

Niemand
zeugt für den
Zeugen.
(*GW* 2:72)

(no-one
bears witness for the
witness.)

NOTES

Epigraph: "Die Erste Elegie," in *Die Duineser Elegien*, in *Sämtliche Werke*,
ed. Rilke-Archiv (Frankfort: Insel, 1955–56), 2:685. "For Beauty's nothing / but
beginning of Terror we're still just able to bear, / and why we adore it so is
because it serenely / disdains to destroy us." "The First Elegy," in Rainer Maria
Rilke, *The Duino Elegies*, trans. J. B. Leishman and Stephen Spender (New York:
Norton, 1939), 21.

1. "Zwei / Mundvoll Schweigen" (*GW* 1:167). Throughout, the translations will be my own; however, I have consulted those of Michael Hamburger
and Rosmarie Waldrop, as well as Katherine Washburn and Margret Guillemin.

2. "Phaëton-Segmente," in *Sämtliche Werke*, ed. D. E. Sattler (Frankfort:
Luchterhand, 1984), 9:26. See also Hölderlin's remark that poetry is the "simple
advance of the unthinkable." *Sämtliche Werke*, 5:266.

3. *L'Écriture du désastre* (Paris: Gallimard, 1980), 94. *The Writing of Disaster*,
trans. Ann Smock (Lincoln: University of Nebraska Press, 1986), 57.

4. See, for instance, the second section of "Die Sprache im Gedicht. Eine
Erörterung von Georg Trakls Gedicht," in Martin Heidegger, *Unterwegs zur
Sprache* (Pfullingen: Neske, 1975), 52–76. Henceforth this work will be cited
as *US*.

5. "Phaëton-Segmente," 26.

6. George Steiner speaks eloquently of the problem facing those writing in
German after the Holocaust:

For let us keep one fact clearly in mind: the German language was not innocent of
the horrors of Nazism. It is not merely that a Hitler, a Goebbels, and a Himmler
happened to speak German. Nazism found in the language precisely what it needed
to give voice to its savagery. . . . A language in which one can write a "Horst Wessel
Lied" is ready to give hell a native tongue. (How should the word "spritzen" recover

a sane meaning after having signified to millions the "spurting" of Jewish blood from knife points?)

And that is what happened under the Reich. Not silence or evasion, but an immense outpouring of precise, serviceable words . . . Words were committed to saying things that no human mouth should ever have said and no paper made by man should ever have been inscribed with. . . .

Languages have great reserves of life. . . . But there comes a breaking point.

"The Hollow Miracle," in *Language and Silence* (New York: Penguin, 1967), 140–43.

7. "Le langue des fleurs," in *Oeuvres Complètes*, intro. Michel Foucault (Paris: Gallimard, 1970), 1:176. "The Language of Flowers," trans. Allan Stoekl, in Georges Bataille, *Visions of Excess*, ed. Allan Stoekl (Minneapolis: University of Minnesota Press, 1985), 13.

8. "Lecture de Strette. Essai sur la poésie de Paul Celan," *Critique* 27, no. 288 (1971), 388.

9. This is a point at which one might begin to discuss Celan's language in terms of the sublime. See, for instance, Kant's *Critique of Judgment*, where he remarks that the sublime "only reveals itself aesthetically through sacrifice." *Kritik der Urteilskraft*, ed. Karl Vorländer (Darmstadt: Meiner, 1968), Ak. 271. For an interesting discussion of thinking as sacrifice, a discussion which leads to remarks on language in the poem, see Martin Heidegger, "Nachwort zu: 'Was ist Metaphysik?,'" in *Wegmarken* (Frankfort: Klostermann, 1978), 307–9.

10. Heidegger, "Das Wesen der Sprache," in *US*, 203. Here one finds a special resonance with the first words of Elias Canetti's autobiography:

My earliest memory is dipped in red. I come out of a door . . . , the floor in front of me is red, and to the left a staircase goes down, equally red. . . . A door opens, and a smiling man steps forth, walking toward me in a friendly way. He steps up to me . . . and says: "Show me your tongue." I stick out my tongue, he reaches into his pocket, pulls out a jackknife, opens it, brings the blade all the way to my tongue. He says: "Now we'll cut off his tongue." I don't dare pull back my tongue, he comes closer, the blade will touch me any second. In the last moment, he pulls back the knife, saying: "Not today, tomorrow."

The Tongue Set Free, trans. Joachim Neugroschel (New York: Seabury, 1979), 3.

11. Theodor W. Adorno defines the living relevance of philosophy with much the same sensibility when he begins his *Negative Dialektik* (Frankfort: Suhrkamp, 1977) with the remark that "philosophy, which once seemed to be overcome, remains alive because the moment of its realization was passed by" (15). Likewise, in the epilogue of "Der Ursprung des Kunstwerkes," Heidegger defines the situation of art in terms of its own destination in what Hegel defined as its death. See "Nachwort" to "Der Ursprung des Kunstwerkes," in Martin Heidegger, *Holzwege*, 6th rev. ed. (Frankfort: Klostermann, 1980 [1950]), 65–67.

12. In what follows, I will not address the question of how appropriate it is to speak of "the" body, as if one could not legitimately raise the question of the body only as already a gendered body. I regard the question of writing and sexual difference as a serious question to be asked, and prescind from it here only

because my intention is to unfold the topic of language and body according to the specificity given it by Celan and Heidegger.

13. One regard in which the body extends itself through its relation to language is suggested by Osip Mandelstam, who writes that "the *Inferno* and especially the *Purgatorio* glorify the human gait, the measure and rhythm of walking, the foot and its shape. The step, linked to breathing and saturated with thought: this Dante understands as the beginning of prosody." Quoted in Bruce Chatwin, *Songlines* (New York: Viking, 1987), 230. See also Heidegger, "Das Wort," where he speaks of "step," "call," and "breath" in the poem, ultimately leading him to say that "step . . . and call and breath hover around the rule of the word" (*US* 235).

14. "Aus einem Gespräch von der Sprache," in *US*, 74.

15. This is a point which is basic to what I hope to say, yet one which I will assume rather than belabor.

16. See Katherine Washburn's introduction to her translation of Celan, where she cites Celan's inscription (presented to Michael Hamburger), stating that he was "ganz und gar nicht hermetisch." "Introduction," in *LP*, vi.

17. See, for instance, Hans-Georg Gadamer, "Celans Schlußgedicht," in *Argumentum e silentio*, ed. Amy D. Colin (Berlin: de Gruyter, 187), 60. For a detailed reading of Celan's "Atemkristall," see Hans-Georg Gadamer, *Wer bin Ich und wer bist Du?* (Frankfort: Suhrkamp, 1976). There are many remarks in this reading which would be worth careful attention: in particular, see the comments on "readiness for death" in the poem (17) and those on the "wound" and "pain" of reading (78).

18. *GW* 3:202. Cf., e.g., Heraclitus, fragment 51: "How a thing agrees at variance with itself; it is an attunement turning back on itself." *Die Fragmente der Vorsokratiker,* trans. Hermann Diels, ed. Walther Kranz, 5th ed. (Berlin: Weidmann, 1934), 1:162.

19. "Die Sprache im Gedicht," 37.

20. Quoted in Heidegger, "Der Weg zur Sprache," in *US*, 241. Novalis, "Monolog," in *Schriften*, Die Werke Friedrich von Hardenbergs, ed. Paul Kluckhorn and Richard Samuel (Stuttgart: Kolhammer, 1960), vol. 2, Das Philosophische Werk I, ed. Richard Samuel, 672.

21. Such stretching of language beyond itself is equally the effort of the translator. Celan's work as translator should not be neglected, but rather regarded as a practice belonging to his poetic practice. For a discussion of the intersection of poetry and translation, see Dennis J. Schmidt, "Hermeneutics and the Poetic Motion," *Translation Perspectives* 5 (1990), 5–18.

22. *Vorlesungen über die Philosophie der Geschichte*, Part 1, Theorie Werkausgabe, ed. Eva Moldenhauer and Karl Markus Michel (Frankfort: Suhrkamp, 1970), 18:12.

23. *Phänomenologie des Geistes* (Hamburg: Meiner, 1952), 470.

24. Here one could compare Freud's comment that all works of art bear a "date-stamp" as the enduring trace of memory in all poetic practice and as raising the question of the repetition at work in all art. Sigmund Freud, "The Relation of the Poet to Daydreaming," in *Collected Papers* (New York: Basic Books, 1977), 4:177.

25. *Schibboleth pour Paul Celan* (Paris: Galilée, 1986), 87.

26. Cf., for instance, Gianni Vattimo, "The Shattering of the Poetic Word," in *The End of Modernity* (Cambridge: Polity Press, 1988), 65–78.

27. *Gesammelte Schriften*, ed. Rolf Tiedemann and Helmut Schweppenhäuser (Frankfort: Suhrkamp, 1980), 1(2):701. "Theses on the Philosophy of History," in Walter Benjamin, *Illuminations*, ed. and intro. Hannah Arendt, trans. Harry Zohn (New York: Schocken, 1969), 261. See also Dennis J. Schmidt, "Heidegger and the Greeks: History and Catastrophe," in *Heidegger Toward the Turn: Essays on Texts of the 1930s*, ed. James Risser (Albany: State University of New York Press, 1993).

28. Cited in Otto Pöggeler, *Spur des Worts. Zur Lyrik Paul Celans* (Freiburg: Alber, 1986), 250. For discussions of the two meetings between Celan and Heidegger, see 259–71. See also Gerhard Neumann, *Erinnerung an Paul Celan* (Frankfort: Suhrkamp, 1986), 65–70.

29. Others who felt an equally deep kinship also must be read as having dedicated themselves to interrogating the possibilities of political and historical life after Heidegger. I refer especially to Hannah Arendt and Emmanuel Lévinas, and, to a lesser extent, Hans-Georg Gadamer, each of whom pursued such political concerns long before the present furor released by the publication of Victor Farias's researches. Much of the recent "breast beatings" and "eye openings" that have dominated political questioning by those working in Heidegger's wake work more to close the possibility of political questioning than to pursue its possibilities. I am suggesting that Celan numbers among those to whom we might turn in pursuit of such possibilities.

30. Amy D. Colin, "Celan's Poetics of Destruction," in *Argumentum e silentio*, 167.

31. The genealogy of these texts is worth noting: Jünger's text, itself an answer to Nietzsche, was written for the occasion of Heidegger's birthday. See "Über die Linie," in Ernst Jünger, *Sämtliche Werke* (Stuttgart: Klett-Cotta, 1980), 7:239–80. Heidegger's text was retitled and published as "Zur Seinsfrage," in *Wegmarken*, 379–419. Also relevant is Jünger's "Über den Schmerz," in *Sämtliche Werke*, 7:145–91.

32. Martin Heidegger, *Beiträge zur Philosophie (Vom Ereignis)* (Frankfort: Klostermann, 1989), 510. The full sense of silence in Celan, however, is related to many other specific concerns not present in Heidegger. See, for instance, Shira Wolosky, "Mystical Language and Mystical Silence in Paul Celan's 'Dein Hinübersein,'" in *Argumentum e silentio*, 364–74.

Epigraph: *L'Écriture du désastre*, 219. *The Writing of Disaster*, 145.

33. *Ästhetische Theorie* (Frankfort: Suhrkamp, 1981 [1970]), 477. Theodor W. Adorno, *Aesthetic Theory*, trans. Christopher Lenhart (London: Routledge & Kegan Paul, 1984), 444.

34. One knows this simply in knowing that a poem cannot be read silently, but must be sounded by some voice, even a soundless one. This relation of voice and body is also felt as the curious alienation from one's own voice when one is speaking a "foreign" language. Nowhere else is the alien element of another language felt as palpably as in the voice of the speaker.

35. "Das Wesen der Sprache," 205.

36. "Die Sprache im Gedicht," 62.

37. *The Body in Pain* (London: Oxford University Press, 1985), 33. One of

the many interesting aspects of the reflections on the relation of language and
pain in Scarry's study is the one in which a torturer is described as "a colossal
voice" and the victim of torture as "a colossal body" (57). These remarks lead
to further insight about the relation of voice and power.

38. Heidegger, "Das Wesen der Sprache," 215. This is the point from
which one can understand the full significance of Heidegger's remark that "anxiety robs us of words." "Was ist Metaphysik?," 111.

39. "Das Wesen der Sprache," 159.

40. *Götzen-Dämmerung*, in *Werke*, ed. Karl Schlechta (Frankfort: Ullstein,
1976), 3:477.

41. "Die Sprache im Gedicht," 62.

42. Ibid., 64. The discussion of "blue" in this text on Trakl needs to be
called into question. Here it would be helpful to refer to Gottfried Benn's remarks on "blue" in the essay "Probleme der Lyrik." See *Gesammelte Werke in
vier Bänden*, ed. Dieter Wellershoff (Stuttgart: Klett-Cotta, 1977), 1:504 and
512. One of the curious features of both Heidegger's and Benn's very curious
remarks on "blue" is that at some point both give lists of colors and then proceed to attach "meanings" to these colors; both include blue on their lists; and
both omit only blue from the subsequent list of determinate meanings. See "Die
Sprache im Gedicht," 74–75; and "Probleme der Lyrik," 504. I am indebted to
Werner Hamacher for the reference to Benn. See his unpublished essay "Political Blue."

43. "Die Sprache im Gedicht," 72.

44. "Das Wesen der Sprache, 208 and 205.

45. "The Mother of God," in William Butler Yeats, *Collected Poems* (New
York: Macmillan, 1979), 244.

46. *Kritik der Urteilskraft*, Ak. 277.

47. Heidegger, "Die Sprache im Gedicht," 63.

48. "Das Wort," in *Unterwegs zur Sprache*, 235. Cf. Martin Heidegger,
Hölderlins Hymnen "Germanien" und "Der Rhein" (Frankfort: Klostermann,
1980), 87.

49. Derrida, *Schibboleth*, 83.

50. Heidegger, "Das Wort," 235.

51. *Cahiers* (Paris: Gallimard [Pléiade], 1973), 1:1126. Quoted from Jean
Starobinski, "Monsieur Teste Confronting Pain," in *Fragments for a History of
the Human Body*, ed. Michel Feher (Cambridge: MIT Press, 1989), 2:371.

52. "In the Forest," in Friedrich Hölderlin, *Hymns and Fragments*, trans.
Richard Sieburth (Princeton: Princeton University Press, 1984), 226. Friedrich
Hölderlin, "Im Walde," in *Sämtliche Werke*, ed. Friedrich Beißner (Stuttgart:
Kolhammer, 1951), 2(1):325.

3

Catastrophe

Philippe Lacoue-Labarthe
Translated by Andrea Tarnowski

"Tübingen, January": the Patriarchs' beard of light, the stammering. Might it not be, asks A. R., an allusion to Moses?[1]

Not for a moment had I thought of this. But rereading pages devoted as if despite themselves to the oedipal motif of blinding, as I had to today, I became aware that they may indeed secretly have only one object: the interdiction against representation—or rather, they are haunted solely by: the unfigurable or unpresentable. In the end they are subjugated, more or less unknowingly, by the type of metaphor (or image) destruction that seems to attract Celan's poetry as its last requirement. "Tübingen, January" literally shatters an image (the reflection); "Todtnauberg," a poem about the disappointment of poetry, no longer contains any image, unless it is—this should be checked, supposing it could be—the "starred die," the "Sternwürfel" of the third stanza. The extenuation, one might say, of the tropic.

The "Meridian," appropriately, provides some explanation of this.

Appropriately: the title itself, or more precisely, the word, when it makes its appearance in the course of the speech, does not do so without crossing or intersecting, without "encountering" a certain *Witz* on tropes and (the) tropics. On the plural of "Trope": "Tropen." Virtually the last words are: "Ladies and gentlemen, I find something which offers me some consolation for having traveled the impossible path, this path of the impossible, in your presence. / I find something which binds and which, like the poem, leads to an encounter. / I find something, like language, abstract, yet earthly, terrestrial, something circular, which traverses both poles and returns to itself, thereby—I am happy to report—even crossing the tropics and tropes. I find . . . a *meridian*."[2]

The "tropic," then. On the "dialogue" that is the poem, a dialogue with beings but also with things, we can read:

When we speak with things in this manner we always find ourselves faced with the question of their whence and whither: a question which "remains open" and "does not come to an end," which points into openness, emptiness, freedom—we are outside, at a considerable distance.

The poem, I believe, also seeks this place.

The poem?

The poem with its images and tropes?

Ladies and gentlemen, what am I really speaking of, when, from *this* direction, in *this* direction, with *these* words, I speak of the poem—no, of *the* poem?

I am speaking of the poem which does not exist!

The absolute poem—no, it does not exist, it cannot exist.

But each real poem, even the least pretentious, contains this inescapable question, this incredible demand.

And what, then, would the images be?

That which is perceived and to be perceived one time, one time over and over again, and only now and only here. And the poem would then be the place where all tropes and metaphors are developed *ad absurdum*. (199/37–38/78–79)

How should we understand this?

To even begin to see our way clear, we must consider things from a greater distance.

———

The poem, Celan had said earlier—this is my point of departure—the poem is alone: "Das Gedicht ist einsam" (198/87/78). "Alone" is a word which says singularity—or at least, it makes no sense here but in reference to singularity, to the singular experience. "The poem is alone" means: a poem is only *effectively* a poem insofar as it is absolutely singular. This is undoubtedly a definition of poetry's essence (that which, by itself, is decidedly nothing "poetic"): there is no poetry, poetry does not occur or take place, and is therefore not repeatedly questioned, except as the event of singularity.

In a way, it is the effort to say this singularity, or at least designate it, that underlies the whole "Meridian" speech—and is ever ready to break through. Aligned to this effort, as dictated by circumstances,[3] is the debate or discussion, the *Auseinandersetzung* with Büchner.

The locus of the discussion is the question of art. More precisely: the question of art in relation to poetry. Jean Launay circumscribes the issue in these terms:

Art is strange to poetry—that is, at first, at the time to which the poet's mood always returns when he despairs, or hopes too much. And then: art is the strange for poetry. And thus, art is fascinating for poetry. It indicates the possibility of spectacle; it indicates a window; it invites one to jump. This is also why, in art, there is always the hum of a country fair, the drumroll preceding an artist's performance, that is, always more or less the "death-defying leap" which, barring a foolish accident, always ends well. The artist lands on his feet. That is what makes him an artist.[4]

This is certainly not incorrect, in any case from the point of view of "theme," as Launay says when justifying comparisons of Celan with Kafka and Egon Friedell.[5] But one sees that it is also a complete response, already organized: the question Celan bears with him and tries to articulate, literally out of breath, no longer resonates. Thus Launay does not entirely do justice to the way Celan proceeds, to the road followed, to the difficult (if not completely "impossible") journey; nor to Celan's precise but complex strategy vis-à-vis Büchner. And above all, *dialectically* re-treating the opposition between art and poetry, reducing the strange to the fascinating by mediation of a "for" and appropriating it as such (art is *the* strange for poetry), takes into account neither singularity itself, nor poetry as Celan desperately seeks to understand it.

What does the "Meridian" actually say?

Not, exactly, that art is strange to poetry, but that yes, poetry is the interruption of art. Something, if you will, that "takes art's breath away" (I am thinking of the motif of *Atemwende*, of the turn-of-breath,[6] which makes its first appearance in Celan here). Or, to recall another of Celan's words, the "step" (*Schritt*) outside art; in French one could say, following Derrida's reading of Blanchot closely, *le pas—d'art* or *le pas—"de l'art."*[7] The event of poetry (and as such, poetry is event, and there *is* poetry) is thus a "setting free," a "Freisetzung" (194/34/75). It is a liberation, not in the sense—common in German—of dismissal, but in the sense of deliverance. And, as we shall see, of a free act. This is perhaps, in a phrase I leave to its own ambiguity, art liberation. And very probably, a certain kind of "end of art."

But the idea that poetry occurs in this manner, when art gives in, and that the poem is said to be "itself" when it is "art-less" or "artfree" (196/35/76), does not mean merely that for poetry, art is a form of supervision or oppression. Nor even that art is, strictly speaking, the alienation of poetry. Certainly, art is "strange" ("fremd"). One can thus call it "other," but Celan prefers to say that it is elsewhere or that it is distant, that it is *the* distant and *the* elsewhere (195/35/75). Yet in reality, art is only so because it is first uncanny, *unheimlich*: strangely familiar, or, in other words, disorienting, unusual, disquieting. Art is even the Disquieting, as such: *das Unheimliche*. Its strangeness or alterity is thus not a pure alterity. Nor is it a "determinate" alterity in the sense that Hegel speaks of "determinate negation." In relation to a "same" or to a "self," to a "near" or to an "own,"[8] art exists in a strangeness which is itself strange, another alterity. The difference it makes differs from itself; it is unassignable. For this reason it is disquieting rather than "fascinating." It could not be fascinating unless it occupied its own place, exercised attraction in a particular direction. But that is just the point: art has no place of its own. Indeed, it is nothing one can call art proper or properly itself. Without a stable identity, everywhere present but always elsewhere (Celan says that "it possesses, aside from its ability to transform, the gift of ubiquity" [190/31/71]), it is not "the strange for poetry." This is moreover why, if the task or destination of poetry is to liberate itself from art, this task or destination is nearly impossible. With art, one is never done.

It is clear that Celan's discourse on art has to do with mimesis. This should at least be noted. So should the choice of *unheimlich* (or its equivalent: *ungeheuer*), the word used by Hölderlin, then Heidegger, to translate the Greek *deinos*, with which Sophocles names the essence of *techne* in *Antigone*. For Heidegger, art and the work of art are equally *unheimlich*. Celan was no doubt fully aware of this—one respect (though certainly not the only one) in which the "Meridian" is a response to Heidegger. Yet I think it would be more enlightening for a reading of the speech (and for the question I am asking) to focus on art in the—explicit—debate with Büchner.

Thus defined as *unheimlich*, art is indeed, initially, art as Büchner understands it, or rather as he contests it: artifice and the artificial. It is the marionette or puppet Camille Desmoulins denounces in *Der Tod des Dantons*: "you can see the rope hanging down that jerks it, and . . . the joints creak in five-footed iambics at every step"; it is the monkey of *Woyzeck*, dressed in coat and trousers, or the robots in *Leonce und Lena*, announced "in a pompous tone" as "Nothing but art and mechanism, nothing but cardboard and watch springs" (188/30/69). In this sense, Launay is right to evoke barkers, circuses, and fairs. But with literature and poetry, with *Dichtung*, which is Büchner's business, art is really also eloquence; we again find it here, but this time as bombast and turgidity, grandiloquence with its inevitable effects of *déjà-entendu* and a repetitive, wearisome aspect. Art, says Celan, is an old problem ("hardy, long-lived . . . that is to say, eternal"), a "problem which allows a mortal, Camille, and a person who can be understood only in the context of his death, Danton, to string words together at great length. It is easy enough to talk about art" (188/30/69).

Yet this kind of determination is not enough; it assigns art too easily, appropriates the *Unheimliche* too rapidly (and in an entirely classical mode, with marionettes, robots, and artificial bombast). This is why for Celan, art remains what Büchner opposes to this notion of art, namely—according to that most ancient, indestructible model—the natural: Creation, as Camille says in his great speech on art ("They [the people] forget God himself, they prefer his bad imitators").[9] So art is simply nature once one takes pains to imitate it. That is, once nature presents a spectacle, enters the realm of representation—in short, when it aligns itself with art. Thus the *tableau* of the two girls in the valley that Lenz evokes when he speaks of art and defines his (or rather Büchner's) poetics: "At times one would like to be the Medusa's head so as to be able to transform such a group into stone, and call out to the people so that they might see" (191–92/32/69). Celan comments on these lines in the following terms: "Ladies and gentlemen, please take note: 'One would like to be the Medusa's head,' in order to comprehend that which is natural as that which is natural, by means of art!" (192/ 32/72). And he adds, a little further on, "as you can see, whenever art makes an appearance . . . [the] pompous tone cannot be ignored" (192/33/73).

Behind Büchner's Lenz stands Büchner himself. But behind Büchner, there is the historical (literary historical) Lenz, "Reinhold Lenz, the author of the 'Notes on the Theater.'" Behind him, in turn, the Abbé Mercier, with his phrase "Elargissez l'art." That this was naturalism's *mot d'ordre*, that it contains "the social and political roots of Büchner's thought" (191/32/71), is here without any real importance. But in its most general sense, wrenched from historical inscription and context, *Elargissez l'art* tells the very secret of art; it indicates art's movement—and the obscure will presiding over this movement, or animating it from within. Art wants to expand itself; it clamors to be expanded. It wants its difference from the things and beings of nature effaced. In a way, that which is art's own, "proper" to art (to the *Unheimliche*), is the tendency to mitigate differentiation, and in so doing invade and contaminate everything. Or mediate everything, according to Lenz-Büchner's dialectical formulation (nature is only nature by means of art). Thus, to "dis-own" everything. Art is, if the word can be risked, generalized "estrangement"—the Medusa's head, the robots, the speeches—without end.

When he brings up this theme, Celan well knows that he is echoing very ancient rumors about art. So ancient, that they precede even the philosophical (Platonic) designation of mimesis, and its execution or appropriation as representation, reproduction, semblance, or simulation. As imitation. And Celan not only acts as an echo—he says he "listens to the noise persistently" (192/33/73), but seems to lend it a favorable ear, bringing back, along with the rumors, the old fear and the old condemnation of the mimetic (which very well can be, and has been, conjoined with the interdiction against representation). All Heidegger's force is needed—and even that may not suffice—to dissipate the evil aura of the *Unheimliche*, to lift the harmful and demonic to the level of the *daemonic*.[10] Not simply to succumb and oppose it—in the end, dialectically—to the *Heimische-Heimliche*, the *Zuhause*, even the *Heimkehr*, to all the figures and values of the own, the familiar, the "at home," the native land, etc.—the way Celan seems to do when, near the end of the "Meridian," he marks the close of the poetic journey as "Eine Art Heimkehr," "A kind of homecoming."[11]

And it is true that for poetry, what Celan opposes or seems to oppose to the *Unheimliche*, to art (at least "at first," as Launay would say) is, under various names, the own—the own-being: the "self" or "I," even the "he" of singularity (he, Lenz, Lenz himself, and not "Büchner's Lenz"), the "person" Celan also curiously calls the "figure" ("Gestalt") (194/34/74). Or, using a word which, though borrowed from Büchner, does not lack religious resonance, the "creature" (197/36/77). Nevertheless, despite appearances, what is at issue is not simply the subject in the metaphysical sense of the term. One word condenses all these names: the human, *das Menschliche*. The human, not man. And not the humanity of man. But the human as that which allows there to be one man or another—*that* man there, singular—in the here and now, says Celan. The human, then, as the singular essence (a pure oxymoron, philosophically untenable), the singularity of man or of being-man. It is Camille in *The Death of Danton*, as he is perceived by Lucile when he discourses on art and she does not listen to what he says, but hears him, him particularly, for "language is something personal, something perceptible" (189/31/70). Or rather, we suspect, it is Lucile herself, "the one who is blind to art" (189/31/70) but who still "perceives" (I will return to this word).

The *Unheimliche*, estrangement, is estrangement of the human taken in this sense. It affects existence, undoes its reality. The *Unheimliche*, despite what Celan's formulations imply, does not open up an *other* domain. It takes us "outside the human" (192/32/72), but opens up a domain "turned toward that which is human." Existence itself, but "made strange": "the human feels out of place [*unheimlich*]" (192/32/72). Life in art or in light of art, life in the preoccupation with art—even more simply, life benumbed and carried off by art, what I would call life in mimesis or representation, is the life in which *one* "forgets oneself" (193/33/73). The result is that Lenz gets lost in his speeches (on literature), that Camille and Danton "spout grand phrases" all the way to the scaffold. And that the Revolution is theater. Again, the motif of eloquence. And dramatization.

But in reality, eloquence precedes dramatization and provides a reason for it: theater and theatricalized existence only *are* because there is discourse. Or rather, *discoursing*. This means that the *Unheimliche* is essentially a matter of language. Or that language is the locus of the *Unheimliche*, if indeed such a locus exists. In other words, language is what "estranges" the human. Not because it is the loss or forgetting of the singular, as by definition language embraces generality (this is a frequent refrain, and an old motif derived from the so-called philosophies of existence); but because to speak, let oneself be caught up and swept away by speech, to trust language, or even, perhaps, be content to borrow it or submit to it, is to "forget oneself." Language *is* not the *Unheimliche*, though only language contains the possibility of the *Unheimliche*. But the *Unheimliche* appears, or rather, sets in (and no doubt it is always there, already there)—something turns in man and displaces the human, something in man even overturns,[12] perhaps, or turns around, expulsing him from the human—along with a certain posture in language: the "artistic" posture, if you will, or the mimetic. That is, the most "natural" posture in language, as long as one thinks or pre-understands language as a mimeme. In the infinite series of cross purposes of the "artistic" and the "natural," and the misprision of language, the *Unheimliche* is, finally, forgetfulness: forgetting who speaks when I speak, which clearly goes together with forgetting to whom I speak when I speak and who listens when I am spoken to. And, always brought about by these, forgetting what is spoken of.

Indicated here in the motif of forgetfulness and turnaround (reversal) is that the *Unheimliche*, because of language, is the catastrophe of the human.[13] And this is what explains that poetry—that which Celan calls poetry or tries to save with the name of poetry, removing and preserving it from art—is, "every time," the interruption of language: Lucile's absurd "Long live the King!" (189/31/70) cried out in despair over Camille's death, and above all Lenz's "terrible silence" (193/35/76), the silence that fragments Büchner's narrative, stops it (and stops art, including naturalism), but which already enigmatically signaled its presence in a phrase (without grandiloquence) that says the catastrophe's most secret essence: "now and then he experienced a sense of uneasiness because he was not able to walk on his head" (195/34/75).

The interruption of language, the suspension of language, the caesura ("counter-rythmic rupture," said Hölderlin)[14]—that is poetry, then: "[robbed] . . . of breath and speech," the "turn" of breath, the "turn at the end of inspiration" (195/33/76). Poetry occurs where language, contrary to all expectations, gives way. Precisely at inspiration's failing—and this can be understood in at least two senses; or, even more precisely, at retained expiration, the holding of breath: when speaking (discoursing) is about to continue, and *someone*, suddenly free, forbids what was to be said. When a word occurs in the pure suspension of speech. Poetry is the spasm or syncope of language.[15] Hölderlin called the caesura "the pure word."[16]

It would seem, then, that poetry is appropriation: of speech, and, indissociably, of the human? Yes, in a sense. And this would mean that poetry is properly speech, as speech attests to the "presence of the human"? Yes, again, this is indeed what Celan says when he comments on Lucile's "Long live the King!," which he calls—not without philosophical and political risk—a "counter-word" ("Gegenwort"):

After all the words spoken on the platform (the scaffold)—what a word!

It is a counter-word, a word that severs the "wire," that refuses to bow before the "loiterers and parade horses of history." It is an act of freedom. It is a step.

To be sure, it sounds like an expression of allegiance to the *ancien régime*—and that might not be a coincidence, in view of what I am venturing to say about the subject now, today. But these words—please allow one who also grew up with the writings of Peter Kropotkin and Gustav Landauer expressly to emphasize the point—these words are not a celebration of the monarchy and a past which should be preserved.

They are a tribute to the majesty of the absurd, which bears witness to mankind's here and now.

That, ladies and gentlemen, has no universally recognized name, but it is, I believe . . . poetry. (189–90/31/70)

One should not hurry—let us use Celan's own political clarification as a model—to stress the philosophical overdetermination of these remarks, which is in any case undeniable. It would be, I think, to fail them. It would almost be to commit them an injustice.

What Celan calls Lucile's "counter-word" does not properly oppose anything, not even the speeches delivered beforehand (Camille and Danton's "grand phrases" at the foot of the scaffold). Not even discourse in general. The counter-word approves nothing either: it says nothing in favor of the monarchy, is not a political word—nor even an anarchic one. It is "absurd"; it does not mean anything. But this does not make it "neutral," or if so we would have to agree on the meaning of the term. It is a gesture. It is only a *counter*-word insofar as it is such a gesture and follows, as Büchner says, from a "decision": the gesture or decision to die. By shouting "Long live the King!" Lucile simply kills herself. Here, the word is suicidal; it is, as Hölderlin said of Greek tragic speech, "deadly-factual, for the body which it seizes truly kills."[17] As pure provocation, it signifies (the decision to die), but in a mode other than signification. It signifies without signifying: it is an act, an event (though I would hesitate somewhat to use the word "performative").

Here is the scene:

A PATROL enters.
A CITIZEN. Who's there?
LUCILE. Long live the King!
CITIZEN. In the name of the Republic.
She is surrounded by the WATCH and led away.[18]

If Lucile's cry—poetry—properly says what is proper to the human, we must understand the proper here as being like the own of "own death." In the counter-word, or rather through the "counter" of the counter-word, the possibility of death "resolutely" opens up, and indeed, something like what Heidegger calls, with respect to *Dasein*, its "ownmost possibility." And from there on exist—these are Celan's words—"fate" and "direction" (188/30/69). That is, liberty. Exactly like the sky opening "as an abyss" beneath Lenz.

Poetry, then, *in effect* says existence: the human. It says existence, not because it takes the opposing course to discourse or because it upsets the *unheimlich* turnaround, the catastrophe of language (the catastrophe that is language); poetry is in no way a catastrophe of catastrophe; but, because it aggravates the catastrophe itself, it is, one might say, its *literalization*.[19] This is what the "figure" of Lenz signifies: existence suddenly "released" at the height of catastrophe, the "mortal's" sudden revelation of himself as the one whose existence rests on the abyss—the bottomlessness—of the heavens.

This is why poetry does not take place outside art, in some elsewhere supposed to be the other of art or of its strangeness. It takes place in the "strange place" itself. And if Celan says of this place that it is "the place where a person [succeeds] in setting himself free, as an—estranged—I" (195/34/75), we must not lose sight of the fact, whatever the dialectical cast of such a remark (very close, as it happens, to Hölderlinian formulations), that the I which thus releases and frees itself, which "comes home," which perhaps even hopes to have reached the "occupiable realm,"[20] this I is in the vicinity of death, silence, and insanity: it falls, it frees itself in the void. If there is appropriation, it is, as in Hölderlin, abysmal. One could almost say that it does not take place as such—and the poetry does not occur unless it is by default, as the *pas—d'art* in art's greatest intimacy, in the very difference of art from itself or in the strangeness to self of strangeness: at the unassignable heart of the *Unheimliche*.

This explains why Büchner—the poet, not the poetician—can occasion, can even be the opportunity—obviously paradoxical—of attempting to say the essence of poetry, and thus calling art into question:

> And I must now ask if the works of Georg Büchner, the poet of all living beings, do not contain a perhaps muted, perhaps only half conscious, but on that account no less radical—or for precisely that reason in the most basic sense a radical—calling-into-question of art ... ? A calling-into-question, to which all contemporary poetry must return if it is to continue posing questions? To rephrase and anticipate myself somewhat: may we proceed from art as something given, something to be taken for granted, as is now often done; should we, in concrete terms, above all—let us say—follow Mallarmé to his logical conclusion? (192–93/30/73)

And this also explains, but in reverse, why Celan, before that which is "so difficult" (200/38/80)—not to say impossible—to distinguish (in the last pages he speaks of the "impossible path," the "path of the impossible"), is forced to use a double language. Now, the language of simple opposition, which is—though ironically—the language of hope (poetry is understood to free art, be the end of art):

> Perhaps . . . perhaps poetry, in the company of the I which has forgotten itself, travels the same path as art, toward that which is mysterious [*unheimlich*] and alien [*fremd*]. And once again—but where? but in what place? but how? but as what?—it sets itself free?
>
> In that case art would be the path travelled by poetry—nothing more and nothing less. (193–94/33–34/74)

Now, in the midst of difficulty, of the impossible: the language of difference, which is not—ironically—the language of despair (poetry is understood as the liberation of art, art goes on endlessly):

> Poetry: that can signify a turn-of-breath. Who knows, perhaps poetry travels its path—which is also the path of art—for the sake of such a breath turning? Perhaps it succeeds, since strangeness [*das Fremde*], that is, the abyss *and* the Medusa's head, the abyss *and* the robots, seem to lie in the same direction—perhaps it succeeds here in distinguishing between strangeness and strangeness, perhaps at precisely this point the Medusa's head shrivels, perhaps the robots cease to function—for this unique, fleeting moment? Is perhaps at this point, along with the I—with the estranged I, set free *at this point* and *in a similar manner*—is perhaps at this point an Other set free?
>
> Perhaps the poem assumes its own identity as a result . . . and is accordingly able to travel other paths, that is, the paths of art, again and again—in this art-less, art-free manner?
>
> Perhaps. (195–96/35/76)

Or yet, and this time in the most demanding, that is to say, the most desperate fashion possible (but always with suitable irony):

> Ladies and gentlemen, I have reached the conclusion—I have returned to the beginning.
>
> *Elargissez l'Art!* This question comes to us with its mysteries [*Unheimlichkeit*], new and old. I approached Büchner in its company—I believed I would once again find it there.
>
> I also had an answer ready, a "Lucilean" counter-word; I wanted to establish something in opposition, I wanted to be there with my contradiction.

Expand art?

No. But accompany art into your own unique place of no escape. And set yourself free.

Here, too, in your presence, I have travelled this path. It was a circle.

Art—and one must also include the Medusa's head, mechanization, robots; the mysterious, indistinguishable, and in the end perhaps the only strangeness [nur *eine* Fremde]—art lives on. (200/38/79–80)

If the difference can ever be made, if there exists the slightest possibility of a separation of poetry, then we must think this difference and this separation as internal to art itself. It would be inside art that poetry would succeed—perhaps—in withdrawing from art; it would exit art within art. We must thus think, in art's greatest intimacy and as this intimacy itself, a sort of spacing or hiatus. A secret gaping. Perhaps the intimacy—the "heart" of the same—is, as the possibility for the same to be itself and to join within itself to itself, always such a gaping, the pure—empty—articulation of the same. And perhaps, as concerns art (the *Unheimliche*), this intimate gaping would be precisely what ceaselessly "estranges" the strangeness of art (of the strange): precisely the caesura of art, the spasm—furtive, hardly felt—of the strange. In which case poetry would not be, in art-outside-art, the flaw or failing of art, of language: let us say, silence. But rather the pain of art (of language). Hence the aggravation of the catastrophe, which is, strictly speaking, a revolt (Lucile, Lenz).

This is why poetry, if it ever occurs, occurs as the brutal revelation of the abyss which contains art (language) and constitutes it, after all, as such, in its strangeness. Poetry takes place, can take place, in art. But this place is not any place. The place of poetry, the place where poetry takes place, every time, is the place without place of the intimate gaping—something that must certainly be thought as the pure spacing which places (do not) sup-pose and which upholds them, with no hold.

No doubt this is what Celan rigorously calls u-topia:

Topos study?

Certainly! But in light of that which is to be studied: in light of u-topia.

And human beings? And all living creatures?

In this light. (199/38/79)

Poetry, by this account, can be called the abyss of art (language): it makes art (language) abysmal. In all senses. This mode of occurrence, advent, is "proper" to it.

But it does not occur, if ever it does occur, as Poetry, even if, afterward, it can be (with difficulty) recognized as such. "The absolute poem—no, it does not exist, it cannot exist" (199/38/79). It occurs, then, every time, in the time or betweentime of the caesura, in a syncope, as *a* poem, that is to say as a word—singular, unique. It occurs in "this unique, fleeting moment" (196/35/76), in the "instant" (*Augenblick*), the wink of an eye or the head's inclination (Celan speaks of "the angle of inclination of . . . existence" [197/36/77]), in the blink of "release," of the "free act": in the instant of the catastrophe, the revolt—the conversion of the I which opens to existence and allows the human to take "place" within it.

Every time, this instant makes a date—it is date-making. The poem keeps date memories:

> Perhaps one can say that every poem has its "20th of January"? Perhaps the novelty of poems that are written today is to be found in precisely this point: that here the attempt is most clearly made to remain mindful of such dates?
>
> But are we all not descended from such dates? And to which dates do we attribute ourselves? (196/35/76)

In a way which differs altogether from the standard expression, and thus in its strongest sense, poetry is *occasional poetry*.[21] It is on this account that it keeps, if you will, a dates register, or that it is the search, poem after poem, for the dates an I can ascribe to itself (Celan plays on *schreiben*, "to write," and *zuschreiben*, whose primary meaning is "to note on an account"). It is thus the memory of events, that is, every time, of the singular, though certainly not unique, advent into existence. Yet this memory is not pure. Likewise, it is probable that there are neither pure events nor pure advents: they are numerous, repeatable, already brought in by language. Thus the singular, unique word is, precisely, not unique: the *poem* is always already carried away in the *poems*, which is to say in the infinite approximation of existence that is art, and language. Whatever task or absolute vocation it assigns or accords itself as regards existence (the human), poetry is language. It speaks: "But the poem," says Celan, "does speak! It remains mindful of its dates, but—it speaks" (196/35/76). Poetry is thus the memory of dates just strictly insofar as it is *mnemotechne*: after all, an art—of memory. And thus, after all, an art of language: *logotechne*.

Certainly—we must not be afraid of always having to travel the same circle—memory is here, irreducibly, the memory of a single one. As soon as it speaks and must speak (for this is also its imperative, the "you must" which commands it), the poem can do so only in "its own, its own, individual cause": *in seiner eigenen, allereigensten Sache*, in what properly concerns it (196/35/76). This is why, at the limit of its own possibility, "at the edge of itself," wrenching itself from its "now-no-longer" toward its "as-always" (197/36/77), the poem must clear a way between silence and discourse, between mutism's *saying nothing* and the *saying too much* of eloquence. It is the poem's narrow path, the *straitening*: the path which is "most narrowly" that of the I (200/38/80). But this path does not lead to speech or to language. This path leads to only *one word*, to a "language become reality, language set free under the sign of an individuation which is radical" (197–98/36/77). Irreducibly, to the language of a single one: "Then the poem would be—even more clearly than before—the language of an individual which has taken on form; and, in keeping with its innermost nature [*seinem innersten Wesen*], it would also be the present, the here and now" (197–98/36/77).

Such is, in sum, the "solitude" of the poem, and what obliges it, with as rigorous an obligation as the obligation to speak, not to "invent" a singular language or build an idiolect from start to finish, but to undo language (semantically and syntactically), disarticulate and rarefy it, cut it up according to a prosody which is neither that of spoken language nor that of earlier poetry, to condense it until one comes to the hard center, the muted resistance where one recognizes a voice which is singular, that is, separated from language, as is a tone or a style.

Here, clearly, resides what I have called, for lack of a more judicious term, the "idiomatic" threat: the threat of hermeticism and obscurity. Celan has, if I may put it thus, a very clear awareness of this. He even demands the risk. What is surprising, though, is not that he demands it. The surprise is that this demand is in fact, once again, absolutely paradoxical; for if it is indeed made, as one might expect, in the name of catastrophe itself (in the name of abysmal conversion, or even revolt), that is, in the name of existence, it is rightfully justified or authorized by only one thing: the hope of what Celan calls the "encounter," *die Begegnung* (198/37/78).

Just after evoking the one who "walks on his head" and the abyss of the heavens beneath him, Celan says, without any lead-in:

> Ladies and gentlemen, nowadays it is fashionable to reproach poetry with its "obscurity." Permit me now, abruptly—but has not something suddenly appeared on the horizon?—permit me now to quote a maxim by Pascal, a maxim that I read some time ago in Leo Schestow: *Ne nous reprochez pas le manque de clarté puisque nous en faisons profession!* That is, I believe, if not the inherent obscurity of poetry, the obscurity attributed to it for the sake of an encounter—from a great distance or sense of strangeness possibly of its own making. (195/35/75)

Obscurity, in poetry, is thus not at all native (does not in the least belong to its essence). But it comes upon poetry, is or can be conjoined with it. That it *can* thus come upon poetry is only, Celan says precisely, "for the sake of" (*um . . . willen*) the encounter, at once in the name of and for the love of an encounter, which itself befalls "from a great distance or a sense of strangeness." The paradox here is that obscurity originates in taking the encounter into consideration, and not in the demand for solitude. Celan does not say obscurity is destined to prepare to provoke the encounter, that it is a call to the encounter, or that the encounter is its final aim. He says obscurity is, on the contrary, a mark of attention—even respect—with regard to the encounter. This means the encounter is the occasion, or rather the very *circumstance* of the poem: only once there is an encounter is there the poem's "solitude," and thus obscurity. And in fact:

> The poem is alone. It is alone and underway. Whoever writes it must remain in its company.
>
> But does not the poem, for precisely that reason, at this point participate in the encounter—*in the mystery of an encounter*? (198/37/78)

It is difficult to conceive the encounter, its secret or mystery (*Geheimnis*: a word in which the *Heim* of the near and the own, of the familiar and intimate, still resonates).

In what is perhaps the most striking twist of the "Meridian" (the moment when Celan recognizes that after all, the poem "does speak," even if "in its own . . . individual cause"), the *other*, indeed, the *wholly other*, abruptly appears to replace the elsewhere and the alien, which until this point had been the only terms in question. It is here that the encounter, in its essence and possibility, is decided:

> But I think—and this thought can scarcely come as a surprise to you—I think that it has always belonged to the expectations of the poem in precisely this manner to speak in the cause of the strange—no, I can no longer use this word—in precisely this manner to speak *in the cause of an Other*— who knows, perhaps in the cause of a *wholly Other*.
>
> This "who knows," at which I see I have arrived, is the only thing I can add—on my own, here, today—to the old expectations.
>
> Perhaps, I must now say to myself—and at this point I am making use of a well-known term—perhaps it is now possible to conceive a meeting of this "wholly Other" and an "other" which is not far removed, which is very near. The poem tarries, stops to catch a scent—like a creature when confronted with such thoughts. (196–97/35–36/76–77)

This is not, contrary to what one might think, a "forced passage." At the most, on the "path" which never stops closing off, coming to nothing or leading back to the same point, it is an attempt at a new clearing. We already know that at any rate there will be no "passage" in the "Meridian."

Nor is this a simple "profession of faith": the "who knows," which is itself *dated* ("at which I see I have now arrived"), is purely suspensive. In any case it leaves open the question of existence, or of the possibility of the "wholly other" thus designated. Moreover, the justification for recourse to such an expression is itself particularly discreet and reserved: there is not one word too many; and nothing, anyway, to flatter the "old expectations" too much.

Yet this said, how is the encounter decided in the substitution of alterity for strangeness? And how is such a substitution possible?

The logic we have already seen at work is still the same: catastrophic and paradoxical. Speaking in its own name or its own individual cause, speaking the language of singularity, of "an individuation which is radical," the poem hopes, has always hoped, precisely in this manner, in *this* language (though it is so difficult to reach), to speak "in the cause of the strange," in the name of the strange and the alien. That is, to use, in and as one's own, proper language, the alien language, the language of estrangement. Celan's brutal reversal here of the movement which until this point has straitened his gait is simply the sign that between proper and not-proper, near and far, familiar and strange, the exchange is always reversible, and for this reason never stops: it is not fixed and has no determined direction. It is at the very heart of estrangement or disappropriation that, by way of an enigmatic trope or turn, appropriation occurs. But this also means that such an appropriation takes place "outside the self." The appropriation, the singular appropriation, is in no way the appropriation of the self within itself. The self—or the singular I—reaches itself within itself only "outside." Reapplying one of Heidegger's formulas, we can say the "outside self" is the self's origin. It is thus, for example, that in the last poem of *Die Niemandsrose*, "In der Luft" ("In the Air"), it is said of "die Entzweiten" ("the dis-united"): "heimgekehrt in / den unheimlichen Bannstrahl / der die Verstreuten versammelt" ("come home / in the estranging ban ray / that assembles the dispersed" [*GW*, 1:290]).

And in fact, the volt or revolt of appropriation does not take *place*. The "here and now" of singular existence is immediately an elsewhere and another time (a date whose memory must be kept). If appropriation occurs, we know that it is in u-topia itself. This is why it is necessary to substitute for the topological division of here and strange, near and far, which—no matter what one says—assigns places, the unlocatable division of difference or alterity. In the place (without place) of the elsewhere, an "other" occurs, that is, a singular existent in whose name—and this time, the expression is apt—the poem maintains the hope of speaking. Estrangement yields ground to the encounter.

But the encounter is no less abysmal than estrangement. As soon as other occurs, as such, there is the threat of an alterity which is absolute—that is, ab-solute: which forbids or renders impossible all relation. The other, if it is indeed other, is immediately the wholly other. But at the same time, the other, even if wholly other, is, insofar as it is *other*, unthinkable without relation to the same: as soon as other appears, detaching itself from the same, the same, in advance, has already recovered it and brought it back. It is impossible to think a total unbinding.

Alterity is, in its essence, contradictory. From precisely this paradox, Western onto-theology up to Hegel and beyond—one might as well say, all our thought—has developed. Here, it underpins Celan's entire discourse. But with a very particular accent—once again close to Heidegger's—which aims to remove it from all structuring of a dialectical type, to suspend in it the movement of resolution, to maintain it as pure paradox.

For the same, in turn, is itself only in relation to the other: the beginning of *Die Wissenschaft der Logik* says, in substance, that the simple and immediate position of the same (of Being) is pure no-thingness or empty no-thingness. Between the same and the other there is necessarily a relation, a reciprocal relation, or rather, as Hölderlin said, an exchange. One could say that this double relation, which simultaneously divides the same and the other to put them, chiasmatically, in relation to the other than what they are, stems *equally* from the sameness of the same and the alterity of the other. But this is not at all so. In the "to relate to," it is by definition the movement of alteration which predominates. Or, if one prefers, it is difference which is always more primitive. So that in the relation of the same and the other there is an imbalance. This means that it is the alterity of the other, the being-wholly-other of the other or a certain "duplicity" in the other that institutes the same as a relation to the other, and thus, always differentiates it. The same is Heraclitus's "the one differentiated in itself"—a phrase moreover "rediscovered" by Hölderlin at the dawn of Speculative Idealism.[22] This is why the wholly other—whether or not this word, for Celan, designates God—de-parts the other, that is, approaches it: re-lates it to the same, which receives it in, or rather *as* its most intimate difference. The wholly other is the gift of the other as the possibility of the same, that is, as the possibility for the same of establishing itself as differ*a*nce (I use Derrida's spelling here for what it indicates as to temporality and the origin of time). There is not, as speculative logic believes, an exit by the same (the Subject) outside the self and passage into its other, with a view to returning and relating itself back to the self so as to establish itself as such. But beneath the (original) gift of the other to which it already always relates itself, the same is the pure movement that allows the intimate gaping, which is, within the self, its "original outside self" (time), to hollow itself out, to open and spread.

I may be wrong, but in the first part of *Die Niemandsrose* there are two poems, "Dein Hinübersein" ("Your Being Beyond") and "Zu beiden Händen" ("On Either Hand"), which in fact appear one right after the other, and which speak, it seems to me, not *of* this (they in no way say this very thing), but *from* this. In the first one reads:

Gott, das lasen wir, ist
ein Teil und ein zweiter, zerstreuter:
im Tod
all der Gemähten
wächst er sich zu:

Dorthin
führt uns der Blick,
mit dieser
Hälfte
haben wir Umgang.
          (*GW* 1:218)

(God, so we read, is
a part and a second, a scattered one:
in the death ·
of all those mown down
he grows himself whole.

There
our looking leads us,
with this
half
we keep up relations.)
          (*P* 161)

And in the second:

ich
finde hinaus.

O diese wandernde leere
gastliche Mitte. Getrennt,
fall ich dir zu, fällst
du mir zu, einander
entfallen, sehn wir
hindurch:

Das
Selbe
hat uns
verloren, das
Selbe
hat uns
vergessen, das

Selbe
hat uns—
    (*GW* 1:219)

(I
find my way out.

O this wandering empty
hospitable midst. Apart,
I fall to you, you
fall to me, fallen away
from each other, we see
through:

One
and the same
has
lost us, one

and the same
has
forgotten us, one
and the same
has—)
    (*P* 163)

    The substitution of the other and the wholly other for the strange and the elsewhere thus produces an extreme thought of difference. And it is this thought which in turn permits one to think singularity as the secret—we can also say as the intimacy—of the encounter. What Celan calls the encounter is thus first the hollowing out, the intimate gaping of singularity. The encounter is the original intimate ecstasy according to which singular being exists. This is why, of the poem which is "alone," one can simultaneously say that it takes place "in the mystery of an encounter." It is also why Celan can say, when he evokes the two texts in which he "started to write from a '20th of January'" near the end of the "Meridian"—the "catastrophic" quatrain I have already cited ("come on your hands to us") and the "Conversation in the Mountains" ("Gespräch im Gebirg"): "In each instance I started to write from a '20th of January,' from my '20th of January.' / I encountered . . . myself" (201/39/81).

    It is true that in the encounter (*Begegnung*), the value of the "against" (*gegen*), of the "across from" or "vis-à-vis," seems to predominate. Thus, a value of opposition. And this certainly seems to be the way

Celan understands it when he determines the poetic act as "attention," "perception," and "dialogue":

> The poem wants to reach the Other, it needs this Other, it needs a *vis à vis*. It searches it out and addresses it.
>
> Each thing, each person is a form of the Other for the poem, as it makes for this Other.
>
> The poem attempts to pay careful attention to everything it encounters; it has a finer sense of detail, of outline, of structure, of color, and also of the "movements" and the "suggestions." These are, I believe, not qualities gained by an eye competing (or cooperating) with mechanical devices which are continually being brought to a higher degree of perfection. No, it is a concentration which remains aware of all of our dates.
>
> [. . .]
>
> The poem becomes—and under what conditions!—a poem of one who—as before—perceives, who faces that which appears. Who questions this appearing and addresses it. It becomes dialogue—it is often despairing dialogue. (198/37/78)

But at the same time, the value of opposition is clearly not the determining value here. It is, as is always inevitable, attached to the motif of alterity. Yet nothing indicates that it constitutes the concept.

What these lines really seek to say is the poetic act as an act of thought. It is no accident that Celan's definition of attention is, via Benjamin, that of Malebranche: "'Attention'—permit me at this point to quote a maxim of Malebranche which occurs in Walter Benjamin's essay on Kafka: 'Attention is the natural prayer of the soul'" (198/37/78).

Again, it is no accident that the encounter is defined as a "perceiving" and a "questioning": the "perceiving" (*wahrnehmen*)—and once more we must consider Heidegger, who here, as it happens, is both very far from and near to Benjamin—is the Greek *noein*, thought, the very essence of reason (*Vernunft*); and as for the questioning—but here, the proximity is very strange—we well know that Heidegger, in a famous text, said it was nothing less than the "Frömmigkeit des Denkens."[23]

Yet thought supposes what I am calling, of course for lack of a better term, intimacy or the intimate difference. It supposes, or more precisely, it originates in intimacy as the possibility of *relating to* in general. It is in this sense that the poem thinks or is a dialogue. The dialogue is a speaking and a naming (which one would have to call "pure" if remembering Benjamin, "essential" if thinking of Heidegger). But speaking and naming are, in turn, a "letting speak." To speak to the other—being or thing—to address him or it, is to let what speaks in him or it occur, and accept this word in the very heart of the poem (in its "immediacy and proximity") as the gift of the other. It is to prepare, ecstatically, for the "presence" of the other within oneself; to let intimacy open up.

> Only in the realm of this dialogue does that which is addressed take form and gather around the I who is addressing and naming it. But the one who has been addressed and who, by virtue of having been named, has, as it were, become a thou, also brings its otherness along into the present, into this present.—In the here and now of the poem it is still possible—the poem itself, after all, has only this one, unique, limited present—only in this immediacy and proximity does it allow the most idiosyncratic quality of the Other, its time, to participate in the dialogue. (198–99/37/78)

The "counter" of the encounter or the against is thus not simply the "counter" of opposition. Rather, in the very vis-à-vis that is the encounter, it is what rids itself of opposition. It is the "counter" of proximity, that is, of de-parting. The other de-parts, close against a proximity such that it makes the very space of intimacy which renders possible thought and word, that is, dialogue. For this reason the poem turns, within itself, to the appearing, to what is "in the process of appearing": it questions the very coming into presence. The poem (the poetic act), in this mode which is proper to it (dialogue), is the thought of the presence of the present, or of the other of what is present: the thought of no-thingness (of Being), that is to say, the thought of time. "Soviel Gestirne" ("So Many Constellations"):

> in den Schluchten,
> da, wo's verglühte, stand
> zitzenprächtig die Zeit,
> an der schon empor- und hinab-
> und hinwegwuchs, was
> ist oder war oder sein wird—,
>
> ich weiß,
> ich weiß und du weißt, wir wußten,
> wir wußten nicht, wir
> waren ja da und nicht dort,
> und zuweilen, wenn
> nur das Nichts zwischen uns stand, fanden
> wir ganz zueinander.
>   (GW 1:217)

> (in chasms,
> and where they had burnt out,
> splendid with teats, stood Time,
> on which already grew up

and down and away all that
is or was or will be—,

I know,
I know and you know, we knew,
we did not know, we
were there, after all, and not there
and at times when
only the void stood between us we got
all the way to each other.)
(*P* 159)

Of course, Celan is not saying *time*, but, speaking of the other who is, every time, such and such an other: *his* time. The poetic act (the poem) is a singular experience, the dialogue is a singular dialogue. And this is of course what distinguishes poetry from thought proper, from the exercise of thought, even (and especially) if poetry thinks. But I do not think one can make this an argument, as Lévinas does a bit hastily, in favor of who knows what improbable "beyond" of "ontology." In favor of a pathos, in the strict sense, of the "otherwise than Being."[24] Certainly, poetic questioning begins with a singular address: to the other, in fact *envisaged* as a "you." But this address to the you is an address to the alterity of the you—of *this* other—it is the address, obscurely arisen from intimacy (from the intimate difference), to the being of the other, which always "is" and can only "be" Being. How would it be possible to speak in the slightest if Being was not involved? There is no "otherwise than Being," unless, once again, one understands Being as being, and misses, in the other, precisely its alterity. Poetry's "you-saying," its naming, is a way of "Being-saying" other than that which properly belongs to thought, but still a way of "Being-saying." It is possible that from such a naming, another space opens up, or that naming sheds a different light on the space opened up by any saying. To say this, Heidegger uses Hölderlin's word: "the holy" ("das Heilige"). But the other space or the space on which a different light is shed is in no way "beyond" Being. The experience of the You, the encounter, opens onto nothing other than the experience of Being: of the no-thing of being—which Celan designates, precisely in Hölderlin's terms (not Rilke's), as "openness," "emptiness," "freedom." I again quote the decisive passage:

> When we speak with things in this manner we always find ourselves faced with the question of their whence and whither [*nach ihrem Woher und Wohin*]: a question which "remains open" and "does not come to an end," which points into openness, emptiness, freedom—we are outside, at a considerable distance.
> The poem, I believe, also seeks this place. (199/37/78–79)

In other words, poetry's questioning is meta-physical questioning itself, in the sense that it is the repetition of the meta-physical as Heidegger understands it. It questions in the direction of being as "transcendence as such" ("das transcendens schlechthin").[25] In the singular thing or being it is incumbent upon poetry—upon the poem—to perceive (think), just such a "transcendent" is sought: it is the "wholly other," the *arche* and the *telos* of the other, and nothing here permits us to simply identify this wholly other with God. This is why Celan can say of poetic questioning, of the demand or pretension (*Anspruch*) there is in all poems, even the least pretentious (*anspruchsloseste*), that they are at once "inescapable" and "incredible." The question the poem carries is, as Launay correctly translates, "exorbitant" (199/38/79).

It is in this sense that the poetic act is ecstatic. The exorbitant is the pure transcendence of being. It follows that the poem, as a questioning, is turned toward the open, offered up to it. And the open is itself open, after a fashion, to u-topia, to the place without place of the advent. In other terms: the poetic act is catastrophic: an upsetting relation to what is an upset, in being, in the direction of no-thingness (the abyss).

This is just what justifies the idea that poetry is the interruption of art, that is, the interruption of mimesis. The poetic art consists of perceiving, not representing. Representing, at least according to some of the "ancient rumors," can only be said of the already-present. What is "in the process of appearing" cannot be represented, or if so, we must give a completely different meaning to representation. For poetry, representation is organized starting with what one might call the ontic comparison (the comparison of the already-present with the already-present), from which arise figures or images, "metaphors and other tropes," all the turns of phrase that allow a certain use of language to be defined as "poetic." Measured against the requirements of the questioning toward Being or presence, the ontic comparison, and therefore the "poetic," have to do with what Heidegger denounced as "idols" ("Götzen") and problematized as "thinking in models" ("Denken in Modellen").[26] There is nothing to which one can compare Being: Being is, purely and simply, the unrepresentable.

Poetry as Celan understands it is thus in this sense the interruption of the "poetic." At least, it is defined as a battle against idolatry. All "real" poems, all that are effectively poems, seem to aim at nothing other than being the place where the "poetic" collapses, becomes abysmal. And the task of poetry would be to tirelessly undo the "poetic": not by "putting an end" to figures and tropes, but by leading them *ad absurdum*, as Lucile's "Long live the King!" in the sharp light of death suddenly makes the theatricality and grandiloquence of "historic" discourses absurd. In the highly rigorous sense this term has in Heidegger, poetry would thus be the "deconstruction" of the poetic, that is to say, both of what is recognized as such (here there is a closely fought confrontation with the poetic tradition) and of the spontaneous "poeticity" of language (which supposes the strictest possible language work).

Such a task, which amounts to extenuating the "poetic," is perhaps impossible—Celan is the first to say so. Nevertheless, this is what his poetry strives to do. It strives as "poetry of poetry." But it also strives inasmuch as it seeks to reduce the image to pure perception, that is, inasmuch as it seeks to empty or hollow out the image. To the question: "And what, then, would the images be?," once the poem condenses in "exorbitant" questioning, the response is: "That which is perceived and to be perceived one time, one time over and over again, and only now and only here" (199/38/79). Poetry would thus measure itself against the impossibility of a language without images or the impossibility of what Benjamin calls "pure language," that is, the language of names.[27] Two remarks to close:

1. In its impossible combat with art, where it exhausts itself (the motif of panting, babbling, or stammering), what poetry would like to rid itself of the beautiful. The poem's threat is the beautiful, and all poems are always too beautiful, even Celan's.

The beautiful is obviously closely linked to mimesis. This is particularly visible in Benjamin, who defines the beautiful "as the object of experience in the state of resemblance." He quotes Valéry on this: "Beauty may require the servile imitation of what is indefinable in objects."[28] If one went so far as to say: the servile imitation of that which is *inimitable* in things, one would reach what makes the essence of poetry for Celan, that is, what does not destine it for the beautiful—or for mimesis. But at the same time this pure oxymoron, the imitation of the immitable, marks the impossibility of poetry. In Celan, this is the tragic.

2. I do not know, finally, if "Tübingen, Jänner" contains the slightest allusion to Moses and the interdiction against representation. All I know is that it did indeed happen that Hölderlin, more than has been believed and more than the Heideggerian commentary leads us to think, evoked the Patriarchs. "Am Quell der Donau," for example, says this:

And think of you, O valleys of the Kaukasos,
Whatever your antiquity, paradises far,
And your patriarchs and prophets,

O Mother Asia, and your heroes
Without fear for the signs of the world,
Heaven and fate upon their shoulders,
Rooted on mountaintops days on end,
Were the first to understand
Speaking to God
Alone. . . .[29]

Patriarchs and prophets are named here: those who have known an encounter—a dialogue—with God. Celan would perhaps have said: with the wholly other. And perhaps he would have thought such a dialogue as poetry itself.

Perhaps.

Another poem from *Die Niemandsrose*, "Bei Wein und Verlorenheit" ("Over Wine and Lostness"), speaks in this direction. It says:

ich ritt durch den Schnee, hörst du,
ich ritt Gott in die Ferne—die Nähe, er sang,
es war
unser letzter Ritt über
die Menschen-Hürden.

Sie duckten sich, wenn
sie uns über sich hörten, sie
schrieben, sie
logen unser Gewieher
um in eine
ihrer bebilderten Sprachen.
    (*GW* 1:213)

(I rode through the snow, do you hear,
I rode God into farness—nearness, he sang,
it was
our last ride over
the human hurdles.

They ducked when
they heard us above their heads, they
wrote, they
lied our whinnying
into one
of their be-imaged languages.)
    (*P* 154)

NOTES

1. *Translator's Note.* "Stammering" translates the French "bégaiement," which corresponds to Celan's "lallen" in " Tübingen, Jänner" (*GW* 1.226). Michael Hamburger, Whose translations of Celan will be used wherever they do not prejudice Lacoue-Labarthe's text, translates *lallen* as "babble"(*P* 177).

2. *T.N.* "Der Meridian" (*GW* 3:202). "The Meridian," trans. Jerry Glenn, *Chicago Review* 29, no. 3 (1978), 40. Henceforth page references to the "Meridian" will be given in the main body of the text: first to the German; then to Glenn's English translation; and lastly to the French translation by Jean Launay,

used by Lacoue-Labarthe ("Le Méridien. Discours prononcé à l'occasion de la remise du prix Georg Büchner," *Po&sie* 9 [1979], 68–82). At times, the English translation has been modified to coincide with Lacoue-Labarthe's use of Launay's French version of Celan's text.

3. The acceptance speech for the Georg Büchner Prize customarily addresses Büchner's work.

4. "Une lecture de Paul Celan," *Po&sie* 9 (1979), 7.

5. In the same issue of *Po&sie* (9 [1979]), Launay includes, along with his translation of the "Meridian," translations of Kafka's "Ein Bericht für eine Akademie," *Gesammelte Werke in sieben Bänden* (Frankfort: Hanser 1983), *Erzählungen*, 139–47, and Egon Friedell's *Talents zur Wahrheit* (1910), in order to clarify the tone proper to the "Meridian."

6. *T.N.* Glenn's translation of the "Meridian" gives three different versions of *Atemwende*: "reversal of breath," "turn of breath," and "breath turning."

7. "Pas (préambule)," in *Gramma* 3–4 (1976). *T.N.* This text is reprinted in Jacques Derrida, *Parages* (Paris: Galilée, 1986), 19–116. *Pas* in French means both "step" and "not."

8. *T.N.* this is Lacoue-Labarthe's first mention of "propre," a word to which he will frequently return. I have given it in English as "own," or, when possible, as "proper."

9. *T.N. Dantons Tod*, in Georg Büchner, *Werke und Briefe*, ed. Fritz Bergemann (Wiesbaden: Insel, 1949), 41. *The Death of Danton*, trans. Howard Brenton and Jane Fry, in Georg Büchner, *The Complete Plays*, ed. Michael Patterson (London: Methuen, 1987), 40.

10. Connections should be made here between the commentary on Sophocles in Martin Heidegger, *Einführung in die Metaphysik* (Tübingen: Niemeyer, 1953) and the 1942 lectures on "Der Ister," in Martin Heidegger, *Hölderlins Hymne "Der Ister"* (Frankfort: Klostermann, 1984), "Der Ursprung des Kunstwerkes," in Martin Heidegger, *Holzwege* (Frankfort: Klostermann, 1950), 7–68, and the "Brief über den Humanismus," in Martin Heidegger, *Wegmarken* (Frankfort: Klostermann, 1967), 145–94 (the passage on the translation of Heraclitus's maxim: *ethos anthrope daimon* [185–94]).

11. 201/39/81. Or when, on the contrary—but it amounts to exactly the same thing—he seems to appropriate the *Unheimliche* as the "realm in which the monkey, the robots, and accordingly . . . alas, art, too, seem to be at home" (192/32/72).

12. *T.N.* Lacoue-Labarthe's words are "quelque chose . . . se renverse," with *renverser* as the echo of "catastrophe" (from the Gr. *katastrephein*, "to turn down," "overturn"). Although I have used "overturn" here, the three other instances in which a form of *renverser* occurs seem to require "upset."

13. Once again we are very close to Hölderlin—"language, most dangerous of possessions"—even to the Heideggerian interpretation of this proposition. See "Hölderlin und das Wesen der Dichtung," in Martin Heidegger, *Erläuterungen zu Hölderlins Dichtung* (Frankfort: Klostermann, 1981), 33–45. Heidegger thinks of danger as that which threatens Being rather than the human. But Hölderlin's proposition derives from a fragment which seeks to respond to the question "Who is man?" And as for Celan's determination of the human, what would it/he be without a relation to Being, that is—I will come

to this—to time? Even if the "Meridian" is, as we may plausibly allow, partially addressed to Heidegger, that is not sufficient reason to hastily read into it an "ethical" response to "ontology." The human is in no way an "ethical" category, and moreover, no category of this kind can resist against the question of Being. *T.N.* Lacoue-Labarthe quotes Hölderlin from the fragment "Im Walde," in *Sämtliche Werke*, ed. Friedrich Beißner (Stuttgart: Kolhammer, 1943–85), 2(1):325. Cf. "In the Forest," in Friedrich Hölderlin, *Hymns and Fragments*, trans. Richard Sieburth (Princeton: Princeton University Press, 1984), 57.

14. *T.N.* "Anmerkungen zum 'Ödipus,'" in *Sämtliche Werke*, 5:196. "Remarks on 'Oedipus,'" in Friedrich Hölderlin, *Essays and Letters on Theory*, trans. Thomas Pfau (Albany: State University of New York Press, 1988), 102.

15. Jean-Luc Nancy's term. See *Le Discours de la syncope* (Paris: Aubier-Flammarion, 1976).

16. *T.N.* "Anmerkungen zum 'Oedipus,'" 196. "Remarks on 'Oedipus,'" 102.

17. *T.N.* "Anmerkungen zur 'Antigonä,'" in *Sämtliche Werke*, 5:269. "Remarks on 'Antigone,'" in *Essays and Letters on Theory*, 113.

18. *Dantons Tod*, 86. *The Death of Danton*, 80.

19. This is the case in the quatrain Celan quotes at the end of the "Meridian": "Voices from the path of the nettles: / *Come on your hands to us*. / Whoever is alone with the lamp / has only his palm to read from" (*GW* 3:201).

20. Celan's words are: "when I attempted to make for that distant but occupiable realm which became visible only in the form of Lucile" (200/38/80).

21. *T.N.* In French, "poésie de circonstance." There is further reference to circumstance later on.

22. *T.N. hen diapheron eauto*. See *Hyperion*, pt. 1, bk. 2, in *Sämtliche Werke*, 3:81. Cf. Heraclitus, fragment 51, in *Die Fragmente der Vorsokratiker*, trans. Hermann Diels, ed. Walther Kranz, 5th ed. (Berlin: Weidmann, 1934), 1:162.

23. These are the last words of "Die Frage der Technik," in *Vorträge und Aufsätze* (Pfullingen: Neske, 1954), 36. Heidegger defines this piety as "Weise, in der das Denken dem Zu-Denkenden *entspricht*." In this way, it is itself a product of dialogue (*Gespräch*) as the essence of language (of thought). See "Hölderlin und das Wesen der Dichtung," 38–40. Celan himself thinks perception and questioning as dialogue.

24. *T.N.* A play on the title of Emmanuel Lévinas's *Autrement qu'être ou au-délà de l'essence* (Haag: Nijhoff, 1974).

25. *Sein und Zeit*, 11th ed. (Tübingen: Niemeyer, 1967), 38.

26. The denunciation concludes "Was ist Metaphysik?," in *Wegmarken*, 19. The problematization is in "Protokoll zu einem Seminar über den Vortrag 'Zeit und Sein,'" in Martin Heidegger, *Zur Sache des Denkens* (Tübingen: Niemeyer, 1969), 54.

27. Cf. "Über Sprache überhaupt und über die Sprache des Menschen," in *Gesammelte Schriften*, ed. Rolf Tiedemann and Hermann Schweppenhäuser (Frankfort: Suhrkamp, 1977), 2(1):140–57. "On Language as Such and on the Language of Man," in Walter Benjamin, *Reflections*, ed. Peter Demetz, trans. Edmund Jephcott (New York: Schocken, 1986), 314–32.

28. Walter Benjamin, "Über einige Motive bei Baudelaire," in *Gesammelte Schriften*, 1(2):639. "On Some Motifs in Baudelaire," in Walter Benjamin, *Illu-*

minations, ed. Hannah Arendt, trans. Harry Zohn (New York: Schocken, 1969), 199. The quotation from Valéry is from *Autres Rhumbs.*

29. *T.N.* Hölderlin, *Sämtliche Werke,* 2(1):126–29. Hölderlin, "At the Source of the Danube," in *Hymns and Fragments,* 57.

FIGURE AND TIME

4

The Realities at Stake in a Poem

Celan's Bremen and Darmstadt Addresses

Christopher Fynsk

In reading Celan's prose statements, and particularly the speeches delivered in Bremen and Darmstadt, I cannot escape an impression Celan himself may have sought to prompt with his choice of language: *here is what must be said about poetry after Heidegger.* "Must be said" in that Celan seized the essential elements of a meditation on poetic language that still remains crucial to any reflection on the historicity of the poetic text; but "must be said" also in that Heidegger's writing on language and poetry fails to answer fully to a time after the "terrifying silence" to which Celan, evoking the Second World War, refers in his Bremen address.[1] Celan recovers in these texts something of the engagement with history that initially prompted Heidegger to turn to Hölderlin's poetry in 1934 and that informed all of his thought of the late twenties and thirties. He recovers it through an effort to think our time *from our time* (the time given to us in the assumption of our finitude), and in recognizing, with the later Heidegger, that such a task implies thinking from language. Yet he also recovers it *for* our time in a reflection on what poetry must be after terrifying silence and under the ever-expanding reign of *Technik.*

In the following, I will document the impression (or claim) I have described by offering partial readings of both Celan's "Speech on the Occasion of Receiving the Literature Prize of the First Hanseatic City of Bremen" (January 20, 1958) and the "Meridian" (October 27, 1960). Although I will discuss them separately, it should become apparent that the two speeches touch upon the same possibility of *passage* in language (toward oneself and toward the other, in time) and thus on the poetic experience of history. Together, they point powerfully to what was at stake in Heidegger's meditation on language and history, and what is at stake there for us today. They mark an engagement and an affirmation to which I believe we would do well to attend—now, when the question of history assumes a new, essential urgency, and is all too frequently closed by those who, for ideological purposes, evoke "history" most loudly: as though we knew where we stand today (amidst the distractions of socioeconomic systems that work powerfully to suspend a knowledge of time), as though "history" could speak for itself.

––––––––––

Celan begins his Bremen speech in terms that immediately evoke Heidegger. He invites his auditors to refer what he says about the path that has brought him to Bremen both to what Heidegger suggests in *Was heißt Denken?* concerning the relations between thought, memory, and thanks, and to Heidegger's development of the concept of remembrance in his reading of Hölderlin's "Andenken."[2] He will answer the honor accorded to him by the city of Bremen by recalling the experience that has brought him to Bremen *as a poet*. Out of this remembrance, he will offer a reflection on the "realities" and (as we will see in the "Meridian") the thought at stake in the poem—for him and for those who are coming after him: "other, younger poets" (*GW* 3: 185/ *CP* 35).

He will commemorate a movement—a movement involving topographical displacements, to be sure, but more essentially an experience of time that comes to him in and through language. It begins in a region "now dropped from history" (Celan will not give its name—as though this closest name remains most distant as the "details" come back to him): a kind of literary landscape (or a landscape of the letter) from which comes "many of the Hassidic stories which Martin Buber has retold in German . . . a region [*Gegend*] . . . where both people and books lived" (*GW* 3:185/*CP* 35). There, the name of Bremen traces its distant outline for Celan through his encounter with the names of authors associated with the city and through the shape of books published by the *Bremer Presse*. In the literal topography drawn in the imagination of the young Celan, Bremen is brought near, but still sounds distant, "unreachable" (*GW* 3:185/*CP* 33). In reach (*Das Erreichbare*: Celan will use some form of the word four times) is Vienna, a literary site that Celan can hope to attain and inhabit.

But in the years to come, this imaginary topographical construction defining what is "reachable" is destroyed. We know what detours this destruction occasioned.[3] And we know that the fact that Vienna, for example, can no longer be attained is certainly not without relation to the possibilities of access offered to Celan by the German language. Yet language—"his" language (the same German language in which he wrote his poetry) and, in a sense to be determined, language itself (for Celan appears to invoke in this passage something like what Heidegger would term the essence of language)—remains reachable, "unlost." The possibility of a different kind of topography—or rather, the possibility

of finding a bearing, of marking out paths and pursuing a direction—
will continue to hold itself out to Celan:

> Only one thing remained close and reachable amid all losses: language.
>
> Yes, language. In spite of everything it remained unlost. But it had to go
> through [*hindurchgehen durch*] its own lack of answers, through terrifying
> silence, through the thousand darknesses of murderous speech. It went
> through and gave no words for what happened; but it went through this
> event. It went through and could resurface, "enriched" [*"angereichert"*] by
> it all.
>
> In this language I tried, during those years and the years after, to write
> poems: in order to speak, to orient myself, to find out where I was, where
> things were going, to sketch for myself a reality.
>
> It meant, as you see, something happening [*Ereignis*], movement [*Be-
> wegung*], being under way [*Unterwegssein*], it was an attempt to find direc-
> tion. And when I ask about the sense of it, I feel I must tell myself that this
> question also speaks to the question as to the sense of the clock's hand.
> (*GW* 3:185–86/*CP* 34)

I cite this passage in its entirety because Celan describes in it an
experience with language that is fundamental for his poetry. The "Meridian" will in fact provide a more precise description of poetic self-
discovery; it will offer more precise "dates." But what Celan terms a
"date" in that text—a "turning" in an individual's existence that involves
an experience of mortality and of the abyss to which the singular human
Dasein opens in its freedom, a turning remarked, but also in some sense
accomplished in the language of the poem—is not dissociable from the
experience with language he describes here. And no knowledge of mortality, for Celan, can come without the memory of the losses to which
he refers in the passage I have quoted. Or more precisely, all knowledge
of mortality for him, after the war, entails knowledge of what became
of death in the time of "terrifying silence" and murderous speech—a
time for which language gave no words (thus a time where death loses
meaning).

Yet if language gives no words for what happens in the time of murderous speech, it nevertheless gives itself. Despite its silence, and perhaps even through its silence—much as when Heidegger says that we
only come to have a knowledge of language itself, that is, in its essence,
through some kind of failure or suspension of speech[4]—language gives
itself as the persistence of the possibility of relation. A pure possibility,
we might say, for in its silence it gives no relation other than a relation
to itself as "reachable" (which will offer to Celan, as we will see, another
form of relation). Any other relation as Celan has previously known it
is destroyed. There are no words for what is happening (no words that
hold), no meaning; there is only "murderous speech," which is *of* lan-

guage, certainly, but unspeaking, and of a strange negativity that destroys relation and meaning.[5] Still, silence and the din of "murderous speech" remark a kind of presence of language itself ("reachable, near and unlost" [GW 3:185/CP 34])—language remaining, persisting in its nearness, and as Celan puts it, "going through" its own lack of answers, terrifying silence, and the darknesses of murderous speech (thus a kind of death of its own). Six times in the second paragraph of the passage quoted, Celan uses the term hindurchgehen to describe the survival of language. Its presence thus comes to be marked by a mode of temporality.

We should pause to consider what it might mean to try to write poems in a language that "gives no words" for what is happening and at a time when a world of signification has collapsed (a world of symbolic relations). Such a poetry cannot signify or pretend immediately to rebuild relations as they have previously been known. It would necessarily be a poetry of language in a previously unheard-of form: for again, of living symbolic relations, only language remains, and as the relation language offers to itself in its survival. An effort, then, to bring a mute language into speech (but in its muteness), to work in its proximity, and to bring forth from this proximity (which is also a distance) what language still offers of relation, what remains. "Singbarer Rest," Celan writes in a later poem, and then from the same poem in lines shortly thereafter:

Entmündigte Lippe melde
das etwas noch geschiet, noch immer,
unweit von dir.[6]

The effort to write in and from this language (to discover where he stands, to find a direction) will entail, Celan says, not a naming but a movement (Ereignis, Bewegung, Unterwegssein [GW 3:186/CP 34]). And Celan may well be suggesting that from language's very mode of remaining or surviving, of going through a kind of death, there comes a knowledge of time. Relation, he discovers, is a reaching through time ("durch die Zeit hindurchzugreifen" [GW 3:186/CP 34]). To project a reality and to sketch out a direction toward this reality is to move in time. Continuing with the passage I have been commenting on, we read:

And when I ask about the sense of it, I feel I must tell myself [so glaube ich, mir sagen zu müssen; the lesson is not easy] that this question also speaks to the question as to the sense of the clock's hand [Uhrzeigersinn].

For the poem is not timeless. True it lays a claim to the infinite and tries to grasp through time—but through it, not above it [durch die Zeit hindurchzugreifen—durch sie hindurch, nicht über sie hinweg].

Thus when language resurfaces, or returns to the "day," as Maurice Blanchot would say, when it begins to speak again and thus to give a relation to what is, the relation it offers is one of approach or reaching through. The notion of relation has undergone a change for Celan, and with it the nature of the poetic task. Whereas the region of his origins constituted a kind of narrative space (the space of the Hassidic stories), and whereas it was possible for the aspiring writer to construct a topological distribution of "literary" names marking distance and proximity (the reachable and the unreachable), the destruction of this essentially linguistic region and the accompanying experience of language in which this destruction issues lead Celan to conceive of an entirely different structure of relation, one that is fundamentally temporal in character.

Language is "enriched" by its passage through silence and murderous speech, Celan says, *"angereichert."* He writes the term in quotation marks—and surely not without a measure of irony.[7] For if language might be termed "richer" after passing through silence and emerging in its essence as the ground of any possible relation (perhaps in an entirely new manner in a historical perspective—in this sense, we would indeed have to do with a transformation), this enrichment involves a most paradoxical gain. Language is "enriched" by time—not in the manner of a regeneration, or through a dialectical sublation of the "death" through which it has gone (no *meaning* is given to this death or to the losses of the time through which it has passed—language is in no way more meaningful, no richer in any traditional sense of the term), but rather in the emergence of its temporal essence. Language now offers itself in its historicity and as the ground of a relation that is radically finite. When it begins to speak, its richness does not inhere in the words or the names it offers, but in the manner in which these words are marked by time. Accordingly, we see that if it offers the poet a new possibility of poetic relation, namely as address to an other in dialogue or conversation ("A poem, being one of the forms in which language appears, and thus dialogical in essence . . ." [*GW* 3:186/*CP* 334–35]), this possibility is attenuated to an extreme degree—for Celan compares the poem's effort to reach across time to throwing a letter in a bottle out to sea, "with the—surely not always strong—belief that it could somehow wash up somewhere, perhaps in a shoreline of the heart" (*GW* 3:186/*CP* 35). The poetic relation, we might say, is grounded in time and exposed to time: the letter may not reach its destination.

Nonetheless language as it now offers itself does give something like "approach." It offers to the poet the possibility of a kind of self-situation in and through movement toward an other: a "reality," perhaps a "you," he writes, that is approachable or addressable ("ansprechbar") inasmuch as it stands open in its essence and offers itself in a proximity that may be inhabited (*GW* 3:186/*CP* 35). In other words, inasmuch as language gives it to be approached (renders it "addressable"). For the approach, Celan says, is in "dialogue": the poem answers to what it approaches or it broaches a "conversation" (as Celan will write in the "Meridian") in a manner that is already response, already the answer to an opening.

In the "Meridian," Celan will develop this structure more fully in terms of his notion of encounter and a kind of countering movement. Here, Celan stresses simply that he has come to understand the task of the poet as one of seeking paths in the direction of what language gives of an opening to the other. He stresses that this opening is in no manner guaranteed, just as language itself, even if it remains "near and unlost," is in no manner a possession, and something quite other than a world of names the poet might inhabit or build upon. When Celan suggests, after comparing the poetic effort of reaching to another to tossing a letter out to sea, that what is at stake for the poem is an addressable "you" and an addressable reality ("Um solche Wirklichkeiten geht es, so denke ich, dem Gedicht" [*GW* 3:186]), he clearly means that these are no more than possible realities. Language offers relation, it offers the possibility of approach, but this approach is not simply given, any more than the place from which this movement starts out.

On the contrary, we start today, Celan suggests, in a situation of loss and exposure which requires the same kind of movement he undertook in the years of "terrifying silence." His own efforts, Celan says, are to be compared with efforts of "younger poets," "those who, with man-made stars flying overhead, unsheltered in this hitherto unanticipated manner and thus exposed in the most uncanny way in the free, carry their existence into language, racked by reality and in search of it" (*GW* 3:186/*CP* 35).

Following the remarkably affirmative character of the Bremen address, we may say that Celan takes the experience of "uncanny exposure" to be the condition of poetry in the second half of the twentieth century. For such exposure also exposes language, gives language as the possibility of relation and thus the possibility of a reality. In the most extreme danger, Heidegger wrote in his meditation on *Technik*, and in memory of Hölderlin, there grows what saves.[8] Celan intends something comparable with his notion of a language "enriched." It is enriched in that it is given anew (it gives itself) in its temporal essence *as the possibility and necessity* of poetry in this time of radical loss—that is, as the sole ground of relation. Pierre Joris has suggested to me that Celan turned Adorno's remarks concerning Auschwitz and poetry in such a manner as to suggest that *only* poetry is possible after Auschwitz. Celan's statements in his Bremen address would seem to bear out this reading. Furthermore, if we take "poetry" in a large sense—that is, as an approach to a reality in and through an experience with language (an approach in and through language that is also found in thought and in each of the arts, though in always specific ways)—then I think we may accept Celan's response as a decisive "counterword" to Adorno's assertion.

Celan follows tradition when he accepts the Georg Büchner Prize with a speech that situates his work in relation to that of Büchner, but he does not offer his audience a literary history. Rather, he engages with Büchner's text in a manner that Heidegger terms *Auseinandersetzung* (Heidegger's notion of *Erörterung* is also germane), taking the problem of self-situation as a kind of lever for this critical confrontation. Moreover, Celan performs this confrontation, rather than describing it. As he indicates with the choice of title, the speech *describes a movement* of self-situation. It demonstrates in its very structure that its concern is not with literary history, but with literature and history—with the historicity of literature. The accent, as Celan puts it, is on the present (*GW* 3:190/*CP* 40–41).

That Celan's accent is on the present means initially that he starts from the point where Büchner's text concerns us today. Poetry, he says, must return to the question Büchner poses to art if it is to question further on its own; for in the "muted," half-conscious questioning he finds in Büchner, Celan hears something that evokes "the oldest uncanny things" about art—something that is also "in the air today" (*GW* 3:192/*CP* 43), the air we have to breathe. Büchner broaches a question that concerns our historical element (breath, Celan remarks, involves "direction and destiny"), an element that Celan finds stifling.

Celan starts from Büchner, then, and if he seeks a distance and a certain liberation from the uncanny side of art to which Büchner points with his question (a muted, half-conscious question in that Büchner's own voice bespeaks, and is to some extent in the grips of, the uncanny),[9] he does so from within Büchner's text. This is why Celan's confrontation with Büchner is properly an *Auseinandersetzung*. He takes his distance from Büchner *from Büchner*, and by carrying through Büchner's question: "I am not looking for a way out, I am pushing the question farther in the same direction which is, I think, also the direction of the *Lenz* fragment" (*GW* 3:193/*CP* 44). To *carry through* the question, as we will see, is to effect a turn and to follow the text back to its most proper object of concern (what Celan will describe as "seiner eigenen, aller eigensten Sache" [*GW* 3:196/*CP*48]). Here, before "Büchner,"[10] Celan finds the place from which poetry may proceed in a step that liberates it from "art"—poetry in general, today, and his poetry. From here, and from an extraordinary statement of what poetry may "hope for," Celan will cite lines of his own, lines that mark a self-encounter and what Celan calls "a kind of homecoming" (*GW* 3:201/*CP* 53). The "step back" in and from Büchner's text liberates the possibility of self-citation and the poetic naming of this movement of self-situation which the speech has described.

Celan begins the confrontation to which I have referred after introducing the "eternal problem" of art (in its uncanniness), and after describing the interruption of art by poetry, illustrated by Lucile's "counterword." The "turn" begins when Celan locates Büchner's question regarding art in his evocation of the means by which art serves "the natural and the creaturely" (*GW* 3:191/*CP* 42). He foregrounds in Lenz's description of the scene he has witnessed of "two girls sitting on a rock" a kind of disjunction or incongruity between the admired natural beauty and the expression of a desire to capture it: "Sometimes one would like to be a Medusa's head to turn such a group to stone and gather the people around it" (*GW* 3:191–92/*CP* 42). The strangeness, even the perversity of Lenz's expression (perverse already by virtue of the figural transactions occurring between the Medusa's head and the girl on a rock "putting up her hair"), allows Celan to remark the distance implicit in Lenz's—and Büchner's—aesthetic effort, which is "to seize the natural *as* the natural by means of art" (*GW* 3:192/*CP* 42 [my emphasis]). Such an effort, Celan remarks, "means going beyond what is human, stepping into a realm that is turned toward the human, but uncanny—the realm where the monkey, the automatons and with them . . . ah, art, too, seem to be at home" (*GW* 3:192/*CP* 42–43). Büchner's question would seem to involve the extent to which the human can be served by such a transcending movement, and perhaps even the extent to which art is even about the human or the "creaturely," in the sense of the naturalism evoked by Lenz.

Celan draws out this question by further remarking the uncanny form of Lenz's reference to art's uncanny means. For as I have noted, in Lenz's words, he hears "Büchner's own voice" (*GW* 3:192/*CP* 43). Here, the mimetic character of the *Lenz* fragment betrays itself in such a way as to reopen the questions about the uncanny nature of art already posed by Plato ("the old and oldest uncanninesses"). Philippe Lacoue-Labarthe has identified what is essentially at stake in this implicit reference to the uncanny aspect of mimesis—namely its alienating character, its capacity to make persons involved in it (the artist and the commentator, reader, listener, or observer) "forget" about themselves.[11] Büchner has forgotten himself, Celan suggests, and this is why his questioning is "half-conscious." But he has engaged with the question of mimesis enough, or has gone far enough with art's antimimetic means, to have exposed another possibility in art. The very instability by which the Lenz fragment betrays its mimetic character points to a presence of the artist that cannot be grasped with any notion of representation.

At the outset of his speech, Celan had located such a presence of the human in the figure of Lucile in *Danton's Death*: Lucile, who does not listen to what is said, but who "hears the speaker, 'sees them speaking,' who has perceived language as a physical shape and also—who could doubt it within Büchner's work—breath, that is, direction and destiny" (*GW* 3:188/*CP* 39). He now listens to Büchner's text as Lucile might ("I think of Lucile when I read this," he says, speaking of the way the artist forgets himself [*GW* 3:193/*CP* 44]), and seeks Büchner as a "person" in the figure of Lenz.

Lucile testifies to the presence of the human with her defiant "Long live the King"—an act of freedom, Celan writes, a step, that draws its force from its mortal character inasmuch as with this "counterword" Lucile commits herself to death. Celan finds an indication that the *Lenz* fragment is also written out of an experience of mortality (Lenz's experience of mortality as grasped by Büchner) in its interrupted last sentence: "His existence was a necessary burden for him.—Thus he lived on . . ." (*GW* 3:194/*CP* 45). By reading this final sentence in the light of Lenz's end (the historical Lenz), he is able to give it a kind of Heideggerian— and even more appropriately, perhaps, a kind of Hölderlinian—tonality. In other words, Celan is able to inscribe the fragment under the sign of poetry, which, he says, "rushes ahead" and seeks to "see the figure in its direction" (*GW* 3:194/*CP*45); that is, as it emerges as a figure, as a "sign," advancing under the unthinkable, as Hölderlin says, and toward death. From this end, he can find the "person" of Lenz ("that is—Büchner") in lines that appear near the beginning of the fragment—his presence as an "'I' become strange" (*GW* 3:195/*CP* 46) in an opening upon the abyss whose condition, Heidegger tells us, lies in an authentic confrontation with mortality. Lucile's words, honoring the "majesty of the absurd," and thus testifying to the presence of the human, now find their counterpart in a line expressing Lenz's regret that he cannot walk on his head. As Celan remarks: "A man who walks on his head, ladies and gentlemen, a man who walks on his head sees the sky below, as an abyss" (*GW* 3:195/*CP* 46). Lenz ("that is—Büchner") has gone further than Lucile, however, in that his "step" is no longer a word: It is a "terrifying silence [*ein furchtbares Verstummen*]," Celan writes, which "takes away from him—and us—breath and the word" (*GW* 3:195/*CP* 47).

In the Bremen address, Celan had used the same words to describe the suspension through which language had passed during the war. It had gone through "its own lack of answers, through terrifying silence, through the thousand darknesses of murderous speech." As we saw, for Celan this silence was something like the condition of poetry as he came to practice it. Here, in the "Meridian," poetry is identified with a turn back to such a suspension of the word and of the breath:

Poetry: this means perhaps an *Atemwende*, a turning of our breath. Who knows, perhaps poetry goes its way—the way of art—for the sake of just such a turn? And since the strange, the abyss *and* Medusa's head, the abyss *and* the automaton, all seem to lie in the same direction—it is perhaps this turn, this *Atemwende*, which can sort out the strange from the strange? It is perhaps here, in this one brief moment, that Medusa's head shrivels and the automatons run down? Perhaps, also with the I, estranged and freed *here, in this manner,* some other thing is also set free?

Perhaps from there the poem can be itself . . . can in this now artless, art-free manner go its other ways, including the ways of art, time and again. (*GW* 3:195–96/*CP* 47)

Büchner's phrase ("only, it sometimes bothered him") thus *remarks a silence* that echoes beneath Lenz's steps in the mountains, a silence in which the poetry of the *Lenz* fragment takes its own step. *Against this silence,* "Büchner" here appears in the shape of Lenz. The event (*Ereignis*) marks a date: the 20th of January. Celan notes here that perhaps every poem is marked by such a date and that what constitutes the "newness" of poems today is that they seek to be "mindful" ("eingedenk") of such dates (*GW* 3:196/*CP* 47). But this "newness" is not what he referred to as "in the air." On the contrary, it is what interrupts the ubiquity of art and the spread of the uncanny.

It would be worthwhile to pause at greater length over Celan's treatment of the uncanny. He tells us near the end of his address that he set out to counter the contemporary demand for an extension of art, and it would seem to follow that he is attempting to counter a contemporary form of art's alienating tendencies. Celan may be referring to a specific movement or movements, or he may be thinking more generally of *la societé du spectacle* (a reference that may be justified by Celan's allusion to the reign of *Technik*);[12] most likely, he had both possibilities in mind. But whatever his specific reference, we should observe that Celan's concern is with art's uncanny character *in relation to the human.* His stated purpose is to free poetry from art, but it must be emphasized that this also means freeing art from its subservience to a notion of representation that is indissociable from a representation of the human and "what is natural for the creature" (a representation no less stifling today than in 1960). By freeing the possibility of recognizing poetry in art, and thus the presence of the human—in other words, by delimiting art (and the uncanny) and making it possible to approach art from another direction ("Perhaps after this the poem can be itself . . . can in this now artless, art-free manner go other ways, including the ways of art, time and again" [*GW* 3:196/*CP* 47]), Celan is able to entertain the possibility of relaxing the distinction he has attempted to achieve between the strangeness proper to poetry and the strangeness of the uncanny and assert that "art, the uncanny strangeness which is so hard to differentiate and is perhaps only one after all—art lives on" (*GW* 3:200/*CP* 52). Carrying through Büchner's question in the *Lenz* fragment and finding "Büchner," Celan can consider the uncanny side of art as the way of access to the strangeness from which poetry takes its departure, and thus as the way of access to self-encounter ("take art with you into your innermost narrowness. And set yourself free" [*GW* 3:200/*CP* 52]). The uncanny both alienates *and* affords a poetic experience of mortality and the abyss.

Jacques Derrida has remarked in his reading of Celan that we learn about death and mourning from language, not the other way around,[13] and in *Schibboleth pour Paul Celan*, he has gone far in defining the potential in language that creates the ambiguity of the uncanny around which Celan's speech pivots. To carry Celan's question any further, we would have to dwell longer on this question of language and the strangeness of art. At this point, however, I want only to emphasize the "pivoting" movement itself and to suggest that it makes possible the essential turn in Celan's text, a turn away from the aesthetic, mimetic tradition by which art is conceived as the imitation of reality. This turn is a movement back from the transcending (albeit "uncanny") movement by which the natural is seized as natural and in which the existence of the writing subject is effaced; it is a turning back in which the poetic self situates itself in relation to a reality toward which it "reaches" in its otherness and *in its time*.

In a discussion of this movement "back," Celan will evoke an attention to "detail, outline, structure, color," and to the "tremors and hints" (*GW* 3:198/*CP* 50) of the creature described by Lenz. In other words, Celan will describe a no less precise—indeed, a far more "realistic"—attention to the "natural and the creaturely," but he will do so from the perspective of the finitude or "finite transcendence" of the singular (writing) Dasein. He will describe a poetry that would proceed from the turn of an *Atemwende*, and thus a poetry that would proceed from *difference* in its approach to the other. In so doing, he will describe how poetry effects the "push" into historical existence that Heidegger described in *Sein und Zeit*.[14]

I will try to stress essentially two points in Celan's remarkable statement of his poetics and what he hopes to add to the "old hopes": these concern the time of the poem and the structure (also temporal) of the encounter it seeks. I will stress the first point, because I believe we find in Celan's statement a forceful appropriation of Heidegger's description of the structure of the work of art. By emphasizing the second point, I hope to bring forth the way in which Celan begins to depart from Heidegger by pushing Heidegger's thought of the singularity of existence (or of the work of art) in the direction of a very radical understanding of the relation to the other.

The time of the poem, of course, is that of an *Atemwende*; and as we have seen, the poem marks a date, even commemorates a date (it is "mindful," Celan says), as it proceeds from this pause of the breath and the word. It speaks from out of this date, "its date," and as such it speaks of its own concern ("in seiner eigenen, allereigensten Sache"). As Celan will emphasize, this concern, or "matter," is the concern of an individual; indeed, in these pages in which Celan exposes his poetics, he will return repeatedly to the fact that the poem is the "language become shape of a single person" ("gestaltgewordene Sprache eines Einzelnen") (*GW* 3:197–98/*CP* 49). In doing so, however, he will also always return to his notion that that self comes to itself in relation to an other. The poem thus marks the advent of a self to itself in the "present" of the poem—but this is the presence of a self as open to an other and as heading or reaching to this other. In his description of the poem's structure and "object," Celan will move back and forth between the presence of the solitary "I" and the other toward which the poem moves, but in the interweaving of these motifs, he will make it clear that the poetic self comes to itself and comes forth or steps forward in its finitude only in and by its movement toward the other. Poetry, as Celan writes in moving to identify "Lenz," "rushes ahead" and "tries to see the figure in its direction." This direction is the direction of the figure in its mortality. Yet in the opening given in and by this "being toward death," the movement is also toward the other. Thus, Celan adds that in its *Atempause*, in the present of the poem opened by its "pause for breath," the poem also "heads straight for the otherness" which it considers "reachable." Its movement from its date is also to an other (date)—it marks its date *in this movement*.

The time of this movement is the time of hope and thought. The poem has always hoped, Celan claims, to speak from a different matter ("in einer Anderen Sache" [*GW* 3:196/*CP* 48]) even as it speaks only its own; once again, to speak its own concern is to give a "voice" to the other. Celan "merely" adds to the "old hopes" a different understanding of this other (a notion that leads him to speak of an "altogether other" [*GW* 3:196/*CP* 48]), and speculates that the poem "dwells or hopes" ("verweilt oder verhofft") (*GW* 3:197/*CP* 48) with the thought of an encounter between this entirely other and a quite close other (which we may take, I believe, to be the freed and estranged "I"). The poem commits itself to a thought (with hope, "a word for living creatures," Celan adds, indicating that the time of the poem is distinctly human [*GW* 3:197/*CP* 48)—it is the poem *of a thought* (the conception of a relation between self and other) that is "conceivable, perhaps, again and again."[15] The poem gives its thought to be thought repeatedly, just as it goes its way "time and again." Its time, the time of a pause for breath ("Nobody can tell how long the pause for breath—hope and thought—will last") is one constituted in repetition.

The repetitive character of the poem's particular presence is remarked again by Celan when he recognizes that the poem "shows a strong tendency to silence" (*GW* 3:197/*CP* 48), but then asserts—as if to characterize more precisely the poem's "abruptness"—that the poem "holds its ground on its own margin": "In order to endure [*um bestehen zu können*], it constantly calls and pulls itself back from an 'already no more' into a 'still here' [or 'yet still,' *ein Immer noch*]" (*GW* 3:197/*CP* 49). These are difficult lines, but I believe we may understand them by remembering that the poem commemorates an event (a date) that *has happened*, and that is nothing other than the emergence of a singular Dasein in its finitude. The poem proceeds from this event ("we all write from such dates," Celan observes [*GW* 3:196/*CP* 47]), but the event only happens in the language of the poem. It happens in the poem, as Heidegger says of the event of truth in the work of art, as *having happened*.[16] The poetic self steps forward *against* the difference that opens with this step, and that is ontologically prior to it, as a kind of origin. In structural terms, we may speak of a delay of the Dasein with respect to its origin. But this stepping forward as it occurs in the poem *draws out the event* which is the opening of difference, or the opening of a relation between Dasein and everything that is, including other Dasein. It draws it out (makes it come about, makes it perdure) and brings it forth (re-marks the date: this manifest re-marking constitutes what Heidegger calls the "createdness" of poetry) in an initiatory fashion. The repetitive structure of the poem derives from the fact that the poem re-marks its origin in such a way as to bring it about as having been. And the more forcefully (the more "abruptly") it asserts itself (*sich behauptet*), the more it remarks the origin from which it proceeds, thereby standing out or standing forth more distinctly against this origin. It stands out, then, as Celan observes, through the singularity of the poet's language: "The still here can only mean speaking . . . In other words: language actualized, set free under the sign of a radical individuation" (*GW* 3:197/*CP* 49).

"Still here," or "yet still"—a word that corresponds to the *Das* ascribed by Heidegger to the work of art[17]—marks the presence of the poem. The essence of the poem, Celan claims, is the presence of something present ("seinem innersten Wesen nach Gegenwart und Präsenz" [*GW* 3:197–98/*CP* 49]). It marks a here and now ("Even in the here and now of the poem—and the poem has only this one, unique, momentary present—even in this immediacy and nearness" [*GW* 3:198–99/*CP* 50]) that in its repetitive structure turns both forward and back, anticipating and recollecting (forward to the other, back to its date), in such a way as to remark relation and a movement, a passage in time. I should perhaps reemphasize that the presence in question is not the presence of the metaphysics of presence, for the presence is that of a sign that does not signify, but rather, in its very distinctness (Hölderlin spoke of its "firmness"), points beyond itself in an allegorical mode—thus marking relation to an alterity.

Celan remarks that the "yet still" is language "corresponding," language that is *Entsprechung*—"and not simply verbally."[18] This last qualification, "and not simply verbally," refers undoubtedly to what he has said about Lucile's perception of language, for he goes on to emphasize that the language of the poem is the language of a "radical individuation," the language of poets "who do not forget that they speak from an angle of reflection which is their own existence, their own creaturely nature" (*GW* 3:197/*CP* 49). This is a language, then, that "corresponds" to the person (though not in the mode of signification, since the person first emerges in this language). While Celan's focus in this paragraph is on the singularity and solitude of the individual, as of the poem, the turn of the paragraph ("Does this very fact not place the poem already here, at its inception, in the encounter, *in the mystery of encounter?*" [*GW* 3:198/*CP* 49]) reminds us again that the "correspondence" of the poem's "still here" must also be conceived more broadly. "Corresponding," the language is *commensurate* with the event that has happened (that it draws out) and *answering to* something to which it gives itself over, which it "needs" and which it addresses as an other "over against it." Once again, this is simultaneously recollection and a reaching forward—a reaching forward out of recollection:

> The poem intends another, needs this other, needs an opposite. It goes toward it, addresses it.
>
> For the poem, everything and everybody is a figure of this other toward which it is heading.
>
> The attention which the poem pays to all that it encounters, its more acute sense of detail, outline, structure, color . . . all this is not, I think, achieved by an eye competing (or concurring) with ever more precise instruments, but rather, by a kind of concentration mindful of all our dates. (*GW* 3:198/*CP* 49)

We have seen that the date marks the emergence of the poetic self in its mortality—against the possibility of its death, and thus against the opening that occurs in this assumption of mortality. For Dasein, this is the opening of a spatio-temporal disposition that defines its time and its place, and thus the opening of the possibility of relation to an other (in other words, the event of truth). The poem thus gives expression to the movement of an individual existence *in and from its time.* Yet this time is given to it (the event is drawn out in the poem) only as this existence emerges in its movement *toward an other* with which it seeks to engage. In seeking the other, then, the poem is seeking its own (and its author's) truth: its truth, in relation (understood always temporally).

For the poem, Celan writes, everything and everybody is a figure of this other. The altogether other is u-topic—for it is other than every other (everything that is). It is precisely that which gives the other to be perceived in its precise outline—in other words, it is its essence or what is most proper to it: most fundamentally, Celan suggests, its time ("Even in the here and now of the poem . . . even in this immediacy and nearness, the poem lets the other speak with what is most proper to it: its time"). Yet we might ask here: if Celan is insisting so markedly on the singularity of the self that emerges in the poem, would not every "you" be a singular "you" in the same manner, and would not that which is most proper to it also have the same unique character? In which case, how could every other be a figure of the altogether other which the poem seeks?

The answer to this question, I believe, derives from Celan's elaboration of the notions of finitude and singularity. The essence sought by the poem, what constitutes the "otherness" of the other, has its origin in what must be understood not as a substantial ground, but as difference. This difference is the "same" out of which beings emerge in their difference—over against one another, as Heidegger puts it, *gegeneinanderüber*. Thus we may speak appropriately in these terms of *the* other or *the* difference the poem seeks. But Celan underscores the radically temporal character of this difference, and in view of his emphasis on the solitude of the poem (and its author), as well as the radical individuation of the poet, we may conclude that he is pushing Heidegger's thought of finitude to the point of recognizing that the difference can only be thought as occurring or opening *in relation*, in always singular relations (and thus thought as always differing from itself). The difference, then, is to be understood in the manner of what Jean-Luc Nancy refers to as a *partage*.[19] It is other than any other—"transcendent," one might say (thus it is the u-topic out of whose "light" the poem seeks "the human being" and "the creature")—but other *only in relation*, thus a "quasi-transcendental," to use Derrida's term.[20] "Truth," Heidegger argued in "The Origin of the Work of Art," happens nowhere other than at the site where it is drawn out, in always singular articulations; that to which the poem points (allegorically) is other than it, but also occurs nowhere other than in it.

We may understand better now what it means to say that the poem is seeking its truth—its truth, in relation. Its truth is the opening of a possibility of relation realized in the movement of reaching poetically for an other. This is not its truth in the sense that this possibility would be something it brings to the other or institutes *from itself*. Rather, it would be something that comes about or occurs as it proceeds, in and from an experience of mortality, toward the other (other beings in their singularity). The poem *seeks* its truth in going to the other, it *draws out* a relation, a relation that is open-ended like the question posed by the poem: "Whenever we speak with things in this way we also dwell on the question of their wherefrom and their whereto . . . a question pointing to the Open, Empty, and Free, a question that remains open and has no end" (*GW* 3:199/*CP* 50).

Once again, it is difficult not to hear Heidegger in these lines. Also, it is difficult, in this context, not to recall another one of Heidegger's terms for the site of difference or what he calls here the "Open," *Das Gegend*, a term that appeared in Celan's Bremen address, meaning "country" or "region." In its engagement or encounter (*Begegnung*) with the other, the poem would be pointing with its "question" to the *Gegend*. *Gegend* does not in fact appear in this passage (though we find, in addition to "Begegnung," "Gegenwart" and "ein Gegenüber"), but it comes immediately to mind when we recognize the extent to which Celan is following Heidegger in thinking relation with the preposition *gegen—working* the term in such a way as to subvert its dialectical determination. A brief consideration of Heidegger's employment of *gegen* in "The Nature of Language" will help to show what is at stake here, and also allow me to introduce my final points about the reading of Heidegger contained in the "Meridian."

In "The Nature of Language," Heidegger proposes to move from the neighborhood of poetry and thought (defined in relation to the "divergence" of their modes of saying and the relation that opens out of the tracing of this difference, a relation that Heidegger defines as a *Gegeneinanderüber*) back to the "region," the *Gegend*, in which this neighborhood stands. The "way back" is provided by the region itself, Heidegger suggests, because all encounter (as in the relation between poetry and thought, taken in this essay as an exemplary case of the "face to face encounter of things") takes its possibility from the countering, the way-making movement of the region:

> Speaking allusively, the country [*Gegend*], that which counters, is the clearing that gives free rein, where all that is cleared and freed, and all that conceals itself, together attain the open freedom. The freeing and sheltering character of this region lies in this way-making movement, which yields those ways that belong to the region.
>
> To a thinking so inclined that reaches out sufficiently [*hinreichend Gedacht*], the way is that by which we reach [*was uns gelangen läßt*]—which lets us reach what reaches for us by concerning us, by suing us.[21]

What concerns and summons, what puts underway, is essence, understood in its temporal character. Heidegger brings out this temporal determination with the phase, "Es west" (literally, "it essences"): "*Es west* means it presences, in persisting it regards us, moves us and concerns us [or "sues" us: *be-wëgt uns und be-langt uns*]. Essence, so understood, names the persisting, what concerns us in all things, because it moves and makes a way for all things."[22] Heidegger then adds that if essence can thus summon or "sue" us, it is because language is what is most proper to it: "What moves all things moves in that it speaks."[23] Essence "counters," then, in speaking. All encounter with that which concerns us or regards us (in the manner of the other which *in its otherness*—in its essence—is "turned toward the poem," as Celan says) is made possible by language, understood in its most originary manner as a "Saying" that opens "ways" and thus articulates the "region," the *Gegend*, as the differential relation structuring all relations of things as they stand "over against one another" (*gegeneinanderüber*).

Yet essence counters, Heidegger suggests, only as it is drawn out in and by a "rejoining" ("entgegnende") word—a word which "corresponds" ("entspricht") to that which it draws forth (the speaking of language itself).[24] For Heidegger, such a rejoining word occurs in all language where truth is at stake, but it occurs most manifestly in poetry. Might we say, then, that this "rejoining word" is equivalent to Lucile's "counterword" ("Gegenwort") and Lenz's silence ("His 'Long live the King!' is no longer a word, but rather a terrifying silence")? Explicitly designating Lucile's word as "poetry," Celan suggests that all poetry has its source in the turn, the turning against (art) that occurs with such a speaking (even Lenz's silence is a kind of "speaking"—it is the same as a "Long live the King"). To the extent that all poetry is encounter, for Celan, we may presume that it proceeds from and embodies such a countering word which opens the possibility of relation by opening to the other in its otherness.

The detour I have taken through Heidegger's meditation on relation by way of the preposition *gegen* should throw light on the structure of what Celan understands by poetic relation. Yet most importantly, perhaps, it should underscore the point that the relation in question is a relation *in and of language*, for the relation to the other toward which the poem moves and which it seeks to bring to speech is given essentially in language and in what Heidegger calls the speaking of language. As we saw already in his Bremen address, Celan conceives of poetry as *engaging with language*—with the essence of language understood as that which gives relation. With its "counterword," the poem opens the paths that are the ways of relation given by language itself (as Saying) when it is brought to "speak," that is, when something other is brought forth in its singular presence "over against," a "speaking I" as something that "concerns and sues" in its otherness. The way is opened in the tracing of what Heidegger calls the *Riß*, a differential relation that both separates and draws together—it is the *difference* that "lets us reach what reaches for us by concerning us, by suing us."[25] We have seen that the poem traces out such ways with its initiating counterword, but this counterword must be understood also as a response, or understood as *becoming* a response in the time of the poem (as it is poised between recollection and advance toward an other)—a response that allows the unfolding of a poetic relation that is *given* by language. It is in this sense, finally, that the poem is "conversation"—it is a conversation *in and from language*.[26]

Such a conception of the poetic conversation does not—or should not—elide the "creaturely" existence of the speaking subject or that of the other (thing or human being) over against which the "I" comes to stand. But it is true that Celan succeeds in the "Meridian" in carrying a thought of the singularity of existence—as Heidegger himself began to develop it in *Being and Time*—into a meditation on poetic language that Heidegger perhaps only approached in his readings of Hölderlin (we do not find it, for example, in "The Origin of the Work of Art"). He does so in a manner that effectively challenges in its very radicality the thought of finitude and historicity which Heidegger pursued in the existential analytic, because he thinks singularity *always in relation* (as is required, in fact, by the very notion of singularity). By introducing his concept of *Mitsein*, Heidegger recognized the necessity of thinking Dasein in relation, but he failed to carry through this concept in any manner adequate to his own description of the facticity of Dasein. He failed, in effect, to think through sufficiently the relation to the other in its otherness, and to take the measure of what this might mean for a thought of the historicity of Dasein.[27]

This last assertion will have to stand without development, for it would require, to begin, a lengthy commentary of section 74 of *Being and Time*, on "The Basic Constitution of Historicality."[28] If we consider Celan's own description of poetic "conversation," however, it is possible to hear something of the radicality to which I want to point in the very *questioning* character of the conversation as Celan understands it:

> The poem becomes—under what conditions! [Celan would appear to be referring to the "increasing speed" of *Technik*, in a time after the experience of "terrifying silence"—C.F.]—the poem of one who—yet still—perceives, one who is turned toward what appears, questioning and addressing what thus appears. The poem becomes conversation—often desperate conversation.
>
> Only in the space of this conversation does that which is addressed constitute itself, gather itself around the naming and addressing I. But this addressed, also become a "you" through naming, brings its being-other into this present. Even in the here and now of the poem—and the poem has always only this one, unique, momentary present—even in this immediacy and nearness, it lets what is most proper to this other, its time, speak along with it.
>
> Whenever we speak with things in this way, we also dwell on the question of their wherefrom and whereto, a question "remaining open," "coming to no end," and pointing toward the Open, the Empty, and the Free. —We have ventured far out.
>
> The poem also searches for this place. (*GW* 3:198–99/*CP* 50)

This relation is tenuous, this passage seems to suggest, because it is a relation in time: the "abyss" for Celan, lies in time itself. I have said that the poetic "I" seeks its truth (and thus its time—the time in which it situates itself, mindful of its dates) in relation to the other, in and from the difference between self and other. But this difference in which time occurs for Dasein can only be thought, if we follow Celan's text, in such singular relations, in always singular instantiations (single "instants," *Augenblicke*), and cannot be thought as *gathering* the terms it draws into relation (as would a third term that provides a common measure).[29] To put it schematically: the time I must assume as Dasein is not your time, though I know my time only in opening to yours, in relation. Properly speaking, this is not "my" time, but a time given in this relation, "our" time, shared. Yet as "shared," this time differs from itself with each occurrence in which it is drawn out and instantiated (your time is not my time). I ask "wherefrom and whereto" in this encounter in order to situate myself in the present, a "shared" time—I can know (encounter) myself only by going beyond myself in search of this time. But the time I seek will never constitute a grounding destiny or even a shared condition, precisely because it is "shared" in an originary fashion and because the other remains other, even as relation is drawn out.

Hence, the conversation is "often desperate," for I may situate myself only in relation to an other, but my reach is toward an otherness of the other that I can never appropriate and that exposes me always to an alterity ("La poésie ne s'impose plus, elle s'expose" [*GW* 3:181/*CP* 29]). This alterity is marked in the poem—brought to "speak" there—but its voice is fundamentally unsettling, *because always other.*

I believe we hear something of the unsettling character of the relation to the other in the quatrain Celan offers as an example of poetry written from his own "20th of January." Of this poem, and of "Conversation in the Mountains," Celan affirms (with the same sureness with which he announces that he has "touched" a meridian with his audience): "I had . . . encountered myself" (*GW* 3:202/*CP* 53). Both texts are about being under way and about encounter; they each evoke in some manner "the paths on which language becomes voice." Indeed, "Conversation in the Mountains" contains a reflection on language that complements the turn against naturalism that Celan develops in relation to Büchner's aesthetics. The "encounter" in this text unfolds in a linguistic space that is declared to be incommensurable with the "language" of nature, a language "without I and without You." This text also mirrors the assertions of the "Meridian" in that the encounter unfolds through a movement of recollection that allows something like an opening by which the speaking I comes to describe itself as "accompanied." I will not try to read the text any further here, however, because its complex linguistic structure and its evocation of Judaic motifs re-

quire quite lengthy analysis—an analysis that could well force us to re-
consider in depth the somewhat "Greek," Heideggerian, character of
the phenomenology which the "Meridian" seems to offer, but which
could only reinforce my suggestion that Celan is trying to think a less
gathered essence of time than the one developed by Heidegger, and
thus necessarily a very different kind of "homecoming." Rather, and by
way of conclusion, I will focus on the quatrain Celan chooses to cite in
the "Meridian." Its irony might be said to reflect some of the instability
he finds in Büchner's *Lenz*, and it points to the uncertainty out of which
Celan—"Celan"—proceeds in seeking relation to the other in its otherness. In German, the quatrain reads:

> Stimmen vom Nesselweg her:
> *Komm auf den Händen zu uns.*
> Wer mit der Lampe allein ist,
> Hat nur die Hand, draus zu lesen.
> (*GW* 3:201 [*GW* 1:147]/*CP* 53)

In a literal translation:

> Voices from the nettle-path:
> *Come to us on your hands.*
> One who is alone with the lamp
> Has only the hand to read from.

The irony at play in the quatrain derives already in part from the way
in which it echoes its context in the "Meridian." It recalls to us, for
example, the line regarding Lenz's desire to walk on his head: to walk
on one's head is, after all, to walk on one's hands (the figures are of
course very different, but Celan seems to be working with this echo in
order to point back to Lenz, as he will do in referring to his use of
"a man like Lenz" in "Conversation in the Mountains"). Moreover,
the abruptness of the quatrain cannot but prompt us to look to it as a
Gegenwort. Yet is the *Gegenwort* in the challenging, italicized call, or is
it in the sardonic character of the second couplet which might evoke for
us an absurdity that "bespeaks the presence of human beings," but this
time in anything but a majestic manner?[30]

Within the quatrain, and through the ironic play of *both* couplets,
we find a rather sharp reflection on the unsettling character of the encounter and on the difficulty experienced in moving toward the other. I
am amplifying the tone of the quatrain somewhat, but I believe one
cannot avoid hearing the one addressed as the object of a kind of teasing
aimed at dislodging it from a solitude to which the second couplet refers; indeed, I would suggest that the subject of this quatrain—actually
elided in it—is a subject "dislodged," but barely under way, or under

way hesitantly. The call, we might say, evokes the hesitance of the addressed subject; it speaks to that hesitancy in asking that this subject undertake with the hands what is hardly a tempting path. We may well read the path as the path of poetry "on which language becomes voice" (*GW* 3:201/*CP* 53): a path that *the poet* is invited to undertake inasmuch as poetry is a craft and thus "a matter of hands"—"the hands of one person, i.e., a unique, mortal soul searching for its way with its voice and dumbness.[31] But there is something mildly cruel or mocking in these voices which invite the poet[32] to proceed by hand over a path through *nettles*. Had Celan written "thorns," for example, this couplet would have taken on a far different tonality in that the poet would be called to a kind of ritual suffering. To be sure, "nettles" are also not without their ritual connotations, but their *annoying* character upsets any possible gravity in their appearance in this couplet.

Of course, the voices are calling for either trust or humility, or both, inviting the one addressed to follow the voices by feeling the way along a "blind " path (where sight will somehow not suffice to direct an erect gait), or inviting the one addressed to come in a kind of supplication or even humiliation. They require a kind of openness or exposure, and a form of self-renunciation. Yet, obeying this call (at least as it is heard from the position of the one addressed) will be something more than difficult—it will also be irritating and unpleasant. In this way, "nettles" undoes or unsettles any too pious or easy evocation in this context of the attention to which Celan refers in quoting Malebranche by way of Walter Benjamin: "Attention is the natural prayer of the soul" (*GW* 3:198/*CP* 50).

After the first couplet, the second also takes on something of an ironic, stinging character. The couplet could be read as part of the address by the voices, but the italics distinguish the second verse in such a way as to suggest that the couplet is spoken by one who has heard their call (in which case—which is certainly the most probable and interesting—the quatrain embodies a movement of self-reflection). In either case, in the image of one who in solitude—let us say, "Celan"—has only the lines of his hands in which to read a figure of his destiny ("solitary" in that he is proceeding under what we might call the light of conscious understanding), there is a subtle but quite effective inversion of *finding one's way with one's hands* (poetically). The "reader" (the poet) is impoverished, and somewhat pitiful, not because he has no book with him; he is impoverished because he is following the solitary path of reflection and interpretation, along which no lines will ever confront him with a destiny. In this solitude, he will never see or hear the trace of the other—he might as well read his hands. He can know his destiny only by going out toward the other in a mode of encounter that exceeds any traditional hermeneutic relation. He cannot "read" the other; he must "invent" the other by reaching poetically for the other in a language that projects a reality and is thus "under way" toward an addressable "you."

In "Engführung," Celan writes:

Lies nicht mehr–schau!
Schau nicht mehr—geh!
(*GW* 1:197)

(Read no longer—look!
Look no longer—go!)

The quatrain, I would suggest, embodies such an invitation—an invitation and a *response* that draws out the invitation as an invitation coming from an unsettling alterity. The irony of the quatrain remarks the otherness of the voice and the necessity of a movement toward the other, even as it evokes its difficulty. It remarks that the other *has been heard*; thus it marks a date.

Beyond *Nesselweg*, and "voices," there is no "figure" of the other here, and the speaking "I" is all but elided, appearing only in a turn. The quatrain offers no more than a sketch of encounter and a movement that is no more than the condition of conversation (a movement of self-reflection *in response to the other*). Nonetheless it underscores the fundamentally unsettling character of exposure to the other; thus it gives some sense of the instability of the opening from which poetic questioning proceeds. When Celan invokes the presence of the person and the distinctness of the figure it takes as images of the other, we must not forget that they are traced out against *such* a date.

The irony at work in the quatrain, I want to suggest, cannot but spill over into the argument of the "Meridian" and prevent us from any too triumphant celebration of the possibility of self-discovery. Through its re-evocation of Lenz, it reminds us that the freedom of the estranged "I" lies in the opening to an abyss: "only it sometimes bothered him that he could not walk on his head." If the obscurity and strangeness of this last phrase—deriving from its opacity as the "actualized language" of an existent being—appears "for the sake of an encounter," the encounter occurs only over this abyss. The abyss, we have seen, is time as it is given *with* the possibility of relation to the other, that is, *with* language when it is brought to speak in the "actualized speech" of the individual (language, once again, that is a *sign*) as a difference that holds one over to another (but as other). Language, the language which Celan experienced as "near and unlost," and to which the poem turns in its *Atemwende*, gives relation only in and through time. More simply, it gives time: the irreversible time of a singular existence as it seeks itself in reaching to an other. Here, then, is what I wanted to suggest must be said today about poetry (after Heidegger): its language gives time, and only in this time—a time we know today as irreversible and disjunctive—can we speak of something like an encounter with reality. What is at stake in poetry is the possibility of a reality: from language and in time.

NOTES

1. *GW* 3:186/*CP* 34. Where my reading of Celan's texts has required a more strict translation, I have modified existing English renditions.

2. See in particular lecture 3, part 2 of *Was heißt Denken?* (Tübingen: Niemeyer, 1962), 91–95. Martin Heidegger, *What Is Called Thinking?*, trans. Fred Wieck and J. Glenn Gray (New York: Harper & Row, 1968), 138–43. The reading of "Andenken" appears in Martin Heidegger, *Erläuterungen zu Hölderlins Dichtung*, Gesamtausgabe (Frankfort: Klostermann, 1981), vol. 4, and in lecture form in vol. 52.

3. "Detours" is Celan's word—one that he immediately puts in question. For the history Celan is commemorating has radically altered any thought of destination or of homecoming.

4. See in particular Heidegger's discussions of the everyday occurrence of words failing us and of Stefan George's poem "Das Wort." "Das Wesen der Sprache," in Martin Heidegger, *Unterwegs zur Sprache*, Gesamtausgabe (Frankfort: Klostermann, 1985), 12:147–204. "The Nature of Language," trans. Peter D. Hertz, in Martin Heidegger, *On the Way to Language* (New York: Harper & Row, 1955), 55–108. Celan's experience of silence is incomparably more severe than anything described by Heidegger in his essays on language, but the experience is essentially the same. Language gives itself (or gives a relation to itself in its nearness/withdrawal) in a suspension of speech that is indissociable from an experience of mortality.

5. A strange negativity because negativity has always been thought as the source of meaning. The negativity of "murderous speech," however, destroys meaning. In relation to the essence of language, it occupies a place not unlike that of evil in relation to the divine logos. It is a possibility in the logos—again, it is necessarily *of* language—that is destructive of the logos in that it turns against the capacity of the logos for holding in being. "Murderous speech" destroys the relation that it is of the essence of language to give.

6. *GW* 3:36. Cited by Maurice Blanchot, *Le Dernier à parler* (Montpellier: Fata morgana, 1984), 35. Maurice Blanchot, "The Last One to Speak," trans. Joseph Simas, in *Acts* 8–9 (1988), 235. The lines I have cited appear there in translation by Pierre Joris: "Singable remnant"; "—Unmouthed lip, announce, / that something's happening, still, / not far from you" (235).

7. In what hardly seems an accidental manner (though the echo does not seem conceptually active), "*angereichert*," "'enriched,'" echoes Celan's use of *Erreichbar* in the first part of his speech (*Klang des Unerreichbaren*; *Erreichbar*; *das zu Erreichende*; and *Erreichbar*). This linguistic echo, working by etymology, is then further developed at a semantic level with the term *hindurchgreifen*. James K. Lyon remarks in an essay that "*angereichert*" is a term drawn from mineralogy, as is "*zutage treten*" (translated above as "resurface"). See "Paul Celan's Language of Stone: The Geology of the Poetic Landscape," *Colloquia Germanica* 8, nos. 3–4 (1974), 298. The quotation marks around *angereichert* might be

signaling this technical reference—but this would not exclude the fact that the term is used with some irony.

8. Cf. "Die Frage nach der Technik," in *Vorträge und Aufsätze* (Pfüllingen: Neske, 1978), 32 and 39.

9. Celan writes: "This is not the historical Lenz speaking, but Büchner's Lenz. Here we hear Büchner's own voice: here too art holds something uncanny for him." And shortly thereafter: "But you see: we cannot ignore the 'rattling' voice Valerio gets whenever art is brought forward. These are—Büchner's voice leads me to this supposition—old, the very oldest uncanninesses" (*GW* 3:192/ *CP* 43).

10. Which I write in the manner of Heidegger when he describes the object of his *Auseinandersetzung* with Nietzsche's thought: "Nietzsche." Cf. *Nietzsche* (Pfüllingen: Neske, 1961), 9.

11. My reading of the "Meridian" will pass close at times to the one offered by Lacoue-Labarthe in *La poésie comme expérience* (Paris: Bourgois, 1986)—a reading with which I fully concur. In retrospect, I see that our major point of agreement concerns the fact that the "Meridian" develops a notion of singularity, and that what is at stake in this reflection is a thought of the possibility of relation. I also arrive at an understanding of Celan's notion of dialogue similar to the one offered by Lacoue-Labarthe, though I follow a direction noted, but not followed by him (Heidegger's thought on language). This path was indicated to me by Celan's very Heideggerian notion of a *Gegenwort*. Lacoue-Labarthe reaches a similar reading of Celan's use of the preposition *gegen*, but he expresses concern regarding the possible dialectical or representational overdetermination of the term. For my part, I am struck by the extent to which Celan pursues Heidegger's textual work with it in an effort to produce a nondialectical, nonrepresentational thought of relation. In the "Meridian," Celan offers (intentionally or not) a very precise and rich reading of Heidegger's "The Nature of Language."

I might add that the reading offered here is also essentially in agreement with the one proposed by Jacques Derrida in *Schibboleth pour Paul Celan* (Paris: Galilée, 1986). In fact, it was undertaken in part in order to work through Derrida's suggestions concerning the notion of encounter. See esp. 19–28.

12. Cf. "'Speed,' which has always been 'outside,' has gained yet more speed" (*GW* 3:197/*CP* 48).

13. "One cannot say that we know [about the spectral quality of words] *because* we have the experience of death and mourning. This experience comes to us from our relation to this ghostly return of the mark, and then of language, of the word, of the name." *Schibboleth*, 96.

14. 15th ed. (Tübingen: Niemeyer, 1979), 384. Martin Heidegger, *Being and Time*, trans. John Macuarrie and Edward Robinson (New York: Harper & Row, 1962), 435.

15. *GW* 3:197/*CP* 48. The fact that the *Atempause* marks the time of a thought and hope is another indication that Celan associates breath (in accordance with an ancient, etymological tie) with spirit. Lucile, we remember, "perceives language as a physical shape and also . . . breath, that is, direction and destiny." From this line, however, we also see that if spirit is thought in its historicity, it is also embodied thought—thought that exists only as the "language

become shape of a single person." If Celan confesses to a "u-topian" drive in speaking of the poem, he nevertheless makes it clear that the "non-site" of encounter toward which he seeks to move "exists" only in and by language. There is no metaphysics of presence in this text, if such a metaphysics presupposes a notion of a transcendental signified and the presence to self of mind or spirit. Rather, presence is understood here as occurring in and by a relation to alterity, and spirit breathes only in the letter, conceived "bodily."

16. Indeed, Celan is describing the same event as does Heidegger in "The Origin of the Work of Art"; for when the singular Dasein comes to itself in its finitude, it also stands before—more properly it traces out: when it remarks its own limits it *opens upon* and *draws out*—the difference that Heidegger thinks in this text as the relation between world and earth, and more originally, between concealment and unconcealment. Cf. "Der Ursprung des Kunstwerkes," in Martin Heidegger, *Holzwege*, Gesamtausgabe (Frankfort: Klostermann, 1977), 5:53. "The Origin of the Work of Art," trans. Albert Hofstadter, in Martin Heidegger, *Poetry, Language, Thought* (New York: Harper & Row, 1971), 65.

17. Cf. "Der Ursprung des Kunstwerkes," 53.

18. An *Entsprechung* is a "corresponding case or instance," or can be an analogous or equivalent word. The poem's *Entsprechung*, we might say, is its "ana-logy." The verb *entsprechen*, which Celan is activating here, means "to answer to," "to conform to," "to correspond to," or "to be commensurate with."

19. This notion is developed in Nancy's *Le Partage des voix* (Paris: Galilée, 1982). *Partager* means "to share," and this can be either in the sense of "dividing" or "communicating." We will see that this last sense of the term is quite appropriate to Celan's discussion of difference.

20. In *The Tain of the Mirror: Derrida and the Philosophy of Reflection* (Cambridge: Harvard University Press, 1986), Rodolphe Gasché has developed the meaning of this term extensively.

21. "On the Way to Language," 95. Celan would appear to be thinking of essence along these lines—that is, as what "regards" us or concerns us (*angehen*)—when he speaks of the poem's other as "reachable [*erreichbar*], as able to be freed, as perhaps vacant and at the same time turned—like Lucile, let us say—toward it" (*GW* 3:197/*CP* 48). Later, in speaking of the *Atemwende* that punctuate his address, Celan writes: "Twice, with Lucile's 'Long live the King' and when the sky opened as an abyss under Lenz, there seemed to occur an *Atemwende*, a turning of breath. Perhaps also while I was trying to head for that inhabitable distance which, finally, was visible only in the figure of Lucile" (*GW* 3:200/*CP* 52). Lucile thus offers not only an example of a *Gegenwort* with her "Long live the King," but she is also taken as a figure of the other toward which the poem moves and which comes to its encounter.

22. "The Nature of Language," 95 [trans. modified].

23. Ibid.

24. I have drawn the terms *entgegnen* and *entsprechen* from the last pages of Heidegger's essay, "Die Sprache" (in *Unterwegs zur Sprache*, 29), an essay in which Heidegger focuses primarily on poetic speaking. For a reading of the structure of "rejoinder," see Christopher Fynsk, "Noise at the Threshold," *Research in Phenomenology* 19 (1990), 101–19.

25. Cf. "The Nature of Language," 95.

26. In the sense in which Heidegger speaks of language's "monological" character. See "The Way to Language," 111 and 134. I should underscore, however, that this "monologue," as the articulation of difference, is not a kind of immanent conversation of language with itself; Heidegger does not turn language into a ground.

27. Precisely because it might mean that no gathering or grounding measure might be found for existence, I cannot help but suspect that Heidegger's concern for the gathering character of relation (or difference) prohibited him from carrying far a radical thought of singularity. Such a thought is certainly present in his text—it is there to be read and developed, but remains largely latent.

I might note here that the direction taken by Celan is anticipated in a remark made by Emmanuel Lévinas in an early essay on Blanchot. See *Revue des Sciences Humaines* 51–52 (1948), 117. In speaking of a possible "philosophical exegesis of art" that would fulfill the task of criticism, Lévinas writes, one "would have to introduce the perspective of the relation with the other [*autrui*] without which being could not be told in its reality, that is, in its time." This remark is cited by Paul Davies in a forthcoming book on Heidegger, Blanchot, and Lévinas.

28. *Being and Time*, 434–39.

29. Thus the *gegen* relation, the "over against," *gegeneinanderüber,* is disjunctive: the relation of one Dasein to an other is not the same as the relation of the other to this Dasein, though each is only in relation to the other. Blanchot has developed a notion of such a disjunctive relation. See, for example, *L'Entretien infini* (Paris: Gallimard, 1969), 103–5.

30. Here, I suspect that "countering" can only be thought as occurring *between* the two couplets. The countering challenge of the first couplet comes forth in its unsettling character when it is answered with the irony of the second—the challenge occurs *with* the answer. Only with this second couplet does it emerge as *having been heard,* thereby marking the presence of the other.

31. In the letter to Hans Bender from which this line is taken, Celan continues: "Only truthful hands write true poems. I cannot see any basic difference between a handshake and a poem" (*GW* 3:177/*CP* 26).

32. The one addressed in this couplet could also be the reader—in the succeeding paragraph, Celan refers to poetry as "paths from a voice to a listening you." Thus this quatrain could also be saying something about the countering character of the poem for a reader—a countering that must be answered in some other manner than "reading under a lamp." Inasmuch as Celan speaks of encountering himself in this quatrain, however, it is clear that the addressed subject—at least here, in the "Meridian," here in this recollection of dates—must be "Celan."

In memory of Manfred Hoppe

5

Reading Celan

The Allegory of "Hohles Lebensgehöft"

and "Engführung"

Joel Golb

In "Hohles Lebensgehöft," from the 1967 collection *Atemwende,* Paul Celan offers a self-reflective landscape, both simile and metaphor, which is also a conundrum:

HOHLES LEBENSGEHÖFT. Im Windfang
die leer-
geblasene Lunge
blüht. Eine Handvoll
Schlafkorn
weht aus dem wahr-
gestammelten Mund
hinaus zu den Schnee-
gesprächen.
    (GW 2:42)

(HOLLOW HOMESTEAD OF LIFE. In the *Windfang*
the lung, blown
empty, blossoms.
A handful of
sleepgrain
wafts from the true-
stammered mouth
out to the snow-
conversations.)

On the one hand, we have here a naturalistic scene, tinged with bleakness: an abandoned homestead (*Gehöft*), snow blanketing its tranquil surrounding country. On the other, the homestead is a "lifestead," and the paradox of the poem's title is doubly rendered living: first, as the smoke drifting over the countryside from the (empty) dwelling; then, in the identity of this movement with a fused biological and pneumatological process. The "lifestead" is—the homestead is analogous to—the hollow of the poet's chest, and the smoke is "sleepgrain" that his lungs blow through his mouth. These imaginative, transformative kernels are wafted (or, in a parallel metaphor, scattered outward by the poet's hand in the act of writing) toward the "snow conversations" signifying communion with the reader. *Lesen* is the poem's absent double entendre, meaning both "read" and "glean"; like the wordplay, the reader is absent from the text, yet moving toward it.

But what, in fact, is the nature of our reading/gleaning (*Lesen*) of the poem? We might stop at this point, perhaps citing the significance of Martin Buber's I/Thou relation for Celan, seeing the poem's message in the stammered communion itself: the "message in a bottle" by which he defines poetry in his Bremen-prize address (*GW* 3:186). Such a reading touches on a Buberian theme that is, indeed, at the heart of Celan's sense of his poetic purpose. It does not, however, touch on the "truth" he states is hiding here, inside the poem. Celan describes this "true stammered" truth as "blooming" or "blossoming," along with the poet's and poem's "lung," deep within what, in Heideggerian fashion, we might call the hollow homestead of Celan's and the poem's being: in what the German calls a *Windfang*. Looking up *Windfang* (literally: "wind-trap") in a modern dictionary, we find something like the "porch" or "portal" of a house—a definition demanding that we reconcile the poem's existential pathos with the image (risking bathos) of Celan's hollow home caught fire, smoke pouring over the snowy landscape, not from its hearth-fed chimney, but its "porch" (*P* 235).

In fact, *Windfang* is an old and venerable word, exemplified in the Grimm brothers' historical dictionary by a rich variety of citations. For instance, we have its sixteenth- and seventeenth-century meaning as "bellows," used commonly for an organ, but also, humorously, in a medical text of Johann Dryander published in Cologne in 1537, to signify the lungs. Similarly, it is used in Johann Sommer's *Aenigmato-graphia rhythmica* of the late sixteenth century to signify the throat. Below this, we find Wolfgang Hohberg's use of the word in the *Georgica Curiosa* of 1682 to denote "an air hole, used to strengthen the draft in an oven, particularly a furnace"; and Goethe used the term for a "movable implement in a chimney, used for food that smokes."[1]

The reality of Celan's *Windfang* is that of the word's historicity. By acknowledging this historicity, we supply Celan's analogy with its narrative coherence. The secret, stammered "truth" of "Hohles Lebensgehöft" hides in the entire range of the word's historical usage, most particularly in the presence inside the poem of an oven's air hole; it surfaces in the word's contemporary, rural designation of the outside flue to a hearth. Keeping in mind its connection with Latin *venticax*, we might translate the word as "vent." The meaning of the analogy now emerges, or "blossoms," in our interpretive awareness, having penetrated the false front of "porch." On the one hand, there is the poet-sleeper, muttering "true" words in a dream-text. These words, an inscribed "handful of sleepgrain," move from the poet's lungs through the mouth into the night air and a snowy countryside, observed, perhaps, one night from the window of Celan's Norman country home, but also representing the poet's Bukovinian past and a utopian future (the "hope" embedded in *Lebensgehöft*)—the "snow conversations" of an ongoing dialogue on death and poetry. On the other hand, there is Celan's house, with its fireplace or old-fashioned stove. Inside this metaphoric dreamscape, the stove becomes a horrific oven, with an infernal bellows pumping air up through its chimney. As glowing coals and ash, the bellows "blossoms" in the chimney vent, a smoke trail wafting over the European night—a process that Celan, disturbingly, identifies with the transformation of poetic pneuma into text.

Our reading of this dream-text is enriched with an awareness that it may well interact with Freud's; speaking of Scherner's *Das Leben des Traumes* in the *Interpretation of Dreams* (the section on "The Somatic Sources of Dreams"), he offers the following observation:

Scherner did not merely depict the psychical characteristics unfolded in the production of dreams in terms charged with poetic feeling and glowing with life; he believed, too, that he had discovered the principle according to which the mind deals with the stimuli presented to it. On his view, the dream-work, when the imagination is set free from the shackles of daytime, seeks to give *symbolic* representation of the nature of the organ from which the stimulus arises and of the nature of the stimulus itself. Thus he provides a kind of "dream book" to serve as a guide to the interpretation of dreams, which makes it possible to deduce from the dream-images inferences to the somatic feelings, the state of the organs and the character of the stimuli concerned. . . . The human body as a whole is pictured in the dream-imagination as a house and the separate organs of the body by portions of a house. . . . A variety of such symbols are employed by dreams to represent the same organ. [Freud now cites from Scherner:] "Thus the breathing lung will be symbolically represented by a blazing furnace, with flames roaring with a sound like the passage of air."[2]

Keeping in mind Scherner's German Neoromantic fusion of the somatic and the psychic, and—following Johann Sommer—Celan's use of the word *Windfang* as "throat," we reach a deeper, radically somatic dimension of the poem's central analogy: the "hollow homestead" as the corpse-text of a (gassed) gallows-poet, word-kernels, chanting a mouth-organ's *Galgenlied*, propelled outward by dying breath to then blossom as death-crystals.

Celan's linguistic ascesis, his poetics of strangeness, reflects a desire to remove the veil of habit from a radical evil linking the present to a repetitively remembered past. It thus not only articulates a manichean conflict between the realm of ordinary language and another, unpolluted realm, but also focuses on an ethical obsession. Connected to this, Celan writes in a revelatory vein, and his revelatory message is almost always cryptically embedded, to one or another extreme, in a kind of code. Consequently, his texts belong to a generic tradition often called hermetic allegory, distinguished, in the words of Morton W. Bloomfield, "from Biblical, Classical, and other allegories . . . in the attitude it creates in its adepts and readers—one of awe at a hidden secret meaning which presumably is not open to the profane and vulgar."[3]

Let us here recall Quintilian's "vertical" definition of allegory in the first-century *Institutio Oratoria* (I will make use of Maureen Quilligan's revisionary, "horizontal" definition below): it is always a kind of extended metaphor, saying one thing through another in some form of narrative sequence or story with a distinct structure of action, thus having time as one of its constitutive elements.[4] Furthermore, such stories must signal their need for systematic reinterpretation and therefore the *intentionality* of the tenor's "presence" in the vehicle or text. These signals may range from the explicit indication in a text of the allegorical nature of part of its narrative—what Quintilian calls *permixta allegoria*—to an obviously symbolic pattern or schema embedded or lurking in a larger narrative context (for example, this would be the case with Hawthorne's or Melville's novels), to a chain of self-contained metaphors transparently requiring decoding (this would be the case with Celan). Finally, in both the latter varieties of what Quintilian calls *tota allegoria*, decipherment depends on the initiation of the reader into an absent, implicit interpretive context shared with the text, its stable "hierarchy of values."[5]

Despite a growing recognition of the densely allusive and multivalent nature of Celan's language, its relation to allegory has not been sufficiently examined.[6] And yet such a conceptual framework is extremely useful for reading Celan—an insight emerging *a posteriori* from a growing awareness that, frequently, using Grimm's dictionary and other reference works makes sense of words and poems that otherwise would lack referential value. Nonetheless, resistance to such an approach is not surprising. To begin with, there is a traditional widespread resistance to genre, linked to what Richard Wollheim has termed the "presentational" approach to the work of art, whose most orthodox expression in literary studies was probably New Criticism. Presentationalism, according to Wollheim, consists of the belief "that a work of art possesses those properties, and only those, which we can directly perceive or which are immediately given,"[7] with an attending rejection of a vital role in criticism for biographical, historical, psychological, and related factors. In part, the presentationalist rejection of genre has its source in Croce's argument against genre in the *Aesthetic*; but this argument (viz., that genre distinctions violate the uniqueness of the individual aesthetic act) is a form of Romantic Expressivism refuted by an acknowledgment of the crucial role various conventions play in deciding how to read a text.[8] Just as important for our purposes is the functionalist insight that genres are identifiable units in a total system (i.e., "literary discourse"), that they are "quantities of attribution" gaining sense in relation to one another and thereby giving the system coherence as a whole.[9] Such pragmatic considerations, rather than essentialist ones, inform my understanding of allegory. In this manner, I will argue that various approaches to the mode or genre claimed (implicitly or explicitly) by their authors as mutually exclusive are in fact not so, being useful in different ways for making sense of Celan's poems.

Complicating an approach to allegory as genre, however, is a tension between two views of what allegory is. As Lloyd Spencer has recently suggested, Walter Benjamin's discussion of allegory in *Ursprung des deutschen Trauerspiels* has opened a gap between an understanding of "allegory as a rhetorical figure or trope—basically writing or saying one thing yet meaning another," and allegory as articulating a way of seeing, pointing to the "*dissolution* of the stable, hierarchized and meaningful existence which most allegory [i.e., allegory in the former, generic sense] seems to imply."[10] Ultimately, we can uncover such dissolution in every text, now read as a chain of differential signifiers negating its own intentional structure. Such ontological anti-intentionalism, a radical counter to the formal anti-intentionalism of the New Critics, argues for an irrevocable absence of the author from the text. And this dismissal of authorial presence seems to conflict with the nature of allegory, understood as a distinct form of literature. To begin with, autobiographical allusion, recognizable only by means of anecdotal *a priori* knowledge, can in principle play a significant role in the unfolding of an allegory's narrative and in the construction of its abstract, iconic system of self-reference—a generic feature sometimes found in Celan's poems. Beyond this, as indicated, acknowledging authorial intent plays a role in recognizing the presence of an allegorical tenor, particularly in the *tota allegoria* that lacks generic markers (such as transparent personification), and in defining the various "pragmatic presuppositions" that allow us to interpret symbols, ciphers, and allusions, forming them into a coherent narrative.[11]

Are we left, then, with an irreconcilable conflict between two allegories? I think not, once we recognize (with Stanley Cavell) that an au-

thentic skepticism is deeply dialectic in nature—the same as an awareness that skepticism defines itself by a movement toward the world of
ordinary human experience (the ground beneath our feet we never
grasp), an acknowledgment of the claims of the skeptic being an outcome of the movement.[12] In the case of Celan, it is important to acknowledge a repetitive self-questioning that undermines the desire he
articulates for mnemonic plenitude—and even a corrosive doubt, drawing us into Benjamin's allegorical void. But what gives Celan's doubt its
interest is the experience he has hoped to grasp—a movement we can
only (in a sense) recover through a pragmatic determination of how his
poems are meant to be read.

Another, very different, argument against reading Celan's poems as
(generic) allegory involves the association of allegory with narrative, as a
genre suitable for both narrative prose and poetry with strong narrative
elements like the epic and elegy, but not for the dense, elliptic, and
highly personal texts of Celan. Still, particularly in light of Winfried
Menninghaus's taxonomy of Celan's imaginary universe, which shows
how metaphors from different realms (botanical, mineral, etc.) syntheti-
cally represent both the anti-utopian origin and utopian goal of each
poem's poetological movement, it becomes clear that Celan is, indeed,
repetitively telling a kind of story: that of the poem's own movement,
or the writing of the poem, or, as I have described it, the poet's quest to
master a traumatic past by evoking a utopian point of its recovery.
Hence Celan's hermetic allegory is also an allegory of writing. As
we have learned to expect in modern poetry, the points of this narrative sequence unfold as a self-reflexive temporal process: in "Hohles Lebensgehöft," for example, the discursive passage from the poem's opening words on itself represents the process of the lung blossoming and
the "handful" of written "sleepgrain" wafting toward the border of
snowy utopia and horror, the "snow conversations" at the poem's end.
The oven vent itself is located in the hollow space between HOHLES
LEBENSGEHÖFT and *Eine Handvoll,* so that the poem becomes a kind
of "hollow homestead," within whose vent the lung verbally blossoms—the resulting "sleepgrain" thus moving outward in its long
final phrase.

But this formal process has its counterpart in a process taking place
within the reader's consciousness, here as a blooming of insight inside
the oven vent—that is, "inside" the word *Windfang.* Gerhard Kurz has
emphasized the heuristic nature of allegory's second level of meaning,
or tenor. Particularly in *tota allegoria,* we must ourselves attach this
meaning to the allegorical vehicle, thus enriching it with a second dimension, on the basis of an unarticulated knowledge shared with the
author (what Kurz calls allegory's "pragmatic presuppositions"). For
Celan's readers, this involves not only an *a priori* knowledge of the historical, psychological, and poetological framework of his code, but also,

in general, the semantically overdetermined nature of his language, and in particular, a recognition of its diachronic depth. By diachronicity, I mean the potential of Celan's words to thematize their own history at certain intended moments—in this case the history of the word *Wind-fang*. Once entered into, this turns out not to be a homey porch or portal, but the vent of a ghastly oven, into which the reader is tossed by his or her discovery, re-creating, in disturbing communion, the imaginative process by which Celan "remembers" the fate of his friends and family—or rather only partly "remembers," in a correlative to the stammered hope, germinating in the poem's hollow *Lebens-gehöft*, for the full communion or "blossoming" of a utopian moment ending history. As a presence in *Windfang*, this is concretized as German history; we can thus understand the movement of the poem as a "stammered" effort to transcend its origins in the history encoded by this word.

In uncovering layer after historical layer of words of this sort, often signaled to the reader by their obscurity or strangeness, we reconstruct the history from which each of Celan's poems formally, or on its synchronic surface, enacts the desire to escape. They thus exploit, by means of their hermeneutic dynamic, the dependence of allegory on an understanding of its unexpressed dimension: it is the reader's active, extratextual labor which must supply the poem with the full story behind its poetological program, often by means of an "ordinary" excavation of Grimm.

As I have suggested, this process works not only by supplying the text with diachronic depth. Rather, this is one aspect of a constant, systematic, and obsessive encoding of various allusive realms into the text. Among such realms are the symbolic universe of Germanic superstition, of Jewish ritual, and of the Kabbalah as interpreted by Gershom Scholem; various specialized lexicons such as geology, botany, physiology, astrology, and astronomy; other works of imaginative literature including Celan's own poetry and translations, whose significance is lurking in the text as paraphrase or citation; a range of historical events to which Celan attaches deep personal meaning; the life histories of other poets as well as details from Celan's personal history; the hermetic worlds of number-magic and naming-magic, with secret sequences, anagrams, acrostics, and hidden proper names—along with a pronounced propensity for punning. This semantic overdetermination reflects the heuristic possibilities built into allegorical language and is related to the process of etymological wordplay Maureen Quilligan discovers at the heart of allegory.[13] Its astonishingly systematic and detailed nature represents Celan's contribution to the history of a certain kind of writing—the extent of the detail tends to be limited or even entirely absent for those who do not read Celan's poetry in a manner corresponding to its allegorical nature.

It is thus apparent that even the most elliptic of Celan's poems has the potential to generate complex, spatially and temporally extended hermeneutic encounters, with different allusive realms and narrative planes interacting with and reflecting one another. This is something separate from the extended vehicle/tenor relation (i.e., between two stories; one written, the other not) on which all allegory, including Celan's, is based. It is an open rather than a closed system, allowing an infinite variety of implicit "stories," yet still an exploitation of possibilities inherent in the genre.

By the same token, Celan's refinement of the genre interacts with a temporal theme rendering his allegory "allegorical" in Benjamin's particular metaphysical sense. In other words, it evokes the pathos of the essential human need for plenitude, for symbolic closures. Within the interpretive process, we reexperience Celan's pathos as a loss of any final "ground" to our subjective judgment. On the one hand, even when remaining within the periphery of the poem's rhetorical logic, in perusing Grimm's *Wörterbuch* or hunting down the symbolic resonance of a word, we do not know when to stop or at what point our reading slips beyond Celan's cryptographic intent—a potential plunge into an interpretive abyss tensely interacting with our engagement in the reflective hermeneutic process. On the other hand, Celan usually either represents the "hope" of the past's recovery or of a magic "grounding" of his language inside his poems as a formal space or silence (here, the hollow of his "homestead")—or, often, describes it as something that might have happened somewhere in the reading or writing of the poem, but probably did not. In Celan's poetry, then, as in the entire tradition of language mysticism and pietist meditation, the thematization of temporality and of breaks in the temporal process reflect one another as reverse sides of a linguistic mirror.

Celan's reduction of temporal allegory to its bare, schematic bones, the underlying structural framework of virtually all his poems, is nevertheless a process we can trace out through his oeuvre as an increasing ellipticism, cryptic brevity, and allegorical "density" as it progresses. In this light, we can understand the meaning of the later poetry as "recompressed" or "repacked" into the base of which traditional allegory is an unpacking; these poems retain their rhetorical impact because their cryptic quality gives them great heuristic force, which is one of the chief criteria involved in evaluating the strength of any given poem of Celan. Hence, despite the technical virtuosity of their composition, poems such as "Todesfuge" (*GW* 1:39–42) or even "Psalm" (*GW* 1:225) articulate their sense of loss on too overt a level and find their integrity threatened by sentimentality—a problem Celan was acutely aware of and which contributed to his poetry's ever-greater ellipsis: as it moves toward an increased embedding of meaning beneath its semantic surface, it becomes more and more elliptic. This is paralleled by an ever-greater linguistic ascesis, reflecting, in the end, an intense malaise at the tainted nature of the phenomenal world. On both counts, Celan's poetry slides toward an eventual null-point of elliptic density or semiotic death.

Inversely, Celan's allegory is unfolded, or "unpacked," in certain longer poems from what, in retrospect, we may consider his middle period, covering the 1959 volume *Sprachgitter* and the 1963 volume *Die Niemandsrose*, and marking the attainment of his creative mastery. These poems—"Engführung" from *Sprachgitter* (*GW* 1:195–204) and a series comprising most of the fourth part of *Die Niemandsrose*, ending with what is perhaps Celan's most masterly single poem, "Und mit dem Buch aus Tarussa"—all thematize temporal process as the mnemonic movement toward a traumatic past. Because of their length, they do not achieve their rhetorical impact through heuristic density, but by accumulating it in the course of a quasi-narrative sequence. Among these poems, Celan lays out the terms of his allegory most fully in "Engführung," his longest and perhaps strangest poem, which directly, if cryptically, calls attention to its generic nature from the first.

The stature of "Engführung" in Celan's oeuvre is by now well established. Along with numerous brief discussions scattered through the criticism of the past decade, there have been several efforts to interpret the poem in its entirety, the most well known and influential being Peter Szondi's "Durch die Enge geführt."[14] This essay remains the first important attempt to read Celan by way of Russian Formalist and French structuralist insights into the nature of poetic language. On the one hand, along with offering a rigorous structural analysis of "Engführung," Szondi succeeds in demonstrating the crucial role played by formal elements (linguistic mimesis; Celan's fugal architecture) in conveying the poem's meaning. On the other hand, more than fifteen years after the publication of the essay, it may be time to consider the limits of Szondi's approach. These limits are marked off by a contradiction in the commentary becoming more evident as it proceeds: as an underlying methodological premise, Szondi insists that Celan's text "speaks itself"; hence its rigorous reading is a strict tracing of its own self-contained, self-reflexive, formal, and thematic universe. Yet in order to arrive at the text's meaning, Szondi is in fact forced to resort to precisely the "outside," real, historical world—the signified—that, he explains, we are now aware has no place within the text.

This inconsistent effort to treat the poem as an entirely immanent linguistic entity may be one source of a striking oversight: namely, that the poem is an anomalous, postwar manifestation of the German Classical elegy, being a carefully contrived, formal, and thematic refutation— or *Widerruf*—of Hölderlin's "Brod und Wein."[15] Like Hölderlin's elegy,

"Engführung" has nine sections; like the earlier text, it has a central "turning point" facilitating, on a thematic level, the movement of a (here radically fractured) contemplative consciousness toward a (here radically problematized) illuminating moment at the poem's end; where Hölderlin's elegy is structured on an elaborate system of tonal modulations, a *Wechsel der Töne*, with subterranean tones emerging to the text's semantic surface at the end of each section, Celan mimics the surface tones with verbal echoes of the previous section at the start of the one that follows; finally, there is a striking duplication of the unfolding vocabulary of "Brod und Wein" in Celan's poem, from one section to the next.[16]

Similarly, Szondi does not note that "Engführung" is also Celan's most programmatic lyric enactment of the poetics he formulated in the same period as the poem's composition, articulated in his 1960 Büchner Prize address, the "Meridian" (*GW* 3:187–202). Briefly summarized, Celan sees the poem as a movement toward a transcendent "other," achieved as authentic "poetry" (*Dichtung*), taking place along the "path of art" or "artifice" (*der Weg der Kunst*). With this quasi-idealist schema evoking Hölderlin's "eccentric path" (*exzentrische Bahn*), Celan's poem suggests a relationship between itself and the "Meridian" formally similar to that between Hölderlin's major elegies and the elaborate poetics they exemplify. In this manner, the premise of an illusory textual immanence here leads to the elision of a literary-historical theme fundamental to the text's semantic structure: Celan's charged and ambivalent relationship to the German Romantic and Idealist tradition, and to Hölderlin, his strong poetic "brother."[17]

The presence in "Engführung" of a pronounced and deliberate intertextuality dramatizes the difficulty of using the notion of a "zero-degree" text as a basis for starting to read Celan. The difficulty becomes more acute when we consider the manner in which Szondi approaches Celan's *language*. For, while on the one hand "Engführung" is a kind of elegy, on the other its elegiac themes and structure, along with Celan's self-citations, are intentionally encoded into a fully realized allegory. (The poem thus condenses strongly allegorical elements of the German elegiac tradition, that is, the elegy's "story" as the constant thematizing of another, greater story: the eschatological movement of consciousness and culture.) It is the very nature of allegorical language to establish a systematic dialectic between its immanent, synchronic textual presence and a temporal unfolding, in this sense text-transcendent "signified"—a temporal dynamic Celan's obsessive ambiguity exploits and that he carries to an extreme in "Engführung." The conflict between Szondi's methodological premise and the results of his reading reflects a failure to recognize the systematic way in which Celan's language plays out this dialectic in his poem.

In *The Language of Allegory*, Quilligan speaks of allegory's capacity to stimulate in the reader an "understanding [of] the act of reading as itself an ethical action."[18] For Quilligan, a basic characteristic of allegory is what she calls "a sensitivity to the polysemy in words," with the allegorical narrative consisting of an unfolding investigation into the meaning of its own "threshold text" and the "verbal implication of the words used [therein] to describe the imaginary action." Hence the basic plot of the "Book of Holiness" in *The Faerie Queene* involves an investigation into the meaning of the word *error*, unfolding as a complex series of etymological puns that gradually reveal Spencer's underlying ethical intent. Strikingly, we can see a similar process at work in Celan's poems—a "horizontal" dimension to his allegory that, contrary to what Quilligan's revisionist argument implies, does not conflict with, but rather compliments its "vertical," vehicle-tenor dimension. Once we understand his customary use of uppercase letters for their opening words as more than a convention, these words, in fact, often constitute a kind of "threshold text" whose meaning is explained by the rest of the poem.[19]

Thus "Hohles Lebensgehöft" ultimately explains what is meant by this threshold metaphor in terms of a self-reflexive linguistic "wafting" out from an etymologically grounded understanding of *Windfang*. Although what Celan does here is not precisely what Quilligan describes, it is very close, and "Engführung," being a more traditionally allegorical text, conforms more closely to her description. We could consider the entire poem as an explanation of the meaning of the first word of the first strophe, "BROUGHT [VERBRACHT] to / the scape / with the unmistakable trace," but we can just as easily discover its "threshold text" in an actual threshold text: the allegorical textual landscape inscribed on the stony, white page in this strophe and the one following:

Gras, auseinandergeschrieben. Die Steine, weiß,
mit den Schatten der Halme:
Lies nicht mehr—schau!
Schau nicht mehr—geh!
    (*GW* 1:197)

(Grass, written apart. The stones, white,
with the shadows of grassblades:
Read no more—look!
Look no more—move!)

The rest of the poem unfolds as an explanation of what it means to really read such a text, focusing on the pun at play in the injunction between *lesen* as "read" and *lesen* as "pluck."[20] From the perspective of the pun, *lesen* means something like merely gleaning stray verbal "grass" the way we do in an ordinary reading, that is, remaining on the surface of the text's semantic soil. Celan's intensifying injunctive sequence (that is, first picture the poem's scene, then step right in) is both a statement of the text's ideality and its generic contract.[21] Ideally, being fully "transported" to its time and place would involve a full identification with its verbal movement (*geh!*). The third strophe describes this movement as that of a self-propelling verbal wheel; really reading the text would involve "moving" along the palimpsestic circular, self-reflexive surface of the pagescape and into its temporal, deathly subtext, which surfaces in the images of this strophe:

Geh, deine Stunde
hat keine Schwestern, du bist—
bist zuhause. Ein Rad, langsam,
rollt aus sich selber, die Speichen
klettern,
klettern auf schwärzlichem Feld, die Nacht
braucht keine Sterne, nirgends
fragt es nach dir.
    (*GW* 1:197)

(Move, your hour
has no sisters, you are—
are at home. A wheel, slowly,
rolls on its own, the spokes
clamber,
clamber up a kind of black field, the night
doesn't need stars, no asking
for you anywhere.)

The play between "read" and "pluck" is itself a threshold contract for this kind of reading. It sets us up for the same play in the poem's sixth section, not in relation to grass but to a beech tree (*Buche*), with the analogy between grass and letter (*Buchstabe*) taken over in an etymological punning between book (*Buch*) and beech. In this way, the grass "becomes" a beech, a process continuing throughout the poem, turning it into a strange, evolving verbal plant.

By a movement toward a magic turning point or internal closure, sections two through five of the poem prepare us for a proper "reading" of the terms of its threshold contract. The story told in these sections is of a pair of characters who enact, in the second section, the reader's inability to "read" the text of their lives and contextualize their locus by giving it a "name." They do this as a failure to penetrate a verbal barrier between them, or use words as a path to one another rather than as a way of "talking about words" ("Sie ... redeten von / Worten" [*GW* 1:198]), or awake from somnolence. The language of this section is grammatically, stylistically, and rhetorically awkward, mimicking the alienation it thematizes. In the third section, the surfacing of a first-person voice (an *ich*) marks the possibility of a magic breakthrough of the barrier—a possibility moving through the text beneath its surface; in the fourth, "stitchings" (*Nahtstellen*), a word both for scars and points where temporally distinct sections of a text are fused, describes this possibility as a literal closure to the text, touched on in the mnemonic probing of the poet's pen-hand; and in the fifth it becomes a magic, formal presence in the text as a space between the two parts of this central section, the poem's elegiac "turning point," indicated as such by the inversion of the last words of the previous section in the verbal echo that follows.

Thematically, this turning point or magic space marks the point in the poem's narrative where the reader can begin to read its allegorical inscription, or discover the name of an anonymous locus (*Ort*) linked to its characters earlier, at the beginning of the second section. In the second strophe of the sixth section, Celan then picks up the play on "reading" and "plucking," this time in terms of his text or "book" as a beech, whose reading branches out through the rest of the poem, generating its fundamental meaning. In fact, this section is an elaborate, if cryptic, comment on the nature of the poem's threshold text, rooted in a transformative process taking place, in a sense, under the surface of the four sections linking the threshold grass-blade letters with Celan's beechy book.

The strophe—with its

Orkane. Orkane, von je,
Partikelgestöber, das andre,
du
weißt ja, wir
lasens im Buche, war
Meinung
    (*GW* 1:200)

(Cyclones.
Cyclones, since always,
Particle flurries, the other,
you
know, we
read it in the book, was
opinion)

—centers on a citation from Democrites that Celan inscribed in a copy of *Sprachgitter* given to Hans Mayer: "Nothing exists except atoms and empty space; everything else is opinion."[22] This inscription is linked to a passage from Dante's *Inferno* (5.94–142), most directly to verse 138: "quel giorno più non vi leggemo avante" ("on this day we read no further"). The book involved is the Arthurian romance, with the story of Lancelot and Genevra, read in Dante's work by Paolo and Francesca, who fall in love through it.[23] It seems, then, that "the other" (*das andre*) signifies love, and the question of the next strophe, "how did we hold each other with these hands?," means something like: "If the world around us [or: the text] consists merely of 'particle flurries,' what caused the magic turning we have just experienced in section five, offering us, the poem's characters, a breakthrough of the barrier that has kept us apart and a voice in the poem about us?" The answer to this question would be something like: "The claim to any 'turning point' is grounded (merely) in the poem's verbal particles, and what 'happened' in the turn will surface in a reading of the rest of this section as well as the rest of the poem."

The shift to a meaning apparent only with anecdotal help indicates an advance in a mnemonic process represented by the poem's total movement. Nonetheless, the process is encoded more radically as the embedding of Celan's personal history within this anecdotal content. It is, first of all, a romantic history: the love of Paolo and Francesca is that of Paul Celan and the gentile Frenchwoman Gisèle Lestrange, and the name Lancelot is a play on Celan-Ançel, with Genevra perhaps a reference to Gisèle.[24] In this light, Celan's beech (*Buche*) evokes his birthplace, Bukovina, the "land of beeches," along with Buchenwald, an emblem of the destruction of the childhood world.

Celan's linking of book and beech is etymologically sound.[25] The term *Buch* comes from the *Buche* originally used for writing tablets (as does "book" from "beech"), hence *Buchstabe*, "letter," literally "book-staff." Grimm's dictionary, noting the tree's rare appearance in the masculine (thereby grounding in grammar a double reading of "wir lasens im Buche"), clarifies Celan's play with the linkage: "In fact, since individual runes are named for trees and books have 'leaves,' the relation between 'book' and 'beech' seems well based and very fitting." Under "Buche," Grimm also helps us grasp the linkage as one encoding of Celan's poetological movement, from historical source to utopian endpoint: "Like the oak, the beech is mostly a German tree and grows most magnificently in our soil; the Finns call it 'the German oak,' *saksan tanni*. Heathen sacrifices mostly take place in beech woods [*im buchenwald*]. The beech furnishes the wood for bonfires and runes." Grimm also notes that "one should not overlook the fact that the meaning of 'beech' extends to the fruit, like *fagum* in relation to *fagus, malum, po-*

mum to *malus, pomus*: 'my nourishment was nothing but "beeches" [*buchen*] that I plucked along the way [*die ich unterwegs auflase*].'"[26]

In light of Grimm's citation from *Simplizissimus*, it becomes clear that the kind of "reading" the characters in the sixth section of "Engführung" do in their book is lapsarian—a "plucking" from the Tree of Knowledge involving, as yet, no conscious awareness of the Fall determining the fragility of love or its status as mere "opinion." This Fall, as crystalline Zyklon B or death camp gas, and floating ash, is conveyed by the cyclones (*Orkane*) and particle flurries that open the section. Such awareness, arrived at, as it were, only after the text's complete reading, links the sort of reading referred to as the "plucking" of a grassy text in the first section with the "reading" of a booky beech in the sixth.

Celan's linguistic lapsarianism and the theme of two kinds of reading are also at play in the section's fourth strophe:

> Es stand auch geschrieben, daß.
> Wo? Wir
> taten ein Schweigen darüber,
> giftgestellt, groß,
> ein
> grünes
> Schweigen, ein Kelchblatt, es
> hing ein Gedanke an Pflanzliches dran—
> (*GW* 1:200)

> (It also stood written that.
> Where? We
> placed a silence upon it,
> poison-stilled, large,
> a
> green
> silence, a sepal, a
> thought of plant-stuff clung to it—)

"Es stand auch geschrieben, daß" is a typical biblical locution, inscribed in Celan's "book" with an authority like the Bible's. But the line's incompletion reflects an inadequate or "poisonous" reading of the silent, heavy, green, poisonous leaves hanging from the Tree of Knowledge, linked to the line as Celan's "standing" textual beech. Here, we find a fusion of the topos of the Book of History with that of the Book of Nature (*liber naturae*), and the latter's inversion: Celan's Heavenly Author is both absent and, as suggested in the section's fourth strophe ("grün, ja, / hing, ja, / unter hämischem / Himmel" ["green, yes, /

clung, yes, / under a gloating / heaven"] [*GW* 1:201]), full of malice. At the same time, in its role as part of the poem's narrative process, Celan's vegetative world marks a metamorphosis of the *liber naturae* into an object of pantheistic identification, as articulated, say, in the following observation of Jakob Grimm: "The poetry of nature can be called life in its pure enactment, a *living book* full of true history, which we can begin to read [*lesen*] and understand on every page [*Blatt*], but never read through [*auslesen*; also "cull" or "pick clean"] or understand completely. On the contrary, the poetry of art [*Kunstpoesie*] is life's labor, already philosophical in the first bud."[27]

As the initial result of an effort by the poem's characters to linguistically and mnemonically master historical trauma, their "reading" of the Book of Nature, contrary to Grimm's assertion, is lacking its historical—hence ethical—dimension. It can only operate tautologically, as a loss of memory and a failure of the effort. Celan inscribes this incoherence in his poetic "book" through linguistic mimesis: a phonetic monotony, stylistic awkwardness, and repetitiveness that is particularly pronounced in the fourth, fifth, and sixth strophes of the poem's long sixth section. The text here reproduces the "poison" to which it is responding; in doing so, it addresses the relation between a debased romanticism and a "poisoned" ideological tradition. But also, as the concentration of an awkward, poisoned rhetoric at work throughout the poem from one section to the next, it signifies, in a quasi-gnostic mode, both the fallen condition of the language Celan has inherited from tradition and of language in general as a sign of the Fall. The poem's opening shift from "read" or "pluck" to "move" (or "go") thus initiates a quest within the text of the whole tradition by which the book-topos is conveyed.

In the second half of the section, the quest continues as a shift from something inscribed on a tree to something inscribed on a stone ("es blieb / Zeit, blieb, / es beim Stein zu versuchen—er / war gastlich" ["there was still / time, still / time for seeking the stone—he / was welcoming"] [*GW* 1:201]): the other medium, less subject to temporal wear, upon which the original *Buchstaben* were written. This stone links the poem's narrative to the white stones of its threshold text. On the one hand, then, its history is still unarticulated, or dormant in it; on the other, however, as a metamorphosis of the poisonous silence clinging to the beech-book's leaves into a kind of language later called "petrified" or "fossilized" leprosy,[28] the stone offers an opening to the poem's utopian end point, here captured in the romantic metaphor of the rune, magically transforming the links in an abstract verbal chain, meant to be "read," into objects of cultic worship, meant to be "seen." The stone thus offers a sort of petrified solace; it is "welcoming" to the poem's personae. The string of adjectives then describing the stone in the next strophe turn it back into a multibranched allegorical tree, petrified into a weird string of *-ig* or *-icht* endings:

> Körnig,
> körnig und faserig. Stengelig,
> dicht;
> traubig und strahlig; nierig,
> plattig und
> klumpig; locker, ver-
> ästelt
>   (*GW* 1:201)

> (Grainy,
> grainy and fibrous. Stalky,
> dense:
> clustery and radial; renal,
> lamellated and
> clumpy; loose, ram-
> ified)

With this further metamorphosis of the beechy book, Celan carries his technique of lexical allegorism to an extreme. In order to properly "read" his vegetal stone, we need to consider the semantic resonance of each of its adjectives—the diachronic soil in which their atemporal surface is rooted.

Turning again to Grimm's dictionary, we note that while apparently some of the adjectives apply more to stone (*körnig, plattig, klumpig, locker*), others to plants (*faserig, stengelig, traubig, verästelt*), and the rest (*dicht, strahlig, nierig*) to both,[29] from a diachronic perspective, and that of a specialized geological and crystallographic lexicon, virtually all of them in fact belong to both realms. Hence each becomes a metaphor of the poem's "petrified leprosy"; in turn, each is a sort of linguistic crystal, reflecting different facets of the poem's central meaning, clustered by grammatical breaks into larger units, condensed into the self-contained "solidity" of extreme ellipsis. This condensation is signified by *dicht* ("thick," "dense"), which also, anachronistically, is identical to *das Gedicht*, "the poem," with its source in Low German *ticht* ("lament and secret thought"). Celan's *dicht* thus condenses the etymologies of *carmen cantare* and *dicht machen, condensare*. In the latter sense—often, Grimm notes, referring to vines and branches (here to the adjectives "traubig . . . ver- / ästelt" [*GW* 1:201])—the word is linked with the old German *dihan: gedeihen, heranwachsen, procedere, pollere*.[30] Here, the "growth" or "potential" at work within Celan's intertwining adjectives is itself a signifier of the poem's movement. Thus the stony plant is not only "dense"

(*dicht*), but also "loose" (*locker*)—or put in another way: the most allegorically packed point in the poem offers access to its "secret thoughts"
or meaning, formally preparing the way for their proper "reading" in
the following sections.

This meaning determines the liminal quality shared by all the adjectives, defining the border area between the horror from which the
poem departs and the utopia toward which it heads. To begin with, such
liminality is present in *körnig*, on each of its levels of meaning. In general, particulate matter such as sand or hail signifies for Celan a dialectic
union of this source and goal,[31] emerging again here in the adjective's
equal application to the poisonous world of plants and to stone, in the
stone itself, and in another of Celan's elemental metaphors: the crystal
("Grainy: consisting of grains, in granular form: showers of granular ice
[hailstones] [Goethe]. Those forms that align their sections in crystalline and granular fashion [Humboldt]").[32]

Along with an abstract connotation—similar to Mallarmé's—of purity, clarity, self-reflective illumination, and also (like snow, glaciers, and
whiteness) of its polar nullity in death, there is a more concrete deathly
reference at work in Celan's allegorical crystal: both to *Kristallnacht*,
and, as I have already suggested, apocalyptically to crystalline Zyklon B.
This death is at play, in turn, in an entry from Grimm under *körnig* as
"siliginous": "barley jew [*kornjude*]. m. jew as barley merchant [*kornhän-
dler*], then barley userer [*kornwucherer*] in general. [Moser:] in the writing of a barley merchant. the so-called barley jews. relating thereto barley judaism [*kornjudenthum*] [J. Paul]."[33] Captured in the figure of the
Kornjude is a double liminality: the socioeconomic liminality defined by
the nature of his trade (a hovering between the world from where he
comes and the gentile world that sustains him), and an existential liminality which was such an ingrained quality of traditional European Judaism—a life centered upon the grubby necessity for material sustenance, but also upon writing and the letter. In both these senses Celan
is a sort of *Kornjude*, expressing his desire for a vanished origin by means
of a fragmented language—the "writing of a barley-merchant"—
steeped in the tradition responsible for its extinction, hence itself polarized between the corrupt nature of its materiality and the transcendence
toward which it strives.[34]

In this regard, it is worth noting that *körnig* has frequently been
applied to language (for instance in Herder's "naiv körnicht deutsch");
here, then, it functions as a first linguistic crystal, crystallizing not only a
cluster of related meanings in the way we have seen, but also the hidden
meaning of the other adjectives attached to the stone. Hence, in the
following line, it divides itself up into *körnig* and *faserig* ("fibery"), with
the *fibrae* in *faserig* being attached to both rock and plant—a liminality central to their identity with *Faden* ("threads," another key term in
Celan's imaginary universe) and also strongly present in the etymol-

ogy of *Faser* (Middle-High German *vase, Faser, Franse, Saum eines Ge-
wandes*), which can be traced back to Indo-European *pes, blasen, wehen*,
thus linking it to the pneumatological mysticism at the heart of Celan's
poetics.[35] Keeping in mind the additional, anatomical sense of *faserig*
(i.e., "muscle fiber"), we can understand the term's utopian aura, like
that of *nierig* below it, as containing a horror at work throughout the
passage.

After this first adjectival clump or cluster follow a string of others,
set off, not by periods like this one, but semicolons: hence each the unit
of a further atomization of the "particles" of the initial phrase. *Stengelig*
("stalky") is denoted in Grimm as both "of plants" and "of the crystalline form of certain minerals."[36] It thus signifies the verticality of Celan's
petrified poem (or *dicht*), an articulation of artifice (*Kunst*) or difference
also pointing the way toward authentic "poetry" (*Dichtung*). *Traubig*
("grapey") has a more specialized use in mineralogy, for "one sort of
round, external form,"[37] and in crystallography, where—in an intensi-
fication of the atomizing process that is also a deepening of the poem's
allegorical narrative—it is linked lexically to "kidney-like," or *nierig*.[38]

Through crystal and opal, *traubig* and *nierig* also possess the quality
of *strahlig*, containing the radical ambivalence of its function as part of
Celan's "optics of names": both a blinding "force of light" (*Lichtzwang*)
and the purity of a utopian radiance or *Ausstrahlen*. Likewise, *strahlig*
has its place in the lexicon of mineralogy, botany, and anatomy, and also
describes a particular sort of fossil (or "petrified leprosy").[39] Along with
the use of *nierig* cited above, an additional entry from Grimm (under
"niere") is important: "like heart, liver, and lungs to signify the interior,
the site of the power of life and the emotions [*lebenskraft und affecte*], a
biblical notion . . . usually related to 'heart.'" Thus we might understand the term as linked to Celan's metaphors of heart and breath: like
these, it signifies a polar fusion, here as a secret presence of spirit within
matter.[40] *Plattig* ("platey") applies equally to layers of stone and to
plants;[41] along with their functions as statements about the nature of the
poem, *klumpig* ("clumpy") and *locker* ("loose") link the scene of its inner
narrative to the textual surface of its threshold landscape.[42] In this manner, Celan's stony plant is *ver- / ästelt*, etymologically "ramified." It
branches out through the poem's various allusive layers, while on the
surface—equivalent to the somnolent surface of its characters' consciousness, or the inadequacy of their "reading"—it seems merely a
mirroring of linguistic petrification.

In the sixth section of "Engführung," Celan uses this technique of
"lexical allegorism" as a way of exploiting to its fullest allegory's tendency to comment on a threshold text (in this case, the poem's opening
injunction). As a result of Celan's exploitation of the ambiguity built
into the phrase "wir lasens im Buche," the reader's "plucking" from a
Bukovinian tree means that this section occupies a much greater portion

of the poem than an ordinary reading (the kind meant by *lies nicht mehr*) would involve. This points to another kind of "reading" as the thematic focus of Celan's narrative, metamorphosed from one part of the text (or chapter of his "book") to the next. While in the remainder of the poem the play on "reading" and "plucking" become embedded once again under its semantic surface, the narrative still proceeds as a further metamorphosis of the vegetal stone.

The "hospitality" of the sixth's section's lithoglyph does not overcome the poem's "silence," but its allegorical density possesses a transient eloquence. This is expressed in the lines referring to the stone, immediately following the adjectival cluster, and culminating in the poem's only distinctly metered line: "es / sprach / sprach gerne zu trockenen Augen, eh es sie schloß" ("it / spoke, / spoke gladly to eyes that were dry, before it closed them") (*GW* 1:201). This muted dactylic echoing of the harmony of classical aesthetics, cut off from the poem's discordant tenor, points to a shift in Celan's literary-historical "book" from late Romantic, organicist "poison" to "petrified" Classical harmony. The shift continues in the next section as a linguistic "thousandfold crystal" (*Tausendkristall*), a group of colored geometric forms emerging from the crystalline metaphors attached to the vegetal stone:

> und
> die Welt, ein Tausendkristall,
> schoß an, schoß an.

> *

>   Schoß an, schoß an.
>   Dann—

> Nächte, entmischt. Kreise,
> grün oder blau, rote
> Quadrate: die
> Welt setzt ihr Innerstes ein
> im Spiel mit den neuen
> Stunden.—Kreise,
> rot oder schwarz, helle
> Quadrate, kein
> Flugschatten,
> kein
> Meßtisch, keine
> Rauchseele steigt und spielt mit.
>   (*GW* 1:202–3)

(and
the world, a thousandfold crystal
shot on, shot on.

*

      Shot on, shot on.
             Then—
nights, decomposed. Circles,
green or blue, red
squares: the
world stakes its innermost in
a playing with the
most recent hours.—Circles,
red or black, bright
squares, no
flight-shadow,
no
measuring table, no
smoke-soul rises and plays.)

While the language in the seventh section of "Engführung" occupies a dehistoricized, eternal present—what Celan calls a "playing with the most recent hours," emphasized by the arbitrary choice and mingling of the colors of the geometric forms—history still starts to surface as a horror lurking in the "flight-shadow," "measuring table," and "smoke-soul" he cites as *absent* from the scene (*GW* 1:203). The "rise and play" of these terms with the language of their repression prepares the way for the rise and play of memory in the following sections—a process condensed into the plant, the crystal, and the geometric forms.

That this process is not only cognitive and poetological, but also one of literary history, is the thematic motivation for setting off the last stage of the crystallization of the beech-book in a section of its own. Where the beech's *Kelchblatt* is attached to an organicist language and poetics, the following Platonic forms emerge from the universe of Mallarmé. As a link between Celan and Mallarmé we have a passage from the "Meridian" address where Celan asks whether Mallarmé ought to be "thought through" to the end (*GW* 3:193)—a question he indirectly answers in the talk by affirming, then radically historicizing, Mallarmé's aesthetic imperative: an estrangement of his language from the corrosion of contingency and habit. In this sense, Celan both thinks "through" and "beyond" Mallarmé—an homage and critique implicit in his only citation of the master in "Engführung": the pattern of single asterisks inscribed into the space between its sections.[43] As Leo Bersani has suggested, Mallarmé "was fascinated by an analogy between poetic structures and stellar structures,"[44] inscribing—"according to exact laws"[45]—a constellative pattern into "Un coup de dés," and thereby drawing an analogy between poetic and cosmological creation.[46] At the same time, Celan's asterisks represent Stars of David, isolated and typographically hollow, hence extinct or extinguished, yet pointing "beyond" their emptiness—itself an allegorical historicizing of Mallarmé's *disposition typographique*[47]—toward a tenuous illumination in the poem's eighth part: the metaphor of fragile moral presence conveyed by Celan's mnemonic-historical inscription.[48]

The play of geometric forms in the seventh section of the poem thus involves a literary-historical metamorphosis of Celan's "book," corresponding to an advance in its formal movement and the quest of its characters, remaining equally inadequate on this level. Likewise, the shift to the eighth section, initiated as a "rising" and "playing" of the horror "absent" from the seventh in its transitional echo, involves a shift from Mallarmé's text to Celan's own. Celan indicates this in the most cryptic fashion, by inscribing his name in his "book" just after the echo, in the section's second strophe:

> In der Eulenflucht, beim
> versteinerten Aussatz,
> bei
> unsern geflohenen Händen, in
> der jüngsten Verwerfung,
> überm
> Kugelfang an
> der verschütteten Mauer[.]
>   (*GW* 1:203)

> (In the owl's flight, by the
> fossilized lepra,
> by
> our fled hands, in
> the most recent rejection,
> above
> the shooting-butt at
> the demolished wall[.])

Grimm defines the *Eulenflucht*—"owl's flight," evoking Hegel's owl of Minerva and everything it says about the West—as a coinage for *crepusculum*, hence evoking the shadow and obscurity of the poem's opening landscape; but it also obscurely encodes the anagram of Ancel, Celan, by means of Celander, cited by Grimm as next in line from the metaphor's source.[49]

We have a further metamorphosis of the play between "beech" and "book" in the next four terms linked to the string of prepositions "naming" the second section's unnamed place (*Ort*). *Aussatz* as "leprosy" connects the petrified horror of Celan's verbal plant to the tree leprosy (or leprosy of the *Buche*) denoted in the less common usage of the word for botanical scurf; in its link with *aussetzen* (*exponere*), it reveals the leprosy's "reading" as something petrified in the poem-tree's verbal artifice, and also as something "edicted" (cf. *Aussatzung*) by the authors of violence in history. "Our fled hands," taking up the *Eulenflucht*, marks the formal "flight" of the plucking, probing, mutually touching hands of the poem's earlier sections to this place in the narrative question. The hands are also Celan's, fashioning mnemonic detritus into a "book" after a flight from Bukovina to Paris, by way of Vienna. Finally, this personal ordeal attests to the Eastern European Jewish ordeal of which it was a part, "the most recent rejection [*Verwerfung*]," which has now gained interpretive transparency.

Along with its usually meaning of "rejection" or "condemnation," *Verwerfung* also means a geological displacement, the vertical offset of rocks by movement along a fault. As a reappearance of the fissure probed by the poet's finger, the fault is here a radical principle of difference: a temporalization splitting or shattering the petrified plant turned crystal, objectified in the rubbly wall, covered with blood (the adjective *verschüttet* has both connotations) at the strophe's end. Most transparently, this wall is the Black Wall at Auschwitz; it also seems to be that focal point of the Jewish eschatological consciousness, the Wailing Wall or Wall of Lamentation. The grooves (*Rillen*) that are "newly visible" in the eighth section's second strophe, etched by bullets in the shooting butt of the Black Wall, would then be the same as cracks in the Wall of Lamentation, into which pious Jews stuff message-scraps to God. Simultaneously, the Wall is a page from Celan's beechy book, the groove-cracks being lines of verse—"unmistakable" printed tracks or traces of the text's threshold deportation. Their circular-cylindric (*kugelig*) mnemonic movement thematically renders the poem into a bullet catch or shooting butt, a *Kugelfang*.

With the eighth section of "Engführung," we can "read" the inscriptions on the white (tomb)stones of the poem's threshold text, in a way identifying Celan's book with the mnemonic locus or deathly time and place, toward which its characters are moving. In the remainder of the poem, the achievement of their quest is marked by a pronounced ambivalence. It is proposed—as a choric and psalmic, resurrectionary moment; as an illumination, close to the poem's end, of one of the inscribed David's stars declared marginal, or useless, at its beginning; as a full, formal closure offered by the last section's repetition of the first. And it is revoked: as a *damals* looking back, in part, to death-rattle psalms and gas-chamber choruses ("die / Rillen, die // Chöre, damals, die / Psalmen" ["the grooves, the // choirs, back then, the / psalms"]); as both the immediately following, chopped up, death's grin "ho, ho- / sianna" and a "wohl" ("Ein / Stern / hat wohl noch Licht" ["A / star / may still have light" (*GW* 1:203–4)]) paling the new-lit star's conviction; lastly, as a grammatical bracketing of the entire ninth, and final, section. This ambivalence is characteristic of the German Classical elegy and, in particular, of the formal-thematic "pretext" for "Engführung," Hölderlin's "Brod und Wein." Likewise, Celan's "bracketing" will not fail to remind us of Derrida's notion of *rature* and what it stands for: the straddling of an inside/outside border demarcating the Western metaphysical quest, both repeating its terms (say, as the German Romantic version of the quest) and challenging its foundations. But Celan's ambivalence also points to the intense ambivalence Angus Fletcher has suggested is at the heart of allegory as a symbolic mode.[50] Let us shift now to this more general perspective, confronting, in the process, the problem of the nature of the allegorical imagination.

As thematizations of its temporal nature, perhaps the most prevalent signs of traditional allegory are travel and the quest.[51] Whereas in "Hohles Lebensgehöft" Celan's quest is cryptically embedded, in "Engführung" its presence is more direct: the poem's "reading" is one dimension of a fractured subject's search for a sense of self, or the total surfacing of a repressed, traumatic past. The implicit psychoanalytic analogue of this mnemonic movement is revealed in the gradual "narrowing" by which the past surfaces in the central consciousness uniting all the poem's sections and perspectives. This takes place in a series of steps that link the opening and closing scenes of the poem in a complex temporal unfolding, operating on parallel levels. The formal linkage of each section to the next by an echo, and the end to the beginning; the gradual identification of the reader with the poem's characters and story, reflected in the shift from "you" at its start to "we" at its end; the effort of the characters to break through the barrier between them; the struggle of an "open," "ticking" word to penetrate a world of ash and fog; the allegorical unfolding of Celan's "book" and the literary history and love story within it—each is a different expression of an identical quest, occupying a single narrative "scape" or *Gelände*.

In different ways, this painstaking, embedded reenactment of a single quest dramatizes the obsessive purposiveness Fletcher sees at work in allegorical texts. Ultimately, this purposiveness is transcendental, in a manner implicitly challenging Goethe's and Benjamin's distinction between allegory and symbol: symbolic moments are often incorporated into allegorical systems as ecstatic, apocalyptic breaks in the temporal process. Inversely, when an allegory becomes purely visionary, it does so after a struggle to reach that goal. "The stage prior to final vision," Fletcher writes, "seems to be qualitatively unlike that final vision; the latter is a moment of liberation. The former is a sequence of difficult labors, often taking the form of the hero's enslavement to a fatal destiny. The *psychomachia* and the progress are narrative images of this struggle. They are battles for, and journeys toward, the final liberation of the hero. If a temporary liberation occurs along the way, it is but the precursor of one final victory." [52]

In his "Meridian" address, Celan offers a poetological schema fully consistent with the structure described in this passage. Celan speaks of "poetry" traveling the "path of art." In other words, poetic language strives to transcend its "artful," artificial or inauthentic state (its fall through history), with "poetry" signifying such a breakthrough: a "moment of liberation" Celan calls a "breath turn" (*Atemwende*). "Engführung," Celan's most poetological poem, thematizes the "path of art" by a variety of "labors": the poem's to give birth to memory, its characters' to break through the barrier between them, along with all the other quest enactments we find in the text. It thematizes the movement from "art" to "poetry" as a "final [illuminatory, choric] vision" in the eighth section; the movement is also present in key elements of the poem's linguistic universe, such as stone and crystal, as a polarization of utopian goals and historical source.

Celan's "magic of form," in Menninghaus's phrase, present in the poem in many modes, also represents the liberation from "art" and "artifice." On the one hand, the (near) identity of the poem's first and final sections marks a closure to (or "final liberation" from) its temporal movement, turning it into a self-reflexive circle. On the other, we have a formal counterpart to the "temporary liberation" of the poem's characters when they contact one another within the poem, the magic "breath turn" in the sixth section that heads it back to its starting point. This "turn" is present as an atemporal moment between the two strophes of the poem's central section (a nine-line section of a poem with nine sections). Its static, atemporal nature is mimicked in the polar balance of the strophes between the two worlds comprising the poem's dialectic content (word and light facing night and ash)—a balance reflected in the rare rhyme between the strophe's final words ("leuchten / feuchten").

The "path of art" also has its generalized formal presence in the poem, both as a distinct syntactic, stylistic, and thematic awkwardness in certain passages, mirroring the alienation they describe, and as a monotonous *a*-sound, particularly prevalent in section two, but droning on from one section to another, making the entire poem a "talking about words." [53] This is a phonetic manifestation of a self-censuring thematic at play throughout Celan's oeuvre: the creative impulse as a reflection of the fall from grace. Carried to an extreme, Celan expresses this as a moralistic condemnation of his own work as pornographic *Kunst*. [54] He encodes such a condemnation in "Engführung," as part of the engendering of memory in the sixth section, where the "thousandfold crystal" marks the emergence of a new linguistic cosmos:

> Wir
> ließen nicht locker, standen
> inmitten, ein
> Porenbau, und
> es kam.
>
> Kam auf uns zu, kam
> hindurch, flickte
> an der letzten Membran,
> und
> die Welt, ein Tausendkristall,
> schoß an, schoß an.
> (GW 1:202)
>
> (We
> held our place firmly, stood
> in the center, a
> structure of pores, and
> it came.
>
> Came up upon us, came
> right through, stitched
> invisibly, stitched
> on the last membrane,
> and
> the world, a thousandfold crystal
> shot on, shot on).

At this point in the text, there is a disturbing, implicit interweaving of the poetological and pornographic: in the talk of a "membrane," in the similarity of *flicken*, intentional or not, with the obscene *ficken*. The pornography is of history, of the world, of all language in the world (and the poem). It is played out by the poem's characters as they engender its movement toward its own "inside," and is also something both inside and outside the crystal: outside (or on the surface) as the fetishized balance and perfection of a textual "world" reflecting its own form; inside as a hidden horror from which it claims to escape. Hence the "thousandfold crystal" marks the formal crystallization (*Anschießen*) of the crystal verbal world hidden in the stony plant, and also signifies the deadly "crystallizing" of countless human souls. We find a similar ambivalence in the word *Anschießen* itself: along with "crystallize," it has a more plainly murderous valence. This ambivalence is then mimicked in the form of the strophe as well: the movement of *kam* to *flickte* to *schoß an* is mimed by a verbal doubling that also constitutes a balance. The balance is mirrored by the balanced, rhymed movement from *kam* to *Membran* to *schoß an*, which at the same time marks phonetically the continued fall from grace of the poem's own discourse—its continued movement along the "path of art."

Applying a vocabulary in debt to Freud, as well as to Kenneth Burke, in order to offer what is, finally, a phenomenological-taxonomical (as opposed to a genetic) perspective on a symbolic system, Fletcher locates the source of allegorical ambivalence in "ambivalence of emotion": a clash between opposing authoritative ideals resulting from intense moral conflict. Such conflict, "if radical and stubborn, results in a division, an inflexible dualism, in all branches of feeling and thought, which so influences the sufferer's apperceptions, that every significant object become ambivalent to him, being composed, as he sees it, of two contrary elements, one good and one evil, which cannot be reconciled or blended."[55] This observation about Melville is relevant to Celan's allegorical imagination, firmly grounded in a "radical and stubborn" moral conflict, the result of a rooting of his language and literary tradition in a Jewish locus. Apocalyptically condemning the former as the vehicle of the latter's extinction (the underlying "story" told in "Engführung"), Celan's creative enterprise thus articulates a polarization between two internalized, authoritative ideals—the metaphysical German ideal incarnate in his self-identity as *Dichter*, and an intense nostalgia for an ideal, utopian, Jewish "other," attached to the destroyed world of his past—the one running into conflict with the other in the very process of articulation. Keeping in mind Freud's discussion of what he terms "projection" in *Totem und Tabu*, our tendency to settle inner conflicts through their symbolic externalization in the real world, we may thus regard the constitutive elements of Celan's imaginary universe—the magic names, culled from anthropological, astrological, and other realms, each encoding the polarized terms of the poem's programmatic movement—as "antithetical primal words," formally encapsulating intense emotional ambivalence, translated into a symbolical world as a "double cathexis": the endowment of such words with that which is at once the taboo of things contaminated, poisonous, or filthy and the magic aura attached to objects of utopian desire.[56]

More generally, such ambivalence determines the diachronic schema reflected in the polarity of *Kunst* and *Dichtung*, from which the primal words emerge. The poem's quest for self-identity is also for identity with a radical principle of difference: the horror that the poetic spirit desires to "remember." Inversely, the horror would only be repeated, as a kind of suicide, in any overcoming of the distance from its origin—such suicide hence lurking in the transcendental purpose of

Celan's primal words. In this manner, Celan simultaneously locates death and resurrection at the final outcome of his allegorical quest, where traditional allegory offers a choice, depending on ideology and moral intent, between one and the other.[57]

The allegorist's transformation of the outer world into a mirror of his inner spiritual condition—a "filtering" process explaining the extraordinary, and perhaps unique, rigor of Celan's allegorical imagination—points to the close connection between allegory and paranoia, as well as to the link between paranoia and compulsion. Fletcher defines the "agency" of allegorical compulsion as obsessional anxiety—the desire (or need) of an allegorical agent to reach a goal (home or the Celestial City), combined with a fear of the obstacles along the way or of not reaching it at all. Attempting to deny or destroy evil, the allegorist, in a "search for pure power," sends a "daemonically empowered agent of death against the camp of the evil doers." The agent is termed "daemonic," Fletcher points out, in that he acts "as if possessed by a daemon, since by definition if a man is possessed by an influence that excludes all other influences while it is operating on him, then he clearly has no life outside an exclusive sphere of action." The obsessiveness of the quest of the daemonic agent, revealing a sense that "there is no such thing as satisfaction in this world," thus involves a *manie de perfection*—"an impossible desire to become one with an image of unchanging purity. The agent seeks to become isolated within himself, frozen in an eternally fixed form, an 'idea' in the Platonic sense of the term."[58] In this light, we can understand Celan as the daemonic agent of his own poetry, repetitively questing for full poetic plenitude by transforming the impurity of his language's source into the purity of its goal: a mono-obsessive theme at work within Celan's individual primal words as well as in each poem's formal-thematic movement. In fact, it is present in the movement of the oeuvre as a whole, essentially excluding all other influences and themes from its reductive force (which gradually moves the poetry toward silence), and reflecting Celan's profound moral horror at the state of a world "read" under the sign of the extinction of the Jews.

The anxiety at the heart of allegory is kept in check, controlled and contained, by the very terms of its expression: an unbroken compulsive surface, the "rigid sequence of events leading to the winning of the quest." Making use of different kinds of ritualistic schemes such as double plots and psychomachia, the allegorist "slows and regulates the pace of the existence his fiction represents."[59] Even the strongly marked syntax—paratactic or hypotactic—characteristic of allegorical texts, and often mapping out the course of Celan's "language curves,"[60] reveals such regulatory intent. In a manner reminding us of Freud's linkage of compulsive and religious ritual, the form of allegorical symbolizing thus tends to alleviate allegorical tension or ambivalence,[61] and such texts become elaborate ritual constructs, "the narrative equivalent of visual, geometric designs."[62] As such static, iconic systems of reflexive reference, they represent formally or reify the "images of unchanging purity" which are the objects of their thematized desire. We have already come across a number of ways in which Celan encodes such "ritualistic schemes" in "Engführung." The textual weave of both the "echoes" at the end of each section and of the *a*-sounds representing the "path of art" offers (in the latter case paradoxically) a synthetic unity to the poem's fracturing of voices, person, and tense. Interacting with the magic closures at its inside or center and outside or end, they help make of it a carefully contrived, rigidly elaborated iconic structure. In a sense, then, what the ritualistic sexual theme in the sixth section of "Engführung" reveals is Celan's ambivalent awareness of this "icon making" process: in the end, an enactment of the desire to penetrate and fuse with the text's image.[63]

Citing both Huizinga's characterization of the waning Middle Ages as a period marked by "the extremes of brutality and moral chaos on the one hand, and ornamental refinement and rigid cosmology on the other," and Wilhelm Worringer's theory of the mind's discovery of shelter from "a world of hardly controlled flux" in aesthetic abstraction, Fletcher has pointed to the context from which the allegory's formal magic emerges.[64] Like all language mysticism, the allegorical propensity is most active in periods of historical crisis, and its encoding of formal ritual is one reflection of the desire to master history.[65] Otto Fenichel's observation that "he who knows a word for a thing, masters the thing,"[66] is relevant here, applying as much to the nature of Celan's ritual enactments as Langland's or Spencer's. Celan's allegory, refining characteristics of the symbolic mode already manifest in its medieval Christian form, is the ritual mastery of a radical, internalized historical crisis: the moral disorientation and psychic chaos left in the wake of the Holocaust.

In "Engführung," Celan lays out the terms of this psychological-historical dynamic, and I would like to conclude by briefly pointing to its presence in the threshold text as obsessional anxiety. Reread, this text constitutes a deathly landscape into which the reader is not only "brought" or "deported," but where he or she is also killed—an alternative meaning of *verbringen* in Grimm. This sense, however, is only present in Middle-High and -Low German; in other words, Celan's threshold word, VERBRACHT, is defined by the same historicity as *Windfang*. This word points to the presence of a specific, anxious image lurking in the threshold scene: that of an allegorical hearse in a textual graveyard ("the stones, white . . ."), "bringing" (or "rolling") us there to decipher the inscriptions on a tombstone. As with the circle, the topos of the wheel has its place in the history of German mysticism, particularly in the writings of Jakob Böhme and Comenius, where it is based on the eschatological vision of Ezekiel. Through its presence in "Engführung,"

Celan enacts the deathly movement lurking in the history of its threshold word, identifying this movement with the text's "proper" reading. Thus the qualities of the poem as part of a literary genre correspond to the needs of a specific sort of literary imagination, both these elements informing the heuristic nature of allegory: the task it gives the reader to construct or unfold its moral message.

NOTES

1. Jacob and Wilhelm Grimm, *Deutxches Wörterbuch* (Leipzig: Hirzel, 1854-1961), bol. 14, pt. 2, cols. 299-301. My German citations from Grimm will retain original orthography throughout (viz., lowercase initial letters on nouns).

2. Sigmund Freud, *The Standard Edition of the Complete Psychological Works* ed. and trans. James Strachey (London: Hogarth Press 1953), 4:225.

3. "Allegory as Interpretation," *New Literary History* 3, no. 2 (1972), 306.

4. Cf. Gerhard Kurz, "Zu einer Hermeneutik der literarischen Allegorie," in *Formen und Funktionen der Allegorie*, ed. Walter Haug (Stuttgart: Metzler, 1979), 15.

5. Lloyd Spencer, "Allegory in the World of the Commodity: The Importance of Central Park," *New German Critique* 12 (1985), 62.

6. Several writers have described his poems in a broad way as "allegorical": cf. Renate Böschenstein-Schäfer, "Allegorische Züge in der Lyrik Paul Celans," *Etudes germaniques* 25, no. 3 (1970), 251–65, and Henriette Beese, *Nachdichtung als Erinnerung. Allegorische Lektüre einiger Gedichte von Paul Celan* (Darmstadt: Agora, 1976). Winfried Menninghaus, in his book on Celan's "magic of form" and the metalinguistic movement he sees Celan as thematizing from poem to poem, omits any talk of allegory—a particularly striking omission in that Menninghaus stresses the affinity between Celan's poetics and Benjamin's theory of the relation of language to history, with which the latter's belatedly influential notion of allegory is aligned. See *Paul Celan. Magie der Form* (Frankfort: Suhrkamp, 1980).

7. *Art and Its Objects* (Cambridge: Cambridge University Press, 1980), 44.

8. Cf. Wollheim, *Art and Its Objects*, 66–73.

9. Cf. Jürgen Fohrmann, "Remarks Towards a Theory of Literary Genres," *Poetica* (Amsterdam) 7, no. 3 (1988), 273–85.

10. Spencer, "Allegory in the World of the Commodity," 62.

11. Cf. Kurz, "Zu einer Hermeneutik," 16. The response to the skeptic's query regarding allegory's interpretation—"Can you prove it?"—should thus be something like: "No, but since the evidence is strong, it may diminish things to see them otherwise." For example, *arbitrarily* assigning *random* entries from Grimm to Celan's "surface" lexicon would not result in narratives that cohere to the "pragmatic presuppositions" we bring to the poems.

12. Cf. Stanley Cavell, *In Quest of the Ordinary* (Chicago: University of Chicago Press, 1988), 132–36, esp. 117. On literary texts as intentional systems, see Thomas Pavel, *Le Mirage linguistique. Essai sur la modernisation intellectuelle* (Paris: Minuit, 1988), 170–78.

13. See *The Language of Allegory: Defining the Genre* (Ithaca: Cornell University Press, 1964).

14. In *Celan-Studien* (Frankfort: Suhrkamp, 1972), 47–111. See also Marlies Janz, *Vom Engagement absoluter Poesie* (Frankfort: Syndikat, 1976), 74–88; Heinz-Michael Krämer, *Eine Sprache des Leidens. Zur Lyrik von Paul Celan* (Munich: Grünewald, 1979), 96–118. Cf. a more recent effort—unavailable at the time of this essay's writing—to interpret the poem in light of passages from Nietzsche, Jean Paul, Franz Rosenzweig, and Shakespeare, among others: Otto Lorenz, *Schweigen in der Dichtung. Hölderlin—Rilke—Celan* (Göttingen: Vandenhoeck & Ruprecht, 1989), 171–243.

15. Cf. Götz Wienold, "Paul Celans Hölderlin-Widerruf," *Poetica* (Amsterdam) 2, no. 2 (1968), 216–28 (on "Tenebrae"). On the elegy of German Classicism, see Theodore Ziolkowski, *The Classical German Elegy, 1795–1950* (Princeton: Princeton University Press, 1980).

16. Briefly cited, for example: "Brod und Wein," strophe 1, line 2, "rauschen die Wagen hinweg" = "Engführung," section 1, lines 10–13: "Ein Rad, langsam, / rollt aus sich selber, die Speichen / klettern," etc.; "BW" 1.4–5, "und Gewinn und Verlust waget ein sinniges Haupt / Wohlzufrieden zu Haus" = "E" 1.9–10; "du bist—bist zuhause"; "BW" 1.14, "das Schattenbild" = "E" 1.5: "die Schatten der Halme"; "BW" 1.15–17, "die Nacht / kommt / Voll mit Sternen und wohl wenig bekümmert um uns, / Glanzt die Erstaunende," etc. = "E" 1.13–15: "die Nacht / braucht keine Sterne"; "BW" 2.25–26, "Aber zuweilen liebt auch klares Auge den Schatten / Und versuchet zu Lust, eh' es die Noth ist, den Schlaf" = "E" 2.21–28: "Sie / sahn nicht hindurch / . . . Keines / erwachte, der / Schlaf / kam über sie"; "BW" 2.33, "das strömende Wort" = "E" 5.49–50: "Kam, kam. / Kam ein Wort"; "BW" 3.41, "das Offene" = "E" 3.32–33: ich war / offen; "BW" 4.61, "wo leuchten sie denn, die 'fernhintreffenden Sprüche'" = "E" 5.49–52: "Kam . . . / ein Wort . . . / durch die Nacht, / wollt leuchten, wollt leuchten"; "BW" 8.132, "der himmlische Chor" = "E" 8.146–47: "die Chöre"; "BW" 8.137, "Brod ist der Erde Frucht, doch ists vom Lichte gesegnet" = "E" 8.151–53: "Ein / Stern / hat wohl noch Licht"; finally, "BW" 9.147–48, "er bleibet und selbst die Spur der entflohenen Götter / Gotterlosen hinab unter das Finstere bringt" = "E" 1.1–3 and 9.164–68: "Verbracht ins Gelände mit der untrüglichen Spur." Likewise, three key terms in the "Meridian" address—*das Offene, das Eigene, die Fremde*—are each found in "Brod und Wein" (3.41–42; 4.67).

17. Cf. Joel Golb, "Translating Tradition: A Reading of Paul Celan's 'Huhediblu,'" *Acts* 8–9 (1988), 168–80. (See also note 20 below.)

18. Quilligan, *The Language of Allegory*, 153, 33, and 53.

19. That they are not only a convention is suggested by the difference between various first lines regarding how many words are capitalized—a difference appearing to reflect Celan's decision as to how many of the opening words he wants to "announce" or dramatize (for instance, "DIE EWIGKEITEN TINGELN" [*GW* 2:159] versus "DIE EWIGKEITEN fuhren" [*GW* 2:283]). In some poems, the capitalization extends into the second line; in the titled poems ("Engführung" excepted) there is no such capitalization—thus pointing back to the convention.

20. Along with its implicit presence in "Hohles Lebensgehöft," the vast majority of Celan's poems with *lesen* in any of its forms or derivatives makes use of this double entendre. Cf. for example "Dein Hinübersein" (*GW* 1:218) ("Your Being Beyond" [*P* 161]): "Gott, das lasen wir" ("God, so we read") (1.

10). Here, a recognition of the double meaning—the reference to both a "reading" of the text and a "plucking" from God's (transcendental) "beanstalk"—calls into question any interpretation of the poem as supporting the contention that Celan's texts, being Judaic, do not articulate, even as a possibility, Augustinian transcendence. See Shira Wolosky, "Mystical Language and Mystical Silence in Paul Celan's 'Dein Hinübersein,'" in *Argumentum e Silentio*, ed. Amy D. Colin (Berlin: de Gruyter, 1987), 364–74. It is similarly crucial to recognize that with "Bruder / Geblendet, Bruder / erloschen, du liest, / dies hier, dies: Dis- / parates" ("Brother / blinded one, brother, / extinguished one, you read / this here, this: / dis- / parate stuff") in "Huhediblu" (*GW* 1: 275), Celan is referring to both the poem's "reading" and a mandrake's murderous/suicidal "plucking." (Interestingly in light of "Engführung," in here addressing his "blind brother," Celan is citing Trakl's cipher for Hölderlin in "Untergang" and elsewhere.) Not carefully considering the pun's role is one source of a failure by several commentators to grasp the poem's organic narrative unfolding, and the key to its rhetorical coherence—it's expression of its *own* "fallen," polluted, and simultaneously transcendental movement (shared most intimately with Hölderlin, but also with Mandelstam, Trakl, the reader, and others). See Ulrich Konietzny, *Simneinheit und Sinnkohärenz des Gedichtes bei Paul Celan* (Bad Honnef: Bock & Herchen, 1985), 117–37; Edith Horowitz-Silbermann, "Paul Celan: Huhediblu: Versuch einer Deutung," *Literatur für Leser* 2 (1988), 84–97; and Amy D. Colin, *Paul Celan: Holograms of Darkness* (Bloomington: Indiana University Press, 1991), 113–33.

21. On the generic contract, establishing the reader's "horizon of expectation," see Gérard Genette, *Palimpsestes. La littérature au second degré* (Paris: Seuil, 1982), 11.

22. Cited in Krämer, *Eine Sprache des Leidens*, 108, from Hans Mayer, *Der Repräsentant und der Martyrer. Konstellationen der Literatur* (Frankfort: Suhrkamp, 1971), 182.

23. The reference to Dante is found in Szondi ("Durch die Enge geführt," 77), where it is limited to verse 138. Szondi notes that "Celan has repeatedly pointed to this 'source' for the passage in 'Engführung.'" Krämer, not citing Szondi but information Celan gave Janz, cited in her book, expands the reference and thus relates it to the meaning of *das Andere*.

24. Cf. Janz, *Vom Engagement absoluter Poesie*, 223, who omits the last of these parallels.

25. In this context, cf. Joel Golb, "Celan and Heidegger: A Reading of 'Todtnauberg,'" *Seminar* 24, no. 3 (1988), 258n and 264n.

26. *Deutsches Wörterbuch*, vol. 2, col. 470.

27. Cited in Ernst Robert Curtius, *Europäische Literatur und Lateinisches Mittelalter* (Bern: Francke, 1969), 238–39. Quoted from Anton Emanuel Schönbach, *Gesammelte Aufsätze zur neueren Literatur* (Graz: Leuschner & Lubench, 1900), 100.

28. Krämer, *Eine Sprache des Leidens*, 25, points out that the *Kelchblatt* evokes the poison in a poison-cup (*Giftkelch*).

29. Cf. Szondi, "Durch die Enge geführt," 84.

30. Cf. *Deutsches Wörterbuch*, vol. 2, col. 1055.

31. Cf. Menninghaus, *Paul Celan*, 101–16.

32. *Deutsches Wörterbuch*, vol. 2, col. 1826.

33. Ibid., vol. 5, pt. 2, col. 1827.

34. The problem discussed may be considered from the inverse perspective: any historical dictionary being a record of the violence of history, and much of its lexicon suitable for Celan's linguistic eschatology, it is always a matter of judgment whether or not he is intentionally thematizing a particular entry from Grimm. But Celan was a most scrupulous encoder of the mammoth work, and for this reason we cannot discount even the obscurest citations. In this passage, it seems likely that *Kornjude* is a presence; less so, for instance, that the following lines from Lessing are at work in *dicht*: "wenn alle diebe gehängen würden / die galgen müßten dichter stehn" (*Deutsches Wörterbuch*, vol. 2, col. 1056). But our very recognition of this interpretive problem dramatizes allegory's heuristic potential.

35. Cf. Gerhard Wahrig, *Das große deutsche Wörterbuch* (Gütersloh: Bertelsmann, 1968), col. 1218.

36. *Deutsches Wörterbuch*, vol. 5, pt. 2, col. 2363.

37. *Deutsches Wörterbuch*, vol. 11, pt. 1, col. 1323; quoted from Zappe, *Mineralhandlexikon* (1817).

38. As in the following citations: "Complex combinations (of crystals) whose single parts tend to form half cylinders [*halbkugeln*—an embedded allusion, apparently, to the *Kugelfang* (bullet-catch) that will surface in the poem's eighth section]. These are kidney-shaped [*nierenförmig*] and grapelike [*traubig*] combinations . . . the kidney-shaped ones combine smaller into larger clusters." "(Opal) is kidney-shaped and grapelike." *Deutsches Wörterbuch*, vol. 11, pt. 1, col. 1323, citing Tschermale-Becke, *Lehrbuch der Mineralogie* (1921), and A. G. Werner, *Oryktognose* (1792). Parallel to its semantic hovering between the mineral and botanic, we find, in the application of *traubig* to hardened tree-resin, a fusion of dryness—that of the eye's contact with the stone at the end of the strophe (*GW* 1:201)—and liquidity—that of the earlier damp eye. This is the same as a "hardening" (crystallization, icing over) of the "ground-water traces" ("Grundwasserspuren") toward which the poem is moving (*GW* 1:204). The suggested etymology for *Traube* leads back to Low German *drubbel*, "stack of humans." Cf. Wahrig, *Das große deutsche Wörterbuch*, col. 3600.

39. *Deutsches Wörterbuch*, vol. 10, pt. 3, cols. 808–10.

40. Cf. ibid., vol. 7, col. 832, where its use in crystallography also has an equivalent in mining—a buried lexical "treasure" linking the term with the mining metaphors of the Romantics, especially Novalis.

41. Cf. *Deutsches Wörterbuch*, vol. 10, pt. 3, cols. 809–10.

42. Cf. ibid., vol. 10, pt. 1, col. 1111.

43. Cf. Aris Fioretos, "Nothing: Reading Paul Celan's 'Engführung,'" *Comparative Literature Studies* 27, no. 2 (1990), esp. 163–66.

44. *The Death of Stéphane Mallarmé* (Cambridge: Cambridge University Press, 1982), 77.

45. Stéphane Mallarmé, *Oeuvres complètes* (Paris: Gallimard, 1945), 1582.

46. Paul Valéry evokes this analogy impressionistically in "Le coup de dés," a piece Celan probably knew well. See *Variété II* (Paris: Gallimard, 1930), 195–96.

47. Valéry, "Le coup de dés," 197.

48. Cf. Fioretos, "Nothing," 164–65.

49. "In der ulenflucht kam ek erst weer in" (Schambach); "in der späten eulenflucht zu ihnen gieng" (Celander, *Verliebter Student*). Cf. *Deutsches Wörterbuch*, vol. 3, col. 1194. Szondi, "Durch die Enge geführt," 96, notes the Grimm citation in passing. Hegel's owl appears at the end of the preface to the *Grundlinien der Philosophie des Rechts* (Berlin: Akademie-Verlag, 1981 [1833]), 28.

50. See *Allegory: The Theory of a Symbolic Mode* (Ithaca: Cornell University Press, 1964), esp. 220–78.

51. On the allegorical quest and voyage, see Fletcher, *Allegory*, 147–80.

52. Ibid., 22.

53. This serves as a countervoice to the "great many radiant *a*-sounds" Hölderlin uses to signify the descent of the Gods to earth in "Brod und Wein." Cf. Jochen Schmidt, *Hölderlin's Elegie "Brod und Wein"* (Berlin: de Gruyter, 1968), 88–89.

54. The most extreme expression of this "pornodialectic" is in "Spasmen," contained in *Atemwende* (*GW* 2:122).

55. Fletcher, *Allegory*, 301. Fletcher cites Henry Murray's introduction to Melville's *Pierre* (New York: Hendricks House, 1949), xv.

56. On antithetical primal words and double cathexis in relation to allegorical compulsion, see Fletcher, esp. 293–303.

57. Fletcher, *Allegory*, 174–75.

58. Ibid., 286–87, 339, 49, and 65.

59. Ibid., 228 and 161–74.

60. Cf. Menninghaus, *Paul Celan*, 230–48.

61. Cf. Fletcher, *Allegory*, 346.

62. Ibid., 69.

63. This process is connected with what Joseph Frank, combining insights of New Criticism with Wilhelm Worringer's historicism, has suggested is a quality of modernist narrative in general. See "Spatial Form in Modern Literature," in *The Widening Gyre: Crisis and Mastery in Modern Literature* (New Brunswick: Rutgers University Press, 1964). In *La révolution du langage poétique* (Paris: Seuil, 1964), Julia Kristeva views the modernist shift from traditional rhetorical-discursive structures, not as reflecting a desire to establish symbolic "power systems" à la Fletcher, but (inversely?) as undermining the power-code of bourgeois culture.

64. Fletcher, *Allegory*, 284n and 58n.

65. See Vera Calin, *Auferstehung der Allegorie* (Vienna: Europaverlag, 1969).

66. Cited by Fletcher, *Allegory*, 295.

6

The Second of Inversion

Movements of a Figure through Celan's Poetry

Werner Hamacher
Translated by Peter Fenves

Under the sign of the semantic function to which language, according to the classical doctrine formulated by Aristotle, should reduce itself in the course of its only veridical mode of expression—predicative assertions—language appears caught in an aporia that admits only an aporetic solution: it is explained away as an empty gesture that must evanesce before the power of the factual, or it is accorded all the weight of the only ascertained reality, whose types are stamped onto the entire region of objectivity and constitute objectivity itself. In the first case, language is destined to disappear before the presence of the world of things and their movements; it is nothing in itself, a mere instrument, in the crudest instance an instrument of deixis, a means of reference that should disappear precisely where the things themselves appear. In the other case, language is exalted into the schema of all reality, and so it encounters in reality only itself; it employs objects to confirm the efficacy of its figures and runs into a virtually endless process of repeating, without resistance, its preestablished types. In one case, language makes statements about reality to which it cedes all rights in order, as the shadow-like image of reality, to recede before its light, whereas in the other case reality only retains the rights of language in whose image it was created. The infinitude of the real in one case confronts the infinitude of language in the other. In both cases, language and its inherent epistemological forms are denied the power to be a reality with its own rights and its own structure, a reality that could not be exhausted by any relationship of analogy, representation, or of typifying other realities. Both interpretations of language, which essentially define it according to its semantic and referential functions, must therefore end up in a paradox: once language reaches its ends and thus the site of its definition, it no longer means anything and no longer refers anywhere; on this destined site, it would make room for whatever has been meant by language, or it would only be purely itself in whatever has been modeled after its image. At the end of every semantic theory of language and its truth stands the aporetic verdict: language does not speak; it has nothing to say, only itself or its disappearance. But the basis of this aporia lies in the assumption that reality only shows itself as objectivity, that this objectivity fulfills itself in its being present and that, under the conditions of its absence—an absence projected according to the image of objectivity fulfilling itself in presence—language intercedes in order, as either substrate or prototype, to preserve or to reserve the possibility of objectivity. According to this idea of a transcendental semantics, which organizes not only classical philosophical systems but also the most unreflective linguistic theories, language would be the proper place of origin for reality interpreted as objectivity.

But the very notion that reality takes its lead from language—and not the other way around—will be construed by the naive, normal, and natural understanding of the world as a malicious presumption. Once this notion is accepted, the world appears upside-down, perverted, stood on its head. In the texts of Kant and Hegel, as the culmination of the theories of absolute subjectivity, the metaphors of turning, of overturning and transforming, of perverting, reverting, and returning make their entrance together with those of reflection and speculation, and they do so with unprecedented density. Joining the Platonic figure of epistrophe and the evangelic one of metanoia, they gain an obligatory power that was to become mythical for subsequent philosophical and literary texts.

The Kantian "revolution in the mode of thought" attempts experimentally, as it were, and with an explicit appeal to the Copernican turn, to make a plausible argument that, for there to be *a priori* knowledge, objects must first be stamped by the forms under which they are known. In such knowledge the subject, as form of representation, gives its objects the rule according to which they can be objects of knowledge in the first place. The inversion of the traditional mode of thinking that Kant sets into motion therefore secures access to reality, since it assigns to knowledge the form of objectivity and thereby brings the entirety of the given under the epistemic premises of subjectivity. The *ordo inversus* induced by Kant's critique—an induction in which this critique is by no means exhausted—is the figure of totalized subjectivity. On this point Hegel appointed himself the executor of the legacy of Kant's critique, since he saw not only the world of nature but equally that of history placed under the principle of representing, conceptualizing, and thinking spirit. The *locus classicus* of his corresponding formulations refers once again to a revolution, the one that took place in France, and imparts to this revolution a significant turn of speech whose fragility would deserve a detailed analysis. It is to be found in his *Lectures on the Philoso-*

phy of History: "Never since the sun stood under the firmament and planets revolved around it had it come to pass that human beings stood on their head, that is, in their thoughts and built reality according to such thoughts. . . . This was indeed a glorious dawn."[1] If human beings and their reality stand on their heads when the light of reason first arises, it is because their life and their history only attain a stable foundation for their significance in the head. Only in thought does reality and its historical process come to itself, and only standing on its head does reality reach its first true stance, the stance of truth in which nothing alien opposes it any longer; the other, on the contrary, shows itself to be the other of its *self*. In taking its stand on the principle of subjectivity, historical reality stands up and stands upright: it thereby shows that the objectivity of finite spirit is already inhabited by the infinite self-relation of subjective spirit.

But Hegel's speculative inversion does not simply bring the objective reality of history to itself and thus to reason. Inversion Hegelian style performs its greatest feat—and does so against the deepest intentions of the Kantian inversion—in the arena of nonreality, in death as the abstract negation of entities as such. Spirit thereby shows itself as substantial subjectivity by turning its own nonreality—its dismemberment and absence—into being. In the preface to the *Phenomenology of Spirit* Hegel writes: "Death, if that is the name we want to give this unreality, is the most dreadful thing of all, and the greatest strength is required to hold fast what is dead." Spirit is the power in which absolute dismemberment finds itself again, "only when it looks the negative in the face and dwells there. Such dwelling is the magical force that turns the negative into being.—It is the same as what was earlier called the subject, . . . the true substance . . . that does not have mediation outside itself but rather in this mediation itself."[2] Death, "if that is the name we want to give to this unreality," can only be held fast, looked in the face and turned into being, if it has been transformed from death into something dead, from an unreality—by prosopopoeia—into a face, from the negation of the "I" into the pure energy of the "I." It can only be turned into being after it has been assigned a determinate place in the circle of speculative inversion. The point is not to censure a *petitio principii*—but this petition, this *petitio principii*, is perhaps *the* problem of philosophy; the point is, rather, to make clear that the life of spirit can only turn the unreality of death into objective reality because its absence comes into view as the hollow mold of its own shape, as a death in the image of life, as a negative according to the model of "absolute position or positing," as Kant defines being. Meaning can only be affixed to a death for which subjectivity has lent an aspect, a countenance, a face according to the pattern of its own shape. The process of prosopopoeia—the lending of a face or a mask—and thereby the roots of possible meaningfulness in finite life became a problem for Kant—most clearly so in the paragraphs of the third *Critique* devoted to the Analytic of the Sublime—but turned into a problem for Hegel only in those places which he himself considered peripheral to the system. The dominant figure of Hegelian philosophy—negation of the negation, speculative inversion—holds sway over a domain already sheltered by the principle of subjectivity against the abyssal shapelessness of death, "if that is the name we want to give this unreality." Only because nothingness, as Hegel writes in his critique of skepticism, always figures as the "nothingness of something" and thus already assumes the figure of objective being, can the figure of inversion be brought to bear against it and can it—or "nothingness"— be returned to being. Turning in this way, the being of the subject is mediated with its nonbeing and is itself nothing other than the movement of this mediation with its other as itself. By virtue of the mediating and converting character of the substantial subject, a meaning attaches itself to each linguistic sign it posits—we indeed "want to name" this unreality (even after a certain pause) death—and this meaning remains indispensable for the interaction among the sign, what it signifies, and the communicative interaction between different speakers, because the very thing signified is already drawn into the shape of subjectivity as a moment of mediation. To the degree that everything which falls under the domain of language becomes, through the movement of mediation, a means of semiocentric inversion, everything also—at least such is Hegel's intention—steps into the middle of its meaning: it no longer means anything but is itself the process of meaningfulness; it not only refers to something absent but is itself the process of its presentation, pure energy of subjectivity as it presents and thereby objectifies itself.

One could demonstrate the efficacy and determining power of the figure of inversion, here sketched only with reference to two standard philosophical texts, over a wide range of philosophical and literary texts from romanticism and classicism to Feuerbachian and Marxian materialism as well as so-called poetical realism up through neo-romanticism; one could make this demonstration in the macrostructure of the novel of *Bildungsroman* as well as in the syntactical details of lyric poetry.[3] However diverse the intentions controlling this figure may be, inversion remains—with the great exception of the Hölderlinian inversion, which sets the resistance to the meaning of finite linguistic material against the universalization of its semantic energy[4]—inversion still remains the dominant rhetorical and epistemological figure for the consolidation of meaning and for the universalization of subjectivity.

———

In this sense inversion is also the canonical shape of the lyric. It reaches its culmination in Rilke's *New Poems*.[5] In the "Archaic Torso of Apollo," which is placed as an emblem at the opening of its second part and thereby occupies roughly the center of the entire book, the remains of Greek plastic art turn into precisely what time has taken away from it: they turn into eyesight, *Augenlicht.*

Wir kannten nicht sein unerhörtes Haupt,
darin die Augenäpfel reiften. Aber
sein Torso glüht noch wie ein Kandelaber . . .

(We did not know its unheard-of head,
in which its pupils ripened. But
its torso still glowed like a candelabrum . . .)[6]

Contrary to the impression awakened by the prosaic temporality of "still," the torso's blinding brilliance does not radiate as residue of a shape that was whole at its origin; rather, this brilliance arises only by virtue of its fragmentation. Only because this God of phenomenality lacks eyesight does that which is absent wander into its torso, bringing the mutilated body to light as an extinguished one, making the "stone" into a "star," material obscurity into the foundation of the phenomenal world of objectivity and the poetic one of sound—the world, that is, into which Rilke's poetry installs itself as its own stele and presents itself in its melodious perfection. Just as the viewer of Apollo's torso becomes something seen because this torso itself has become its missing "unheard-of head"—"denn da ist keine Stelle, / die dich nicht sieht" (for there is no place / that does not see you)—so this "unheard-of head" becomes in the poem something heard: in its place the poem states the imperative of the glance that falls from the torso to the reader: "Du mußt dein Leben ändern" (You must alter your life). But how alter your life other than according to the canon of inversion—an inversion, moreover, that the reader, having come under the imperative of art, has experienced in the shape of an Apollo turned into sound and appearance through his fragmentation? The language of the poem and its object have so thoroughly permeated one another that the one, in a further inversion, has taken the place of the other: the object of the poem has turned into the poem, the poem into its object. "You must alter your life." Alter life you must—and the imperative is here at the same time a constative of necessity—because the resonant glance of the poem has itself become the subject of life blinded in its finitude, and its finitude turns into the fulfillment of sound and shape. The poem is imperative, because it is *strictu sensu,* by virtue of the figure of inversion that it describes and runs through, *not-wendig:* nimbly turning away misery. It transforms its misery of being merely fragmentary into the virtue of presenting itself the law of the whole. Only where the artwork is ruined can its sheer shape, *ordine inverso,* come forth. With this turn, the ethical mandate of the poem has been established. For the life of that which is seen, apostrophized in the "you," already stands, as finite, under the law that the poem establishes for its object: having to be, as a broken piece, already another, namely, the generation of the whole. The imperative that states the necessary consequence of the figure of inversion is therefore also the *restitutio ad integrum* of the center of the "Archaic Torso of Apollo"—"jener Mitte, die die Zeugung trug" (the center that bore procreation). That it was once there, although as little known as the "unheard-of head," and that only a smile the torso aims at the place which "bore" it still remains—these things lend the entire text a nostalgic trait; the fact, however, that this center captures undistorted hearing in the imperative to regenerate the whole and guarantees the whole energy of subjectivity turned into sound and appearance precisely in its absence lends Rilke's inversion-poem the pathos of a finitude that knows itself capable of virtually endless procreative acts. In this poem the phallic substrate of subjectivity emerges in an almost compulsive fashion. The archaic torso of Apollo is the arche of a *whole* generation of art. Only the very last poems of Rilke turn toward a finitude that no longer allows for pathos, toward an absence that cannot be inverted into a pure presence and so withstands its transformation into shape and resounding meaning.

Paul Celan, whose precise familiarity with Rilke's poetry has been copiously documented, adheres to this tradition. Hardly a figure of his early and middle lyrics asserts itself with such open insistence as inversion. But it is characteristic for the historico-philosophical position of this poetry—if it is still possible to speak in an unaltered way, with reference to Celan, of history, philosophy, and position—that it radicalizes this figure to abstract purity, no longer tolerating any ornamental glow and seeks ultimately to surpass and to abandon this figure by means of a procedure to which the formulation "inversion of inversion" hardly does justice. In the early collection of aphorisms and parables Celan published in 1949 in the Zürich journal *Die Tat* under the programmatic title *Gegenlicht* ("Counter-light"), the sentence "Their embrace lasted so long that love despaired of them"[7] takes up a position against the concept of unification on behalf of its concrete realization, and this realization has the power to drive the general concept into despair and division. In the sentence "The day of judgment has come, and in search of the greatest of desecrations the cross was nailed to Christ,"[8] the apocalypse appears as that turnabout in which the cross—mere instrument of desecration—becomes itself the object of desecration and the human being becomes irredeemably devalued through instrumentalization; furthermore, in the sentence "'Everything flows': even this thought, and does it not bring everything again to a standstill?"[9] the Heraclitean dictum is turned against itself: if everything flows, then so does this thought, and this thought, having now turned into another, can only maintain the flow of all things if at the same time it lets this flow stand still: this dictum can therefore be a universal statement only when its performance denies the universality of what it states. In this inversion and in the other ones that *Gegenlicht* pursues, the possibility and the constancy of general sentences and concepts in which a truth, an insight, or even just a stable meaning is supposed to be preserved are drawn into doubt by their own inner logic. If murder and movement present themselves as negations of dignity and constancy, then Celan's inversions negate the positive remainder that inhabits their negativity and thereby prevents every harmonizing mediation. In this respect, they do not amount to inversions of inversions in the sense of a dialectical setting aright of a perverted world, and they are not a return to its authentic form. As the thought of the cross nailed to Christ bears witness, Celan's world is one of perfect desecration, and the light that his texts cast on the world owes its existence to this very world: it is only light as counter-light, and that means darkness as well. In a meditation that recalls the Kabbalistic theory of *zimzum*, the self-limitation of nothingness, Celan writes: "Don't confuse yourself: this last lamp no longer gives off light—the enveloping darkness has absorbed itself into itself."[10] If there is still a light and if there is still a language in which this light imparts itself, then it is not as positive phenomenality and not as a remainder of the original logos but, rather, as a lucidity out of emptiness, out of the space left by the self-absorption of darkness. There is no light that would not be, in this sense—and contrary to ordinary representations of naive consciousness, even if it is given a dialectical spin—merely the lack of darkness. Linguistic signs are not referential indicators coordinated by autonomous subjects with their representations, nor are they the self-presentation of their objectivity. In the ellipsis of Celan's inversion, they are only the barren space opened up by a muteness lost in itself. Like the site of language, so its presence—even the apocalyptic presence of its last instant—is not a primary fact of reason but rather the secondary effect of a self-contraction of absence.

The second to the last cycle in Celan's second volume of poems, *Mohn und Gedächtnis* (Poppies and Remembrance), bears the same title as the early collection of aphorisms: "Gegenlicht," "Counter-light." The last poem in this cycle, a love poem, concerns the very site of the language of love:

Der Tauben weißeste flog auf: ich darf dich lieben!
Im leisen Fenster schwankt die leise Tür.
Der stille Baum trat in die stille Stube.
Du bist so nah, als weiltest du nicht hier.

Aus meiner Hand nimmst du die große Blume:
sie ist nicht weiß, nicht rot, nicht blau—doch nimmst du sie.

Wo sie nie war, da wird sie immer bleiben.
Wir waren nie, so bleiben wir bei ihr.
    (*GW* 1:61)

(The whitest dove flies off: I can love you!
In the soft window swings the soft door.
The still tree steps into the still room.
You are so near as though you did not linger here.

From my hand you take the great flower:
it is not white, not red, not blue—yet you take it.
Where it never was, it will always remain.
We never were, so we remain with it.)

The poem describes in a relatively classical fashion and, with regard to its lay-out, in a rather didactic way the linear progression of convergence and joining. Following the seemingly late romantic metaphor of elevation contained in the rising dove, the poem, quoting the image of reflection in the windowpane, brings together first two spatial openings, window and door, and then outer and inner space, nearness and distance, so as to address in the last line of the first stanza the nearness of the beloved as the appearance of a distance: "You are so near as though you did not linger here." The law of inversion—the greater the distance, the nearer the figure—finds no less pronounced formulations in *Niemandsrose* (No One's Rose) than in *Mohn und Gedächtnis*. In "Chymisch" (Chymous) the large, gray shape of the sister is said to be "wie alles Vorlorene nahe" (near as all things lost) (*GW* 1:227); in "Stumme Herbstgerüche" (Mute Autumn Smells) the second stanza runs:

Eine fremde Verlorenheit war
gestalthaft zugegen, du hättest
beinah
gelebt
    (*GW* 1:223)

(A strange lostness was
present as shape, you might have
almost
lived)

Whereas a severity in tone is produced in these later texts by abstractions, by the adversative connotations of *zugegen* ("present") and the mere *beinah* ("almost") of the living shape—a tone that indicates a change in the figure of inversion—the harsh distance in the text from

"Gegenlicht" is dissolved into the obliging melos of its plain language. Yet the flower that the beloved receives from the hand of the speaker becomes by virtue of its thoroughly negative attributes—at least on the semantic level of the poem—almost a nothing flower, a no one flower. In this flower, the inversion of distance into nearness is radicalized to the point where absence turns into presence: a radicalization that manifests itself in the line "where it never was, it will always remain," even if it appears to have been softened by the tense shift from "was" to "will remain." The poem reaches the extreme of radicality in its final line, where it asserts the nonexistence of the "we" and draws the consequence from this assertion—in accordance with the law of inversion— that we remain in the flower that always remains: the annihilated "we," analogous to the nothing flower, have changed into the ever-lingering constancy: "We were never, so we remain with it." If the "blue flower" of Novalis was still a symbol of the universal poeticization of the world, so this early flower of Celan—which is not blue and indeed bears no other color but rather could dazzle by its absence like none but those collected by Mallarmé—is no less a symbol: that of the poeticization of lack. In the best symbolic tradition, the remaining presence of poetry and the unification of I and You into We climbs out of this *flos rhetoricus negativus.* In the language of this flower, which is indeed not metaphorical in the traditional sense but, rather, meta-metaphorical, laying bare the mechanism of carrying-over of imagistic language at its extreme, thus trope, turn, and reversal par excellence: in the language of this flower, separated things have been brought together and what never was has turned into ever-remaining existence, because this very language came from a nothing and became something that remains. But this change is indebted to the categorical certainty of being perceived, received, and retained, and only in this perception that institutes the unity between giver and receiver does the gift of nothingness change into substantial being: "From my hand you take the great flower / it is not white, not red, not blue—yet you take it." Were this per-ception, this taking-in, to remain outstanding, were the gift not to arrive at its destined site, there would be no language, no change, no remaining. Were the nothing of language not received and perceived, its inversion into being would not be possible. This possibility of the impossibility of its own existence breaks open in Celan's poem only in the dash before the *doch* ("yet"), in the interruption of tropic language, in the mute hesitation of receiving and perceiving. This graphic pause—Celan later found for a similar moment the word *Verhoffen,* a state of expectancy to which the alternative of hope and despair does not apply, as in the alarm of animals when faced with a hunter—opens in poetic speaking a hole whose closure is not in the power of the logic of inversion to perform; it opens a distance that cannot be transformed into a nearness, a difference that cannot turn into a unity, a mute site that cannot change into a topos of an eloquent image. This is the site of an absence that must still remain unreachable for every absence that could change into our own, into the presence of our language.

However meager this hole in the tropological system of Celan may be, it makes clear a danger that threatens many of this early texts: the danger of making nothingness into a positive, of allowing for absence merely as the negative of presence and of wanting to change absence, by virtue of language, into ever-lasting being. However desperately and mockingly certain texts may at times deny the possibility of such a reversal, they nevertheless remain unquestionably committed to its idea. The emphatic closing lines of "Spät und Tief" (Late and Deep) show this:

> es komme . . .
> der geharnischte Windstoß der Umkehr,
> der mitternächtige Tag,
> es komme, was niemals noch war!

> Es komme ein Mensch aus dem Grabe.
> (*GW* 1:35–36)

> (let come . . .
> the armored gust of reversal,
> the midnight day,
> let come what never yet was!

> Let come a man from the grave.)

This commitment is shown in oxymorons of the "rostgeborene Messer" (rust-born knives) (*GW* 1:68), the 'gesteinigten Stein' (lapidated stone) (*GW* 1:51) and the "Flor der abgeblühten Stunde" (bloom of withered hours) (*GW* 1:55). All these oxymorons, paradoxes, and inversions have—and thereby they take up in a radicalized manner the problems of subjectivity in philosophy and literature since romanticism—the movement of time as their subject. The transcendental-aesthetic foundation for the figure of inversion is given in time, as the formal unity of contradictory predicates. The rhetoric of inversion is the rhetoric of temporality to the extent that the latter is represented as the finite form of unity for that which differs from itself. This concept of time permeates the lyrics of the young Celan even in those passages that expose it to its utmost limit.

Under the Nietzschean title "Lob der Ferne" (Praise of Distance) Celan weaves an entire mesh of antinomic formulations whose intention is not simply the presentation of unity but, dialectically, the presentation of the unity of unity and division:

> Abtrünnig erst bin ich treu.
> Ich bin du, wenn ich ich bin.
> [...]
> Ein Garn fing ein Garn ein:
> wir scheiden umschlungen.
>
> Im Quell deiner Augen
> erwürgt ein Gehenkter den Strang.
> (*GW* 1:33)
>
> (Only disloyally am I faithful.
> I am you when I am I.
> [...]
> A net caught in a net:
> we part entangled.
>
> In the source of your eyes
> a hanged man strangles the rope.)

Only apostasy, betrayal, and separation bind together; only the dynamic of difference gives force to unification, and only in the sundering of itself that characterizes time do the separated parts come together. "Im Quell deiner Augen / hält das Meer sein Versprechen" (In the source of your eyes / the sea holds its promise): the promise, once delivered to its redemption in temporal distance, is "held" by the sea in the eyes of the beloved; it is already fulfilled and is the—oxymoronically—fulfilled speaking of the poem in which everything subjected to temporal dissociation stands together in the formula of a negative unity. Celan's poem attempts to speak from the negativity of time itself, but a negativity that, however deeply it may have buried the traits of transience in the words spoken and distorted them into a mere allegory of speaking, nevertheless remains the center of the mediation between source and sea, presence and past, I and you, the promise and its redemption in the poem. The promise is held because past and presence are held together by the threads that run through time and that split them asunder. Because time—by virtue of its negativity and not in spite of it—is the most powerful force of synthesis, it is also the foundation for all figures of inversion that are collected in Celan's early volumes of poetry and that find their greatest concentration in *Mohn und Gedächtnis*. For inversion is nothing other than the negative positing of the negative and, by virtue of its negativity, the strict binding together of that which has been separated: it is the movement of time itself to the extent that time—as with

Hegel but not only with him—is determined as the continuum of negativity referring to itself and, furthermore, as the negative unity of difference. The language of inversion is the language of time represented as a continuum of negativity. In it, the I becomes the You at the precise moment when it disavows its loyalty to the You; the I departs from the You at the precise moment when they become entangled in one another: I and You in their relation to one another and in their self-relation are conceived as temporal moments, as moments of time for which a positive unity is as unreachable as the negative unity of their binding separation is compelling. The same negativity also stamps the speaking that the poem helps to express: in this speaking a promise is held only in such a way that the corresponding oath is breached: "Hier werf ich/[. . .]/von mir[. . .]den Glanz eines Schwures" (Here I cast . . . from me . . . the glow of an oath). Only apostasy from the already given word can fulfill it; only the breached word holds the promise of language. And so the central metaphor of the "Garne der Fischer der Irrsee" (Nets of the Fishermen of the Sea of Error), which organizes the entire texture of the poem, may be read as the spinning out of the metaphor of the "seaman's yarn," a turn of speech that refers to lying, fraud, and fantastical fabrications. The promise of which Celan's poem speaks and which Celan's poem gives itself is a fraudulent one—a promise that, like the Sea of Error, leads into errancy, a promise that only fulfills what it betrays and is only fulfilled in revealing itself as a fraud.

The language of time is not that of simple reference, which, because of its own consistency, could then refer to constant substances. The language of time is also not that of deception, which allows one to maintain the illusion that there is a region free from deception. The language of time is the one that denies for itself the denial of its truth-content and fulfills the false promise in its very breach.[11] It is, in sum, the language of a temporality that—by virtue of the negation it can repeat infinitely and on the basis of the continuity secured by such negation—remains in a position to speak the truth under the conditions of deception and in a position to speak this remaining under the conditions of disappearance: the remaining of time and its language. To become one with the movement of time—of negativity—in such a way it would become the continuum of time itself probably did belong to the deepest intentions of Celan's language in *Mohn und Gedächtnis*. The loving unification of time and language can only succeed because both, by virtue of their negativity, are energies of unification. The exhausted, the failed, the buried: "blind wie der Blick, den wir tauschen, / küßt es die Zeit auf den Mund" (blind as the gaze we exchange, / it kisses time on the mouth) (*GW* 1:57). It is time itself that sings and speaks; it is no longer an object of discourse but a subject who speaks: "Die Zeit, aus feinem Sande, singt in meinen Armen: . . . noch einmal mit dem Tod im Chor die Welt herübersingen" (Time, from fine sand, sings in my arms: . . .

once again in the chorus with death to sing the world hither) (*GW* 1:69). The imago of the beloved that Celan's poems projects bears the traits of time as much as it bears all the other subjects that find their way into his texts. But this very temporal structure suits them only because time is the subject and form of the process of the language in which these subjects are presented: "ein Wort, von Sensen gesprochen" (a word, spoken by scythes) (*GW* 1:70). With every word spoken, the time of the things this word means not only passes away; the word—or the name— is itself the cut with which time does away with the consistent subsistence of representations. And yet, in its negativity the language of time is essentially positive: it brings what is said into a finite world and into earthly life. The death that the word brings about belongs to the conditions of life:

> Aus Herzen und Hirnen
> sprießen die Halme der Nacht,
> und ein Wort, von Sensen gesprochen,
> neigt sie ins Leben.
>   (*GW* 1:70)

> (Out of hearts and brains
> sprout the blades of night
> and a word, spoken by scythes,
> bends them into life.)

The semantic potential of language whereby it can refer to objects and objective relations in the world of experience is as indebted to its temporalizing as the world of experience itself. A ripening and temporalizing function accrues to language even before its referential function. What Kant said of time is no less valid for temporal language in Celan: it is the formal condition *a priori* of representation in general. In this way, Celan's poems speak—in transcendental manner like only those of Hölderlin and, to a lesser degree, those of Rilke—of the conditions of their own possibility. They do not name something determinate but bring the very determining ground of speaking into language: its temporalizing character. In a significant departure from Kant, however, the temporalizing language in Celan is not the form of representation that makes possible the projection of world-pictures and of particular representations but is, rather, the form of transformation that makes subjects themselves into figures of time and thereby robs them of the possibility of relating themselves, as stable subjects of language, to the world and its appearances: "Stumm wie . . . [die Halme der Nacht] / wehn wir der Welt entgegen" (mute as . . . [the blades of night] / we waft toward the world) (*GW* 1:70). We *have* no language we could utilize as an instrument; rather, we *are* only that which has been spoken, wafted into a world by the cut of language—a world in which we must remain mute because, here too, time takes the words out of our mouths:

> was wir jetzt sind,
> schenken die Stunden der Zeit ein.
>
> Munden wir ihr? Kein Laut und kein Licht
> schlüpft zwischen uns, es zu sagen.
>   (*GW* 1:70)

> (what we now are,
> the hours pour in for time.
>
> Does it savor us? No sound and no light
> slips between us to say so.)

The word of time does not refer to objective data or abstract meanings; it *is* only as the withdrawal of objectivity and meaning. The language of finitude is the chronic retreat of the referential and semantic functions of language, because with each one of its words, which all bend representations into life, the world and the very being of the things thus spoken are brought to the point of disappearance. In turning to speak to its own ground, Celan's poetry can assert the condition of its possibility only as the condition of the impossibility of its stable semantic subsistence, and so it opens up the abyss of its own futility. "Poetry," as Celan will formulate it in his "Meridian" address, "poetry, ladies and gentlemen—: this pronouncement of the infinite of mere mortality and in vain!"[12]

The temporalization of language—and of all that can enter into its domain—shakes the place of the subject and the stability of its discourse, which were supposed to be secured by the transcendental turn. If it can be said and must be thought that the scythe—this allegorical prop of death and time—wields language, the *ordo inversus* that was supposed to give a foundation for the order of subjectivity and that had already fallen into difficulties with Kant's discovery of finitude and of a merely finite faculty of human presentation no longer offers any reliable guarantee for the presentation and the linguistic fixation of a world and its possible meaning. The only unity and the only continuum that can, from now on, yield to speech are those of disappearance, of a negativity without center and without sublation. All the same, the lyrics in Celan's *Mohn und Gedächtnis* draw their formal unity from this structure of negativity. A figure of inversion such as "Blicklos / schweigt nun dein Aug in mein Aug sich" (sightless / your eye now goes silent in my eye) (*GW* 1:70)—despite the negation of language and appearance expressed in it—still holds onto the rigorous relation between my eye and yours, and in their intimate unity it maintains that communication beyond language and sight reaches its mark. While the figure of the inverse order along with the form of communication persists, its substance, as sheer transience, is however consumed: its content is emptied, and its basis is turned into an abyss. The inverted world is not, as in Hegel, a world stood on its head as its unshakeable ground but is a world held in the abyss of temporality, a world so held that no one can hold onto it any longer. In his 1960 "Meridian" address, Celan lays open this same abyss in a formulation drawn from Büchner's *Lenz*, which, like many lines in his dramas, takes aim at Hegel, for he imparts a spin onto a trifling turn of speech that had already become a "classical" figure of inversion during Büchner's time. In Büchner's text it is said of Lenz: "He went forward with indifference; nothing stood in his way, now going up, now going down. He had no trace of weariness; only he sometimes felt irritated that he could not walk on his head."[13] Celan's justly famous comment on this turn of speech runs: "he who walks on his head, ladies and gentlemen,—he who walks on his head has the sky beneath him as an abyss."[14] This abyss—not the bottomlessness of heaven and what a deteriorating philosophy would like to intuit therein and call transcendence but, instead, the untenability of the transcendental forms of our representation itself—opens up with ever less concealment in Celan's linguistic mode of procedure and his poetological reflection during the late fifties and sixties.

If language is nothing more than the articulation of the withdrawal of the world, then it becomes itself a figure of falling, no longer able to designate this withdrawal as an object; if it is unable to stand the world on the head of its poetic presentation, if it is, instead, nothing more than the cut and strut of an incessant passing away, then it is itself drawn into the turnings and becomes the vertiginous vortex of disfiguration in which nothing can any longer mean what it says. Just as the functions of the sign break down in the face of an "object" such as the abyss, death or nothingness, conventional units of meaning—words and sentences, strophes, which are also turns—likewise dissolve, having been infected, as it were, with this death, and thus they leave room for an altered form of speaking and for the interruption of speaking itself. One of the destructuring figures Celan privileges in his poetry is paranomasia.[15] In explicit instances of paranomasia—as when "Zangen" (forceps) is placed alongside "Zungen der Sehnsucht" (tongues of longing), the "Verbrannte" (incinerated) alongside the "Verbannten" (exiled), "Schläfe" (temples) alongside "schlaflos" (sleepless), "Erzväter" (patriarchs) alongside "Erzflitter" (the glitter of ore), and "das blutende Ohr" (bloody ear) alongside "blühselige Botschaft" (blessed tidings)—the phonetic proximity of the word whereby one affects the other with its semantic potential sets a verbal unity into oscillation. In "Huhediblu" the lines themselves tell how they came into being and how they are to be read:

> du liest,
> dies hier, dies:
> Dis-
> parates—: . . .
>   (*GW* 1:275)

> (you read,
> this here, this:
> Dis-
> parates—: . . .)

The lines come into being and are read as *disparation*: as the diversification and dispersal of the monosemic body of the word. In implicit instances of paranomasia a minimal alteration of the phonetic or graphic form of a word that does not itself appear produces another word, and this other word acts as the distorted echo of the first: "rauchdünn" (smoke-thin) thus replaces "hauchdünn" (filmy) (*GW* 1:288); "Morgen-Lot" (morning plumb-line) stands in for "Morgenrot" (dawn); "Ferse" (heels) for "Verse" (verses) (*GW* 2:25); "Pestlaken" (plague shroud) for "Bettlaken" (bedsheet) (*GW* 2:153); and "Datteln" (the dates one eats) for "Daten" (the dates of a calendar) (*GW* 2:134). If in explicit paranomasia the alteration is manifest and the semantic destabilization is confined to the localized zone of the word as it appears in the text, the corresponding word in implicit paranomasia remains latent, its shape uncertain, exposing every word in the text to the possibility of being an alteration of some lost paradigm, which stubbornly withdraws from rational or divinatory reconstruction. Each of these words presents itself—if not exclusively, then at least primarily—as the disfiguration of that which has gone silent, *a limine*, as the translation of that which does not give rise to voice, as the carrying over of everything muted. What Celan writes elsewhere of a forgotten word goes for these words as well: "Dies ist ein Wort, das neben den Worten einherging, / ein Wort nach dem Bilde des Schweigens" (This is a word that walked along with the words, / a word in the image of silence) (*GW* 1:92).

In the programmatic opening sequence of the volume *Sprachgitter* from which Celan, in his "Meridian" address, cited the second section—"Komm auf den Hände zu uns" (come on your hands to us)—as a parallel to the abyssal maxim drawn from Büchner's *Lenz*, the opening text reads:

> *Stimmen*, ins Grün
> der Wasserfläche geritzt.

Wenn der Eisvogel taucht,
sirrt die Sekunde:

Was zu dir stand
an jedem der Ufer,
es tritt
gemäht in ein anderes Bild.
    (*GW* 1:147)

(*Voices*, into the green
of the water surface etched.
When the kingfisher dives,
the second buzzes:

What stood to you
on each of the banks,
it steps,
mowed into another image.)

The figure of inversion that the next text of the sequence will explicitly set into an image is latent in this one as well: the objective world of the embankment whose image has benevolently turned toward the "you" addressed in the poem enters, like the voices that have etched the surface of the water, into the image of the water-mirror inadvertently, averted and unfamiliar, having been inverted and stood on its head. This transformation—a metamorphosis like the one Alcyone undergoes when she is turned into a "kingfisher" during her dive after her drowned husband[16]—is occasioned by a cut: what is trusted and familiar is "mowed" into another image—mowed, that is, by the cut of the *Sekunde* understood now in its etymological sense, as the *secare* of time. Time transforms the voices into the writing of the water-mirror and turns the trusted image of the objective world into the averted, inverted, and afflicted images of the literary text, which no longer offers them a ground beyond that of an *unda* in which they sink. But the same displacement underlies the language in which the poem articulates this transformation of a stable image into one that is overturned. Not only is the metaphor of reaping drawn from a metaphor lying dormant in a foreign word (in the *secare* of *Sekunde*)—a procedure Celan abundantly employs[17]—but this word, *die Sekunde*, is itself cut and read as *diese Kunde* (this message, this conduit for information).[18] This possibility is suggested in the phonetic combination of *s* and *i* in *sirrt*, which provokes a corresponding contamination of the *ie* and *Se* that follows, and it is also suggested by the very colon after *Sekunde*, which allows the second quatrain to appear as the content of a message, indeed as a conduit. *Die Sekunde—diese Kunde*; the second—this conduit: it is time, the cutter, that conducts its message in the inversion of the world of images, but this message accomplishes the inversion only by subjecting the second itself—the temporal atom—to its own principle of fission, by splitting the unity of the message, cutting off the conduit. The very principle of separation by which an "other image" is generated brings together whatever stands on separate banks—"on each of the banks"—and so *DieSeKunde* is not simply a metamorphosis but also a metaphor, the very movement of metaphorization: conducting across and carrying over. All images and all turns of speech in Celan's text follow the alteration dictated by its eccentric center—*dieSeKunde*, the second, this conduit: they are not metaphors for representations but metaphors for metaphorization, not images of a world but images of the generation of images, not the transcription of voices but the production of the etched voices of the poem itself. They inscribe themselves as the script of alteration when they let themselves be exposed to this very alteration: they write, they are *dieSeKunde*, this second, this conduit: the incisive word-exchange in which the phenomenal and linguistic world is opened on to a caesura that not a single shape of this world can exorcize, since every one of these shapes results from it. The second—this conduit—of Celan's poem is the self-interrupting, self-dismembering, distributing and redistributing, communicating and imparting speaking of language. The differentiation and varying distribution of linguistic segments do not so much articulate a particular meaning or nexus of meaning—although it does this too by expressing the rigorous connection between linguisticity and temporality—nor does it turn toward an earlier and primary meaning that it, being secondary, would help bring to light; rather, this differentiation and distribution articulate the condition of possible meaning—language—by opening themselves to that which does not correspond to themselves. The privative *se* of *SeKunde* cuts this conduit—this *Kunde*, the word for language—and takes from it the indubitable capacity to mean something that it, as a conduit of a message, could still claim, dividing its language as it divides language from itself. *SeKunde* is the secession of *Kunde* from itself, the rift or etch in the conduit at which point its language interrupts and exposes itself as finite, as not in agreement with itself. *Die Sekunde*—this second, this conduit—dictates the law of "originary" secondariness; it is the cut that precedes everything primary, the rift that opens in every principle, including that of universal linguisticity, and it disperses every unit and every condition that makes unity possible. *DieSeKunde* is, from the first, second in relation to itself: "Sekunde"—it "buzzes"—in the musicological sense of interval, an interval between different meanings, an interval between different languages, an interval in language itself that first gives the speaking of language space and time. Whatever steps into it, into this interval, this speaking, becomes other than it is.

The conduit—*ordine inverso*—is not one; it has no message to impart. It asserts nothing more than this: that is has nothing to assert but its own secession from itself, and is, as self-revocation, the movement of turning about. In so turning, it does not turn toward an empirical or transcendental other but rather steps, itself "mowed," into another image, one that no longer stands in for a You and no longer belongs to anyone. Nothing could be more foreign, for it is the etched image of a fundamental alteration, the alteration of every basis into an abyss.

––––––––

If the semantic function of language, which the figure of inversion was supposed to secure under conditions of finitude, is suspended and if this suspension, as the radicalization of inversion, implies that language turns into the image of its own interruption, then the very communicative performance of language is likewise put into question. It can no longer be conceived as an exchange between two or more already constituted subjects of a linguistic community; since, on the contrary, there can only be language by virtue of its division from itself, communicative performance must be thought as the im-parting of language through which its subjects, however unstable they may be, are first constituted. The fact that this im-parting[19] can no longer be a mediation at a mid-point held in common and cannot be a communication in an already given common medium; the fact that there is no place in such im-parting either for the substantialization of language or its instrumentalization into a means—all this comes into language in one of the longer texts of *Die Niemandsrose*, "Radix, Matrix." Precisely what step lies between this text and the earlier ones becomes evident when one reflects on the attribution in *Mohn und Gedächtnis* of an instrumental character to language and indeed to the language of the mother, to the mother-tongue[20]—the character, that is, of help and protection. Celan is most outspoken in the poem "Reisekamerad" (Traveling companion):

Deiner Mutter Seele schwebt voraus.
Deiner Mutter Seele hilft die Nacht umschiffen, Riff um Riff.
Deiner Mutter Seele peitscht die Haie vor dir her.

Dieses Wort ist deiner Mutter Mündel.
Deiner Mutter Mündel teilt dein Lager, Stein um Stein.
Deiner Mutter Mündel bückt sich nach der Krume Lichts.
(*GW* 1:66)

(Your mother's soul hovers on ahead.
Your mother's soul helps navigate the night, reef after reef.
Your mother's soul whips the sharks in front of you.

This word is your mother's ward.
Your mother's ward shares your couch, stone by stone.
Your mother's ward stoops for the crumb of light.)

This poem—"this word"—stands under the guardianship of the mother who helps it steer clear of the danger of being struck dumb, helps it turn away from darkness and helps it preserve the remnants of light: it is one of the most lucid poems Celan ever wrote. But it is also one of the most spellbound inasmuch as the maternal tutelage of which it speaks is realized by the mastery of one and the same syntactical paradigm, and this paradigm only allows the most minimal variation. Such a paradigm—the matrix of language that guarantees the strength of coherence and of mutual comprehension—is given up in "Radix, Matrix." It is a poem devoted to the loss of the mother tongue, of the middle and its capacity to mediate.

RADIX, MATRIX

Wie man zum Stein spricht, wie
du,
mir vom Abgrund her, von
einer Heimat her Ver-
schwisterte, Zu-
geschleuderte, du,
du mir vorzeiten,
du mir im Nichts einer Nacht,
du in der Aber-Nacht Be-
gegnete, du
Aber-Du—:

Damals, da ich nicht da war,
damals, da du
den Acker abschrittst, allein:

Wer,
wer wars, jenes
Geschlecht, jenes gemordete, jenes
schwarz in den Himmel stehende:
Rute und Hode—?

(Wurzel.
Wurzel Abrahams. Wurzel Jesse. Niemandes
Wurzel—o
unser.)

Ja,
wie man zum Stein spricht, wie
du
mit meinen Händen dorthin
und ins Nichts greifst, so
ist, was hier ist:

auch dieser
Fruchtboden klafft,
dieses
Hinab
ist die eine der wild-
blühenden Kronen.
       (*GW* 1:139–40)

(RADIX, MATRIX

As one speaks to the stone, as
you
to me from the abyss, from
a homeland, con-
genial, cata-
pulted, you,
you to me long ago,
you to me in the nothingness of a night
you in the counter-night encountered, you,
counter-you—:

Then, since I was not there,
then, since you
paced off the plowland, alone:

Who, who was it, that
race, the murdered one, the one
standing black in the sky:
rod and testicle—?

[Root.
Root of Abraham. Root of Jesse. No one's
root—o
ours.]

Yes,
as one speaks to the stone, as

you
with my hands over there
and into nothingness grasp, so
is what is here:

even this
receptacle gapes:
this
downward
is one of the wild-
blooming crowns.)

"Radix, Matrix" describes the figure of an impossible dialogue. The attempt undertaken in the first clause to determine the speaking by placing the impersonal "one" in relation to the anorganic "stone," is already
suspended with the insertion of the second part of the sentence, and
this suspension is accomplished by an almost luxuriating digression in
which the lyrical I apostrophizes this "you" in a series of pronomina-
tions that all touch on the forms of relation between the I and the "you,"
until the I inverts the direction of speaking: whereas at the beginning
of the clause it still ran from the "you" to an indeterminate addressee,
at its end it runs—inverted—along the line of illocution from the I to
that "you." The second clause—"as / you," and with it, the determination of the addressee of the discourse of the "you"—remains open even
after the end of the first strophe: the sentence it begins finds no conclusion. One finds only implicit indications of the possibility that the I
could itself be the addressee of the discourse of the other. For the series
of apostrophes speaks of this "you" as congenial, catapulted and encountered exclusively in its relation to the I. But this virtual addressee,
I, this virtualized I is characterized by its parallelism with the stone—
the other addressee of the discourse—as mute, as voiceless and without
determination: not something that can be the subject of the poem's discourse. In "Gespräch im Gebirg" (Dialogue in the Mountains), which
may have originated contemporaneously with "Radix, Matrix," Celan
writes of the stone: "It does not engage in discourse, it speaks, and whoever speaks, cousin, engages in discourse with no one; that one speaks,
because no one hears it, no one and No one." [21] Since the determination
of the discourse of the "you" remains suspended in the first stanza,
something can be read in the second stanza that jumps, as it were, into
the gap of the first—a new attempt at determination undertaken by the
I, which at the same time expresses the reason why this I did not become
the addressee of the discourse of the "you": "Then, since I was not
there, / then, since you / paced off the plowland, alone: . . ." The "you"
that paces off the plowland according to an archaic form of measure-
ment and that accomplishes the determination of its site with this pace

is without an addressee, without the I to whom it could turn its discourse. Yet the second stanza could be read as a continuation of the discourse of the I, who, without a voice or at least with an indeterminate voice, asserts its own absence, and it could also be read—with equal justification, especially if one considers the colon at the end of the first sentence—as the discourse of the "you" who "then . . . was not there" and who left the I alone during its attempt at determination. This double character of discourse, being both continuation and alteration; this double character of the two points of the colon, signaling both continuity and interruption; these two double characters not only have as their consequence the wandering and diffusion of the "you" and the I of this text; they also yield the ineluctable indeterminacy in the structure of speaking—a structure with which the very discourse of the text is concerned and therefore an indeterminacy in the discourse of the text itself which strikes its subject and its addressee as well as its illocutionary character. Nothing of this discourse is certain any longer, nor can anything in the discourse be subjected to logical rules or their linguistic correlates, especially since the reciprocal determination of the "you" and the I, which appeared to classical metaphysics and even to dialogics to be possible as an intersubjective event, is referred to its lack of an object by means of interruption and immanent muteness. The ineluctable ambiguity of Celan's formulation whereby the absence of the You suspends the I and the absence of the I suspends the You and, accordingly, suspends discourse itself—this unsublatable ambiguity realizes on the level of composition what the apostrophe says about the You when it links up with the terminology of dialogistics: that it is, namely, the one encountered "in the nothingness of the night." This nothingness is, however, just as much the space in which the You encounters the I as it is that which, as the You, encounters the I: nothingness encountered; nothingness speaks, and it speaks—the I is also a form of that You—to nothingness. As one speaks to the stone, so too does the stone speak: to no one and to nothing. But so then does the poem make itself into the stone and into nothingness.

This, the most radical version of inversion whereupon language no longer turns its own nothingness into the substantial being of appearance, sound, and consciousness, as in Hegel and Rilke, but rather turns its literary existence, compositionally and semantically, into nothingness is grounded in the third stanza's questioning after the murdered race, the murdered *Geschlecht*. This question, opened once again by the colon of the preceding stanza, could pertain just as well to a "you" asking the I or asking after the I as it could pertain to the I asking the "you" or asking after the "you." This question questions undecidably from both to both and asks for the ground of their communality, inquiring after that "race," after that *Geschlecht*, in which familial, genealogical, social, sexual, and linguistic unity would be given and, in this gift of

unity, the reciprocal determination of the subjects of speaking in dialogue as well as the determination of speaking and of language would
first be made possible. But this question is not only undecidable in the
sense that neither its subject nor its addressee can be discerned; it is also
undecidable in the sense that it is an impossible question, a question
not possible to answer, for it asks after the essence of a race—of a
Geschlecht—that was murdered, destroyed, annihilated and stands
"black" in the sky like the "nothingness of a night." The question itself
reacts to the indeterminacy of its object, to its virtual loss of an object,
and does so by ending up once again after a colon—"who was it, that
race"—in an explicit apposition that could very well be the attempt at
an answer that it itself has put into question: "Rute und Hode—?" (Rod
and testicles—?) Rod and testicles isolate the sexual aspect of the *Geschlecht* but not, as it might appear, its phallic aspect. For *Rute* is the
word for the *radix*, which stands in Latin not only for vegetable root,
for origin, source, firm ground, and soil, but also, as in *radix virilis* for
the masculine member. *Hode*, on the other hand, derives from the Latin
cunnus, the pudenda, and so corresponds to *matrix*, which just as much
as *radix* means source, origin, and stem, but in its feminine aspect as
progenitrix, womb, uterus.[22] Only together, as *Rute* and *Hode*, and
brought still closer in the asyndeton of the title, as *radix, matrix*: as the
coupling of the masculine and feminine sexes are they "that *Geschlecht*,
that murdered one, the one / standing black in the sky." Only in this
coupling do they fulfill the figure of immanent inversion that the
erected abyss presents.

The question directed at this *Geschlecht*, at this coupling of *Ge-
schlechter*—and it cannot be concluded from the text of the poem
whether this coupling is not itself its murder—does not allow for an
answer, because it is without an object, because the murdered *Geschlecht*
after which it asks is not an object of possible presentation, even though
it and it alone demands its presentation. For only in the *radix, matrix*
would language have gained not only an object and an addressee but
also its own ground, its origin and its source, its provenance and the
possibility of a future, and only by means of the *Geschlecht* and the commonality guaranteed in it could there be not only a dialogical mediation
between "I" and "you" but also a communicating, determinate, and determining language. In asking after *radix, matrix*, the poem asks after its
own ground. In presenting its question as objectless, it delivers itself up
to the abyss of possible meaninglessness, indeterminacy, and incomprehensibility. With the open question whose openness is not accidental
but indeed structural, the one who questions—"I" or "you" and their
two languages—places itself in question and wrenches open that which
could have counted as a ground: opens itself as an abyss. In the open
question, the poem makes itself into that speechless tone whose mute-

ness is renounced by every community of language—of every *Geschlecht*—and announces nothing more than this renouncement. The language of this poem is *die Sekunde des Geschlechts*—the second of the race, this conduit of the sex—in which it, cut, murdered, no longer communicates nor mediates but, instead, im-parts that which, along with the *Geschlecht*, is cut in its nothingness. This "second" itself is the mark of castration, and in its historical, its most intolerable form, it is the mark of the murdering of European Jewry in the extermination camps of the Nazi regime. If, according to Adorno's dictum "After Auschwitz . . . it became impossible . . . to write poems"[23]—and if Szondi made this more precise with the dictum that "after Auschwitz no poem is any longer possible except on the basis of Auschwitz"[24]— then, faced with "Radix, Matrix," it is necessary to add that this basis of the poem is an abyss, that it is not the condition of its possibility but of its impossibility and that the poem can still speak only because it exposes itself to the impossibility of its speaking. It no longer speaks the language of a race or a sex, which could be the ground, center, origin, father and mother; rather, it speaks—deracinated, dematricated—the language of the murdered *Geschlecht*. For this reason, Auschwitz does not become for it a historically limited fact; the murder does not become an unproblematical object of speaking but the objection of a question that concedes its muteness and thereby admits that it itself has been struck by that murder.

Not even the fourth stanza offers an answer. It stands—the parentheses around it indicate this—outside the discourse; it is the very discourse of the eradicated root, its parentheses having retracted and curtailed its significance and its determinacy. "No one's / root—o / ours." No one's root is not a root and at the same time the root of personal nonexistence. In the doubleness of this root—being both no root and the root of no one—the doubleness of "radix, matrix" refracts the doubleness of the nothingness of night that is a counter-night (*Aber-Nacht*), of the You that is a counter-You (*Aber-Du*): an again-You and an against-You, a You and a not-You. So, as the immanent revocation of its name, its concept, and its linguistic sign, the nothingness at the root of language asserts itself within language, but against it and its semantic function. As the You always doubles and reduces itself to the counter-You for the I, so the root is our own only so long as it is no one's root, and it is no one's root only so long as it is ours. The commonality of the I and the You that first finds its word—"ours"—in this (parenthetical) place; this commonality, which is that of the sexes and is therefore the race, is attained only where it is suspended in the loss of personal, generic, sexual, and historical existence. Only in their separation from one another and from the *Geschlecht*, as the ground of secure being and of stable communication, can they be and be open to one another; only in the dispersal, dismemberment, and destruction of language's historical continuity and of the *Geschlecht*'s homogeneity does it—abandoned to its finitude, to its nothingness—impart.

This im-parting no longer underlies the figure of inversion, however little it can renounce it, for this figure is itself struck by division: "(Root. / Root of Abraham. Root of Jesse. No one's / root—o / ours.)" The terse genealogical catalog, which contains an infinite genealogical promise, is—after "Jesse"—no longer subject to a chiasmus alone, to an inversion of the syntactical elements that sets "no one" in the place of "root," but this chiasmus is itself subjected by the line-break to an interruption that opens in the place of "root" an empty place—a "pause," a "hiatus," a "lacuna."[25] It is the pause in the meaning of the *Geschlecht*'s language—a pause that can no longer be characterized according to morphological oppositions. Only by virtue of such morphological oppositions, however, are linguistic signs and their meaning generated. This pause could be characterized as a zero-opposition, to use a concept Jakobson develops, and it could thus be understood as a linguistic event whose distinguishing mark consists in presenting no opposition to already established linguistic forms but nevertheless—and indeed against Jakobson's definition of this concept[26]—persists in *not* neutralizing these oppositions. The lacuna between "no one's" and "root" cannot be brought down on either side of the opposition between meaning and meaninglessness: it maintains itself between the poles of this opposition, as it likewise maintains itself between the negative pronoun "no one's" and the noun "root," which—and here is a remarkable convergence between the formal and semantic structure of this line—designates the root of meaningfulness as such. Neither semantically nor asemantically cathected, the lacuna—and not only this one—holds open the space between negation and the negated, keeps it open for their relation and at the same time for the possibility of nonrelation. Thus the pause between "no one's" and "root" stands between the nothingness of the *Geschlecht*'s language, which can still be asserted and thereby become the negative referent of this language, on the one hand, and its sheer absence, on the other: between mere muteness and the possibility of saying or writing "mute." In the pause is nothing and is not nothingness. This pause is "the weight that holds back emptiness," as the text that precedes "Radix, Matrix" in *Niemandsrose* puts it: it holds the emptiness up, detaining it and delaying it; the pause holds the emptiness fast and exorcises it; this pause hampers—be it only for the second of writing or reading—its arrival and its disappearance. The second of emptiness interrupts the inversion of the genealogical discourse of *radix, matrix* and holds it back. So held back is the "root" that it neither disappears *into* the discourse of origin nor *out of* it. Root: it becomes a root of no one's *Geschlecht* and of no one's language only by traversing its pause and therefore only as a suspended root. Only when this lacuna and loophole separate language from itself does language impart as ours; as language held in common, it only imparts as one held back by the collapse of communication.

Once this commonality is articulated in the suspension of commonality, the speaking of the poem again takes up the attempt at determination that was already interrupted in its second line, and it does so with the paradoxical amplification that, just as one speaks to a stone, so "you / with my hands over there / and into nothingness grasp." Speaking is grasping with the hands. In his letter to Hans Bender, Celan had written of poetry as hand-clasping[27] and had thereby taken up once again the dead metaphor of grasping a concept, of making oneself capable of being grasped and, held in this grasp, of being understood. Because of its parallelism with nothingness (*Nichts*), the stone (*Stein*) shows itself to be anagrammic inversion: *Niets*. Just as the language of the murdered race gropes into nothingness and says nothing to no one, so

is, what is here:

here, in the very *hic et nunc* of the poem; here is neither the site of sheer *nihil negativum* nor the locus of its reversal into fulfilled being of present language. Here is articulated the linguistic being—and being *is* only thus articulated—in which language reaches out to its own nothingness, to the nothingness of its reference, its meaning, and its determination. Language relates to nothingness as to its own no-longer; it is—and this is its *thus*, its mode, its genre, its kind, and its *Geschlecht*—the already-there of its no-longer, the relation to its nothingness in which it withdraws from itself the relation that makes it into language. As the withdrawal of relation, however, it still is this reference to the possibility of its own impossibility; as the already-there of its no-longer, it is at the same time the still-there of its no-longer, so that the gap it opens up in itself, as the gap of its own nothingness, is also—while it holds open the *possibility* of this impossibility—the gaping of the vegetative receptacle. The collapse of the poem into the abyss of its impossibility in the *summum* of the possibilities of its speaking. Thus, cut by a caesura, speaking with the lacuna between its words, as its impossible You and its impossible I, the poem imparts—deracinated and robbed of the matrix of its determinations, without ground and without a law that would stand above it—: the poem imparts as "one of the wild- / blooming crowns."

even this
receptacle gapes:
this

downward
is one of the wild-
blooming crowns.

Two impulses may have had a hand in the elevated pathos of this metaphor, the content of which nevertheless remains perfectly discreet. The
first is Psalm 132:18: "His [David's] enemies will I clothe with shame:
but upon himself shall his crown shine." The other is a formulation
from the *Book of Bahir*, which Celan may have known through Scholem's
book on the symbolism of the Kabbalah; according to this work, "holy
Israel" forms the "crown" of the tree of both the world and God.[28] From
the same work of Scholem it emerges that, according to the *Zohar*, with
which Celan must have been familiar, the "root of all roots" from which
the tree draws nourishment is the nothingness that, as an aura, surrounds *En-Sof*: the non-basis and abyss of God.[29] However influential
these biblical and Kabbalistic metaphors may have been on "Radix, Matrix," they are altered when they enter into Celan's text. In the poem
there is no longer a root about which it could be absolutely said that it
is nothingness, for nothingness appears only in a verbal form breached
by a pause, as counter-nothingness, as non-nothingness and double-
nothingness, as a vacancy and a holding back of its lin- guistic presentation. But the crown that is announced to David and his *Geschlecht* is here
no longer one that blooms over him and that could be imparted to him
from outside. The poem itself—"what is here . . . this /downward"—is
one, but it is only one, not the only one; one but not the only wild-
blooming, insubordinate, insubstantial crown.

There is—where no matrix remains—no longer any poem that
could claim the privilege of being able to articulate the lacuna that the
loss of this matrix opens up. For there is no longer the one lacuna that
could stand alone at the end of the attempt to determine it. At the point
where the support that speech could find in its object or in its own figures fails, speaking itself steps forward, altered. No end and no aim, no
object—even a negative one—and no subject—even if this subject is
said to be absent—organizes the poem; organization, rather, comes
only from what is, here, *is*: a path, a movement *downward*, without further determination, destination, or definition. This downward *without*
ground is the crown. Where, however, the ground fails—and even the
ground of *a* nothingness objectified, the ground of nothingness determined as *one*—there is also no longer the one, no longer *the* crown and
no longer *the* poem that could correspond to this failure. Not only the
subject and figure of speaking but also this speaking itself loses its totalizing power. The inversion, which is no longer merely a rhetorical
figure that this speaking would employ to present its objects but is,
rather, the procedural form that is supposed to secure its own possibility, is disempowered. There is no longer the one and only inversion, *the*

inversion whereby the poem's descent without determination could turn into a climax and its objectless question after the *Geschlecht* could convert into its highest pronouncement. The version the poem passes through is one of the inversions: one of two. Just as the grasp of the You, "with my hands," blossoms as one of the crowns into the nothingness of the I and its *Geschlecht*, so the other one blossoms in the grasping of the I, with your hands, into the nothingness of the You. I and Thou, which, according to dialogical theories, should reciprocally constitute each another, deconstitute one another in the chiasmus—it too an inversion—of their crossed attempts to get a grip on themselves and to make them into figures of an encounter with nothingness. Each one encounters in the other his own nothingness, and the discourse of the other opens itself to each one as the abyss of his own. "What is here" does not therefore only mean the poem in which "you / with my hands over there / and into nothingness grasp," and so does not only mean the chiastic crossing of I and You in the foundering and, by its foundering, the blooming grasp for the commonality of the *Geschlecht*: "what is here" acknowledges in the almost imperceptively minor detail of the phrase "*one of the* crowns" that it is still the discourse of the I, that the poem thus remains bound to its primacy, and "what is here" also refers, in turn, to the missing complement that would be the *other* one of the crowns: the crown that does not bloom *here* and that does not blossom out of the I. The inversion does not offer itself as the entire inversion, as a total one. "Wurzelkrone: / gescheitelt" (crown of roots: / parted) (*GW* 2:196)—thus is the movement of "Radix, Matrix" expressed with extreme concentration in a later text from the volume *Fadensonnen*. One crown remains apart from the other, because there is no You for which the I would not once again be a You, and other whose strangeness the poem respects by declining to speak in its place. Its alterity remains insusceptible to sublation in the inversion. Only what is rootless—and even is without the root of the one nothingness—can be a crown. And only that other for whom even this crown is no root is itself a crown.

There are always, at least, two crowns. They do not submit to a common matrix by way of inversion. The inversion that was for a long phase of Celan's lyric production the very form of movement with which the I and its language could claim to mediate whatever eluded their grasp has ceased to be its rhetorical and epistemological matrix. It no longer constitutes the commonality of the one language of *Geschlecht* but rather—itself merely one of two, partial—only institutes the commonality of the reciprocal indeterminacy of I and You as they fail to encounter one another. Being-with-one-another is a gaping—of at once the abyss and the receptacle—which rips open the gap of being-oneself and its inversion into a thematic You. The parting of the two crowns that hold themselves together and apart no longer has a positive figure in the poem. The poem is the movement in which I and You impart each other without being able to gather together in the one crown that is the positive figure of *this* poem. The poem—and, with it, the logic of inversion—imparts itself: to that which (it) cannot be. Only as the im-parting and this parting of speaking in which it exposes (itself) does the poem carry out the *encounter* with the alterity of the You, which is at the same time its own alteration. It speaks as the movement of alteration and thereby stops being merely *this* poem and merely a *poem*. It is the carrying out of the difference between itself and the other— not the carrying out therefore of the difference between its being and its non-being no longer spoken according to the voice of subjectivity— not the carrying out therefore of the difference between its determin- ation by the one *Geschlecht* and its indeterminacy written from the position of objectified being—no longer therefore fixed to the arche- teleological line of communication; it is the carrying out of the differ- ence between its meaning and the incapacity of meaning in view of nothingness—and it is therefore a poem that withdraws from the sche- matisms of semantics, and only by virtue of its parasemantic character does it attain the peculiar gravity of its speaking. "Radix, Matrix" is a poem that departs from the radix and the matrix of every provenance and parts ways with itself.[30] Only as a movement of its deracination, dematrication, dissemination is it a speaking that has nothing above it, nothing about it and does not speak *about* anything. It is the experience of freedom from its own language. And only in giving up the grounding figure that organizes its movement—that of inversion—and, in cross- ing out its own trope, is it on a path that neither it itself nor its basic figure dominates. The radicalization of inversion leads to the giving up of inversion as a matrix.

Since the time of the transcendental turn in philosophy and litera- ture at the very latest, the figure of inversion has been tied to the idea of turning back, of returning and restoring the self. The immanent re- versal of history, represented as a process of disintegration, is supposed to allow the subject to grasp once again its authentic shape and to attain an undistorted understanding of itself and its language. Inversion can thus be characterized as the figure of the historical, aesthetic, and her- meneutic self-relation of the subject, as the privileged trope of subjec- tivity in general. In this figure, language not only relates to itself and refers to itself; in it and as it, it *is* real and effective in the first place. Peter Szondi has spelled out the consequences of this theory of subjec- tivity for one part of Celan's lyrical production, without, of course, com- mitting himself to this theory. In "Poetry of Constancy—Poetik der Beständigkeit," at the end of his analysis of Celan's translation of a Shakesperian sonnet, he writes that Celan has "replaced the traditional symbolist poem, which is concerned only with itself and which has itself as its subject-matter, with a poem that is no longer concerned with itself but that is itself."[31] Szondi's formulations have the merit of insisting on a trait of Celan's lyrics that threatens to be concealed by the theories of negativity advanced by much of scholarship devoted to Celan. His formulations have the corresponding disadvantage of disregarding the specific constitution of the poem so as to affirm their self-being. Celan's texts do not part ways with subjectivity by adhering to the sphere of sheer objectivity located in their linguistic being in order to find therein a new home and a guarantee for their constancy, as so-called concrete poetry tries to do through the technical organization of language reduced to material; rather, they depart from subjectivity by articulating the structure of self-relation and self-reference as that of a linguistic act which, once dissolved from the self and the logic of its positing, attains an altered relation to itself in the very movement of dissolution. Language is not posited but projected: in accordance with a graphic paranomasia, a paragraphism that corresponds to the one in Greek between λογος and λογχη, "word" and "javelin"—the word (*Wort*) is a throwing stick (*Wurf-holz*), a boomerang, a projectile with the ability to turn on itself and return to its place of departure if it is thrown in the right way. In Celan's poem "Ein Wurfholz" (A Boomerang), which describes the movement of the word to itself, its point of departure no longer is taken up in the discourse, as it had been in the poem "Aber" (But) from *Sprachgitter*, where, relying on the classical poetic emblem of the swan, he has the boomerang to which it is compared whiz by "from nothingness":

> die Schwäne,
> in Genf, ich sah's nicht, flogen, es war,
> als schwirrte, vom Nichts her, ein Wurfholz
> ins Ziel einer Seele: . . .
>   (*GW* 1:182)

> (the swans,
> in Geneva, I didn't see it, flew, it was,
> as if, from nothingness, a boomerang whizzed by
> into the target of a soul: . . .)

The reference to this initial nothingness first installs itself in the later text from *Niemandsrose* at the site where the word arrives—in its relation to itself:

> EIN WURFHOLZ, auf Atemwegen,
> so wanderts, das Flügel-
> mächtige, das
> Wahre. Auf

Sternen-
bahnen, von Welten-
splittern geküßt, von Zeit-
körnern genarbt, von Zeitstaub, mit-
verwaisend mit euch,
Lapilli, ver-
zwergt, verwinzigt, ver-
nichtet,
verbracht und verworfen,
sich selber der Reim,—
so kommt es
geflogen, so kommts
wieder und heim,
einen Herzschlag, ein Tausendjahr lang
innezuhalten als
einziger Zeiger im Rund,
das eine Seele,
das seine
Seele
beschrieb,
das eine
Seele
beziffert.
      (*GW* 1:258)

(A BOOMERANG, on breath-ways,
so it wanders, the wing-
powered, the
true. On
astral
orbits, by world-
splinters kissed, by time-
kernels grained, by time-dust, co-
orphaned with you,
Lapilli, be-
littled, dwarfed, an-
nihilated,
deported and thrown away,
itself the rhyme,—
thus it comes
flown, thus it comes
back and home,
for a heartbeat, for a millennium,
to pause as
lone hand on the dial,

by one soul,
by its soul
inscribed,
by one
soul
ciphered.)

A boomerang—this word—is, thrown, already on its way with the first word of the poem, therefore not at home but grasped in the flight of its displacements and transformations, "on breath-paths." It is under way along not one but several elliptical or circular orbits which traverse the domains of the living (*Atemwege* also means "respiratory ducts"), the mythical ("the wing / powered" not only contains an allusion to Hermes, the wingèd messenger-god of Greek mythology, but also one to angels, the messengers of God in Judaic and Christian mythology), and the cosmic ("astral / orbits"), and, as it wanders through these do-mains, it turns into another: from the collisions with the shards of the world and of time that it undergoes on these orbits, it is increasingly diminished, "be- / littled, dwarfed," in order finally to be "an- / ni-hilated." Only thus—"an- / nihilated, deported and thrown away"—in such a way that it is brought to the point of disappearing, brought away from the path of living breath, deported, despised, not made familiar and, thrown in the wrong direction, not brought to the target for which it was destined: only thus does it come, "it comes / back and home." Not by corresponding to something else, to another *Wort* (word) or an-other *Ruf* (call); not by reaching the intentions bound up with its throw or by reaching out to the intended addressee, but by corresponding to nothing and to no one, by speaking to nothing and to no one as to itself; only therefore by being "itself the rhyme" can it be said of the *Wurfholz*, this boomerang, that "it comes / flown . . . it comes / back and home." But it does not come to itself as if it were a given, objective being; anni-hilated, it comes to a nothingness whose place is not the grounding point of departure of its movement, nor the target of its meaning but is, instead, the false, the failed, the site of failure reached only in the displacement and distortion of the general topography of intentions by way of its de-portation and its throwing away. This is not the site of a positive nothingness, for *ver- / nichtet* does not simply mean *vernichtet* but, as the severing the *ver-* brings out its intensifying as well as its di-gressive and dissimulative connotations (as in *verschreiben*, "miswrite," or *versetzen*, "displace"), it also means the failure of this annihilation; it is not the site of a nothingness that corresponds with itself. The site on which the word, the call, the topos come back and come home is the u-topos found wherever it does not itself arrive as word, call, and topos. The word comes to itself as to nothing. In "Deine Augen im Arm" (Your Eyes in the Arm), from *Fadensonnen* (*GW* 2:123), Celan makes it clear that the negation of "where" (*wo*) is at the same time the negation of the stupification of the "word" (*Wort*), when he writes this negation as *entwo*.[32] This poem—itself this word, "a boomerang"—does not write this coming-to-itself by positing itself as an objective entity that it itself grasps but, rather, by exposing itself to the movement of its disappearance. It exposes itself to damage, to being thrown away, to annihilation; it sets out to disrupt itself by exposing itself to the distance from its destination and to the rejection of its form, and it ex-poses itself by interrupting its discourse: in every one of its word-breaks and line-breaks, in every one of its alterations of images; in its central line, it so ex-poses itself that it characterizes its linguistic self-reference not as identity but as paranomasia, as *Reim* ("rhyme"), and it makes this outcome even more precise through the rhyme-word *heim* ("home"), therefore through a further alteration. And in its central line it ex-poses itself even more: this pivotal line is interrupted with a dash that disrupts the discourse precisely where it comes to itself. Celan's poem, where it comes to itself, is the rhyme, the paranomasia of its an-nihilation. Its word is the ex-posure—the setting out, interruption, and breaking down—of its being. "La poésie," as it is said in the sole French maxim of Celan that has so far been transmitted, "la poésie ne s'impose plus, elle s'expose."[33]

The return and the homecoming of the word to itself, traditionally thought as the awakening of the potencies exhausted by conventional usage or as the "metapoetic" reflection of its contents and thus, once again, as the inversion that sets things in order, take a strange turn in Celan's poem, since it does not return in restituted form to its authentic and proper site but returns, rather, in a scarred, dismembered, and finally an-nihilated form at a site that is now its own and where it is not itself. But the word just as little is itself here as it means itself. It refers only in orphaning: its *Verweisung* (reference) is always a *Verwaisung* (orphaning). It separates itself from its provenance and from the intentions to which it is bound; it mortifies what is meant by it and addressed with it, and so it is the movement of infinite singularization. The sole interconnection it maintains is the one—expressed in a lapidary fashion, like everything in Celan—with what is likewise on the way to becoming an orphan: "co- / orphaned with you, / Lapilli." This "Lapilli," the only apostrophe in this poem, evokes the whole series of stones and rock formations with which Celan's texts, true lithographs, calculate; it evokes the alchemical philosopher's stone, *der Stein der Weisen*, as well as that of the orphans, *des Steins, den der Waisen* (*GW* 2:283); it evokes the white stone of the apocalypse, which resembles the hidden manna and in which a new name is written, a name that no man knows saving that he receive it (Rev. 2:17); it evokes the voting stones of Artemis that save Orestes; it evokes the white stones of Hänsel and Gretel which failed to show them the way home; it evokes "The Stone," from Mandelstam's first volume of poetry, and it evokes the pebble that—like "language," the "three-year-land of your mother" and the "bud on her breast"—"your thoughts carried to Prague, / to the grave, to graves, into life" (*GW* 1:285).[34] It evokes with these and so many other memorials and headstones the black ballot-pebbles called *lapilli*, from the fifteenth book of Ovid's *Metamorphoses*,[35] which condemned the one named Myscelus—not so far from Celan—to death and which later, having been transformed into a white stone under the influence of Hercules, freed him and allowed him to leave his fatherland to found a new city at the site designated by God, at the grave of Croton. This absolving and expiating trait of Ovid's *lapilli* is even more pointed in Celan's poem, since the orphaning of its "Lapilli" knows neither a God nor a homeland beyond its own nothingness.

Following the syntactical ambiguity of the lines "by time- / kernels grained, by time-dust, co- / orphaned with you, / Lapilli, be- / littled, dwarfed," this orphaning can be an orphaning *by* the boomerang as well as an orphaning whose object is the boomerang itself. The word, orphaned, itself becomes that from which it was orphaned. It becomes a kernel of time: the smallest segment of time and the seed of time, isolated as the "lone hand on the dial" which points, as the linguistic or graphic atom of the elapsing of time (the form of the boomerang in fact resembles that of the hour-hand); it becomes an index, a script, and a cipher of time and history, which marks its own passing away (the crooked figure of the boomerang, as a *C*, presents not only a Roman numeral but also the first letter of Celan's name: one can read the entire poem as a "C élan," as a hypogram, a signature, an autobiographical stenogram).[36] The word—the poem—is, as self-orphaning, "the second" in which it separates itself from itself. As orphaning that is itself orphaned, it lacks every semantic or communicative reference; as an orphaned, objectless orphaning that has become selfless, its coming to itself, its homecoming, and return stand under the sign of non-arrivability. The boomerang comes to itself, to language—but, orphaned by itself, it does not arrive. Only because and as long as it does not arrive, does it come home. Its homecoming and return are this: not arriving. Being, being-oneself, and being-with-one-another is a coming without arrival. "A Boomerang," however much it turns on itself and describes its trajectory as a circle, is not and cannot mean—metapoetically—itself; rather, it refers, out of the distance necessary for this referral, to itself as a distancing reference that can never reach home—its literal sense, intended meaning, the thing meant, the desired word—without confronting therein that distancing, that referring altered into an orphaning and thus confronting the fact that the orphaning is not present in the reference itself. The relation of every reference to itself writes itself necessarily—and so the "boomerang" is not called true but "the / true"—as the spatio-temporal distancing of reference and as its self-withdrawal. As language without language. Its speaking of itself is this conduit, the second in which it departs from itself and is with itself, with the parting, the difference. Its being—being is orphaning. Its inversion is the trope that, traversing itself, gapes open.[37]

For a better understanding of "A la pointe acérée," Celan reported in a conversation[38] that he borrowed the title of the text from a note by Baudelaire, cited in Hofmannsthal's journal under the date June 29, 1917: "Il est de certaines sensations délicieuses dont le vague n'exclut pas l'intensité, et il n'est pas de pointe plus acérée que l'Infini."[39] Celan's poem, as its ambiguous title indicates, is written *on* this point of the infinite and *with* it. Immediately before this citation from Baudelaire one finds in Hofmannsthal's notes a second citation, taken from Paul Claudel's *Les Muses*, which runs as follows: "O mon âme! Le poème n'est point fait de ces lettres que je plante comme des clous, mais du blanc qui reste sur le papier."[40] Hofmannsthal adds this remark: "Here is the very image of the emptiness that persecutes me." After the citation there follows a stylistic observation about Claudel's "highly peculiar prose" which ends up affirming that he ties down the rush of the sentence by a "sudden freezing." In Celan's poem, it is not the overflowing of language but rather the "blanc qui reste sur le papier" that crystallizes itself; it is the "unwritten" that hardens into language in accordance with another saying of Hofmannsthal, the final words Death speaks in *Der Tor und der Tod*: human beings are the ones "who interpret the uninterpretable, / Who read what was never written."[41] With the pointers Hofmannsthal has given him, Celan reads in the opening lines of his poem the "pointe acérée de l'Infini" about which Baudelaire speaks as the "clous plantés de ces lettres" to which Claudel refers; against Claudel's intentions, therefore, he reads them as the high point in which the unwritten, instead of remaining outside of writing, contracts into writing. Writing concentrates the *blanc*. The infinite emptiness that crystallizes into language remains effective in language and through language as the intermittent movement of laying bare and setting free.

Es liegen die Erze bloß, die Kristalle,
die Drusen.
Ungeschriebenes, zu
Sprache verhärtet, legt
einen Himmel frei.

(Nach oben verworfen, zutage,
überquer, so
liegen auch wir.)
    (*GW* 1:251)

(The ores are layed bare, the crystals,
the druses.
The unwritten, into
language hardened, sets
a sky free.

[Rejected upward, into daylight,
crisscross, so
lie we too.])

However much Celan's poetry may be quoting in these lines, it always quotes only the unwritten, the empty, the holes, the *blanc*. No topos, not even the topoi it employs, determines the site, none of its tropes determine the movement, and no method defines the path of the poem: the *loci communes* of "ore" and "crystals" open in the hollows of the "druses" an emptiness that no writing, however hardened, can capture except in circum-scription and trans-scription; the metaphor of petrifying the unwritten into language, itself written, brings to light that it misses the unwritten; the "Wege dorthin. / ... der blubbernden Radspur entlang" (the ways hither ... along the spluttering wheeltrack) (*GW* 1:251) follow, by paranomasia, "der Spur einer Rede" (the trace of a discourse) that lays bare in the explosion of its bubbles something it conceals. These are the ways of the poem—"spluttering ways hither." Something is under way along these ways, not to come into language but to lay bare what must remain vacant in its petrification, unwritten in the poem and unattainable in its progress toward the "unrepeatable": it is under way toward that which has not come into language, on its way to the undeterminable, along a trace, as a reading:

Auf-
gelesene
kleine, klaffende
Buchecker: schwärzliches
Offen, von
Fingergedanken befragt
nach——
wonach?
    (*GW* 1:251)

(Col-
lected, read
open,
small, gaping
beechnuts: blackish
Open, by
finger thoughts questioned
after——
after what?)

The seed capsule "col- / lected" from a beech—from a book—is, with respect to its "Open," that which is read open (*offen-gelesene*): interpretation is setting free, *Auslegung* is *Freilegung*. Reading, as *lectio* and *Lesen*, is not so much a collecting and storage, nor a recollecting and sublation, as an opening of language onto what remains unsaid in it, what indicates itself in it of the unrepeatable bygone, what merely announces itself as coming. This co-lectio is the questioning movement of thought along a way that cannot, however, lead to the unrepeatable as long as it is a way cleared by conventions of discourse and of reading. Insofar as it relates to the unrepeatable, the reading of the poem does not give back a pregiven reality; it does not detain any hidden or remote sense in the house of language; rather, it opens itself onto a coming that no intentional act can bring about. The poem therefore takes a turn in its last stanza and no longer speaks of its going or the goings-on of a reader but, inversely, of a coming.

Etwas, das gehn kann, grußlos
wie Herzgewordenes,
kommt.
   (*GW* 1:252)

(Something that can go, without greetings
as what has turned to heart,
comes.)

What comes here can, however, be double. From the viewpoint of the reading that gropes along, what comes is the unwritten, that which is interrogated in all reading, and the unwritten must impart from itself to interpretation by way of its coming, since it could not otherwise become an object even of the most abstract thought. On the other hand, from the vantage point of the unwritten, what comes is the poem with its questioning reading.

Etwas, das gehn kann, grußlos
wie Herzgewordenes,
kommt.

As the movement of writing, the poem approaches itself as the unwritten—the unwritten comes to the poem as the experience of the interruption of its writing. Its going is the coming of the unrepeatable. It comes as the disfiguration of the figures into which writing has conjured its language. Selfless, it writes itself only in writing the coming of an other, of the poem; it writes itself only in writing itself otherwise and in ascribing itself to another. As for the poem, what is coming in its writing is not itself but that which it does not write. It is always the other that comes. This two-turned coming—the implicit inversion of writing and the unwritten, of reading and the unreadable, in every poem, every speaking and reading—is itself the movement of alteration in which even the most hardened and petrified self opens itself toward an other. The "ores" (*Erze*) of the beginning are then "turned to heart" (*Herzgewordenes*).

What comes, always the other, must be able to set out on a way, to go and also to go away. It has not been said that what is coming also arrives. But the possibility that whatever comes goes away belongs to the conditions of coming—of the poem and of what it does not write, of reading and what it does not read. Without greetings, without a word, in a going even prior the alternative of coming and going, in the linguistic movement prior to the choice between the word *come* and the word *go*, it is there and gone away. It writes itself, it reads itself—it comes—free.

NOTES

1. G. W. F. Hegel, *Werke in zwanzig Bände*, Theorie Ausgabe, ed. Eva Moldenhauer and Karl Markus Michel (Frankfort: Suhrkamp, 1970), 12: 529; *The Philosophy of History*, trans. J. Sibree (New York: Dover, 1956), 447. All citations, including those of Celan, are newly translated for this essay; references to standard English translations are given for the convenience of English-speaking readers.

2. G. W. F. Hegel, *Phänomenologie des Geistes*, ed. Johannes Hoffmeister (Berlin: Ullstein, 1973), 29; Preface, § 32. Cf. *Phenomenology of Spirit*, trans. A. V. Miller (Oxford: Oxford University Press, 1977), 19.

3. Manfred Frank and Gerhard Kurz have begun to carry out a portion of this task, though not with uniform persuasiveness; see "Ordo Inversus: zu einer Reflexionsfigur bei Novalis, Hölderlin, Kleist und Kafka," in *Geist und Zeichen*, Festschrift für Arthur Henkel (Heidelberg: Winter, 1977), 75–97.

4. These thoughts are given theoretical formulations in a series of notes bearing the title "Reflexion" in Friedrich Hölderlin, *Sämtliche Werke*, ed. Friedrich Beißner (Stuttgart: Kohlhammer, 1961), 4:233–36. Here one finds the sentence: "One has inversions of words in the period. Yet the inversion of the periods itself, then, must prove greater and more effective." Friedrich Hölderlin, *Essays and Letters on Theory*, trans. Thomas Pfau (Albany: State University of New York Press, 1988), 45.

5. Paul de Man has shown this in his text on Rilke. See "Tropes (Rilke)," in *Allegories of Reading* (New Haven: Yale University Press, 1979), 20–56.

6. Rainer Maria Rilke, *Sämtliche Werke*, ed. Ernst Zinn et al. (Frankfort: Insel, 1955), 2:557.

7. "So lange währte ihre Umarmung, daß die Liebe an ihnen verzweifelte" (*GW* 3:163).

8. "Der Tag des Gerichts war gekommen, und um die größte der Schandtaten zu suchen, wurde das Kreuz an Christus genagelt" (*GW* 3:163).

9. "'Alles fließt': auch dieser Gedanke, und bringt er nicht alles wieder zum Stehen?" (*GW* 3:165).

10. "Tausche dich nicht, nicht diese letzte Lampe spendet mehr Licht— das Dunkel rings hat sich in sich vertieft" (*GW* 3:165).

11. In connection to this, see Paul de Man, "The Rhetoric of Temporality," in *Blindness and Insight: Essays in the Rhetoric of Contemporary Criticism*, 2d rev. ed. (Minneapolis: University of Minnesota Press, 1983), 187–229.

12. "Die Dichtung, meine Damen und Herren—: diese Unendlichsprechung von lauter Sterblichkeit und Umsonst!" (*GW* 3:200).

13. See Georg Büchner, *Werke und Briefe*, ed. Fritz Bergemann (Wiesbaden: Insel, 1958), 85. Cf. *Lenz*, trans. Michael Patterson, in Georg Büchner, *The Complete Plays*, ed. Michael Patterson (London: Methuen, 1987), 249. One can assume that Büchner was familiar with the "Walpurgis Night's Dream" in the first part of Goethe's *Faust*, where the following words are put into the mouths of the "clever ones"—and, as the text suggests, the converted ones: "Going by foot doesn't work any more / so we go by our heads" (ll. 4369–70).

14. "Wer auf dem Kopf geht, meine Damen und Herren,—wer auf dem Kopf geht, der hat den Himmel als Abgrund unter sich" (*GW* 3:195). Celan's commentary on Büchner's sentence once again recalls Hölderlin's "Reflexion": "Man kann auch in die Höhe fallen, wie in die Tiefe" ("One can fall upwards as well as downwards"). *Sämtliche Werke*, 4:233; *Essays and Letters on Theory*, 45. Without referring to Hölderlin, Heidegger took up this thought in his first study of Trakl, "Die Sprache," and he used it for the determination of his gnomon, "Die Sprache spricht [Language speaks]." One can assume that Celan knew Hölderlin's text as well as that of Heidegger. In "Die Sprache," Heidegger writes: "Wir fallen in die Höhe. Deren Hohheit öffnet eine Tiefe. Beide durchmessen eine Ortschaft, in der wir heimisch werden möchten, um den Aufenthalt für das Wesen des Menschen zu finden [We fall upwards. The height of this fall opens up a depth. Together, they measure out a site in which we would like to become at home, so as to find the dwelling-place for the essence of man]." Martin Heidegger, *Unterwegs zur Sprache* (Pfullingen: Neske, 1971), 13; *Poetry, Language, Thought*, trans. Albert Hofstadter (New York: Harper & Row, 1975), 191–92.

15. Peter Szondi was the first to recognize it as such. See "Poetry of Constancy—Poetik der Beständigkeit," in *Schriften*, ed. Jean Bollack et al. (Frankfort: Suhrkamp, 1978), esp. 2:338; "The Poetry of Constancy: Paul Celan's Translations of Shakespeare's Sonnet 105," in Peter Szondi, *On Textual Understanding and Other Essays*, ed. Michael Hays, trans. Harvey Mendelsohn (Minneapolis: University of Minnesota Press, 1986), 165. Although not unjustly in this context, Szondi places paranomasia, as "phonological near-identity," under the rubric of unification and constantiation. I read in paranomasia, as it is used by Celan, a mode of the diversification of linguistic units (syllables, words, syn-

tagms) through which they open themselves to a multiplicity of other—and indeed, *a limine*, not determinable—unities, thereby, under the appearance of correspondence, making room for a limitless play of alteration.

Ferdinand de Saussure, in his search for a suitable concept for the principle of construction of "saturnine" verses, finally designated as "anagrammic," considered the term "hypogram" and made the fragmentary remark: "Paranomasia comes so close with its principle that . . ." Jean Starobinski gives the following commentary: "It is curious that Saussure . . . should not have fixed his attention more closely to paranomasia. Perhaps he feared . . . that this 'figure of speech' might imperil the aspect of *discovery* which, for him, was attached to the theory of anagrams." *Les mots sous les mots* (Paris: Gallimard, 1971), 32; *Word upon Word: The Anagrams of Ferdinand de Saussure*, trans. Olivia Emmet (New Haven: Yale University Press, 1979), 19. Paul de Man has extensively commented and expanded on Saussure's considerations of the hypogram in "Hypogram and Inscription." See *The Resistance to Theory* (Minneapolis: University of Minnesota Press, 1986), 27–63.

16. See Ovid, *Metamorphoses*, trans. Mary M. Innes (New York: Penguin, 1955), bk. 11, ll. 720–48. In this connection one also thinks of Celan's remark (September, 1966) that naming takes place in the depth of language, that *taufen* ("baptize") and *tauchen* ("dive") stand in an intimate relation to one another. Reported by Dietland Meinecke in *Wort und Name bei Paul Celan* (Bad Homburg: Gehlen, 1970), 189.

17. See, for example, the informative studies of Elizabeth Petuchowski, which are devoted to the polylingual wordplay in Celan: "A New Approach to Paul Celan's 'Argumentum e Silentio'" and "Bilingual and Multilingual *Wortspiele* in the Poetry of Paul Celan," both in *Deutsche Vierteljahrsschrift für Literaturwissenschaft und Geistesgeschichte* 52 (1978): 111–36 and 635–51, respectively. The young Celan's proclivity for wordplay with inversion is well documented by Petre Solomon, "Paul Celans Bukarester Aufenthalt," in *Zeitschrift für Kulturaustausch* (Stuttgart), 32, no. 3 (1982): 222–26.

18. One finds a comparable treatment of words in "Ein Tag und noch einer" (A Day and One More), also in the volume *Sprachgitter*: the expression "der Ast / rasch an den Himmel geschrieben" [the branch, / quickly scrawled on the sky] (GW 1:179) contains the word *Astra*, written apart and dismembered by the line break and the comma. Before it finds in "Leuchter" [chandelier] a relatively unambiguous semantic equivalent, it is repeated in disguise once more: "ein Morgen / sprang ins Gestern hinauf" [a tomorrow / leapt up into yesterday]: "Gestern" can also, in this context and with its reference to "hinauf," be read as "Ge-Stern" (the collection of stars). Cf. Celan's pun *per c-aspera ad astra*, reported by Israel Chalfen in *Paul Celan. Eine Biographie seiner Jugend* (Frankfort: Suhrkamp, 1983), 96.

In a poem from *Fadensonnen*, Celan gave the poetic recipe for the preparation and reading of his texts, and not just his own: "Kleide die Worthöhle aus / mit Pantherhäuten, // erweitere sie, fellhin und fellher, / sinnhin und sinnher, //gib ihnen Vorhöfe, Kammern, Klappen / und Wildnisse, parietal, // und lausch ihrem zweiten / und jeweils zweiten und zweiten / Ton" (Dress the wordcaves /with pantherskins, // expand them, infur and outfur, toward sense and away from sense, // give them vestibules, chambers, shutters / and wilderness, parietal, // and overhear their second / and at each time second and second /tone) (*GW* 2:198). Here, too, we have an inversion of familiar ideas. Aside from the duplicity of the word *auskleiden*, which in isolation can mean both "dress" and "undress," the outside—the skin, the pelt—is displaced as sense into the inscape of the word; sense is only one—and indeed an alien, second—skin, an inner mask. Tone, as "that which is always second," is in each case distanced further than the audible tone, infinitely secondary; it too is a second. Celan's later poems are written out of this second and for its sake; they are dated, as finite language, on the second. The inversion of the secondary into the "primary," of the outer into the "inner," is always effected in them so that they expand the character of the secondary, *in fine*, instead of domesticating it. Thus, as he himself stressed, we can only "understand" his texts "from a distance."

In addition, *auskleiden* is one of the possible meanings of *auslegen* ("to interpret," "to lay out"). Insofar as the poem takes on this—second—sense in the image, in the clothing, in the pelt, it itself practices the "hermeneutic" operation it recommends: the whole becomes feline, *fellhin und fellher*, although not without falling into what would count as failure for a normative understanding.

19. Helpful indications for the problem of language as a *Mit-teilung* ("imparting") that precedes every reduction and idealizing into communication—indications, however, that have to be elaborated—are given in Walter Benjamin, "Über die Sprache überhaupt und über die Sprache des Menschen," in *Gesammelte Schriften*, ed. Rolf Tiedemann and Hermann Schweppenhäuser (Frankfort: Suhrkamp, 1980), 2(1):142 ("On Language As Such and on Human Language," in Walter Benjamin, *Reflections*, trans. Edmund Jephcott [New York: Harcourt Brace Jovanovitch, 1978], 315–16); in Martin Heidegger, *Sein und Zeit*, 11th ed. (Tübingen: Niemeyer, 1967), § 34, 160–64; and in the untitled introductory text to Maurice Blanchot, *L'Entretien infini* (Paris: Gallimard, 1969), ix–xxvi. The problem of *Mit-Teilung* is also developed masterfully by Jean-Luc Nancy, *Le Partage des voix* (Paris: Galilée, 1982); and *La Communauté desoeuvrée* (Paris: Galilée, 1986); "Sharing Voices" in *Transforming the Hermeneutic Context*, ed. Gayle L. Ormiston and Alan D. Schrift (Albany, N.Y.: State University of New York Press, 1990), 211–59; *The Inoperative Community*, ed. Peter Connor, foreword Christopher Fynsk (Minneapolis: University of Minnesota Press, 1991).

20. Israel Chalfen writes in his biography that for Celan's mother "the German language was the more important, and throughout her life she made sure that a correct, literary German was spoken in her house. She had no patience with the everyday language of Bukovina." *Paul Celan*, 40. And "she especially liked to read the German classics, and in later years she would compete with her son Paul in citing from the authors they most loved" (31).

21. "Er redet nicht, er spricht, und wer spricht, Geschwisterkind, der redet zu niemand, der spricht, weil niemand ihn hört, niemand und Niemand." (*GW* 3:171).

22. In this connection it is not unimportant that in the mystical speculations of Jacob Böhme, a few of which may have been known to Celan, *matrix* is given outstanding significance. See, in particular, "*De tribus principiis matrix* oder Beschreibung der Drei Prinzipien Göttlichen Wesens," chapters 5–13, in

Jacob Böhme, *Sämtliche Schriften*, fac. of 1730 edition, ed. Will-Erich Peuckert (Stuttgart: Frommann, 1955–61), vol. 2. See also further references in volume 11 (index).

23. "Kulturkritik und Gesellschaft," in *Prismen* (Frankfort: Suhrkamp, 1955), 31; "Cultural Criticism and Society," in Theodor W. Adorno, *Prisms*, trans. Sidney and Shierry Weber (Cambridge, Mass.: MIT Press, 1981), 34.

24. Peter Szondi, "Durch die Enge geführt," *Schriften*, 2:384.

25. *Pause, Wortlücke*, and *Leerstelle* are concepts employed by Celan in "Gespräch im Gebirg": "es schweigt der Stock, es schweigt der Stein, und kein Schweigen, kein Wort ist da verstummt und kein Satz, eine Pause ists bloß, eine Wortlücke ists, eine Leerstelle ists, du siehst alle Silben umherstehn" (the stick goes silent, the stone goes silent, and no silence, no word is struck dumb here, nor any sentence; it is only a pause, a lacuna, a hiatus, you see all the syllables stand about) (*GW* 3:170). One encounters the "same" inversion and the "same" hiatus between "Wurzel Jesse. Niemandes Wurzel" to "Wurzel—o / unser," where the "o"—placeholder for the "Wurzel"—is to be read not only as a plaintive sound but also as the graphic sign of the annulment of the root and of ours.

26. See "Sign Zéro," in *Selected Writings* (The Hague and Paris: Mouton, 1971), 2:219.

27. "Only true hands write true poetry. I see no difference in principle between handclasping and poetry." Letter to Hans Bender dated 18 May 1960 (*GW* 3:117).

28. See Gerschom Scholem, *Zur Kabbala und ihrer Symbolik* (Frankfort: Suhrkamp, 1973), 124; *On the Kaballah and Its Symbolism*, trans. Ralph Mannheim (New York: Schocken, 1965), 92.

29. See *Zur Kabbala*, 138; *On the Kabbalah*, 103.

30. Bernard Böschenstein's fine sentence on "Sperrtonnensprache" points in a similar direction: "The poem has outlived and survived itself." *Leuchttürme* (Frankfort: Insel, 1977), 305.

31. Peter Szondi, *Schriften*, 2:344; "The Poetry of Constancy," 178.

32. Cf. Winfried Menninghaus's analysis in *Paul Celan. Magie der Form* (Frankfort: Suhrkamp, 1980), 62–67.

33. "Poetry no longer imposes, it exposes itself" (*GW* 3:181).

34. Cf. Chalfen, *Paul Celan*, 30.

35. "Mos erat antiquus niveis atrisque lapillis, / his damnare reos, illis absolvere culpa" ("It was the practice, in days of old, to condemn prisoners with black pebbles, to acquit them with white"). Ovid, *Metamorphoses*, bk. 15, p. 336, ll. 41–42.

36. Among the palimpsests of "EIN WURFHOLZ" may be the "Speech of Christ, after Death, from the Cosmos, that there is no God," the "First Flower-Piece" from the *Siebenkäs* of Jean Paul, whom Celan held in high esteem. Its central theme is that the atheist is orphaned—"No one is so much alone in the universe as a denier of God. With an orphaned heart, which has lost the greatest of fathers, he stands mourning" (270, 279)—and that the son of God who denies God has ceased to be himself (a son of God) and is in fact fatherless—"'We are all orphans, I and you; we are without a father'" (273, 282). The path the dead Christ traverses in search of his father is not unlike the one taken by the boomerang: "'I traversed the world. I ascended into the suns, and flew the milky

ways through the wilderness of the heavens; but there is no God'" (273, 281–82). The "I" finds itself annihilated, in "frozen, dumb Nothingness" (274, 283). It is the fate of the particular poetic figures in Jean Paul's "Speech," like that of the boomerang, to announce their own dissociation and destruction. They are allegories in the strict sense, the sense given by Benjamin: they signify the non-being of what they present. See Walter Benjamin, *Der Ursprung des deutschen Trauerspiels*, in *Gesammelte Schriften*, 1(1):406; *The Origin of German Tragic Drama*, trans. John Osborne (New York: Verso, 1985), 233. The proximity and distance between Jean Paul's "speech" and Celan's poem emerge with the greatest clarity in the fact that, in Celan's Democritean universe, orphaning no longer refers to God, but only to itself, thereby annulling its own indexical function; in the fact that the "dial" which the boomerang—its / soul"—"described" and whose "solitary hand" it is displays the same *O*, the same untimely conditioning of time and of the sign as does the "dial-plate" of eternity in Jean Paul: "Aloft, on the church-dome, stood the dial-plate of Eternity; but there is no figure visible upon it, and it was its own index [*Zeiger*, hand]; only a black finger pointed to it, and the dead wished to read the time upon it" (273, 281). Page numbers refer to Jean Paul, *Werke*, ed. Norbert Miller (Munich: Hanser, 1971), vol. 2; *Flower, Fruit and Thorn Pieces*, trans. Edward Henry Noel (Leipzig: Tauchnitz, 1871), vol. 1.

37. At the end of the "Meridian" address, Celan writes: "Ich finde etwas—wie die Sprache—Immaterialles, aber Irdisches, Terrestrisches, etwas Kreisförmiges, über die beiden Pole in sich selbst Zurückkehrendes und dabei—heitererweise—sogar die Tropen Durchkreuzendes—: ich finde. . . . einen *Meridian*" (I find something—like language—immaterial yet earthly, terrestrial, something circular, returning to itself over the two poles and thereby—cheerfully—even traversing the tropics. I find. . . . a *meridian*) (*GW* 3:202). Marlies Janz has stressed the possibility that the address on the "meridian" could represent a greeting to Adorno, who refers to a meridian, if only very casually, at the outset of his essay "Valérys Abweichungen" (Valéry's Aberrations), published in 1960 and dedicated to Celan in gratitude for his "Gespräch im Gebirg." Cf. *Vom Engagement absoluter Poesie. Zur Lyrik und Ästhetik Paul Celans* (Frankfort: Syndikat, 1976), 115–16. With equal—if not more pertinent—justification, one could venture the conjecture that the address on the "meridian" refers to Heidegger's "Zur Seinsfrage," in *Wegmarken*, 2nd and rev. ed. (Frankfort: Klostermann, 1987), 379–419, which was first published as a response to Ernst Jünger's "Über die Linie," in *Sämtliche Werke* (Stuttgart: Klett-Cotta, 1980), vol. 7, Essays I, pp. 239–80, with the title "Über 'Die Linie.'" This text, like the one of Jünger, characterizes the 'line' as the *Nullmeridian*, the prime meridian. These two references are not mutually exclusive; in accordance with Celan's usual procedure, they may be thought as concentrated into the single word *Meridian*. As far as I know, the only serious discussion devoted to the problem of Celan's relation to Heidegger is to be found in Philippe Lacoue-Labarthe, *La Poèsie comme expérience* (Paris: Bourgois, 1986), 11–58.

38. The conversation was with Dietlinde Meinecke; see *Wort und Name bei Paul Celan*, 229–30.

39. "There are certain delicious sensations whose vagueness does not exclude intensity, and there is no sharper point than Infinity." Hugo von Hofmannsthal, *Aufzeichnungen*, ed. Herbert Steiner (Frankfort: Fischer, 1959),

181. Hofmannsthal quotes from the third piece in Baudelaire's *Spleen de Paris*, entitled "Le *confiteor* de l'artiste." "The sharpest point of the Infinite" is quoted again in Hofmannsthal's 1924 prose poem "Erinnerung" ("Remembrance"), as the "point of a lance" that destines the one whose heart is hit—Hofmannsthal speaks here of his own experience—to be a poet. *Gesammelte Werke*, ed. Bernd Schöller (Frankfort: Fischer, 1979), 7:155.

40. "O my soul! The poem is not at all made of these letters that I plant like nails but of the white that remains on the paper."

41. "Die, was nicht deutbar, dennoch deuten, / Was nie geschrieben wurde, lesen." Hugo von Hofmannsthal, *Gesammelte Werke*, 1:297–98; "Death and the Fool," in Hofmmansthal, *Three Plays*, trans. Alfred Schwarz (Detroit: Wayne State University Press, 1966), 65.

INSCRIPTION AND MATERIALITY

7

Spectral Analysis

A Commentary on "Solve" and "Coagula"

Anders Olsson
Translated by Hanna Kalter Weiss in collaboration
with the author

SOLVE

Entosteter, zu
Brandscheiten zer-
spaltener Grabbaum:

an den Gift-
pfalzen vorbei, an den Domen,
   stromaufwärts, strom-
abwärts geflößt

vom winzig-lodernden, vom
freien
Satzzeichen der
zu den unzähligen zu
nennenden un-
ausspechlichen
Namen aus-
einandergeflohenen, ge-
borgenen
Schrift.
    (*GW* 2:82)

(SOLVE

De-Eastered, grave-
tree split into
logs for burning:

past the poison-
palatinates, past the cathedrals,
floated upstream,
downstream

by the tinily flaring, the
free punctuation marks of
the sequestered writ that
has dis-
persed
into the
countless, un-
utterable,
to be uttered
names.)
(P 257)

COAGULA

Auch deine
Wunde, Rosa.

Und das Hörnerlicht deiner
rumänischen Büffel
an Sternes Statt überm
Sandbett, im
redenden, rot-
aschengewaltigen
Kolben.
(GW 2:83)

(COAGULA

Rosa, your
wound as well.

And the hornlight of your
Romanian buffaloes

instead of stars above
the sandbed, in
the talking, red-
ember-powerful
butt.)

      (*P* 259 [trans. modified])

Paul Celan's poems "Solve" and "Coagula" appeared in the 1967 collection *Atemwende*. "Solve" on the left and "Coagula" on the right, combined they are a diptych which separates them from their surroundings. Unique in the context of *Atemwende*, their titles suggest a common denominator: the Latin formula *solve et coagula*, indicating two opposing phases of the alchemical process. The first separates and dissolves, the latter recombines. Nicholas Valois stated its cyclical meaning in his procedural description: *solvite corpora et coagulate spiritum*, "dissolve the body, and render the spirit rigid."

It is not surprising that Celan associates his poetry with the alchemical tradition. Traceable throughout his oeuvre, it is perhaps most apparent in the 1963 volume *Die Niemandsrose*, the collection preceding *Atemwende*, where Celan begins the poem "Chymisch" (*GW* 1:227) with the words "Schweigen, wie Gold gekocht, in / verkohlten / Händen" ("Silence, cooked like gold, in / charred / hands" [*P* 179]). He may have encountered a similar interest in the surrealists, well known to him through his translations of the works of Desnos, Eluard, and Char—or in Rimbaud. In his study *Alchemie*, the alchemist Eugéne Canseliet, who was close to the surrealists, discusses in detail Rimbaud's "Alchemie du verbe."

"Solve" and "Coagula" stand within a sequential alchemical framework. The solve-phrase, by way of the "red- / ember-powerful / butt," describes the breaking-up of the *prima materia*. It denotes the phase of death and disintegration in which the wasted matter turns black. Hence the name of this phrase: *nigredo*. Similarly, Celan breaks down the primal matter, symbolized by the grave tree—a combination of Christ's cross and Adam's tree, frequently cited in alchemical speculation and planted "East of Eden" at the dawn of Creation (Gen. 2:8). Already the poem's first word—one of Celan's many new coinages, the negative *Entosteter*, "De-Eastered"—implies the cruel dispossession of the tree from its origin. The Christian-mystical, even the kabbalistic, elements in Celan's work are not uncommon in alchemy. Nor does the apostrophe in "Coagula," *Auch deine Wunde, Rosa*, break with the traditional alchemical framework. The wound metaphors and the drama of mystical suffering of traditional alchemy can be found already in the work of Zosimos, a Greek alchemist in Alexandria during the fourth century. *Rosa*, most often a synonym for Mary, corresponds with what Yeats in a series of poems called "the secret rose" or "rosa alchemica,"[1] the bride whom the Red King unites in the final phase. This last phase is red, traditionally called *rubedo*, and clearly the model for Celan's poem: it forms the basis for the relation between the coagulation of the title, Rosa's wound, the buffalo horns, and the red ashes.

In Celan's oeuvre, the word *Rosa* appears only on this occasion, but it relates closely to the rose mysticism inherent in his earlier poetry, especially in *Die Niemandsrose*, with its confession to a flowering Nothing, as in "Psalm" (*GW* 1:225). A further reference to the alchemical code occurs in the line "instead of stars above." A star ignites in the sky at the end of the *nigredo* phase, indicating a promise of rebirth after the destruction. Celan alters the sign. In his poem the buffalo horns shine over the sandbed, on which the bolt is traditionally placed in the alchemist's furnace.

What, then, does Celan do with this alchemical framework? First of all, he eliminates the conjunction from the formula *solve et coagula* and writes two separate, independent poems—as autonomous as two parts of a diptych can be. It makes little sense to interpret the contents of "Coagula" as sequential to "Solve." There is a definite break between the two, bridged by the parallelism of the sacrificial motif: the grave-tree and Rosa's wound. As compared to alchemy, there is also another difference to be noted in the absence of beginning and end. Unlike the alchemists, Celan fails to restore the paradisiacal primal state: Ouroboros does not bite its tail, and the dragons do not devour one another, as they ought to in a formula from the alchemical tradition proposed by the forefather of alchemy, Hermes Trismegistos—*terra enim est mater elementorum; de terra procedunt et ad terram revertuntur,* "The earth is the mother of the elements; they rise from the earth and to the earth they return." In Celan, the origin is lost from the very start, and the end, indiscernible, is not reached. Thus both parts of the diptych lend themselves to a dual interpretation: open or closed, mildly or harshly ironical, or preferably a combination of partially contradictory perspectives.

In a single, complexly fragmented sentence, "Solve" describes how the grave-tree, sequestered from its origin, floats away, past the symbols of mundane-sacred power ("Gift- / pfalzen, Domen") aided by "the free punctuation marks" that are part of the finally saved or hidden writing. This writing is purportedly "dis- / persed" into innumerable, unutterable names. Whose names are these if not those of the annihilated victims, also dispersed? The writing seems to be inseparably intertwined with the fate of humanity, crystallized in the portrayal of the splintered, doomed grave-tree.

The two stanzas following the colon seem to recapitulate syntactically the floating of human wreckage in a laborious movement forward. Everything is subject to the same "Solve"—the cloven grave-tree, the active punctuation mark, the diffused writ—submitted to the same, destructive imperative. Celan's texts are always open to a historical interpretation, and if applied to this phase of dissolution, it takes on a more concrete and brutal significance: *Solve* may be read as *Endlösung*; *Brandscheiten* may refer to "corpses trudging like sticks of firewood in Treblinka"; and *Giftpfalzen*, by a strangely archaic circumlocution, may be read as "gas chambers."

Yet the death process seems incomplete in "Solve." The writing is *ge- / borgen*, the word division underlining that it is not only hidden, but maybe saved *because* it can be kept secret, *because* it can be regarded, like the Sefiroth of the Kabbalah, as the emanation of the invisible Godhead, *Ein-sof, Deus absconditus*. Frequently the Sefiroth is pictured as a tree, or a human being, thus incorporating the idea of language and names emanating from the Godhead. The Kabbalah provides the background for understanding Celan's association of tree, humanity, name, and writing into one thought. It is difficult, then, to avoid reading "Solve" as a compression of the story of Creation, beginning with Adam's sin, the curse of exile, and the ensuing destruction of the human race.

The question remains, however, as to what is "saved" in this slaughter. The free punctuation mark blazes with tiny flames—a counterpart to the alchemical fire—not only causing destruction, but floating and propelling ahead, perhaps in an act of participation or solidarity. The world process is a linguistic process, and the poem takes on a self-referential character: it is that of which it speaks. With tiny flames, Celan's poem blazes and splits lines, words, and syllables into something like a diabolical mimesis of annihilation.

By addressing the other—the movement toward a you characteristic of Celan's poetry—the other poem, or the other part of the poem, "Coagula," indicates an opening toward another order. In so doing, Celan follows the alchemical transition from death to life—from *nigredo* to *rubedo*. The difficulty here is that there appears to be no key in either the alchemical or the Judeo-Christian tradition. Replacing the star, the horns' light derives from the Romanian buffaloes of the you. There is also an echo of David's mention of his "saving horn" in Psalm 18. In addition, it may imply a fertile encounter between the buffalo horn and the red Rosa, the ensuing wound functioning as a testimonial. The "Romanian" is too specific, however, indicating yet another layer—not an occult, but rather a spectrally expanding codification, as is often the case in Celan.

In fact, without the supplemental consideration of the word "Romanian," the reading of the poem would lead to grave misunderstanding from the outset. A beautiful and memorable passage in a letter from Rosa Luxemburg to Sonja Liebknecht, written from her prison

cell on December 24, 1917 while detained by the Breslau police, provides the necessary clue. Celan's poem addresses not only the *rosa alchemica*, but also the revolutionary Rosa Luxemburg:

> Ach, Sonitschka! I have experienced an acute pain here. In the yard where
> I walk, military wagons often arrive, packed full with sacks, or old uniforms
> and shirts often spotted with blood. . . . They are unloaded here, passed
> out in the cells, mended, then reloaded, and delivered to the military. The
> other day, such a wagon came drawn by water buffaloes rather than horses.
> This was the first time that I saw these animals up close. They are built
> sturdier and broader than our oxen, with flat heads, their horns bent flat,
> their skulls rather black with large soft eyes. They come from Rumania,
> they are trophies of war. . . . The soldiers who drive the wagon say that it
> was a very hard job to catch these wild animals and even more difficult to
> use them, who were so used to freedom, as beasts of burden. They were
> beaten frightfully to the point where the words apply to them: "Woe to the
> defeated." . . . About a hundred of these animals are said to be in Breslau
> alone. Moreover, used to the luxuriant pastures of Rumania, they receive
> miserable and scant fodder. They are mercilessly exploited in dragging all
> kinds of loads, and so they perish rapidly.
>
> Anyway, a few days ago, a wagon loaded with sacks drove into the prison.
> The cargo was piled up so high that the buffaloes could not make it over
> the threshold of the gateway. The attending soldier, a brutal character, be-
> gan to beat away at the animals with the heavy end of his whip so savagely
> that the overseer indignantly called him to account. "Don't you have any
> pity for the animals?" "No one has any pity for us people either!," he an-
> swered with an evil laugh, and fell upon them ever more forcefully. . . .
> Finally, the animals started up and got over the hump, but one of them was
> bleeding. . . . Sonitschka, buffalo hide is proverbial for its thickness and
> toughness, and it was lacerated. Then, during the unloading, the animals
> stood completely still, exhausted, and one, the one that was bleeding, all
> the while looked ahead with an expression on its black face and in its soft
> black eyes like that of a weeping child. It was exactly the expression of a
> child who has been severely punished and who does not know why, what
> for, who does not know how to escape the torment and brutality. . . . I
> stood facing the animal and it looked at me; tears were running from my
> eyes—they were *his* tears. One cannot quiver any more painfully over one's
> dearest brother's sorrow than I quivered in my impotence over this silent
> anguish.
>
> How far, how irretrievably lost, are the free, succulent, green pastures of
> Rumania! How different it was with the sun shining, the wind blowing;
> how different were the beautiful sounds of birds, the melodious calls of
> shepherds. And here: this strange weird city, the fusty stable, the nauseat-
> ing mouldy hay mixed with putrid straw, the strange, horrible people—
> and the blows, the blood running from the fresh wound. . . . Oh! My poor

buffalo! My poor beloved brother! We both stand here so powerless and spiritless and are united only in pain, in powerlessness and in longing.[2]

These lines certainly support more than one way of interpreting the poem, but the Romanian buffaloes provide an additional focal point where the lives of two Jews may converge—the exiled Romanian Paul Celan and the murdered Rosa Luxemburg. The alchemical code not only proves insufficient for a reading of the poem, but also turns out to be merely one of several possible—albeit necessary—supplements. Underlying it is Rosa Luxemburg's stark experience described in her letter: the buffalo's wound, the reversed address by which Celan turns Rosa's expression of solidarity with the buffalo to mean herself, the horns, even the sandbed and the butt are obvious correlations in the letter. Rosa describes how sleepless and lonely she is in her dark cell, stretched out on a stone-hard mattress and listening hopelessly to the crunching of gravel under the sentry's footsteps. Yet at the same time she imagines herself lying in a grave with a strange feeling of happiness. Her cell is undoubtedly like an alchemical butt. Unable to glimpse the stars, she can still see the light of the buffaloes, her brothers and fellow-sacrifices, enter her cell.

In Celan's poem the butt is "talking" (*redend*). In the butt/cell Rosa's address is born, that which Celan in his Büchner speech, the "Meridian," called "the mystery of an encounter" (*GW* 3:198). "Coagula" is not the only poem in which Celan expresses his interest in Rosa Luxemburg's fate. He also does it in "Du liegst," a poem contained in *Schneepart* from 1971, but written in Berlin in 1967 (*GW* 2:334). As Peter Szondi has shown in his well-informed analysis, it is primarily the naming of places that here reveals the concrete basis.[3] The question remains, however, as to how much this supplementary reading helps us to understand Celan's text. The danger is that we remain in a circular and totalizing reading, in which we discover that the poem moves between two layers of meaning, the general (alchemy) and the particular (Rosa Luxemburg), as if it were concretizing some general idea, or generalizing something concrete. This kind of synthesis, however, would contradict Celan's spectral method of composing, memorably described in a conversation with Hugo Huppert:

And as regards my alleged encodings, I would rather say: ambiguity without a mask, it expresses precisely my feeling for cutting across ideas, an overlapping of relationships. You are of course familiar with the manifestation of interference, coherent waves meeting and relating to one another. You know of dialectic conversions and reversals—transitions into something akin, something succeeding, even something contradictory. That is what my ambiguity (only at certain turning-points, certain axes of rotation present) is about. It stands in consideration to the fact that we can observe several facets in one thing, showing it from various angles, "breaks" and "divisions" which are by no means only illusory. I try to recapitulate in language at least fractions of this spectral analysis of things, showing their *varying* aspects and interrelationships with other things: related, succeeding, contradictory. Because, unfortunately, I am unable to show these things from a comprehensive angle.[4]

Continuing this discussion, Celan denies emphatically any supernatural gift or connection with the occult. "I reject any oracle."[5] Celan's multilayered, precise concreteness has all too often been disregarded and has made him hermetic in a Mallarméan sense. For Celan the poem stands by itself, with its own, inexorable, metathetic, or in other ways worked through logic. Nevertheless one of its most essential characteristics is its openness toward a multiplicity of worlds and references, superimposed in a way impossible to unify in a harmonious whole.[6]

The multiplicity of layering is possible to follow only by analyzing the first two lines of "Coagula," the address "Auch deine / Wunde, Rosa." Israel Chalfen's biography of the poet's early years provides material in this respect. At the university, in 1940, Celan became acquainted with Rosa Leibovici, whose Communist sympathies had brought her from the Romanian Jassy to Czernovitz, controlled by the Soviets. He helped her establish herself, and their relationship led to a short but intense love affair. After the war, Rosa married a high-ranking Romanian politician, but contracted tuberculosis and died in the early sixties. According to a witness in Paris, Celan received the news of her death with deep sorrow. Chalfen suggests a guilt-complex, since it was in all probability Celan who broke off their relationship. His short love affairs, which suddenly blossomed up only to fade away just as suddenly, were well known to his friends. Chalfen tells us: "It is therefore not impossible that his poem 'Coagula,' which begins with the words *Auch deine / Wunde, Rosa,* refers to Rosa Luxemburg as well as Rosa Leibovici, biographically important for him, who came from Moldavia, home of the *Romanian buffalo* mentioned in the poem."[7] As far as I can see, there is nothing that contradicts this reading. Presumably, the poem was written in the early or mid sixties; further research may decide whether or not this poem may even have been composed in connection with the news of Rosa Leibovici's death.

If correct, Chalfen's explication nevertheless ought not to hide the fact that Rosa Leibovici's presence in "Coagula" is even more enciphered than that of Rosa Luxemburg. In a peculiar, spectral manner, the poem in its address expands from the general to the cryptic, from *rosa alchemica* to Rosa Luxemburg, and then to the yet more obscure Rosa Leibovici. The fact that the "Romanian buffaloes" also lend themselves to a reading on the personal level indicates that Celan was highly conscious of the precise extension of focus when he wrote the poem.

Chalfen's information stresses an important dimension of Celan's technique: it does not preclude one reading at the cost of another; it does not become less "personal" when it opens itself to the flood of voices and addressees; Celan puts layer on layer, some of which may never be recognized in a reading. In this way, his poem moves from clarity to obscurity, from obscurity to clarity, in transitions where the different layers partly interact and partly contradict one another.

An analogous example is offered by the last stanza of the poem "Schibboleth," collected in the volume *Von Schwelle zu Schwelle* from 1955:

Einhorn:
du weißt um die Steine,
du weißt um die Wasser,
komm,
ich führe dich hinweg
zu den Stimmen
von Estremadura.
    (*GW* 1:131–32)

(Unicorn:
you know about the stones,
you know about the water,
come,
I shall lead you away
to the voices
of Estremadura.)
    (*P* 97)

Here, too, the address fans out in various directions. The initially hidden meaning connects the word *Einhorn*, which in addition to its literal appeal to the unicorn's mythical significance also functions as a proper name: the name of a dear friend, Erich Einhorn, who shared Celan's political involvement in the Republican cause during the Spanish Civil War, to which the poem refers.[8]

Celan's work is born in a dialogue with another. The enciphering of his poetry has numerous aspects, but the one I have in mind here, paradoxically, has to do with a fundamental urge to communicate, a wish to establish a relationship with someone else, although this may not necessarily be with the reader. Or, rather: it concerns relationships which *in principle* may be established during the reading, yet which retain an element of unreadability, a seal that can never fully be broken because it always seems capable of provoking yet another possibility of interpretation.

Again we need to ask how the choice of addressee influences the interpretation of the poem as a whole. If we have a number of different addresses side by side, as is the case here, does this imply that the poem contains equally many directions of intention? Are they compatible or incompatible in that case? I find it reasonable to doubt that they can all fit into *one* integrated whole in the classical hermeneutic sense. If we replace Rosa Luxemburg with Rosa Leibovici, it seems prudent to emphasize less the utopian ideal, and more the mourning aspect of "Coagula." Even if the alchemical code is irreducible and necessarily interacts with the other layers, we must regard "Coagula" as several poems in one, impossible to conform to a single interpretation. Thus it is as if the rigorous "contraction," to use an expression of Jacob Böhme, so characteristic of Celan's poetry (at least after *Atemwende*), is related with an equally extreme ability to fan out. It is as if the poem wanted to be maintained in its diffused form, reifiably unreadable, as if open and closed at the same time. The paradox in an analysis which supplies the poem with multiple layers of meaning in this manner is that the additive readability precisely underscores the poem's fundamental unreadability. The more one reading is realized, the more other dimensions are pushed aside.

For the sake of clarity, I would like to show yet another plausible concretization of the addressee, which has an even more compelling intertextual significance than is the case with Rosa Leibovici. There is in fact a possible connection with Kafka's story "Ein Landarzt" in Celan's poem.[9] As Werner Hamacher has pointed out, this is a story "about the wound, Rosa. Perhaps this may explain the word 'Auch' in 'Auch deine Wunde, Rosa.'"[10] Read in this manner, the wound becomes less symbolic. In Kafka's story, Rosa is the maid who is sacrificed to the savage farmhand when the doctor leaves to attend to a sick man one night during a severe winter storm. She is left alone with her terror and the wound that the farmhand has inflicted on her in an act the doctor has been the witness to: while she is helping the farmhand to harness the horses, he throws himself over her, and sinks his teeth into her cheek so that "the red marks of two rows of teeth" become visible.[11] The doctor ignores the incident, however, and only after he arrives at the sick man's house, ten miles from the scene, does the thought of Rosa begin to haunt him. She becomes a wound on *his* conscience, a devastating reminder of his moral guilt, which remains unatoned until the end. Eventually, the farmhand takes command of the household, and Rosa is his victim.

There is yet another wound in the story, however—the wound of the sick man, described with the same horror-filled fascination and perspicuity. It is striking that at this point the word "Rosa" reappears both as a color and as a flower. "Coagula," with its *Auch*—that is, with its call for plurality—may well be read as a dialogue with Kafka, an act of shared suffering for which there is no remedy:

> In his right side, near the hip, was an open wound as big as the palm of my hand. Rose-red, in many variations of shade, dark in the hollows, lighter at the edges, softly granulated, with irregular clots of blood, open as a surface mine to the daylight. That was how it looked from a distance. But on a closer inspection there was another complication. I could not help a low whistle of surprise. Worms, as thick and as long as my little finger, themselves rose-red and blood-spotted as well, were wriggling from their fastness in the interior of the wound towards the light, with small white heads and many little legs. Poor boy, you were past helping. I had discovered your great wound; this blossom in your side was destroying you.[12]

As plausible as this additional reading may be, it should perhaps be noted that it involves fewer of the elements in "Coagula" than do the readings discussed above.

Let us turn, finally, to the diptych as a whole and to a closer look at Celan's way of writing. If the analysis of "Solve" and "Coagula" showed a plurality in the singular, then this applies to an even greater degree to Celan's treatment of syntax and word formation. In "Solve" there is mention of a floating which uses the deadly separation as if it were the only act of freedom possible. The writing, at once saved and hidden, encompasses an endlessly expanding multiplicity of addressees and directions of meaning. The world becomes writing, and writing becomes a world. It is remarkable how the alchemical process itself becomes a linguistic course of events, orally and in writing. The butt is also the place for the poem's coming-into-being. In this way, it would be possible to regard Celan himself as an alchemist who breaks down and reassembles. Only his re-creations are never without visible seams. In his poetic butt there is never a final fusion of bride and groom, no synthesis of opposites. There is only the act of painful participation, a deposit of red ashes.

The terrible and, in a positive sense, provocative aspect of Celan's poetry is that this participation also contains an element of contamination and confusion. It is as if Celan took it upon himself to brutalize his own writing. And if this writing is "alchemical," the alchemical code is itself already deformed and made suspect by the brutal experiments of history. It seems to imply a profoundly ironic, if not sarcastic, commentary on the dreams of perfection of alchemy (and other doctrines); the butt, which is the egg of the universe, a microcosmic reflection of the macrocosmos, is at once the scene of destruction and of spilled blood. Alchemy, then, is a sacrificial process.

Thus one should also perceive an element of the non-negotiable in the spectral construction of Celan's poem. It is not enough to link together varying and often even contradictory readings *one by one*; rather, it is a question of retaining at least some of them in one and the same procedure. Only then can the particular effect of over-layering come about. This layering is achieved by differentiation already on the micro level. A fusion like "rot / aschengewaltigen / Kolben" is not splice-free. Here, Celan differs from the surrealists, who in their fusion of opposites nevertheless strive to create a new image. Celan always retains the wall between the spliced parts, and just as in the splitting of verses in "rot- / aschengewaltigen," comparable to the one of "ge- / borgenen" in "Solve," he marks his monstrously diptychal vision by division. Evil can turn into good, good into evil; the red can turn violently into ashes, ashes into red. There may even be a connection here with the coagulated, healed wound, or the red sulfur, which the alchemical process has made resistant to any annihilating fire. We must thus conclude that in Celan the butt speaks, *at least* doubly. And the world remains unreadable.

NOTES

1. Cf., e.g., *Collected Poems* (New York: Macmillan, 1956), 67.

2. Rosa Luxemburg, *Gesammelte Briefe*, ed. Georg Adler et al. (Berlin: Dietz, 1984), 5:349–50. *The Letters of Rosa Luxemburg*, ed. Stephen Eric Bronner (Boulder: Westview Press, 1978), 241.

3. "Eden," in *Celan-Studien* (Frankfort: Suhrkamp, 1973); now contained in Peter Szondi, *Schriften*, ed. Wolfgang Fietkau (Frankfort: Suhrkamp, 1978), 2:390–98.

4. Hugo Huppert, "Spirituell. Ein Gespräch mit Paul Celan," in *Paul Celan. Materialien*, ed. Werner Hamacher and Winfried Menninghaus (Frankfort: Suhrkamp, 1988), 321.

5. Ibid.

6. There are a few studies showing how Celan limits and outlines this layering—not only structurally, but also rhetorically—through inversions and chiasms. Cf., e.g., Christoph Perels, "Erhellende Metathesen," in *Paul Celan*, ed. Hamacher and Menninghaus, 127–38; and Håkan Rehnberg, "Krasis," *Kris* (Stockholm) 34–35 (1987), 140–49. Nevertheless, there remains much to be done.

7. Israel Chalfen, *Paul Celan. Eine Biographie seiner Jugend* (Frankfort: Suhrkamp, 1979), 151.

8. Cf. ibid., 114–15.

9. *Gesammelte Werke*, 7 vols., ed. Max Brod (Munich: Fischer, 1983), *Erzählungen*, 112–17. "A Country Doctor," in Franz Kafka, *The Penal Colony: Stories and Short Pieces*, trans. Willa and Edwin Muir (New York: Schocken, 1976), 136–43.

10. Correspondence to the author, August, 1986. Cf. also Dietlind Meinecke, *Wort und Name bei Paul Celan. Zur Widerruflichkeit des Gedichts* (Bad Homburg: Gehlen, 1970), 215.

11. "Ein Landarzt," 112. "A Country Doctor," 137 (trans. modified).

12. "Ein Landarzt," 115. "A Country Doctor," 141.

For Lore

8

Intertextuality in Celan's Poetry

"Zwölf Jahre" and "Auf Reisen"

Hans-Jost Frey
Translated by Georgia Albert in collaboration with
the author

ZWÖLF JAHRE

Die wahr-
gebliebene, wahr-
gewordene Zeile: . . . *dein*
Haus in Paris—zur
Opferstatt deiner Hände.

Dreimal durchatmet,
dreimal durchglänzt.

. . . .

Es wird stumm, es wird taub
hinter den Augen.
Ich sehe das Gift blühn.
In jederlei Wort und Gestalt.

Geh. Komm.
Die Liebe löscht ihren Namen: sie
schreibt sich dir zu.
        (*GW* 1:220)

(TWELVE YEARS

The become-
true, remained-
true line: . . . *your*
house in Paris—to
your hands' place of sacrifice.

Three times breathed through,
three times shone through.

. . . .

It gets dumb, it gets deaf
behind the eyes.
I see the poison bloom.
In every word and shape.

Go. Come.
Love erases its name: it
writes itself to you.)
    (P 165)

AUF REISEN
Es ist eine Stunde, die macht dir den Staub zum Gefolge,
dein Haus in Paris zu Opferstatt deiner Hände,
dein schwarzes Aug zum schwärzesten Auge.

Es ist ein Gehöft, da hält ein Gespann für dein Herz.
Dein Haar möchte wehn, wenn du fährst—das ist ihm verboten.
Die bleiben und winken, wissen es nicht.
    (GW 2:45)

(ON JOURNEYS

It is an hour which makes dust into your residue,
your house in Paris into your hands' place of sacrifice,
your black eye into the blackest eye.

It is a farm, there a team stops for your heart.
Your hair would like to blow when you ride—it is not allowed to.
They remain and wave, do not know about it.)

An empty line splits the poem "Zwölf Jahre" into two parts. When
reading, one skips over it. But what does one skip over? The series of

dots is not a compact obstacle, as a drawn line would be, but it also cannot be simply overlooked like a mere blank space. It stops one's glance, yet is permeable. This porous border encourages the passage from the first section, whose end it indicates, to the second, whose beginning it marks. That end and beginning can occur in the middle of a poem is familiar to us from any number of strophe sequences. Here, however, the falling silent and the resumption of speech do not simply happen, but are made visible by the dots. The dots say the lack of language. They are the sign for the fact that here speech has both ceased and not yet begun. The dots mean. Thanks to them the space is not simply a speaking cue for the reader, but rather the thematization of the lapse into silence, the written end of speech, but also the marking of the silence that precedes it.

One would like silence to surround a poem. By beginning and ending, the poem seems to surface out of silence and to fall back into it. But precisely this simple view of the poem's unity is what is torn apart by the dotted line. In it, the beginning and the end of the poem are brought into its middle. This causes a revolution or inversion of all relations. That the beginning and the end of the poem are transferred into its middle means that it is the second part that begins and the first that ends. But this in turn means that the beginning is not the beginning and the end is not the end. Although the second part begins out of the silence of the empty middle, it also follows upon the first part, which has fallen silent in it. And when the first part ends, the end has not yet been reached; instead, a second part follows. Something precedes the beginning, and something comes after the end. One can apply these observations to the situation of the poem, which thematizes its own starting and ending through the marked empty line. The silence that surrounds a poem is always only an interruption. The beginning of a poem always follows upon an end, just as a beginning follows upon its end. Thus the relationship between the two parts of "Zwölf Jahre" is at the same time the representation of every poem's relation to what comes before and after it. The empty line within the poem stands for the intertextual relationship. This poem is about intertextuality.

This is also clear from the fact that at the beginning the poem refers back to what precedes it and at the end points beyond itself. Through the citation about which the first section talks, the poem refers to something that precedes its beginning. The citation introduces into the poem what is prior to it. In a similar way the *Du* to which love addresses itself (*sich zuschreibt*) at the end anticipates in the poem what comes after it. This also means that the poem will have been what is prior for what follows upon it, and that it has become an answering *Du* for the poem "Auf Reisen" quoted in it, the answering *Du* toward which that poem has traveled. The pre-text and the post-text are also part of the text. A poem is not isolated: it is an excerpt from a text without beginning or end. It derives from a text and is directed toward another text. This excerpt-character of the poem, which becomes visible in the punctuated empty line, is represented a second time in the citation, which is split into two halves by a dash absent in the original. The citation, however, does not simply repeat the structure of the whole poem, but also represents the poem's excerpt-character by being a line taken out of its context and given without what comes before and after it.

Line, part of poem, poem are excerpts which depend on context. If one looks at it in this way there is no basic difference between, on the one hand, the relationship between parts of a text and, on the other, the relationship between two texts. The intertextual relationship is in turn an intratextual one. Here, however, the question is bound to arise of how text-borders are constituted. It is not that texts begin and end, but rather that they are interrupted. The interruption is what makes beginning possible, but also that which, as pause in the flow of speech, allows for the crystallization of the text's shape. Otherwise there could be, for example, no citation. A citation is the repetition of a text within another text. Repetition presupposes an interruption. If something is to be repeated, it must be finished in some way. In quoting, one goes back to an earlier beginning, one bridges over a gap, which "Zwölf Jahre" perhaps alludes to in its title. Not only the citation, but every intertextual relation is the bridging over of an interruption and therefore the production of a new, more encompassing text.

In "Zwölf Jahre" the overcoming of the interruption is not only displayed in the course of the text through the empty line, but it is also discussed in that it is said of the quoted line what has happened to it (it is "wahr- / geblieben, wahr- / geworden"). But these two manifestations of the interruption and its bridging stand in a difficult relation to one another. Although the statement constitutes itself in the course of its expression, so that discourse and statement are a single movement, they contradict one another. The initiation and suspension, the taking place of speech, opposes what it says. The first part of the poem falls silent in the empty line and therefore proceeds in such a way that it does the opposite of what it says. For in it an earlier poem is resurrected which, insofar as it has remained and become true, has precisely not fallen silent. The second part of the poem, seen from the point of view of the empty middle, is the new beginning of speech. Yet at the very point where silence makes the transition back into speech, the poem speaks about falling silent. On both occasions there is tension between what happens and what is said. The poem proceeds in such a way that it simultaneously disproves what it says.

This contradictoriness, which the poem itself expresses concisely in the line "Geh. Komm," can also be illustrated in another way. If one looks at it from the perspective of the movement of the text, the first part of the poem points forward. The poem steps forward word by word. But in this process text is accumulated which is the precondition for what is coming, so that one can say (simplifying somewhat) that the poem is turned backwards even as it moves forward. The text does not run a simply linear course, but transforms itself retrospectively from the end. On the level of the arrangement of the text, the first part points forward toward the second and the second backwards toward the first. This is the reversal of what happens on the semantic level. Here the first part refers back to an earlier text which is quoted, while the second part points forward beyond itself. Once again the statement and the arrangement of the text run counter to one another. The text itself shows this quite clearly. Put in a general manner, the question concerns the relationship between the two halves of the poem. Since on the level of the statement the first part points backwards and the second part forward, the empty line in the middle becomes a gaping void out of which the two halves strive to pull away from one another. If this is not merely to remain on the level of assertion, it must be possible to show to what extent the two sections of the poem are not only separate but also connected, or, more precisely, to what extent the first part points not only backwards to the poem quoted in it, but also forward to the second part, and to what extent the second part is not only turned toward the addressee (*Du*), but also reflects on the first.

The question must be answered on the basis of the opening words of the poem. "Die wahr- / gebliebene, wahr- / gewordene Zeile" is a qualification of the citation that follows—a qualification that remains to be understood. In any case, remaining (*Bleiben*) and becoming (*Werden*) are the defining elements of the very linguistic process in the course of which they are named. In the transition from *wahr-geblieben* to *wahr-geworden* everything has remained except for the element [*b*]*lieb*, which has become *word*. This refers ahead to the second part, where the words *Liebe* and *Wort* appear, but remains hidden from the linear glance ahead and becomes accessible only retrospectively from the second section. It is only when the second part refers back to the first that the first becomes recognizable in its pointing forward. This relationship cannot be reduced to a question of sound. Although the transformation, in the transition from *wahr-geblieben* to *wahr-geworden*, initially consists only in the substitution of one sound sequence for another ([*b*]*lieb-word*), once the relationship to the words *Liebe* and *Wort* appears the meaning of this transformation can no longer be ignored. It then becomes manifest that love becomes word. The question thus posed about how language arises is complementary to the one about falling silent. Both processes are ambivalent in a way that remains to be unfolded.

At the end of the poem, two linguistic attitudes are opposed to one another: "Die Liebe löscht ihren Namen: sie / schreibt sich dir zu." That love becomes word can mean first of all that it is named. The word *love* is the name of love. Love erases it because it does not recognize itself in it. The word that love becomes when it is named is empty. It is the freezing of the flux of life into conceptual generality. This form of linguistic definition thus results in the loss of what it would like to appropriate, and is a kind of falling silent. It is for this reason that the name is erased and that a different discourse is opposed to it: "sie / schreibt sich dir zu." *Sie* is the noun erased in the pronoun. *Sie* does not simply stand for love, but rather for the erased name. For this reason it is impossible to decide what it stands for, if indeed it stands for anything at all. Now there is no longer something (love) that becomes language by being named, but rather something that takes place, namely, the movement (*Sichzuschreiben*) toward the *Du*. The line-break, which emphasizes the pronoun, serves to isolate the *schreibt sich dir zu* as the movement which is the only concern of this discourse. Here, too, love becomes word, yet not as something given, which is then also named, but rather in such a way that it happens as the discourse of the poem that writes itself toward the other.

Yet this is not true either: the text that says this does not itself fulfill it. Love must be named so that one can say about it that it erases its name. And address (*das Sichzuschreiben*) itself is talked about rather than actually performed. Although in the transition from noun to pronoun the announced erasure of the name also actually takes place, the text is, as a whole, naming. It alienates itself from what it says precisely to the extent that it says it. In order to become what it understands itself to be, it would have to give up saying what it is. It would have to erase itself as the empty name which, by constituting itself as the naming of the erasure of name, it has become. Thus the two linguistic attitudes, which in the poem apparently follow each other as though the one could replace the other, cannot in fact be separated. All discourse that finds its way back into motion by dissolving what is solidified lapses in turn into congealment.

The conclusion of Celan's poem leaves no doubts as to the unavoidability of this ambivalence. Both sides of the discourse are bound together in the ambivalence of the *sich zuschreiben*. "Sie / schreibt sich dir zu" means not only the movement of the poem toward an addressee: *zuschreiben* also means to ascribe, to attribute something to someone. To the extent that the poem is not what it says, since it says what it is, it only attributes the gesture of address to itself. Attribution (*die Zuschreibung*) is always uncertain. Its relation to what it says remains one of claim and is the arbitrary pinning down of something that is open and cannot be grasped.

In the divergence between its parts, the poem represents the inner contradictoriness of its course, in which crystallization takes place as dissolution. The crystallization of the words *Liebe* and *Wort* out of *gebliebene* and *gewordene* goes together with the erasure of the name, and at the end the poem dissolves once again what it has constituted itself to be. A certain temptation now arises to settle the ambivalence of the poem's discourse in a specific direction by way of a value judgment. The poem's conclusion encourages this by making the possibility of the address to the *Du* dependent on the erasure of the name. That this address (*Sichzuschreiben*) is, at the same time, once again attribution (*Zuschreibung*) would not detract from the validity of the value judgment, but only from the possibility of moving beyond the devalued solidification once and for all. Yet such a solution is not possible. Even in the realm of values there is only ambivalence. This is proven by the only passage in the poem that seems to be unambiguously evaluative: "Ich sehe das Gift blühn. / In jederlei Wort und Gestalt." The Grimms' *Deutsches Wörterbuch* says: "the close relationship between *blühen* and *blasen*, both in letter and concept, is not to be missed, the flower breaks and comes out of the bud like air from the mouth."[1] Blossoming has to do with breathing, which in Celan stands again and again for the discourse of the poem. But here what blossoms in the words that "originate like flowers" is poison (*Gift*). It blossoms in breath-crystal, or "Atemkristall" (*GW* 2:31/*P* 231), in the shape into which breath solidifies. This is the process in the course of which *Liebe* shapes itself out of *gebliebene*, *Wort* out of *gewordene*. What is poisonous in the blossoming of words is the solidification into concept—which itself appears in this poem as the name that must be deleted.[2]

But the crystallization of words, however fateful, is also necessary for any utterance to be able to occur at all. It is only insofar as breath takes shape in words that language comes to be and that it can occur as address to an other. For this reason, the solidification is not only the poison that suffocates breath, but also the gift (*Gabe*) that the word *Gift* means etymologically: the gift of what is to be said in its being said. So here, too, it is impossible to break away from indecision.[3] Solidification and motion are both gift and poison. Poison is what is always opposed to what is understood as a gift. If the balance between the two opposite meanings is upset by the fact that in current linguistic usage the poison (*Gift*) carries more weight than the gift (*Gabe*), it is nonetheless restored on the level of the overall structure of the poem, since the first section stresses more the bright side, the second more the shadowy side of language.

The ambivalence of the linguistic movement which solidifies as the gift of what is to be said, but in which, however, poison always already blossoms, and by destroying the shape on its way to congealment keeps open the possibility of taking shape, can be read in reference to the movement of the poem. The poem falls silent in the first part, where it speaks of the permanence of what was once said, and in the second part, where it starts to speak again out of silence, it speaks of falling silent: this is the manifestation of the ambivalence of the linguistic process in the shape that it has taken in "Zwölf Jahre." Now, since the relationship between the two halves of the poem is the representation within the poem of its own intertextuality, it is possible to apply what can be read in the relationship between its parts to its relationship to other poems. Poems then appear as a series of constellations which replace and dissolve one another, transitory solidifications which are brought back into motion by what follows them. Thus what happens inside each of the poems repeats itself on the level of the series of poems. In "Zwölf Jahre" the step from the intertextuality *inside* the text to the intertextuality *of* the text is made by way of a citation. By incorporating a line from "Auf Reisen," the poem places itself explicitly in a relation with another poem that calls for further reflection.

What is quoted has remained. It takes part in the solidification. The quoted text stays, and one stands by it. However, it has not only *remained*, but also *become* true; it has therefore changed despite the fact that its wording has remained the same. This is already made visible by the typographical arrangement of the citation: the text explicitly designated as a "line" is divided between three lines and again cut in half by a dash. But the transformation that a text undergoes when it is quoted can also be deduced from general considerations. One does not know where a citation belongs. As a text that is displaced into another text, it belongs both to the one from which it has been taken and to the one in which it is inserted. Since it is marked as a citation, it is only incompletely integrated in the text that incorporates it. It belongs in it to the extent that it depends on the new context, but it does not belong in it to the extent that it is recognizable as a foreign text and thereby refers to an earlier text which on the one hand is absent, but on the other is also alluded to in the quoting text as the absent origin of the citation. Thus the citation is a sort of intertext. It connects the text from which it comes to the text into which it enters. It belongs at the same time in two different contexts. On the one hand this means that these two contexts must be read together and that the relationship between the two texts connected by the citation can itself be read as text; on the other hand, however, the citation becomes uprooted by having its place in two different contexts and falls out of its secured relationship to its contexts into an isolation which requires that it be self-sufficient. Therefore, the citation must be read not only in connection with two different contexts, but also in its not belonging with either of them—as an excerpt without context, which represents, within the quoting poem, the poem's own separateness from other poems.

It is said of the quoted line that it has remained true and become true. Since the line has not remained as such, but only in its wording, its truth can only extend to what it says. But the line no longer says the same thing it used to say and has therefore not remained true in the sense that it proclaims a fixed truth, valid once and for all, but rather in the sense that what has happened in the meantime has enriched its wording, which has remained the same, with a different meaning. The line has remained true precisely in the sense that it has not remained tied to what it once meant, but is now open to new possibilities of meaning. It has *remained* true because it has *become* true. The poem offers here with the greatest concision a formula for the historicity of texts. They remain, transforming themselves, in being read—and that also means in being quoted. The citation is a moment in the history of the text and is perceived as such in the poem "Zwölf Jahre."

That the line has remained true having become true can, in this particular case, also be understood biographically. In "Auf Reisen" the line is part of a sentence: "Es ist eine Stunde, die macht dir . . . / dein Haus in Paris zur Opferstatt deiner Hände." Since "Auf Reisen" was written before Celan's move to Paris, one can understand this sentence retrospectively as a prophecy that was fulfilled. From this perspective it makes sense that in the citation the time specification disappears, since in the meantime what the sentence attributed to the prophesied hour has actually happened. What has remained true is not the sentence, which as prediction is out of date, but the line that names what has been predicted, and which still remains true when what has been predicted becomes true. The syntactical coherence of the sentence falls apart when the line is detached from it. The consequences of this for the text become meaningful from the point of view of the changed situation. First of all, the particle *zu* becomes incomprehensible, since without a verb it cannot be said that the house changes *into* a place of sacrifice [*zur* Opferstatt wird]. The dash that in the citation divides the line into two seems to indicate that the connection between the house and the place of sacrifice is destroyed and that the two halves should be read each in isolation. Their relationship, however, has only become a different one: while according to the prophecy the house *will* become a place of sacrifice, after the fulfillment of the prophecy it *has* become one. The house *is* now the place of sacrifice, and "zur / Opferstatt deiner Hände" announces the name of the house like an inn sign.

But what does it mean that "your house in Paris" has become "your hands' place of sacrifice"? In *Opfer*, "sacrifice," survive the two Latin words *operari* and *offerre*. The work and the gift. The place of sacrifice of the hands is the workshop for the handiwork. And the handiwork is the hand that gives itself [*die sich selbst gibt*; also, that offers itself for a handshake]. "Nur wahre Hände schreiben wahre Gedichte. Ich sehe keinen prinzipiellen Unterschied zwischen Händedruck und Gedicht" ("Only true hands write true poems. I see no fundamental difference between a handshake and a poem").[4] Read in this way, the citation has a biographical and a poetological side. It binds the writing of poetry to the place where it happens. This bond is a fully private one and arises from the fact that Paris became Celan's residence and thereby the city and site of his writing. This coincidence could not have been meant at the time that "Auf Reisen" was written, but only arose from the later course of Celan's life. This increase in meaning due to changed life circumstances has something unsatisfying about it. In order to be able to do something with the name "Paris" one must recur to outside information to which the poem itself provides no access. The text seems to remain impenetrable without this extra-textual knowledge. Given the way it appears in "Zwölf Jahre," however, the line not only evokes something to which the text provides no access, but also, as citation, refers to itself as text and to the text from which it is quoted. This emphasis on textuality peculiar to the citation is a hint to the fact that it is not enough to relate the line's remaining and becoming true to extra-textual events, but that the quoted words also change their meaning in that other texts have occurred between "Auf Reisen" and "Zwölf Jahre" which influence the citation's semantic field. Certain of these texts make it possible to read the quoted line in such a way that it not only refers to something entirely personal, but also justifies the presence of the personal and singular in the poem. This becomes clear if one takes into account the connection Celan establishes elsewhere between the hands and the irreducibly singular.

In the same text that speaks of the poem as handshake, one also finds the following passage: "Handwerk—das ist Sache der Hände. Und die Hände wiederum gehören nur *einem* Menschen, d.h. einem einmaligen und sterblichen Seelenwesen, das mit seiner Stimme und seiner Stummheit einen Weg sucht" ("Handiwork—that is the hands' business. And the hands in their turn belong only to *one* person, i.e. a unique and mortal being who looks for a path with its voice and its silence") (*GW* 3:177). Thus the handiwork of poetry is only possible out of the singularity of the person to whom the hands belong. A similar relationship establishes itself in the "Meridian," the address delivered by Celan on the occasion of his reception of the Georg Büchner Prize. There, Celan quotes four lines from *Sprachgitter*: "Stimmen vom Nesselweg her: / Komm auf den Händen zu uns. / Wer mit der Lampe allein ist, / hat nur die Hand, draus zu lesen" ("Voices from nettle-way: / Come to us on your hands. / He who's alone with the lamp / has only the hand to read out of") (*GW* 3:201). The citation is made in connection with Büchner's Lenz and his desire to walk on his head. To walk on one's hands: through this association, this acquires the entire meaning that Celan ascribes to the personal and singular, which "remains inscribed" in the poem as given, the date (*Datum*), the "20. Jänner" (*GW* 3:196). Here Celan reads his own poem's palm. In connection with his reading of Büchner's text, the hands that appear in it mean something more and other than they did before. From now on they can be read in terms of the "date." This possibility has repercussions for "Zwölf Jahre" and has something to do with the 'becoming true' of the line, since it did not exist at the time of "Auf Reisen" and changes the meaning of the unchanged wording. The citation in "Zwölf Jahre" refers, in the ultimate impenetrability of its personal background, to a date, a January 20. But because the hands appear in it, this citation comes upon the meridian which Celan traces in the "Meridian" through his own and Büchner's text, and moreover becomes the sign for the inaccessibility of the date that is named in it. Thus to the poetological side of the quoted line belongs the justification of the opaque personal date in the poem.

The use of other Celan texts is not an unreflected recourse to parallel passages to explain the poem: rather, it is an attempt to follow the interpretive guidelines that "Zwölf Jahre" gives through its way of thematizing its own intertextuality. This happens not only by way of the quoted line, but also through the way it is described. If the line has remained true as what has become true, it is, among other things, because it has come under the spell of texts such as the letter to Hans Bender or the "Meridian," and has been charged with meanings and connotations that it did not have before. In the case of the "Meridian," however, the relationship goes even further, since what is demonstrated in the passage concerned is the same process of becoming true of a text by way of the transformation of its context that is expressed in "Zwölf Jahre." On both occasions, we are dealing with a commented self-citation. An earlier poem is reinterpreted in the light of the new contexts into which it enters, and becomes true in a new way. The earlier text—since it has become true—proves itself retrospectively to be predictive. Celan called this *a posteriori* prophetic quality of the poem the "Sichvorausschicken zu sich selbst" ("sending oneself ahead to oneself") (*GW* 3:201). Thus the quoted and the quoting text stand in a metonymical relationship to one another.

However, this metonymical relationship between texts is found both in the "Meridian" and in "Zwölf Jahre," and therefore these two texts, since both produce a metonymical textual relationship by quoting, are metaphorically related to one another. This is not all, however: the "Meridian" is also a station on the way that leads from "Auf Reisen" to "Zwölf Jahre." By virtue of the fact that the hands are read here in a particular way in connection with Büchner, the passage from *Sprachgitter* appears retrospectively as an anticipation of the line from "Auf Reisen" quoted in "Zwölf Jahre." This relationship is metonymical. This means that the relationship between "Zwölf Jahre" and the "Meridian" repeats the textual relationship with other texts that is produced inside these two texts. When read together, these two texts are the metaphor of their relationship.

The transformation that the line from "Auf Reisen" undergoes through contact with the meridian is a possibility of its "becoming true." What is so called in Celan's poem is part of an understanding of language according to which there are no fixed meanings. Meaning originates without ever remaining stable. The process of becoming true seems to know no stabilization. It is textual history as continuous change. But with the becoming true belongs also—in a way not discussed until now—the falling silent which is opposed to it in the second section of "Zwölf Jahre," not in such a way that the two follow upon one another as isolated motions, but so that they are the two aspects of a single process. Two considerations on citation may serve to explain in what way becoming true and falling silent are simultaneous and indivisible.

A text becomes true by signifying in a new manner again and again. However, each transformation is a restriction, since it can only come about by way of the privileging of a certain contextual relation at the expense of others. The process of becoming true is a history of meaning which necessarily proceeds in such a way that the different meanings replace one another, that one falls silent in order to make the other possible. Every new interpretation of a text is based on the neglect of certain relationships and the emphasis on others that have remained unnoticed and which are now discovered as those which transform the text. As they substitute for one another, the meanings silence one another again and again. Yet there is a silence that lies even deeper. When the becoming true is understood as change of meaning, one is only attentive to what is said. The communicative function of language stands in the foreground and obscures one's sense for the movement of language as process. In the becoming true as a constant movement of transformation, the return to the text as a stable linguistic shape is secured, since otherwise it would not be *this* text that could become true as remaining true; every time a meaning is produced, however, the text tends to fall silent as linguistic process in that to which it refers. What falls silent in the poem that is only read for its meaning is the verse. The breaking-up of the line in the citation is the destruction of the verse from "Auf Reisen." What is called a "line" (*Zeile*) is dismembered and divided into three lines that have no rhythmic consistency. At the same time, the verse is nonetheless preserved, not only because the citation is designated as a *line* and therefore as a unit, but also through the italics, which put the fragments back together. This means that the verse here is not simply destroyed, but rather appears in the poem as destroyed. The typographical arrangement means the falling silent of the verse. The quoted line has not only become true; it has also at the same time fallen silent as verse insofar as its content has gained the upper hand. But this is again precisely not the case in "Zwölf Jahre," since the verse is remembered, named, and represented as having fallen silent. The graphics of the poem prevents the inherent danger of content-focused reading from taking place. It corrects the disintegration of the verse, which it makes visible, precisely by representing it and thus preserving the lost verse as lost. The line that, by no longer being a verse, has fallen silent and become past is the *war*-gewordene, "the one that has become 'was.'"

The second consideration concerns citation in general. A citation is the repetition of a wording. A text must remain unchanged in order to change its meaning. The quoted line can only become true because it is still the same. What becomes clear here about the citation as repetition of text is valid for all speech. In speaking, one quotes language. Words are always already given, and can only be quoted. If a word is to become true and if one is to say something new through it, it must be recognizable as the same word, which has changed its meaning with use. That words remain the same while their meaning shifts is a loosening and calling into question of the firm bond between wording and meaning. When the wording breaks loose from the meaning, however, it must be thought of independently. There are extreme phenomena like echolalia, which is also well known as the clown act in which the one simply keeps repeating what the other one says, and in which the repetition causes the words to lose all meaning and finally their very characteristic as language. Something like this is also at work in the act of citation. The becoming true as shift in meaning requires the emptying out of the words one uses, or at least the suspension of their connection with a particular meaning. The wording must fall silent in order to mean. It can only mean something new because it might also not say anything. It renews itself by temporarily ceasing to mean. In "Huhediblu" (*GW* 1:275), this conflation of transformation and emptying out of meaning is presented in an extreme form.

The loosening of the connection between wording and meaning makes the shift in meaning of texts and words possible. Repeating them does not ensure consistency of meaning for them. The mute wording releases different meanings, granted to it by its new contexts. The same goes for the quoting of "Auf Reisen" in "Zwölf Jahre." In order to read these two poems in their relation to one another, one must detach oneself from the desire to preserve them as individual poems. Far from being unconnected, they belong together just like the two sections of the poem "Zwölf Jahre." By quoting a line from the earlier poem, and by qualifying it as having remained and become true, the later poem thematizes the relationship between texts on the level of the wording, which starts to mean again in a new way through the change in its context. Through the citation, the two poems become each other's context. It must therefore be possible to show how the wording of each is reinterpreted through the context of the other.

In trying to carry this out, we come upon the beginning of the second section of "Zwölf Jahre," which we have not yet examined: "Es wird stumm, es wird taub / hinter den Augen." Among the possible ways of reading this sentence, one leads back to the beginning verse of "Auf

Reisen": "Es ist eine Stunde, die macht dir den Staub zum Gefolge." The most obvious image here is that of a carriage that turns up dust. In addition, the dust that we become in the poem "Psalm" (*GW* 1:225), and which "no one discusses," might be meant here as well. In both cases, the dust is the trace that remains of what has disappeared. In "Zwölf Jahre," it could be the reading eyes which journey in the text, and behind which "it gets deaf and dumb." The becoming deaf and dumb ("das Stumm- und Taubwerden"), however, has to do with dust (*Staub*) in multiple ways. The dust that is mentioned in "Auf Reisen" becomes visible in "Zwölf Jahre" as the empty line whose dust specks are what the reading eyes have just left behind. But the empty line stands for the lack of speech, just as the dust stands for the missing carriage. Thus the dust in "Auf Reisen" can retrospectively become a metaphor for the lapse into silence.

But the matter does not rest there, with this intertextual metaphorization of dust. The text read by the eyes behind which "it gets deaf and dumb" is not only the poem "Zwölf Jahre," which is now on its way, but also the poem "Auf Reisen" and particularly its first line. This line falls silent not only because the reading eyes leave it behind, but also in the sense of the previously indicated reinterpretation of the wording. The word *Staub* has the words "*stumm*" and "*taub*" hidden in its sound configuration and releases them into the poem "Zwölf Jahre." For this to be possible, the wording must be isolated and its meaning suspended. Only out of this word *Staub* that no longer communicates meaning can the latent meanings *stumm* and *taub* within it be retrieved and crystallized into words. These words do not mean just anything, however, but precisely what has shown itself through the intertextual relationship to be the metaphorical meaning of the dust. Thus "Es wird stumm, es wird taub / hinter den Augen" is the translation of the metaphorical meaning of the first line of "Auf Reisen," a metaphorical meaning which, however, can only come about through this translation. The word *Staub* not only designates the dust, but also refers, as sound, to the two words which say the falling silent (*das Verstummen*) in "Zwölf Jahre," and thereby reveal the metaphorical meaning of the dust as a sign for dumbness (*das Verstummtsein*). This is true of the dust specks in the empty line in "Zwölf Jahre" as well as of the word *Staub* and the dust it designates in "Auf Reisen." The metaphorization of the dust is a process that corresponds exactly to what the poem calls the "becoming true." The becoming true is possible because there is no consistency in the meaning of texts. When it is impossible to pin a wording down to a meaning, however, the wording can become productive. It does not stand for a meaning that preexists it: rather, it produces meaning. The group of sounds in *Staub*, on the one hand, and *stumm* and *taub*, on the other, can mean that the dust becomes a metaphor for dumbness—just as the dots in the empty line, which mean silence, can evoke dust and therefore help produce the word chain *Staub-stumm-taub*. It is not possible to decide what is prior and what is caused, since there is only the permanently fluctuating relationship between wording and meaning.

What is peculiar about "Zwölf Jahre"—but is it peculiar?—is that it prolongs the play between words and meaning beyond the individual poem into the intertextual relationship. This means that the poem as final shape, that is, as a result which comes to rest and stabilization, is called into question, and in its place an infinite text is postulated which neither begins nor ends, but rather is caught up in constant transformation and, by moving on, constantly effaces what it posits. "Auf Reisen" and "Zwölf Jahre" are *one* text which reinterprets itself by extending itself, but which only gains the possibility of this reinterpretation by interrupting itself and thereby making it possible to come back to itself in repeating—that is, in reading—through the dust of the empty line and of the years.

NOTES

1. (Leipzig: Hirzel, 1854), vol. 2, col. 155.

2. *Name* appears here to name—also—the opposite of what is called thus in Winfried Menninghaus, *Paul Celan. Magie der Form* (Frankfort: Suhrkamp, 1980). This is no doubt why "Zwölf Jahre" is not in the catalog of passages (see 9–12) which "easily" identify "the word 'name' as the fundamental subject of every Celan interpretation" (9).

3. The same indecision is further exemplified in "Auf Reisen": "Es ist ein Gehöft, da hält ein Gespann für dein Herz." *Herzgespann* is an illness, but also the plant that was used for its cure. And does one not already see the *Gift* blossoming in the *Gehöft*? The reference to the plant name *Herzgespann* can be found in Barbara Wiedemann-Wolf, *Antschel Paul—Paul Celan. Studien zum Frühwerk* (Tübingen: Niemeyer, 1985), 213.

4. Celan in a letter to Hans Bender on May 18, 1960 (*GW* 3:147).

9

Nothing

History and Materiality in Celan

Aris Fioretos

"This mere nothing of voice," Kafka writes in his last text, "asserts itself and finds its way to us; it is well to think of that."[1] It would be no exaggeration to claim that such "nothing of voice" has an importance for the manner in which the poetry of Paul Celan is articulated. In it, the tiniest fibers and elements of articulation may make a difference. Celan's poems stutter, interrupt or repeat themselves, catch their breath and begin again, but they also have a remarkably fluid character which conveys the impression that most of his texts since the 1959 *Sprachgitter* are written as complex articulatory movements in which the poem's syntax approaches the swells of breathing, its turns, twists, and sudden pushes—as in "Frankfurt, September," for example, written in conjunction with a visit to the Frankfurt Book Fair in 1967, where the final alliterative inscription of *Kafka* paradoxically speaks of song with the help of dominant plosives ("Der *Kehlk*opfverschlußlaut / singt" [*GW* 3:114]).

Celan's poetry comes into being in such conflictual interpenetration of speech and writing, seriously investigating not only the aspects of language traditionally attributed to the realm of voice (tone, phrase, timbre), but also phonetic manipulations such as devoicing as well as graphematic elements and compounds distinctly part of written discourse. Indeed, his poetry, in which "the glottal stop" may prove paradoxically to sing, offers one of the most incisive and informed explorations in post-Romantic poetry of a doctrine of literature grounded on the distinction between spirit and letter. In this regard, Celan's treatment of what Kafka termed "this mere nothing of voice" extends beyond mere thematization: that to which his poems do not give voice but which nonetheless takes place in them is as much a determinant of their manner of signifying as that which is in fact explicitly stated. His poems, then, contain not only the representative traits of vocalization, but also something which resists oral expression—a materiality of writing, which cannot be translated into the spoken language of voice without an unaccountable remainder.

The 1960 prize address, the "Meridian," contains a treatment of the relationship between literature, history, and materiality, and thus by extension also a theory of poetic temporality of interest in this context. The poem, Celan claims in his speech, is not so much "language as such" as "a speaking," "language actualized, set free under the sign of a radical individuation which, however, remains as aware of the limits drawn by language as of the possibilities it opens" (*GW* 3:197/*CP* 49). What emerges here may seem a familiar distinction between linguistic passivity and activity, or language and the act of speech. Yet Celan's discussion of *Sprache schlechthin* and *ein Sprechen* is no conventional retroping of the Saussurian difference between *langue* and *parole*. For one thing, it maintains that the poem's "speaking" remains contingent upon the possibility of addressing another, a "you," who "brings its otherness into the present," an "otherness [which] gives voice to what is most its own: its time" (*GW* 3:199/*CP* 50). For another—which may seem like the same thing, but ultimately amounts to an enactment of this insertion of the time of the other into the Now of poetic discourse— Celan's discussion blends the act of linguistic production with that of its reception.

This crossing, with its emphasis on *another* temporality, is of particular significance for the poetological statements advanced in the "Meridian." Construed as a reading of other texts, primarily those of Georg Büchner, the prize address not only offers but also performs a set of comments on that which most properly amounts to the marking of poetic temporality: accents. Speaking of the "acute" that he argues should be put on the reading of Camille's sarcastic exclamation "—ach, die Kunst!" in Büchner's *Dantons Tod*, Celan opposes the "acute of today" and the grave of history—also of literary history. "'—Oh, art!,'" he exclaims with Büchner:

> You see I am stuck on this word of Camille's.
>
> I know we can read it in different ways, we can give it a variety of accents: the acute of today, the grave of the historical—also the literary historical—, the circumflex—marking length—of the infinite.
>
> I give it—I have no other choice—I give it the acute. (*GW* 3:190/*CP* 40–41 [trans. modified])

To trace the "acute" character of Celan's own poetry would mean reading the way in which it offers a radicalized conception of the relationship between literature and history at the same time as it "remains as aware of the limits drawn by language as of the possibilities it opens."

This acuity pertains to the intention toward language conventionally attributed to Celan's poetry—a context in which the texts' treatment of the relationship between spoken and written language is of particular importance. A quotation culled from the work of one of Celan's elective affinities, Novalis, may provide access to the issue. "Most writers," Novalis observes in his so-called "Telpitz Fragments,"

> are at the same time their *readers*—in writing—and thus so many traces of the reader occur in the works—so many critical considerations—some things befitting the reader and not the writer. Dashes—words in bold print—highlighted passages—all of this belongs to the domain of the reader. The reader puts the *accent* arbitrarily—he actually does what he wants with a book.[2]

The following discussion will be devoted to a few such "traces of the [writer as] reader" in Celan, marking that which is not strictly linguistic in written language, but which nonetheless takes on an inscriptional value (for instance, dashes, the typography of certain words, and highlighted passages). It will begin with some remarks on the "Meridian" in light of Celan's theory of accents and touch briefly on a poem written around the time of the prize address, "Beim Hagelkorn" in the 1967 *Atemwende*. An analysis will follow of a text in which history—also literary history—is at stake: "Tübingen, Jänner" in the 1963 *Die Niemandsrose*. The kind of memory that this poem thematizes will then be considered in a reading of Celan's position vis-à-vis hermeticism. Kafka's "mere nothing of voice" may serve as the guiding star for the analysis of a poem of particular significance in this regard, "Engführung" in *Sprachgitter*, whose traces of the writer as reader could contribute to a more precise reading of the way in which history occurs, acutely, in Celan.

Celan's traces of the writer as reader are the elements of a dense poetry in which the most minor textual detail may make a difference. A slippage in the poem's structure of reference will often render its utterances as much about the manner in which they are phrased as about that which they are about. Reading Celan's German translation of Shakespeare's Sonnet 105, for example, Peter Szondi considers it a "poetry of constancy" bringing about "a shift in accent from the person who is being praised to the act of praising or composing." Yet such a shift from signified to signifier, Szondi goes on to say, not only amounts to that "bolder display" of which Hölderlin spoke in conjunction with his Sophocles translations, but also constitutes what is (with Benjamin's by now institutionalized phrase) labeled an "intention toward language."[3]

In the "Meridian," there are several references not only to accents, but also to the materiality of language, which certainly makes it feasible to speak of a "poetry of constancy" and thus of a turn away from things to their signs (as Jean Paul did with regard to "intellectual freedom" in his *Vorschule der Ästhetik*),[4] but which perhaps more accurately could be termed a punctuation of constancy. At one point, for instance, Celan mentions "somebody who hears, listens, looks . . . and then does not know what it was about. But who hears the speaker, 'sees him speaking,' who perceives language as a physical shape and also . . . direction and destiny" (*GW* 3:188/*CP* 39). At another, he refers to the poem's "more acute sense of detail, outline, structure, color, but also of . . . 'tremors and hints'" (*GW* 3:198/*CP* 50).

This attention to the nonsemantic aspect of language, what Celan considers its "physical shape" and acute character, is intimately bound up with that form of memory which Benjamin, in a neologism, termed "Eingedenken."[5] In the Bremen address, "eingedenk sein" is explicitly linked to a cluster of words centered upon "denken" and "danken," "thinking" and "thanking" (*GW* 3:185/*CP* 33), and much of the argument of the "Meridian" is aimed at underscoring the importance of this remembrance while destabilizing conventional doctrines of the relationship between text and reading. Indeed, Celan's poetics may seem to insist on an encounter as unlikely as it is patently utopian. "The poem intends another," it claims; it "needs this other, needs an opposite" (*GW* 3:198/*CP* 49); and in the Bremen address, it is said in no uncertain terms that "poems are *en route*: they are headed toward. / Toward what? Toward something open, inhabitable, an approachable you, perhaps, an approachable reality" (*GW* 3:186/*CP* 35).

Yet if traditional poetics—*pace* Benn—ascribes a similar, fixable intention to poems, Celan's discussion makes it clear that the poem of which the "Meridian" speaks implies a radical rather than a conventional incompletion—a "still-here" or "Immer-noch" (*GW* 3:197/*CP* 49)—which, apart from the poem's directedness toward a you, makes its "being *en route*" (and thus implied future) a defining trait. If this *Unterwegssein* also implies a taking-shape—a sort of formal inchoative of poetry—then outlines and contours, but also tremors and hints, arguably become decisive elements of the poem's orientation. In this regard, it is less important to determine the direction of the address than to make out its shape and contour—in other words, to "see" the poem "speak."

A first instance of a trace of the writer as reader already occurred in the passage from *Danton's Death* on which Celan got stuck in his discussion of accents: Camille's cursing expletive "—ach, die Kunst!" is preceded by a dash signaling direct speech. As convention stipulates, this dash does not contribute to meaning, but rather amounts to the inscription of voice. In Celan, where poetry is "one person's language become shape and, essentially, a presence in the present [*Gegenwart und Prä-senz*]" (*GW* 3:198/*CP* 49), such inscription is also the survival of breathing in the materiality of punctuation.

Yet the dash does not always signal that breathing voice which the "Meridian" spoke of as "direction and destiny." A poem written several years after the Büchner speech, but constituting an instance of that *Gedicht* of which the address speaks, provides a particularly telling case in which the dash no longer amounts to the sign of actual speech but rather marks the materiality of direction itself. In its concluding stanza, the poem, titled "Beim Hagelkorn," mentions an "arrow-script" sent off from a "heart-thread":

BEIM HAGELKORN, in
brandigen Mais-
kolben, daheim,
den späten, den harten
Novembersternen gehorsam:

in den Herzfaden die
Gespräche der Würmer geknüpft—:

eine Sehne, von der
deine Pfeilschrift schwirrt,
Schütze.
　　　(*GW* 2:22)

(WITH THE HAILSTONE, in
the rust-blighted ear
of maize, at home,
obedient to the late, the hard
Novemberstars:

woven into your heart-thread, the
conversations of worms—:

a bowstring, from which
your arrow-script whirrs,
archer.)
　　　(*65 Poems*, 54)

Quite clearly an affair of the heart, even more so if one recalls that the first version of the poem spoke of the "wishes of worms [*Wünsche der Würmer*],"[6] this text seems troped on that fatal destiny for which the "Meridian" contains much of the poetological matrix. The poet is here figured as an archer, and his writing takes off like an arrow from a bowstring woven of the conversation of worms. To take part in this writing as a reader seems to imply that one expose oneself to its sharp point—a highly dangerous business, which turns the writing of poetry into a possibly fatal activity.

One could indeed wonder about the consequences of this for the relationship between sender and receiver, but if one considers the tendency toward oblique self-reference in Celan's texts—and the fact that the "Meridian" claims that the author of a poem "stays with it" (*GW* 3:198/*CP* 49), speaking moreover of a "kind of homecoming" (*GW* 3:201/*CP* 53)—one may recall not only that "Beim Hagelkorn" was written in that month of which it speaks, November, but also that Celan himself was born under the stellar sign mentioned in the text, the *Schütze* or Sagittarius.[7] "Obedient" to those "late" stars of November, in Celan's case hardening time into the sideral image of destiny, the poem's *Pfeilschrift* thus remains at once faithful to that constellation, of which it must be thought an extension, and bound to a future the precarious nature of which can only coincide with reading.

Yet Celan's particular *Pfeilschrift* is not just an image for a fatal—albeit poetic—message; it quite literally takes off from a "bowstring" inscribed as a dash in the seventh line of the poem and graphically marking its textual condition. In contrast to Camille's dash, this *Gedankenstrich* has nothing to do with voice, but nonetheless marks the material extension of poetic temporality. It is a trace of the writer-as-reader, signaling transition as a form of binding and distantly invoking the etymology of *religio*. In the "Meridian," a text in which the dash could be argued to be if not the most frequent, then certainly the most important—because argument-bound—marker of punctuation, this form of binding is glossed as "the connective [*das Verbindende*], which, like the poem, leads to encounters" (*GW* 3:202/*CP* 54).

Marked by more than one such "trace of an arrow" ("Pfeilspur" [*GW* 2:84]), Celan's writing remains on the way toward a readability which can only coincide with a time coming. Its illocutionary mode is that of the promise, which is prospective but nonetheless assumes a particular date at which it was once incepted. Only there, in a delayed future over which writing has no control, does the script of the arrow seem to be made clear—a condition of writing which has its most rigorous theorization in Benjamin's reflections on "the historical index of images." In the work on the Parisian Arcades, Benjamin claims that this temporal index "does not simply say that they [the images] belong to a specific time, it says above all that they enter into readability at a specific time. And indeed, this 'entering into readability' constitutes a specific critical point of movement inside them." And he adds: "Every Now is determined by those images that are synchronic with it: every Now is the Now of a specific recognizability. In it, truth is loaded to the bursting point with time. (This bursting point is nothing other than the

death of *intentio*, which accordingly coincides with the birth of authentic
historical time . . .)."[8]

By taking off from a bowstring into which a conversation of worms
has hardened materially, Celan's *Pfeilschrift* seems to demonstrate this
death of intention and birth of historical time. The poet is no longer in
command of his poem, even if he "stays with it," as the "Meridian" puts
it. Authorial intention dies out at the moment when the poem enters
history, and is directed toward a constant and constantly repeatable posteriority. Future legibility—albeit dangerous and uncertain—is inscribed in the *Pfeilschrift* as the material condition for its "specific critical point of movement"—only in this manner may the script of the
arrow at some infinite point turn into that read image of which Benjamin writes. Indeed, it seems like a premonition that Celan's script, when
contracted to its initials, becomes *PS*—a postscript legible only in that
coming After which is the Now, the always only acute Now, of reading.

At the end of his address, Celan remarks: "I am coming to the end,
I am coming, along with my acute accent, to the end of . . . *Leonce und
Lena.*" "And here," he adds, "with the two last words of this work, I
must be careful [*muß ich mich in acht nehmen*]" (*GW* 3:201/*CP* 53). The
reason for this need to be cautious, *sich in acht zu nehmen*, Celan claims,
is the danger of reading *kommode* ("comfortable") at the very end of
Büchner's play as *kommende* ("coming")—as Celan's fellow native, Karl
Emil Franzos, erroneously did in his first edition of Büchner's complete
works. "And yet," Celan asks, reflecting on such an arbitrarily put accent, "is *Leonce und Lena* not full of words which seem to smile through
invisible quotation marks, which we should perhaps not call *Gänsefüßchen*, or goose feet, but rather rabbit's ears, that is, something that
listens, not without fear, for something beyond itself, beyond words?"
(*GW* 3:202/*CP* 54).

Here, we are offered yet another image of a practice of reading-
while-writing which turns the focus from the objects not so much to
their signs as to the materiality of those signs. Rather than calling quotation marks *Gänsefüßchen* in accordance with the colloquial German
idiom (such "goose feet" are the kind of quotation marks, usually referred to as guillemets, which look like arrows: « and »), Celan prefers
to picture them as rabbit's ears, that is, as a faculty with the capacity to
perceive the most notable trait of language when actualized in speech:
its audibility. In the case of the penultimate word of *Leonce and Lena*,
kommode, this listening for something "beyond itself" proves possible
only when attention is paid to the word's homophonic "outline," what
Celan also calls its "physical shape."

Yet the "Meridian" not only speaks of a listening "beyond itself,"
but also of something that listens "beyond words." Celan's caution
against Franzos's reading of *kommode* as *kommende* not only concerns an
adjective erroneously read as a present participle, but also a shift of

stress: in the transition from *kommode* to *kommende* there is a shift from a grave or possibly circumflexial accent to an acute (*kommôde* becomes *kómmende*). Celan seems to prefer to be literal and thus to stay with what is *kommode* (conventional or given)—that is, to "remain within the limits of language" as the Meridian" put it—yet, as his theory of rabbit's ears suggests, the change from a piece of literary history actualized in a quotation to the Now of reading implies a material shift from convention (or "comfort," *das Kommode*) to the inscription of the always-ahead or "coming" of the poem (its *Kommendes*).

What Celan here leaves unread and to come, as it were, what his quotation of Franzos on Büchner only points toward as something literally «beyond» the quoted *kommende*, is the second of the two words he claims to end up with, coming to the end of *Leonce und Lena* with his acute accent. In Büchner's play, this word beyond words is *Religion*.[9] In Celan's materialist conception of transition and mediation—which argues "that the poem has always hoped . . . to speak . . . *on the behalf of the other*, who knows, perhaps of an *altogether other [in eines* ganz Anderen *Sache]*" (*GW* 3:196/*CP* 48)—this left-out or coming "religion" should not be read in the sense of the *ganz Andere*, with which Rudolf Otto designated the divine being,[10] but rather in its strong etymological sense: as binding.

Conventionally one of the dominating tropes of religious discourse, hope is voided of any form of cognitive force—or "belief"—in the "Meridian." If at all, it is maintained in the dash, as the material inscription of that *pneuma* which for Celan amounted to "direction and destiny." "But who knows," Celan adds in his address: "this 'who knows' is all I can add here, today, to the old hopes" (*GW* 3:196/*CP* 48). The reservation is telling: Celan quotes his own uncertainty and sees himself only arriving at a hope which has not yet been transformed into certainty—whose illocutionary mode, like that of the promise, consists of an open direction toward something other, perhaps altogether other.

It is significant, then, that the inscription of the dash in the poetic text is available solely in a "language actualized" in which writing "gives voice," as the "Meridian" puts it, "to that which is most its [the other's] own: its time." When read anagrammatically, the *Sache* in the phrase "in eines *ganz Anderen* Sache" gives voice to "in eines *ganz Anderen* Asche," "in the ashes of the wholly other"—those ashes for which Celan never ceased to speak.[11] If this shift of accents seems to take Novalis too much at his word ("the reader," it was claimed in the Telpitz fragment, "actually does what he wants with a book"), one should consider the inscription of *z-Andere* in "ganz *Andere*." In one of those multilingual wordplays of which Jean Paul spoke in his *Vorschule der Ästhetik*, and for which Celan's intention toward language has become so famous, *z-Andere* would be the homonym of the French *cendre*, "ashes."[12]

Celan's name has often been associated with a negative poetry approaching such an ashen articulation, in which metatheses, multilingual anagrams, and various forms of verbal contraction are used in order to give voice to that to which voice was once denied. Not infrequently, his name has been understood as a signature for the paradoxical movement of poetry between a dangerous, impending Never and a considerably weaker, nonetheless tough Still. Grounds for such a view have often—and rightfully—been culled from Celan's own poetological statements. In the "Meridian," for example, it is said that "the poem today . . . clearly shows a strong tendency towards silence" (*GW* 3:197/*CP* 48); and also that "the poem holds its ground on its own margin. In order to endure, it constantly calls and pulls itself back from an 'already-no-more' into a 'still-here'" (*GW* 3:197/*CP* 49).

It is difficult to deny such statements their exposedness; indeed, it would be far from wrong to consider Celan's poetry to be inscribed between the poles of extinction and survival, patiently noting language's signs of negativity. In this poetry, at once painful memory and shivering novelty, an experience of the limits of language is rendered evident. One could also say that it is in the gray passage between effacement and salvation, between Already-no-longer and Still-here, that Celan's poetry comes into existence. His poems—being instances of that "'grayer' language" mentioned in Celan's response to a questionnaire in 1958 (*GW* 3:167/*CP* 15)—thus necessarily speak of their own conditions of possibility.

Yet it would be one-sided, if not misleading, to take the crystalline terseness of Celan's poems as a sign of a negative practice for which the ultimate end would be the sublation of poetry in the empty exactness of beauty. Celan's texts may take form at the border to the lost; they speak for it and approach the ashen articulation of extinction—what an early text on Edgar Jené calls "the ashes of burned-out signification" ("die Asche ausgebrannter Sinngebung" [*GW* 3:157/*CP* 6 (trans. modified)]). But even if this articulation may seem enciphered and difficult to ascribe conventionally organized meaning to, it is never wholly sealed off. On the contrary, Celan often inverts the attributes of interiority and exteriority whose paradigm generally constitutes esoteric doctrine in a manner which seriously puts into question a definition of his poetry as hermetic.[13]

"Tübingen, Jänner" is organized according to an inversion that is particularly interesting in light of an attempt to define Celan's poetry as esoteric.[14] Granted, the poem does not explicitly thematize a resistance to understanding the way "Engführung" does, for example, yet the manner in which it renders conventional modes of elucidation problematic is distinctly in evidence and could well be read, for instance, in relation to the thematization of historical disjunction in Hölderlin's German rendition of *Antigone*—though it is colored by other experiences and, above else, by other memories:

Zur Blindheit über-
redete Augen.
Ihre—"ein
Rätsel ist Rein-
entprungenes"—, ihre
Erinnerung an
schwimmende Hölderlintürme, möwen-
umschwirrt.

Besuche ertrunkener Schreiner bei
diesen
tauchenden Worten:

Käme,
käme ein Mensch,
käme ein Mensch zur Welt, heute, mit
dem Lichtbart der
Patriarchen: er dürfte,
spräch er von dieser
Zeit, er
dürfte
nur lallen und lallen,
immer-, immer-
zuzu.

("Pallaksch. Pallaksch.")
    (*GW* 1:226)

(Eyes talked into
blindness.
Their—"a riddle is
the purely
originated"—, their
memory of
Hölderlin towers afloat, circled
by whirring gulls.

Visits of drowned carpenters to
these
submerging words:

Should,
should a man,
should a man come into the world, today, with
the shining beard of the
patriarchs: he could,
if he spoke of this
time, he
could
only babble and babble
over, over
againagain.

["Pallaksch. Pallaksch."])
        (*P* 177 [trans. modified])

Customarily understood as a *Widerruf* to literary history in general
and to Hölderlin in particular, "Tübingen, Jänner" has been read as a
critique of the notion of the poet as prophet, performed by one of the
post-Auschwitz representatives of poetry at the very end of intelligible
history.[15] Much, of course, would speak in favor of such an interpretation: among other things, the poem's thematics, word order, and curiously hypothetical structure. The details it mentions have more or less
factual correlatives; the events alluded to have demonstrable contexts;
and the blindness it thematizes has an array of literary antecedents.
    Indisputably, "Tübingen, Jänner" is one of Celan's clearest intertex-
tual *Auseinandersetzungen* with literature, history, and literary history—
not necessarily in that order. Yet formally, the particular blindness of
which the poem seems to speak is not so much an allusion to or a repetition of a Homeric or Sophoclean topos (the blind prophet, singer, or
riddle-solving king)[16] as a blindness occurring in a linguistic transition:
a blindness "talked into." Celan's breaking up of his unusual use of the
German *überreden* underscores such a reading by distributing the elements of this transport onto different metric levels and structurally
marking the transition by means of a kind of lexical enjambment. What
seems to take place in the opening lines of the text thus signals not so
much an instance of (literary historical) commentary, alluding to a former past of literature and constituting its own modernity by reformulat-
ing the meaning of what precedes it, as it indicates an essentially linguistic act, marking the transition from perception and visuality to
cognition and blindness.
    There may well be an intertextual relation to Hölderlin's ode "Der
blinde Sänger," as well as to the self-willed blindness of Oedipus—returning from Hölderlin's translation of *Oidipos Tyrannos*, his notes on
the Sophocles translations, and the perhaps apocryphal fragment "In
liebliche Bläue" to prophetic discourse in the Sophoclean texts them-

selves.[17] Yet what organizes the opening of "Tübingen, Jänner" is a transition which can only be understood as a linguistic or rhetorical act (*überreden* being the conventional formula for rhetoric as *persuasio*) marking the moment when the agents of vision are "talked into" a blindness which will soon turn out to necessitate cognition in linguistic rather than visual terms—a blindness, that is, thematized by a turn from things which can be perceived visually to language.

If one wants to determine the relationship of Celan's poem to that which precedes it, one would thus first have to consider this peculiarly verbal blindness relying on an initial speech act prior to the possibility of conveying an understanding in intertextual terms. It is not until after this inaugural act which has in fact already taken place (Celan uses the preterit) that the poem can be said to allude to literary history and to proceed to quote Hölderlin from the patriotic hymn "Der Rhein." "The power that takes one from one text to the other," as Paul de Man argues in a different but related context, "is not just a power of displacement, be it understood as recollection or interiorization or any other 'transport,' but the sheer blind violence that Nietzsche, concerned with the same enigma, domesticated by calling it, metaphorically, an *army* of tropes."[18]

In Hölderlin, the passage cited reads in its immediate context (the fourth stanza of "Der Rhein"):

> Ein Räthsel ist Reinentsprungenes. Auch
> der Gesang kaum darf es enthüllen. Denn
> Wie du anfiengst, wirst du bleiben,
> So viel auch wirket die Noth,
> Und die Zucht, das meiste nemlich
> Vermag die Geburt,
> Und der Lichtstral, der
> Dem Neugebornen begegnet.[19]

"The Rhine" has elicited many commentaries, usually pointing out the significance of its fourth stanza, especially of that stanza's first line, but more infrequently tracing the implications of its reversibility.[20] It is in this much discussed line that one finds the clearest formulation of the relation between origin and expression, genesis and language, crucial to Hölderlin's poetics and also to be found in "Tübingen, Jänner." In order to better appreciate the difference taking place between the poems and how the enigma of this difference is thematized in the latter text, it may be worth first briefly considering the former.

Hölderlin's hymn is a meditation on the geographical appearance of the Rhine and the possibility of an interpretation in teleological terms. The course of the river—as it flows eastward, deviating from its source in the Zapport glacier in the Swiss Alps and driving "toward

Asia," then turns north in the direction of Lake Constance, and, "after leaving the mountains," "quietly" moves "through German country"—is traced in the first six stanzas, devoted to the Rhine understood generatively as a growing maturity, a coming-into-its-own, and a fulfillment of destiny. Thus the course of Hölderlin's "demi–god" (l. 31)—a designation the river shares with Promethean rebels in stanzas seven through nine, as well as with Rousseau, referred to in stanzas ten through twelve—is perceived as a spatial (i.e., geographical) evolution shading into a temporal (in this case, explicitly genetic) development with the potential for fulfillment. In this crossing of space and time, the fourth stanza takes on a central importance, since it is here that the origin of the river is discussed—that is, the moment rendering possible spatio-temporal terms.

In the latter portion of the fourth stanza, the origin of the Rhine is said to be a "holy womb" (l. 59) and the river is mentioned in the narrative third person singular, whereas in the former part, it is twice expressly addressed as a *reinentsprungenes* "you." This you, coded as apostrophe, figures a certain recurrence, but also a progression: not only is it repeated, but moreover, and perhaps more importantly, the sentence in which it occurs states the essential (genetic) constancy binding origin to future ("as you began, so you will remain").

This designation of the origin as something *reinentsprungenes* is the axis around which a large part of the poem moves.[21] The adjectival morpheme *rein* constituting part of the word *Reinentsprungenes* is repeated thrice in the hymn, on each occasion in conjunction with language: apart from the affiliation of "riddle" and "the purely originated" in line 45, one finds mention of "the pure voice of youth" in line 95, and in lines 144 through 148 it is said of Rousseau "daß er aus heiliger Fülle / Wie der Weingott, thörig göttlich / Und gesezlos sie die Sprache der Reinsten giebt / Verständlich den Guten, aber mit Recht / Die Achtungslosen mit Blindheit schlägt."[22] In each of these instances, purity is linguistic if not properly a purity *of* language. The "language of the most pure," said to be spoken by an apostrophized Rousseau, is the language of that which is close to the origin and exists in the proximity of the sacred, being the only entity with reference to which it can be fully understood. The "pure voice of youth," in its turn, speaks untainted by the corruption and forgetting of this origin (explicitly conjoined with "the pure voice" of the preceding line). Finally, the "riddle"—connected to birth, the moment when cause and effect have not yet been severed from one another—is itself "purely originated."

The particular interest of *Ein Räthsel ist Reinentsprungenes*, however, giving the locution an urgency absent in the other two mentions of *rein*, lies in its reversibility. Constructed as a predicative statement, both the sentence's "riddle" and "the purely originated" can take the position of predicative complement. Thus the statement must not only be read as

signifying that the pure origin is enigmatic, as seems to be the case with
the Rhine and Rousseau later on, but also in the sense that a riddle has
originated purely, much like the "words originating like flowers" in the
fifth stanza of "Brod und Wein."[23] This duplicity, and the impossibility
it asserts in settling for one semantic alternative at the expense of another, points to the attempt to destabilize the traditional ontological
hierarchy between natural and linguistic realities peculiar to Hölderlin.
Not only can that which springs or descends from a pure source be
articulated enigmatically, but a verbal construct such as a riddle may
also originate purely, as a linguistic phenomenon with the ontological
status of a natural object.

Yet whereas in the former case the source has the permanence of a
natural principle of emanation, always and clearly—albeit mysteri-
ously—identical with itself (the mystery of virgin birth providing the
referential analogy), in the latter the riddle may well originate purely,
immaculately articulated, but will never coincide with itself like a natural source, providing the meaning of its own riddling nature. It "is in
the essence of language," as de Man points out in a reading of "Bread
and Wine," "to be capable of origination, but never of achieving the
absolute identity with itself that exists in the natural object. Poetic language can do nothing but originate anew over and over again; it is always constitutive, able to posit regardless of presence but, by the same
token, unable to give foundation to what it posits except as an intent of
consciousness."[24]

Language has the power of originating and becoming, to follow de
Man, but unlike its source (the natural object from which it supposedly
draws its signifying strength), it has no recourse to that which it never
was but should have been in order to be itself. In contrast to a natural
entity such as a river or its source, capable of providing access to a fundamentally immutable origin, a linguistic entity such as the riddle can
only be posited without providing the meaning of its mysterious essence, always in error as to the understanding of its own origin. For this
reason the statement *Ein Räthsel ist Reinentsprungenes* should be read not
so much with reference to the following "For as you began, so you will
remain . . . for birth can accomplish most," as to the last sentences of
the previous stanza:

> Die Blindesten aber
> Sind Göttersöhne. Denn es kennet der Mensch
> Sein Haus und dem Thier ward, wo
> Es bauen solle, doch jenen ist
> Der Fehl, daß sie nicht wissen wohin?
> In die unerfahrne Seele gegeben.[25]

In Hölderlin's hymn, it is not a question of a nostalgic longing for a source, as of an erring movement toward a "whither" (*wohin?*) posited in "the inexperienced souls" of "the blindest." The difference of direction offers an explanation for the blindness of such demigods as the Rhine, who conform to their spatial and temporal limits or accept the fact that they are finite consequences originating in a transcendent source, constituting their infinite cause—yet who because of the elusive nature of this confinement seek an answer, or "fulfillment," by a movement toward experience and consciousness necessarily unfolding in time. In Hölderlin's poem, this accounts for the thematic as well as the strophic transition from inanimate natural entities such as mountains and rivers to half-animate and half-conscious Promethean rebels in order finally to arrive at such exactingly self-conscious creatures as Jean-Jacques Rousseau.

The particular blindness of the young Rhine and his godly peers, as a superlative blindness, lies in its initial, inexperienced desire to move "toward Asia" in the face of a fate which can be realized only gradually. The riddle of the source remains a mystery. Rather than moving backward toward their cause—a movement as impossible as the rewinding of time—they can only distance themselves further from it in the hope of becoming what they seem no longer to be or realize they are, thus acquiring "destiny." Yet the fact that they do not know where to go (*daß sie nicht wissen wohin*) is an "error" (*Fehl*) imparted to their inexperienced souls (*In die unerfahrne Seele gegeben*)—a "given," in other words, marking the date of the inception of their ignorance.

In this regard, the statement that a "riddle is the purely originated" takes on another significance: not only does it say that the pure source toward which the Rhine seems at the outset senselessly to strive is enigmatic, and that a riddle has originated immaculately, but it also indicates that this reversibility belongs to that which makes the language of poetry, while always in error, particularly telling as an instance of the nonlinear unfolding of cognition in time. The text, then, is not "asserting the existence of a transcendental experience that lies beyond the reach of language."[26] Rather, the reversibility that denies the possibility of this extralinguistic experience demonstrates the extent to which Hölderlin's poem must be thought of as a problematization of those referential models depending on a translatability between natural and linguistic realities.

In "The Rhine," error does not happen *après-coup*, as the result of inexperience: it is *given* in the souls of "the blindest," marking the moment of birth as much as it does purity. To err or lack a sense of direction in time or space—to "not know whither"—is the condition of possibility of cognition. The reversibility of Hölderlin's gnomic statement thus points to the structural ordering of language as the most certain element in which the absence of clear direction may be observed. That this reversibility no longer returns us to the extra linguistic riddle or mystery of an ultimate cause or reference, but rather folds us back on language itself, as the medium of erring, is the particular enigma that Hölderlin's poem forces us to consider.

While the source itself may remain pure and riddling in "The Rhine," establishing a sacred domain inaccessible to thought since it remains outside temporality, and while language moreover seems to be treated as the medium of its purity, it is equally clear that the purity of the enigmatic statement in which this is asserted ("Ein Räthsel ist Reinentsprungenes") is highly doubtful. Not only does a riddle belong to that category of rhetorical figures with a particular propensity for obscurity, but the sentence's assertion is achieved through a pun as bold as it is problematic. The homophonic adjectival segment *Rein* plays on the name of the river whose name the poem bears, thus establishing an assertion of purity with the help of what conventionally might be defined as an impure form of language—a joke. The very language in which language is implied to be the privileged medium of purity turns out to be anything but pure. Thus, as a consequence, the riddle said to originate immaculately must be phrased in a way that contaminates its own linguistic cleanliness.

It is true that Hölderlin's poem represents a figure (the Rhine as a riddle), but this representation is itself achieved by wordplay, articulated figuratively, forcing us not only to read the adjective *rein* homophonically as a noun or proper name (*Rhein*), but also to search for the meaning of that which is *Reinentsprungenes* in the different operations of the text itself. What we read is, in fact, a figure of figure. If the distinction de Man makes between riddle and enigma in "Allegory (*Julie*)" is applicable in the case of "The Rhine" (which he discusses in the earlier essay "The Riddle of Hölderlin"), one would have to read the *Räthsel* in *Ein Räthsel ist Reinentsprungenes* as a riddle, but the statement in which it occurs as an enigma.[27] That is, the riddle which originates purely in Hölderlin's poem hides, as de Man puts it, "a definite answer known from the beginning," an ultimate cause said to rest in a "holy womb," thus engendering a text which defers the answer in order to provide a narrative of hermeneutic fruition—much in the same manner as the river, moving away from its origin, is in search of a destiny able to provide it with "fulfillment." This riddle is not, "in itself, out of reach of knowledge," as de Man observes, "but is temporarily hidden from knowledge by a device of language that can, in turn, be deciphered only by another operation of language."[28] With the de Man of "Allegory (*Julie*)," we may now infer that this device of language, rather than constituting a riddle which it is ultimately possible to convert into knowledge by giving it a signified (for example, a sacred or extralinguistic origin) must be an instance of irresolvable textual complexity in the poem—a case of that linguistic predicament which he on more than one occasion calls "enigma."[29] Hölderlin's text thus seems to be something as paradoxical as the enigma of riddle.

The riddle that Hölderlin's poem thematizes and that carries the promise of an answer by narrating how the Rhine moves from a mystery toward a fully conscious fate is thus complicated by the enigma that the text construes by way of the pun on *Rhein* and *rein*. This later enigma "sullies" it in a way which is far from uninteresting: in contrast to a conventional pun, which changes meaning by changing articulation, Hölderlin's pun does not occur *as* sound. A shift in meaning comes about only by the arbitrary play of a letter, or the inscription of the most noiseless of alphabetical signs, the consonant *h*. Theorized by Hölderlin's near-contemporary Hamann in his "Neue Apologie des Buchstaben h von ihm selbst" and poetically mystified in Goethe as well as in Rilke, this elusive *h* has long haunted the German branch of theologically inclined linguistic speculation with its intimated nearness to *Hauch*, "breath."[30] Indicating an inaudible difference within an homophonic identity, it seems to amount to the pure spirit of the letter.

Neither semantically buried nor rhetorically veiled, either in Hölderlin or for that matter in Celan, the secret of this enigma is completely evident yet inaccessible to any hermeneutic excavation which would desire to bring it to light out of the semantic depths of language. It is no wonder that "Even song may hardly disclose it," as the poem goes on to say, since the nonaspirated *h* in *Rhein* is only buried in the impurity of a potentially ambiguous syllable, *Rein-*, in which it cannot be perceived when it is articulated, but only read as the elusive difference it makes by inscription. In contrast to the aspirated *h* in the verb *enthüllen*, "disclose," which is precisely *not* hidden when spoken but disclosed, this *h* is the pure silence occurring between *r* and *ein* in *Rein-*, troped in the most impure of linguistic mannerisms. It directs us, then, to that enigma of language of which Adorno, in his notes toward a theory of the hermetic work of art, allusively says that it is something that has originated but also absconded (*Entsprungenes*).[31]

In "Der Rhein," the movement described in genetic historical terms as a development in time and space is undermined by the medium in which the gradually arrived at knowledge of destiny is articulated. The riddle Rhine can always be interpreted, since it is built on a principle of depth and surface which is also thematized in the narrative of the poem. The enigma Rhine, however, does not permit such interpretation; rather, it demonstrates that the language constituting the story of the river's course toward its destiny undoes the genetic tropes at the disposal of such hermeneutic operation.

This problematic is rewritten by "Tübingen, Jänner," but in a way which no longer can be understood as a paraphrase of Hölderlin. On the contrary, Celan's poem seems to focus primarily on the enigmatic traits of the "Rhine" hymn. Its title, situating the text in time and space, draws attention to one of the poem's more intriguing details: the poem's manifest abundance of umlauts.³² Both *ü* and *ä*, already noticeable in the place (*Tübingen*) and time (*Jänner*), recur throughout, in particular in words of potential action—that is, in subjunctive verbs. Thus we have *käme* in lines 12, 13, and 14; *dürfte* in lines 16 and 19; and *spräch* in line 17. These subjunctive verbs, marking an action that *could* take place, revocalize the sonorous purity prevalent in "The Rhine," a text which in fact presents hardly any subjunctives, and turn "Tübingen, Jänner" into a poem written in an anything but pure idiom.

As muted, impure sounds, these umlauts seem to signal that something has happened in the transition from one text to the other. Exactly what has happened must remain putative, given the subjunctive tense, yet it can only with difficulty be understood by way of that "deobjectification" which Hugo Friedrich proposes as a characteristic trait of modern poetry, in which referential reliance is replaced by the language magic of *poésie pure*.³³ If there is a "deobjectifying" principle at work in Celan's poem, it would concern not a tendency of the poem to be uninterested in anything but its own euphonic euphoria, but an irreality having an important, though far from facile bearing on the particular (subjunctive) temporality created by its muted verbs.

In "Tübingen, Jänner," the umlauts tell a rather paratactic story of what would happen if "a man" came "into the world" of "today." Not only does the clarity of articulation seem to have undergone drastic change in comparison with Hölderlin's hymn (with its spontaneous confidence in the stability of the indicative), but blindness rather than clarity of sight seems to reign as well. This visual darkness is something that takes place in a transition identical to the one in the poem's opening, characterized by a blind violence. Should Celan's "man" arrive in such a grimly obscure world, he would be an *infans senex* already wearing a luminous beard (oddly reminiscent of the "blind, light- / bearded display wall" in "Frankfurt, September" ["Blinde, licht- / bärtige Stellwand"] [*GW* 2:114]). This curious being would be unable to speak in "the pure voice of youth" of Hölderlin's hymn, but only "babble and babble" in a tongue deprived of all reason, though not of all rhyme.

This inversion of the genetic pattern of understanding, informing "The Rhine" on the level of description if not on the level of figuration, has both acute complications and grave historical implications in "Tübingen, Jänner." If a man were to come into the world of today, the poem claims, he would be born at the end of his life—that is, he would already have (personal) history behind him. In this almost mock-apocalyptic scenario, the language spoken by Celan's *infans senex* could be redemptive only insofar as it sounded as sheer gobbledegook, devoid of the signifying power usually ascribed to language in order for it to be language. Instead of engraving his speech with the temporal deepening of meaning, the capacity of which is customarily attributed to history, the particular history constituting the ground for Celan's text would make the language of this man collapse into something like a pre-articulate but post-empirical gobble. A possible apocalypse, then, for which there would only be a language of incomprehensibility.

With history already behind him, the *lallen und lallen* of Celan's man would nevertheless not be the pure babble of an infant, unexposed to sign systems and inexperienced in language. Rather, it would be a seemingly unending string of sounds, impurely stuttering over and over again, deprived of semantic dignity but nonetheless carrying the empirical weight of an experience in all respects inarticulable. The source of this experience seems to rest in a loss of the sense of selfhood which has been claimed to run parallel to the loss of the representational function of poetry. Thus, as de Man puts it in an essay partly devoted to "Tübingen, Jänner," "ultimately, the function of representation is entirely taken over by sound effects."[34] In contrast to Friedrich's assumption, however, this mimetic collapse does not bring an end to reference or meaning in Celan. On the contrary, his babbling figure is articulated by repetitions and anacoluthons which, rather than denying him representationality, turn him into an exemplary figure of doubling and fragmentation.

In Hölderlin, the emphasis falls on the narrative of a consciousness originating in the (paradoxically) high depths of the Swiss Alps and unfolding in time and space. The poem describes the coming forth of its subject, the Rhine, as an origination out of an "abyss": "Im kältesten Abgrund hört' / Ich um Erlösung jammern / Den Jüngling."[35] The obscure power and significance of the river receives its momentum in an analogy of the way in which meaning is brought forth from the semantic depths of language. In the flow of time, this significance may stiffen into the consciously employed signs of poets, if we follow the dictum of "Andenken."[36] The mimetic aspect of Hölderlin's poem here lies in the text's dependency on an analogous relation between theme and narrative: the description of how the infant Rhine issues from the abyssal womb of the Swiss Alps, wrenches toward Asia in his early youth in order to stabilize according to his destiny, and wanders through the German lowlands as a mature man, able to found civilization along his path, is paralleled by a narrative which moves from the depths of an original and utterly incomprehensible mystery toward a notion of language that is less prey to a doctrine of spontaneity than susceptible to a notion of consciousness, ultimately incarnated by the perhaps most insistent literary agent of intentionality, Rousseau.

In Celan, this metaphysical movement, which in spatial terms is informed by a striving from depth to surface and in temporal terms by a movement from mysterious inception to a conscious fulfillment of destiny, is complicated to the point of reversal. Instead of a growing—if enigmatic—lucidity granted to us by language's power of mediation, we are provided with a linguistic movement leading into blindness. Furthermore, in contrast to "The Rhine," this blindness is entirely deprived of a syntactic proprietor, since the initial sentence of "Tübingen, Jänner" lacks a nominal subject. This syntactic incompleteness spills over into the next sentence: as in Hölderlin's "never, never does he forget it" in the seventh stanza of "The Rhine," something surely remembers in Celan, but there seems to be no person present as the agent of this memory.[37] At best we can say that it is language itself that remembers. What is remembered most clearly in Celan's poem is obviously the history of literature—that is, the line from Hölderlin inscribed in the text as quotation. Yet even if language remembers this fragment from its literary past, Celan's poem retains the otherness of this inserted piece of text and thus indicates an alterity not completely interiorized. Significant, too, is the fact that the line from Hölderlin inserted in "Tübingen, Jänner" is not only remembered, albeit blindly, but also indicates that which makes language historical: citationality.

In the "Visits of drowned carpenters to / these / submerging words" of the next stanza, the most important moment in Celan's reversal of the movement in Hölderlin is manifested. Instead of language originating purely, if not properly *in* purity, as in "The Rhine," Celan's poem has words dive into water on the surface of which fragments of memories are floating. This surface is linked to *Erinnerung*, or interiorizing memory, as an instance of remembrance that symbolically tries to incorporate that which belongs to a temporal anteriority—like the Rhine (of whom it was said in Hölderlin that "he will never, never forget" his past) carries within itself the riddling origin out of which it once sprung. Oddly, then, Celan's *Erinnerung* is associated not with the unfathomable depth of waters—that reservoir of meaning from which poetry archetypically wells up its inspiration—but explicitly with its surface. His *Erinnerung* thus takes on the character usually ascribed to *Gedächtnis*, that technical memory which made it possible for the miserable Paul Valéry, for example, unable to commit to memory any poetry, to memorize the strange poems of Mallarmé. But this is far from saying, as Friedrich does of the mnemotechnically impotent Valéry, that the insistence on a sonority disconnected from meaning, promoting recollective staying power, "characterizes the works of any number of twentieth-century poets and is often the only standard for measuring the quality of a poem."[38]

By way of the inversion of *Erinnerung* and *Gedächtnis*, "Tübingen, Jänner" allows interiorizing memory to be manifested on the surface and exterior or mechanical memory to reside in the depths. In effect, language seems to interiorize itself according to the logic of precisely that principle which does not permit interiorization. It pierces—or dives—through the surface of *Erinnerung*, but only comes up with words phrased in a halting diction marked by its mechanical repetition of locutions and syllables. These stuttering repetitions take on the qualities of the hypothetical babble which is said to be the only way for its "man" to speak of "today," the poem becoming a symptom of that for which it fails to account.

Thus in "Tübingen, Jänner," the mechanically tainted, impurely stuttering chatter—which in Friedrich's reading of hermeticism amounted to a "faddish gesticulation ... chattering away at random"[39]—is the experience of time in and through language. If he spoke of "this / time," the nonsensical drivel of Celan's *Mensch* would be organized in accordance with the principle of syntax rather than of semantics: devoid of content, the speech of this "man" would lack meaningful depth, only able to reiterate itself "over, over / againagain." In this syntax, only repetition, an essentially temporal movement of figuration, seems able to permit an experience of time which secures the possibility of memory.

Through the mechanical memory of language itself, the *Lallen* of "Tübingen, Jänner" may also be distantly reminiscent of some words by August Stramm, the Expressionist and latter-day aspirer to Cratylic language theory. In a letter to Herwarth and Nell Walden on February 25, 1915, Stramm, describing himself as "trunken" and repeatedly referring to himself with the deictic "dieser," writes with the usual paratactic verve: "I am a riddle. Who unriddles the riddle. Am I a riddle, you the one feeling [*Empfinder*]. You are the solver. It does not solve any riddle. It only carries it on into further riddles." And he continues, in part untranslatably: "Wo sind Worte für die Worte. Ich bin trunken. Ich habe keine Worte, nur Lallen. Lallen! Ich lall das Weltall an und das Weltall lallt."[40]

While it would be foreign for Celan to espouse the holistic onomatopoeia of Stramm, the constellation of tropes organizing his pseudo-poppycock moves sufficiently close to the tropological movements of "Tübingen, Jänner" to suggest an affinity if not on the level of *Erinnerung*, then on the level of *Gedächtnis*. Thematically, "Tübingen, Jänner" reiterates several of the elements informing Stramm's letter, but it may be the mechanical remembering of language itself that most persuasively stresses its point—demonstrating, as it does, that there are only babbling words for words, only their disfiguring, mutilating repetition in ever-new syntactic constellations.

Resisting the tendency to synthesis and certainly withstanding the effacement of distinction implicit in Stramm's letter, the mechanical repetitiveness of Celan's "man" undermines the category of meaning traditionally secured through *Erinnerung* and underscores a memory which can only remember by pointing to the impossibility of maintaining in words the stable meaning of phenomenal events. It is, as Celan says himself in the Bremen address, an "enriched" language, a language which has gone "through its own lack of answers, through terrifying silence, through the thousand darknesses of murderous speech (*GW* 3:185–86/*CP* 34).

Naming occurs in the depths of language, Celan is reported to have said in conversation with Dietlind Meinecke.[41] This observation, which can be brought to bear on many poems in his oeuvre, takes on a crucial significance in "Tübingen, Jänner." In Celan, it is through the paradoxical submerging into that which nevertheless remains external that words seem to receive their identity and can in turn name.

Language is the medium of remembrance, but a medium which does not interiorize the remembered so much as it repeats it figuratively. This logic may recall that of Hölderlin's *Ein Räthsel ist Reinentsprungenes* in that it, too, allows for a reversal—here of surface and depth. One could thus observe that the subjunctive prolepsis of "a man [coming] into the world, today," hinges on the second stanza's "bei / diesen / tauchenden Worten." The augury literally consists in "these . . . words," in fact, since the deictic *diesen* with the subsequent colon clarifies a relation which must be read as a predication. The "babble" that may emerge "today" thus seems to be the prattle before baptism of a baby born very old. This babble exists in a state prior to naming and hence to the legal formation of identity, but does not possess the purity of an ordinary infant, not yet cognizant of the particular memories which come with words. On the contrary, the *lallen und lallen* of Celan's *infans senex* is charged with history and experience, "enriched," as the Bremen address has it, yet it is not until "these . . . words" of the poem have plunged into the superficial depths of language that this "babble" can acquire its name.

Not capable of conserving the natural entity or event it names, this mechanical memory nonetheless assures us of a constancy similar to that analyzed by Szondi in his interpretation of Celan's German rendition of Shakespeare's Sonnet 105. In contrast to "The Rhine," in which language originated purely and untainted, the oblique baptism performed by the diving words in "Tübingen, Jänner" attempts to conserve not so much the meaning of language as its structural movement. Thus the disfiguring syntax of the poem is not history in the sense of time conceived of as progressive disintegration, but paradoxically as that which defies temporality. Far from wishing to forget the grave significance of historical events, Celan's poetry attempts to maintain its constancy in the ordering of language.

In this poetry, there seems to be little nostalgia for an Adamic tongue ignorant of linguistic arbitrariness and originating in the same pure fashion as flowers. Words can only acquire their name by piercing the shimmering surface on which memory floats. Only by submerging into the interior exterior of experience can language project—and in "Tübingen, Jänner" memory is in an uncanny sense projected toward the future. The language constituting it is already impure prior to its nominalization—that is, before its solidification into names—and seems to hover in the suspension between a past which it can only repeat figuratively, from afar, and a hypothetical future which it is merely able to articulate as the wounded syntax of babble.

Hence the "today" of which Celan's poem speaks could indeed constitute that "dürftige Zeit" of which Hölderlin spoke in the seventh stanza of "Bread and Wine."[42] That this designation is not bereft of reason—though its temporal reference may be—is indicated by the paranomastic inscription of *dürft' Zeit* in the poem's statement "er *dürf*te, / spräch er von dieser / Zeit." The subjunctive prediction *er dürfte* contaminates the future *Zeit* which it hypothesizes, thus paranomastically becoming part of the crisis it seeks to foresee.[43]

Yet perhaps the most interesting interpenetration of interiority and exteriority in "Tübingen, Jänner" occurs at the very end of the poem, in its concluding single-line stanza *("Pallaksch. Pallaksch.")*. As many critics have pointed out, Bernhard Böschenstein being first, the word *Pallaksch* is reported to have been used by the mad Hölderlin during the years of illness in the tower by the Necker in Tübingen. The young poet Christoph Theodor Schwab noted in his diary that, depending on the context, Hölderlin expletive expression could mean either "yes" or "no."[44] This "non-word," to borrow the designation offered by Schelling,[45] is a curious fold in the texture of Celan's poem. The quotation marks maintain the foreign nature of the words, thus signaling something exterior to the text signed by Celan, while the parenthesis not only brackets the repetition of an already ambiguous word, but also marks the interiorization of this locution, inscribing it further into the poem.[46] As in the reversal performed by the "diving words," again we have an exterior imbedded in an interior, an outside brought deeper into the text to which it nevertheless remains external.

In comparison with the quotation from "The Rhine," which was still liminally, albeit ambiguously, integrated into Celan's poem, the ending parenthesis of "Tübingen, Jänner" is more rigorously set apart from the remainder of the text; and whereas the earlier quotation stemmed from something written during Hölderlin sanity, the latter originates from the realm of language spoken during the years of his madness. What is remarkable, however, is that both insertions make a difference only when read, since the poem's traces of the writer as reader—dashes, quotation marks, parentheses—will never be perceived if it is spoken. The graphic distinction is thus not complemented by an auditory one, yet through the concluding repetition of *Pallaksch*, Celan allusively relates the second quotation to the first: by means of ono-matopoeia—that is, by means of figuring the coinciding of name and reference in sound—the splashing of the Necker against its banks re-calls the tumultuous Rhine whose banks, according to Hölderlin's poem, "slink to his side."[47] Aligning the mechanical production of sound with the submerging words in the second stanza (the exact point of reversal in a poem numbering twenty-two-plus-one lines, where the twenty-second line ends as the first one begins, though in duplication), the repetition of *Pallaksch* also figures the sound of these diving words into the superficial depths of language where they are given name.

Celan's onomatopoeia, literally "name-making," takes on the qual-ity of a word which anagrammatically ties together "*Pa*triarchen," "*lal*-len," "*k*äme," and "Men*sch*," and indicates the way in which Celan in-scribes that which makes a difference without being reducible to volatile meaning. The interiorization necessary for the constitution of individu-ation is here turned inside out, with the result that the effacement of proper subject in the poem—connected with the violently blinding transition performed by language in the opening lines ("über- / re-dete"), and possibly also with drowning—gives the mention of *Mensch* a generality which cannot be assigned to any determinable historical person (Moses, Hölderlin, or anyone else).[48] While the repetition of *Pallaksch* remains exterior, it nevertheless operates in the interior of the poem, constructing an utterance of insoluble undecidability—doubly signifying here yes, there no. Its enigmatic quality resists solution, since it is inextricably bound up with a mechanical duplicity of language which makes it impossible to decide whether the expression borrowed from Hölderlin only repeats its meaning (yes or no) or corrects itself the second time (sounding the same, but meaning the opposite). Being "these ... words," Celan's diving vocables effectively act out what "Sprich auch du" imperatively requests: "Speak—/But do not split no from yes" (*GW* 1:135/*P* 99).

This is the baptizing speech act that Celan's diving words perform: they name undecidability. The particular name that these submerging words emerge with—*Pallaksch*—is a quotation, an idiomatic remnant from a time of the loss of a legal selfhood, marking a historical linguistic event. Yet by surviving in the form of quotation, this name also implies the absence of that which is quoted—thus pointing to a sense of future which has already been. It marks a *futurum exactum*, paradoxically hypo-thetical—as the coming of Celan's *infans senex*, who, if he spoke of this time of dearth, could only continually repeat (that is, quote) himself, surviving his own time through the scanty but uncanny temporality of language.

"Tübingen, Jänner" may be read as an *Auseinandersetzung* with that literary historiography built on a belief in development, in which poetry gradually becomes more and more preoccupied with its own internal problems until it ultimately refers only to itself in hermetic—albeit negative—self-indulgence. In such a historiography, the final or at least "modern" stage is a linguistically "magic" *poésie pure* devoid of ambition to refer to anything at all.

In Celan's poem there may be a destruction of the conventional ways for language to refer to history, but the result is no sweet, though rather pointless song. On the contrary, "Tübingen, Jänner" demonstrates a poetic language marked by history whose ability to foresee coming time visionarily must be considered highly dubious. Not only does blindness reign, but the genetic metaphors usually articulating the understanding of the historical development of literature from a mimetic to an allegorical mode are also thrown into doubt: if anyone would be born today, it would be an old man who could only "babble" incomprehensibly "if he spoke of this / time." Moreover, there is a radical inversion in the text of the spatial paradigm of interior and exterior, essential and superfluous, conventionally determining the organizing role of memory for existence. Celan's poem is no example of hermetic poetry locked into an ivory tower, but rather a way of writing marked by that unnameable linguistic "enrichment" constituting its particular history. The text may be allegorical, but then it is an allegory which "can only blindly repeat its earlier model, without final understanding," as de Man points out, revealing "the paradoxical nature of a structure that makes lyric poetry into an enigma which never stops asking for the unreachable answer to its own riddle."[49]

In his *Aesthetic Theory*, Adorno alludes to this complication when he writes:

> Hermetic poetry thematizes a problem that was unconsciously present in art earlier on, namely the problem of interdependence between artistic production and the way in which this productive process is reflected in itself. . . . In the more than eighty years since Mallarmé, the history of hermetic poetry has undergone considerable change, reflecting change in the social realm. The cliché about ivory-tower art certainly fails to do justice to the windowless creations of hermetic poetry. In the beginning there was some half narrow-minded, half desperate ebullience: hermetic poetry was a religion of art trying to convince itself that the only purpose in life was a beautiful verse or a perfect period. This has changed. In Paul Celan, the greatest exponent of hermetic poetry in present-day Germany, the experiential content of the hermetic is the opposite of what it was previously. His poetry is permeated by a sense of shame stemming from the fact that art is

unable either to experience or to sublimate suffering. Celan's poems articulate unspeakable horror by being silent; their truth content itself becomes something negative. They emulate a language that lies below the helpless prattle of human beings—even below the level of organic life as such. It is the language of dead matter, of stones and stars.[50]

This observation is important and underlines what cannot be emphasized enough: Celan's poetry tries to speak for the dead. Nonetheless, it may be asked to what extent dead matter, such as stones and stars, has the capacity to speak without being animated through figuration—thus being promoted rhetorically, by means of prosopopoeia, to the level of organic life. What seems questionable in Adorno's interpretation of Celan, however, is the way in which it confers a sense of shame on Celan's poetry said to stem from is inability to "experience or sublimate suffering." It may indeed be true that the experience of death cannot be mediated in living language, except perhaps in texts such as Kafka's "Gracchus der Jäger," and it may also be true that one of the emotive codes at work in Celan's poetry is shame. Nonetheless, many of his poems, "Tübingen, Jänner" being one example, do in fact render accessible an experience of suffering—albeit in a manner different from the one intended by Adorno: linguistically.

Adorno is certainly right in claiming that the "truth content" of Celan's poetry situates itself in relation to negativity. Yet many of his poems seem nourished by a contradictory hope moving toward an unlocated light for which they propose ever-new designations—laying out a topology to be read "in light of what is still to be searched for: in light of u-topia (*GW* 3:199/*CP* 51 [trans. modified]). Celan's poetry may emulate the language of stones and stars, but it remains an open question whether it thus "brings to completion Baudelaire's task, which according to Benjamin was to write poetry without an aura."[51] The stones of Celan's poems are understandably different from the material shaping Apollinian torsos in *Neue Gedichte*, for instance, and their stars do not constitute auratic points of sideral fixation as in the tenth of the *Duineser Elegien*—to use the examples of a post-Baudelairean poet in German. Yet as "Engführung," among other poems, indicates, Celan's poetry contains its own version of light—a more negative and less immaterially ethereal light than that of Rilke. And it is here that Celan's singular treatment of that "nothing of voice" of which Kafka spoke takes on its particular significance, since the "truth content" of this light itself becomes something negative.

"How can one write nothing?," asks Derrida in his reading of Celan, implicitly addressing the possibility of understanding such negativity in light of historically determinable *topoi* in literature.[52] This question, the subject of which is historicized by Friedrich as a thematic category of post-Romantic writing, may remain more posed than answered by Derrida; yet by remaining open, it points to a way of approaching nothingness different from the one offered in Friedrich's reading of Mallarmé, where it is aesthetically recuperated by a notion of *poésie pure*.

In Derrida's reading, nothingness is irreducibly linked to writing in a way which has little to do with the free, sonorous sway of language magic. Perhaps the most important poem from Celan's middle period, "Engführung" points to this juncture of writing and nothingness with exemplary precision (*GW* 1:197–204/*P* 136–49). It has been interpreted as a critical reading of its euphonically more naive precursor, "Todesfuge" (*GW* 1:41–42/*P* 60–63), with which it shares a fugal composition. Raising the question of readability, however, it reinscribes a set of deeply troubling problems in a manner which obliquely undoes whatever uncomplicated, albeit coolly desperate faith in the salvaging power of naming may have been prevalent in "Todesfuge." Both poems are concerned with the Holocaust, but while "Todesfuge" still participates in a tradition the poetic assumptions of which are essentially aesthetic, "Engführung" must be read as a critique of the ideology constituting this *via regia* of eloquence in literature. In contrast to "Todesfuge," it chooses a language essentially at odds with a tradition based on the verbal fluency of beauty, in which the salvation of poetry—the extent to which it exists—resides in a beautiful verse or a perfect period.

Instead, "Engführung" chooses the language of the deprivation of language in an attempt to circumscribe the incomparable. A certain marker of punctuation shows this with particular exactness, and in order finally to trace the material inscription of history in Celan, I will conclude by focusing on the acute importance of punctuation for the organization of "Engführung." To limit the reading of a poem of some eight to ten pages to markers of punctuation leaves almost nothing left, one might feel compelled to object, and rightly so, though in this particular case nothing makes all the difference. I will, however, also be concerned in passing with a chiasmus already encountered in the crossing of interior and exterior articulated by "Tübingen, Jänner." This chiasmus demonstrates the precarious way in which Celan grounds his poetry; and the poem's punctuation may indicate how he tries to write that nothing which lacks comparison.

As a technical term, *Engführung*, or "stretto," refers to a device employed in the composition of fugues. An artifice by which theme and figure overlap, it gives a "direction," in the definition proposed by the *Oxford English Dictionary*, "to perform a passage, especially a final passage, in quicker time."[53] The definition, by underscoring the elliptical way in which the poem is written, also points to that passage from content to structure which Renate Böschenstein-Schäfer has suggested is characteristic of Celan's mature poetry, which Szondi noted when he observed "a shift in accent from the person who is being praised to the act of praising or composing," and which the "Meridian" indirectly points to when speaking of "the faster flow of syntax or a more awakened sense of ellipsis" in "the poem today."[54]

Derrida touches upon the latter feature of "Engführung" in referring to "the rhythm of its own caesuras,"[55] and Szondi, in what may still be the most attentive reading of the poem, speaks of the former as a renunciation of discursive speech, suggesting that the textual links "are realized musically."[56] Both remarks emphasize the importance of transition; already in the poem's first stanza we encounter its tropological significance. By opening with the assertion

> VERBRACHT ins
> Gelände
> mit der untrüglichen Spur
>   (*GW* 1:197)

> (PASSED into the
> terrain
> with the unmistakable trace
>   (*P* 137 [trans. modified])

Celan's poem attempts to create in allegorical form a relation between the deportation which leads to the death camps and the deportation which carries the reader not only from the exterior to the interior of the text, but also allows him or her to experience this violent transition in an act of reading reminiscent of the one offered by "Tübingen, Jänner."

Relying on the subsequent imperatives

> Lies nicht mehr—schau!
> Schau nicht mehr—geh!
>   (*GW* 1:197)

> (Read no more—look!
> Look no more—go!)
>   (*P* 137 [trans. modified])

and proposing "that there is a path the text opens," Szondi concludes: "it is the path the reader should take."[57] This observation is paralleled theoretically in the distinction between reading and interpretation that Szondi tries to elaborate.[58] Of the "premise" of this enterprise, he writes that the poem "demands less that the meaning of words be taken into consideration than that their function be considered." Involving the reading of the text as a musical score rather than the interpretation of it in terms of the representation of a given semantic content, this distinction indicates that Szondi is more interested in the "in-between" or the material of which relations are made.

Advancing the idea that, "fundamentally, there is no representation," Szondi emphasizes: "Poetry is not *mimesis*, no longer representation"; "it becomes reality. Poetic reality, to be sure—text—and no longer follows any reality, but lays itself out and constitutes itself as reality." Accordingly, he prefers to interpret the reading and seeing mentioned in the passage above as activities corresponding to the mimetic aspect of the poem, whereas walking amounts to an allegorical activity which permits us to experience that which the text is. Relying on the fugal composition of "Engführung," where the semantic weight of the text is less crucial than the pattern of its syntactic texture, he remarks: "the reading subject coincides with the subject of the poem that is read."[59] What the poem demonstrates is in some way also the reading of its text.

But if Celan's poem proposes an allegory of reading, this would imply that the conception of writing as a reproduction of speech be reassessed—not least because it is precisely writing that the poem thematizes. Nonetheless, Szondi seems to read the written text as reproduced speech: the distinction between text and extralinguistic reality on which he bases his interpretation in order to define the relationship between mimetic and allegorical poetry is not matched by a corresponding distinction between spoken and written language. One could thus pose the question, as one critic does: "Why would the written character [*Schriftlichkeit*] of a poem, which among other things speaks of that which is written, not belong to the reality as which it constitutes itself?"[60]

Stating in the opening stanza: "PASSED into the / terrain / with the unmistakable trace," "Engführung" directs attention to the textual character of the area it lays out to read. Aware of the catastrophic tonality of the poem, Szondi develops the idea that what it unfolds "is the terrain of death and mourning."[61] Reading here becomes an experience allegorically troped on the walking through the *Gelände* of a death camp. Yet this experience is only made possible through an act which we are nonetheless asked to give up—the development from reading to seeing to walking being the result of an activity the poem demands be overcome. Reading becomes a question of not obeying the imperative of the text ("Do not read"), and thus must exert violence in each step of its process.

The disadvantage of Szondi's compelling view—where a "poetic reality" guarantees a resistance to extinction that is of a linguistic order— is that it does not seem able to account for this complication. Despite its sense for "shape" and "contour," to use the terms of the "Meridian," it overlooks the materiality of Celan's poem. This materiality or *Schrift-lichkeit* cannot be understood as the representation of speech. Is there, then, a more text-centered way of reading the development from reading to seeing to walking which can account for the intricate self-reflexivity of Celan's poem, while at the same time not disregarding the implications of the fact that reading, by not obeying the imperative of the text, exerts hermeneutical violence?

Hans-Jost Frey, who partly poses this question, points to the "trace" of the first strophe and claims that where there is a trace, there is no longer any walking: "The trace is not where one walks, but where one has walked. It is what remains and has become visible after the walking. The trace is writing."[62] In such a process, reminiscent of Novalis's reflections in the Telpitz fragment quoted earlier, the relationship between the markers of an irretrievable anteriority (traces) and a Now consisting of that act of reading we are nonetheless asked to give up is primarily a question of the poem's temporality. As an "allegory of absolute terror,"[63] "Engführung" poses this question in all its acuity. Not only can it be noticed in the stenographic arrangement of the poem, in which the text's elliptical character is signaled by the *Eng* of the title (corresponding to the Greek word for "narrow" or "strict," *stenos*), but in its third strophe time is also thematized explicitly. With reference to a sleep which "came over them," it is there said:

> Kam, kam. Nirgends
>   fragt es—
> Ich bins, ich,
> ich lag zwischen euch, ich war
> offen, war
> hörbar, ich tickte euch zu, euer Atem
> gehorchte, ich
> bin es noch immer, ihr
> schlaft ja.
>   (*GW* 1:198)

> (Came, came. Nowhere
>   anyone asks—
> It is I, I,
> I lay between you, I was
> open, was
> audible, ticked toward you, your breathing
> obeyed, it is
> I still, but then
> you are asleep.)
>   (*P* 139 [trans. modified])

As Szondi remarks, the verb *ticken* signifies both "to tick" and "to touch with fingers." That which ticks and touches, he therefore concludes, is "at the same moment the emblem of time," the clock, and "time itself, temporality."[64] Time is thus phenomenalized through anthropomorphism, *ich tickte euch zu*. This anthropomorphized temporality—given hands, as it were, to indicate itself and phenomenalized in audible ticking—places an invisible equal sign between life and listening, which allows for an exchange of attributes, not only perforating the boundaries that separate innate substance from a limitless movement devoid of materiality, but also piercing the bar that keeps sound, always prey to disappearance, separate from mute durability.

Temporality becomes "listenable" ("ich war . . . hörbar, ich tickte euch zu"), and the listenability refers to an act of touching. Szondi interprets this listenability of time as life approaching those who are deprived of hearing, the deaf, the lost souls, enveloped in the diminutive of death: sleep. A series of oppositions is thus construed—between life and death, speech and muteness, that which can walk and move around (and possesses phenomenal traits) and that which can only be read in "traces" (that is, material markers). This polarization may be brought to bear on the earlier distinction between spoken and written language, and its implications may be best pursued in the structural composition of the poem.

"Engführung" consists of nine stanzas, developing a "contrapuntal bringing-together of themes."[65] Szondi distinguishes a pattern, based on the formula 4+1+4, in which the first five stanzas are governed by a temporal succession from present to past, and the last five stanzas reverse this succession, going from past to present.[66] The formula allows the middle section to belong to both temporal movements, from present to past to present. This periodic structure—already codified in Hermogenes, who talks of "chiasmatic periods"[67]—is clearly reminiscent of Hölderlin's theory of the alternation of tones and periods. In his notes to the translation of *Oedipus*, Hölderlin addresses the concerns of "today's poets" and outlines a fragmentary theory of "lawful calculation." Although he specifically discusses the nature of tragedy, limiting his observations to the genre of drama, his understanding of the caesura, which is explicitly borrowed from the discursive realm of "poetic meter," gives it a bearing on poetry as well.

In "the rhythmic sequence of the representations," Hölderlin writes, "wherein *transport* presents itself, there becomes necessary *what in poetic meter is called caesura*, the pure word, the counter-rhythmic rupture; namely, in order to meet the onrushing change of representations at its highest point in such a manner that very soon there does not appear the change of representation but the representation itself."[68] This caesura does not express anything it itself; it only does so *that* something appears. It amounts to the form of representation, but not the representation itself. Not having a determinable content, it consists in a stasis in time, as sudden as empty, in which the past is separated from the future in a manner which does not allow the realms of anteriority and posteriority to unite in a temporal integrity. The caesura is pure rupture; it marks a moment of the expressionless, to use Benjamin's reflexion in his essay on Goethe.[69]

In this regard, the passage immediately preceding the middle stanza of "Engführung," which Szondi variously nominates as being "the focus of the composition" and its "central part,"[70] takes on a particular importance. It is literally the turning point of the text at which the grammatical temporality of the poem is acutely disrupted. The fourth and fifth stanzas read:

> Bin es noch immer—
> Jahre.
> Jahre, Jahre, ein Finger
> tastet hinab und hinan, tastet
> umher:
> Nahtstellen, fühlbar, hier
> klafft es weit auseinander, hier
> wuchs es wieder zusammen—wer
> deckte es zu?
>
> *
>
> Deckte es
> zu—wer?
> Kam, kam.
> Kam ein Wort, kam,
> kam durch die Nacht,
> wollt leuchten, wollt leuchten.
>
> Asche.
> Asche, Asche.
> Nacht.
> Nacht-und-Nacht.—Zum
> Aug geh, zum feuchten.
> (*GW* 1:199)
>
> (It is I still—
> Years.
> Years, years, a finger
> gropes down and up, gropes
> around:
> seams, palpable, here

it is split wide open, here
it grew together again—who
covered it up?

*

        Covered it
           up—who?
Came, came.
Came a word, came,
came through the night,
wanted to shine, wanted to shine.

Ashes.
Ashes, ashes.
Night.
Night-and-night.—Go
to the eye, the moist one.)
(*P* 139–41 [trans. modified])

What was put previously in the mode of subjectivity—"Ich bins . . .
ich tickte euch zu"—has now become a category of calculable time,
Jahre. This measure of time, thrice repeated, is then paratactically extended to *ein Finger.* The subjectivity which was one of pure and phenomenalized motion in the earlier section, "ich tickte euch zu," has now
frozen into semantic concretion at the expense of fluid temporality: "ein
Finger / tastet." The description of the moving finger is then further
transformed. The two subsequent lines end with *hier,* changing the figure of the finger into a deictic gesture—which allows language to turn
itself into something which is taking place and can be referred to,
"here."
In "Engführung," this act of pointing has to do with *Nahtstellen.*
Indicating a wound at once open and sewn together, these "seams" are
the stitches by which the sensuous, or "palpable," and the abyssal are
tied together. Not wanting to ask the meaning of this, Szondi expresses
the discreet wish to read what thereafter occurs as an inversion between
the fourth and fifth stanzas of the poem: "wer / *deckte es zu? // * //*
Deckte es / zu—wer?" Congruent with Hölderlin's thoughts about the
"tragic transport," he reads it as an "abyss" and a "rupture."[71] If one
follows Hölderlin, however (which Szondi does not do explicitly), it
may be noted, too, that the inversion of syntagms in this abyssal passage,
"here," performs a syntactically perfect chiasmus. The text asks "who
covered it up?," a question inverted in the subsequent stanza: "Covered
it / up—who?"

Considered as speech acts, these anguished questions seem enacted unknowingly. As all nonrhetorical questions, they are in fact non-constantive since they do not provide any answer. They find their ground in groundlessness—a fact which has its direct correlate in the temporal structure in whose "abyss" Szondi likes to find the focus of the poem's two chiasmatical questions, in the transition from the fourth to the fifth strophe. This chiasmus—the crucial significance of which did not elude Celan, who writes in an adjacent note to the "Meridian," contained in the unpublished *Nachlaß*: "In the chiasmus, the cross is closer than the theme 'cross'"[72]—describes a cross–shaped arrangement over an abyss which does not seem possible to fill with meaning. Having its root in a letter and not a word (the Greek—and ultimately Phoeni-cian—letter *chi* [χ]), the figure literally lacks grounding in semantics. Acquiring significance only in the performative, as a figure, Celan's chi-asmus marks the tropological movement over an abyss which cannot be endowed with meaning. This abyss gapes open, grows together again, but lacks the meaningful ground that could answer the chiasmatically arranged questions. Open but not accessible, veiled but not sealed, this is the "abyss" out of which Celan's poem seems to speak.

Whereas a poem such as "Todesfuge" retreats into surrealistic sym-bolism, juxtaposing the golden blond Margarethe and the ashen haired Sulamith, "Engführung" is a renunciation of naming that which cannot be named, a refusal to utter that which resists articulation. Szondi clearly perceives this crux in reading Celan. Yet something seems lost in his reading: strictly speaking, *nothing* is lost. Klaus Voswinckel touches upon this point indirectly when he writes that in "a manner of elocution" such as that of "Engführung," "the extinction of the starlike word turns into an immediately shattering occurrence."[73] It is crucial to stress this turn into a disruptive transition—this *gegenrythmische Unter-brechung*, in Hölderlin's words—executed through the annihilation of a "starlike word." What occurs at the turning point of "Engführung" is a figure, a chiasmus, through which the temporal movement of the text is dramatically inverted. Granted, no "starlike word" is uttered at the heart of this expressionless caesura, but a sign does occur: an asterisk.

This graphic marker, used nine times, silently punctuates the ellip-tical course of "Engführung."[74] Asterisks, however, are also stars. Al-though they can hardly be said to carry meaning, devoid as they are of semantic ambition, they serve a function. Compositionally they make a difference, giving the text "the rhythm of its own caesuras," as Derrida puts it, or they "write apart," as "Engführung" itself has it when twice referring to grass that is "auseinandergeschrieben" (*GW* 1:197 and 204). Yet the asterisks occur in between, in the chasms separating the stanzas of the poem. It is not surprising, then, that Szondi passes over these graphic markers: after all, alphabetically speaking, they amount to noth-ing. They cannot be uttered in any other form than through the refusal to utter, in silence, as something that goes without saying. Contrary to Adorno's assertion, in "Engführung" Celan's poetry does not speak the language of stars: at this point, it is strictly expressionless.

"Es stand auch geschrieben, daß" (*GW* 1:200) ("It was written too, that" [*P* 143 (trans. modified)]), as the poem puts it rather abruptly in the sixth stanza, paraphrasing biblical locutions and perhaps alluding to the *Daß* of Martin Buber.[75] By means of anacoluthon, breaking off at a point where nothing can be stated, it questions itself and continues in an instructively interrogative mode: "Wo? Wir / taten ein Schweigen darüber" (*GW* 1:200) ("Where? We / passed a silence over it" [*P* 143 (trans. modified)]). Reminiscent of the covering of the chiasmatically arranged questions, the prepositional *darüber* ("over," "thereover") indicates that the answer to *Wo?* cannot be given other than through silence—a silence which nonetheless will veil precisely nothing in terms of speech acts. This nothing cannot be articulated, yet it is not identical with the silence passed over it. The asterisks mark a positional act, it is true, but what they posit is negative, an absence of language. They function as the material inscription of this unspeakability, bereft of the semantic dignity which always goes along with speech.

If the manner of writing in "Engführung" is stenographic, a reading invited by the elliptical construction of the poem, the analogy could be developed further: as stenography, the poem prompts us to read its text as the transcription of a dictation. Not only does a stenography respond to something which is dictated (by a voice no longer present), but that which dictates may well be the imperative to remember those particular "data of remembrance," in Benjamin's phrase,[76] which constitute the poem and the loss they intimate. After the "All-burning," in Derrida's literal translation of Holocaust,[77] nothing remains, only "the ashes of burned-out meaning," as Celan's text on Jené has it—or "Asche. / Asche, Asche," in the painful conjuration of "Engführung," unable to express anything but the impossible name of that which was once denied voice.

In Celan, the Holocaust is never mentioned by name. Unable to give this event adequate designation, his poetry can only refer to "that which happened" ("das, was geschah") (*GW* 3:186/*CP* 34 [trans. modified]). Yet precisely in the materiality of the poem, one finds the traces of this nothing as something irreducibly written, neither audible nor transcribable, yet curiously, singularly, translatable—something which could never have been dictated and is only to be read: "*."

Celan demonstrates that poetry after Auschwitz is possible, but solely when grounded on an impossibility. The signs of this possible impossibility are inscribed in the text as the constellation around which the poem is grouped and in the sign of which its data of remembrance must be read. Szondi, who attentively cites Mallarmé from "Crise de vers," could also have quoted the "alphabet of stars" in the section on

"L'action restreinte" in *Variations sur un sujet*, of which "Crise de vers" is a part. In effect, this alphabet would be the closest we come to Adorno's language of stars. But he could also have quoted some other lines of this poet of the abyss. In "Un coup de dés," it is said with a dictum as famous as enigmatic: "Nothing may have taken place but the place except perhaps a constellation."[78]

The particular constellation created in "Engführung," whose sideral constancy coincides with the poem's own materiality, constitutes an image like the one in which history becomes readable according to Benjamin. Only marking the rhythm of the poem's caesuras, the asterisks put an accent on the text which must be that of reading. They are "traces" in a strict sense and as such historical, yet their particular history is one which only occurs in an act of reading enforced against the expressed will of the poem. Their inscription must be observed in a highly paradoxical Now, an actual history dependent on that *Schriftlichkeit* which is the condition of possibility of the text. This constellation would finally amount to an inscriptional occurrence—or a graphic example of what de Man enigmatically terms "the materiality of actual history."[79]

Celan's poetry, aspiring "to chart . . . reality," as the Bremen address puts it (*GW* 3:186/*CP* 34), can only posit "ein blindes // E s s e i" ("a blind // L e t t h e r e b e"), in the phrase of "Die Silbe Schmerz" (*GW* 1:281). There may be a fiat, able to posit regardless of presence, but it remains unable to give luminous foundation to what is instituted. As "Die Silbe Schmerz" indicates, this blind fiat can only be written in outline, as a *gesperrter Schrift* which forever "bars" the access to that which it has blindly posited, but by the same token prevents it from being deported from the text into which it has been inscribed. Out of this resistance to elucidation, out of this barred fiat, which is one with the text's materiality and has to do neither with the concealment of meaning nor with the phenomenality of light, Celan's poetry abysmally spells itself forth in a sarcastically apocalyptic scenario:

> . . . ein
> Knoten
> (und Wider- und Gegen- und Aber- und Zwillings- und Tau-
> sendknoten) an dem
> die fastnachtsäugige Brut
> der Mardersterne im Abgrund
> buch-, buch-, buch-
> stabierte, stabierte.
> (*GW* 1:280)

(... a
knot
[and contrary- and against- and but- and twin- and thou-
sand-knot], which
the Shrove Tuesday eyed bride
of the marten stars in the abyss
spelled, spelled, spelled
out, out.)

The pain thematized throughout Celan's poetry here becomes the wounding of syntax, the cutting agony of language itself. The abyssal stars from which it is brought forth are not the stars of any maternal generation, but of theft and deprivation (*Marder* carrying the double weight of "marten" and "thief"). Celan deftly rewrites the tenth of Rilke's *Duino Elegies*, in which it is said:

Und höher, die Sterne. Neue. Die Sterne des Leidlands.
Langsam nennt sie die Klage:–Hier,
siehe: den *Reiter*, den *Stab*, und das vollere Sternbild
nennen sie: *Fruchtkranz*. Dann, weiter, dem Pol zu:
Wiege; *Weg*; *Das Brennende Buch*; *Puppe*; Fenster.
Aber im südlichen Himmel, rein wie im Innern
einer gesegneten Hand, das klar erglänzende '*M*',
das die Mütter bedeutet. . . . .—[80]

In Rilke, writing is troped on fictive star constellations bearing names such as *Der Stab* and *Das Brennende Buch*. The final yet originating constellation, as pure and immaculate as the interior of a blessing hand, is the "clearly-resplendent '*M*,' / standing for Mothers." In Celan, this initial of life and language is neither genetic nor blessing anything; it only stands for repeated murder and deprivation (*Mardersterne*).[81] Violently undercutting Rilke's *Stab* and *Buch* in writing "buch-, buch-, buch- / stabierte, stabierte," Celan's poetry comes into being as the pain of language itself: a syntactically wounded stutter breaking down language into its smallest elements: *Buch-staben*.

In "Engführung," this monstrous process is reflected in the paratactic progression of its verse, for example in the twice chopped-up "Ho, ho- / sianna" and "Ho- / sianna" of the penultimate stanza (*GW* 1:203–4/*P* 147). This disfigured cry of acclamation and adoration, *Ho, ho-*, is linked to the cry of the owl whose flight the poem then proceeds to mention ("Eulenflucht"). It marks an intersection not only of the owl in Rilke's tenth elegy, incidentally the only one of the *Elegies* incorporating an asterisk, but also with the famous owl of Minerva in Hegel's *Philosophy of Right*. In contrast to Hegel, however, where the owl is said to spread "its wings only with the falling of the dusk,"[82] the dusk in Celan does not coincide with that of nightfall but with that of day ("taggrau"). In Hegel, history was the realization of a purpose, the actualization of a free self-consciousness. In Celan, the *Ho-, ho-* of the owl signals the violently abbreviated "Pray, save (us)!" of a subject deprived of name. Here we are not at the nightly end of history, but rather at the end of the history of the end of history—on a day that is "the seventh and not the last," as "Gespräch im Gebirg" puts it (*GW* 3:172/*CP* 21).

Bracketed by the travestying hosannas of the next-to-last stanza of "Engführung," we read:

> Also
> stehen noch Tempel. Ein
> Stern
> hat wohl noch Licht.
> Nichts,
> nichts ist verloren.
>> (*GW* 1:204)

> (So
> there still stand temples. A
> star
> probably still has light.
> Nothing,
> nothing is lost.)
>> (*P* 147 [trans. modified])

Relying on the initial *Also*, Szondi reads these lines as the "lesson" of "Engführung." Something remains; nothing is lost. Nothing, but nothing. The first, solitary *Nichts* posits the lack which the second *nichts* assures us is not lost. Only by repetition, nothing can be lost. "Here there is only existence," Szondi summarizes, "if it transforms itself into memory, into 'trace,' of non-existence."[83]

If one reads this observation together with the poem's mention of *darüber*, as well as the *zudecken* of the chiasmatically arranged questions quoted above, the singular resistance to hermeneutic unraveling exerted by Celan's text becomes apparent. "Engführung" discloses the trace of that which can never be converted into language. By passing silence over it, however, the poem also veils this trace. Nothing is paradoxically inscribed in the text, and nothing resists articulation. The stars, strictly graphical, write the text apart. By marking only *that* it takes place—and as the caesura is a matter of pure form in Hölderlin, so is the "constellation" in Mallarmé—the asterisks resist exegetical unfolding.

Celan's stars thus defend themselves against interpretive operations aimed at laying bare the text with words and silences and endowing it with meaning. (To interpret them as stars of David would be to repeat the violence of the very gesture, founded on a confounded hermeneutics, for which designation seems only another name for disposal.) They cannot be converted into speech, the medium par excellence of hermeneutics, yet they are nevertheless experienced in and through their resistance to such procedures. Strictly speaking, Celan's particular "nothing of voice" cannot be deported, annihilated, or lost. The asterisks can only be read—read, that is, in a certain, perhaps "utopian" light. As graphic stars they shed written or material light on that which has been lost: "Ein / Stern hat wohl noch Licht." But with "the dark light of this nothing," as Derrida remarks in one of his essays in memory of de Man, "we learn that the other resists the closure of our interiorizing memory."[84]

Generally, asterisks function as signs of a name whose fullness has been omitted (Mr. A***, for example, or Ms. S***). In that sense, Celan's graphic stars may be taken as the material "contour" of such omission or nothing. Taken in another of their formal capacities, they become footnotes without a text, signs divorced from their signification—or sheer referentiality, referring to that which will always remain other and impossible to interiorize in an act of cognition. Rather than encoding history in a poetry of constancy, as Szondi suggests, "Engführung" inscribes this always-other in its mute, nine-times-repeated punctuation.[85]

Derrida's question of how nothing can be written receives a profoundly divided answer in Celan's poem. The graphical stars of "Engführung" mark that something radically other than language takes place in the poetic text, materially inscribing a constellation which resists hermeneutic excavation. Terribly, such a resistance makes no semantic difference—in that sense, it is like a shibboleth. Occurring only in texts and thus making a difference, writing the text apart, Celan's stars shed light on that which can never be given words. They realize this nothing, and thus mark the actuality of a history to which only reading can attest. They speak, as the "Meridian" puts it, *"on the behalf of . . .* an *altogether other,"* graphically giving it "its time." Hence the particular image in which they are read, as Benjamin says, "bears to the highest degree the stamp of that critical, dangerous moment that lies at the source of all reading."[86] It is this which makes Celan's poem such incomparable, and incomparably acute, reading: nothing, nothing makes a difference.

NOTES

1. "Josefine, die Sängerin oder das Volk der Mäuse," in *Gesammelte Werke,* 7 vols., ed. Max Brod (Munich: Fischer, 1983), Erzählungen, 207. "Josephine the Singer, or The Mouse Folk," trans. Willa and Edwin Muir, in Franz Kafka,

The Complete Stories, ed. Nahum N. Glatzer (New York: Schocken, 1983), 367 (trans. modified).

2. *Schriften*, Die Werke Friedrich von Hardenbergs, ed. Paul Kluckhorn and Richard Samuel (Stuttgart: Kolhammer, 1960), 2:609.

3. "Poetry of Constancy—Poetik der Beständigkeit. Celans Übertragung von Shakespeares Sonett 105," in Peter Szondi, *Schriften*, ed. Wolfgang Fietkau (Frankfort: Suhrkamp, 1978), 2:325. "The Poetry of Constancy: Paul Celan's Translation of Shakespeare's Sonnet 105," in Peter Szondi, *On Textual Understanding and Other Essays*, trans. Harvey Mendelson (Minneapolis: Minnesota University Press, 1986), 164.

4. Cf. *Werke*, ed. Norbert Miller (Munich: Hanser, 1971), 5:199. *Horn of Oberon: Jean Paul Richter's School for Aesthetics*, trans. Margaret R. Hale (Detroit: Wayne State University Press, 1973), 138. The reference to Jean Paul in this context has become a commonplace in Celan scholarship. It was first given by Adelheid Rexheuser. See "'Den Blick von der Sache wenden gegen ihr Zeichen hin'. Jean Pauls *Streckverse* und *Träme* und die Lyrik Paul Celans," in *Über Paul Celan*, ed. Dietlind Meinecke, 2d ed. (Frankfort: Suhrkamp, 1973), 174–93. In keeping with the Romantics, in particular with Celan's elective affinities, one might also recall Novalis's definition of "magic" as a "mystical theory of language": "the sign's *sympathy* with the signified." *Schriften* 2:499.

5. See, e.g., "Über den Begriff der Geschichte," in Walter Benjamin, *Gesammelte Schriften*, ed. Rolf Tiedemann and Hermann Schweppenhäuser (Frankfort: Suhrkamp, 1980 [1972]), 1(2): 701 and 704 ("On the Concept of History," in Walter Benjamin, *Illuminations*, ed. and intro. Hannah Arendt, trans. Harry Zohn [New York: Schocken, 1968], 263 and 266); "Zum Bild Prousts," in *Gesammelte Schriften*, 2(1): 311 ("The Image of Proust," in *Illuminations*, 204); and "Das Passagen-Werk," in *Gesammelte Schriften*, 5(1): 589 ("N [Re the Theory of Knowledge, Theory of Progress]," trans. Leigh Hafrey and Richard Sieburth, in *Benjamin: Philosophy, Aesthetics, History*, ed. Gary Smith [Chicago: University of Chicago Press, 1989], 61). In several places, Benjamin distinguishes *Eingedenken* from *Erinnerung* and *Gedächtnis*—interiorizing memory and mechanical memory, respectively. See, e.g., "Der Erzähler," in *Gesammelte Schriften*, 2(2): 453–54 ("The Storyteller," in *Illuminations*, 97–98).

6. Paul Celan, *Werke*, text-critical edition, ed. Beda Allemann, Stefan Reichert, Axel Gellhaus, and Rolf Bücher (Frankfort: Suhrkamp, 1990), 7(2): 76.

7. Celan was born on November 23, 1920. The manuscript of "Beim Hagelkorn" is dated November 8, 1963. See *Werke*, 7(2): 75. Much discussed, the importance of Celan's name in and for his poetry is still in need of an extensive treatment. Of particular significance, of course, is the inversion of syllables—from *An–cel* to *Cel–an*—which not only created a new identity, but also substituted a family name for a poetonym with no immediately obvious national or ethnic traits of identification. Anagrammatic encodings, paranomastic inscriptions, and biographical allusions of different kinds (not only to his own last name, but also to his first name, and to his synagogal name, Pessach, as well as to his father's, mother's, and wife's names) are frequent in Celan's poetry, in particular with regard to words and conceptual entities such as *Amsel*, *Asche*, *Lanze*, and even *Cello*. The three former ones have often been pointed out in secondary literature; the latter not. In his account of the "Romanian dimen-

sions" of Celan's poetry, Petre Solomon describes how he and Celan, both very young at the time, used to spend hours at the same desk piled up with dictionaries. Constituting "a sort of musical formation," in Solomon's words, Celan is said to have referred to this duo as a "solo by the Petronome, with accompaniment by the Pauloncello." *Paul Celan: l'adolescence d'un adieu*, French trans. Daniel Pujol (Castelnau–le–Lez: Climats, 1990), 25. For Celan's poetics, with its intimate relationship to projection and projectiles (arrows, lances, boomerangs), it may not be incidental that a poem such as "Cello-Einsatz," containing the letters spelling "Celan," also mentions a "beyond hit by arrows" ("das von Pfeilen getroffene Drüben" [*GW* 2:76/*P* 253]).

Among the many poems incorporating anagrams of the poet's name, it might suffice here to single out only the two texts treated in this essay. In "Tübingen, Jänner," the mention of "Pallaksch" may contract the syllables of Paul Antschel (*GW* 1:226/*P* 177); and in "Engführung," it is hard not to hear the resonances of the same name spelled in Romanian (Ancel) in the sixth stanza's "Gedanke an Pflanzliches dran," words which are repeated a little later, "An, ja, / Pflanzliches" (*GW* 1:200–201/*P* 143).

8. "Das Passagen-Werk," 577–78. "N [Re the Theory of Knowledge, Theory of Progress]," 50. Elsewhere, I engage in a more extensive reading of this passage, in particular as it relates to the literally *infinite* character of the "zur Lesbarkeit gelangen" ("entering into readability") of historical images. See Aris Fioretos, "Avbrottet," *Det kritiska ögonblicket. Hölderlin, Benjamin, Celan* (Stockholm: Norstedts, 1991), 71–133.

9. Georg Büchner, *Werke und Briefe* (Munich: Deutscher Taschenbuch Verlag, 1980), 118. "Leonce and Lena," trans. Anthony Meech, in Georg Büchner, *The Complete Plays*, ed. Michael Patterson (London: Methuen, 1987), 146.

10. Cf. *Das Heilige* (Stuttgart: Perthes, 1917), e.g., 28. Rudolf Otto, *The Idea of the Holy*, trans. John W. Harvey (London: Oxford University Press, 1923), e.g., 26.

11. Cf. Mikael van Reis, *Celans aska* (Göteborg: Litteraturvetenskapliga institutionen vid Göteborgs universitet, 1987), 44. Van Reis gets the German spelling wrong, however.

12. Cf. van Reis, 45. For a discussion of multilingual wordplay in Celan, see Elizabeth Petuchowski, "Bilingual and Multilingual *Wortspiele* in the Poetry of Paul Celan," *Deutsche Vierteljahrsschrift für Literaturwissenschaft und Geistesgeschichte* 52, no. 4 (1978), 635–51.

13. It may be worth remembering that Celan himself emphatically rejected this description when he inscribed a copy of *Die Niemandsrose* given to Michael Hamburger with the words "absolutely not hermetic" ("ganz und gar nicht hermetisch"). Michael Hamburger, "Paul Celan: Notes Towards a Translation," *PN Review* 6, no. 6 (1980), 59. Celan's inscription was prompted by an anonymous review of *Die Niemandsrose* in the *Times Literary Supplement*, which he erroneously thought was written by Hamburger. Scores of studies of Celan rely on a definition of his poetry as hermetic. The most eloquently stated, if not most compellingly argued, of these may be one by Hans-Georg Gadamer. See "Sinn und Sinnverhüllung bei Paul Celan," *Poetica* (Frankfort: Insel, 1977), 119–34. Most recently, Thomas Sparr has tried to argue the case in a study mostly devoted to establishing the theoretical and methodological boundaries for a definition of hermeticism. See *Paul Celans Poetik des hermetischen Gedichts*

(Heidelberg: Winter, 1989). The only solid interpretation Sparr provides is of the poem "Blume" (*GW* 1:164/*P* 115), already treated in this context by Bernd Witte. See "Zu einer Theorie der hermetischen Lyrik. Am Beispiel Paul Celan," *Poetica* (Amsterdam) 13, nos. 1–2 (1981), 133–48.

14. Cf., e.g., Witte, "Zu einer Theorie der hermetischen Lyrik," esp. 141–45.

15. See, e.g., Martin Anderle, "Sprachbildungen Hölderlins in modernen Gedichten (Celans 'Tübingen, Jänner' und Brobowskis 'Hölderlin in Tübingen),'" *Seminar* 8, no. 2 (1972), esp. 100–7; Paul Coates, "Flowers of Nothingness: The *Spätwerk* of Paul Celan," in *Words After Speech: A Comparative Study of Romanticism and Symbolism* (London: Macmillan, 1986), esp. 145–57; Hans Meyer, "Sprechen und Verstummen der Dichter," in *Das Geschechen und das Schweigen* (Frankfort: Suhrkamp, 1969), esp. 11–15; and Hartmunt Müller, "Das lyrische Paradoxon," in *Formen moderner deutscher Lyrik* (Paderborn: Schönigh, 1970), esp. 35–37.

More general readings of the relationship between Celan and Hölderlin are provided by, e.g., Sieghild Bogumil, "Celans Hölderlinlektüre im Gegenlicht des schlichten Wortes," *Celan-Jahrbuch* 1 (1987), 81–125; and Götz Wienold, "Paul Celans Hölderlin-Widerruf," *Poetica* (Amsterdam) 2, no. 2 (1968), 216–28.

16. Cf., e.g., Witte, "Zu einer Theorie der hermetischen Lyrik," 142.

17. For this intertextualization, cf., e.g., Jochen Börner, "Zweierlei Blindheit—Hölderlin, Celan und die entstellte Sprache. Zu Celans Gedicht 'Tübingen, Jänner,'" *Die Drei* (Stuttgart) 56, no. 3 (1986), 181–84; Bernhard Böschenstein, "Paul Celan: 'Tübingen, Jänner,'" in *Studien zur Dichtung des Absoluten* (Zürich: Atlantis, 1968), 179; Manfred Geier, "'Zur Blindheit überredete Augen'. Paul Celan / Friedrich Hölderlin: Ein lyrischer Intertext," in *Die Schrift und die Tradition. Studien zur Intertextualität* (Munich: Fink, 1985), 19–25; and Witte, "Zu einer Theorie der hermetischen Lyrik," 142.

18. "Anthropormorphism and Trope in the Lyric," in *The Rhetoric of Romanticism* (New York: Columbia University Press, 1983), 262. De Man discusses this "army" at the outset of his essay (239–43), as well as in "Rhetoric of Tropes (Nietzsche)." See *Allegories of Reading: Figural Language in Rousseau, Nietzsche, Rilke, and Proust* (New Haven: Yale University Press, 1984), 110–12. It marches in, of course, from "On Truth and Lie in an Extra-Moral Sense." See "Über Wahrheit und Lüge im außermoralischen Sinn," in Friedrich Nietzsche, *Werke*, ed. Karl Schlechta (Frankfort: Ullstein, 1981), 3:1022.

19. *Sämtliche Werke*, ed. Friedrich Beißner (Stuttgart: Kolhammer, 1951), 2(1): 143. Henceforth I will use the abbreviation *SW.* "A riddle is the purely originated. Even song may hardly disclose it. For as you began, so you will remain, much as need can accomplish, and breeding, for birth can accomplish most, and the ray of light that meets the new-born infant." Friedrich Hölderlin, *Selected Verse*, trans. Michael Hamburger (London: Anvil, 1986), 162 (trans. modified).

20. Cf., however, Paul de Man, "The Riddle of Hölderlin," in *Critical Writings, 1953–1978*, ed. Lindsay Waters (Minneapolis: University of Minnesota Press, 1989), 206 and 209–10. Cf. also John W. Erwin, "Wenn wir Harmonia Singen: Projections of Community by Hölderlin and Celan," in *Lyric*

Apocalypse: Reconstruction in Ancient and Modern Poetry (Chico: Scholars Press, 1984), 97.

21. Cf. de Man, "The Riddle of Hölderlin," 205.

22. Höderlin, 2(1): 146. "That [he] from holy profusion like the wine-god ... foolishly, divinely, and lawlessly lavished it, the language of the most pure, comprehensible to the good, but rightly struck with blindness the irreverent." *Selected Verse*, 166.

23. Hölderlin, *SW,* 2(1): 93. Hölderlin, *Selected Verse*, 109 (trans. modified). The proximity between the two poems is underscored by the fact that the former is dedicated to Hölderlin's friend Wilhelm Heinse, which originally was to be the case with the latter as well. We also know that the mention of "Rousseau" in the tenth strophe of "The Rhine" first read "Heinse."

24. "Intentional Structure of the Romantic Image," in *The Rhetoric of Romanticism*, 6.

25. *SW* 2(1): 143. "But the blindest of all are the sons of gods. For a man knows his own house and in the animal's soul where it must build was implanted, but in their inexperienced souls the defect of not knowing where to go." *Selected Verse*, 161 (trans. modified).

26. De Man, "The Riddle of Hölderlin," 210.

27. Cf. *Allegories of Reading*, 203. "Riddle" possesses a cryptical content which de Man views as already "known" and therefore only engendering a text by postponing its open secret. "Enigma," however, is seen as a case of figural complexity in the text, characterized by an obscurity which cannot be taken to imply a postponement of an already known but for the moment veiled meaning. As a "knot which arrests the process of understanding," as de Man writes elsewhere, "enigma" takes on an allegorical character absent in "riddle." "Shelley Disfigured," in *The Rhetoric of Romanticism*, 98. It thus comes close to the rhetorical definition proposed by Heinrich Lausberg: "Enigma is a non-ironic . . . allegory." *Handbuch der literarischen Rhetorik*, 2d rev. ed. (Munich: Hueber, 1960), 444.

28. "The Riddle of Hölderlin," 206.

29. Cf., e.g., "Semiology and Rhetoric," in *Allegories of Reading*, 10; "Genesis and Genealogy," in *Allegories of Reading*, 79; "Shelley Disfigured," in *The Rhetoric of Romanticism*, 99 and 103; "Anthropomorphism and Trope in the Lyric," in *The Rhetoric of Romanticism*, 262; "The Resistance to Theory," in *The Resistance to Theory* (Minneapolis: University of Minnesota Press, 1986), 13 and 18; "Hypogram and Inscription," in *The Resistance to Theory*, 47; "Reading and History," in *The Resistance to Theory*, 70; and "Pascal's Allegory of Persuasion," in *Allegory and Representation*, ed. Stephen J. Greenblatt (Baltimore: Johns Hopkins University Press, 1981), 1.

30. Cf. Johann Georg Hamann, *Sämtliche Werke*, ed. Josef Nadler (Vienna: Herder, 1951), 3:104–7. The I of Hamann's curious piece of text, explicitly calling itself a *Hauch*, insists on the invisible *pneuma* of *gramma* and polemicizes against the reductive literalism governing the lexicological enterprise of the Grimm brothers. Hamann argues that the endeavor of the Grimm brothers— whose worldliness is said to imply the possibility of binding in an "image-word" (*Bildwort*) that which is not of this world—does not take into account the fact that it rests on "custom and tradition," that is, on human history, and is

thus prey to the arbitrariness and volatility of time. In Hamann, the letter *h* seems to be the only—or at least the most certain—remnant and remainder of an unmovable, atemporal essence in an otherwise corrupt and materially impure language—the roots of which will never tell us anything about the principle of liveliness, that is, never answer the question of why we breathe.

31. "Der Rätselcharakter ist ein Entsprungenes." *Ästhetische Theorie* (Frankfort: Surhkamp, 1981 [1970]), 192. Adorno's English translator, Christopher Lenhardt, "translates" this untranslatable remark as: "It is a product of history." Theodor W. Adorno, *Aesthetic Theory*, ed. Gretel Adorno and Rolf Tiedemann (London: Routledge & Kegan Paul, 1984), 185.

32. Cf. Geier, "'Zur Blindheit überredete Augen,'" 18–19, who does not elaborate on the issue.

33. Cf., e.g., *Die Struktur der modernen Lyrik* (Hamburg: Rowohlt, 1988 [1956]), 135–36. Hugo Friedrich, *The Structure of Modern Poetry: From the Mid-Nineteenth to the Mid-Twentieth Century*, trans. Joachim Neugroschel (Evanston: Northwestern University Press, 1974), 103.

34. "Lyric and Modernity," in Paul de Man, *Blindness and Insight: Essays in the Rhetoric of Contemporary Criticism*, 2d enl. ed. (Minneapolis: University of Minnesota Press, 1982 [1971]), 172. De Man explicitly polemicizes against Friedrich's genetic historiography, underscoring the problems involved in arguing that, in modern poetry, mimetic modes of writing are superseded by allegorical ones much like a child following upon parents.

35. *SW* 2(1):142. "In the coldest abyss I heard the youth wail for release." *Selected Verse*, 160–61.

36. Cf. *SW* 2(1): 189. *Selected Verse*, 211.

37. Cf. Erwin, "Wenn wir Harmonia Singen," 100, who adopts a different reading of the first stanza.

38. *Die Struktur*, 135. *The Structure*, 102. For a more extensive treatment of Friedrich's theorization of hermeticism, in particular in regard to the category of obscurity, see Aris Fioretos, "Obscuritas," *Tidskrift för litteraturvetenskap* (Stockholm) 22, no. 1 (1993), 35–58.

39. *Die Struktur*, 182. *The Structure*, 142.

40. Quoted in *Literaturrevolution 1910–1925. Dokumente, Manifeste, Programme*, ed. Paul Pörtner (Darmstadt: Luchterhand, 1960), 1:52–53.

41. Cf. *Wort und Name bei Paul Celan. Zur Widerruflichkeit des Gedichts* (Berlin: Gehlen, 1970), 189. Celan relies on the etymological link binding *tauchen* ("submerge") to *taufen* ("baptize"), and farther to *Tiefe* ("depth").

42. *SW* 2(1):94.

43. In a certain sense, then, "Tübingen, Jänner" also stages a series of future readings, allegorically troped on the "visits" (*Besuche*) of the pluralized "carpenter" Ernst Zimmer, the caretaker of Hölderlin during his madness. It carries its own acute now into the future, projecting it as that arrow or lance of intention which for Celan was inextricably as well as anagrammatically entwined in his own existence as a poet. (Most likely, Celan was aware of the anagram of his name contracted in the German *Lanze*, "lance," mentioned for example in the early poem "Der Stein aus dem Meer," in *Mohn und Gedächtnis* [*GW* 1:27].) One may also note, in this context, the "whirring" sound of the "arrow script" in "Beim Hagelkorn," returning in the description of gulls "whirring" around "Hölderlin towers" in "Tübingen, Jänner."

44. *SW* 8(3): 203. Schwab's diary entry is dated January 14, 1841. Cf. Böschenstein, "Paul Celan: 'Tübingen, Jänner,' " 180.

45. Cf. Hölderlin, *SW* 8(3): 453.

46. Cf. Erwin, "Wenn wir Harmonia Singen," 101, with whom I am otherwise in disagreement.

47. *SW* 2(1): 144. *Selected Verse*, 162.

48. Wilhelm Höck has argued for the identification of Celan's *Mensch* with Moses by way of Hölderlin's "Am Quell der Donau" (*SW*, 2[1]: 128; *Selected Verse*, 147). See "Von welchem Gott ist die Rede?," in *Über Paul Celan*, 2d enl. ed., ed. Dietlind Meinecke (Frankfort: Suhrkamp, 1973), 270.

49. "Lyric and Modernity," 186.

50. *Ästhetische Theorie*, 476–77. *Aesthetic Theory*, 443–44 (trans. modified).

51. *Ästhetische Theorie*, 477. *Aesthetic Theory*, 444.

52. *Schibboleth pour Paul Celan* (Paris: Galilée, 1986), 110.

53. 1933 ed., 10:1117.

54. *GW* 3:197/*CP* 48. Cf. Böschenstein-Schäfer, "Traum und Sprache in der Dichtung Paul Celans," in *Argumentum e silentio*, ed. Amy D. Colin (Berlin: de Gruyter, 1987), 226.

55. *Schibboleth*, 84.

56. "Lecture de Strette. Essai sur la poésie de Paul Celan," *Critique* 27, no. 288 (1971), 393. Peter Szondi, "Reading 'Engführung': An Essay on the Poetry of Paul Celan," trans. David Caldwell and S. Esh, in *Boundary 2* 11, no. 3 (1983), 231–64. Since this translation relies on the German translation of Szondi's text ("Durch die Enge geführt," in *Schriften*, 2:345–89), rather than on the French original, I will use my own translation.

57. "Lecture de Strette," 389.

58. In recent time, this distinction has been theorized by Andrzej Warminski. See *Readings in Interpretation: Hölderlin, Hegel, Heidegger* (Minneapolis: University of Minnesota Press, 1987).

59. "Lecture de Strette," 399, 390, and 388.

60. Hans-Jost Frey, "Verszerfall," in Hans-Jost Frey and Otto Lorenz, *Kritik des freien Verses* (Heidelberg: Schneider, 1980), 63.

61. "Lecture de Strette," 389.

62. "Verszerfall," 67.

63. Stéphane Moses, "Quand le langage se fait voix. Paul Celan: *Entretien dans la montagne,*" in *Contre-jour. Etudes sur Paul Celan*, ed. Martine Broda (Paris: Cerf, 1986), 128.

64. "Lecture de Strette," 358. Szondi refers to Grimm, *Deutsches Wörterbuch* (Leipzig: Hirzel, 1935), vol. 11, col. 480.

65. *Der große Brockhaus*, cited in Szondi, "Durch die Enge geführt," 351.

66. Cf. "Lecture de Strette," 399–400.

67. See the section "on the period" (*peri periodou*) in *Opera*, ed. Hugo Rabe (Stuttgart: Teubner, 1969 [1913]), 176–83.

68. "Anmerkungen zum 'Ödipus,'" in *SW* 5:196. Friedrich Hölderlin, "Remarks on Oedipus," in *Essays and Letters on Theory*, ed. and trans. Thomas Pfau (Albany: State University of New York Press, 1988), 102.

69. Cf. "Goethes Wahlverwandschaften," in *Gesammelte Schriften*, 1(1): 181.

70. "Lecture de Strette," 393.

71. Ibid., 400.

72. "Im Chiasmus ist das Kreuz näher als im Thema 'Kreuz.'" Reported by Böschenstein-Schäfer, "Traum und Sprache in der Dichtung Paul Celans," 226.

73. *Paul Celan. Verweigerte Poetisierung der Welt* (Heidelberg: Stiehm, 1974), 101. Voswinckel is close to interpreting the "starlike word" as the word of those who wore the yellow star.

74. As Marlies Janz has pointed out, the ninth asterisk was missing in the first edition of *Sprachgitter.* See *Vom Engagement absoluter Poesie. Zur Lyrik und Ästhetik Paul Celans* (Frankfort: Syndikat, 1976), 223, n 97.

75. Cf., e.g., Exod. 17:14; Luke 24:46; and John 19:22.

76. Cf. "Über einige Motive bei Baudelaire," in *Gesammelte Schriften*, 1(2): 639. "On Some Motifs in Baudelaire," in *Illuminations*, 182.

77. *Schibboleth*, 83.

78. "Rien n'aura eu lieu que le lieu excepté peut-être une constellation." *Oeuvres complètes*, ed. Henri Mondor and G. Jean-Aubry (Paris: Gallimard [Pléiade], 1945), 474–77. Stéphane Mallarmé, *The Poems*, trans. Keith Bosley (New York: Penguin, 1977), 292–97. For brevity's sake, I quote the text, which is spread over six pages, in compressed form and without capital letters. For "l'alphabet des astres," see *Oeuvres complètes*, 370.

79. "Anthropomorphism and Trope in the Lyric," 262.

80. *Sämtliche Werke*, ed. Rilke-Archiv (Frankfort: Insel, 1976 [1955]), 2:725. "And, higher, the stars. New ones. Stars of the Land of Pain. / Slowly she names them: 'There, / look: the *Rider*, the *Staff*, and that fuller constellation / they call *Fruitgarland.* Then, further, towards the Pole: / *Cradle, Way, The Burning Book, Doll, Window.* / But up in the southern sky, pure as within the palm / of a consecrated hand, the clearly-resplendent *M*, / standing for Mothers. . . . .'" Rainer Maria Rilke, *The Duino Elegies*, trans. J. B. Leishman and Stephen Spender (New York: Norton, 1939), 85.

81. Cf. James Rolleston, "Consuming History: Celan's 'Die Silbe Schmerz,'" in *Psalm und Hawdalah. Zum Werk Paul Celans*, ed. Joseph P. Strelka (Bern: Lang, 1987), 47.

Earlier we read: "Es fuhren / wortfreie Stimmen rings, Leerformen, alles / ging in sie ein, / gemischt / und entmischt / und wieder / gemischt" (*GW* 1:280) ("Wordless voices / travelled around, empty-forms, everything / went into them, / mixed / and unmixed / and mixed / once again")—words bringing us back not only to "Engführung," which mentions "Nächte, entmischt" (*GW* 1:202) ("Nights, demixed" [*P* 145]), but also to the finale of Hölderlin's "The Rhine": "Bei Nacht, wenn alles gemischt" (*SW* 2[1]: 148) ("by night, when all is mingled" [*Selected Verse*, 169]).

82. *Grundlinien der Philosophie des Rechts*, Theorie Werkausgabe, ed. Eva Moldenhauer and Karl Markus Michel (Frankfort: Suhrkamp, 1970 [1821]), 7:28. G. W. F. Hegel, *The Philosophy of Right*, trans. T. M. Knox (New York: Oxford University Press, 1945), 13. Cf. Rilke, "Die zehnte Elegie," 724. "The Tenth Elegy," 99. In Leishman and Spender's translation, the asterisk is curiously omitted.

83. "Lecture de Strette," 416.

84. "Mnemosyne," in *Mémoires pour Paul de Man* (Paris: Galilée, 1988), 53. "Mnemosyne," in *Memoires for Paul de Man*, trans. Cecile Lindsay (New York: Columbia University Press, 1986), 34.

85. It remains a task to read the way in which the nine asterisks of "Engfüh-rung," the last poem in *Sprachgitter,* may or may not relate to the first poem of the collection, *"Stimmen"* (*"Voices"*), in which seven asterisks occur. See *GW* 1:149 / *SG* 80–84.

86. "Das Passagen-Werk," 578. "N [Re the Theory of Knowledge, Theory of Progress]," 50–51 (trans. modified).

PURE LANGUAGE AND SILENCE

10

The Relation between Translation and Original as Text

[The Example of Celan's Version of Shakespeare's Sonnet 137]

Hans-Jost Frey
Translated by Georgia Albert in collaboration with the author

One feature of translation is that it is not the original but its repetition. Within the framework of a system in which the faith in the originality (*Originalität*) of the original holds, the translation, like everything derivative, is classified from the beginning as something inferior, and its relative worth is measured by the attained degree of closeness to the original. The highest goal set for a translation seen in this perspective would be for it to annihilate itself and coincide with the original, embodying it. Such a conception of translation runs into a dilemma: to the extent that the translation approaches what it should be, it stops being what it is. In the moment of its full realization it should disappear. The essence of the translation would be to be something other than itself. The translation, that is, would be essentially a non-essence, something inessential which has to be gotten rid of.

What bars access to translation as such is the unquestioned value judgment and preference granted to the original and to the translation's closeness to it. So long as this system of values, which is based on originality (*Ursprünglichkeit*), is not called into question, the danger exists that what is specific to the translation is repressed in favor of what it has in common with the original. If the translation is better the smaller its distance from the original, then this distance measures only the degree of incompleteness of the translation and becomes unimportant to the extent that the translation is successful. Against such a view stands the fact that there is translation only insofar as it differs from the original.

Difference is an essential characteristic of translation, and translation as such can never be reflected upon so long as a task is assigned to it the fulfillment of which would be the denial of what it is.

Difference is not only a deficiency of the translation; it is also what allows it to set itself off from the original as another discourse, and to become self-sufficient with respect to it precisely because it does not have the independence of the original but rather refers to it. Renouncing the value judgment that considers difference a deficiency of translation makes it possible to discuss translation on the basis of difference and not of its repression.

All attempts to understand translation by measuring it against the original are based on the assumption that the original is available as a fixed standard of measure. They presuppose a conception of reading which includes the possibility of taking possession of a text by ascertaining its meaning. If one gives up this assumption, the original can no longer function as a standard of measure, but becomes itself dependent on its relationship with its translation. Then, its being translated does not leave the original unaffected, but rather takes part in the constitution of its meaning. Like every reading and interpretation, a translation affects the original as a moment of its history, in the course of which new layers of meaning keep adding themselves to the original through the change in its context. Seen thus, the relationship between original and translation is no longer hierarchical, because it can no longer be anchored to a fixed point; rather, it becomes a suspended constellation in which the original and the translation mutually determine one another.

To translate is to speak second-hand. What is to be said is only accessible by way of the detour through the text that is to be translated. The translation, taken as such, refers not only to what it says, but also and at the same time to the text that it translates, which has already said what the translation has to say. Because the translation is always already repetition, it always already says everything for the second time. Because it is, from the start, repetition, the translation can never lay claim to originality (*Ursprünglichkeit*) without disowning itself as translation and becoming a lie. Instead, it attains what is particular to its status as derivation from an original precisely by repeating the original. The "originality" ("*Originalität*") of the translation is not to have any and to refer to another text as its precondition.

The result of this is that the translation reaches its self-sufficiency with regard to the text that it reproduces precisely when it makes the most of its independence and thereby of its discord from it. But the question is how this can happen. The elementary prerequisite for this is that the translation be recognizable as translation. That this possibility exists is less obvious than it seems. There are translations which, as we say, read like an original. This means that nothing in them betrays the fact that they are the reproduction of another text. The possibility of such translations is disquieting because they throw suspicion on the texts that pass for originals. If it is possible to take a translation for an original, then we can no longer be certain that what passes itself off as an original is not a translation. For a translation to be recognized as such, the original must also be available at the same time. But the situation in which both texts are given simultaneously is not a usual one. It is, of course, the situation of the translator and also holds for those who are concerned in some way with questions of translation, but not for the reader to whom the translation is destined and who would like to read in his language what he does not understand in the foreign tongue. The translation does not become an object of reflection for the reader for whom it is intended. He reads it like an original. The translation can only become a problem for someone who does not need it. Thus the possibility of asking about the relationship between translation and original arises only when the instrumentality of translation has become irrelevant because original and translation are read side by side and with one another. Only their being side by side makes accessible their relationship and thereby what is peculiar to the translation.

The difference between original and translation can only be seen when they are simultaneously present. When the texts are available at the same time, their chronological sequence and thereby the priority—in every sense of the word—of the one to the other is called into question. In the extreme case in which both texts belong to the same period and contain no clues that help identify one of them as the later one, it can become uncertain which of the two is the original and which the translation. Even when this is not doubtful, however, the relationship between the two contiguous texts must be seen as a reciprocal one. The text that appears together with its translation is not the same as it would be if read in isolation or in a different context. The original is not something that is established once and for all: being translated modifies it. The modified original is not only the translation, in which the differences can be found, but also the original itself, in which new possibilities of meaning are opened up by the fact that the translation could transform it in this particular way. For this reason it is necessary not only to read the translation from the point of view of the original, but also to read the original from the point of view of the translation, and further to read the original with an eye to the fact that it has been translated.

Once the interrelationship between original and translation is established through the simultaneous presence of the two texts, the situation of translation becomes relevant for the understanding of both texts. The translation appears in the context of the original and the original in the context of the translation. If the translation is read in reference to the context, that is, from the point of view of the original, then what it says is no longer to be referred only to the internal context of the text of the translation; rather, this text is referred, as a whole, to the original of which it is a translation. If one proceeds from the assumption that the original and the translation say the same thing, then this "same thing" in the translation is something different, because it is in a translation. As soon as the translation is read as such, that is, in the context of the original, this difference must be accounted for. To read a translation as translation means that everything it says must also be read with an eye to the fact that it is said in translation. Since what is said in the translation read in the context of the original is always related to its being said in a translation, new possibilities of meaning arise. The same is true for the original that is put in this relationship with the translation. Because the original is now read from the point of view of its context (the translation), what it says is no longer to be understood on the basis of itself only, but must also be related to its being translated.

The relationship between original and translation, as their simultaneous co-presence, is a text. The formulation according to which the translation stands in the context of the original and the original in the context of the translation means that both together, in reference to one another, form a third text which is constituted by their relationship to one another. This text is not under the authority of any author. Even if one assumes that the author of the original and the translator can each take responsibility for his own text, neither has authority over the other's. For this reason, both of them are deprived of power over the intertextual relationship, and since this relationship transforms the texts that it connects, each also loses his mastery over his own text. Thus the text constituted by the relationship between original and translation is a space in which the relationships between the two texts play independently of any controlling authority.

One of the possible ways in which translation and original can relate to each other when they are read together is by thematizing their reciprocal relationship in what they say. Such a thematization does not necessarily have to occur, and one can consider it accidental since it cannot be traced back to any intention. Yet chance, as lack of an authorial instance, is precisely what is playful about the play constituted by the relationship between original and translation as text. It can happen that situating the original in the context of the translation makes it possible to read what it says with an eye to its being translated and as metaphor for its own translatability, and that what the translation says when read from the point of view of the original becomes the metaphor for the process of translation. This possibility of reading original and translation as metaphors for their interrelationship can only arise when the two texts' relationship to one another is recognized and read as a text in which all possible connections that produce meaning are permissible. What emerges in this case is a reading of the relationship between translation and original in which differences in rank and worth disappear in favor of the shifts in meaning that occur in the original expanded by the translation as well as in the translation expanded by the original. Read as text, the relationship between a text and its translation is no longer a hierarchical one but one of reciprocal reference. This is most easily visible where the relationship between the two texts makes itself explicit by turning original and translation into figures for itself, so that the two texts represent both themselves and their relationship to one another. Since this cannot be predicted in advance, does not always happen, and always only happens in individual cases, here the transition to an example is theoretically justified. Since the theory does not prove that the described metaphorization of original and translation is necessary, but only that it is possible, the proof that this possibility actually realizes itself can only be gained through individual texts and their translations.

Shakespeare's Sonnet 137 and Paul Celan's translation of it (*GW* 5:356–57) may serve as example. The thematization of the translation relationship should here become visible in three places.

Thou blind fool, Love, what dost thou to mine eyes,
That they behold, and see not what they see?
They know what beauty is, see where it lies,
Yet what the best is take the worst to be.

If eyes corrupt by over-partial looks
Be anchor'd in the bay where all men ride,
Why of eyes' falsehood hast thou forgèd hooks
Whereto the judgment of my heart is tied?

Why should my heart think that a several plot
Which my heart knows the wide world's common place?
Or mine eyes, seeing this, say this is not,
To put fair truth upon so foul a face?

In things right true my heart and eyes have err'd,
And to this false plague are they now transferr'd.

Narrsts Aug mir, Blindling Liebe, fort und fort!
Es schaut, nimmt wahr—sieht nicht, was es gewahrt,
erkennt die Schönheit, sieht der Schönheit Ort,
siehts Beste—hälts für dessen Widerpart.

Verschautes Aug, solls nun vor Anker gehn
in jener Bucht, wo festmacht alle Welt:
mußt, Liebe, Trug zum Haken schmieden, den
das Herz fühlt, wenn es Herzensurteil fällt?

Kanns dies sein eigen nennen, da es sah:
Allmend is diese Flur und nimmer sein?
Mein Aug, dies schauend, sagts, dies sei nicht da?
Läßts wahr sein, schön, und weiß: es ist gemein?

Mein Herz, mein Aug: verirrt im Wahren, beide,
und heimgesucht nun von dem Lügen-Leide.

At the end of Celan's translation appears the term *Lügen-Leid* (literally: "lie-suffering"), which stands for the English "false plague." Several things can be meant by this: the suffering from false seeing, which in Celan is called *Verschauen* ("to mis-see") (l. 5); or the suffering from the fact that one holds on to the illusion although one knows the truth (ll. 11–12); or finally the "dark Lady" herself, about whom the poem speaks, and from whose untruthfulness the speaker suffers. Celan's translation encompasses the first two possibilities, but excludes the third. Yet the *Lügen-Leid* is not to be questioned only for its degree of fidelity to the original. This word combination can be interpreted in two ways: it can mean the suffering from the lie, and through this meaning it fulfills the function of reproducing the possibilities given in the original; however, it can also designate the suffering itself as lie, as false suffering, which is out of the question in the English text, but becomes meaningful as soon as one takes into account the status of the translation. The I as speaker of the original ascribes to himself experiences, feelings, and thoughts which are discussed in his speech. The truth content of this discourse need not be discussed here. Even if it is a fiction, the fact remains that the speaker can make it without being given the lie by the situation in which he speaks. The I of the translation must likewise ascribe to himself the feelings expressed in the original, since he must play the role of the I of the text that must be translated. Yet as soon as the translation is no longer read as if it were an original, but is seen as translation, a difficulty arises, because the difference between the I of the translation and the I of the original becomes clear. Behind the I of the translation one cannot assume the presence of a person who can lay claim to the statement of the original, since the translation reproduces someone else's discourse. The I of the translation only pretends to be the I of the original.

Nonetheless there are also things that the I of the translation can rightly ascribe to himself: namely, all that constitutes what is particular about his situation as distinct from that of the I of the original. But to this belongs also the untruthful appropriation of the feeling taken over from the original discourse. The suffering (*Leid*) about which the translation speaks is a *Lügen-Leid*, because insofar as the translation is identified as translation, the suffering is only a pretense to which no feeling corresponds. Like the actor, the translator must repeat what someone else has said and is excluded from what he mimes. But precisely this being excluded can be the motive for the real suffering of the translator as translator. The *Lügen-Leid* as suffering from the lie which belongs to the essence of translation may thus be understood as a thematization, in the translation, of the particular condition of the I of the translation. *Lügen-Leid* is therefore not only the translation of "false plague," but at the same time the firsthand expression of the condition of the translator excluded from "original" feeling.

While here the situation of translation is thematized in the translation, in the second example it is the original that makes explicit its translatability. The possibility for this is already present in the theme of the poem. Shakespeare's poem is about a woman who grants her love quite generously and therefore does not deserve the speaker's love for her. Love, to which the poem is addressed, deceives him over and over again into forgetting the unworthiness of the loved object, and blinds him to the fact that this object will not be restrained by his love and therefore cannot belong to him. The poem, however, is not spoken from the point of view of this illusion, but rather opposes to it the recognition of the unworthiness and unfaithfulness of the beloved. This happens particularly clearly at the beginning of the third stanza: "Why should my heart think that a several plot / Which my heart knows the wide world's common place?" (ll. 9–10). The imagery here is that of real estate. "Several plot" is the private plot of land, "common place" the open village square. Yet the customary designation of this square is the substantive "common." "Common place," on the other hand, is a rhetorical concept designating what is understandable to all and thus banal. From the context one can conclude that the commonplace here is the woman, whom everyone knows because she is at everyone's disposal.

What is important, however, is that with the concept "common place," even if it is only there as allusion, one's attention is called to the discourse, and in a way that is also relevant for the translation. In fact, the commonplace can also be read in reference to the situation of translation. The commonplace is what is common to all, what everyone can say, and what can be carried over from the discourse of one into the discourse of the other, just as the "dark Lady"'s liking goes from one lover to the next. The commonplace is what cannot be tied down to the discourse in which it occurs, just as the speaker's love is unable to bind the "dark Lady" to him. The commonplace is what is translatable. Translation is a sort of prostitution of the content. This would suggest that the situation described in the poem can be read in reference to its own translatability: "common place" is not only a metaphor for the unworthy beloved, but also for the translatability of the text itself.

In our last example, again from the last verse of the poem, the thematization of the translation relationship takes place both in the translation and in the original. "To transfer" means to modify, to bring something from one situation to another, and therefore also names the process of translation. Read strictly in the framework of the text that the translation relationship constitutes in the simultaneous presence of the two adjacent texts in the bilingual edition,[1] this verse can also be read to talk about the poem's being translated as the passage to the *Lügen-Leid* of the facing page. This passage takes place "now," that is, every time that the original and the translation are perceived together in the simultaneity of their relation of exchange. The allusion, found in the original, to the poem's being translated disappears in the translation. "Heimgesucht nun von dem Lügen-Leide" (literally: "afflicted [or: 'looked for at home'] now by the lie-suffering") appears to be a quite inaccurate rendering of the English text. The most important difference is the inversion of direction in the German version. "To be transferred" says that something is taken from here to there, while the *Heimsuchung* is a movement from there to here. From the point of view of the situation of translation this reversal becomes significant, especially against the background of the results of our discussion of *Lügen-Leid*. If one considers the process of translation to be a movement, then the original is its beginning and the translation its end. The *Lügen-Leid* is that toward which the original is set in motion ("transferred"), but also that which afflicts the translation [von dem die Übersetzung heimgesucht wird], and which is at home in it. What is thus thematized in the last line of the two versions is the particular situation which arises for the original on the one hand and for the translation on the other when they are associated with one another in the translation relationship. As soon as they are taken out of this relationship, the context-dependent layer of meaning which has been uncovered here disappears. But as long as the two poems in their correlation are read as text, the first is as much "transferred" into the second as the second "afflicts" the first.

NOTE

1. *Translator's Note*. Celan's Shakespeare translation first appeared in a bilingual edition. William Shakespeare, *Einundzwanzig Sonette*, trans. Paul Celan (Frankfort: Insel, 1967). For Sonnet 137, see pp. 46–47.

For Ernst Prelinger and Werner Hamacher

11

Er, or, Borrowing from Peter to Pay Paul

Further Notes on Celan's Translation of

Shakespeare's Sonnet 105

Thomas Pepper

In the course of a given rhetorical reading, there is a paradoxical relation between the reasons for the choice of a particular text or passage
for reading and the micrological or histological reading which follows
upon this initial choice. This initial decision—the rhetoric of intention
is particularly dangerous here—may be an ideological matter (in the
technical sense, a question about the *logos*, the meaning of a text), for
example in the case where it seems that a given passage is a crux and
that a successful interpretation of this text depends upon its resolution.
Yet that which follows in the rhetorical analysis has more to do with
lexical considerations: *how* is this text (dis)organized, and what does this
(have to) do (with) (to) the presupposition of meaning? My question,
then, concerns how the lexical reading relates to the original choice of
reading material by means of logical (read thematic) considerations.
What is the *thematic scar* left by the necessity of the initial choice upon
the lexical reading which ensues from it, and how does this scar structurally limit the scope of the reading, or its extension (in the logical
sense of entities covered by the predicate, what we might call the reading's power)? I call the thematic scar the mark left by the initial choice
of a text to be read on the rhetorical procedure which treats signifiers
(and not concepts). How does this scar necessitate the proviso that
comes with any reading, namely, that it is a reading only of *this* text, a

particular reading, but one which also confers exemplarity upon the choices it makes and forecloses?

After these initial considerations, why choose to talk about the poetry of Paul Celan? To bring Celan into a discussion of the limits of the thematic today? One might, after all, choose Kafka or Blanchot, Pseudo-Dionysios the Areopagite or Nicholas of Cusa, or any one of a number of others. Perhaps because in reading Celan's work one does not know so easily what he is talking about, and this thematic disorientation comforts itself by determining the power of this negativity in a particular thematic, in a concern with a very particular historical fact, the extermination of the Jews. I do not at all want to suggest that Celan's poetry is not marked by this event. It can (also) be read as an extended name for that event, as an epithet or an epitaph. While my primary concern here has to do with some of the intrinsic, linguistic features of Celan's poems themselves, I hope to suggest not only some ways in which these poems may well, in their very resistance to reading, contribute to the frantic search for extrinsic, extratextual causes or occasions, but also how these poems—as well as the recourse to the historical they somehow seem to encourage—may have something to tell us about their own historical positing and about the occurrence of texts in general.

Peter Szondi, whose last book (still incomplete at the time of his death) is a study of Celan, attempts in this monograph an examination of Celan's poetry based largely on lexical considerations.[1] Not that Szondi sees his work in terms of a rarified, hyperformalized textual aestheticism, as an attempt to remove the serious study of Celan's poetry, which at the time of Szondi's writing was still in its infancy, from historical considerations. On the contrary, Szondi wants to suggest that the approach to Celan's texts provided by reading might bring critical awareness closer to an understanding of Celan's historical importance through the consideration of his treatment of signification in his poetic practice. Yet certainly these readings by Szondi, like those of his earlier *Hölderlin-Studien*,[2] have a strong polemical moment which is bound up with the attempt to bring German studies away from the weight of the primitive accumulation of empirico-biographical data (though not at all to dispense with them) into a productive encounter with American New Critical and also with more recent French structuralist and poststructuralist analyses of poetry.

In each of Szondi's three written essays on Celan, the occasion for the choice of the particular poem to be read is thematically centered. The extended reading of "Engführung," commissioned by *Critique* and written in French,[3] attempts to show a kind of parallelism between two deportations. The one leads to the death camps, while the other carries the reader—from the first line or even from the very title on—from the outside to the inside of a poem. It is no accident that Szondi chooses "Engführung" for this purpose, since it is itself Celan's major attempt to write himself out of the more thematically accessible language of his earlier "Todesfuge," the publication of which canonized its author immediately but also vitiated the reading of his work by placing it under the rubric "poetry of the Holocaust," thus treating it simply as a form of historical documentation to be cited in a pious manner on state occasions. It takes only the most cursory inspection of Celan's work to imagine his contempt for such a use of his—or anyone else's—poetry, and his equal or greater contempt for poetry written for such a purpose. "Engführung" was a provocative declaration: *harter Stil, nicht glatter.*

"Eden," the last and incomplete essay in Szondi's book (the editor's apparatus also contains notes for two unwritten essays), is a reading of a late Celan poem, written during one of the poet's rare visits to Berlin. In this final essay, the critic-witness makes explicit many of the recondite references in the poem to the celebration of the Christmas holiday and to the police reports of the murders of Karl Liebknecht and Rosa Luxemburg. While Szondi was with Celan during much of his stay in Berlin and reports on many of the events which took place at that time, he warns at the same time that a narrative containing all the *facts* of which he speaks, while apparently helpful, does not amount to a reading of the poem. Still, the body of the discursively written-out part of the essay is devoted to a presentation of these facts, while the lexical considerations with which a close reading of the poem would itself have to begin remain only in note form, and have been reproduced for us by the editors as such.

Szondi reports that a manuscript version of this poem bears the title "Wintergedicht," which has been effaced, along with the date of composition, from the version published in the posthumous volume *Schneepart* (1971).[4] What remains to be done in order to complete Szondi's essay on this poem, which he was writing at the time of his death, is to pick up where he leaves off, at his assertion that to relate as much as possible of the context or of the occasion of the poem's composition is not to perform a reading of it.

At the very moment where the written-out part of the book breaks off, in the "Eden" essay on Celan's Berlin-winter poem, at the moment where Szondi relates and must relate—must relate because he has related them[5]—the facts that he and only he knows about the circumstances surrounding Celan's composition, his testimony is written in the decorous third person: he refers to himself as "someone," "a friend," etc. We will return to this strange third person, the apparent decorum of which may call attention to a different necessity. Szondi's modesty, as well as his sense of embarrassment at not being able to complete the task, may account for the fact that he has given us an eyewitness account written in the curious impersonality of this third person. Yet the fact remains that while his essay ends—curiously enough in a manner similar to the poem's (non)ending in "Nichts / stockt"—with this injunction to the necessity of intrinsic criticism, the matter of the essay which leads up to that (non)ending relates for the most part a piece of biography, an episode in the poet's life to which the critic was a witness. Thus what is called for—an internal analysis of the poem which would concentrate on morphology rather than semantics—is preceded by an account of phenomenal, and not of textual, events.[6]

The other complete essay, and perhaps the most successful one, is devoted to a historical inscription of another kind: here Szondi turns his attention to one of Celan's translations from Shakespeare's *Sonnets*, to sonnet 105, "Let not my love be called idolatry." And in his reading it is a matter of making explicit, of thematizing the way in which Celan's *version* acts out lexically, or performs a linguistic constancy, where Shakespeare's poem *describes* the constancy of his poetic attention to his beloved as the theme of the verse. Thus the relation between Shakespeare's poem and Celan's illustrates what I have already called a thematic scar, that (non)site or opening/closing which takes place between Shakespeare's melodic model of epideictic verse and, as I will argue in the following pages, Celan's potentially de-thematizing, lexically disarticulating (Szondi would say performative) reading of it.

In each of Szondi's three essays, then, there is a constant grappling with a thematic scar—that is, with the seal[7] which provides the occasion for the thematic choice of the particular poem for reading and which has some kind of relation (even if it is that of a nonrelation) to the lexical or morphological analysis which ensues upon it.[8]

Szondi's analysis of Celan's Shakespeare translation is meticulously morphological—to a point. And here a revisionary—but not in Harold Bloom's sense of the word—reading of Szondi reading Celan could properly begin.

> Let not my love be call'd idolatry,
> nor my beloved as an idol show,
> Since all alike my songs and praises be
> To one, of one, still such, and ever so.
>
> Kind is my love today, tomorrow kind,
> Still constant in a wondrous excellence;
> Therefore my verse, to constancy confin'd,
> One thing expressing, leaves out difference.

"Fair, kind and true" is all my argument—
"Fair, kind and true" varying to other words;
And in this change is my invention spent—
Three themes in one, which wondrous scope affords.

"Fair, kind and true" have often liv'd alone,
Which three till now never kept seat in one.

Ihr sollt, den ich da lieb, nicht Abgott heißen,
nicht Götzendienst, was ich da treib und trieb.
All dieses Singen hier, all dieses Preisen:
von ihm, an ihm und immer ihm zulieb.

Gut ist mein Freund, ists heute und ists morgen,
und keiner ist beständiger als er.
In der Beständigkeit, da bleibt mein Vers geborgen,
spricht von dem Einen, schweift mir nicht umher.

"Schön, gut und treu", das singe ich und singe.
"Schön, gut und treu"—stets anders und stets das.
Ich find, erfind—um sie in eins zu bringen,
sie einzubringen ohne Unterlaß.

"Schön, gut und treu" so oft getrennt, geschieden,
In Einem will ich drei zusammenschmieden.⁹

Borrowing a celebrated expression from Walter Benjamin, Szondi characterizes the difference between the Shakespeare poem and Celan's translation as a difference in "intention towards language."¹⁰ In trying to isolate what he wants to call the enacting—as opposed to the descriptive—elements of Celan's version of the sonnet, Szondi speaks a great deal about minimally varied repetition, the *Dauer im Wechsel* which has become the staple food of the Jakobsonian version of poetics in this century: *treib / trieb* in line 2; *ihm / ihn / ihm* in line 4; *singe / singe* in line 9; *stets / stets* in line 10; and so on. But what he himself identifies as the most risky move in his reading, as well as the emblem of Celan's success, has to do with line 11. With the *ich find, erfind*, the critic insists that the reader of the poem must draw an artificial hiatus, and read not *ich find, erfind*, "I find, invent," but *ich find, er[ ]find*, "I find, he finds." Beginning with Celan's boldness, he proceeds with his own assertion that these lines show the most violent break with a traditional notion of translation which would depend on the presupposition of interlinguistic allosemes.¹¹

For Szondi, the departure from a view of translation as paraphrase into one of translation as performance is yet another way in which Celan's poem exhibits linguistic constancy in the lyrical chanting, or the dead repetition, of a linguistic paradigm. Having done this, however, what the critic fails to do is to see that once he has separated this small piece of *Er-Sprache* from the poem in order to bolster a notion of linguistic constancy, the automatisms which pervade the entire linguistic structure are made manifest. *Er* is one of the most common diphones to be found in German, perhaps the most common, and seeing it draw attention to itself here in this line (Szondi's move should hardly be considered a risky one) must lead us to perform a recursive scanning of the poem, which Szondi does not do.

To choose an example which is not merely one among others, Szondi's discovery of *er* does not take him back to line 6, *Und keiner ist beständiger als er,* which demands now to be read as *und kein[]er ist beständig[]er als er.* Not: "And no one is more constant than he," but: "and no he is more constant than he"—or even: "and no he is he-constanter than he." But as translation is precisely the problem here, and having already admitted that it is not a question of an allosemic plugging-in of equivalent, translinguistic values, and hence that there are no equivalent translations of *faits bruts de langue,* we must write, finally: "And no er is constant-er than er": Er, er, er.[12] In answer to the question "*Wer* ist er?," we cannot even say "*Der* ist er!," maybe only "Er ist er," or better yet: "Das ist er"—for even the pronominal function itself has dissolved in its specificity, leaving only the stuttering automatism of the marks on the page.

While this translation thus makes it difficult to see any particular face on the portrait of Mr. W. H., we should not rush to say that this pronominal profusion empties the poem of meaning. Such a move has perhaps become a shibboleth of contemporary criticism, and a point could also be made through the opposite formulation, that this er-proliferation over- or hyper-means, has one meaning, making explicit a kind of verbal-apophantic boy-craziness on the part of Shakespeare-Celan. All one meaning, no meaning—neither one of these is my point, which I choose to express in the tension of a question: what can be said to be the referent of such massive over-in(si)stance of such a general, deictic, almost syncategorematic word—if it be one or a word?

Lest these er-findings seem arbitrary or trivial, one should point out that while there is not a single occurrence in Shakespeare's poem of a first, second, or third person pronoun in any grammatical case—no I, no me, no you, not a single he or even a him, only my—all three "persons" are present in Celan's version, which is so bold as to open with the lyrically speaking highly egregious second person plural, *Ihr,* which we can read in one way as an almost-er. Yet to the extent that this *Ihr,* which, of all the German personal pronouns most resembles er, does *not* enter into a rhyme with another er, and thus is not being phonetically pushed into a near er-identity, we can say that this *Ihr* points out the complete absence of the second person throughout the rest of the poem, calling attention to the fragility of its own second-personhood, even in this abstract world of pronouns.

Metrically, Celan could have written *du* without any problem, as he does, for example, in his translation of the first line of the first sonnet. In addition to being phonemically closer to er, the *Ihr* is also capable, thematically speaking, of encompassing the company of an entire future history of readers in a move which would not have been too bold for Shakespeare himself. And this despite the fact that while er may be the most common of German syllables, the second person plural is the least common grammatical person to be found in the written language. Perhaps, then, we can say something more about *Ihr*.

As Szondi duly notes, the quotation marks around the three epithets "Fair, kind, and true" may have been deliberately chosen by Celan, who was the most meticulous of poets when it came to the mechanical. At the level of our argumentation, however, this is an irrelevant point. Why does it matter whether Celan chose an edition which used the quotation marks, or if he just happened to be working from the English text opposite some handy copy of Schlegel-Tieck translations, or from a dime-store copy? The point is that the consideration of what is going on in Celan's poem does not depend on his intention, in the same way that the frequency of the occurrence of er (or of re) does not depend on his intention. In attributing an intention toward language to Celan which is different from that of Shakespeare, Szondi makes Celan an allegorical name for something like language or language power. Intention toward language here must rather be taken in a thoroughly non-intentional, non-consciousness-oriented sense, as the *poem's* slant on language. Speaking psychologistically, Szondi has lost a friend and been left with a poem, and what he has done—as reader—in his essay is to transfer the constancy of the friend into a property which he can save by attributing it to the poem. This forces him to misread Benjamin's notion and to give an all too intentional account of intention. While the quotation marks are included in numerous editions of Shakespeare, and thus are not Celan's invention, they do not appear in the Quarto of 1609 and have been dropped from contemporary critical editions. They, too, can be read as intentional *stricto sensu*, or as without intention, forcing a question similar to the one posed above about the instance of er. In fact, Szondi points to what I would call the ontological transformation of the three epithets accomplished by the quotation marks, which call attention to the merely verbal existence of these allegorical names.

Stephen Booth, whose annotated critical edition of the *Sonnets* is as good a standard as any, speaks of sonnet 137 as being playfully and mockingly engaged in a parody of Trinitarian language. He opens his commentary on the poem with the following paragraph, before proceeding to gloss it line by line:

> The wit of this playful experiment in perversity derives from the false logic resulting from the speaker's studiously inadequate understanding of idolatry. Idolatry has traditionally been almost synonymous with polytheism: in Shakespeare's England its commonest occurrence was in self-righteously puritan attacks on Roman Catholics; it referred not so much to *substituting* worship of idols or other false gods (such as the golden calf of Exodus) for worship of the Christian god as to real or apparent worship of other gods (e.g. the saints—Mary in particular—and relics), *in addition to* the Christian god. . . . However, although all polytheism is idolatrous, it does not therefore follow that any and all monotheisms are orthodox as the speaker here pretends. In the narrow and misleading sense of *idolatry*, the poem makes its case, but the diction of the poem is ostentatiously reminiscent of Christian doctrine (lines 12–14 cap the litany-like repetition of the suggestively triple *Fair, Kind and True* with a specific echo of the doctrine of the Trinity), and of the forms of Christian devotion (line 4 echoes the *Gloria Patri*: "Glory be to the father, and to the sonne, and to the holy ghost. As it was in the beginning, is now, and ever shal be: worlde without ende"). Thus the same rhetoric that strengthens the argument for innocence of idolatrous polytheistic beliefs not only testifies to the idolatrous nature of the speaker's allegiance to the beloved but sharpens the evidence with overtones of active sacrilege.[13]

My own recourse here is not precisely to the Trinity, but to a motif which is ever-present in Renaissance literature, which prefigures the Trinity in a conventionally historical sense and which has been compendiously documented by Edgar Wind in his *Pagan Mysteries in the Renaissance*.[14] That is to say, we are here involved with the personification of the dynamic triad of the Three Graces, an illusion to which opens Szondi's own essay.

That to which Wind's iconography returns, in its patient tracing of the depiction, both verbal and pictorial, of the Three Graces, is the ambiguity of the position of the Third Grace. Debates on the use of the allegory always seem to center on the role of this third figure. There is giving and there is receiving, but how does one best represent returning so as to keep the tableau *vivant*, that is, so as to keep the economy in circulation? I do not know if there is an answer to this question, except to say that the story Wind tells is an objective historico-textual account of the recurrent difficulties in reading a figure, and is thus a second or third level narrative, or allegory.[15] In our account of Celan's poem, however, the *sprachontologische* shadiness does not relate to the grammatical *third* person which is, in this poem, omnipresent, but to the strangeness of the second, which flickers into whatever existence it may have in and as the opening of the poem and just as quickly disappears. The ambiguity that centers on the figure of the third grace (who is also the second, however, in the sense that she often stands between giving and receiving as the figure of their relation—that is, as returning) also centers on the second person of Celan's poem.

To whom is the sonnet addressed? When Paul Celan wants to speak to a reader, he most often writes *du*, although the ontological status of the *du* in many of his poems could not possibly be interpretatively foreclosed in such a manner. *Ihr* is perhaps an address to these three verbal nonentities, these three words *schön, gut, und treu*—"you [three] should not call the one whom I loved there an idol, nor idolatry what I do and did"—but its secondness is also a kind of thirdness.

While the *Ihr* would thus be foregrounded, I would like to conclude with some more remarks in the field of the automatism of the impersonal or grammatical opened up above. As noted, Szondi comments on Celan's repetitions as performing linguistic constancy. Continuing in our recursive reading of the poem, and moving one line further up to "Gut ist mein Freund, ists heute und ists morgen," we may now have to take seriously the (in German rather conventional) fading out of er into the contracted *es*, as a shading off into the neutrality of the third person, which is not really a person at all. A noun may (pretend to) be the name of a person, place, or thing, but what is a pronoun?

We can say of pronouns what we can say of other shifters as well as of deictic marks in general, such as "this," "here," "now," and so forth, precisely what Benveniste, who translates the most traditionally Hegelian philosophemes into something like a linguistics, says: their abstract generality phagocytes the particularity of each speech event in which they are spoken.[16] The linguistic necessity of allegory—the necessity to speak the other, because that is all that can be spoken—exists if anywhere most clearly in the occurrence of deictic language, for it is in deictic language that apparently referential statements can be seen most clearly to lose their referential moment in the very act of being uttered.[17] The reading of the predications consequent to the utterance of any pseudodeictic act of the form "this is x," where x is any predicate whatever, narrates the fall of positional language into abstraction, which is hence an inextricable part of any referential statement or description, no matter how "definite" it may hope to be. Thus the fall into the thematic to which I alluded in the opening remarks is a necessary linguistic moment which accompanies every positional speech act, and which embeds thematization as a structural moment in predicative utterance. Thematization is the name for this fall, for the fated process that befalls the (non)moment of positing of any utterance, which utterance can be spliced in as a moment of some account—such as is the case in Szondi's as well as in the present essay—and thus be made into the matter or theme of that account. Such is the disjunction at the core—or on the surface; it is the same—of all speech acts considered in the linguistic truth of and as allegory.[18] What occurs here is prior to any consideration of a conflict between codes or between natural languages; it is the rupture attendant to syntactic structure which constitutes and inhabits the code as such.

To return to the poem, however. Speaking of *ich*, *ihr*, and *er*, we are principally concerned with the first and third, inasmuch as the second, according to our analysis, reveals itself as an address to the constituent figures of an allegorical tableau which already has something of the third person about it. Its secondness, considered as a plurality of phenomenal addressees, of singular yous, drops out, as it were. *Ich* and *er*, "he" and "I": the *und* unites and divides. Yet to maintain our pursuit of the automatisms at the heart of this poem, of the *er*s, *und*s and *ist*s, we should now draw the logical conclusion of our argument thus far: namely, that *ich*, I, in its abstract, (non)positional generality, is no more personal than the so-called third person. In his "Meridian" speech in acceptance of the 1960 Georg-Büchner Prize (*GW* 3:187–202), speaking of the day on which Büchner's Lenz went into the mountains, Celan writes of that Lenz who thus goes: "er als ein ich." This was first translated into French as "Lui en tant que Moi,"[19] then corrected as "Lui en tant qu'un moi."[20] But it should perhaps be even "Lui en tant que je," "He as an I." Having gone through an analysis of the asymmetrical symmetry of the relation between the first and third persons, we can now say, inverting Celan's maxim: *ich als ein er*, "I as a he."

While Szondi reads Celan's couplet as the expression of a hope, the hope the fulfillment of which would be the performance of the constation of line 7, "In der Beständigkeit, da bleibt mein Vers geborgen" ("In constancy, there remains my verse sheltered"), it would be more accurate to say that the expression of the wish "In Einem will ich drei zusammenschmieden" is precisely the correlate of a kind of failure, although the failure here is a necessary and linguistic one, and not one that should be interpreted in the register of the pathetic. It is a failure in the sense that it is the disjunction of Celan's translation, of the disjunction which *is* his translation; that is, it is the very achievement of this poem, of the translation of Shakespeare's song without a singer into his—Celan's—prose poem which overflows with impersonal personalities.[21] It is this success/failure (I would not try to subordinate one of these terms to the other), this *Fehlleistung*, which results in the impossible wish of the last line, which speaks a hope of something that cannot be, rather than the satisfaction of a desire already gratified. With its exhortation, the first line of Shakespeare's poem speaks of a present love, whereas Celan's speaks not only in the simple past of a perfected action, but also of another place, "den ich *da* lieb," of a *da* which is *fort*. This *da* occurs three times in Celan's poem. Where or what is this place?

First, it is the place of the one whom I loved; second, of the activity which I do and did; and third, where my verse remains sheltered. Critics perhaps too numerous to count have interpreted the first and greater portion of Shakespeare's *Sonnets* as consisting, for the most part, of the narrative of the Bard's love for a young man. In this reading, the narrative is often taken referentially, as the story of a chain of events, beginning with the so-called procreation sonnets and ending with a sequence of poems in which the speaker's idealization of his love into an abstract object, as opposed to a love object, leads to the waning of the relationship. In keeping with this fabular reading, we could say that the place of this *da* is the place of the preceding poems in which the poet spoke of his beloved, and not so much of his love. Yet this would be to miss the point of (our analysis of) Celan's poem, as well as to efface the one occurrence of the *da* in a line where it relates both to present as well as to past activity: "was ich da treib und trieb."

Once we have said that this is a poem about er, if not about him or about my or his love, we will no sooner realize that we cannot say this. For this level of analysis is not "about" anything. The question of the "about" which we posed at the beginning is the question from which we departed when we left behind the considerations of the theme of the theme. Instead of saying that this is a poem about er, we might want to adopt—in a move that appears to be at first glance a pathetic attempt at the recuperation of the *melos* purported to exist at the root of the lyric— the more musical expression and say that this is a poem in er. This would be no melocentrism in the traditional sense, but rather some kind of asymmetrical inversion on the order of "the birth of music from the dead letter of poetry," or from the illusion of the existence of poetry. Thus here, in the kingdom of *ich, ihr*, and er, in which there is no *du* (as there is no you in Shakespeare's poem either—the poet at this point being fully engaged in his activity of writing, which activity is not being addressed, as in many of the earlier sonnets, to a singularly beloved you), a kingdom from which all "persons" have been deported, the poet's activity is always already accomplished in the preterite of "den ich da lieb." There are more reasons than one why one always fails to speak of whom—or of what—one loves.

NOTES

1. *Celan-Studien* (Frankfort: Suhrkamp, 1972); now in Peter Szondi, *Schriften*, ed. Jean Bollack et al. (Frankfort: Suhrkamp, 1978), 2:319–98; "Poetry of Constancy—Poetik der Beständigkeit. Celans Übertragung von Shakespeares Sonett 105," 321–44; "Eden," to which I will also refer, 390–98.

2. Now in *Schriften*, 1:264–412.

3. "Lecture de *Strette*. Essai sur la poésie de Paul Celan," *Critique* 27, no.

288 (1971), 387–420; reprinted as "Durch die Enge geführt," trans. Jean Bollack et al., in *Schriften*, 2:345–89.

4. Apparently this kind of effacement of dates and titles between the fair copy of the single poem and the book manuscript was not an uncommon practice for Celan.

5. The point here is that the only necessity that can be attributed in literary history has to do first with the occurrences of texts, and only secondarily with the narrative-temporal order within which such events are incorporated into a history after the fact. There is no prediction in literary history because there is no principle of sufficient reason for the occurrence of texts. The necessity of any relation construed between given texts is a necessity constructed after the fact, even if such explanation often occults this by telling a story of genesis, decline, regression, or whatever, as though it were a relation between texts themselves—as though such entities were imaginable. In this respect, much literary history is more formalist than supposedly hyperformalist readings which insist on the positing, occurrence, or eventhood of texts. On the crucial question of how and why what is called deconstruction is *not* a formalism, see Paul de Man, "Kant and Schiller," in *Aesthetics, Rhetoric, Ideology*, ed. Andrzej Warminski (Minneapolis: University of Minnesota Press, forthcoming).

6. An intrinsic reading of Celan's poem might want to take account of the way in which the "nichts / stockt" at the end of it not only stops the poem (among Szondi's notes for the Celan essays occur the following two fragmentary lines: "Darüber, das nichts stockt, stockt das Gedicht" and "Das nichts stockt, macht das Gedicht stocken" [*Schriften*, 2:429]), but, by forcing the poem to spill over onto the fourteenth line of type on the page, makes this poem which begins with an unnamed *du* into a kind of degenerate sonnet that stops/does not stop. Celan's poem, originally entitled "Wintergedicht," cannot have been written without that other twentieth-century lyric in mind, that is, Trakl's "Ein Winterabend," the sacramental final line of which ("Auf dem Tische Brot und Wein") has been transposed into the "DU LIEGST im großen Gelausche" of Celan's first line, as well as into the center of the later poem, in the verses "Es kommt der Tisch mit den Gaben / Es biegt um ein Eden." The Trakl poem is one of the ostensible subjects of an essay by Heidegger. See Martin Heidegger, "Die Sprache," in *Unterwegs zur Sprache* (Pfullingen: Neske, 1959), 9–33.

7. Celan's poetry contains both the figure of the scar as well as that of the seal in prominent places. See, for example, "Engführung" (*GW* 1:199/*P* 139) and the opening of "Mit Brief und Uhr" (*GW* 1:154/*P* 107).

8. It would not be uninteresting to describe this relation—that between Szondi's essays and Celan's poems—in terms borrowed from the description of psychic structures, as emblematic of the paradoxes of mourning considered as a narcissistic wound, of the necessity of a subject's divestment of whatever value it has—not necessarily previously—put into an object. In a preliminary fashion, it would not be wrong to characterize Szondi's monograph as his own kind of textual mourning to and for Celan. And it would be neither wrong nor monstrous to try to write an account of this relation which would tell the story of two suicides, and to read Szondi's interrupted text as enacting the paradox of mourning—as being always necessary and inevitable, on the one hand, and, on the other hand, impossible and "in error." "Dem gleich fehlet die Trauer" is the

last line of Hölderlin's "Mnemosyne," which looms large over the work of Paul Celan and which Richard Sieburth has translated as "For him, mourning is in error." Friedrich Hölderlin, *Sämtliche Werke*, ed. Friedrich Beißner (Stuttgart: Kolhammer, 1951), 2(1): 196. Friedrich Hölderlin, *Hymns and Fragments*, trans. Richard Sieburth (Princeton: Princeton University Press, 1984), 119.

Lest these comments provoke a knee-jerking accusation of the worst form of psychologizing, I would add that the kind of situation within which such a *Trauerarbeit* would take place would be one in which any psychoanalytic terminology employed would be thought through in terms of the linguistic structures which have proven so useful in being taken up by analytic theory and practice. It is neither a question of assimilating psychoanalysis to linguistics nor vice versa, and the kind of work to which I am alluding has progressed a great deal since Lacan's seminar on the psychoses, and his reflections there on pronominal fadeouts in relation to subjective fadeouts. See Jacques Lacan, *Le séminaire, livre III: les psychoses* (Paris: Seuil, 1981); or Derrida's work with Abraham and Torok: "Fors," preface to Nicolas Abraham and Maria Torok, *Le verbier de l'homme aux loups* (Paris: Aubier, 1976), 7–73. Jacques Derrida, "Fors: The Anglish Words of Nicolas Abraham and Maria Torok," trans. Barbara Johnson, in Nicolas Abraham and Maria Torok, *The Wolf Man's Magic Word: A Cryptonymy*, trans. Nicholas Rand (Minneapolis: Minnesota University Press, 1986), xi–xlviii.

9. *GW* 5:344–45. A rough translation of Celan's poem reads: "You [plural] should not call the one whom I loved there an idol, / nor idolatry what I do and did. / All these singings, all these prizes: / from him, to him, and ever for the love of him. // Good is my friend, is't today and is't tomorrow, / and no one is more constant than he. / In constancy, there remains my verse sheltered, / speaks of the One, does not waver about. // 'Fair, good and true,' I sing it and sing. / 'Fair, good and true'—always otherwise and always thus. / I find, invent—in order to bring them into one / To harvest-them-into-one without remainder. // 'Fair, good and true' so oft separated, sundered / In One I want three to forge."

10. "Die Aufgabe des Übersetzers," in *Gesammelte Schriften*, ed. Rolf Tiedemann and Hermann Schweppenhäser (Frankfort: Suhrkamp, 1980 [1972]), 4(1), ed. Tillman Rexroth, 9–21. "The Task of the Translator," in Walter Benjamin, *Illuminations*, ed. and intro. Hannah Arendt, trans. Harry Zohn (New York: Schocken, 1968), 69–82.

11. Szondi writes:

> Celan's translation of [this] verse evinces the same rejection of the traditional conception of language, according to which different signifiers can correspond to the same signified. Indeed, we can sense a desire to abolish the distinction between signifier and signified altogether. In this verse, Shakespeare explicitly mentions that *change* (i.e., the replacement of one word by another, while the intended meaning remains the same) whose premise is precisely this traditional conception of language:
>
> And in this change is my invention spent.
>
> Celan refuses to concede that words may be interchangeable in this way, just as he successfully avoids using a word derived from the familiar rhetorical term *inventio* to designate the poet's activity and capacity. Designation is replaced by speaking: *Ich*

find, erfind. In linguistic terms, this is one of the boldest passages in Celan's version, surpassed perhaps only by the immediately following one. For here the repetition of the verb, that is, of the word for the activity, does more than simply convey the activity's constancy (which was its sole function in the case of the expressions *Gut ist mein Freund, ists heute und ists morgen* and *das singe ich und singe*). Furthermore, to understand the phrase *Ich find, erfind*, it is not sufficient to read the expansion of "find" in the repetition (*erfind*) as a delayed translation of "invention"; nor should it be viewed as a substitute for the dimension of "change" that Celan refuses to mention explicitly or even to accept a possible means of expressing variation. To be sure, it is all that. At the same time, however, with the phrase *Ich find, erfind* Celan pierces the façade of linguistic performance, that is, of *parole* (speech), making it possible to glimpse the inner workings of the linguistic system, of *langue* (language). (He already did this, although in an incomparably less bold fashion, in verse 2: *was ich da treib und trieb*.) What is thereby revealed are parts of the conjugation paradigm, once with respect to tense (*was ich da treib und trieb*) and once with respect to person: *ich find, erfind* (= *er find*). Admittedly, this reading is not compelling in the first case (the change of tense, accompanied by lexical constancy, has its own function, as was seen above); it becomes so only when the first case is considered together with the second (*Ich find, erfind*). Our interpretation of the second case presupposes that, in this position, the prefix *er* carries the connotation of the personal pronoun *er* ("he").

"Poetry of Constancy—Poetik der Beständigkeit," 334–35. "The Poetry of Constancy: Paul Celan's Translation of Shakespeare's Sonnet 105," in Peter Szondi, *On Textual Understanding and Other Essays*, trans. Harvey Mendelson (Minneapolis: Minnesota University Press, 1986), 170–71. It is perhaps more than amusing to note a change that takes place between the title of Szondi's essay, "Poetry of Constancy—Poetik der Beständigkeit," and the English translation, which is simply called "Poetry of Constancy," and thus effaces the interlinguistic tension present in the original title.

12. We should cease to underline 'er' at this point, since, according to our argument, while belonging to language, it does not belong to any particular language, hence not to the impure German language. Being further than foreign, it is not simply a foreign word, or even a word at all. It is as though it were a piece of pure language in Benjamin's sense.

13. *Shakespeare's Sonnets*, ed. with an analytic commentary by Stephen Booth (New Haven: Yale University Press, 1977), 336–37.

14. (New York: Norton, 1968 [1958]).

15. In precisely the sense which Paul de Man gives to the term in "Allegory (*Julie*)." See *Allegories of Reading* (New Haven: Yale University Press, 1979), 205. When de Man speaks of allegory as a second or third level narrative, the ambiguity in the ordination must be accounted for, which I propose to do in the following way, following de Man's discussion: if the figure in the text is level one, then the text being read is assigned to level two, and the critical reading thereof level three. Yet a naked figure as such is not something which is given to be read, so alternately the figure could be conceived of as a zero-level, after-the-fact construction which the reader has abduced from the text (level one) in the course of the reading (level two). This may be a heuristic device for the

understanding of one sentence in the paragraph in question, but it is important to remember that de Man's greater point is that the levels, as is particularly the case in Rousseau (whose *Julie* is being discussed in the passage in question), are always contaminating each other and that an *unambiguous* scheme such as the one just proposed would pertain only to a model or ideal, that is, to a nonexistent language. Another way of saying this would be to say that in the case of a text for which an un-double account could be given, reading would not be necessary—or to put it in de Man's own words from "The Resistance to Theory": rhetorical readings are "consistently defective models of language's impossibility to be a model language." *The Resistance to Theory* (Minneapolis: University of Minnesota Press, 1986), 19.

16. The section of Benveniste's *Problèmes de la linguistique générale* (Paris Gallimard, 1974), vol. 1, entitled "L'Homme dans la langue" (223–76), is largely a recounting of Hegelian commonplaces, a fact which does not, however, invalidate it as a set of observations about language or about linguistics, given that it is not at all assured that any linguistics could ever emancipate itself from any such ideological translation, even and especially in its founding gestures, such as those which would try to define its object.

This does not make linguistics false or irrelevant. If anything, such a structuralist observation concerning structuralist linguistics only makes more evident the depth of the relation between linguistics and other discourses which may or may not be considered to be linguistically oriented. Lacan's work is an example of an attempt to introduce linguistic models into a domain (psychoanalysis) which had not necessarily previously seen the need to lean on such a model.

17. De Man makes this point most forcefully in a reading of Hegel. See "Sign and Symbol in Hegel's *Aesthetics*," in *Aesthetics, Rhetoric, Ideology*. See also his "Hypogram and Inscription," in *The Resistance to Theory*, esp. 41–43.

18. An exemplary analysis of such disruption at the grammatical level occurs in Lacan's analysis of the difference between the sentences "tu es celui qui me suivras" and "tu es celui qui me suivra." See *Le Séminaire, livre III: les psychoses*, 281–91 and 307–20. I would like to thank Debra Keates for calling my attention to this passage in Lacan.

This moment of Lacan's text, which concerns a node of contiguity between the registers of the imaginary and the symbolic, is an expansion of Benveniste's cliché (*pace* Riffaterre) concerning the way in which the personhood of the second grammatical person is just as "imaginary," as it were—that is, symbolic— as the purported specificity, the haecceity of the first or third. All poems or letters written in the intimate second person might as well, in this sense and according to this line of thinking, be addressed "dear occupant." But the rhetorical irreplaceability of the *you* has to do with the very *attempt at* address, even if, in technical-linguistic terms, the pronominal function effaces the specificity of any given addressee. Anyone knows that he or she cannot address a lover as a "second-person function," but it is precisely this nexus of (ir)replaceability which makes the transference, and hence psychoanalysis, possible—and, *a fortiori*, all interpersonal relations, according to Freud and Lacan, inasmuch as all of our relations are based on what Freud calls *Anlehnung*, or anaclitic object choice. The theory and practice of psychoanalysis could be said to exist in the space between the need to have an address for any given second person and the actual linguistic leveling impersonality of the structure of that—and of all other—"persons." De Man has written an intriguing commentary on this: "Rather than being a heightened version of sense experience, the erotic is a figure that makes such experience possible. We do not see what we love but we love in the hope of confirming the illusion that we are indeed seeing anything at all." "Hypogram and Inscription," 53 n.

19. Paul Celan, "Le Méridien," trans. André du Bouchet, in *Strette* (Paris: Mercure de France, 1971), 188.

20. Paul Celan, "Le Méridien. Discours prononcé à l'occasion de la remise du prix Georg Büchner," trans. Jean Launay, *Po&sie* 9 (1979), 75.

21. It is a prose poem, in this account, because it highlights, or backlights, the craft-work of grammar, and not the art-work conceived of in symbolic terms.

O könnt ich doch, mit meinem Munde,
solch erstes Schweigen sein
—Mandelstam, translated by Celan

Dies ist ein Wort, das neben den Worten einherging,
ein Wort nach dem Bilde des Schweigens
—Celan

12

Poetic Mutations of Silence

At the Nexus of Paul Celan and Osip Mandelstam

Leonard Olschner

One of the most consequential paradoxes surrounding Paul Celan's work, one allied to its patent resistance to a feared adulteration by misused, euphemistic, and outworn, obsolete metaphorical language, originates in the silences from which his poetry emanates, the silences inherently belonging to Celan's sense of language. To be sure, this situation does not pertain to Celan uniquely—Hölderlin and Rilke, both formative influences, paradigmatically faced related problems[1]—but his work came early on to be associated with *Verstummen*, as though this reductive term, taken alone, were an insightful and hence hermeneutically productive label. This differs fundamentally from a coy preciosity or the infamously forbidding blank sheet of paper. In his 1960 "Meridian" address, Celan wrote:

> Poetry today . . . exhibits an unmistakably strong tendency toward silence [*Verstummen*] . . . Poetry maintains its ground at its own margins; in order to exist, it must summon and extract itself from its state of no longer existing [*Schon-nicht-mehr*] to one of its still existing [*Immer-noch*]. (*GW* 3:197)

This observation summarizes a substantial part of Celan's experience as a poet to that date, formulates a central aspect of his poetics, and functions as a point of departure for the reader. Displaced to the periphery of their own existence and threatened equally by distorting articulation from the inside and inarticulable silence from the outside, Celan's poems work to overcome these seemingly insurmountable obstacles simultaneously. Striving for, or directed toward, unheard-of lucidity, they appear to become—or in fact do become—fractured, obscure, and hermetic (this last a necessarily problematic term and one that Celan himself vigorously rejected for his work). In the course of Celan's development, the texts become increasingly inaccessible and also more numerous, even if generally more terse—as though the poet were writing, futilely, to stem a threatening flood of silence. The final surrender, Celan's suicide in 1970, is also the final silence. His poetic texts are left to understanding and misunderstanding and to the threat of becoming silenced themselves through critics' dismissal and readers' disregard, as exemplified by the position that hermeticism represents a solipsistic rejection of communicative acts or a willed flight from "reality" and from responsible social consciousness (positions which can be and have been shown to be misinformed).

How do we define such resistance to engulfing silence, resistance which consists of designating the unspeakable, not in metaphysical categories, although perhaps in metalinguistic ones? Of Celan's poetry Adorno wrote:

> This poetry is imbued with the shame of art in view of the suffering that withdraws from both experience and sublimation. Celan's poems attempt to express the most extreme horror [*das äußerste Entsetzen*] through remaining silent [*durch Verschweigen*]. . . . The language of lifelessness becomes the final consolation over a death bereft of every meaning. The transition to the inorganic cannot only be observed, through motifs and themes, but the path from horror to silence can also be reconstructed in the self-contained structures.[2]

If *Verschweigen* implies knowledge that its possessor suppresses, for whatever reason, then Celan is searching for a mode of language that takes prelinguistic perception into account.[3] (Celan's translation of Valéry's "ce silence complice" with "dies Schweigen und Verschweigen" [*GW* 4:134–35, l. 198] exemplifies this move.) This form of perception occurs at poetic levels, while the poet attempts to avoid all "poeticizing" of experience (cf. *GW* 3:167), since poeticizing entails at best the making harmless of unspeakable but unforgotten events and is at the least tasteless and odious after the Holocaust. Thus Adorno's *das äußerste Entsetzen* refers to the horrors of persecution under National Socialism, and *Verschweigen* to the inherent failure of language to comprehend this catastrophe as one of the most abject manifestations of human imagination. For this reason *äußerst* may be understood both as "extreme" and *in extremis*, in the throes of death. It was presumably the poetry of Celan which moved Adorno to retract his pronouncement, written in 1949, "to write a poem after Auschwitz is barbaric";[4] for the provenance of Adorno's understanding of poetry had evidently included conservative figures such as Stefan George and Rudolf Borchardt, whose aesthetics he perforce abandoned after the Nazi atrocities became known, but to whom he later returned in essays.

The thematization of *schweigen* and *verstummen* occurs with explicit reference to language itself—which is not to state a truism[5]—in Celan's collections from *Mohn und Gedächtnis* (1952) to *Die Niemandsrose* (1963) as well as in equally relevant translations of poetic texts by Paul Valéry, Jules Supervielle, and especially Osip Mandelstam. The dialectic of silence and language—each attempting to overcome the other, despite their interdependence—is nearly ubiquitous for this period. Later work shifts away from this dichotomy and toward different configurations of themes and problems significant on their own ground. "Argumentum e silentio" (*GW* 1:138), to cite an especially conspicuous example—whose title, a term taken from logic, refers to suppressing knowledge for rhetorical purposes—argues literally from silence: from the language of silence to the silencing of language:

> Lege,
> lege auch du jetzt dorthin, was herauf-
> dämmern will neben den Tagen:
> das sternüberflogene Wort,
> das meerübergoßne.
>
> Jedem das Wort.
> Jedem das Wort, das ihm sang,
> als die Meute ihn hinterrücks anfiel—
> Jedem das Wort, das ihm sang und erstarrte.
>
> Ihr, der Nacht,
> das sternüberflogne, das meerübergoßne,
> ihr das erschwiegne,
> dem das Blut nicht gerann, als der Giftzahn
> die Silben durchtieß.
>
> Ihr das erschwiegene Wort.
>   (ll. 6–20)
>
> (Place,
> now you should also place what wants to
> dawn beside the days:

the word overflown by stars,
poured over by sea.

To each the word.
To each the word that sang to him,
when the pack attacked him from behind—
To each the word that sang to him and froze.

To her, the night, [the word]
overflown by stars, poured over by sea,
to her, [the word] acquired by silence,
whose blood did not clot when the poison fang
penetrated the syllables.

To her, the word acquired by silence.)

The opposition between day and night corresponds to one between worn, quotidian talk and poetic speech, between *sang und erstarrte* and *erschwiegen*, the latter of which implies an active and initial attainment of speech through and on the basis of silence. *Jedem das Wort* appears to echo scornfully the Ciceronian phrase "Jedem das seine" (*suum cuique*)—the expression made into a grim and derisive welcome on the gate of Buchenwald. It is unlikely Celan would have unwittingly, not to say consciously, used this expression with a neutral reference after a lapse of attention to involuntary associations.

Celan's own experience with persecution and the murder of his family and his raw sensitivity toward neo-Fascism made him suspect intrigues at every turn; the quickly refuted charges of plagiarism by Claire Goll and the ensuing "critical" demagogy and pedantry are a case in point. This helps to explain Celan's own ambivalence toward the Federal Republic, to which he seems to refer as the "Stummvölker-Zone" (*GW* 1:288), contained in "Und mit dem Buch aus Tarussa" ("And with the Book from Tarussa" [*GW* 1:287–91):

mit
geatmeten Steppen-
halmen geschrieben ins Herz
der Stundenzäsur—in das Reich,
in der Reiche
weitestes, in
den Großbinnenreim
jenseits
der Stummvölker-Zone, in dich

Sprachwaage, Wortwaage, Heimat-
waage Exil.

(with
breathed steppe-
grass written into the heart
of the hour-caesura—into the realm,
the widest of
realms, into
the great internal rhyme
beyond
the zone of mute nations, into yourself
language-scale, word-scale, home-
scale of exile.)
(*SG* 209)

The word *stumm* can be read as a submerged translation of the Russian
немой, and this in turn is etymologically related to немец (German, a
speaker of German).[6] Speaking from Paris, Celan considers himself outside the regions where German is spoken, which makes him foreign,
alien (in Old Slavic немец was used to refer to every "stranger"), an exile
writer with affinities to Russia and particularly to Mandelstam, Sergej
Esenin, and Marina Cvetaeva.

The poet who was most influential and later became an alter ego to
Celan was of course Mandelstam,[7] whose poetic and prose works Celan
read intensely in the mid- to late fifties and some of whose poetic texts
on the existence or preexistence of poetry in silence or music Celan
translated. Markings in the margins of Celan's copy of Mandelstam's
essays indicate a careful reading of texts which would become important
for his own poetics.[8] An only recently discovered manuscript of a radio
essay by Celan on Mandelstam testifies to the direct influence the Russian poet had on him; for in explicating Mandelstam's poetics, Celan
articulates his own poetics by paraphrasing or directly quoting from the
radio essay in the "Meridian," the speech he gave upon receiving the
Büchner-Prize.[9]

Key texts for the understanding of the complex in question are "Silentium" (*GW* 5:5–57), which lends itself to comparison with Celan's
"Argumentum e silentio," and "Das Wort bleibt ungesagt" (*GW* 5:114–
15). Both texts speak of the poetic word by postulating, respectively, its
preexistence and its movement toward and then retreat from incarna-
tion. In "Silentium," Mandelstam attempts to trace the path of poetic
speech back to its origins in silence and chaos, thereby considering music to assume a transitional or mediating position; it expresses a longing
to regain a linguistic Arcadia, the silence from which language issues

forth. This is in itself a model of translation analogous to that of the translation of poetry from one language to another.[10] Without knowledge of Mandelstam, Benjamin noted in the mid-1930s: "Boundary: lacking need for translation. Poetry: nearest to music—greatest difficulties in translation.[11] Mandelstam's text "Silentium" reads in Celan's translation:

Sie ist noch nicht, ist unentstanden,
Musik ist sie und Wort:
so lebt, verknüpft durch ihre Bande,
was west und atmet, fort.

Im Meer das Atmen, ruhig, immer,
das Licht durchwächst den Raum;
aus dem Gefäß, das bläulich schimmert,
steigt fliederblaßer Schaum.

O könnt ich doch, mit meinem Munde,
solch erstes Schweigen sein,
ein Ton, kristallen, aus dem Grunde,
und so geboren: rein.

Bleib, Aphrodite, dieses Schäumen,
du Wort, geh, bleib Musik.
Des Herzens schäm dich, Herz, das seinem
Beginn und Grund entstieg.

(Она еше не родилась,
Она и музыка и слово,
И потому всего живого
Ненарушаемая связь.

Спокойно дышат моря груди,
Но, как безумный, светел день,
И пены бледная сирень
В мутно-лазоревом сосуде.

Да обретут мои уста
Первоначальную немоту,
Как кристаллическую ноту,
Что от рождения чиста!

Останься пеной, Афродита,
И слово в музыку вернись,

И сердце сердца устыдисб,
С первоосновой жизни слито!)

(It [fem.] is not yet born,
it is both music and word,
and hence the unbroken bond
of all that is alive.

Quietly breathe the breasts of the sea,
but, like a madman, the day is bright,
and the pale lilac of the foam
is in the cloudy azure vessel.

May my lips find
primeval silence
like a crystal tone
that is pure from birth.

Remain as foam, Aphrodite,
and word, return to music,
and heart, be ashamed of the heart,
united with the source of life.)

The theme of "Das Wort bleibt ungesagt" complements "Silentium" by assuming the same neo-Romantic premise—analogous to Benjamin's concept of "reine Sprache"—that language exists in the cosmos before it becomes degraded and violated through the metamorphotic translation into human speech. In a complex metaphorical and intertextual structure,[12] centering on the swallow as an image of the poetic word, Mandelstam describes the near-entry of poetic speech into recognizable existence. Celan does not take the interplay of biographical and literary allusion into consideration (assuming he was aware of it), but attributes a more singular voice to the text—while relegating, inadvertently or not, the other voices to silence anew—and then constitutes a "dialogue" with it through translation:

Das Wort bleibt ungesagt, ich finds nicht wieder.
Die blinde Schwalbe flog ins Schattenheim,
zum Spiel, das sie dort spielen. (Zersägt war ihr Gefieder.)
Tief in der Ohnmacht, nächtlich, singt ein Reim.

Die Vögel—stumm. Und keine Immortelle.
Glashelle Mähnen—das Gestüt der Nacht.
Ein Kahn treibt, leer, es trägt ihn keine Welle.

Das Wort: umschwärmt von Grillen, unerwacht.

Und wächst, wächst wie es Tempeln, Zelten eigen,
steht, jäh umnachtet, wie Antigone,
stürzt, stygisch-zärtlich und mit grünem Zweige,
als blinde Schwalbe stürzt es nieder, jäh.

Beschämung all der Finger, die da sehen,
o die Erkenntnis einst, so freudenprall.
O Aoniden, ihr—ich muß vor Angst vergehen,
vor Nebeln, Abgrund, Glockenton und Schall.

Wer sterblich ist, kann lieben und erkennen,
des Finger fühlt: ein Laut, der mich durchquert . . .
Doch ich—mein Wort, ich weiß es nicht zu nennen,
ein Schemen war es—es ist heimgekehrt.

Die Körperlose, immer, Stund um Stunde,
Antigone, die Schwalbe, überall . . .
Wie schwarzes Eis, so glüht auf meinem Munde
Erinnerung an Stygisches, an Hall.

(Я слово позабыл, что я хотел сказать.
Слепая ласточка в чертог теней вернется,
На крыльях срезанных, с прозрачными играть.
В беспамятстве ночная песнь поется.

Не слышно птиц. Бессмертник не цветет.
Прозрачны гривы табуна ночного.
В сухой реке пустой челнок плывет.
среди кузнечиков беспамятствует слово.

И медленно растет, как бы шатер иль храм,
То вдруг прокинется безумной Антигоной,
То мертвой ласточкой бросается к ногам
С стигийской нежностью и веткою зеленой.

О если бы вернуть и зрячих пальцев стыд,
И выпуклую радость узнаванья.
Я так боюсь рыданья Аонид,
Тумана, звона и зиянья.

А смертным власть дана любить и узнавать,
Для них и звук в персты прольется,

Но я забыл, что я хочу сказать,
И мысль бесплотная в чертог теней вернется.

Всё не о том прозрачная твердит,
Всё ласточка, подружка, Антигона . . .
А на губах как черный лед горит
Стигийского воспоминанье звона.)

(I have forgotten the word that I wanted to say.
The blind swallow returns to the palace of shadows,
on cut wings, to play with the transparent ones.
In nocturnal unconsciousness a song is sung.

Birds cannot be heard. The immortelle is not in bloom.
Transparent are the names of the nocturnal herd.
In the dry river an empty boot swims.
Among grasshoppers the word becomes unconscious.

And slowly grows, like tent or temple,
suddenly strikes, crazed Antigone,
throws herself down with the dead swallow
with Stygian tenderness and green branch.

O to retrieve the shame of seeing fingers
and the swollen joy of knowledge.
I fear the wailing of the Aonids,
the fog, the tingling, the abyssal opening.

And to mortals is the power given to love and perceive,
for their sake sound is poured into fingers.
But I have forgotten what I want to say,
and the incorporeal thought returns to the palace of shadows.

Constantly the transparent one speaks of the same thing,
Constantly the swallow, friend, Antigone . . .
But on the lips there burns like black ice
a tingling of the Stygian memory.)

Apart from negating the first-person pronoun я, the transposition of
Я слово позабыл ("I have forgotten the word") to *Das Wort bleibt ungesagt*, betrays both a similar conception of the poetic word for the two poets
and a major difference. Whereas Mandelstam had sensed the word almost within his grasp before it elusively returned to its origin, Celan
assumes the *a priori* existence of the same word; that is, in this transla-

tion, he has actual knowledge of this word, or rather, it is assumed (since no agent is mentioned in the initial phrase) that this word will not be spoken, *es wird verschwiegen*. This difference is identical to the difference between poetic amnesia (Mandelstam) and sublimated poetic anamnesis (Celan). The shift remains consistent with Celan's own poetics as revealed in lines such as the following from "Selbdritt, selbviert" (*GW* 1:216):

> Diese Stunde, deine Stunde,
> ihr Gespräch mit meinem Munde.

> Mit dem Mund, mit seinem Schweigen,
> mit den Worten, die sich weigern.

> (This hour, your hour,
> their talk with my mouth.

> With the mouth, with its silence,
> with the words that resist.)

For here the unspoken although explicitly postulated words define the nature of *Schweigen* as a linguistic phenomenon containing congenitally the potential for speech, expression, verbalization, and hence perception and possibly communication. These situate the poem, analogous to its author, within historical time (as in the words of the Bremen address: "poetry is not timeless" [*GW* 3:186]), an aspect of Celan's poetics which he equally ascribed to Mandelstam. The poem, he says in his essay, is "the site where what is perceivable and attainable through language is collected around that center from which it acquires shape and truth: around this individual's existence, which questions the hour—one's own and that of the world—the heartbeat and the aeon" (*GW* 5:623/*CP* 63). *Diese Stunde, deine Stunde* and *die Stunde, die eigene und die der Welt* appear to be interchangeable for both Celan and Mandelstam.

Toward the end of his poem, Mandelstam varies line 1 by eliminating *слово* ("word") and changing the modal verb expressing volition from past to present (*хотел* ["wanted"] to *хочу* ["want"]); Celan, however, appears to stutter, a sign of imminent speechlessness in the form of a linguistic gesture:

> Doch ich—mein Wort, ich weiß es nicht zu nennen,
> ein Schemen war es—es ist heimgekehrt.

> Но я забыл, что я хочу сказать,
> И мысль бесплотная в чертог теней вернется.

(But I have forgotten what I want to say,
and the incorporeal thought returns to the palace of shadows.)

Celan's variation on Mandelstam's *чертог теней* ("palace of shadows")
in lines two and twenty avoids the image of the palace, presumably for
ideological convictions,[13] and speaks instead of *Schattenheim* and *heimgekehrt*. According to this reading, poetic speech is at home in silence,
perceptible and by some approximation retrievable—the implication
being, however, that it should stay there, in its silence, unless absolutely
vital reasons justify its being called away.

The words "mein Wort, . . . es ist heimgekehrt" recall the opening
and closing lines of Celan's poem "Unten" (*GW* 1:157), written concur-
rently or shortly after the Mandelstam translation:

Heimgeführt ins Vergessen
das Gast-Gespräch unsrer
langsamen Augen.

Heimgeführt Silbe um Silbe, verteilt
auf die tagblinden Würfel, nach denen
die spielende Hand greift, groß,
im Erwachen.

Und das Zuviel meiner Rede:
angelagert dem kleinen
Kristall in der Tracht deines Schweigens.

(BELOW

Led home into oblivion
the sociable talk of
our slow eyes.

Led home, syllable after syllable, shared
out among the dayblind dice, for which
the playing hand reaches out, large,
awakening.

And the too much of my speaking:
heaped up round the little
crystal dressed in the style of your silence.)
    (*P* 111)

"Heimgeführt ins Vergessen / das Gast-Gespräch" and "Doch ich—
mein Wort, ich weiß es nicht nennen, / ein Schemen war es—es ist

heimgekehrt" become two variations or paraphrases of a single movement (or withdrawal) of language from explicit articulation, with the
initially insignificant distinction that Mandelstam's text thematizes poetic speech, whereas Celan's only implies it in *Rede. Heimgeführt* and
heimgekehrt are not semantically congruent, however, since *heimführen*
denotes the taking home of a newly wed wife by the husband—this suggests a different kind of unification which may be a beginning, in contrast to the homecoming, a return to a beginning.[14]

Celan's poem "In Mundhöhe," probably written in 1957, operates
with oppositions closely analogous to those active in Mandelstam's text
"Das Wort bleibt ungesagt":

> In Mundhöhe, fühlbar:
> Finstergewächs.
>
> (Brauchst es, Licht, nicht zu suchen, bleibst
> das Schneegarn, hältst
> deine Beute.
>
> Beides gilt:
> Berührt und Unberührt.
> Beides spricht mit der Schuld von der Liebe,
> beides will dasein und sterben.)
>
> Blattnarben, Knospen, Gewimper.
> Äugendes, tagfremd.
> Schelfe, wahr und offen.
>
> Lippe wußte. Lippe weiß.
> Lippe schweigt es zu Ende.
> (*GW* 1:180)

> (ON MOUTH-LEVEL
>
> On mouth-level, palpable:
> dark-growth.
>
> [Light, you need not seek it, you remain
> the snow-snare, you hold
> your prey.
>
> Both are valid:
> Touched and Untouched.
> Both speak with quilt about love,
> both want to be and die.]

Leaf-scars, buds, ciliation.
A glimpsing, alien to day.
Husk, true and open.

Lip knew. Lip knows.
Lip dumbs it to the end.)
    (*SG* 129)

Here *Mundhöhe* signifies the locus where speech emerges from silence, as poetry or as discourse. That which is "palpable" (*fühlbar*), however, is also sinister (*Finstergewächs*), a formation of speech threatening to extricate itself from silence (thus the organic aspect *-gewächs*, later the botanical terms *Blattnarben, Knospen, Gewimper,* and *Schelfe*). *Äugendes* suggests a collective and nonspecific consciousness, a metaphorically understood organ striving for perception. As a present participial noun it is in the imperfective aspect, thus leaving any finality of successful perception questionable, or at the least open to revision of observation. Being *tagfremd*, it does not reveal itself to light, that is, to illumination, enlightenment, or explication, since light remains a mere *Schneegarn*, a net for capturing partridge in the winter and thus ironically a metaphor not for enlightenment but for closure and confinement. The *Beute* may be understood to mean those perceptions which the beholder believes to be accurate representations of reality and of cognition.

In a move toward a new dichotomy, Celan returns to his earlier poem "Sprich auch du" (*GW* 1:135), which states centrally: "Sprich— / Doch scheide das Nein nicht vom Ja" ("Speak— / But keep yes and no unsplit" [*P* 99]). "In Mundhöhe" varies this idea:

Both are valid:
Touched and Untouched.
Both speak with guilt about love,
both want to be and die.

Rather than committing finality of statement to any observation or perception, the poet prudently recognizes that paradoxical thinking is the only means of approaching reality. The passages addressed to light and to the statement of the dichotomy are in parentheses and are thus an embedded discursive commentary to a minimalist poetic text between the first and fourth sections, which describe, without verbal expressions, a geography of linguistic expression.

The argument culminates in the closing lines, clearly paralleling Mandelstam's "Wie schwarzes Eis so glüht auf meinem Munde / Erinnerung an Stygisches, an Hall":

Lippe wußte. Lippe weiß.
Lippe schweigt es zu Ende.

Lippe, seemingly an advocate of sovereign speech, is simultaneously an image of the tacit presence of speech and a synecdoche for the origin of speech, designating not so much the speech organs themselves as the very process of forming speech within some kind of dialogue ("dialogue" in the broadest sense of the term, but also specifically in the context of Celan's poetics). The poet has perceived that which had been moving toward expression (the illusive *es* in lines three and fourteen); with knowledge of this movement, but also skeptical of its ultimate shape and consequences, he suppresses or withholds speech. The later poem "Singbarer Rest," which one may read as a doublette to "In Mundhöhe," explicitly maintains the hope that poetic speech as conceived by Celan at this point in his development may yet become incarnate:

> —Entmündigte Lippe, melde,
> daß etwas geschieht, noch immer,
> unweit von dir.
> (*GW* 2:36)

> (—Interdicted lip, report
> that something is happening still,
> not far from you.)
> (*SG* 231)

The indirect accessibility of language to silence through poetic cognition defines the utopian potential of poetic language.[15]

The consequences of this for the translation process itself are not insignificant, especially when one assumes that Celan's affinities with mysticism at once do and do not involve a mysticism of the word; that they exist in the unresolved paradox of being metaphysical and literal. Preeminently, though not exclusively with regard to the translation of the texts discussed here, the translation from text to text is virtually the same operation as the translation from silence to speech or—on a different level and not simply as an inversion—from speech to silence. Translation, literally a "carrying-over," surrenders to the larger concept of translatability, the possibility and potential for moving the spoken language of one text to a language spoken differently. Silence is not a "language" as much as it is a medium or a transition, a sluice—anything but a stasis. Of course, the context into which silence is embedded determines both the potential and the limitation of what silence may become. For both cases—silence to speech, speech to silence—Benjamin's conclusion holds relevance when he speaks of the "immense and original danger of all translation: that the gates of such an expanded and thoroughly permeated language slam shut and engulf the translator in silence."[16] The situation may not be so ominous everywhere in Celan's work, although one can sense the danger constantly.

Almost encouraging, by contrast, are the lines from Celan's "Gespräch im Gebirg," published the same year as the Mandelstam translations (1959):

> Das Schweigen ist kein Schweigen, kein Wort ist da verstummt und kein Satz, eine Pause ists bloß, eine Wortlücke ists, eine Leerstelle ists, du siehst alle Silben umherstehn . . . (*GW* 3:170)

> (The silence is not silence, not a word has fallen silent and not a sentence, it is merely a pause, a word-gap, a site of emptiness is what it is, you see all the syllables standing around . . .)

The intermittences, as remnants of original silence, serve to relativize the functions of an uttered language committed to the frailties and finalities of meaning. They threaten poetic speech less than they fertilize it; in this sense they—like the minute dose of poison which heals—help define the path of a poetic thought or text to concretion. The poems are just the opposite of Eliot's "raid on the inarticulate."[17] Ultimately, Celan's texts defy being engulfed by threatening silence, since they attempt to reach the reader—just as the poet himself, haunted by the Holocaust until his death, wrote against overwhelming silence by conceiving of his texts as "messages in bottles" and insisting that his poems were forms of dialogue (*GW* 3:186). As readers, if we are attentive, we will likely corroborate Celan's assumptions concerning his own work and not relegate silence to metaphysical fictions, but assign it to the most fecund prerequisites of poetic creativity. When so much else is at stake, silence need be cultivated, with or without pathos, by neither poet nor critic.

NOTES

Epigraphs: "Silentium," in *GW* 5:57. "This is a word, which came in next to the words, / a word after the image of silence." "Strähne," in *GW* 1:92.

1. See, for example, Andreas Siekmann, "Die ästhetische Funktion von Sprache, Schweigen und Musik in Hölderlins *Hyperion*," *Deutsche Vierteljahresschrift* 54, no. 1 (1980), 47-57; and Joachim W. Storck, "Poesie und Schweigen. Zum Enigmatischen in Rilkes später Lyrik," *Blätter der Rilke-Gesellschaft* 10 (1983), 107-21.

2. Theodor W. Adorno, *Ästhetische Theorie*, ed. Gretel Adorno and Rolf Tiedemann (Frankfort: Suhrkamp, 1973), 477. Theodor W. Adorno, *Aesthetic Theory*, ed. Gretel Adorno and Rolf Tiedemann (London: Routledge & Kegan Paul, 1984), 444. I use my own translation.

3. For a discussion of *das Verschwiegene* in Celan's "Mit Äxten spielend" (*GW* 1:89) and generally in his volumes *Mohn und Gedächtnis* and *Von Schwelle zu Schwelle*, see Georg-Michael Schulz, *Negativität in der Dichtung Paul Celans*

(Tübingen: Neimeyer, 1977), esp. 54: "What was kept silent [*das Verschwiegene*] means to a heightened degree a conscious resistance to communication; something seems to withdraw itself deliberately from language—namely at the point where communication is perhaps possible, but is explicitly denied. Nevertheless it still holds valid that what is kept silent does not signify silence as such, but represents a specific something kept silent, a specific domain of meaning that refuses to make itself accessible to the questioner, which allows the 'words' [*Worte*] to become 'beggary' [*Bettel*] and which attains the 'splendor' [*Prunk*] of an elevated entity sufficient unto itself. This domain is evidently the dimension of death."

4. Theodor W. Adorno, "Kulturkritik und Gesellschaft," in *Prismen. Kulturkritik und Gesellschaft* (Frankfort: Suhrkamp, 1955), 31. Cf. Theodor W. Adorno, *Negative Dialektik* (Frankfurt am Main: Suhrkamp, 1980), 355.

5. One may perceive silence in nature, with Adorno, as a seemingly nonlinguistic characteristic of nature which informs the work of art in its conception and essence. "If the language of nature is mute, then art strives to make silence speak" (*Ästhetische Theorie*, 121). This helps to determine, says Adorno, the autonomy of art: "What in works of art is uninterrupted, connected, well-balanced, is a copy of the silence out of which only nature speaks. What is beautiful in nature is an Other that opposes [any] dominating principle and also diffuse divergence; what is reconciled would resemble it" (115). Thus understood, silence is not a vacuum, static and lifeless, but a dormant potential for an awakening to linguistic expression. The early Benjamin treated this problem more fundamentally in his "Über Sprache überhaupt und über die Sprache des Menschen," in which he claims that all things in both animate and inanimate nature participate in language to the extent that they impart their spiritual (*geistig*) content to the beholder, namely to humans. The communicating process is a "translation of the language of things into that of human beings" as a "translation of the silent into the audible." Walter Benjamin, *Gesammelte Schriften*, ed. Rolf Tiedemann and Hermann Schweppenhäuser (Frankfort: Surhkamp, 1977), 2(1):151.

6. See Christoph Parry, *Mandelstamm der Dichter und der erdichtete Mandelstamm im Werk Paul Celans* (Diss., Marburg, 1978), 186–87.

7. See Gerhart Baumann, "Paul Celan: '. . . Durchgründet vom Nichts . . . ,'" in *Entwürfe. Zu Poetik und Poesie* (Munich: Fink, 1976), 127.

8. See Jürgen Lehmann, "Intertextualität als Problem der Übersetzung: Die Mandelstam-Übersetzungen Paul Celans," *Poetica* (Amsterdam) 19 (1987), 254. See also Leonard Olschner, *Der feste Buchstab. Erläuterungen zu Paul Celans Gedichtübertragungen* (Göttingen: Vandenhoeck & Ruprecht, 1985), 226–50.

9. See Paul Celan, "Die Dichtung Ossip Mandelstamms," in Osip Mandelstam, *Im Luftgrab. Ein Lesebuch*, with contributions by Paul Celan, Pier Paolo Pasolini, Philippe Jaccottet, and Joseph Brodsky, ed. Ralph Dutli (Zürich: Ammann, 1988), 69–81. Celan indicates the approximate date of composition of his radio essay in a letter to Otto Pöggeler on 1 November 1960: "And the Büchner-Prize was an ordeal, to the very end. . . . Now it has been weathered; I even, admittedly at the very last minute, put down on paper a (kind of) lecture—a few formulations from the Mandelstam broadcast . . . had to be included, as islands to other islands." Quoted in Otto Pöggeler, *Spur des Worts. Zur Lyrik Paul Celans* (Freiburg: Alber, 1986), 407.

10. For a detailed interpretation of the poem and translation, see Olschner, *Der feste Buchstab*, 251–59.

11. *Gesammelte Schriften*, 6: 159.

12. Cf. Lehmann, "Intertextualität als Problem der Übersetzung," 242–53, who analyses the intertextual intricacies of Mandelstam's text "я слово позабыл."

13. Cf. "In eins," which implies "Krieg den Palästen!" when citing the Jacobin catchword's other half, *"Friede den Hütten!"* (*"Peace to the cottages!"* [*GW* 1:270/*P* 207), in Büchner's and Weidig's "Der hessische Landbote." Cf. Peter Horst Neumann, *Zur Lyrik Paul Celans*, rev. ed. (Göttingen: Vandenhoeck & Ruprecht, 1990), 63.

14. Schultz's interpretation of "Unten" (42–44) focuses on the notion of the return to a source, without considering the metaphorical implications of the social (nuptial) meaning of *heimführen* and of communication: "the poem demands that we comprehend communication without language as an expression of language."

15. Cf. Schulz, *Negativität in der Dichtung Paul Celans*, 64–65.

16. "Die Aufgabe des Übersetzers," in *Gesammelte Schriften*, 4(1):21. For further discussion of the presence and function of silence in Celan's translations, see Olschner, *Der feste Buchstab*, 133–36.

17. "East Coker," in *Collected Poems 1909–62* (New York: Harcourt, Brace, & World, 1970), 189.

Select Bibliography

This bibliography lists books by Celan in German; translations into English which have appeared in book form; and secondary literature referred to in the contributions of this volume, or else relating to their scope (its aim, then, is *not* to provide an exhaustive account of Celan scholarship). Only last print has been given in the case of secondary literature. If a work exists in English translation, reference has been given only to this edition. In case only the title of a work occurs, other references have already been indicated. It should be noted, finally, that the essays presented in this volume do not appear.

Other bibliographies are provided by: Dietlind Meinecke, "Bibliographie der Werke Paul Celans und der Sekundärliteratur," in *Über Paul Celan*, ed. Dietlind Meinecke, 2d ed. (Frankfort: Suhrkamp, 1973), 293–346; Rolf Paulus and Ursula Steuler, *Bibliographie zur deutschen Lyrik nach 1945* (Frankfort: Athenaion, 1974), 63–78; Stefan Reichert, "Bibliographie zu Paul Celan," in *Text+Kritik* 53–54 (1977), 88–106; and, most extensively, Jerry Glenn, *Paul Celan. Eine Bibliographie* (Wiesbaden: Harrassowitz, 1969); and Christiane Bohrer, *Paul Celan—Bibliographie* (Frankfort: Lang, 1989). A bibliography of Celan in English is provided by Jerry Glenn, "Paul Celan in English: A Bibliography of Primary and Secondary Literature," *Studies in Twentieth Century Literature* 8, no. 1 (1983), 131–50. Glenn also publishes a running select bibliography in the *Celan-Jahrbuch*.

PRIMARY LITERATURE

Single Collections

Der Sand aus den Urnen. Wien: Sexl, 1948.

Mohn und Gedächtnis. Stuttgart: Deutscher Taschenbuch Verlag, 1952. (79pp.)

Von Schwelle zu Schwelle. Stuttgart: Deutscher Taschenbuch Verlag, 1955. (68pp.)

Sprachgitter. Frankfort: Fischer, 1959. (64pp.)

Die Niemandsrose. Frankfort: Fischer, 1963. (94pp.)

Atemwende. Frankfort: Suhrkamp, 1967. (110pp.)

Fadensonnen. Frankfort: Suhrkamp, 1968. (128pp.)

Lichtzwang. Frankfort: Suhrkamp, 1970. (108pp.)

Schneepart. Frankfort: Suhrkamp, 1971. (96pp.)
Zeitgehöft. Frankfort: Suhrkamp, 1976. (67pp.)

Bibliophile Editions

Atemkristall, with eight engravings by Gisèle Celan-Lestrange. Paris: Brunidor, 1965. (85 copies)

Diese freie grambeschleunigte Faust, with six engravings by Gisèle Celan-Lestrange. Paris: Brunidor, 1967. (40 copies)

Fadensonnen. Schlafbrocken, with engravings by Gisèle Celan-Lestrange. Paris: Brunidor, 1967. (100 copies)

Schlafbrocken, with one engraving by Gisèle Celan-Lestrange. Paris: Brunidor, 1967. (100 copies)

Todtnauberg. Vaduz: Brunidor, 1968. (50 copies)

Schwarzmaut, with fifteen engravings by Gisèle Celan-Lestrange. Vaduz: Brunidor, 1969. (85 copies)

Angerufen vom Meer, quotations from poems by Paul Celan, with seven engravings by Gisèle Celan-Lestrange. Private, Paris, 1973.

Bei Wein und Verlorenheit, poems from *Die Niemandsrose* with Italian trans. by Luigi Mormino and some engravings by Gisèle Celan-Lestrange. Luxembourg: Mormino, 1975. (100 copies)

Schneepart 16.12.67–18.10.68. Facsimile edition. Frankfort: Suhrkamp, 1976. (1,000 copies)

Atemkristall and *Schwarzmaut.* Reprint. Frankfort: Suhrkamp, 1990. (980 copies)

Collected Volumes

Gedichte. Ed. and intro. Klaus Wagenbach, in collaboration with the author. Frankfort: Fischer, 1962. (With dates of poems.)

Gedichte. Darmstadt: Moderner Buchclub, 1966.

Ausgewählte Gedichte. Zwei Reden. With Afterword by Beda Allemann. Frankfort: Suhrkamp, 1968.

Ausgewählte Gedichte. Ed. Klaus Reichert with Afterword. Frankfort: Suhrkamp, 1970.

Gedichte. With Afterword by Beda Allemann. Frankfort: Suhrkamp, 1975. 2 vols.

Gedichte. Ed. Richard Pietraß. Berlin, DDR: Neues Leben, 1979.

Die Silbe Schmerz. Ed. Klaus Schuhmann. Berlin, DDR: Aufbau-Verlag, 1980.

Gesammelte Werke. Ed. Beda Allemann and Stefan Reichert, in collaboration with Rolf Bücher. Frankfort: Suhrkamp, 1983. 5 vols.

Gedichte 1938–1944. Ed. Ruth Kraft. Frankfort: Suhrkamp, 1985.

Achtzig Gedichte. Ed. Georg-Michael Schulz. Kornwestheim: EBG, 1986.

Halme der Nacht. Berlin: Handpresse Gutsch, 1986.

Das Frühwerk. Ed. Barbara Wiedemann. Frankfort: Suhrkamp, 1989.

Eingedunkelt und Gedichte aus dem Umkreis von Eingedunkelt. Ed. Bertrand Badiou and Jean-Claude Rambach. Frankfort: Suhrkamp, 1991.

Werke. Historico-critical edition. Ed. Beda Allemann, Rolf Bücher, Axel Gellhaus, and Stefan Reichert. Frankfort: Suhrkamp, 1990–. vol. 7(1), *Atemwende,* and vol. 7(2), Apparatus to *Atemwende,* ed. Rolf Bücher (1990); and vol. 8(1), *Fadensonnen*, and 8(2), Apparatus to *Fadensonnen*, ed. Rolf Bücher (1991).

Celan in English
Death Fugue. Trans. Jerome Rothenberg. Santa Barbara: Unicorn, 1967.
Speech-Grille and Selected Poems. Trans. Joachim Neugroschel. New York: Dutton, 1971.
Nineteen Poems. Trans. Michael Hamburger. Oxford: Carcanet Press, 1972.
Selected Poems. Trans. Michael Hamburger and Christopher Middleton. Harmondsworth: Penguin, 1972.
Breath Crystal. Trans. Walter Billeter. Ivanhoe, Victoria: Ragman Productions, 1975.
Prose Writings and Selected Poems. Trans. Walter Billeter and Jerry Glenn. Carlton, Victoria: Paper Castle Press, 1977.
Poems. Trans. Michael Hamburger. New York: Persea Books, 1980.
Thirty-Two Poems. Trans. Michael Hamburger. Norwich: Embers, 1985.
65 Poems. Trans. Brian Lynch and Peter Jankowsky. Dublin: Raven Arts Press, 1985.
Collected Prose. Trans. Rosmarie Waldrop. Manchester: Carcanet, 1986.
Last Poems. Trans. Katherine Washburn and Margret Guillemin. San Francisco: North Point Press, 1986.
The Poems of Paul Celan. Trans. Michael Hamburger. New York: Persea Books, 1989.

SECONDARY LITERATURE

Collections of Essays and Special Issues
Acts 8–9 (1988).
Argumentum e silentio. Ed. Amy D. Colin. Berlin: de Gruyter, 1986.
Contre-jour. Etudes sur Paul Celan. Ed. Martine Broda. Paris: Cerf, 1986.
Datum und Zitat bei Paul Celan. Ed. Chaim Shoham and Bernd Witte. Bern: Lang, 1987.
die horen 16, no. 83 (1971).
Die Pestsäule 1 (1972).
Etudes germaniques (Paris) 25, no. 3 (1970).
Kris (Stockholm) 34–35 (1987).
La revue des belles-lettres (Geneva) 96, nos. 2–3 (1972).
Paul Celan, "Atemwende". Materialien. Ed. Gerhard Buhr and Roland Reuß. Würzburg: Königshausen & Neumann, 1991.
Paul Celan, Materialien. Ed. Werner Hamacher and Winfried Menninghaus. Frankfort: Suhrkamp, 1988.
Psalm und Hawdalah. Zum Werk Paul Celans. Ed. Joseph P. Strelka. Bern: Lang, 1987.
Revue des sciences humaines 97, no. 223 (1991).
Studies in Twentieth Century Literature 8, no. 1 (1983).
Sulfur 4, no. 2 (1984).
Text+Kritik, 53–54 (1977).
Über Paul Celan. Ed. Dietlind Meinecke. 2d ed. Frankfort: Suhrkamp, 1973.
Zeitschrift für Kulturaustausch (Stuttgart) 32, no. 3 (1982).

Books and Dissertations

Baumann, Gerhart. *Erinnerungen an Paul Celan*. Frankfort: Suhrkamp, 1986.

Beese, Henriette. *Nachdichtung als Erinnerung. Allegorische Lektüre einiger Gedichte von Paul Celan*. Darmstadt: Agora, 1976.

Blanchot, Maurice. *Le dernier à parler*. Montpellier: Fata morgana, 1986.

Bollack, Jean. *Pierre de coeur. Un poème inédit de Paul Celan, "Le Périgord."* Perigueux: Fanlac, 1991.

Brierley, David. *"Der Meridian". Ein Versuch zur Poetik und Dichtung Paul Celans*. Frankfort: Lang, 1984.

Broda, Martine. *Dans la main de personne. Essai sur Paul Celan*. Paris: Cerf, 1986.

Buhr, Gerhard. *Celans Poetik*. Göttingen: Vandenhoeck & Ruprecht, 1976.

Chalfen, Israel. *Paul Celan. Eine Biographie seiner Jugend*. Frankfort: Insel, 1979. In English: *Paul Celan: A Biography of His Youth*. Trans. Maximilian Bleyleben. New York: Persea Books, 1991.

Colin, Amy D. *Paul Celan: Holograms of Darkness*. Bloomington: Indiana University Press, 1991.

Felka, Rike. *Psychische Schrift. Freud, Derrida, Celan*. Vienna: Turia & Kant, 1991.

Gadamer, Hans-Georg. *Wer bin Ich und wer bist Du?* 2d ed. Frankfort: Suhrkamp, 1986.

Glenn, Jerry. *Paul Celan*. New York: Twayne, 1973.

Herrmann, Michael. *Die Büchner-Preis-Rede und das "Sprachgitter": Untersuchungen zur Strukturierung der lyrischen Sprache durch Paul Celan*. Diss., Nürnberg, 1975.

Jabés, Edmond. *La mémoire des mots. Comment je lis Paul Celan*. With two drawings by Gisèle Celan-Lestrange. Paris: Fourbis, 1991.

Janz, Marlies. *Vom Engagement absoluter Poesie. Zur Lyrik und Ästhetik Paul Celans*. Frankfort: Syndikat, 1976.

Kohler-Luginbühl, Dorothee. *Poetik im Lichte der Utopie. Paul Celans poetologische Texte*. Bern: Lang, 1986.

Konietzny, Ulrich. *Sinneinheit und Sinnkohärenz des Gedichts bei Paul Celan*. Bad Honnef: Bock & Herchen, 1985.

————. *"Lesen Sie! Immerzu nur lesen, das Verständnis kommt von selbst." Die Bedeutung von Intention und Rezeption beim Verständnis der Lyrik Paul Celans*. Diss., Utrecht, 1989.

Krämer, Heinz Michael. *Eine Sprache des Leidens. Zur Lyrik Paul Celans*. Munich: Grünewald, 1979.

Kummer, Irene Elisabeth. *Unlesbarkeit dieser Welt. Spannungsfelder moderner Lyrik und ihr Ausdruck im Werk von Paul Celan*. Frankfort: Athenäum, 1987.

Laporte, Roger. *Lectures de Paul Celan*. Plombières-lès-Dijon: Ulysse, 1986.

Luther, Andreas. *'Nach Auschwitz ein Gedicht zu schreiben ist barbarisch . . .' Zur Möglichkeit von Lyrik nach Auschwitz am Beispiel Paul Celans*. Diss., Berlin, 1987.

Mayer, Peter. *Paul Celan als jüdischer Dichter*. Diss., Heidelberg, 1969.

Meinecke, Dietlind. *Wort und Name bei Paul Celan. Zur Widerruflichkeit des Gedichts*. Bad Homburg: Gehlen, 1970.

Menninghaus, Winfried. *Paul Celan. Magie der Form*. Frankfort: Suhrkamp, 1980.

Neumann, Peter Horst. *Zur Lyrik Paul Celans.* 2d rev. ed. Göttingen: Vandenhoeck & Ruprecht, 1990.

Olschner, Leonard Moore. *Der feste Buchstab. Erläuterungen zu Paul Celans Gedichtübertragungen.* Göttingen: Vandenhoeck & Ruprecht, 1985.

Pöggeler, Otto. *Spur des Worts. Zur Lyrik Paul Celans.* Freiburg: Alber, 1986.

Pretzer, Lieselotte Anne. *Geschichts- und sozialkritische Dimensionen in Paul Celans Werk. Eine Untersuchung unter besonderer Berücksichtigung avantgardistisch-surrealistischer Aspekte.* Bonn: Bouvier, 1980.

Rexheuser, Adelheid. *Sinnsuche und Zeichen-Setzung in der Lyrik des frühen Celan. Linguistische und literaturwissenschaftliche Untersuchungen zu dem Gedichtband "Mohn und Gedächtnis."* Bonn: Bouvier, 1974.

Schärer, Margit. *Negationen im Werke Paul Celans.* Zürich: Juris, 1975.

Schulz, Georg-Michael. *Negativität in der Dichtung Paul Celans.* Tübingen: Niemeyer, 1977.

Schulze, Joachim. *Celan und die Mystiker. Motivtypologische und quellenkundliche Kommentare.* Bonn: Bouvier, 1976.

Schwarz, Peter Paul. *Totengedächtnis und dialogische Polarität in der Lyrik Paul Celans.* Düsseldorf: Schwann, 1966.

Sevenich, Gabriele. *Sprache in Person. Versuche authentischen Sprechens am Beispiel Paul Celan.* Diss., Düsseldorf, 1985.

Solomon, Petre. *Paul Celan. Dimensiunea româneasca.* Bucarest: Kriterion, 1987.

Sparr, Thomas. *Celans Poetik des hermetischen Gedichts.* Heidelberg: Winter, 1989.

Szondi, Peter. *Celan-Studien,* in *Schriften,* vol. 2. Ed. Jean Bollack et al. Frankfort: Suhrkamp, 1978.

Terreni, Laura. *La prosa di Paul Celan.* Naples: Libreria Sapere, 1985.

Van Reis, Mikael. *Celans aska. En studie i Paul Celans "Engführung."* Göteborg: Litteraturvetenskapliga institutionen vid Göteborgs universitet, 1987.

Voswinckel, Klaus. *Paul Celan. Verweigerte Poetisierung der Welt. Versuch einer Deutung.* Heidelberg: Stiehm, 1974.

Weissenberger, Klaus. *Die Elegie bei Paul Celan.* Bern: Francke, 1969.

Wiedemann-Wolf, Barbara. *Antschel Paul—Paul Celan. Studien zum Frühwerk.* Tübingen: Niemeyer, 1985.

Zschachlitz, Ralf. *Vermittelte Unmittelbarkeit im Gegenwort. Paul Celans kritische Poetik.* Frankfort: Lang, 1990.

Articles, Chapters, and Essays

Adorno, Theodor W. *Ästhetische Theorie.* Frankfort: Suhrkamp, 1973. Pp. 475–77.

Allemann, Beda. "Paul Celans Sprachgebrauch." In *Argumentum e silentio,* 3–15.

Anderle, Martin. "Das gefährdete Idyll (Hölderlin, Trakl, Celan)." *German Quarterly* 35, no. 4 (1962), 455–63.

———. "Strukturlinien in der Dichtung Paul Celans." In *Über Paul Celan,* 58–68.

Bansberg, Dietger. "Paul Celans 'Sprachgitter.' Eine Interpretation." *Seminar* 12, no. 1 (1976), 2–37.

Baumann, Gerhart. "... durchgründet vom Nichts...." *Etudes germaniques,* 277–90.

Bayersdörfer, Hans-Peter. "Poetischer Sarkasmus. 'Fadensonnen' und die Wende zum Spätwerk." *Text+Kritik*, 42–54.

Bennholdt-Thomsen, Anke. "Auf der Suche nach dem Erinnerungsort." *Celan-Jahrbuch* 2 (1988), 7–28.

Bevilacqua, Giuseppe. "Zu Paul Celans Gedichtzyklus 'Atemkristall.'" In Bernhard Böschenstein and Giuseppe Bevilacqua, *Paul Celan. Zwei Reden*, Foreword by Eberhard Lämmert. Marbach am Neckar: Deutsche Schillergesellschaft, 1990.

Birus, Hendrik. "Celan-wörtlich." In *Paul Celan, "Atemwende,"* 125–66.

Bloess, Georges. "Les silences du discours poétique ou: une autre politique." *Revue d'Allemagne* (Strasbourg) 5, no. 1 (1973), 108–16.

Börner, Jochen. "Zweierlei Blindheit—Hölderlin, Celan und die entstellte Sprache. Zu Celans Gedicht 'Tübingen, Jänner.'" *Die Drei* 56, no. 3 (1986), 180–87.

Böschenstein, Bernhard. "Paul Celan." In *Studien zur Dichtung des Absoluten.* Zürich: Atlantis, 1968.

——. "Erste Notizen zu Paul Celans letzten Gedichten. Zur zweiten Abteilung von *Zeitgehöft.*" *Text+Kritik*, 62–68.

——. "Celan als Leser Hölderlins und Jean Pauls." In *Argumentum e silentio*, 183–98.

——. "Désorientation orientée. Lecture de quelques poèmes de la dernière année." In *Contre-jour*, 151–54.

——. "Hölderlin und Celan." In *Paul Celan, Materialien*, 191–200.

——. "Celan und Mandelstamm. Beobachtungen zu ihrem Verhältnis." *Celan-Jahrbuch* 2 (1988), 155–68.

——. "Gespräche und Gänge mit Paul Celan." in Bernhard Böchenstein and Giuseppe Bevilacqua, *Paul Celan. Zwei Reden*. Foreword by Eberhard Lämmert. Marbach am Neckar: Deutsche Schillergesellschaft, 1990.

——. "'WENN DU IM BETT / auf verschollenem Fahnentuch liegst." In *Paul Celan, "Atemwende,"* 85–92.

Böschenstein-Schäfer, Renate. "Allegorische Züge in der Dichtung Paul Celans." *Etudes germaniques*, 251–65.

——. "Traum und Sprache in der Dichtung Paul Celans." In *Argumentum e silentio*, 233–36.

Bogumil, Sieghild. "Celans Wende. Entwicklungslinien in der Lyrik Paul Celans, I." *Neue Rundschau* 93, no. 4 (1982), 81–110.

——. "Celans Wandern im Wort. Entwicklungslinien in der Lyrik Paul Celans, II." *Neue Rundschau* 94, no. 1 (1983), 88–105.

——. "Celan und Mallarmé. Kontinuität oder Wandel in der zeitgenössischen Poesie?" In *Kontroversen, alte und neue*, ed. Albrecht Schöne, 27–34. Tübingen: Niemeyer, 1986.

——. "Celans Hölderlinlektüre im Gegenlicht des schlichten Wortes." *Celan-Jahrbuch* 1 (1987), 81–125.

——. "'Todtnauberg.'" *Celan-Jahrbuch* 2 (1988), 37–51.

Bollack, Jean. "Pour une lecture de Paul Celan. *Lignes* (Paris) 1 (1987), 147–61.

——. "Paul Celan sur sa langue." In *Argumentum e silentio*, 113–53.

——. Paul Celan sur sa langue. Le poème 'Sprachgitter' et ses interprétations." In *Contre-jour*, 87–115.

———. "Voraussetzungen zum Verständnis der Sprache Paul Celans." In *Paul Celan, "Atemwende,"* 319–44.

Buchka, Peter. *Die Schreibweise des Schweigens. Ein Strukturvergleich romantischer und zeitgenössischer deutschsprachiger Literatur.* Munich: Hanser, 1974. Pp. 45–58.

Buck, Theo. "Mehrdeutigkeit ohne Maske. Zum ästhetischen Modus der Dichtung Paul Celans." *Text+Kritik,* 53–54 (1977), 1–8.

Bücher, Rolf. "Erfahrenes Sprechen. Leseversuch an Celan-Entwürfen." In *Argumentum e silentio,* 99–112.

Buhr, Gerhard. "Von der radikalen In-Frage-Stellung der Kunst in Celans Rede 'Der Meridian.'" *Celan-Jahrbuch* 2 (1988), 169–208.

Caldwell, David. "Interface between Primary and Secondary Translation: The Examples of Celan and Szondi." *Translation Review* 23 (1987), 23–24.

Cameron, Esther Beatrice. "Paul Celan, Dichter des Imperativs. Ein Brief." *Bulletin des Leo Baeck Instituts* 59 (1981), 55–91.

Coates, Paul. "Flowers of Nothingness: The *Spätwerk* of Paul Celan." In *Words after Speech: A Comparative Study of Romanticism and Symbolism.* London: Macmillan, 1986. Pp. 145–82.

Demetz, Peter. "Paul Celan." In *After the Fires: Recent Writing in the Germanies, Austria, and Switzerland,* 39–47. New York: Harcourt, Brace, Jovanovich, 1986.

Erwin, John. "Wenn wir Harmonia Singen: Projections of Community by Hölderlin and Celan." In *Lyric Apocalypse: Reconstruction in Ancient and Modern Poetry,* 83–103. Chico: Scholars Press, 1984.

Exner, Richard. "Paul Celan in English: Remarks on the Limits of Translatability." *Babel* (Amsterdam) 3 (1984), 61–66.

Felstiner, John. "Paul Celan in Translation: 'Du sei wie du.'" *Studies in Twentieth Century Literature,* 91–100.

———. "Kafka and the Golem: Translating Paul Celan." *Prooftexts* 6, no. 2 (1986), 172–83.

———. "Mother Tongue, Holy Tongue: On Translating and Not Translating Paul Celan." *Comparative Literature* 38, no. 2 (1986), 113–36.

———. "'Ziv, That Light': Translation and Tradition in Paul Celan." *New Literary History* 18, no. 3 (1987), 611–63.

———. "Translating Celan / Celan Translating." *Acts,* 108–18.

Figal, Günter. "Gibt es hermetische Gedichte? Ein Versuch, die Lyrik Paul Celans zu charakterisieren." In *Paul Celan, "Atemwende,"* 301–10.

Foot, Robert. "Paul Celan." In *The Phenomenon of Speechlessness in the Poetry of Marie Luise Kaschnitz, Günter Eich, Nelly Sachs, and Paul Celan,* 192–282. Bonn: Bouvier, 1982.

Frey, Eleonore. "'La poésie ne s'impose plus, elle s'expose'. Zu Paul Celans Poetik." In *Psalm und Hawdalah,* 22–36.

———. "Im Herzsinn. Zum Ereignis des 'Sprachwahren' in Celans Gedichten." *Neue Zürcher Zeitung,* 24–25 (November 1990), 67.

Frey, Hans-Jost. "Verszerfall." In *Kritik des freien Verses,* with Otto Lorenz, 61–73. Heidelberg: Schneider, 1980.

Fries, Thomas. "La rélation critique. Les études sur Celan de Peter Szondi." In *L'acte critique,* ed. Mayotte Bollack, 219–36. Lille: Presses Universitaires de Lille, 1985.

Fülleborn, Ulrich. "Rilke und Celan." In *Rilke Heute. Beziehungen und Wirkungen*, ed. Ingeborg H. Solbrig and J. W. Storck, 49–70. Frankfort: Suhrkamp, 1975.

Gadamer, Hans-Georg. "Sinn und Sinnverhüllung bei Paul Celan." In *Poetica*, 119–34. Frankfort: Insel, 1977.

———. "Celans Schlußgedicht," in *Argumentum e silentio*, 58–71.

———. "Phänomenologischer und semantischer Zugang zu Celan?" In *Paul Celan, "Atemwende,"* 58–71.

Geier, Manfred. "Poetisierung der Bedeutung. Zur Struktur und Funktion des sprachlichen Zeichens in einem Gedicht von Paul Celan." In *Paul Celan. Materialien*, 239–71.

———. "'Zur Blindheit überredete Augen'. Paul Celan / Friedrich Hölderlin: Ein lyrischer Intertext." In *Die Schrift und die Tradition. Studien zur Intertextualität*, 17–33. Munich: Fink, 1985.

Glenn, Jerry. "Celans Transformation of Benn's *Südwort*: An Interpretation of the Poem 'Sprachgitter.'" *German Life and Letters* 21, no. 1 (1967), 11–17.

Goltschnigg, Dietmar. "Das Zitat in Celans Gedichten." In *Psalm und Hawdalah*, 50–63.

Greisch, Jean. "Les Fleurs du Rien ('La Rose de Personne' de Paul Celan)." *Le nouveau commerce* 20, no. 55 (1984), 67–83.

———. "'Dieu sans Hauteur' dans la poésie de Paul Celan." In *Qu'est-ce que Dieu?*, Hommage à l'abbé Daniel Coppieters de Gibson, 27–45. Brussels: Publications des Facultés Universitaires Saint-Louis, 1985.

———. "'Zeitgehöft' et 'Anwesen'. La dia-chronie du poéme." In *Contre-jour*, 167–83.

Hamburger, Michael. "Paul Celan: Notes Towards a Translation." *PN Review* 6, no. 6 (1980), 58–59.

Höck, Wilhelm. "Von welchem Gott ist die Rede?" *Über Paul Celan*, 265–76.

Huppert, Hugo. "'Spirituell'. Ein Gespräch mit Paul Celan." In *Paul Celan. Materialien*, 319–24.

Jackson, John E. "Paul Celan." In *La question du moi. Un aspect de la modernité poétique européenne. T. S. Eliot, Paul Celan, Yves Bonnefoy*, 143–240. Neuchâtel: Baconnière, 1978.

———. "Paul Celan's Poetic of Quotation." In *Argumentum e silentio*, 214–22.

Jacottet, Philippe. "Aux confins." In *Une transaction secrète. Lectures de poésie*, 183–85. Paris: Gallimard, 1987.

Kelletat, Alfred. "Accessus zu Paul Celans 'Sprachgitter.'" In *Über Paul Celan*, 113–37.

———. "'Lila Luft'. Ein kleines Berolinense Paul Celans." In *Text+Kritik*, 53–54 (1977), 18–25.

Konietzny, Ulrich. "'All deine Siegel erbrochen?' Chiffren oder Baumläufer im Spätwerk Paul Celans." *Celan-Jahrbuch* 2 (1988), 107–120.

Krolow, Karl. "Das Wort als konkrete Materie." In *Über Paul Celan*, 55–57.

Künkler, Horst. "Die Abgründe streunen . . . Zur Deutung zweier Gedichte des späten Celan." *AION(T)* (Naples) 21, no. 3 (1977), 7–50.

Launay, Jean. "Une lecture de Paul Celan." *Poésie* 9 (1979), 3–8.

Lehmann, Jürgen. "Atmen und Verstummen. Anmerkungen zu einem Motivkomplex bei Mandel'štam und Celan." In *Paul Celan, "Atemwende,"* 187–200.

Lesch, Walter. "Die Schriftspur des Anderen. Emmanuel Lévinas als Leser von Paul Celan." *Freiburger Zeitschrift für Philosophie und Theologie* 12, no. 3 (1988), 449–68.

Lévinas, Emmanuel. "De l'être à l'autre." In *Noms propres*, 59–66. Paris: Fata morgana, 1976.

Lönker, Fred. "Überlegungen zu Celans Poetik der Übersetzung." In *Datum und Zitat bei Paul Celan*, 211–28.

Lorenz, Otto. "Passio. Celans zeitgeschichtliches Eingedenken: 'Engführung.'" In *Schweigen in der Dichtung Hölderlins, Rilkes und Celans. Studien zur Poetik deiktisch-elliptischer Schreibweisen*, 171–243. Göttingen: Vandenhoeck & Ruprecht, 1988.

Lyon, James K. "'Ganz und gar nicht hermetisch.' Überlegungen zum 'richtigen' Lesen von Paul Celans Lyrik." In *Psalm und Hawdalah*, 171–91.

———. "Paul Celan's Language of Stone: The Geology of the Poetic Landscape." *Colloquia Germanica* 8, no. 3–4 (1974), 298–317.

Maassen, Joop P. J. "Tiefimschnee. Zur Lyrik Paul Celans." *Neophilologus* (Groningen) 55, no. 2 (1972), 188–200.

Manger, Klaus. "Die Königszäsur. Zu Hölderlins Gegenwart in Celans Gedicht." *Hölderlin-Jahrbuch* 23 (1982–83), 156–65.

———. "Mit wechselndem Schlüssel. Zur Dichtung Paul Celans." *Euphorion* 75, no. 4 (1981), 444–73.

———. "Paul Celans Gedicht 'Ein Lied in der Wüste'—das Prooimion seiner Dichtung." *Celan-Jahrbuch* 2 (1988), 53–80.

———. "Himmelwracks. Zu Paul Celans Schiffahrtsmetaphorik." In *Paul Celan, "Atemwende,"* 235–52.

Mayer, Hans. "Sprechen und Verstummen der Dichter." In *Das Geschehen und das Schweigen*, 11–34. Frankfort: Suhrkamp, 1969.

———. "Erinnerung an Paul Celan." In *Der Repräsentant und der Märtyrer. Konstellationen der Literatur*, 169–88. Frankfort: Suhrkamp, 1971.

Menninghaus, Winfried. "Wissen oder Nicht-Wissen. Überlegungen zum Problem des Zitats bei Celan und in der Celan-Philologie." In *Paul Celan. Materialien*, 170–90.

Meschonnic, Henri. "On appelle cela traduire Celan." In *Pour la poétique*. Paris: Gallimard, 1973. Vol. 2, pp. 367–405.

Meuthen, Erich. "Paul Celan: *Die Niemandsrose*." In *Bogengebete. Interpretationsansätze zu George, Rilke, und Celan. Sprachreflexion und zyklischer Komposition in der Lyrik der Moderne*, 213–80. Frankfort: Lang, 1983.

Meyerhofer, Nicholas J. "The Poetics of Paul Celan." *Twentieth Century Literature* 27, no. 1 (1981), 72–85.

Moses, Stéphane. "Quand le langage se fait voix. Paul Celan: *Entretien dans la montagne*." In *Contre-jour*, 117–31.

———. "Patterns of Negativity in Paul Celan's 'The Trumpet Place.'" In *Languages of the Unsayable: The Play of Negativity in Literature and Literary Theory*, ed. Sanford Budick and Wolfgang Iser, 209–24. New York: Columbia University Press, 1989.

Myers, Saul. "The Way through the Human-Shaped Snow: Paul Celan's Job." *Twentieth Century Literature* 11, no. 11 (1987), 213–28.

Nägele, Rainer. "Paul Celan: Configurations of Freud." In *Reading after Freud:*

Essays on Goethe, Hölderlin, Habermas, Nietzsche, Brecht, Celan, and Freud, 135–68. New York: Columbia University Press, 1987.

Neumann, Gerhard. "Die 'absolute' Metapher. Ein Abgrenzungsversuch Stéphane Mallarmés und Paul Celans." *Poetica* 3, nos. 1–2 (1970), 188–225.

Olschner, Leonard Moore. "Anamnesis: Paul Celan's Translations of Poetry." *Studies in Twentieth Century Literature* 12, no. 2 (1988), 163–97.

———. "'STEHEN' und Constantia. Eine Spur des Barocks bei Paul Celan." In *Paul Celan, "Atemwende,"* 201–18.

Perels, Christoph. "'Kein Später'. Das Problem der ausgebliebenen 'Erziehung des Menschengeschlechts' in Celans letzten Gedichtbänden." In *Text+Kritik,* 53–54 (1977), 55–61.

———. "Erhellende Metathesen. Zu einer poetischen Verfahrensweise Paul Celans." In *Paul Celan. Materialien,* 127–38.

Petuchowski, Elizabeth. "A New Approach to Paul Celan's 'Argumentum e silentio.'" *Deutsche Vierteljahrsschrift für Literaturwissenschaft und Geistesgeschichte* 52, no. 1 (1978), 111–36.

———. "Bilingual and Multilingual *Wortspiele* in the Poetry of Paul Celan." *Deutsche Vierteljahrsschrift für Literaturwissenschaft und Geistesgeschichte* 52, no. 4 (1978), 635–51.

———. "A New Examination of Paul Celan's Translation of Shakespeare's Sonnet 105." In *Jahrbuch der deutschen Shakespeare-Gesellschaft,* 1985, 146–52.

Pöggeler, Otto. "'—Ach, die Kunst!' Die Frage nach dem Ort der Dichtung." In *Über Paul Celan,* 77–94.

———. "Kontroverses zur Ästhetik Paul Celans (1920–70)." *Zeitschrift für Ästhetik und Kunstwissenschaft* 25 (1980), 202–43.

———. "Poeta theologus? Paul Celans Jerusalem-Gedichte." In *Literatur und Religion,* ed. Helmut Koopman and Winfried Woesler, 251–64. Freiburg: Herder, 1984.

———. "'Schwarzmaut'. Bildende Kunst in der Lyrik Paul Celans." In *Die Frage nach der Kunst,* 281–375. Freiburg: Alber, 1984.

———. "Symbol und Allegorie. Goethes 'Diwan' und Celans 'Atemwende'." In *Paul Celan, "Atemwende,"* 345–60.

Rehnberg, Håkan. "Krasis." In *Kris,* 140–49.

Reichert, Klaus. "Hebräische Züge in der Sprache Paul Celans." In *Paul Celan. Materialien,* 156–69.

Rexheuser, Adelheid. "'Den Blick von der Sache wenden gegen ihr Zeichen hin'. Jean Pauls *Streckverse* und *Träume* und die Lyrik Paul Celans." In *Über Paul Celan,* 174–93.

———. "Die poetische Technik Paul Celans in seinen Übersetzungen russischer Lyrik." *Arcadia* 10, no. 3 (1975), 174–93.

Reuß, Roland. "Schritte. Zu Paul Celans Gedicht 'DU DARFST mich getrost / mit Schnee bewirten'." In *Paul Celan, "Atemwende,"* 13–34.

Rey, Willliam H. "Paul Celan. Das blühende Nichts." *German Quarterly* 42, no. 4 (1970), 749–69.

Rolleston, James. "Consuming History: An Analysis of Celan's 'Die Silbe Schmerz.'" In *Psalm und Hawdalah,* 37–48.

Ryan, Judith. "Die 'Lesbarkeit der Welt' in der Lyrik Paul Celans." In *Psalm und Hawdalah,* 14–21.

Schulz, Georg-Michael. "Individuation und Austauschbarkeit. Zu Paul Celans

'Gespräch im Gebirg.'" *Deutsche Vierteljahrsschrift für Literaturwissenschaft und Geistesgeschichte* 53, no. 3 (1979), 463–77.

———. "'fort aus Kannitverstan'. Bemerkungen zum Zitat in der Lyrik Paul Celans." In *Text+Kritik*, 53–54 (1977), 26–41.

Schulze, Joachim. "Celan and the 'Stumbling Block' of Mysticism." *Studies in Twentieth Century Literature*, 8, no. 1 (1983), 69–89.

Solomon, Petre. "Dichtung als Schicksal." In *Paul Celan, "Atemwende,"* 219–24.

Sparr, Thomas. "Zeichenreflexion in Celans Lyrik." In *Datum und Zitat*, 67–80.

———. "Celan und Kafka." *Celan-Jahrbuch* 2 (1988), 139–54.

———. "Das Gespräch im Gedicht. Paul Celans Gedicht 'Zürich, zum Storchen.'" *Neue Zürcher Zeitung* 24–25 (November, 1990), 67.

Specchio, Mario. "La parola e il silenzio nella lirica di Paul Celan." *Studi germanici* (Rome) 17–18 (1979–80), 339–76.

Speier, Hans-Michael. "Celans Schlußgedicht." *Manna* (Berlin) 326 (1985), 32–34.

———. "Im großen Gelausche. Probleme der Celan-Übertragung," in *Manna* (Berlin) 326 (1985), 34–39.

———. "Zum Verhältnis von Ästhetik, Geschichtlichkeit und Sprachsetzung im Spätwerk Celans." In *Datum und Zitat*, 97–121.

———. "Paul Celan, Dichter einer neuen Wirklichkeit. Studien zu *Schneepart*." *Celan-Jahrbuch* 1 (1987), 65–79.

Stanescu, Heinz. "An-cel-an, ein Dichter und sein Name." *Die Presse* (Vienna) 15–16 (November 1975), 18.

Steinecke, Hartmunt. "Lieder . . . jenseits der Menschen? Über Möglichkeiten und Grenzen, Celans *Fadensonnen* zu verstehen." In *Psalm und Hawdalah*, 192–202.

Steiner, Jacob. "Sprache und Schweigen in der Lyrik Paul Celans." In *Psalm und Hawdalah*, 126–42.

Stephens, Anthony. "The Concept of *Nebenwelt* in Paul Celan's Poetry." *Seminar* 9, no. 3 (1973), 229–52.

Stern, Howard. "Verbal Mimesis: The Case of 'Die Winzer.'" *Studies in Twentieth-Century Literature*, 8, no. 1 (1983), 23–39.

Stewart, Corbert. "Paul Celan's Modes of Silence: Some Observations on 'Sprachgitter.'" *Modern Language Review* 67, no. 1 (1972), 127–42.

———. "Some Problems in Reading Celan." In *London German Studies*, ed. J. P. Stern. London: Institute of Germanic Languages, University of London, 1983. Vol. 2, pp. 135–49.

Strack, Friedrich. "Wortlose Zeichen in Celans Lyrik." In *Paul Celan, "Atemwende,"* 167–86.

Szondi, Peter. "Lecture de Strette. Essai sur la poésie de Paul Celan." *Critique* 27, no. 288 (1971), 387–420.

Tache, Pierre-Alain. "Une parole proscrite." *La Revue de belles-lettres*, 101–03.

Terras, Victor, and Karl S. Weimar. "Mandelstam and Celan: Affinities and Echoes." *Germano-Slavica* (Waterloo, Canada) 1, no. 4 (1974), 11–29.

Turk, Horst. "'Aus einer—vielleicht selbstentworfenen—Ferne oder Fremde'. Zur Sprachmystik Celans." In *Text+Kritik*, 89–92.

———. "Politische Theologie? Zur 'Intention auf die Sprache' bei Benjamin und Celan." In *Juden in der deutschen Literatur*, ed. Stéphane Moses and Albrecht Schöne, 330–49. Frankfort: Suhrkamp, 1986.

Contributors

Jacques Derrida is Professor of Philosophy at the Ecole des hautes études en sciences sociales, Paris, and Visiting Professor of the Humanities at the University of California, Irvine. Among his recent books in English are *Aporias, Cinders, Memoires of the Blind,* and *The Other Heading.*

Aris Fioretos is a Mellon Scholar in the Department of German, The Johns Hopkins University. He is the author of, e.g., *Det kritiska ögonblicket. Hölderlin, Benjamin, Celan*; editor of a forthcoming collection of essays, *The Solid Letter: New Readings of Friedrich Hölderlin*; and translator, into Swedish, of Friedrich Hölderlin, *Hymner.*

Hans-Jost Frey is Professor of Comparative Literature at the University of Zürich. He is the author of *Studien über das Reden der Dichter. Mallarmé, Baudelaire, Rimbaud und Hölderlin* and *Der unendliche Text.*

Christopher Fynsk is Associate Professor of Comparative Literature and co-director of the Program in Philosophy, Literature, and the Theory of Criticism at the State University of New York, Binghamton. He is the author of *Heidegger: Thought and Historicity.*

Joel Golb is a Fellow at the Franz Rosenzweig Research Center, Hebrew University, Jerusalem. He has published essays on Celan in *Acts* and *Seminar.*

Werner Hamacher is Professor in the Department of German and the Humanities Center at The Johns Hopkins University. He is the author of the book-length study *"pleroma." Zu Genesis und Struktur einer dialektischen Hermeneutik,* included in his edition of G. W. F. Hegel, *Der Geist des Christentums*; and editor, with Winfried Menninghaus, of *Paul Celan. Materialien.*

Philippe Lacoue-Labarthe is Professor of Philosophy at the University of Strasbourg and Visiting Professor at the Univeristy of California, Berkeley. Among his books in English are *Typography: Mimesis, Philosophy, Politics* and *Heidegger, Art, and Politics*, as well as, with Jean-Luc Nancy, *The Literary Absolute* and *The Title of the Letter.*

Leonard Olschner is Associate Professor of German at Cornell University. He is the author of *Der feste Buchstab. Erläuterungen zu Paul Celans Gedichtübertragungen.*

Anders Olsson is Assistant Professor of Comparative Literature at Stockholm University. Among his books are *Mälden mellan stenarna. Litterära essäer, Ekelöfs nej,* and *Den okända texten. En essä om tolkningsteori från kyrkofäderna till Derrida;* and, with Håkan Rehnberg, a translation of Celan's late poetry, *Lila luft.*

Thomas Pepper is Assistant Professor of French and Comparative Literature at the University of Miami, Coral Gables.

Otto Pöggeler is Professor of Philosophy at the Ruhr University, Bochum, and the director of its Hegel Archive. Among his books are *Die Frage nach der Kunst. Von Hegel zu Heidegger, Philosophie und Politik bei Heidegger, Hegels Idee einer Phänomenologie des Geistes,* and *Spur des Worts. Zur Lyrik Paul Celans.*

Dennis J. Schmidt is Professor of Philosophy and Comparative Literature at the State University of New York, Binghamton. He is the author of *The Ubiquity of the Finite: Hegel, Heidegger, and the Entitlements of Philosophy;* translator of Ernst Bloch's *Natural Law and Human Dignity;* and editor of the State University of New York Press "Series in Contemporary Continental Philosophy."

Index

This index lists titles or first lines of texts referred to in the original as well as in available English translations. Titles within brackets, [ ], signal translations into German by Celan; titles within single guillemets, ⟨ ⟩, are provided by the editor, following the titles suggested by the editors of Celan's complete works.

GERMAN

Aber, 249
A la pointe acerée, 4–6, 254–57
All deine Siegel erbrochen? Nie, 234
Anabasis, 95–97
Ansprache anläßlich der Entgegennahme des Literaturpreises der freien Hansestadt Bremen, xii–xvi passim, xxn.9, 52, 111–12, 117, 159–65, 167, 174f, 186, 298, 319, 329f, 378, 383
⟨Antwort auf eine Umfrage der Librairie Flinker, Paris (1958)⟩, xxin.16, 303
Argumentum e silentio, 371–73
Aschenglorie, 35, 125
Atemkristall, 104–7 passim, 286
Atemwende, xi, 185, 218n.54, 269, 276, 297
Auf Reisen, 280–94
Aus Engelsmaterie, 89, 92, 247
Aus Herzen und Hirnen, 231

Beim Hagelkorn, 37–38, 297, 299–301, 338n.43
Bei Wein und Verlorenheit, 94, 153
Blume, 336n.13
Brandung, 231
⟨Brief an Hans Bender⟩, xv, xviii, 124, 179, 245, 288–89, 370

Cello-Einsatz, 40–41, 335n.7
Chymisch, 21, 46–47, 226, 269
Coagula, 267–78

Das Leuchten, 93ff
[Das Wort bleibt ungesagt; by Mandelstam], 373, 375–80 passim
Deine Augen im Arm, xxn.14, 251–52
Dein Hinübersein, 145–46, 215n.20
Dein vom Wachen, xviii, 58ff
Der Königsweg, 95
Der Meridian, xiv–xviii passim, 7–14, 15–18 passim, 35, 38, 43, 48–52 passim, 59, 110–24 passim, 130–44, 147–52, 154n.13, 159ff, 164–81, 182n.15, 194, 205, 209, 232ff, 258n.14, 262n.37, 273, 289f, 296–303, 320, 322, 324, 328, 333, 362, 369, 373
Der Reisekamerad, 237–38
Der Stein aus dem Meer, 338n.43
Der Tauben weißeste, 225–26
Die Ewigkeit, 228
Die Ewigkeiten, 215n.19, 252
Die Ewigkeiten tingeln, 215n.19
Die Niemandsrose, 27, 88, 94f, 105, 144f, 153, 193, 226, 237, 244, 249, 269f, 297, 371
Die Pole, 90f
Die Posaunenstelle, 91–93
Die Schleuse, 56–57, 123
Die Silbe Schmerz, 24, 123, 330–31
Die Zahlen, 23
Du gleißende, 97–98
Du liegst, 18–19, 273, 364n.6

Edgar Jené und der Traum der Träume, 303, 329

401

ENGLISH